A Companion to Aristotle's *Politics*

A Companion to Aristotle's *Politics*

EDITED BY DAVID KEYT AND FRED D. MILLER, JR.

BLACKWELL
Oxford UK & Cambridge USA

Copyright © in selection and editorial matter David Keyt
and Fred D. Miller, Jr. 1991

First published 1991
First published in USA 1991

Basil Blackwell, Inc.
3 Cambridge Center
Cambridge, Massachusetts 02142, USA

Basil Blackwell Ltd
108 Cowley Road, Oxford OX4 1JF, UK

Library of Congress Cataloging in Publication Data

A Companion to Aristotle's Politics / edited by David Keyt and
    Fred D. Miller, Jr..
        p.   cm.
    Includes bibliographical references and index.
    ISBN 1–55786–200–1 – ISBN 1–55786–098–X (pbk.):
    1. Aristotle. Politics.   2. Aristotle – Contributions in political
science.   I. Miller, Fred Dycus, 1944–   . II. Keyt, David.
JC71.A7A75   1990
320'.01'1 – dc20   90–35094
                                                            CIP

British Library Cataloguing in Publication Data

A CIP catalogue record for this book is available from the British
Library

Typeset in 10 on 11 pt Baskerville
by TecSet Ltd, Surrey
Printed in Great Britain by Billing & Sons Ltd, Worcester

Contents

Contributors   vii
Preface   x
Acknowledgments   xi
Abbreviations   xiii
Introduction   1

1 Aristotle's Conception of the State   13
   A. C. BRADLEY
2 Aims and Methods in Aristotle's *Politics*   57
   CHRISTOPHER ROWE
3 The Connection between Aristotle's *Ethics* and *Politics*   75
   A. W. H. ADKINS
4 Man as a Political Animal in Aristotle   94
   WOLFGANG KULLMANN
5 Three Basic Theorems in Aristotle's *Politics*   118
   DAVID KEYT
6 Aristotle's Theory of Natural Slavery   142
   NICHOLAS D. SMITH
7 Aristotle and Exchange Value   156
   S. MEIKLE
8 Aristotle's Criticism of Plato's *Republic*   182
   R. F. STALLEY
9 Aristotle's Defense of Private Property   200
   T. H. IRWIN
10 Aristotle on Prior and Posterior, Correct and Mistaken Constitutions   226
   WILLIAM W. FORTENBAUGH
11 Aristotle's Theory of Distributive Justice   238
   DAVID KEYT
12 Aristotle on Natural Law and Justice   279
   FRED D. MILLER, JR.
13 Aristotle's Analysis of Oligarchy and Democracy   307
   RICHARD MULGAN

14 Aristotle on Political Change 323
RONALD POLANSKY
15 Politics, Music, and Contemplation in Aristotle's Ideal State 346
DAVID J. DEPEW

Bibliography on Aristotle's *Politics* 381
Index Locorum 390

Contributors

A. W. H. ADKINS is Edward Olson Professor of Greek and Professor of Philosophy and Early Christian Literature at the University of Chicago. He is author of *Merit and Responsibility: A Study in Greek Values* (1960), *From the Many to the One: A Study of Personality and Views of Human Nature in the Context of Ancient Greek Society, Values and Beliefs* (1970), *Moral Values and Political Behaviour in Ancient Greece* (1972), and *Poetic Craft in the Early Greek Elegists* (1985).

A. C. BRADLEY (1851–1935), a younger brother of the philosopher F. H. Bradley, made his name as a Shakespearean critic rather than as a classicist or philosopher. He was educated at Balliol College, Oxford, where he became a fellow in 1874. He left Oxford in 1881 for a professorship at University College, Liverpool, and proceeded from there in 1889 to a professorship at Glasgow University. In 1901 he returned to Oxford as Professor of Poetry. He is particularly remembered for his books *Shakespearean Tragedy* (1904) and *Oxford Lectures on Poetry* (1909).

DAVID J. DEPEW is Professor of Philosophy at California State University, Fullerton. He is editor of *The Greeks and the Good Life* (1980), and co-editor of *Evolution at a Crossroads* (1985) and *Entropy, Information and Evolution* (1988). He is currently at work on a book entitled *Biology, Politics and Philosophy in Aristotle's Politics*.

WILLIAM W. FORTENBAUGH is Professor of Classics at Rutgers University, where he is currently chairman of the Department of Classics and Archaeology. For ten years he has been Director of Project Theophrastus, an international undertaking whose goals include collecting, editing, and translating the fragments of Aristotle's pupil Theophrastus. He is also editor of the series *Rutgers University Studies in Classical Humanities* and author of *Aristotle on Emotion* (1975) and *Quellen zur Ethik Theophrasts* (1984).

T. H. IRWIN is Professor of Philosophy at Cornell University. He is author of *Plato's Moral Theory* (1977), *Plato's Gorgias* (1979), *Aristotle's Nicomachean Ethics* (1985), *Aristotle's First Principles* (1988), and *Classical Thought* (1989).

DAVID KEYT is Professor of Philosophy at the University of Washington. He has held visiting appointments at Cornell University, the University of Hong Kong, Princeton University, and the Los Angeles and Irvine campuses of the University of California. He has been a junior fellow of the Institute for Research in the Humanities at the University of Wisconsin and the Center for Hellenic Studies in Washington, DC, and a member of the Institute for Advanced Study in Princeton. He writes on both ancient and recent philosophy.

WOLFGANG KULLMANN is Professor of Classical Philology of the University of Freiburg im Breisgau. He is author of *Das Wirken der Götter in der Ilias* (1956), *Die Quellen der Ilias* (1960), *Wissenschaft und Methode. Interpretationen zur aristotelischen Theorie der Naturwissenschaft* (1974), and *Die Teleologie in der aristotelischen Biologie* (1979). He has published numerous articles on various topics in classical philology and ancient philosophy and is co-editor of *Studia Platonica* (1974) and of *Studien zur antiken Philosophie* and *Hermes-Einzelschriften*.

S. MEIKLE is Lecturer in Philosophy at the University of Glasgow. His published work is mainly on Marx, Aristotle, and the 'economic' life of the ancient world. He is author of *Essentialism in the Thought of Karl Marx* (1985).

FRED D. MILLER, JR. is Professor of Philosophy and Executive Director of the Social Philosophy and Policy Center at Bowling Green State University. He is associate editor of *Social Philosophy & Policy*. He has published numerous articles on Aristotle, Plato, and other Greek philosophers and is at work on a book entitled *Nature, Justice and Rights in Aristotle's Politics*.

RICHARD MULGAN is Professor of Political Studies at the University of Auckland. Beginning in Oxford and then in a number of New Zealand universities, he has, at different times, taught philosophy, classics, and political science. He is author of *Aristotle's Political Theory* (1977) and of numerous articles on Aristotle and other aspects of Greek political theory, as well as books and articles on New Zealand politics.

RONALD POLANSKY is Professor of Philosophy at Duquesne University and editor of *Ancient Philosophy*. He is author of many articles on Plato and Aristotle and of a commentary on Plato's *Theaetetus*. His other interests include early modern political philosophy, human character, and the passions.

CHRISTOPHER ROWE is Head of the Department of Classics and Archaeology at the University of Bristol. The research for his paper in this volume was conducted during tenure of fellowships at the Edinburgh Institute for Advanced Studies in the Humanities and at the Center for Hellenic Studies in Washington, DC. He is author of *The Eudemian and Nicomachean Ethics: A Study in the Development of Aristotle's Thought* (1971), *Plato* (1984), and *Plato: Phaedrus* (1986). He is currently completing a commentary on Plato's *Phaedo*.

NICHOLAS D. SMITH is Professor of Philosophy at Virginia Polytechnic Institute and State University. He has published numerous articles in Greek philosophy, many with co-author Thomas C. Brickhouse, with whom he wrote *Socrates on Trial* (1989). Brickhouse and Smith are currently at work on a book on the philosophy of Plato's early period.

R. F. STALLEY is Senior Lecturer in Philosophy at the University of Glasgow. He is author of *An Introduction to Plato's Laws* (1983).

Preface

The papers in this collection focus on the central concepts and arguments of Aristotle's *Politics*. One paper is an influential study from the nineteenth century; four were written specifically for this volume; and the remainder have all been revised and updated for republication. Essay 4 appears for the first time in an English translation. The collection is intended for a wide audience, including students and scholars in social and political philosophy as well as specialists in Greek philosophy.

Greek terms are transliterated except where a point is being made about the Greek text, and nothing in Greek is left untranslated. It should be noted that upsilon is transliterated as "u"; eta as "ê"; omega as "ô"; and iota subscript is either omitted or rendered by an "i" following the subscripted vowel. The word "polis" is treated in this volume as a naturalized word of English having an English plural ("polises") and is thus printed in Latin letters rather than in italics.

We are grateful to the Social Philosophy and Policy Center at Bowling Green State University and its staff for their support for this project and in particular to Mary Dilsaver, Tammi Sharp, Terrie Weaver, and Dan Greenberg. Special thanks are due to Dan Greenberg, Jennifer Lange, and Thomas May for their assistance in preparing the index. We are also indebted to Christopher Shields and Margaret Meghdadpour for help with the translation of Essay 4. We also thank Anthony Raubitschek and Kurt Luckner for assistance on the cover illustration. Fred Miller gratefully acknowledges a grant from the Earhart Foundation, a research leave from Bowling Green, and the hospitality of the Fellows of Jesus College, Oxford, all of which enabled him to work on this volume.

Finally, we much appreciate the patience, encouragement, and expert assistance of Blackwell in bringing this project to completion.

David Keyt, Seattle, Washington
Fred D. Miller, Jr, Bowling Green, Ohio

Acknowledgments

The editors and publishers gratefully acknowledge permission to reproduce the following:

A. C. Bradley, "Aristotle's Conception of the State," originally appeared in *Hellenica*, ed. Evelyn Abbott, (London, 1880 [repr. 1971]), pp. 181–243.

Christopher Rowe, "Aims and Methods in Aristotle's *Politics*," originally appeared in the *Classical Quarterly*, 27 (1977), pp. 159–72.

A. W. H. Adkins, "The Connection Between Aristotle's *Ethics* and *Politics*," originally appeared in *Political Theory*, 12 (1984), pp. 29–49.

Wolfgang Kullmann, "Man as a Political Animal in Aristotle," originally appeared as "Der Mensch als politisches Lebewesen bei Aristoteles," in *Hermes*, 108 (1980), pp. 419–43.

David Keyt, "Three Basic Theorems in Aristotle's *Politics*," originally appeared as "Three Fundamental Theorems in Aristotle's *Politics*," in *Phronesis*, 32 (1987), pp. 54–79.

Nicholas D. Smith, "Aristotle's Theory of Natural Slavery," originally appeared in *Phoenix*, 37 (1983), pp. 109–22.

S. Meikle, "Aristotle and Exchange Value," is a substantially revised version of "Aristotle and the Political Economy of the Polis," which appeared in the *Journal of Hellenic Studies*, 99 (1979), pp. 57–73.

T. H. Irwin, "Aristotle's Defense of Private Property," is a substantially revised version of "Generosity and Property in Aristotle's *Politics*," which appeared in *Social Philosophy & Policy*, 4 (1987), pp. 37–54.

William W. Fortenbaugh, "Aristotle on Prior and Posterior, Correct and Mistaken Constitutions," is a revised version of an article that appeared in *Transactions of the American Philological Association*, 106 (1976), pp. 125–37.

David Keyt, "Aristotle's Theory of Distributive Justice," is a substantially revised version of "Distributive Justice in Aristotle's *Ethics* and *Politics*," which appeared in *Topoi*, 4 (1985), pp. 23–45.

Fred D. Miller, Jr. "Aristotle on Natural Law and Justice," is an expanded version of "Aristotle on Nature, Law and Justice," which appeared in the *University of Dayton Review*, Special Issue on Aristotle, 19 (1988–9), pp. 57–69.

Abbreviations

	Aristotle
An. Post.	*Analytica Posteriora*
An. Pr.	*Analytica Priora*
DA	*de Anima*
Ath. Pol.	*Athênaiôn Politeia*
DC	*de Caelo*
Cat.	*Categoriae*
EE	*Ethica Eudemia*
EN	*Ethica Nicomachea*
GA	*de Generatione Animalium*
GC	*de Generatione et Corruptione*
HA	*Historia Animalium*
IA	*de Incessu Animalium*
DI	*de Interpretatione*
MM	*Magna Moralia*
Met.	*Metaphysica*
Meteor.	*Meteorologica*
MA	*de Motu Animalium*
Oec.	*Oeconomica*
PA	*de Partibus Animalium*
Phys.	*Physica*
Poet.	*Poetica*
Pol.	*Politica*
Probl.	*Problemata*
Protr.	*Protrepticus*
Rhet.	*Rhetorica*
Rhet. Al.	*Rhetorica ad Alexandrum*
SE	*Sophistici Elenchi*
Somn.	*de Somno et Vigilia*
Top.	*Topica*

	Plato
Apol.	*Apology*
Gorg.	*Gorgias*
Parm.	*Parmenides*

Phdo.	*Phaedo*
Phlb.	*Philebus*
Rep.	*Republic*
Soph.	*Sophist*
Theaet.	*Theaetetus*
Tim.	*Timaeus*

Introduction

The two great classics of Greek political philosophy are Plato's *Republic* and Aristotle's *Politics*. They have similar Greek titles, *Politeia* and *Politika* respectively, and share a theme – justice. Along with Plato's *Statesman* and *Laws*, they mark the beginning of political philosophy as a distinct field of study. In the grand scheme of the *Republic* politics is closely intertwined with ethics: Plato seeks justice in the city in order to find justice in the soul and uses the fall of the city to explain the fall of the soul. In Plato's later dialogues and in Aristotle, ethics and politics pull apart. Thus, strictly speaking, the Aristotelian works that correspond to the *Republic* are the *Ethics* and the *Politics*, the two treatises whose joint subject Aristotle at one place calls "the philosophy of human affairs" (*EN* X.9.1181b15; see also I.2.1094a26–b11). Although Aristotle disentangles ethics and politics, he makes no attempt to disconnect them. Both Plato and Aristotle are intent on finding a standard of justice by means of which all the various forms of government may be ranked, and both maintain that a primary aim of a just government is to produce just men and women.

This common ground is contested by the modern tradition of political philosophy stemming from Machiavelli and Hobbes (with roots in the Greek Atomists and Epicurus). Hobbes regards it as a bad mistake on Aristotle's part to claim that certain forms of government such as kingship and aristocracy are correct because they promote the common interest and other forms such as tyranny and oligarchy are deviations because they promote the interest of their rulers only (*Pol.* III.6.1279a17–7.1279b10). "[*Tyranny* and *Oligarchy*] are not the names of other Formes of Government," Hobbes says, "but of the same Formes misliked. For they that are discontented under *Monarchy*, call it *Tyranny*; and they that are displeased with *Aristocracy*, call it *Oligarchy*."[1] Hobbes also disagrees with Plato and Aristotle over the end, or goal, of government. For Hobbes the aim of government is safety, not moral character.[2]

Although the political philosophies of Plato and Aristotle have much in common, there is also a fundamental difference between them springing from

1 *Leviathan* (London, 1651), ch. 19, p. 95.
2 Ibid., ch. 30, p. 175.

a difference in their metaphysics. Both Plato and Aristotle wish to combat the moral relativism of Protagoras, picked up later by Hobbes,[3] by which "whatever things *appear* just and fine to each city *are* so for it as long as it holds by them" (Plato, *Theaet.* 167c4–5). Both seek a true standard of justice. Plato finds it in a transcendent realm of Forms (*Rep.* V.472a8–e6, IX.592a10–b4). Aristotle, who rejects Plato's theory of Forms, must look elsewhere. He finds his standard, not in a supersensible world of Forms, but in the sensible world of nature.

In creating political philosophy, Plato and Aristotle were helped along by the Greek language with its elaborate political vocabulary based on the word "*polis*." The unity of the vocabulary would seem to indicate the existence of a special entity calling for study. The chief items of this vocabulary that appear in the *Politics* are the following:

polis   city, state, city-state
politês   citizen
politis   female citizen
politeia   constitution
politeuma   governing class
hê politikê (sc. technê or *epistêmê)*   political science
ho politikos (sc. anêr)   politician or stateman
to politikon   the citizenry
archê politikê   political office or political authority
politika   things political (title of the *Politics*)
philosophia politikê   political philosophy (III.12.1282b23)
politeuesthai   to engage in politics

The political vocabulary of English is based partly on "*polis*" and partly on "*civis*," the Latin word for citizen. As a consequence, and as the foregoing list makes plain, English does not mark out a special field of study as vividly as Greek.

During Aristotle's lifetime (384–322 BC) the face of the world was changed. The period of his adult life witnessed the rise under Philip II (381–336 BC) of the semi-barbarian Macedon to dominance in the Greek world and the conquest of Persia and the Far East by an army led by Philip's son, Alexander the Great (356–323 BC). In spite of Aristotle's ties to the Macedonian monarchy, these great events are never mentioned in Aristotle's extant treatises.

All of Aristotle's adult life, except for its very end and a dozen years in the middle, was spent in Athens. He was born in Stagira, a city on the east coast of the Chalcidic peninsula later destroyed by Philip. His father, Nicomachus, was the court physician to Philip's father, King Amyntas. As a youth of

---

3 "no Law can be Unjust. The Law is made by the Soveraign Power, and all that is done by such Power, is warranted, and owned by every one of the people; and that which every man will have so, no man can say is unjust" (ibid., ch. 30, p. 182).

seventeen, Aristotle came to Athens and entered Plato's Academy where he remained for twenty years. When Plato died in 347 BC, he left Athens and spent the next period of his life first in Assos in northwest Asia Minor and then in Mytilene on the island of Lesbos. In 343 BC Philip invited Aristotle, now in his early forties, to his court to supervise the education of his thirteen-year-old son Alexander. Although this supervision lasted no more than three years, Aristotle was still in northern Greece in 336 BC when Philip was assassinated and Alexander ascended the throne. He returned to Athens the next year and founded his own school in the Lyceum. During his second residence in Athens he maintained his friendship with Antipater, who was the Macedonian regent in Greece while Alexander was campaigning in Asia. When Alexander died suddenly in 323 BC, the Greek cities rose against their Macedonian masters and Aristotle, because of his Macedonian connections, was forced to flee to Chalcis on the island of Euboea, where he died a year later at the relatively early age of 62.[4]

Aristotle's life is reflected in the *Politics* in a number of ways. First of all, Aristotle's interest in biology, of which the naturalism of the *Politics* is an offshoot, was probably acquired from his father. Second, the cool, dispassionate tone of the outsider characteristic of the *Politics* is perhaps explained by the fact that Aristotle was a resident alien, or *metic*, all of his adult life and had no political rights in any of the cities in which he resided. Third, the trenchant criticism of Plato's three major dialogues on politics – the *Republic*, the *Statesman*, and the *Laws* – as well as his debt to the *Laws* in sketching his ideal city in *Politics* VII and VIII stems directly from his years of study and discussion in the Academy. Fourth, the audience of rulers and statemen for whom the *Politics* is intended reflects the high political circles in which Aristotle moved. Finally, his qualified defense of both democracy (III.11) and absolute kingship (III.17) owes something to his experience of democratic Athens and autocratic Macedon.

The *Politics* is not a well-integrated whole like Plato's *Republic*, where an overarching structure determines the position of every sentence, but a loosely connected set of essays on various topics in political philosophy held together by the inner logic of the subject matter. Indeed, the treatise we have may not have been put together by Aristotle himself, but by an editor after his death. For all we know, Aristotle may never have intended to form a single treatise from the various essays. The table of contents shows the loose structure:

I.1–2   Introduction
I.3–13   Slavery and the family
II   Previous model constitutions (Plato's *Republic* and *Laws*; Sparta and Carthage)
III   General theory of constitutions (citizenship, classification of constitutions and general principles, kingship)

---

4 Ancient texts on the life of Aristotle are collected in I. Düring, *Aristotle in the Ancient Biographical Tradition* (Göteborg, 1957 [repr. 1987]).

IV   The inferior constitutions
V   The preservation and destruction of constitutions
VI   Democracy and oligarchy
VII–VIII   The best constitution (the best life, the best city, education)

The sequence of chapters is awkward in two respects. The natural place for the essay on the best constitution is before the essay on the inferior constitutions, and the natural place for the essay on the preservation and destruction of constitutions is after the essay on democracy and oligarchy. This has led many modern editors and translators of the *Politics* from the fourteenth through the nineteenth centuries to transpose various books. Thus Franz Susemihl, the great nineteenth-century German editor of the *Politics*, adopts the arrangement I–II–III–VII–VIII–IV–VI–V; and W. L. Newman, his great English counterpart, adopts the arrangement I–II–III– VII–VIII–IV–V–VI. That Books VII and VIII were intended to follow immediately after III seems to be indicated by the concluding sentence of III and by a fragment of a further sentence appended to it in some of the manuscripts. The former promises an immediate discussion of the best constitution, and the latter is a slightly altered version of half of the opening sentence of Book VII. But putting VII and VIII before IV does not greatly improve the structure of the *Politics* since the transition from VIII to IV is even more awkward than that from III to IV. The transposition of Books V and VI, proper as it seems at first glance, is ruled out by the fact that Book VI refers back to V four times (VI.1.1316b31–6, 1317a35–8, 4.1319b4–6, 5.1319b37–9).

The network of cross-references linking one passage in the *Politics* with another throws a great deal of light on the structure that Aristotle intended to impose upon his material (on the assumption that these references are all by his hand rather than the hand of an editor or scribe).[5] First of all, every book of the *Politics* except the first and the last refers unmistakably to Book III. As Newman remarks and as the cross-references bear out, "the Third Book is the centre round which the whole treatise is grouped."[6] Second, there are no unmistakable and unambiguous references to passages in Books IV–VI from books outside this group. Finally, although Books IV–VI are laced with cross-references to each other, the only book outside the group that they refer to is Book III. The ten or twelve references to it are strong and numerous enough to tempt one to group it with them. The absence of cross-references between Books VII–VIII and IV–VI suggests that Aristotle never settled the relation of the one group to the other. If this is so, the eight books of the *Politics* do not form a linear sequence. What we have instead is only the following partial ordering:

---

5 The cross references within and between books as well as promises never fulfilled are listed (with a few omissions and many typographical errors) at the end of Susemihl's Teubner edition of the *Politics* (Leipzig, 1894), pp. 365–8.
6 *The Politics of Aristotle*, 4 vols (Oxford, 1887–1902 [repr. 1973]), vol. II, p. xxxi.

This partial ordering follows the internal logic of the treatise, stays within the pattern of cross-references, and emphasizes the central position of Book III.

The latest historical event referred to in the *Politics* that can be identified with confidence is the assassination of Philip II in 336 (V.10.1311b1–3).[7] Thus we know that at least one sentence of the *Politics* was written during the last period of Aristotle's life and after Alexander had ascended the throne. Because of its loose structure, it is difficult to estimate how much of it was written before or after this one sentence. Aristotle may have written the *Politics* in its entirety during the period of the Lyceum; but on the other hand, he may have written its various parts at various times throughout his adult life.

Much ink has been spilled in this century attempting to discover different chronological strata in the *Politics*. The aim of such investigations is to reconcile alleged inconsistencies of approach or of doctrine in a given work. For a philosopher contradicts himself only if he *simultaneously* affirms and denies the same proposition – not if he changes his mind. Thus one way to remove an alleged inconsistency is to assign its different components to different periods of the philosopher's life. But it remains an open question whether there are any major inconsistencies of approach or of doctrine in the *Politics* and, consequently, whether there are any problems that the discovery of different chronological strata could clear up. Although Aristotle does use a variety of different approaches in the *Politics* – historical, aporetic, classificatory, expository – such variety in itself does not pose a problem. Different topics may call for different approaches, so there is no reason Aristotle should not exploit a variety of approaches during a single period of his life.

Although Aristotle devotes different works to ethics and politics, they are closely connected in his view. This is made plain by the references to politics in his ethical works and to ethics in his work on politics. The *Nicomachean Ethics* describes itself in its early chapters as concerned with politics (I.2.1094a27–8, b10–11; 3.1094b14–5, 1095a2; 4.1095a14–17; and compare *EE* VII.1.1234b22) and ends with a transition to a study of politics and the science of legislation (X.9.1180b28–end). Its final paragraph, or epilogue, even outlines the contents of a work on politics:

> Since our predecessors left the subject of legislation unexplored, it is perhaps proper that we should ourselves examine it and the general topic of the constitution, in order that as far as possible the philosophy of man may be

---

7 Events that occurred as late as 333 may be referred to in two passages (II.9.1270b11–12, 10.1272b19–22), but the matter admits of dispute. See Newman, *ad loc.*

completed. First, then, if any particular point has been treated well by those who have gone before us, we must try to review it; then from the constitutions that have been collected we must try to see what it is that preserves and destroys cities and what it is that preserves and destroys each of the constitutions, and for what reasons some cities are well governed and others the reverse. For when these things have been examined, we will perhaps better understand also what sort of constitution is best, and how each is structured, and which laws and customs it uses (1181b12–22).

This outline mentions many of the topics treated in the *Politics*, although the extent to which it describes the treatise that has come down to us is a matter of dispute.

The references from the *Politics* to the ethical works are as numerous as those in the opposite direction. Indeed, Aristotle refers six times to a treatise entitled the *Ethics* (*ta êthika* or *hoi êthikoi logoi*). But the matter is complicated by the fact that three different ethical works are attributed to Aristotle – the *Nicomachean Ethics*, the *Eudemian Ethics*, and the *Magna Moralia* – and it is unclear which of the three the *Politics* is referring to. A further complication is that Books V–VII of the *Nicomachean Ethics* are also claimed as Books IV–VI of the *Eudemian Ethics*.[8] Four of the six references to the *Ethics* are to these common books,[9] and two are most probably to the *Eudemian Ethics*.[10]

The *Politics* is a treatise in practical philosophy (*EN* I.4.1095b5). To grasp the import of this, one must understand how political philosophy on Aristotle's view differs from other branches of philosophy, which in turn involves a short detour through Aristotle's classification of the sciences. All thought, according to Aristotle's classificatory scheme, is either theoretical, practical, or productive (*Top.* VI.6.145a15–16; *Met.* VI.1.1025b25, XI.7.1064a16–19; *EN* VI.2.1139a26–8). These three types of thought differ in their ends or goals. The end of theoretical thought is knowledge; the end of practical thought is good action; and the end of productive thought seems to be useful and beautiful objects such as sandals and poems and good qualities such as health and strength (*Met.* II.1.993b19–21; *EN* VI.2.1139a27–31, b3–4, VI.5.1140b6–7). Theoretical and practical thought are divided in their turn into three subtypes, and productive thought into two. The three kinds of

8 Although the *Nicomachean* and *Eudemian Ethics* are in general agreement, they contain important differences of detail. Scholars dispute about which was written first and about which the common books were intended for. Most regard the *Nicomachean Ethics* as the later and more mature work and the home of the common books, but a few such as Anthony Kenny in *The Aristotelian Ethics* (Oxford, 1978) champion the *Eudemian Ethics* on both scores. It should also be noted that the *Magna Moralia* has been rejected by many scholars as spurious, but some contend that it was really written by Aristotle.
9 II.2.1261a31 refers to *EN* V.5.1132b31–4; III.9.1280a18 refers to *EN* V.3.1131a14–24, III.12.1282b20 refers to *EN* V.3; and IV.11.1295a36 refers to *EN* VII.13.1153b9–21.
10 VII.13.1332a8 most probably refers to *EE* II.1.1219a38–9, b1–2, though it may refer to *EN* 1.7.1098a16–18, 10.1101a14–16. VII.13.1332a22 most probably refers to *EE* VIII.3.1248b26–7, but it may refer to *MM* II.9.1207b31–3.

theoretical thought are first philosophy or theology, natural philosophy, and mathematics (*Met.* VI.1.1026a18–19, XI.7.1064b1–3, and see also *EN* VI.8.1142a17–18), where natural philosophy includes physics, biology, psychology, and astronomy (*Phys.* II.1.192b8–12, *DC* III.1.298a27–32, *DA* I.1.403a27–b2). The three types of practical thought, which deal with the individual, the family, and the polis respectively, are ethics, household management, and politics (see *EN* VI.8 and *EE* I.8.1218b13). Productive thought, or art, is either useful or mimetic. The useful arts are such things as shipbuilding, garmentmaking, gymnastics, medicine, and (presumably) agriculture (*Pol.* IV.1.1288b10–21), whereas the mimetic arts are such things as painting, sculpture, music, dance, and poetry (*Rhet.* I.11.1371b4–8, *Poet.* 1). It is unclear where Aristotle intended to place logic in this scheme. Later Aristotelians pursuing a remark in the *Metaphysics* (IV.3.1005b2–5) regarded logic (since it can be applied equally to any subject matter) not as a science but as the organon, or instrument, of science – as a discipline that is presupposed by the sciences. If one adopts this reasonable idea, Aristotle's classification of the sciences can be diagrammed as follows:

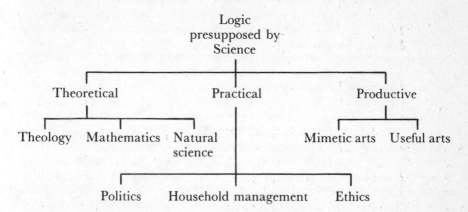

Turning now to the papers in this volume, Essay 1, "Aristotle's Conception of the State" by A. C. Bradley, was originally published over a century ago and may fairly be said to represent the standard interpretation of the *Politics*. This is due partly to Bradley's influence on the great scholars who were producing their large works on the *Politics* as the nineteenth century drew to a close and the twentieth began. W. L. Newman mentions that Bradley commented on a portion of the proof-sheets of his commentary; Franz Susemihl and R. D. Hicks frequently refer to Bradley's essay in their competing commentary; and Ernest Barker, the most influential British writer on the *Politics* during the first half of this century, credits Bradley's essay with arousing his interest in the *Politics*.[11]

11 Newman, *Politics*, vol. I, p. x; F. Susemihl and R. D. Hicks, *The Politics of Aristotle* (London, 1894 [repr. 1976]), pp. 146, 354, 390, and elsewhere; E. Barker, *The Political Thought of Plato and Aristotle* (London, 1906 [repr. 1959]), p. viii.

The problem of relating the various parts of the *Politics* to each other, alluded to earlier, is examined by Christopher Rowe in Essay 2, "Aims and Methods in Aristotle's *Politics*." The classical scholar Werner Jaeger sought to resolve this problem by distinguishing two distinct chronological strata within the *Politics*: on the one hand, there were the "Utopian" books, including VII–VIII, and, on the other, the "purely empirical" books, IV–VI, which belonged to a different and later conception of political theory.[12] Rowe points out, however, that the conception of political theory found in Book IV itself represents the business of constructing ideal states as perfectly compatible with that of addressing actual political problems. In principle these two exercises are, indeed, perfectly compatible; but, Rowe argues, in Aristotle's case, though Aristotle nowhere acknowledges the point, the second exercise necessarily involves a different set of standards from the first. From the perspective of his best constitution, all actual constitutions are merely defective and incapable of improvement. Rowe concludes that there is a real difference between the two groups of books, but that it is not to be explained in chronological terms. According to Rowe, Aristotle is simultaneously committed both to the Platonic ideal of the virtuous city, as represented in the best constitution of VII–VIII, and to the view that political theory should, as Aristotle says, have something to contribute which is of immediate practical use.

In Essay 3, "The Connection Between Aristotle's *Ethics* and *Politics*," Arthur Adkins examines the relation of the *Nicomchean Ethics* to the *Politics*. He focuses on the famous "function." or *ergon*, argument of *Nicomachean Ethics* I.7, in which Aristotle arrives at his definition of happiness (*eudaimonia*) as activity in accordance with virtue (*aretê*) by considering the *ergon* of a human being (*anthrôpos*). After discussing the meanings of the key terms of this argument, especially the term *ergon*, for Aristotle's audience, Adkins examines the gap between the (unspecified) *aretê* of Aristotle's definition and the *aretai* catalogued in the remainder of the *Nicomachean Ethics*. These latter are basically the traditional civic virtues concerned with the defense and administration of the city and household that are possessed by a limited number of adult male Greeks. Thus Aristotle began by seeking the task and excellence of a human being (*anthrôpos*) but ended up discovering instead the task and excellence of a man (*anêr*). Adkins contends that the gap between these two different conceptions of *aretê* is bridged not by argument but by presuppositions and attitudes from the daily life of ancient Greece.

Politics I.1–2 is a sort of preface or introduction to the rest of the treatise, and I.2 contains a detailed defense of three basic theses of Aristotle's political naturalism: that man is by nature a political animal, that the polis exists by nature, and that the polis is prior by nature to the individual. Essay 4, "Man as a Political Animal in Aristotle," by Wolfgang Kullmann, is devoted to the first of these three theses. On the basis of an examination of all the

12 *Aristotle: Fundamentals of the History of his Development*, tr. R. Robinson, 2nd edn (Oxford, 1948), ch. 10.

occurrences of *zôon politikon* ("political animal") in the Aristotelian corpus, Kullmann concludes that it is Aristotle's view that *politikon* is not a specific differentia of man but a property man shares with certain gregarious animals; the political impulse of man is thus genetically ingrained. This does not mean, however, that Aristotle saw no difference between a polis and a colony of honeybees. The existence of a colony of honeybees is due entirely to biological factors; however, according to Aristotle, the existence of a polis is due to a specifically human factor – the conscious striving after gain and happiness – as well as a biological one. Kullmann also contends that within Aristotle's political philosophy the maxim that man is by nature a political animal is primary and the thesis that the polis exists by nature derivative from it. This derivative thesis, moreover, is not to be taken literally. It is not Aristotle's view, according to Kullmann, that a polis is an organic entity or a substance strictly speaking, though it is analogous to such an entity.

Essay 5, "Three Basic Theorems in Aristotle's *Politics*," by David Keyt, which focuses on the arguments Aristotle advances in *Politics* I.2 for his political naturalism, covers some of the same ground as Kullmann's essay, though Keyt's interpretation of the three basic theses diverges to some extent from Kullmann's. Although he agrees with Kullmann's interpretation of *zôon politikon*, he reverses the order of priority between the maxim that man is by nature a political animal and the naturalness of the polis. For Keyt, the former is a corollary of the latter rather than a first principle of Aristotle's political philosophy. Keyt also maintains, in opposition to Kullmann, that for Aristotle the polis is literally, not just analogically, a natural object. Keyt contends, however, that none of Aristotle's arguments for the naturalness of the polis is successful and that in fact Aristotle has good reasons to hold that it is an artificial rather than a natural object.

One reason the polis is natural, in Aristotle's view, is that it is composed of natural communities – most importantly, of households – the household, in turn, is natural because the relations within it are natural. One such relation is that of master and slave. In *Politics* I.4–7 and I.13, Aristotle argues that some individuals are slaves by nature and hence slaves justly. In Essay 6, "Aristotle's Theory of Natural Slavery," Nicholas D. Smith discusses the psychology that grounds Aristotle's theory. Smith contends that Aristotle's theory in fact combines two different psychological models. According to one, the slave is to the master as emotion is to reason: the slave can listen to and obey reason but not initiate a rational course of action. According to the other model, the slave is to the master as the body is to the soul, or as animals are to human beings. Having shown that every aspect of Aristotle's theory can be explained by the application of one or the other of these two models, Smith argues that the two models are incompatible and, as a result, that Aristotle's theory of natural slavery is incoherent.

In *Politics* I.8–11 Aristotle turns to an analysis of the science or art of acquisition, which provides the resources the household needs. This leads Aristotle to a discussion of various economic relations, including commerce. This discussion, along with that of reciprocal justice in *Nicomachean Ethics* V.5, has been of particular interest to economic historians although they have differed widely as to its significance. Some interpreters represent Aristotle's thought as a prototype of the sort of modern economic thinking that arose with market economies. Others reply that Aristotle's grasp of economic relations was too primitive for such an interpretation to be credible: he was engaged in ethical rather than economic analysis, and he was more concerned with defending archaic relationships such as slavery than with studying new ones such as commodity exchange. In Essay 7, "Aristotle and Exchange Value," Scott Meikle argues that Aristotle's discussion contains coherent but incomplete analyses of the commodity, economic value, and the development of exchange. Meikle defends Aristotle's analyses as philosophically deeper than those of Adam Smith and David Ricardo and claims that Marx derived his main criticism of classical political economy from them.

Book II of the *Politics* is devoted to a critical examination of various allegedly ideal constitutions, including those proposed by Plato and other theorists. Aristotle's discussion of Plato's *Republic* in *Politics* II.2–5 has been extensively criticized. Many of Aristotle's comments seem to have little relevance to the *Republic*, and some scholars have thought they show that the empirically-minded Aristotle was incapable of appreciating the thought of his more idealistic predecessor. In Essay 8, "Aristotle's Criticism of Plato's *Republic*," R. F. Stalley argues that we can make sense of Aristotle's comments by seeing them as a discussion of the idea of political community, loosely based on certain sections of the *Republic*, rather than as an attempt at detailed criticism of Plato's dialogue. The main reason Aristotle takes issue with Plato is not that he adopts a purely empirical approach, but rather that his conception of human good is fundamentally different from Plato's.

One point of contention between Plato and Aristotle is over the status of property in the ideal state. Aristotle contends that Plato's abolition of private property among the guardians of his ideal state is more likely to increase than to decrease social conflict and that the moral virtues of generosity and friendship, which are important components of the good life, require private property for their exercise (*Pol.* II.5). In Essay 9, "Aristotle's Defense of Private Property," T. H. Irwin examines this dispute. Irwin argues that although Aristotle's criticism of Plato's abolition of private property identifies some central faults or obscurities in Plato's account of the functions of the state, especially in his treatment of intrinsic goods, it rests on some controversial premises that Aristotle would be hard-pressed to defend without raising difficulties for some of his other political doctrines. Irwin concludes that whereas Aristotle may succeed in defending some sort of individual control over material resources, his defense of anything readily recognizable as private property is seriously defective.

The philosophical core of the *Politics* is Book III, which introduces Aristotle's theory of the constitution. Aristotle defines a constitution as the distinctive form or organization of a polis, which determines its end, or *telos*, and how its offices, especially the highest, are distributed among its citizens. In *Politics* III.7 Aristotle divides constitutions into two groups: those that are correct and those that are mistaken, or deviant. In Essay 10, "Aristotle on

Prior and Posterior, Correct and Mistaken Constitutions," William Fortenbaugh examines Aristotle's claim that correct constitutions are *prior* to mistaken ones. He rejects a temporal interpretation of this ordering and claims that the familiar comparisons of constitutions with numbers, figures, and psychic faculties are more misleading than helpful. He finds an anticipation of Aristotle's analysis in the fourth book of Plato's *Laws*, where correctness is connected with the common interest and constitutions that benefit the entire population are distinguished from those that do not. However, Aristotle does not follow Plato in withholding the label "constitution" from political arrangements that fail to consider the common good. Instead he respects everyday usage while making it clear that some constitutions are better than others. He assigns priority to constitutions directed toward the common good – namely, kingship, aristocracy, and polity – and he establishes an order among these by reference to the virtue of the ruler or rulers.

Since justice is what holds a community together, a constitution is a kind of justice. Accordingly, David Keyt in Essay 11, "Aristotle's Theory of Distributive Justice," claims that Aristotle's political philosophy is essentially a theory about the just distribution of political authority. The basic principle of this theory is introduced in *Nicomachean Ethics* V, but it is only in the *Politics* that the theory is fully developed and applied. In constructing his theory Aristotle was trying, according to Keyt, to avoid Protagorean relativism without invoking the transcendent standards of Platonic absolutism. Keyt also undertakes to show how Aristotle uses his theory of distributive justice to justify three seemingly incompatible constitutions: absolute kingship, true aristocracy, and democracy.

In *Nicomachean Ethics* V Aristotle indicates that the best constitution exemplifies natural justice. Nevertheless, some scholars deny that the doctrines of natural law and justice play any role in the *Politics*. In Essay 12, "Aristotle on Natural Law and Justice," Fred Miller contends that there is a close connection between Aristotle's political theory and his theory of natural law and justice. Miller begins by arguing that a coherent theory emerges from the discussions of *Rhetoric* I, *Magna Moralia* I.33, and *Nicomachean Ethics* V.7, and that this theory should be interpreted in the light of Aristotle's teleological biology. The claim that political justice is partly natural and partly legal is to be understood in terms of Aristotle's idea that the existence of the polis is due partly to nature and partly to human reason. Miller argues, finally, that Aristotle's account of the correct constitution and its laws in the *Politics* should, as *EN* V.7 suggests, be interpreted in terms of natural justice.

Books IV through VI of the *Politics* are often called "realistic" or "empirical" because they are concerned with the establishment, preservation, and reform of actually existing constitutions such as oligarchy and democracy, which fall short of "the constitution of our prayers." In Essay 13, "Aristotle's Analysis of Oligarchy and Democracy," Richard Mulgan argues that Aristotle's analysis of oligarchy and democracy is in fact heavily influenced (and sometimes distorted) by abstract and *a priori* considerations. Oligarchy and democracy form a pair of contrasting poles at opposite ends of a spectrum with polity as the middle or mean. Though oligarchy and democracy provide the elements that are mixed in polity, they are logically posterior to it, as inferior forms or deviations. Furthermore, the subtypes of oligarchy and democracy are ranged along a moderate/extreme continuum and bear little relation to actual historical extremes. Mulgan also argues that the abstract character of Aristotle's method leads him to misunderstand important features of democracy.

Given the prevalence of revolution and other forms of political change in the twentieth century, it is surprising that Aristotle's treatment of the subject in *Politics* V has received so little attention. In Essay 14, "Aristotle on Political Change," Ronald Polansky displays some of the interest and subtlety of Aristotle's thought. Polansky offers an account of this multi-faceted book that shows how it can be both scientific and yet practical. He begins by considering political change in relation to Aristotle's general account of change in the *Physics*, thereby clarifying Aristotle's terms and his view of Greek historical development. Aristotle's understanding of the future of the polis and the role of virtue in constitutions thus emerges. Next, Polansky outlines Aristotle's organization of the mass of material on the causes of change and means of preventing change. This reveals Aristotle's methods for developing exhaustive analyses. Finally, Polansky considers Aristotle's purpose in devoting so much attention to monarchy.

Aristotle's description of the best constitution in Books VII and VIII is the capstone of the *Politics*. In *Politics* VII.1–3 Aristotle maintains that the virtuous life is the best and happiest life for both individuals and states; and then considers whether this is a political or a contemplative life. In Essay 15, "Politics, Music, and Contemplation in Aristotle's Ideal State," David Depew argues that Aristotle in these opening chapters of Book VIII favors a conception of the happy life that ranks contemplative activity over political activity but includes both. Depew contends that this "inclusive ends" conception of the happy life fully informs Aristotle's concrete portrait of an ideal aristocracy in the remainder of Books VII–VIII. Although musical leisure activities are an important part of this city's way of life, Depew disagrees with those scholars who regard music as a surrogate for contemplation in Aristotle's ideal state. Instead, it facilitates the development of both practical wisdom and contemplative virtue (in those citizens capable of attaining it). But Depew sees a fundamental disagreement between Aristotle's ideal and Plato's. Because Aristotle does not make practical wisdom (the intellectual virtue exercised in politics) depend upon contemplation, he has no need for, and considerable distrust of, the rule of philosopher kings.

1

Aristotle's Conception of the State

A. C. BRADLEY

Aristotle's work on *Politics* has a twofold interest – historical and theoretical. If it does not add very materially to our knowledge of facts and events, it throws more light than any other writing, ancient or modern, on the constitutional forms and struggles of the Greek States. It is the result of the political experience of a people, reflected in the mind of one of its wisest men and reduced to theory. Aristotle wrote of life that was going on around him, and the freshness of personal knowledge enlivens his coldest analysis. Thus, in spite of the scientific character of his theory, it is national. He does not write as though Greek civilization were in his eyes something transitory, or a single stage in history. Though he had been tutor to Alexander, he seems unaware that the day of autonomous republics was passing, and that in the Macedonian monarchy a kind of government was arising hitherto unknown in the development of his race. On the other hand, the very fact that he stood on the confines of change gives him a peculiar advantage. His position is not midway in a political development, where the character of institutions and the meaning of movements is obscure. The strength and weakness of Greek society and of Greek civic virtue, the political structure which had protected that virtue and been upheld by it, the gradual decline of public spirit, the corruption of military aristocracy into an oligarchy of wealth at Sparta, of active free government into impotent ochlocracy at Athens, the war of classes which sprang from a social question and became a political one, – all this lay behind him. The prime of Greek life was nearly past when he wrote. What we miss in his work, what would have been of such great interest now, a description of military monarchy and of federal government, would not have touched the life which rises before our minds when we hear of Greek history. And what he *does* describe is fully developed, and therefore capable of adequate analysis.

But it is not merely our desire to understand the past which is satisfied by a treatise like the *Politics*. That which is true of the art and literature of the Greeks is only less true of their political creations. Their most intensely national products are at the same time "purely human." To apply to modern affairs conclusions drawn from Greek history is indeed hazardous, and such reasonings are often as futile theoretically as the imitations of Roman virtue in the French Revolution were practically hollow. The fate of Athenian democracy will not disclose to us the future of the American Republic, for the circumstances are radically different. But in spite of change there are permanent characteristics of social forces and of forms of government, of commerce and agriculture, wealth and poverty, true and false aristocracy, oligarchy and democracy. Not only this: among the subjects of which the *Politics* treats there is something even more permanent and universal, and that is the simple fact of political society. Let a State be the organization of a nation or a city, it is still a State; and what is true of its nature and objects in one case will, up to a certain point, be true of them in another and in every case. It is in the discovery of these truths and the investigation of such ideas as those of justice and right, that the primary business of philosophy in its application to politics consists; and Aristotle is before all things a philosopher. These facts and ideas are so familiar to us that we take little account of them; they seem to us self-evident, and we prefer to deal with more concrete difficulties. But to philosophers the self-evident ceases to be so, and their effort is to know what everybody seemed to know before. Thus Aristotle makes these preliminary problems the basis of all further discussion. It would have seemed absurd to him to attempt the settlement of complex problems, when the elementary conceptions on which they depend have been subjected to no analysis; to blame the State perhaps for overstepping its limits, when we do not know what the State is, and therfore cannot possibly tell what its limits are; or to assert a right to share in government when we can attach no intelligible meaning to the word "right." The fault of reasoning on insufficient data has never been charged on Aristotle's *Politics*; every one knows that he founded his theory on researches into more than a hundred and fifty Greek constitutions, and that he even made a collection of the social and political usages of foreign tribes. But he is equally free from other defects more easily forgiven: he does not use criteria the value of which he has never questioned, nor try to account for one set of human phenomena in total isolation from the theory of all the rest. To him political science is founded on ethics, and ethics on psychology; and all these rest upon metaphysic and its application to nature.

In the following pages I propose to give a sketch of the views which Aristotle held on a few of these preliminary questions. In the nature of things, these questions are less affected than any others by historical changes; and an attempt to show their vital meaning through the forms of Greek thought may have an interest, although it can offer nothing to professed students of antiquity. But the differences which exist between Greek political conditions and those of our own time, and between the ideas associated with each, are so marked that they appear even in the most abstract discussions; and there are some of such importance that, unless they are constantly kept in sight, it is impossible rightly to appreciate Aristotle's views, or to separate what is essential in them from what is merely temporary. In spite of their familiarity, therefore, it will be as well to begin by recalling some of these points of difference to mind, and examining Aristotle's position in regard to them.

First of all, the Greek State was a city, not a nation. If we think of an English county with a single city and its surrounding territory, and imagine it to be independent and sovereign, we shall have more idea of one of the largest Greek States than if we compare it with a modern nation. Political life was concentrated in the capital to such an extent that the same word stands for city and State. In such a community public affairs were as much matters of every day as the municipal politics of an English town, and yet they had all the dignity of national decisions. The citizen, in a State like Athens, took part in politics personally, not through a representative; not once in four or five years, but habitually. His convictions or his catchwords were won not through the dull medium of the press, but from the mouths of practiced orators. The statesmen of his time were familiar figures in his daily life. The opposite party to his own was not a vague collective name to him, but he rubbed shoulders with it in the streets. Thus political life was his occupation and acquired the intensity of a personal interest. The country and its welfare had a vivid meaning to him; he felt himself responsible for its action and directly involved in its good or evil fortune. Under these conditions, the rise and fall of a State visibly depended on the character of its citizens; its greatness was nothing but the outward sign of their energy and devotion; the failure of virtue in them acted immediately on it. Thus the bonds of reciprocal influence, which we can only believe in now, were palpable facts then; and the more direct danger of foreign attack or of civil war was seldom far distant. Hence the vital interest taken by the State in the character of its members and their education. Hence also an amount of governmental inspection and control of private affairs which, even if it suited modern ideas, would be scarcely possible in a nation. Such "interference with liberty" was then not felt to be an interference. In the best days of Greece, to participate in this rapid and ennobling public life was enough for the Greek citizen. If his country was independent and himself an active member of it, this community satisfied him too completely for him to think of "using his private house as a state" (III.9.1280b26)[1] or a castle. "To live as one likes," – this is the idea of liberty which Aristotle connects first with the most primitive barbarism (*EN* X.9.1180a24–9), and then with that degraded ochlocracy which marked the decay of the free governments of Greece (V.9.1310a32–4, VI.2.1317b11–12, 4.1319b30).

---

1 [Editors' note. In referring to the *Politics* and the *Nicomachean Ethics* Bradley does not use the system, which in his day was gradually becoming standard, of citing page, column, and line of Bekker's Berlin Academy edition of 1831. Furthermore, Bradley uses one system for the *Politics* and a different system for the *Nicomachean Ethics*. Under the former he cites only a single line whereas under the latter he cites an entire section. Since the systems he uses are no longer current, all of his references have been transposed to the now standard system of Bekker numbering. An attempt has also been made to determine and to mark the end as well as the beginning of the passages cited from the *Politics*. In making these changes several incorrect references were noticed and corrected. All references are to the *Politics* unless otherwise indicated.

There are two other editorial intrusions. The Greek words and phrases used or mentioned in the original essay have been transliterated, and the footnotes have been numbered consecutively from the beginning to the end of the paper.]

The effects of this one difference on a political theory are incalculable. And Aristotle not only adopts the Greek idea of the State, and consequently thinks of it as a city, but he has expressly raised the question of its proper size. The discussion of this point in the account of the ideal State (VII.4.1326a6– 5.1326b39) contains one or two chance remarks which throw a strong light on the Greek idea and its results. Aristotle mentions an opinion that the State or city should be large; and, while he admits that largeness is an advantage so long as it involves no diminution of that real energy of the State which makes it great and not simply big, he insists that this proviso sets definite limits to the increase of size or population. It is essential that the State should be "easily overseen" (*eusunoptos*, VII.4.1326b24). Just as a boat can no more be two furlongs long than a span long, so a State can no more have 100,000 citizens than ten (*EN* IX.10.1170b29–33). Such a number is possible for a mere tribe (*ethnos*), but not for a political community. And why not? The answer is in the highest degree characteristic. The State implies government; and the function of the governor is to issue orders and to judge. "But if just legal decisions are to be given, and if office is to be apportioned to men according to merit, it is necessary for the citizens to have a knowledge of each other's characters, since, where this is not the case, things must needs go wrong with the appointment of officials and the administration of the law; but it is not right to act off-hand in either of these matters, and that is plainly what happens where the population is over-large." In such a case, again, it is impossible to prevent strangers from quietly obtaining the rights of citizens. And finally, who could be the one general of such a multitude, and who, unless he had the voice of Stentor, their one herald?[2]

A second fundamental distinction is to be found in the social organization of the Greek State. The political life of Sparta or Athens rested on the basis of Slavery. The citizen-body might trace its descent to a conquering race which had reduced the original possessors of the country to a position of more or less complete subjection, and lived upon their agricultural labour, as in the one case; or the slaves might be procured through war and a slave-trade, as in the other. But in both instances the bulk of the necessary work was performed by an unfree population, far outnumbering the select aristocracy of free citizens. This institution and the contempt even for free labour are the most striking proofs that the Hellenic solution of social problems was inadequate; modern writers find in them the "dark side" of Greek life, or even the "blot upon their civilization." But the latter expression at least is misleading, since it implies that such defects had no organic connection with the strength and beauty of this civilization; whereas, in fact, the life of "leisure," devoted to politics and culture or to war, would have been impossible without them, and general conclusions drawn from Greek history which do not take them into account are inevitably vitiated.

On this point Aristotle shares the view common to his countrymen. He recommends that slaves should be kindly treated, and that good conduct on

2 VII.4.1326a35–b22. In III.3.1276a27–9 the size of Babylon is said to fit it for an *ethnos* rather than a polis; compare II.6.1265a13–17.

their part should be rewarded by their liberation. He does not admit that the slavery of men born to be free is justifiable, since, in his view, it is a violation of nature. But he definitely holds that there are men (apparently as a rule "barbarians") whose right and natural destination is servitude; and he adopts the institution in his ideal state. Into his analysis of slavery and his partial justification of it it is unnecessary to enter. Its chief interest is that he attempts to put the question on a moral ground, and therefore in his attempt to defend a bad cause falls into contradictions. He does not base slavery on political utility, nor fortunately has he Biblical arguments at hand which he can call religious. Its morality – and that to him was the deciding question – depends on the fact that some men are destitute of reason in the highest sense of the word; "those men who differ from others as widely as the body does from the soul, or a beast from a man (and men stand in such a relation when the use of their bodies is their function and the best thing that can be got out of them), are by nature slaves" (I.5.1254b16–19); and for them servitude is not merely a painful necessity, but their good. The problem is, then, to find men whose nature is of this kind, and who at the same time are capable of obeying and even anticipating orders (I.4.1253b33–9), of receiving rational instruction (I.13.1260b5–7), and of standing in the relation of friendship to their masters (*EN* VIII.11.1161b5–8). And this is a contradiction which cannot exist. The weakness of the position is brought out in the words which Aristotle adds to his assertion that friendship is possible between master and slave – "not as a slave, but as a man." In other words, to treat a man as a slave is to treat him as though he were not a man.

Another distinction which calls for some remark concerns religion. It would be superfluous to compare the doctrine and spirit of Christianity and Greek religion: superfluous, and perhaps misleading. For the vital differences which really exist between them are liable to be exaggerated by a statement of opposing principles, especially when it is assumed that the "ideal" morality which we describe as Christian is that by which modern Christians, for the most part, really live. But though the actual religious motives and practice of Greeks and Englishmen may be nearer to one another than we are apt to suppose, in the position of religion in the community there is a striking dissimilarity. Greek religion knew no recognized orthodox doctrine and no recognized expositor of that doctrine. A Greek had no church. Consequently one of the most fruitful sources of conflict in modern nations had no existence in Hellas. There is nothing in Greek history even analogous to the struggles of Church and Empire and Church and State, to the religious wars of Germany and France, or even to the semi-theological Great Rebellion, and in Aristotle's list of the causes of *stasis* or civil discord religion is hardly mentioned. A second consequence is this, that the Greek knew little, either for good or evil, of the modern idea that the State is "profane." His religious feelings attached themselves to it. It was not merely the guardian of his property, but the source of right and goodness to him, the director of his worship and guarded by the gods he worshipped. He might not insult its gods, although within certain limits he was left to think and speak of them as he thought right. In the absence of a powerful priesthood, the natural development of the religious ideas of the people was unhampered and could pass easily into corresponding action; a vote of the Legislature might adopt a new deity into the number of those already recognized. Thus, but for the occasional influence of the Delphic oracle, we may say that to the Greek citizen his State was the moral and religious law in one.

It is easy for us to realize the defects of such a relation and the want of truth in the religious ideas connected with it. But it had also a greatness of its own; and this we do not feel so readily. It fostered the social and political virtue of the citizen; and in his devotion to his State, his perception of its greatness and dignity, and the fusion of his reverence for it with that which he felt for his gods, he possessed a spiritual good which the modern world has known only in the scantiest measure, and that only since the Reformation. It is this spirit which breathes through the *Politics*, the spirit which is willing to be guided by the highest authority it knows; which emphasizes its duties to the community, and has not even a word to signify its "rights" against it; which describes the possession of property and the begetting of children not as the private affair of individuals but as services to the State;[3] and which finds in the law, not a restraint but the supremacy of the divine element in human nature, "reason without desire." For the rest, there is nothing specially noticeable in Aristotle's remarks on the religious services of his ideal city. He seems to place this social function first in importance (VII. 8.1328b12–13). It is provided for from the proceeds of the state-lands (VII.10.1330a8–13), and performed by the oldest citizens, who are freed from the duties of war and public life (VII.9.1329a27–34). It cannot be said that Aristotle attributes to religion anything like the importance it has for us. It is characteristic of him that though he certainly did not believe the popular mythology, uses the plainest language respecting it, and even thought that some of it had been deliberately invented by rulers for political ends,[4] he proposes no kind of change in the public worship and contents himself with trying to guard against the moral dangers connected with the celebrations of some deities (VII.17.1336b14–23). What he would have thought of the use of this mythology in education we can do no more than guess, for the book which treats of that subject breaks off long before it can be supposed to be complete. But that his attitude was not due to moral indifference is quite certain. He probably considered the common people incapable of any such exalted monotheism as his own, and thought that their own creed had the sanctity for them that in all cases belongs to the highest form in which the truth is attainable.

It will be already apparent, lastly, that if Aristotle's views represent Greek opinion, we must not expect to find in him our own ideas of the individual. Roman law, with its presumption that every one is a person and capable of being the subject of rights; Christianity, which asserts an identification of the

---

3 *leitourgein têi polei*, VII.16.1335b28, IV.4.1291a33–4. So also of government, IV.4.1291a34–6.
4 *Met.* XII.8.1074a38.

human and divine spirit capable of becoming actual in the soul of the believer, and giving his existence an absolute value; the more popular caricature of this doctrine, which places the end of this individual soul in the attainment of perpetual private pleasure; the romantic preference of personal honour and loyalty to public spirit, and of purity and humility to the social virtues; the principles of the French Revolution and of English liberalism, – all this lies between us and Aristotle. It is natural to us to base our political theories in individual liberty and rights. We look upon man as having a nature of his own and objects of his own, independently of society. We look upon the State as a contrivance for securing to him the enjoyment of his liberty and the opportunity of pursuing his ends, a contrivance which involves some limitation of his rights and ought to involve as little as possible. Even when reflection has shown us that there is something theoretically wrong with these ideas, we remain convinced that a happiness or a morality which is imposed on us from without loses half its value, and that there are spheres of our life and parts of our inward experience into which no one ought to intrude. And if we feel strongly our unity with others, and are willing to admit that social and political institutions have a positive object and not the merely negative one of protection, we emphasize the fact that the character or happiness they are to promote are those of individuals, and are often in danger of falsifying our position by regarding the community and its institutions as something separable from this individual welfare, and a mere means to it. When we read Plato or Aristotle everything seems to be changed. The State is regarded not as a contrivance for making possible the objects of individuals, but as a sun on which the lesser bodies of its system are absolutely dependent, or rather as this system itself. It does not limit private existence; private existence derives its being, its welfare, and its rights from it. The community and even its institutions seem to be regarded as an end in which personal happiness has no necessary place, and to which the existence of any number of individuals is a mere means. We soon discover that the Greek philosophers held no such absurdity as this, that they regarded personal welfare in the highest sense as the sole object of the State, and that they were in far less danger than ourselves of seeking it in conquest or in wealth. But after this has been taken into account, and after we have realized that the modern citizen's patriotism and reverence for law seem to answer more to Greek ideas than to our own theories, there remains a decided difference both in fact and in feeling, a difference which appears again and again in political questions.

For a century or more before the *Politics* was written, the traditional Greek view had been called in question, and ideas had been opposed to it which strike us at once by their modern air. What is the State? Is it something inevitably produced in the development of human nature, or an invention? Is it a whole, the source of all freedom and morality to its members, or a contrivance of individuals, deriving its authority simply from their agreement and from enactment? Is its object something common and equivalent to the end of human life, or is it a mere means to the attainment of the private objects of the individuals who combined to form it? In some such way we may make explicit the questions which decide the character of Aristotle's theory. And they may be summed up in the single inquiry, started by the Sophists, – Is the State natural or conventional?[5] If, with some of them, we hold that it is the latter, that it rests upon custom and enactment, the result seems at first sight to be that the reverence and devotion which it claims from the citizen are misplaced, and that its identification with the moral law is absurd. Yet it is clearly dependent on man's will and intelligence, and neither fixed nor natural as the stars are. If then it is still to be regarded as an absolute moral power, and not the product of fear or force, we must find some way of reconciling this absoluteness with a recognition of the action of man's will in law or custom. Thus we shall find that Aristotle's position towards the question practically amounts to a denial of the antithesis between *phusis* and *nomos*, and an assertion that the State is at once due to man's will and the necessary or "natural" expression of his progress. This result Aristotle reaches not by a refutation of opposing theories, but by his own analysis and interpretation of facts. And the first question, on which all others depend, is: What does the fact of political community mean? What is the State?[6]

"Since all communities or associations are formed for the sake of some good, this must be especially true of that community which is the highest and includes all the rest, and it will clearly have for its object the highest and

---

5 *Phusei* or *nomôi*. It is impossible to render *nomos* by a single word, as it means both enactment and custom. The *Gorgias* and the first two books of the *Republic* contain full illustrations of the Sophistic views referred to.

6 We use the word State in at least two different senses, and to prevent misapprehension it may be as well to define shortly the meaning attached to it in these pages. By State we seem to mean (1) such a community as possesses not only a social but also a political organization, or, in the widest sense, a government. As a State the body politic is not merely a collection of individuals or classes, but is itself an individual or person; as is especially evident in its relations with other States, and in the existence of a monarch or president. In the case of modern States, most of which are already founded upon nationality, the word "nation" expresses this idea; and language which may seem overstrained when applied to the State sounds more natural if we substitute "nation." That word, however, is inappropriate to Greek politics; and even if it were not it does not express clearly the fact that society has a political organization: it is sometimes true to say "the nation does or wills" this or that, when it would not be true to say this of the State. It is in this first sense that I commonly use the expression State. But (2) as this expression lays stress on the organization of the community in *government*, we come to use it as equivalent to government. Thus a single function of the State gets the name of the whole, and acquires a false isolation. Accordingly when language used of the state is understood to apply to the government, it becomes absurd, unless indeed the government is regarded as representing the State and, for the time being, equivalent to it. In such discussions as those on the end of the State, then, it is important to bear in mind that the State is distinct, on the one hand, from *government*, since it is the unity of which government is a single function, and that it is distinct, on the other hand, from *society*, because it is this unity as it expresses itself in political organization and, through the fact of this organization, acts as a person.

most commanding good. This community is the State." With some such words the treatise opens. Their simplicity conceals the extent to which they define Aristotle's position, yet when they are admitted some of the most vexed questions are settled beforehand. In accordance with his fundamental idea that everything is defined by the end it is destined to attain, they lay it down that there is a definite object for which the State exists; that this object is not something accidental, suggested by the chance desires of individuals; and that it is not the merely relative end of making possible the attainment of other ends; but that the State is the highest of human associations, and, instead of being one among others, includes in itself all other associations; and that, as the good at which it aims includes the subordinate objects of desire arrived at by the subordinate communities, this good is nothing short of the final object of human life, the end which alone gives value to all lesser ends and has no end beyond it.

Whatever this chief good which makes life worth living may be, it is the end of *man* and not of an abstraction such as the State is sometimes thought to be. In other words, it is the end of the citizens who compose the community; for the good of the State and that of the individual are, according to Aristotle, precisely the same, although, when we regard this good in the first way, it has a greater perfection and grandeur (*EN* I.2.1094b7–10; compare *Pol*. VII.1.1323a14–2.1324a23). But many men pursue a false end; they give their lives to objects unworthy of a man, such as mere pleasure, or to objects like wealth, which, though they are really desirable, are so only as means to a good beyond them. In the same way there are States which pursue unworthy aims, and Aristotle finds opinions prevalent which either tacitly or openly assign to the State ends which are really beneath it. His opposition to these views brings out his own more distinctly.

There are, for example, certain oligarchic and democratic arguments which assume that the possession of wealth and free birth, respectively, forms such a contribution to the purposes of the State as ought in justice to be rewarded by political privileges. But these arguments, as Aristotle points out, really presuppose that the end of the State is wealth or free birth, positions which he cannot for a moment admit. Not that these elements of life are without importance for the political community; they may even be means necessary to its welfare, but they do not on that account constitute its essence or end. The same is true of other necessary conditions. The State is not a defensive alliance, concluded by individuals who wish to pursue their various objects in security from hostile attacks. Nor is it a device they have adopted for facilitating trade with one another, and insuring themselves against force or fraud. If it were, its object would be (to borrow modern language) merely the protection of person and property; "the law," in Aristotle's own language, "would be a contract and, as Lycophron the Sophist says, a pledge of lawful dealing between man and man;" and two different nations which had formed a defensive alliance, and whose citizens, when their trading led to disputes, could sue and be sued in the courts of either State alike, would only be considered separate States because their territories happened to be distinct. But even if this difficulty were overcome, and to communion in all these points were added the right of legal intermarriage and the existence of societies for holding common festivals and joining in common amusements, the resulting association would still fall short of being "political." "All this must be there if there is to be a State; but even if all this is there, there is not yet a State." For the members of the society would not only lack the single government which is essential to a State, but they would not necessarily have any share in that which alone gives a value to these subordinate bonds of union, the final end of human life (III.9.1280a22–1281a8).

What, then, is this final end or chief good, the pursuit of which and a common share in which is the essence of the State? What additional bond would make this imaginary society political? Aristotle has answered this question in the concrete in the passage before us. This society is a community in mere "living;" and a State is a community in "good living." These associates do not trouble themselves about each other's moral character or wellbeing; and the State aims at nothing short of that. The law to them is a mere contract, protecting their persons and property; but the real law, the law of the State, aims at making the citizens good and just men. "Good living" (I.2.1252b30, III.9.1280a31–2), "noble actions" (III.9.1281a2), a "perfect and self-sufficing life,"[7] "well-being" or happiness, – these are all various names for the chief good of man. The full discussion of it is the subject of the *Ethics*; and we have to do with it here only so far as is necessary to bring out the positive character of the end at which the State is said to aim. It is the full and harmonious development of human nature in the citizen, or, in other words, the unimpeded activity of his moral and intellectual "excellence" or virtue. In the freedom of this activity from hindrances is implied a certain amount of "prosperity" or of "external goods." But the goods of fortune are not goods at all except to the man who can use them aright, and therefore the essence of his wellbeing lies in the activity itself, or in his character, not in what he has, but in what he is. The virtues or excellences in which his true nature is developed are naturally manifold; but in Aristotle's view they fall into two main groups. The soul feels and desires; it thinks and it rules its emotions. In so far as its desires are moulded by reason into harmonious and controlled activities, the soul attains the "moral" virtues in the narrower sense of the word; in the employment of reason itself it reaches what Aristotle calls the intellectual virtues. In both it feels that pleasure which accompanies the free exercise of a function. That all these functions are equally ends in themselves, Aristotle, of course, no more believes than any one else; there is a higher and lower in them, and a greater

---

7 III.9.1280b34–5. *zôês teleias kai autarkous.* One idea connected with the latter word is that of completeness. The chief good must lie in a life which leaves no want of man unsatisfied, whether these wants be external or spiritual, a life in which man's self (*autos*) is fully realised, and which therefore attains his final end (*telos*). "Self-sufficiency" has already a meaning of its own in English, and in many ways "freedom" seems to answer best to *autarkeia*: freedom not in a merely negative sense, but in that in which it is said that the truth makes men free; or, as by Carlyle, that the object of all religion is to make man free; or, as by Hegel, that the idea of mind and the end of history is freedom.

and less desirability in men's lives, according as they develop one kind of excellence or another. It is when the care and the necessary incompleteness of the active citizen life are laid aside, and a man attains to speculative insight into the reason of the world, that the divine element in him approaches nearest to its source, and he touches that highest blessedness which all great philosophers, as well as religious men, have found in union with God. That a whole life of such activity and joy is more than human, and that it can be known only in moments, is no reason for falling back on Philistinism. "We ought not to listen to those who tell us that since we are men, our thoughts should be those of men, and since we are mortal they should be mortal; but, so far as in us lies, we ought to rid ourselves of our mortality and do all we can to live in accord with that which is noblest in us; for though in bulk it be a little thing, in power and preciousness it far surpasses all things" (*EN* X.7.1177b31–1178a2). A life of such happy moral excellence and active "contemplation" is what Aristotle calls "good living." To attain and further this is the end of the State. This itself, community in this, *is* the State.

An inseparable connection of this kind between political society and man's chief good leaves only one possible answer to the question, Is the State natural or conventional? It is man's destination, that in which and through which his end is realized. It is therefore "natural" in Aristotle's use of the word, at least in so far as man is concerned; and if man's end is also an end in the system of the world, the State will be natural in a still further sense. The meaning of these ideas will be clearer if we first consider the steps by which man reaches the stage of political society, and thereby advances towards the goal of his progress. Aristotle's account of the origin of the State (I.2.1252a24–b30) sounds very meagre at the present time; but, besides its historical interest, it contains a further refutation of the view that the relations which connect men with each other are accidental bonds of their own contriving. It destroys beforehand the various theories which found society on an explicit or implicit agreement.

The beginnings of the State, the final community, are to be sought in the most primitive forms of association. These are the unions, Aristotle tells us, of those "who cannot exist without one another;" man and woman, master and slave. Man and woman come together not from any rational resolve, but because in them, as in the other animals and in plants, there is a natural desire to reproduce themselves. Master and slave are united by the desire for security; the master being one whose superior intelligence enables him to foresee the future and fits him for rule, whereas the slave is naturally adapted for simple obedience, because he is only capable of carrying out the orders given him. Thus, we may say, he is a body of which his master is the soul; and owing to the natural division of functions the relation of slavery is for the interest of both parties.[8] It is of these two associations that the household or

---

8 Later on (III.6.1278b33–8), though it is reiterated that "in reality the interests of the natural master and slave are identical," we are told that the master seeks properly his own good, and only accidentally that of the slave.

family consists; and Hesiod's verse, "first of all a house and a wife and an ox to plough" is true, since to the poor man the ox stands in stead of a servant. Thus the origin of the State is to be looked for in the Family. But there is an intermediate step between them – the stage of the *village*. The village consists of several families. Whether it is formed by the aggregation of independent households or by the expansion of a single one, Aristotle does not tell us; but the latter view seems to be favoured by the words, "it seems most naturally to be an offshoot or colony (*apoikia*) of the family (*oikia*), and its members, being the sons and sons' sons [of the family], are called men of the same milk (*homogalaktes*)." In these first beginnings Aristotle finds the explanation of two interesting facts. They show us why the earliest form of political government, like the government of tribes not yet political, is monarchical; for the village from which the State springs is governed by its oldest member. And this explains why the same form of government is attributed to the gods; "for men imagine in their own likeness not only the shapes, but also the mode of life of the gods." Beyond this scanty notice, we have hardly any reference to the village in Aristotle's work. We do not know whether he connected it as a stage in the growth of society with the formation of the *genos* or clan, though the passage quoted above seems to make this probable; and there is a further one in which he speaks of the State first as "a community of families and clans," and immediately afterwards as a "community of clans and villages" (III.9.1280b34, 40). However this may be, and in whatever way he may have imagined the transition from village to city, he mentions no further stage between them. With the union of several villages we have the State.

Thus the individuals who become citizens of a State had already been members in two previous forms of community, each of which involved a definite organization, and, what is more, a relation of government. And in the same way the son of a citizen has his individuality circumscribed or developed by his position not only in the city, but also in these subordinate spheres, which both preceded the State and continue to exist in it.[9] But this is not all. If we look closer, we shall see a deeper connection between the various stages. Each is a preparation for the next; each is produced by the effort of human nature to realize itself; it is because of the failure of each to satisfy this desire fully that a new form is created. And this process cannot cease until that kind of association is reached which gives man the attainment of his true end. Thus the two relations which compose the family are due to the necessity of mere existence; they are formed by those who simply cannot do without each other; and it is obvious that neither propagation nor mere preservation, which are their ends, is any complete realization of human nature. Again, the end for which the family exists is

9 It should be noticed, accordingly, that what is said of the family, as a community *preceding* the State, is not intended to be a satisfactory account of it as a *part* of the State. When the State has come into being, its nature and object must affect its constituent elements; and therefore Aristotle postpones the full discussion of the family until he has examined the political whole with reference to which its relations and education must be arranged (I.13.1260b8ff.).

defined as the satisfaction of daily wants. With the village a further advance is made; the needs which it aims at providing for are more than those of the day. But it is only in the State that the "limit of perfect self-sufficiency" is attained.[10] And if in this passage the imperfection of the lower stages is placed mainly in their failure to reach *autarkeia*, and we are inclined to regard this *autarkeia* as equivalent merely to a complete satisfaction of merely external wants, Aristotle makes his meaning clear by at once adding – "and though the State comes into existence for the sake of mere life, it exists for the sake of good life." For man's end is not reached until his "wellbeing" or "good life" is reached; and it is this which drives him on from stage to stage, and is both the aim and the cause of the whole process of his development.

This process, therefore, and most of all its completion, the State, is *natural*. To say that the State secures or is the end of man is with Aristotle not a *proof* that it is natural: it is simply equivalent to describing it as his nature. For the realization of the nature of anything is its end: that which a thing is when its process of growth is complete, is its nature (I.2.1252b32–4). It is this that defines a thing, or is its formal cause or essence. It is this also that causes its existence, developing it from a merely potential condition to its full actuality. Thus if Aristotle's is a doctrine of final causes, it is not so in the ordinary sense. The final cause is not one imposed on the object from without, an end to which the object is a mere means; it consists in the completed nature of the object itself. In so far as the given thing is "actual," it is equivalent to its final cause; in so far as it is only partially realized, its final cause or end is immanent in it and moves it to its perfection. Thus the final cause of man is realized when his "nature," in the sense of his mere potentiality, is developed into his "nature," in the sense of his end or good. His final cause is to be himself. As a child he is only potentially what he should be or is destined to be; and therefore he grows. And so, as a master, a husband, a father, a member of a village, his possibilities are still in various degrees latent, only partially brought into life. It is only in the State that they come into full play, and therefore the State is "natural" to him.

And this, which is the law of man's being, is the law of the whole world. Throughout the universe this process of the realization of ends is going on; and, what is more, these ends or "natures" are not all of equal value, but form a series of grades of excellence. Thus a lower stage of existence is not merely "for its own sake," but it is also a step to the next highest; and in this sense it is "for the sake of" another, and a means to it. Thus, we may say, to Aristotle all nature is a striving towards its highest form, and what we have seen in the development of man is true on this wider field. One principle, in its impulse to realize itself, produces those lower forms which are the necessary foundation for the higher, and passes beyond them to a less inadequate development, approaching more and more nearly to the divine

10 In *EN* VIII.9.1160a14–30 the State is distinguished from other communities by its aiming at good "for the *whole* of life," which makes the series of the *Politics* complete.

actuality in which no imperfection remains. That man attains only for moments to some likeness of this divine perfection we have already seen; but that he does so even for moments, and for a longer time can produce those activities of the moral life which are the victory of the divine element in him over his lower nature, is enough to place him at the head of earthly things. In him not as a vegetable nor as an animal, but in so far as his true nature, his better self, is active – the highest existence of which the earth is capable is brought into being. In this sense the whole inorganic, vegetable, and animal kingdoms may be said to exist for his sake. And in this final and highest sense the State is natural, and man by nature a "political animal."

Such, in the barest outline, is Aristotle's answer to the Sophistic question. In substance it might almost be expressed by that startling formula of a modern philosopher, that the object of history is the State. This is not the place to criticize it, but, in common with most other metaphysical theories of politics, it is easily misapprehended. Such theories are often accused of annihilating man's will before a spiritual fatality. It is true that Aristotle's ideas lose all their meaing if we suppose that human action is perfectly capricious, or that it is destitute of an "end," or that this end stands in no relation to the order of things. But they are not inconsistent with any sober notion of freedom. When Aristotle said that the State was by nature, he was not denying that it is due to human thoughts and resolutions, any more than Mr Carlyle, when he speaks of an improvement in human affairs as an approach to obeying Nature, means that man would be perfect if he were law-abiding like a stone. To hold that there is within certain limits of deviation a fixed development of human nature – and is not so much as this implied in our calling one change a development or progress, and another the opposite? – is not to hold that this development takes place in as involuntary a manner as does a flower's. And it is those very actions which most further this definite progress that are most free; since that which acts in them is in the fullest sense ourself, and not a distorted fraction of it. But just because they are not assertions of our separate existence, we are apt to speak of such actions as *least* our own. The same apparent contradiction meets us elsewhere. In the creations of art, or in the experience of religion, that which is the most perfect realization of man's higher self abolishes this separate feeling; and so it is with moral action and its concrete products. Thus when we wish to express the freedom of such creations or experiences from our lower selves, or to contrast their absoluteness with the results of our shifting desires, we are apt to use language which takes no notice of the share our will has had in them. It is not the poet who creates, but an inspiration of which he is the mere vehicle; it is not I who act but Christ that dwelleth in me; and the State or justice are due to nature and not to enactment. When language of this kind is used, there is a temptation to fall under its influence, and to separate what we know to be really identical. It is such a separation that is expressed in the antithesis of *phusis* and *nomos*, or in the modern opposition of moral necessity to free-will. But the Greek rose superior to that antithesis; though he might be puzzled when it was put clearly before him, he felt no incompatibility between the origin of the law of his State in the human will and its absolute validity. And Aristotle is only giving a theoretical justification of the position which he could not justify for himself.[11]

It is perhaps hardly necessary to notice another possible misconception. If Aristotle is not abolishing man's will before the moral order of the world, still less does he mean by the "nature" which produces the State what we mean when we contrast the natural and the spiritual. It is true that he not unfrequently uses "nature" in this lower sense, as in the *Ethics*, where he is showing that virtue does not come by nature but through a discipline of the will (*EN* II.1). In this sense those elements of man's being which he shares with the other animals are more natural than his reason and rational desires. In this sense, again, man is by nature "rather a pairing animal than a political one" (*EN* VIII.12.1162a17–18). And the double use of the word may be charged with some of Aristotle's prejudices in questions of political economy. But in the doctrine before us nature has exactly the opposite meaning, and that which is most natural in the lower sense is furthest removed from that nature which is man's end. On the other hand, there is an essential connection between the two; and that connection is teleological. To Aristotle the higher is not so much the result of the lower, as the lower is a preparation and material for the higher. It would be misleading, on his view, to say that man produced the State because he wished to satisfy certain primary needs; those primary needs and instincts are the stirring in him of that immanent end or idea which is expressed in the State. "The impulse to political society exists by nature in all men" (I.2.1253a29–30); but the Aristotelian view is not that man invents the State to satisfy the impulse; he has the impulse because his destination is the State. Thus when it is said that Aristotle's is the first "scientific" view of politics, this assertion may be either true or false. If it means that he considered the laws and productions of human nature to be identical with those of physical nature, it possesses no foundation. It was not in that sense he asserted the unity of the world, for he never held the strange belief that we are to form an idea of nature in abstraction from her highest product, and then to expect no difference between that highest stage and this truncated "nature." If those who propose to treat the State exactly like the objects of physical science are to find an ally in Aristotle, they must adopt the unity of nature in *his* sense; they must admit not merely that man and his works are the *result* of her lower stages, but that the lower stages are (not in a metaphor, but really) the "potency" of man, and that the evolution is determined by its end. When this is admitted, it will be found that Aristotle is by no means averse to recognizing the forms of laws common to man and the lower stages of existence, and that he has little sympathy with that idea of a total breach between the two, in the maintenance of which our spiritual interests have often been supposed to be involved.

Putting metaphysical questions aside, we have now to ask, What is Aristotle's *ground* for regarding the State as man's destination and good?

11 On the conception of Law compare K. F. Hermann, *Ueber Gesetz Gesetzgebung und gestzgebende Gewalt im griechischen Alterthume*.

"Man is by nature a political animal," he tells us; "and he who, owing to his nature and not to ill fortune, has no State, is either morally bad or something more than a man" (I.2.1253a2–4). And again: "He who cannot form one of a community, or who does not need to do so because he is already sufficient to himself, is no part of a State, and is therefore either a brute beast or a god" (1253a27–9). Here we have two characteristics of the State noticed, both of which we have met before; it alone can supply *autarkeia*, and in it alone is morality possible. The reason why it is necessary for morality lies in the imperfection of man, and in the fact that the State has might. "As man in his perfection is the best of animals, so when he is separated from law and justice he is the worst of all," the "unholiest, the most savage, and the most abandoned to gluttony and lust. And justice belongs to political society" (1253a31–7). At the end of the *Ethics*, again, Aristotle has explained how the State is directly involved in the attainment of morality. There are three ways, he tells us, in which men attain virtue. One of these, our natural endowment, is out of our power. Another, intellectual teaching, has little or no effect except on young men of a generous temper, or those who have been schooled in experience. For those who live by their feelings, obeying the dictates of pleasure and pain, it is useless. It is only by the third means, by habituation, that the impulses which lead away from virtue can be trained, and that men can by degrees acquire that love of the good and hatred of the bad without which mere instruction avails little. For the purpose of this habituation, especially if, as is necessary, it is to be exercised throughout the whole of life, we need an authority which must unite two requisites. It must itself be an expression of reason; and it must have the fullest powers to compel and punish. And this union of right and might Aristotle finds only in the State. But it is not only by its direct action, by its compulsory education and its moral guardianship, that the State contributes to "good living." If we examine those virtues in the exercise of which this good living consists, we shall find that they all imply social relations or life in community, and one of the most important, that practical wisdom the possession of which implies the presence of the rest (*EN* VI.13.1144b30–1145a2), has its sphere not only in private life, but also in the ordering of State-affairs: and the *Politics* adds that the virtue of the best man, the perfect virtue, is equivalent to the virtue of the ruler (VII.14.1333a11–12). Thus we find that the individual who realizes his chief good or happiness is necessarily a citizen. And the strongest expression which Aristotle has given to this view is to be found in his statement that the individual is *posterior* to the State, and a part of it.

To say that the State is prior to the individual means primarily no more than that his end is realized in it. By "prior" Aristotle often means not anterior in time, but prior in idea or, as he sometimes says, in nature. Thus in idea or in nature the end is prior to the means, and the actuality to the potentiality. But in the order of time, or again relatively to our knowledge, the means may, and often do, precede the end, and the potential existence is prior to the actual. In one sense of the word, then, the family may be said to be earlier than the State, and in another sense the opposite is true; and in this latter meaning Aristotle might say that the individual is "later" than political society. In the present case, however, this dictum has a further meaning. The State is said to precede the individual not merely as the actual precedes the potential, but as a whole precedes its parts. The part is itself only in relation to the whole, has no existence outside it, and is intelligible only in reference to it. It is therefore said to be posterior to it; for, to take the instance of a living body, "if the whole is destroyed, there will no longer be a foot or a hand, except in name, and as one may call a stone foot a foot; for everything is defined by its function" (I.2.1253a20–23), and with the dissolution of the body the functions of its members have disappeared. Such is the relation of the individual to the State.

Language like this at once recalls the current phrase, "the body politic," and the theories which have attempted to make it more than a phrase. Aristotle has nowhere called the State an organism, and doubtless he did not explicitly connect that idea with it. But, apart from the present passage, there is a close connection between this idea and his view that political society is natural, and he not unfrequently employs in his consideration of it criteria gained from the study of living beings. The use of such criteria no doubt requires caution, and we are sometimes told that the conception of an organism belongs only to the physical world and becomes a mere metaphor when applied to human society. But most of the ideas we use in describing spiritual things are derived from the world outside us, and it is not clear that the categories "thing," "collection," "mechanism," and the like, are any less metaphorically used of a State than the category of life. On the other hand, reasons are not wanting for the view that the latter idea is at least less inadequate than the others; and, if this is the case, what we have to do is only to distinguish in what respects the conception of an organism must differ when it is applied to the animal body and to the political body. It may be interesting, considering the present prominence of this conception in English philosophy, to notice some passages in which Aristotle seems implicitly to regard the State as an organism, and then to ask whether his doctrine recognizes those characteristics in which it differs from living things.

That the State, in the sense of the political community, is a totality or composition (*sunthesis*), admits of no question. Its unity is formed of a multiplicity of parts; it is a number of citizens (III.1.1274b39–41). But there is more than one kind of composition. For example, a heap of cannon-balls is a whole made up of parts. But here the whole is made up by the mere addition of unit to unit: it is a collection. In such a totality the part does not get its existence or character from its relation to the other parts and to the whole; it is the same thing in the pile that it was out of it, and has merely had a relation added to it. If the State were a collection of individuals of this kind it would be absurd to say of it that it was prior to its parts; it would be absurd to compare one of these parts with the hand or foot, which have no existence or function apart from the body to which they belong. A composite body of which this can be said is not formed by the addition of units, and not even the category of whole and parts is in strictness applicable to it. Its "parts" are members; it is a unity which expresses itself in diverse members, functions and organs, and the connection between these members is not mechanical but organic. Apart from the decisive language already quoted, Aristotle insists in more than one place on the diversity of the parts of the State. He is especially emphatic on this head, because he considers that Plato had neglected it and, in his desire to attain a complete unity of the whole body, had disregarded the necessary "differentiation" of its parts. He had wished to see the principle of the whole clearly realized in every member, and, in Aristotle's view, had failed to perceive that this result cannot be obtained by making all the members alike. "The State does not consist simply of a number of men, but of men specifically different from one another;" – these are Aristotle's words,[12] and he at once illustrates his meaning by referring to the distinction between a State and an alliance.[13] In the latter the mere addition of a quantity of men of the same sort is a direct good; but in the State, a community in the functions of good life, the unity to be attained must issue from diversity. It is not true, he insists, that mere unity is its object: if it were, the State would not exist. For the family is, in this sense, more one than the State, and the individual than the family.

In other passages the dissimilar parts of the State are regarded as classes of society, not as mere individuals. These classes are formed of groups of men performing separate "functions," or "works," in the whole. In the description of the ideal constitution these works are enumerated as the agricultural food-providing function, the technical or mechanical, the military, the religious, the function of property, and that of government in its two main branches, according as the decisions arrived at concern the common interest or the administration of justice (VII.8.1328b2–23). In another passage (IV.4.1290b21–1291b2) the list is repeated with some enlargements, and it is pointed out that the reason why different species and sub-species of constitution arise is that, though all these functions or social elements are necessary to a State, the particular forms which each of them takes may vary, and, further, the varieties of each may be combined with those of the rest in different ways. To illustrate his meaning Aristotle refers to the manner in which the various kinds of animals are distinguished. There too we find certain functions which are necessary to animal life, such as those of sense, nutrition and motion; and there are special organs appropriated to them. These appear in various forms, and the varieties of one may be found in combination with those of another. There are different shapes of the mouth, for example, and various developments of the organs of motion; and not only these varieties, but the different combinations in which they are found to coexist, may be made the ground for distinguishing species and sub-species of animals.

---

12 II.2.1261a22–4. The same law which prevents a *commercial koinônia* between two men of the same trade (*EN* V.5.1133a16–18) is active in the political *koinônia*.

13 It will be remembered that Aristotle, in discussing the end of the State, distinguished it from an alliance on the ground that an alliance has no common end, and its law is a mere contract. In other words, an alliance is a collection of homogeneous units, not a unity in diversity.

From this differentiation of functions it immediately follows that inequality among the parts of the State is regarded not as an imperfection, still less as an injustice, but as natural and necessary. And not merely inequality, but a relation of government; "for wherever a single common whole is formed out of a number of elements, a ruler and a ruled is to be found, whether these elements are continuous," as in a physical organism, "or discrete," as in the relation of master to slave, or in a political organism; and an analogue to this relation may be found even in "compositions" not organic (I.5.1254a28–33). But there is a still closer correspondence between the living body and the State in this point. We soon find in reading the *Politics* that all the "parts" or members of the State are not of equal importance; that some of them, as for example the agricultural and industrial functions, are mere means or necessary conditions to others; and that only those which are ends are properly called "parts" at all. Such are obviously those which really share in the life of the whole, or realize its end; in other words, those which are organs of "good living." Accordingly the real parts of the State are, to Aristotle, the citizens alone, who exercise the functions of government and religion, defend the State and possess its landed property. The rest of the population are mere means, or *sine quibus non*. If we turn to the account of the animal body, we come upon a precisely similar distinction. There too the whole body and each of its organs exists for the sake of a certain function or "action" (*praxis*), but only certain parts of the body are regarded as ends. These are distinguished as the specially "organic" parts, and among them are counted the hand and foot, to which at the beginning of the *Politics* Aristotle compares the citizen of the State. To these organic or heterogeneous parts the rest, which are homogeneous, – such as the blood, flesh, fat, bones, and sinews – merely serve as constituents or means. "The living body is composed of both, but the homogeneous are for the sake of the heterogeneous."[14] And so the State is composed both of citizens and of a labouring population; but the one is for the sake of the other.

In Aristotle's treatment of the State as something which has laws of its growth and health, not reversible by man's will except within certain limits, we may trace a further likeness to the conception of an organism. This point of view is especially evident in his remarks, already referred to, on the magnitude of the city. It does not depend simply on the arrangements which the citizens choose to make, how large their State is to be. As a natural existence the State has a definite function, and this function can only be exercised if a certain limit of size is preserved. It is as much subject to this law as other things, – animals, plants, or lifeless instruments (VII.4. 1326a35–7). A departure from the ideal standard in either direction weakens its power to perform its function, and therefore lessens its existence.[15] A still further departure destroys its nature altogether, so that it ceases to be a

14 *PA* II.1; compare in particular, 646b10.
15 Hence, to Aristotle, a *great* State does not mean a large one, but one which vigorously exercises its function.

State. If it has too small a population, it ceases to be "self-sufficing;" and if it has too large a one, it no longer admits of order. But self-sufficience (*autarkeia*) is its essence; and order (*taxis*) is implied in its very existence as a work of nature.

The same point of view is apparent where Aristotle is treating of the necessary equilibrium of the various elements of society. It is only within certain bounds that this equilibrium will bear disturbance. The disproportionate development of one social function is hostile to the wellbeing of the whole, and may destroy the constitution (V.8.1308b10–19, 4.1304a17–38). The illustration is again taken from the living body. "A body is composed of parts, and they ought to grow proportionately, that its symmetry may be preserved; otherwise it perishes;" as it certainly would, if "the foot were six feet long and the rest of the body only two spans." So it is with the State. And as again a certain kind of disproportionate growth may result in one animal form actually passing into another, so one constitution may from the same cause pass into another, and the whole nature of the State be therefore changed (V.3.1302b33–1303a2). The same idea lies at the root of Aristotle's advice to those who wish to preserve either of the two principal "perverted" forms of government, oligarchy or democracy. It is the essence of these constitutions that they represent the preponderance of one social element in the State, whether it be that of the few rich or the many poor, and that this class rules not for the common good but in its own interest. Even so perverted a State has a vital principle of its own. But this principle will not bear straining too far; and Aristotle points out that the worst friends of such constitutions are those who wish to develop their characteristics to the uttermost. "Many of those things that are counted democratic destroy democracies;" and the same is true of oligarchies. The governing class cannot really get on without the opposite element which it strives to suppress, and therefore the pursuance of its main principle beyond a certain point ends in its self-annihilation. "A nose," as Aristotle drily tells us, "may depart from the ideal straightness and tend to be either aquiline or snub, and yet it may still be beautiful and have a charm for the eyes; but if an artist were to push the deviation to excess, first of all the feature would lose its due measure of size, and at last it would not look like a nose at all" (V.9.1309b20–35). The principle of measure or the mean (*to meson*) rules the State, as it does the moral character of the individual.

We may thus reach an important conclusion. That end of the State which is described as good living or happiness is also described as the common interest or good (*to koinêi sumpheron*, III.6.1278b21–2), that noble living (*kalôs zên*) in which each shares according to his ability. In any whole that is "prior" to its parts, in any organism, there is an identity between the general welfare and the particular welfare of each part. It is in the healthy and harmonious development of its organs or functions that the health of the whole body lies, and the interest of the State is nothing but that of its citizens. And conversely, there is no part which really has a separate interest; for its essence and good lie in its function, and this is a function of the whole body. Thus if it appears to have a private interest which is thwarted by its membership in a system and sacrificed to that system, this appearance must be considered a delusion. The disproportionate growth of a single organ, for example, is its real misfortune; for its true nature is not developed, and it injures the whole on which its own health depends. And in the same way we may say that the dependence of one member on the rest is not a sign of bondage but its real liberty, if liberty means "self-sufficiency;" and the growing independence of the parts is equivalent to the loosening of that bond which is the life of the organism and only disappears in its decay.

Such are some of the points in which Aristotle seems to find the characteristics of animal life in the body politic. It is clear that they would not justify us in calling his conception of it organic; but perhaps they amount to something more than analogies, and they give a fuller meaning to his description of the State as a natural existence with laws of its own. If, however, we are to retain this idea at all, it is essential to realize how vitally a political organism differs from a merely physical one; and a few words will suffice to show that Aristotle's view does not obscure the distinction between the two.[16]

"That man is a political animal in a higher sense than the bee or any other gregarious creature, is clear. For nature, as we say, makes nothing in vain; and man is the only living thing that possesses rational speech (*logos*). A mere voice (*phônê*) serves to signify pleasure and pain, and therefore it is possessed by the other animals as well as by man; for their nature goes so far that they feel pain and pleasure, and signify these feelings to each other. But language has for its office to express what is helpful and hurtful, and therefore also what is right and wrong (*to dikaion kai to adikon*). For this is peculiar to man, as compared with the other animals, that he alone has a perception of good and evil and of right and wrong. And it is community in good and right that constitutes a family and a State" (I.2.1253a7–18). Thus, in modern language, the State is more than an organism; it is a moral organism. The soul of man is not a mere principle of growth and nutrition, like that of plants. Its activity is not confined to sense and the desires which depend on sense, like that of the lower animals. It is intelligence and rational will. And therefore man not only has a law of his life, but is capable of knowing the law of his life: he not only knows it, but is capable of living by it. In him therefore appears the separation of what is and what might be, of good and evil, or right and wrong; in a word, morality. And this morality is not something which belongs to each man's private life. It is community in it which constitutes the State or political organism. But the consciousness of this organism, and therefore its morality, can exist nowhere but in its members. The principle of the whole is present in the parts. Its reason and morality are theirs; its end is theirs; it is in them that it feels, suffers and enjoys. And if the converse is not true, if the end of any particular member seems to be something else than the end of the whole, it is because this single function

16 In *MA* 10.703a29 there is an interesting comparison of the animal body to a State, and the fact that the "order" of the latter is due to the human will is pointed out. But it is doubtful whether this treatise is genuine.

attempts to deny the relation in which it stands, and must stand, to the whole.

From what has been already said, it will be evident that Aristotle is in no danger of obliterating these distinctions. The citizen is related to the State as the hand is to the whole body. But the end of the State is happiness or noble action; the State itself is community in this good life, or in the right which language only can express. If the whole then is rational and moral, its highest functions must be rational and moral. But these highest functions are those of its members; and for that very reason those of its parts which fulfil no such function are not, properly speaking, members of it, but merely necessary conditions of its life. For the same reason, however, its true "parts" necessarily attain their own ends in attaining the end of the whole. "Happiness is not a conception like that of evenness in number. That may be predicated of the whole number" (say 10) "without being predicated of its component parts" (say 3 and 7); "but this is impossible with happiness" (II.5.1264b19–22). On the other hand, the welfare of the citizen is not merely bound up with that of the whole, but he is capable of realizing this, and of either devoting himself to the State or making his supposed private advantage his end. His relation to the State is not, like that of the hand to the body, one simply of *fact*, but also one of *duty*. "No citizen ought to think that he is his own, but all that they are the State's" (VIII.1.1337a27–9). And Aristotle does not suppose that, left to himself, a man is likely to identify his good with that of the whole organism in the manner of a healthy animal organ. It is just because he is a

> fool whose sense
> No more can feel but his own wringing,

that the education of the State and the arm of the law are required, to convert him from a life "according to passion" to one of true citizenship and participation in happiness.

The functions of the body politic, then, are moral functions; and the members which exercise these functions are consequently moral agents. It must be remembered, lastly, that the virtue or happiness which is the end of State and citizen alike, is not something distinct from the direct duties of citizenship, but that these duties themselves play a large part in it. A man is not a good citizen in order that he may gain something by it. Happiness is the exercise of "virtue." In being brave and self-controlled and liberal a man is attaining happiness, and at the same time showing the virtues of citizenship. But there are excellencies of a more commanding kind than these. As we have already seen, the crowning talent of moral wisdom, with the possession of which all the virtues are given, has its sphere no less in affairs of State than in a man's own household. It is the virtue of government, the possession of which makes a "good citizen" and a "good man" equivalent terms, while the citizen-virtues of obedience would by themselves not amount to perfect goodness. The citizen must be free from the mere wants of life that he may have time for politics no less than for philosophy; for those are the two main forms of happiness. So far then from the growth or action of the political organism being merely natural, they are to be consciously guided by the most developed character and wisdom. It is as though a plant should be aware of the conditions on which its perfect growth depends, and, making this perfect growth its object, should consciously attempt to realize those conditions. Whether this conscious guidance is a characteristic of the State which renders the conception of an organism radically inapplicable to it, we need not stop to dispute. It certainly is at first sight more in accordance with our common view of government as a mechanism; and to Aristotle it suggests the metaphor of the "ship of State" rather than that of the "body politic." He compares the citizens to sailors (III.4.1276b20), and (by implication) the citizen as ruler to the steersman (III.6.1279a3–4). And there is a psychological fitness in the comparison. For reason, which acts in government, is not in his view connected with the human organism in the same way as the inferior "faculties;" and in the case of this psychical "part," he would have answered in the affirmative the question raised in *de Anima* (II.1.413a8–9), whether the soul is related to the body as "a sailor to his boat."

In any great political theory the comprehension of one main idea makes the rest comparatively obvious. The remaining conclusions on which our space allows us to touch, follow naturally from the general ideas already sketched, and will serve to give them a more substantial shape. With this purpose we may rapidly review Aristotle's teaching on the subjects of citizenship, State-education, the various forms of government, the meaning of political justice and political rights.

Aristotle's view of the nature of citizenship has been already indicated; but it can hardly fail to be misunderstood unless we take into account his judgment as to the political position of the labouring classes. From the conception of the State two main results directly follow: first, that citizenship can mean nothing less than the right or duty of exercising political functions; and, secondly, that this exercise is, in the true State, the activity of those higher virtues which make the good citizen identical with the good man. For practical purposes it may be, though it is not always, true to say that a citizen is one whose father and mother were both citizens. But this is a mere external mark, and does not tell us in what citizenship consists. In what does it consist? Not in the mere possession of civil rights. Just as the State is not merely a community in territory or in the legal protection of person and property, so a citizen does not mean one who resides in a certain city and can be sued in its law-courts. These are not functions of the State, and do not involve participation in its end. If the citizen is to be really a part of the State, he must live its life; and that in the concrete means that he must govern. Thus citizenship may be defined as "ruling and being ruled," and a citizen as one who shares, or has the right to share, in government, deliberative, executive and judicial. In so doing he uses not only the virtues of obedience, not only the common moral virtues, but also the excellencies of moral wisdom and command. His life is pre-eminently one of *aretê*.

But the brain cannot think unless the heart beats; and society cannot exert its highest powers when its lowest needs are unsatisfied. The whole must exist before it can exist well; and it cannot exist well if the organs whose office is to think have to attend to mere living. A life of culture and political *aretê* implies freedom in him who lives it from the necessity of looking after these lower wants (III.5.1278a9–11). It implies what Aristotle calls "leisure," and this leisure must be supported on some one's labour. The life of labour is a mere means to the higher life. It is not a participation in the State-life, but a condition of it, a *sine qua non*. It does not do what is noble, but provides what is necessary. It might produce a joint-stock company, but not a State. It creates mere material prosperity, and "no class has a share in the State which is not a producer of virtue" (VII.9.1329a19–21).

The result of this hard and fast distinction is obvious. So far as *aretê* is concerned, it make no great difference whether the labourer is a slave or a free man. "Those who provide necessaries for an individual are slaves, and those who provide them for society are handicraftsmen and day-labourers" (III.5.1278a11–13; compare I.13.1260a36–b2). And the labouring class includes not only peasants, but all *banausoi*, a designation which covers artisans, professional singers and artists, and no doubt all persons engaged in trade. It is against *banausia* that the reproach of ignobleness is especially directed; and the word, like our "mechanical," has an ethical significance. "That," says Aristotle, "must be considered a mechanical practice or art or subject of study, which makes the body or the soul or the intellect of free men useless for the activities of virtue" (VIII.2.1337b8–11). *Banausia* deforms the body (I.11.1258b37), and renders it unfit for military and political duties (VIII.6.1341a7–8). It accustoms a man's mind to low ideas, and absorbs him in the pursuit of the mere means of life. The *banausos* seeks the satisfaction of other people's wishes, and not the improvement of his own character; and this is the mark of slavery. It is for this reason that the occupation of the professional musician is considered unworthy of a man (VIII.5.1339b9–10). He treats his art "technically" or professionally, practices "amazing and brilliant pieces" (VIII.6.1341a10–12), has to gratify an audience often of vulgar tastes, and therefore practices a kind of day-labour (VIII.6.1341b8–14).[17] If citizenship then means essentially the practice of *aretê*, there can be no question for Aristotle as to the admission of the *banausoi* to political rights. In such perverted constitutions as "democracy" they

---

17 It will be remembered that in Greece not only professional performers but even original artists were considered "mechanical." It is inconceivable that Aristotle, with his high view of art, should have considered his account of *banausia* applicable to Phidias; but probably the following typically antique passage would not have sounded so strange to him as it does to modern ears: "If a man applies himself to servile or mechanical employments, his industry in those things is a proof of his inattention to nobler studies. No young man of noble birth or liberal sentiments, from seeing the Jupiter at Pisa, would desire to be Phidias, or, from the sight of the Juno at Argos, to be Polycletus; or Anacreon, or Philemon, or Archilochus, though delighted with their poems." – Plutarch's *Life of Pericles* (Langhorne's translation)

might find a place, as they actually did; for the principle of that constitution is not the true principle of the State. And in an oligarchy, the "perversion" which substitutes wealth for political virtue, though a day-labourer could hardly attain the property-qualification necessary for citizenship, a *banausos* might (III.5.1278a21–4). Accordingly at Thebes, we are told, a law was in force that a man could not take part in government until ten years after his retirement from the market. But in any true State, in any constitution in which "the honours of office go by excellence or merit," it is impossible that the *banausos* should be a citizen. For his life is "ignoble and opposed to *aretê*" (III.5.1278a18–21, VII.9.1328b40–41).

Aristotle's view is only the reproduction of current Greek ideas. At first sight it is so repulsive to us that we are tempted to condemn it wholesale. But it should be observed that it is due not only to a contempt of labour connected with the institution of slavery, but also to the height of the ideal with which the labouring life is compared. In this point it contrasts favorably with the modern upper-class sentiment which it seems at first to resemble. And it is worth while to ask where its falsity lies.

If we grant Aristotle's premises, no fault can be found with his exclusion of the labouring classes from political rights: their admission would have been a mere inconsistency. It is simply true that, as a body, they could not have possessed the qualities he demands in the citizen, even if they had found the leisure for military, political, and judicial duties. We have given up the idea of professedly apportioning shares in government according to merit, virtue, or culture (words which Aristotle uses interchangeably in this connection); all that we hope for is that, through a political machinery which assigns no superior rights to these qualities, they may yet find their way to the helm. But if we did accept Aristotle's principle in the matter, we should certainly arrive at his conclusion, and should wish to exclude from the suffrage the great majority of those who possess it. Nor again is the idea that this culture depends upon lower labour false. It is a fact which, however painful, cannot be too clearly recognized, that the existence of those excellencies in which Aristotle finds the end of life and the virtues of the citizen, rests upon a mass of mere work as its necessary condition. And is there any modern society which can plume itself on the advances it has made in uniting these two elements, the end and the means, in the same persons or classes? If not, we must admit that, so far, Aristotle's view is not open to reproach. Nor, lastly, will any honest observer deny that there is a moral *banausia* which besets some of the occupations included under that term.

What is disputable in Aristotle's view is the too exalted idea of citizenship, an idea which, with the increase in the size of States, has ceased to be even plausible. What is psychologically untrue is the pre-eminence given to intellect in the conception of man's end, and the hard and fast line drawn between the virtues of government and those of obedience. What is morally repulsive is the consequent identification of the end and means of life with two separate portions of the community, and the feeling that moral lowness has anything to do with labour, as such, or with a professional occupation. Modern civilization, in its best aspects, tends to unite what is here separated.

The intellectual excellencies themselves have become the basis of professions. Payment for performing the duties of government, in Greek democracy the symptom of decay, is the recognized rule of modern States, so far as administration is concerned. Clergymen, artists, poets, authors, philosophers receive, or may receive, wages for their work, and it is not supposed that they necessarily work with a view to their wages. We anxiously avoid even the semblance of contempt for the labouring classes; not only out of deference to their political power, but from a conviction that there is no shame in labour. It is felt that work, be it what it will, may be done in such a spirit that moral character may be developed by it; and that in this character, in family affection, and in religion a happiness is attainable which contradicts the idea that in the mechanical life there can be no production of "virtue," and therefore nothing to make life worth having. Some of our language would even imply that mere labour was the end of life, and not a means to something beyond itself; but this piece of cant is implicitly contradicted by efforts to educate the classes engaged in manual work, and to put suitable "occupations of leisure" within their power.

But it is easy to make too much of these differences, and to imagine a correspondence between the facts of modern society and its best tendencies which does not really exist. Prejudices, resting on old customs and containing half a truth, repose comfortably in our minds side by side with ideas which, if we were thoroughly awake, would destroy them. Aristotle himself has laid down with the greatest clearness that even the most menial services need not be ignoble, and that the slavishness of a pursuit lies not in the things that are done, but in the spirit in which they are done, and in their object. And for this reason he would have some of such services performed by the youthful citizens (VII.14.1333a6–11, VIII.2.1337b17–21). And yet he seems hardly to ask himself whether work which is rewarded in money may not be done for its own sake; and, with ideas of art hardly less exalted than Plato's, he utters no word of protest against the identification of the artist with the *banausos*. Nor, again, can it be said that these old prejudices are wanting in vitality at the present day. If a good many "young men of liberal sentiments" would so far differ from Plutarch that they would desire rather to be Shakespeare than Pericles, most of their relations, and perhaps all their mothers, would take quite another view; and they themselves might not all persist in an ambition which would involve their ceasing to be "gentlemen" and becoming common actors. One of the wisest of Englishmen, when he heard a compliment to the Queen, which Garrick had introduced into a play, characterized as "mean and gross flattery," asked "(rising into warmth): How is it mean in a player – a showman, – a fellow who exhibits himself for a shilling, to flatter his Queen?"[18] Yet Garrick was the greatest actor of the day, and Johnson's personal friend. Again, what does the respectable father of a family think of the boy who turns painter or musician? What does the respectable man of learning think of him? If we do not know from experience how "society" looks

18 Boswell's *Life of Johnson*, vol. ii, p. 215 (edition of 1824 in 4 vols).

upon artists, Thackeray will tell us; what it thinks of "persons in trade," not to speak of the "lower orders," no one can help knowing. But there is a difference between this sentiment and Aristotle's. If he shares our prejudice, he does not share our ideal. The leisure which he thought indispensable for a citizen was not leisure to be stupid, idle, or busy only in amusement. The notion that *that* was the end to which a thousand lives of toil were a mere means would have seemed an astounding one to him. The strenuous exercise of the highest power of body and mind in defending and governing the State, and in striving to quicken the divine reason in the soul, – this is the kind of "high life" with which *banausia* is contrasted, and the citizenship of which it is declared incapable.

If this life is man's personal ideal, there can be little question of the mode in which it is to be approached. Without the gifts of nature not much can be done, and Aristotle hardly seems to find the happy mixture of spirit and intelligence in any race except the Greek (VII.7.1327b20–33). But, given the good material, the rest is the work of *Education*. And Aristotle uses this word in its strict sense. The natural effects of climate, air, water, and the like, are important (VII.11.1330a34–b17). The unconscious influence of a moral atmosphere can do much. The direct action of the Legislature in arranging institutions has its effect. But it is not communism which will cure the moral diseases of society, but education (II.5.1263b39–1264a2, 7.1266b28–31): and when he is describing the ideal city Aristotle's interest in outward arrangements soon flags. He turns abruptly to the question, How shall we make our citizens good men? – and answers, By education.

From the very beginning the child must be definitely trained and guided; and this training has to follow its natural development. Care can be taken of the body before the mind is active, and the desires are in full energy long before the intellect. It is in this early time that the habituation, on which Aristotle lays so much stress, is possible. Pleasure and pain rule the first years of the soul, and the problem of education is to attach these feelings to the right objects; not to teach the reasons of good and evil, but to nurture a love of the one and a hatred of the other. If this has not been done, the cultivation of the intellect will have little moral result; and, if it has been done, reason will afterwards appeal not to a chaos of passions, but to emotions which have taken her own order and colour, and to habits which form a body pliant to her will. A nature which has gone through such a training has a chance of reaching that energy of the soul which is the main constituent of happiness.

To Aristotle then the fundamental problem of politics is one of education. And to him the practical conclusions are inevitable. Education must be *public* and *compulsory*. Aristotle is not blind to the advantages of private instruction, the system followed in most of the Greek States (VII.17.1337a5–6). It has the same advantages which government by a person possesses over government by a fixed law; it can adapt itself to individual differences. But he cannot admit that the State should give up the training of its citizens. That it attended to it, in however narrow a spirit, at Sparta and Crete, was one of the chief claims of those communities to honour. Not only does the State possess a conception of the end which training is to attain, but it, and it alone, has power to enforce this training on unwilling subjects; and, owing to its impersonal character, the compulsion it exercises is comparatively inoffensive (*EN* X.9.1180a18–24). Nor, even if it were possible, would it be right for the State to leave this duty to that private enterprise which means private opinion. It has an end and a moral character exactly as an individual has, and its responsibility is like his (VIII.1.1337a31–2.1337b3). If the object it sets before it is not realized in the persons of its citizens, it is not realized at all. And this object is not something indefinite, but a fixed type of character, or *êthos*. The failure to produce it is the failure of the State, and may be its danger; for the *êthos* is that living spirit which keeps the political body healthy and united. "The greatest of all securities for the permanence of constitutions is what all men now neglect, an education in accordance with the constitution," and the best laws in the world are of no avail if men are not educated in the spirit of the State (V.9.1310a12–14; compare III.11.1282b10 –11, IV.1.1289a13–15).

And this is not all. The same reasoning leads Aristotle to the further conclusion that education must be *uniform* and *universal*. The end of the whole State is one (VIII.1.1337a21–3), and its spirit must be one. Some of the imperfect constitutions might, and naturally would, depart from this rule; for in them the rulers and the ruled form two distinct classes, and would consequently require a different training. But in the true State every citizen at some period of his life takes part in government, and a common culture is the ideal to be sought. Whatever departure from this uniformity might be admitted would be due to that insistence on the absolute universality of education which is one of the most striking features of Aristotle's doctrine. The State is not to content itself with the training of its active citizens. That of its women is hardly less important. It was a fatal error in the Spartan constitution that it educated its men and left its women uncared for, a negligence which bitterly avenged itself in the effect they produced on the moral character of the whole State (II.9.1269b12–1270a15). For the women "form half the free population" (I.13.1260b18–19), and where their condition is not what it should be, "half the State must be considered uncared for by the law." Doubtless, if Aristotle's promise to deal with this subject were fulfilled in the book, as we possess it, we should find that he gave very different regulations for the training of the two sexes; but the same law of conformity to the constitution is insisted on for both.

Nor can the State afford to relax its care with the manhood of its pupil. Its education, in the wider sense of the word, ought to last through life (*EN* X.9.1180a1–5; compare *Pol.* VII.12.1331a37–b1, 17.1336b11–12). For the mass of men, at least in ordinary States, can hardly be expected to live by the light of their own reason. Under the inferior forms of government it is of so great importance that men should live in accordance with the established constitution, that special officials ought to watch and control the lives of disaffected persons (V.8.1308b20–24); and the best of existing governments, we are told, have functionaries to guard the conduct of women

(IV.15.1300a4–6). If we turn from the adult years of the citizen to his very birth, we find the same point of view. If the contribution of nature to man's good lies in part beyond our power, it is only in part that it does so. And with a view to the production of the best material for education the whole arrangements of marriage are placed under the absolute control of government. It is at such points as these that we feel farthest removed from Greek ideas, and are surest of our progress. But there is at least nothing unworthy in the spirit which dictates such interferences with private life. We feel all the moral intensity as well as all the harshness of the ideal statesman (*EN* I.13.1102a7–10) in the rebuke with which Aristotle meets those who wish to live "after their own heart's desire." "But this is base: for one ought not to think it slavery to live in the spirit of the constitution" (V.9.1310a34–5); and, "No man ought to think that he is his own, but all that they are the State's" (VIII.1.1337a27–9).

Of the education which seemed to Aristotle ideal we have only a fragmentary sketch. Its spirit may be conjectured from the end at which it aims, but any account of it would lead us beyond our immediate subject. If we turn now to the perfect city for which this education is intended, a glance at the very scanty account of its political organization will enable us to understand the imperfections of the other form of governments.

All the citizens of the ideal State have received the same education; they are "free and equal." Their education was designed to fit them not only for obedience, but also for government, and for the second by means of the first. Of the virtue implied in this function there is one indispensable condition, – freedom from the necessity of providing the means of life. Accordingly the property of the community is in the hands of the citizens; and though they ought to some extent to permit a common use of it, they hold it as their own, and not in common.[19] Under these conditions what distribution of public rights or duties does justice demand? In virtue of the equality of the citizens, it demands that *all* shall share in civic rights. Of these functions there are two main classes, military and political; and accordingly every one has to take part in each. But the equality of the citizens is not identity; they are unlike as well as like; and in the necessary distinction which nature makes between them Aristotle finds the ground for a difference in rights or duties. Various functions demand various capacities, and these capacities belong roughly to separate periods of man's life. Energy or force (*dunamis*) is the gift of youth, and wisdom (*phronêsis*) of riper years. In the ideal State, then, the citizen in his earlier manhood will perform the military duties, and will only take part in government when they are completed. The remaining function of citizen-

19 One is tempted to suppose that by "property" is meant landed property; since the *banausoi*, who are not citizens, might possess wealth of another kind. But it is possible that Aristotle, who dislikes trade and manufactures, may have intended his State to be almost entirely agricultural. And the agricultural labourers would not be free men (VII.10.1330a25–31).

ship, the care of religious worship, is assigned to those advanced years which relieve men from more active services. We shall see that, as in this distribution of work, so in other respects the ideal State is the image of that perfect justice which in Aristotle goes by a name afterwards applied to a very different conception – natural right.

That every constitution existing in Aristotle's time answered to his idea of the State no one could suppose. Not one fully corresponded to it, and the majority fell far short of it. In this, as in every other work of nature, there are variations and defects. Nature, as Aristotle mythologically says, aims at the best, but she cannot always attain it (compare I.5.1254b27–34, 6.1255b3–4). Her creation is arrested as some point, or it develops itself awry. Thus men do not always reach the stage of political society, and when they do they often form imperfect or even "perverted" States. They mistake the true end, or else they do not take the right means to reach it (VII.13.1331b26–38). Yet the mere beginnings, or the deformed growths, are better than nothing. "Man is by nature so political an animal that, even when men need no assistance from each other, they none the less desire to live together;" and though the common good of a noble life is in the highest degree their end, yet "they come together for the sake of mere life, and form political communities even for it alone. For perhaps it has something of the noble in it" (III.6.1278b19–27). Thus subordinate ends which fall short of man's true development are raised into ultimate ones, and form the bases or fundamental principles (*hypotheseis*) of imperfect constitutions. On the "hypothesis" of wealth arises what Aristotle calls oligarchy, on that of mere freedom what he calls democracy. As we have seen, neither wealth nor freedom is the end for which the State exists; but both are necessary to that end. Hence at once the existence and the weakness of such forms of government. They are States, and so far good; and of neither of them does Aristotle use the language he applies to tyranny, which takes the pleasure of the tyrant for its object. On the other hand, in common with tyranny, they are perversions of the true idea, and therefore contrary to nature (III.17.1287b39–41). Each of them, if it pursues its "hypothesis" to the legitimate conclusion, destroys itself, whereas the true end cannot be pursued to excess. With every step in its development the chance of permanence for the constitution decreases; the extreme forms live a hazardous life, and, like diseased organisms, perish of trifling ailments (VI.6.1320b29–1321a1). The reason is that they diverge from the idea of the State so far, they realize it so little, as hardly to be States at all. And we shall find that this is equivalent to saying that they pursue a false end, that they pervert justice, and that their government is selfish and not public.

When Aristotle thus distinguishes between an ideal State and various perversions of it, he is far from supposing that the existence of bad forms of government is avoidable. He does not dream of framing an ideal scheme of government, the adoption of which would turn a misshapen State into the image of his idea. To him the constitution (*politeia*, a word which has a wider sense than its English equivalent) is inseparable from the nature of the people who live under it – as inseparable as any organization is from the matter organized in it. It is the "order" of the citizens (*taxis*, III.1. 1274b38).

It is the "form" of the State, and constitutes its identity (III.3.1276b1–13): and it is often spoken of as the State itself. But it is possible, and even necessary for our purpose, to draw a distinction between the two. To ask why an imperfect *State* exists is to enter at once on a metaphysical question, and comes at last to the problem of the existence of evil. But there is a more obvious meaning in the inquiry why an imperfect *constitution* exists, although this inquiry must ultimately merge in the other. It exists because it is the natural outcome of a given social condition. Given a certain material, a population of a certain kind and in a definite degree of civilization, and there is a form or order naturally fitted for it; and no other order, however superior it would be in better circumstances, is better for *it*. This fact Aristotle clearly recognizes. There are populations, he tells us, naturally adapted to monarchy, aristocracy, and a constitutional republic (III.17.1287b37–41); and though he adds that all the perversions are unnatural, he does not mean by this that they do not naturally arise under the appropriate social conditions: on the contrary, this is true not only of oligarchy or democracy, but of the various sub-species of those forms (IV.12.1296b24–34, VI.1.1317a23–29). Accordingly, when he is describing his own ideal State, Aristotle does not confine himself to the arrangements of government. He realizes that, if his sketch is to have any verisimilitude, he must imagine also the population for which the constitution is intended, and even the physical conditions under which it lives. In other words, he describes an ideal State, and not merely an ideal constitution. In the same way he recognizes that the approaches which can be made to the constitution of this ideal are very various in degree, and that it is essential for a political theorist to consider all of them. False simplicity he regards as the besetting sin of such theorists. Some of them investigate nothing but the one best constitution, in which things we wish for, and cannot insure, play so large a part; others eulogize a single existing form, like the Spartan, and sweep all the rest out of sight. But it is necessary, Aristotle points out, not only to know what we wish for and to take care not to want impossibilities (II.6.1265a17–18), but also to find out what constitution suits any given population; what is the best constitution that can be framed on a given "hypothesis"; what form is the highest attainable by an average State; and instead of supposing that there is one oligarchy and one democracy, to study all the varieties of each (IV.1). On the other hand, from the fact that for any given people that constitution is best which is fit for *it*, Aristotle does not draw the hasty inference that all constitutions stand on a level. If we consider that people which is fitted for free institutions more civilized than that which is fitted for despotism, we implicitly assert that one form of government is also superior to the other. This is the language which Aristotle commonly adopts: nor is there any objection to it, so long as we bear in mind, as he invariably does, that the constitution is the form of the State, and considered apart from the State, is an abstraction.

Aristotle's main division of the forms of government is into six (III.7). Of these three are good or right, and of each of the three there is a perverted form (*parekbasis*). The first set consists of Kingdom, Aristocracy, and

Republic (*politeia*); the second of Tyranny, Oligarchy, and Democracy. And, according to some passages, the first three are placed in a descending order of goodness, and the second three in a descending order of badness, so that the corruption of the best (kingdom) is the worst (tyranny). But this division, probably suggested by Plato's *Statesman*, undergoes serious modifications in the course of the work. The historical forms of kingdom and aristocracy receive slight attention, mainly because in Aristotle's time they were of little importance. On the other hand, an ideal State, not identical with any of these historical forms, but regarded indifferently as either a kingdom or an aristocracy, though commonly as the latter, becomes a main subject of discussion. In accordance with this point of view, the main division into good and bad States loses its sharpness. The Republic or Politeia[20] is always regarded as markedly inferior to its two companions (compare III.7.1279a37–b4, 17.1288a12–15; IV.8.1293b22–6), and is once roundly called a *parekbasis* (IV.3.1290a24–7). And there is another important change. The three constitutions in each set are at first distinguished according to the number of the government, which may consist of one man, a few or many. But Aristotle has no sooner adopted this principle than he points out that the distinction is in some cases illusory. The number of the governing body is a mere accident of oligarchy or democracy, which are really distinguished by the wealth or poverty of the ruling class (III.8.1279b34–1280a6); and though in the later books Aristotle again modifies his new principle, he never deserts it. In the same way in various passages various causes are assigned for the existence of different forms of government; and the truth is that there is no one principle of division in the *Politics*. This wavering procedure seems to be due in part to the recurrence, at various times, of two distinct points of view, and an indifference to their relation to each other. After what has been said, it will be obvious what these points of view are. At one time Aristotle's endeavour is to fix clearly in what the goodness or badness of a State consists; to discover the fundamental principle of each main form of government, and, by a comparison of it with the standard of the ideal State, to determine its value. At other times the fact that every actual constitution is the expression of a certain social order becomes prominent; and it is found that, though the previous distinction may determine the general goodness or badness of such a constitution, it does not really explain its concrete character. It will be best, without entering into any critical discussion, to separate these methods from each other, and to ask, first, what is the main external difference of constitutions, and afterwards to analyze those characteristics which distinguish any good government from any bad one.

The question what social condition is appropriate to each constitution lies beyond the scope of this Essay. Still less can we reproduce Aristotle's

20 This form of government is, as the reader will see, called simply Constitution. In English we have nothing that is even an apparent equivalent. So far as any Greek State can be called a republic, the Politeia may be called a republic of the middle classes. But there is no single case in all the six in which the use of the designations given to modern States is not misleading.

sketch of the order in which the main forms of government appeared (III.15.1286b3–22), or his explanation of the fact that some of them had ceased to answer to the needs of the time.[21] The doctrine which we have to notice is that the constitution is not merely in general the result of social conditions, but that it expresses the relative power of the different elements or sections of society. Every political community contains a variety of parts, elements, or functions. Translating this into the concrete, we may say that every society is divided into classes, although it does not necessarily happen, and, according to Aristotle, had better not happen, that every function is allotted to a single class. Each of these elements or classes – which are variously enumerated in different passages – contributes something to the State, and so has a certain claim to share in its life, or constitution,[22] or political rights. And, apart from the justice of these claims, as a matter of fact the relative strength of these elements determines the question where the supreme power or sovereignty lies in the community, and therefore settles what the constitution of the State shall be (e.g. III.13.1283b4–8). Thus Aristotle tells us more than once that the variety of constitutions is due to the various *huperochai*, or preponderances of the social parts (IV.3.1289b27–1290a13, 4.1291b11–13); and this must be regarded as his settled view of the existing States, although he does not admit the complete justice of the claim of any class to exclusive power (e.g. III.13.1283b27–8). Thus again the true difference between oligarchy and democracy, the commonest actual forms of government, consists in this, that in the one the element of wealth, which naturally falls into a few hands, is supreme (*kurion*) among the social elements, whereas in democracy the poor multitude has got the mastery. And in the same way the superiority of the Politeia to these two constitutions is that in it neither of these extremes has overpowered the other, but the middle class possesses a social force which results in political supremacy.

These distinctions of fact, however, are only the signs of a difference in moral value. The transition from one point of view to the other is facilitated by the haphazard way in which Aristotle uses abstract and concrete expressions. He speaks of a social element indifferently as wealth or the wealthy, freedom or the free, virtue or the good. Accordingly, instead of saying that one of the classes of society, say the wealthy, predominates in a State, he defines the constitution of that State as one which takes a single social element, wealth, for its standard (*horos*). Thus, he tells us, of the qualifications which can claim to be such a standard there are on the whole three – free birth, wealth, and virtue (since a fourth, nobility, means ancestral wealth and virtue); and these are the standards respectively of democracy, oligarchy, and aristocracy (IV.8.1294a9–25). From the notion of a standard to that of an end the step, especially in Greek, is a short one.

21 See, for example, on the disappearance of the kingly form of monarchy, V.10.1313a3–16; and on the connection of democracy with the increased size of States, III.15.1286b20–22; VI.6.1321a1–2, 5.1320a17.
22 *hê gar politeia bios tis esti poleôs* – IV.11.1295a40–b1. "For the constitution is a [way of] life of a state." [Editors' translation]

Accordingly, we are not surprised to find Aristotle distinguishing constitutions by the *ends* they pursue. And again, since the end or standard determines the rights which are thought to belong in justice to the citizen, we are told that the existence of certain constitutions is due to the fact that men have not a right idea of *justice* (V.1.1301a25–36). But when we come to divide States according to the ends they pursue and the justice they realize, we have left the ground of a mere analysis of social forces, and have entered the region of moral judgement. If we add to these criteria the question what *kind of rule* is exercised in a given State, we shall have found the three tests by which the goodness or badness of a constitution may be tried.

The *first* of these criteria is obvious. The very definition of the State places its whole nature in its end. To pursue a false end is to be a bad State, or even (so far) to fail of being a State at all. The true end, as we know, is that noble life which is identical with happiness or the exercise of complete virtue. But there are various subordinate constituents or various necessary conditions of this end, which may be mistaken for it. And just as a man may take as the object of his life not real happiness, but wealth or pleasure, so may a State. Thus the end of the good State is, as we may suppose, the true end. That of the ideal State is this end in its perfection, so that, in the aristocratic form of it which is really Aristotle's ideal, the virtue of the good citizen is, as such, identical with the virtue of the good man. In the same way the fact that the Politeia is counted among the good States, must mean that its end is virtue; but the virtue at which it aims is that imperfect *aretê* of which a large number of men is capable, the virtue of the citizen-soldier (III.7.1279a39–b4).[23] On the other hand, the ends which define the perverted forms are not merely imperfect degrees of *aretê*, but something subordinate to it. Thus we shall expect to find the object of oligarchy in wealth, and this is implicitly asserted by Aristotle (e.g. V.10.1311a9–10). That of democracy must be freedom, since the other characteristics of that form, poverty, numbers, and low birth, are obviously incapable of being ends (IV.8.1294a9–11, VI.2.1317a40–b2, b40–41). That of tyranny again is not the noble life on which pleasure necessarily follows, but pleasure itself and, with a view to pleasure, wealth (V.10.1311a4–6).

In the perversions, then, the government does not seek the good. But, *secondly*, it does not seek the *common* good (*to koinêi sumpheron*, III.6.1278b19–1279a21). It pursues the end for itself, and not for the whole state. Its rule therefore is not political but despotic; that is, a kind of rule applicable to the relation of master and slave, but not to the relation of citizens to each other.

---

23 In this instance we have an example of the way in which the real conditions of a society are connected with the moral qualities of the constitution. The possibility of attaining the true end depends on a limitation of the number of the body which governs; even in the ideal States only some of the citizens *actually* rule. If a large number are to govern, the end must be lowered, and with it the standard for political rights. Thus the qualification in the Politeia is the possession of arms, or (what comes to the same thing in a Greek State) such a property-qualification as admits only the upper and middle classes to power.

The welfare of the ruled is, like the slave's, only accidentally involved in that of the ruler, in the sense (apparently) that more than a certain amount of ill-treatment destroys the living material or instruments by which the master or tyrant obtains his own objects. Thus the subject, like the slave, is the means to another man's end; whereas it is the essence of political society to be a community of *free* men. In this sense democracy, oligarchy, and tyranny are alike despotic (a20–21). In other words, they are so far not States at all; they are insecure; their vital principle is self-destructive; and their safety lies in suppressing the full development of this principle, or in adopting for a bad end measures which, as a matter of fact, tend to the common good.

Each of these two moral characteristics is indispensable. To seek an end which is common to all the citizens will not make a government correct, if the end is false; and to seek the true end will not do so either, if this end is not sought for all. And Aristotle combines the two characteristics when he defines the common good as the share of noble life which falls to each citizen (III.6.1278b23–4). But beyond this mere *assertion* of their union he does not go; he does not attempt to prove that the pursuit of the true end is necessarily unselfish, whereas that of a false one is not. We may gather such a result from his denial that a mere society of traders would constitute a State. The ground of this denial is, that such a society has not a really "political" end; it seeks nothing more than protection for the endeavour of each man to attain his private end of wealth, an endeavour in which the welfare, and even the wealth, of his fellows is involved, if at all, only accidentally. And to this is opposed the interest of the citizen in the moral character of others, that is, in the attainment of the end of the State by others as well as himself. Or again, we may infer that the true end of the State is necessarily a *common* good, from the account of justice in *Ethics* V.1. In that passage justice is identified with virtue, when virtue is regarded in its relation to other men; and the virtue of the citizen is, as we know, the end of the State. But to seek this justice must be to seek the good of *all* the citizens; for, owing to its relation to others, it may be defined, Aristotle says, as the "good of others" (*allotrion agathon*), and not merely of the just man himself. But we have to find such indications for ourselves. The antithesis of selfishness and disinterested action, which suggests the difficulty, had not such prominence in Greek Ethics as it possesses for good and evil now. Aristotle never explicitly raises the question, so obvious to us, in what relation a man's happiness stands to the realization of the same end in others, and whether it is possible for one to be attained without the other, and, therefore, to be preferred or sacrificed to the other. And in the same way here, there is no attempt to show that the pursuit of the real end is in its nature public-spirited, and that of wealth or mere freedom or pleasure *necessarily* the subordination of the public good to a private or class interest.

We have to ask, *thirdly*, in what way is the State a realization of justice or right.[24] It is so, first of all, in this general sense, that it produces in its citizens

24 On this subject H. A. Fechner's tract, *Ueber den Gerechtigkeitsbegriff des Aristoteles* may be compared. The corresponding passages in the *Politics* and *Ethics* are fully pointed out in the notes to Mr H. Jackson's edition of the fifth book of the *Ethics*.

that virtue for which, as we have seen, justice is another name. But there is also a more special principle of right in political society. This is what Aristotle calls *distributive* justice; and its law is that public honours, advantages, or rights, are distributed among the citizens, not arbitrarily, but in proportion to their contribution to the end of the State, or, in other words, according to their worth (*axia*). Thus this justice may be defined in modern language as the correspondence of rights and duties. A right given, which does not answer, and answer proportionately, to a duty done, is a violation of justice. A duty done, a contribution to the State, which does not meet with its proportionate return in the shape of a right, is equally a violation of justice. Or, again, this justice may be represented as a geometrical proportion. If A and B are two citizens whose worths differ, the rights *a*, which go to A, ought to differ in amount from the rights *b*, which go to B, proportionately to the difference in worth between A and B; or, $A : B : : A + a : B + b$. In the same way Aristotle calls political justice a principle of *equality*. And by this he means not absolute equality, but equality of ratios. Thus if A gets the amount of rights which answer to his worth, and B does the same, they are treated justly; and, although they receive unequal rights, they are treated equally. To give equal rights to unequal worths, or unequal rights to equal worths, is to violate equality. In so far then as a State applies this law of proportion, it realizes distributive justice. On the other hand, although it fairly distributes rights according to worth, it may in reality violate justice by using a false or one-sided standard of worth. Instead of rating the citizen by his capacity of exercising true citizen functions, it may adopt a criterion answering to its own false end. In this case, among others, the justice of the State will, in a higher sense, be unjust. And it is only when this positive justice corresponds to, or expresses, *natural* justice, that the State can be said to be a full realization of right.

This is not the case with the perverted States. Plainly, none of them is likely to produce justice in its citizens. None of them, again, fully satisfies distributive justice. Though all – except, we may suppose, the tyrant – admit that justice means proportionate equality (V.1.1301a26–7, b35–6), in no State except the ideal is political right wholly coincident with natural (*EN* V.7.1134b35–1135a5). The departure from natural justice in oligarchy and democracy is represented by Aristotle in two different ways. A partial equality or inequality is taken as absolute, and a false standard of worth is adopted. Thus in the oligarchy an inequality in one respect is considered a just ground for the exclusive possession of power; and political rights are restricted to those who are superior to their fellow-citizens in one particular, viz., wealth. Here is already an injustice; but it is heightened by the fact that the measure of worth is itself a false one. "What is a man worth?" means in an oligarchy not "What is his *merit*, his contribution to the *true* end of the State?" but "How much *money* is he worth?" The injustice of democracy, though it leads to very different outward results, is in principle the same. Grasping the fact that in one point, freedom, all its citizens are on a level, it takes this partial equality for an absolute one, and gives equal rights to everybody. In other words, it gives equals to unequals, and thereby violates justice. And again, though according to the standard of worth it has adopted it may apportion fairly, this standard is not merit but the imperfect one of free birth. Hence Aristotle can at one time insist that equality is justice, and at another condemn democracy on account of its passion for equality, since the equality it realizes is not proportionate but absolute or numerical.[25] So it comes about that there is an "oligarchical right" and a "democratic right." They are not, in the highest sense, right at all. But to a certain extent they are so; partly because the *axia* which they take as the qualification for political power, although not the true one, still has a subordinate importance for the State; and partly because, on the basis of this standard, they do distribute public advantages and honours according to fixed law. Thus, though Aristotle does not trace the gradual decline of justice in the various stages of these *parekbaseis*, it is not an accident that those extreme forms of oligarchy and democracy, which are furthest removed from right and almost on a level with tyranny, are characterized in his view by contempt of the law, and the substitution for it of the mere will of "dynastic" plutocrats (IV.6.1293a30–33) and the momentary decrees of the despot mob (IV.4.1292a19–20).

Aristotle's application of these ideas to the various grounds on which political power may be claimed is, in the main, very simple. The nearest approach to our modern notion of a "right" is to be found in his discussion of this subject; and, like him, we seem to use this word, as well as "justice," in a double sense. Let us take, as an example of political rights, the suffrage. The poor man, then, claims this privilege as his right; and he bases his claim on the ground that he is equal to, or as good as, those who possess it. The rich man claims a greater or unequal share of power, on the ground that he is superior or unequal to his poorer fellow-citizens. The idea underlying each argument is that of distributive justice, and it is a sound one. If the poor man *is* equal to the rich, he *has* a right to equal powers; and if not, not. But the real question is, What does the equality or inequality of men mean in this connection? In *what* are they equal or unequal? (III.12.1282b23–1283a22). It is evident that equality or inequality in any quality whatever which we choose to take will not give a right to equal or unequal political power. If it did, a man might claim the suffrage because he was the same colour or the same size as those who possess it. An illustration from another field will guide us to the true conclusion. Suppose we had certain flutes to distribute. We should scarcely give the best of them to those players who happened to be of the highest birth; "for they will not play better than other people on that account." And even if the superiority of one man to another in wealth or birth far exceeded his inferiority to him in flute-playing, we should still give the best flute to the poor and low-born proficient. "For it is to the function or

---

25 Hence also Aristotle sometimes says (e.g. VI.6.1321a2–3) that democracy is opposed to "justice according to worth (*axia*)." Its standard of worth is mere freedom, and, therefore, scarcely a standard at all.

work in question that the superiority in birth or wealth ought to contribute; and it contributes nothing." The same principle will apply to politics; and it will not justify either of the claims in question. It is not unjust that a real inequality, a superior contribution to the end of the State, should be rewarded by a superior share in the function. But against the favour shown to *irrelevant* inequalities the democrat rightly protests. On the other hand, the point in which he is equal to every other citizen is not that which ought to settle his political *axia*. The end of the State is no more free birth than wealth; and absolute justice belongs in reality only to claims based on the equal or superior possession of intelligence and moral character. Suppose, however, that a given State pursues a false end, and accordingly adopts a false standard of worth. In this case, whatever the standard may be, he who contributes to it equally with other men may truly be said to have an equal right to political power with other men, although his right would in an ideal State be none. So, again, in an oligarchy a wealthy man has a right to greater privileges than others; and his superior in *aretê*, or the real capacity for government, might be legally treated as inferior to him. In such a case, in one sense the poor man of ability would have no right to the power refused to him, and yet, in another sense, he might be said to have an absolute right to it. Obvious as these distinctions appear, any controversy on the suffrage will show how easily they may still be confused, and that the twofold idea of "rights" is still current. When we say that a man has a right to the franchise, what do we mean? We may mean that according to the constitution, the English political *dikaion*, he can claim it, because he satisfies the conditions laid down by the law as necessary to the possession of it. But when the franchise is claimed as a right by those who do not satisfy these conditions, this cannot be the meaning. They really affirm that the actual law, the English *dikaion*, is not properly or absolutely just and does not express "natural right;" that, according to real justice, they ought to have the suffrage, and that, if they had it, the State would be less of a *parekbasis* and nearer to the ideal. And if the further question were asked, *why* true justice demands the change, would not the answer (unless it were a piece of mere clap-trap) involve the notion that equal rights ought in justice to follow equal duties to the State, and the assertion that those who claim the suffrage contribute equally to the State with those who already possess it?

The result of these principles for Aristotle would seem to be clear; and to a certain extent it is so. That the only true standard of worth for distributive justice is merit, or virtue, or education (*paideia*, "culture"), is obvious. But in the immediate application of this doctrine uncertainties arise. First of all, there is one limitation on all governments, a limitation which has, fortunately for us, become almost too obvious to be worth mentioning. The rule of those who possess *any* superiority, even that of virtue, is to be considered inferior to the rule of law. It is only because the law is too general to meet all the particular cases that arise, that a government is necessary to supplement as well as execute it; and therefore, with one exception to be noticed later, the rule that all governments ought to be subject to it is absolute (e.g.

III.11.1282b1–6). Secondly, an element of doubt is introduced by the true perception that, though wealth or free birth are not direct contributions to the end of the State, they yet constitute elements necessary to its existence (III.12.1283a14–22). There is consequently a certain amount of justice in the demand that the possession of them should be followed by some share in public rights. But what share this should be, and in what rights it should be a share, are questions which Aristotle does not discuss. Lastly, his view of the claims of individuals to political power receive an important modification in the account of the imperfect States. Aristotle tells us (IV.12.1296b17–34) that we have to consider not only quality, but quantity; that is, not only the element or quality on which a claim to rule is based, but also the *number* of those who possess it. It is the comparative power of these factors which settles the constitution of a State. Thus oligarchy means the preponderance of the quality of wealth over the superior quantity of the poor, and democracy[26] the opposite. It is the tendency of either government to push its principle to an extreme. Oligarchy heightens the amount of the "quality" of wealth necessary for political rights, and thereby increases the numbers opposed to it. Democracy extends the franchise more and more, and with its increase of quantity loses more and more all distinctive quality. The further this development goes, and the further these factors are separated, the worse the State becomes, and the nearer it approaches to an internecine struggle between them. Accordingly, it is the characteristic of the Politeia, which is distinguished for its stability, that it combines these elements; and it is in this connection that Aristotle's celebrated eulogium on the middle classes occurs. But it is clear that the application of this idea to the question of political rights will make our previous results uncertain. For those results are based simply on an inquiry into the *quality* which any individual can allege as a claim to power: this doctrine, on the contrary, touches the rights not of an individual, as such, but of a number, or possibly a class, and it expressly admits that their quantity must be considered.

A consideration not quite identical with this, but closely allied to it, is applied even to the good States; and it has a special interest, because it leads Aristotle to discuss the rights of the mass or people (*plêthos*, the whole body of citizens). Let us assume, – so we may state his results (III.11.1281a39–1282a41), that wealth is the standard by which rights are apportioned. Still, it will not follow that "the rich" should rule. The mass might justly dispute their claim; for although the wealth of any rich man might far exceed that of

26 Obviously, according to Aristotle, democracy is absolute government of a quality, viz. free birth, and the oligarchs make up a quantity of men. But then free birth is common to rich and poor, the noble by nature and the noble by birth alike. Accordingly he sometimes speaks as if the essence of democracy were mere numbers, i.e. *mere* quantity, or this united with poverty and low birth, i.e. the *absence* of certain qualities. In the same way, as we saw, he speaks as though democracy recognized *no axia*, because its *axia* is so slight a one.

any poor one, yet the collective wealth of the people might exceed that of the wealthy class. Again, even if we admit that the true standard of justice is *aretê*, it is not certain that the best and ablest man in the State, nor the few best and ablest men, have a right to hold the reins of government. It is possible that the aggregate *aretê* of the people might outweigh that of this individual or class; and then the very arguments on which the latter claim to govern might be turned against them. The man of distinguished *aretê*, we might say, is like the ideal portrait. In it are united the various beauties which in life are distributed among different men, and it is therefore more beautiful than the average man. Yet if we take a crowd, we may find in it here a mouth, and there eyes, and there again another feature, still more beautiful than are the features of the portrait. And so, although each individual of the *plêthos* may be far inferior in political merit to the aristocrat, yet if we take the whole mass, it may contain an aggregate of merit exceeding his. Each member of it brings a contribution to the one vast man, who has many feet and hands and senses. In the same way we find that the judgment of the mass on poetry and music is better than that of a single critic; for one man appreciates one excellence, and another another, whereas the taste of an individual is necessarily one-sided. And again, as a large quantity of water is less easily defiled than a small, so it is harder to corrupt a whole people than an individual; and "it is not easy for them all to be enraged or mistaken at once." For these reasons it may be just to give such powers as those of election and the scrutiny of official actions to the whole people. And if the objection be raised that, if they are not fit to hold office themselves, they cannot be fit to choose officials and judge their conduct, the answer is that in many cases it is not necessary to know how a thing is made in order to judge of it. The head of a household, who could not have built the house, is a better judge of the product than the builder, the man who eats a dinner than the cook who prepared it.

This is Aristotle's version of "the sovereignty of the people;" and his arguments, whether wholly sound or not, have a permanent value. But it is important to recognize clearly on what basis they rest, and to what conclusion they are supposed to lead. We have to remember, first, that the "people," here as everywhere, is not equivalent to the whole male population, and does not include the enormous body of slaves and aliens. Nor does Aristotle suppose that his arguments will apply to any and every mass; for, "by heaven, in some cases this is clearly impossible." And, further, the sovereignty of the people to whom they do apply is doubly limited. It is subject to the ultimate supremacy of the law; and even under the law it is not complete. The very reasons which establish it restrict it to those cases in which the people can act *en masse*, and not individually. In other words, the functions of government in which the *plêthos* can claim a share are the general ones of deliberation and decision, which constitute the definition of citizenship, and not the highest executive offices, for which special ability is required. Lastly, it will be observed that the ground on which these claims are based by Aristotle is not that of simple quantity as opposed to quality. It is a claim based on the superior quantity of a quality. It is not because "all government rests on the consent of the governed," nor because one man is as good as another, nor because the people is a majority, that it has a right to rule; but because, in the case of a high level of civilization, its rule is more likely to realize the government of intelligence and character than any other arrangement. Number stands on no higher level, or even on a lower level, than money or birth. Whatever rights belong to it, belong to it as the sign of something beyond itself.

Partly on account of this discussion, partly through the misinterpretation of various passages in the *Politics*, some readers of the work have identified the Politeia with Aristotle's ideal State. But it is quite impossible to maintain this view. It is true that in both the suffrage is widely extended. But the Politeia is only the practical ideal. It is the constitution adapted to an average good State. It is a government of *aretê* but of imperfect *aretê*. The whole people does not rule; there is a strict qualification for political rights, and, with a view to obtaining a rule of fair *aretê*, the qualification fixed is one of moderate wealth. The ideal State, on the other hand, is the true aristocracy; a government of *complete aretê*, a government of the best men (*aristoi*) for the best end (*ariston*), (III.7.1279a35–7). In the form which Aristotle has given to it the whole body of citizens bears rule. But then he is constructing a State according to his wishes; he supposes all the citizens to be men of high excellence; and even then he does not give the actual functions of government to them until they have reached a certain age. If his "wish" should not be fulfilled, justice would demand a different constitution. A population, in which a small band of men were distinguished to such a degree that their *aretê* surpassed that of the remaining *plêthos*, would, on Aristotle's principle, be governed by that select few. And a still stranger case is not inconceivable to him. It might happen that a man appeared in the State, gifted with a greatness of soul which raised him far above all his fellows. In such an event no love of his own ideal will deter Aristotle from the consistent result of his principles. If the great man really has a spirit so exalted in energy and virtue that these gifts exceed in quantity those of the whole body of his fellow-countrymen, justice demands that he should be held for what he is, "a god among men" (III.13.1284a11). The conditions of common political life cease to be applicable. He is not an equal among equals, to be bound by equal rules. In this single case even the supremacy of law must be abandoned. He is to be recognized as of right an absolute king, governing for the common good. That Aristotle considered such an occurrence extremely improbable is obvious. But that it was conceivable is the reason why he describes the ideal State as either monarchy or aristocracy (IV.2.1289a30–33). And as in the *Ethics* (*EN* VIII.10.1160a35–6), so in the *Politics* he has even given the first place to the former (IV.2.1289a39–b4).[27]

27 The absolute kingship described above is of course the exact opposite of tyranny. It has been supposed that, in speaking of it, Aristotle was thinking of Alexander, and the enthusiasm of his language is certainly striking. But it is almost incredible that such an opinion of the new military monarchy should have left so little trace on the structure of his whole political theory. And it should be observed that the comparison of the rule of law and of an absolute king has throughout a reference to Plato's *Statesman*, and that Aristotle makes use even of Plato's illustrations.

The true State may take various forms; but, whatever form it takes, these two requirements are absolute: it must strive to realize perfect justice by giving power to the natural sovereignty of intelligence and virtue, and it must seek the common good. The Greek constitutions have no more than a historical interest for us now. Our monarchy, our feudal aristocracy, our representative government, were things unknown to them, and the most democratic of their democracies we should call an oligarchy. But these principles remain. The first of them modern States attempt to carry out in various ways. From the very force of circumstances we are even less tempted than the Greeks to translate the truth that reason alone has a "divine right" to rule, into the dictum that philosophers should be kings; but it is still possible to forget that wealth and numbers have no political value except as symbols, and that political machinery is very far from being an end in itself. The second of these principles may be thought, fortunately for us, to have lost the pressing importance it had to Aristotle. For him the ruin of the Greek States was the witness of its violation.[28] The organization of the State, instead of representing the common good and standing above the strife of social parties, had become in many cases the prize for which they fought, and a means which the victorious party used for its own exclusive advantage. Cities were divided into two hostile camps of the rich and poor. In this immediate dependence of the State on society we have one of the most marked characteristics of Greek politics. In modern nations the struggle of classes for political power does not, as a rule, rise prominently to the surface; and, though a change in social conditions – such as the decay of a landed aristocracy, or the rise of the commercial or the labouring classes, – inevitably expresses itself in politics, it commonly does so slowly and, so to speak, unintentionally. The State has a fixity and power such as the Greeks – in spite of the far greater part played by government in their lives – never knew; and, where the opposition of classes begins to pass from the social sphere and to take an openly political form, we recognize a peril to the national welfare and morality which to the Greek, instead of being a rarity, was ever at the doors. But it is impossible to say how far this supremacy of the State is connected with the modern institution of monarchy, and to what extent more popular forms of government, by whatever name they go, may be able to preserve it. That it needs no preservation, that great nations can do without it, and can subsist on nothing but the natural competition of interests modified by public opinion, is a hope which underlies some forms of the democratic faith, and seems to be implicitly adopted by many who have no theoretic convictions on the subject. Yet it seems too probable that, in more than one European country, the irruption of an exasperated social strife into the political arena would follow any weakening of the central power; and it would be a poor change which

---

28 Compare L. v. Stein in the *Zeitschrift für die gesammte Staatswissenschaft* for 1853, pp. 115–182.

freed men from the burden of that power only to bring it back in its least beneficent and progressive form, that of military force. Nor is it possible to confine these doubts to the great continental States. In more than one of the English colonies, unless they are maligned, the interest of a class is predominant in politics, and is susceptible of scarcely any check from above. And if representative institutions are not in other cases to be misused for the same "despotic" purposes, if they are not to produce, instead of the public good and the rule of *aretê*, class-government and the supremacy of the demagogue and the wire-puller, it may be that the sluggish action of public opinion will need to be reinforced by some strengthening of the State and some counterpoise to those tendencies which characterized the extreme democracy described by Aristotle, the gradual weakening of the executive and the grasping of all the powers of government by the popular assembly (IV.4.1292a28–30, 14.1298a29–31, 15.1299b38–1300a1; VI.2.1317b17–35).

There is no fear that modern civilization will abandon the ideas which mark its progress. Unless some gigantic calamity were to overtake it, men who have once conceived of God as identical with the inmost spirit of humanity and bound by no limits of race or nation, who have realized that the breath of morality is freedom, and that voluntary association may be almost as powerful a force as the State, are never likely to find their ideal in the Greek city. The dangers are still on the other side. The process through which those ideas gained strength involved serious losses, and the false antitheses to which it gave rise have not yet ceased to rule our thoughts. To them the spirit of Aristotle's conception may still serve as a corrective. With every step in the moralizing of politics and the socializing of morals, something of Greek excellence is won back. That goodness is not abstinence but action; that egoism, to however future a life it postpones its satisfaction, is still nothing but selfishness; that a man does not belong to himself, but to the State and to mankind; that to be free is not merely to do what one likes, but to like what one ought; and that blindness to the glory of "the world," and irreverence towards its spiritual forces, are the worst of passports to any "church" worthy of the name, – every new conviction of such truths is an advance towards filling up the gulf between religion and reality, and restoring, in a higher shape, that unity of life which the Greeks knew.

So far as opinions have weight, there are not many which more retard this advance than the idea that the State is a mere organ of "secular" force. That it is so seems to be the theoretical, though not the practical, belief of most Englishmen; and Aristotle's fundamental position, that its object is nothing short of "noble living," seems to separate his view decisively from ours. The partial truths that the law takes no account of moral character, and that Government ought not to enforce morality or interfere with private life, seem to be the main expressions of this apparent separation. But, to say nothing of the fact that legal punishments do in some cases habitually consider a man's moral guilt as well as his illegal act, it is forgotten that the reason why this is not the rule is itself a moral reason, and that if, by making it the rule, the good life of the community were likely to be furthered, it would be made the rule. And in the same way the reason why the State does not to any large extent aim at a directly moral result, is not that morality is something indifferent to it, but that it believes it will help morality most by not trying to force it. If we hold to Aristotle's definition, it does not follow that we are to pass sumptuary laws and force men to say their prayers. Every argument that is brought against the action of Government may (so far as it does not rest on a supposed right of the individual) be applied, with whatever truth it possesses, under that definition; and if, in the pursuit of its final object, the State, with a view to that final object, refrains from directly seeking that final object, that does not show that the immediate ends which it pursues are its ultimate and only end. But, apart from this, it is not true that in our own day the State has ceased actively to aim at a positive good, and has restricted itself to the duty of protecting men's lives and property. If the theory that its duty should be so restricted were carried out, it would lead to strange results and would abolish public laws and acts which few would be willing to surrender. We need go for a proof no further than our own country, where the action of Government is certainly not overvalued. A State which, in however slight a degree, supports science, art, learning, and religion; which enforces education, and compels the well-to-do to maintain the helpless; which, for the good of the poor and weak, interferes with the "natural" relations of employer and employed, and regulates, only too laxly, a traffic which joins gigantic evil to its somewhat scanty good; a State which forbids or punishes suicide, self-maiming, the voluntary dissolution of marriage, cruelty to animals, offences against decency, and sexual crimes which, if any act could be so, are the private affair of the persons who commit them, – a State which does all this and much more of the same kind, cannot, without an unnatural straining of language, be denied to exercise, in the broad sense, a moral function. It still seeks not merely "life," but "good life." It is still, within the sphere appropriate to force, a spiritual power, – not only the guardian of the peace and a security for the free pursuit of private ends, but the armed conscience of the community.

2

Aims and Methods in Aristotle's Politics

CHRISTOPHER ROWE

This paper originated in an attempt to come to terms with the problems which arise from the structure of the *Politics*.[1] It is no news to anyone who has the slightest familiarity with the *Politics* that the work reads, to borrow a phrase of Barker's,[2] not as a composition, but as composite. Broadly speaking, it falls into three parts: Books I–III, Books IV–VI, and Books VII–VIII. Books I–III and VII–VIII seem to belong fairly closely together; IV–VI have traditionally been regarded, with no little justification, as interlopers, breaking the essential continuity of the argument between III and VII. Hence the tendency among earlier scholars to place IV–VI after VIII.[3] The main justification for this procedure is that at the end of III, Aristotle clearly promises an immediate treatment of the subject of the best constitution, and that this promised treatment seems to ocur only in VII and VIII; IV–VI are not only not on that subject, but deliberately and explicitly criticize the exclusive preoccupation with the best constitution which seems to characterize both of the other two blocks of books (IV.1.1288b21ff.). There are other considerations, too, which support the view that IV does not belong after III: for example the absence of a connecting particle at the beginning of IV; the manner of the opening of IV; and the mutilated sentence at the end of III.[4]

1 This paper was presented, in different forms, at a seminar at the Center for Hellenic Studies, Washington, DC, in April 1975, and at the 1975 meeting of the Southern Association for Ancient Philosophy in Cambridge. I am grateful for points made in discussion on both occasions. [The paper is reprinted in the present collection with only minor corrections and modifications, which mainly appear in the form of additional footnotes, marked by square brackets. Translations from the Greek are my own unless otherwise indicated. References are to the *Politics* unless otherwise indicated.]
2 E. Barker, "The Life of Aristotle and the Composition and Structure of the *Politics*," *Classical Review*, 45 (1931), p. 167.
3 For a partial list of the arrangements adopted by different editors and commentators, see R. Weil, *Aristote et l'histoire: Essai sur la 'Politique'* (Paris, 1960), p. 60.
4 On which see e.g. F. Susemihl and R. D. Hicks, *The Politics of Aristotle, Books I–V* (London, 1894), pp. 47–8; and W. Jaeger, *Aristotle: Fundamentals of the History of His Development*, tr. R. Robinson, 2nd edn (Oxford, 1948), p. 268.

But the trouble is that although IV officially begins a new approach, it is still itself closely linked with III: thus, for example, the opening discussion in the book is formally presented as a continuation of the description of the various types of constitution begun in III (IV.2.1289a26ff.). It is this combination, not to say confusion, of aims that is the main cause of the even more than usually jumbled structure of the argument in IV. Significantly, too, the number of certain back-references per Bekker page to I–III is far greater in IV–VI than in VII–VIII.[5] In the light of considerations such as these, the fashion for shifting the position of Books IV–VI has waned.[6] The claim of IV–VI to follow III is at least as strong as that of VII–VIII, and probably stronger. But the fact still remains that there is a clear break between III and IV. We are left with a work which is neither a unity in the sense in which we might apply that term to, say, the *Nicomachean Ethics*, nor simply a collection of independent treatises after the manner of the *Metaphysics*. Richard Robinson's suggestion, that it is "a collection of long essays and brief jottings pretending to be a treatise,"[7] seems to me plainly mistaken.

Jaeger's explanation of the state of the *Politics*, from which the argument of this paper will begin, is still perhaps the most plausible of those that have been offered; it has certainly, in its time, enjoyed the most support. In brief, it is that Books II, III, VII, and VIII – which he calls the "Utopian" books – were originally "united and independent,"[8] and that Aristotle later inserted the "purely empirical" books IV–VI, which were now to form the foundation of the discussion of the best constitution. But this arrangement, which is announced, so Jaeger holds, at the end of the *Nicomachean Ethics*, "never got beyond the mere intention, and in point of fact [Books IV–VI] do not in any way prepare for and establish the ideal state, or at least not directly."[9] Jaeger's view of the origin of Book I I shall leave out of account; his reasons for wanting to separate it from II and III seem to me inadequate, as they do, for example, to Moraux.[10] As examples of rival explanations, one may perhaps mention Stark's,[11] which attempts a compromise between the genetic and unitarian views; and Theiler's ingenious solution,[12] according to which the *Politics* as we have it represents a pile of the remains of at least four

5 On my own count, the figures are: for IV–VI, ten certain backward references in 33 pages; for VII–VIII, two in 19 (judgments about what constitutes a "certain" reference may of course differ; but the general conclusion will remain the same).
6 See n. 3 above.
7 *Aristotle's Politics Books III and IV*, tr. R. Robinson (Oxford, 1962), p. ix.
8 *Aristotle*, p. 273.
9 *Aristotle*, p. 268.
10 P. Moraux, in the discussion of R. Stark's paper, "Der Gesamtaufbau der aristotelischen Politik," in Fondation Hardt *Entretiens sur l'Antiquité Classique* XI, *La "Politique" d'Aristote* (Geneva, 1964), pp. 42–3.
11 In "Der Gesamtaufbau der aristotelischen Politik" (*La "Politique" d'Aristote*, pp. 1–35).
12 W. Theiler, "Bau und Zeit der aristotelischen Politik," *Museum Helveticum*, 9 (1952), pp. 65–78.

different, though sometimes overlapping, lecture-courses. Jaeger's hypo-thesis seems clearly superior to both of these. It takes account (at any rate at first sight) of the salient facts, unlike Stark's; and unlike Theiler's, it is also an economical hypothesis.

In what follows, however, I propose to call Jaeger's position into question. Firstly, I shall examine more closely the nature of the contrast between Books IV–VI, on the one hand (the so-called "empirical" books), and Books VII–VIII (the "Utopian" books) on the other. Secondly, I shall consider the extent of the usefulness of the genetic approach as applied in the context of the *Politics* as a whole. There is nothing new in the sceptical tone that I shall adopt on this latter point; so, for example, in the introduction to his translation of the *Politics*, Barker suggests that we should "abandon the attempt to apply a genetic method to the composition and structure of the Politics, and . . . renounce the search for chronological strata." Instead, we should "adopt the view that the six 'methods' of the *Politics* all belong to the period of the Lyceum, and are all – so far as chronology goes – on exactly the same footing. There is really no valid reason why we should adopt any other view."[13] Ross's opinion, too, is much the same.[14] In general, I will claim little originality for my conclusions; only my route to them may be different.

EMPIRICISM VERSUS UTOPIANISM?

It is sometimes denied that Books VII–VIII are Utopian. Stark, for example, claims that the best constitution of VII–VIII (VII.1.1323a14) is essentially the "polity" talked about in the earlier books; it is not simply a matter of "a new experiment in the familiar tradition of the Utopian construction of ideal states," but of the construction of a practical model for the foundation of new states and the reform of existing ones.[15] But this view of VII–VIII does not square well with the text; granted that "polity" (and the "middle constitution" of Book IV, if this is not actually the same thing) is a practical model in the sense Stark has in mind, the constitution of VII–VIII is not a polity. It is, in fact, although Stark denies it, an ideal aristocracy, for all its citizens are to be good men (VII.9.1329a19ff.: see VII.13.1332a28ff.). (Polity, on the other hand, is typically seen as a mixture of oligarchy and democracy – or, in other words, simply as balancing the claims of rich and poor.)[16] In terms of the distinctions made at the beginning of Book IV, the constitution of VII–VIII is best without qualification; whereas polity and the "middle constitution" are constitutions which are "easier and more accessible to all" (IV.1.1288b38–9).

---

13 *The Politics of Aristotle*, tr. E. Barker (Oxford, 1946), pp. xliii–xliv.
14 W. D. Ross, "The Development of Aristotle's Thought," *Proceedings of the British Academy*, 43 (1957), pp. 70–72.
15 "Der Gesamtaufbau der aristotelischen Politik," pp. 32ff.
16 See esp. IV.8, 9.

In Aristotle's terms, then, I would claim that the constitution described in VII–VIII is certainly ideal; it is also nowhere (for no existing state – as Aristotle himself recognizes[17] – educates its citizens for virtue as his state will), and it is plainly based, at least to some extent, on analysis and criticism of existing constitutions (whether it is based on the 158 "collected" constitutions is a separate question which will arise later). The constitution of VII–VIII therefore fulfils the criteria suggested by M. I. Finley for distinguishing Utopian from other kinds of speculation: "The very word Utopia suggests that the ideal society is not actually or wholly attainable. Nevertheless, every significant Utopia is conceived as a goal towards which one may legitimately and hopefully strive, a goal not in some shadowy state of perfection but with specific institutional criticisms and proposals."[18] (Ferguson, on the other hand, seems to identify Utopianism with "building castles in clouds,"[19] and it is in this sense, I suppose, that he declares that "Aristotle was not a Utopian."[20] But in general Ferguson's position seems less than clear.)

It is the second of Finley's two points that I want to stress with regard to Aristotle's description of the ideal constitution in *Politics* VII–VIII: namely that his basic purpose throughout is *critical*. His aim is to provide a standard, either for the reform of existing states, or at any rate for judging them; for as he admits in Book VII, "it happens that some men can partake in happiness [or *eudaimonia*] while others can partake in it only a little or not at all; and it is clear that this is why more than one kind and variety of city and more than one constitution come into being" (VII.8.1328a38–41). As we are told repeatedly elsewhere in the *Politics*, for some communities one of the corrupt types of constitution will be appropriate, because of their make-up – they may, for example, contain a very high proportion of the indigent, in which case some form of democracy will be right for them.[21] No possibility of creating the best constitution here; but at least judgment can be passed – the constitution may be worse or less bad than others, but it is in any case defective, as Aristotle puts it, uncompromisingly (IV.2.1289b9–11).

My point here is that the enterprise of VII–VIII is in principle perfectly compatible with some sort of empirical study of actual constitutions; indeed,

---

17 At *EN* X.10.1180a24–6, he says that "in the city of the Spartans alone, <or> with a few others, does the legislator seem to have paid attention to questions of nurture and habits (*epitēdeumata*)"; at I.13.1102a10–12, the lawgivers of Crete and Sparta are used to illustrate the point that it is the business of the political expert to make the citizens good (see also *Pol.* VIII.1337a31–2, where the Spartans are mentioned alone). But at *Pol.* II.9.1271a41ff., Aristotle explicitly accepts Plato's fundamental criticism of the one-sidedness of Spartan education (compare VIII.4.1338b9ff.).

18 "Utopianism Ancient and Modern," in *The Use and Abuse of History* (London, 1975), pp. 180–1.

19 J. Ferguson, *Utopias of the Classical World* (London, 1975), p. 88. Stark ("Gesamtaufbau") implies a similar view.

20 *Utopias of the Classical World*, p. 80.

21 See esp. IV.12, VI.1ff.

the one is the natural complement of the other. What I want to consider next is whether it is compatible with the kind of enterprise in which we find Aristotle actually employed in Books IV–VI.

I begin by quoting Jaeger:

Over against [the] speculative picture [of Books VII–VIII] stands the empirical part in Books IV–VI. It shows no trace of the old Platonic spirit of constructions and ideal outlines. Aristotle does, however, expressly define his attitude towards the older part when, at the beginning of IV, he explains that in addition to the construction of the ideal it is a no less important task of the political theorist to examine what is good or bad for a particular state in given conditions. The constitution of an absolute ideal, and the determination of the best politics possible under given conditions, are parts of one and the same science. His remarks on this point show that he felt a certain difficulty in combining Plato's Utopian speculations with this purely empirical treatment, although he believed himself able to overcome it. He tried to escape by pointing to the analogy of a double form of medicine and gymnastics, the one concerning itself with the pure standard and the other applying the knowledge thus gained to the given case. Throughout the introduction to the empirical part one can scarcely help feeling that there is an undertone of polemic against the mere construction of ideals, and that Aristotle was very proud of his innovation. The uncompromising assertion of the unattainable ideal could not help the rent and riven actualities of Greek politics.[22]

This characterization of IV–VI and of the contrast between them and VII–VIII is inadequate (nor, I think, is it improved on in the following pages). The political theorist, as Jaeger puts it, is "to examine what is good or bad for a particular state in given conditions," or, alternatively, to determine "the best politics possible under given conditions." But how does this conflict with the construction of an ideal? Knowledge about the ideal and knowledge about how best to approximate to it will surely be *complementary*, for all but the most uncompromising theorist.[23]

22 *Aristotle*, pp. 269–70.
23 On p. 271, Jaeger writes: "in [IV–VI] the unbiased observation of empirical reality has led [Aristotle] to a wholly different mode of treatment, which starts from the particular phenomena and seeks to discover their inner law, like a scientist observing the characteristic motions and emotions of a living thing. The theory of the diseases of states and of the method of curing them is modelled on the physician's pathology and therapy. It is scarcely possible to imagine a greater contrast to the doctrine of an ideal norm, which constituted Plato's political theory and that of Aristotle in his early days, than this view, according to which no state is so hopelessly disorganized that one cannot at least risk the attempt at a cure. Radical methods would certainly destroy it in short order; the measure of the powers of recovery that it can exert must be determined solely be examining itself and its condition." According to this account, as I understand it, the difference between IV–VI and VII–VIII is in the type of treatment proposed for diseased states: whereas in VII–VIII Aristotle had envisaged no alternative to large-scale surgery, in IV–VI he accepts that more moderate measures may be in order; for he now sees that some states will be

The issues emerge rather more clearly in the following passage from G. H. Sabine (who, however, elsewhere follows Jaeger fairly closely):

> Plato's prevailing ethical interest in the subject still predominates; the good man and the good citizen are one and the same, or at all events they ought to be, and the end of the state is to produce the highest moral type of human being. It is not to be supposed that Aristotle consciously abandoned this point of view, since the treatise on the ideal state was left standing as an important part of the *Politics*. At some date not far removed from the opening of the Lyceum, however, he conceived a science or art of politics on a much larger scale. The new science was to be general: that is, it should deal with actual as well as ideal forms of government and it should teach the art of governing and organizing states of any sort in any desired manner. This new general science of politics, therefore, was not only empirical and descriptive, but even in some respects independent of any ethical purpose, since a statesman might need to be expert in governing even a bad state. The whole science of politics, according to the new idea, included the knowledge both of the political good, relative as well as absolute, and also of political mechanics employed perhaps for an inferior or even a bad end. This enlargement of the definition of political philosophy is Aristotle's most characteristic conception.[24]

If Sabine's statement is essentially correct, and I think it is, we are faced with a major puzzle about Aristotle's view of the role of political science in IV–VI. The crucial passage in this connection is at IV.1 1288b21ff.

> So it is clear [Aristotle says there] that it will be the part of the same science both to consider the best constitution . . . and what constitution fits which people . . . and again, thirdly, that which is based on a presupposition (for [the good legislator and the true political scientist] must also be able to consider any given constitution, both how it might come into existence at the beginning, and once it has come into existence, in what way it might be preserved for the most time; I mean for example if it happens that some city is run neither according to the best constitution, but is unprovided even with the necessary resources, nor according to the best constitution possible from the resources it does have, but some worse one), and in addition to all these political science must discover the constitution that best fits all cities; so that the majority of those who have treated of constitutions, even if what they say may be acceptable enough in other respects, fail to hit on what is *useful*.

Now three of these functions of political science seem on the face of it perfectly compatible: consideration of the absolutely best constitution; of the

incapable of being completely cured (through the realization of the best constitution), but that these will nevertheless be able to achieve at any rate a partial cure (some approximation to the best). The basis of this interpretation seems to be IV.1.1288b37ff., which Jaeger takes as self-criticism, but which need not be taken in that way. Even if it is self-criticism, at the worst it would merely suggest a broadening in Aristotle's idea of the concerns of political science – scarcely enough to cause the embarrassment Jaeger detects in IV.1.

24 G. H. Sabine, *A History of Political Theory*, 4th edn (Hinsdale, Illinois, 1973), p. 91.

one that best fits all; and consideration of which constitutions fit which people. It is a standing part of Aristotle's view of science or *technê* that it will not only be concerned with producing ideal results, but also with making the best of the materials at its disposal.[25] So, for example, it is the doctor's business not merely to make people healthy, but to provide the proper treatment for the man who can never be healthy. It follows that the proponent of political science will not be exclusively occupied with ideal constitutions, but also with inferior forms of constitution, where the conditions for the highest form are not present. In these cases, he will have to know what the conditions *do* allow; he will also, so Aristotle suggests, have to set up a more accessible ideal to aim at.

Up to this point, all seems to be much as we would expect. But the fourth of the four functions that Aristotle attributes to political science comes as something of a surprise: the study of any given constitution,

> both how it might come into existence at the beginning, and once it has come into existence, in what way it might be preserved for the most time; I mean for example if it happens that some city is run neither according to the best constitution, but unprovided even with the necessary resources, nor according to the best constitution possible from the resources it does have, but some worse one.

This is Sabine's "political mechanics employed . . . for a bad end." Aristotle uses the analogy of the trainer and the coach: "If a man does not wish to achieve either the physical condition or the knowledge of the competitive skills of which he is capable, it is no less the business of the trainer and the coach to produce this capacity too" (IV.1.1288b16–19).[26] I can see four possible political situations which might come under Aristotle's description, as I understand it: (1) where a city is being founded, and chooses a worse constitution than the one it is capable of; (2) where it changes its existing constitution for a worse one; (3) where it retains its existing constitution, and this is worse than it is capable of; and finally (4) where it changes its constitution for a better one, but this is still worse than it is capable of. This last case is the only one where the parallel with the trainer and the coach will in fact work. There is no parallel at least with the trainer in the first case; everyone is in some sort of physical condition, however bad. As for the other two cases, it will be very odd to say, as the analogy will suggest, that it's the

---

25 *Top.* I.3.101b5ff.; *Rhet.* I.1.1355b10ff.; *EN* I.11.1100b35ff.

26 Strictly speaking, the examples of the trainer and coach are not applied to political science, but are used to illustrate one of the four headings into which all sciences generally are said to divide their subject-matter. But since the particular task of political science in question is obviously intended to fall under that general heading (because (a) the statement about the aims of political science is derived directly from that about the concerns of all sciences (*hōste*, "so that," b21), and (b) the other three tasks assigned to political science correspond to the other three assigned to all sciences), it is reasonable to expect that the example of the trainer and the coach will throw light on it too.

trainer's job to help a man get less fit than he is, or conspire with him to keep him flabby;[27] or that it's the coach's job to help him lose his athletic skills, or stop him improving them if he can. The end or aim of medicine, Aristotle says, reasonably enough, at the beginning of the *Nicomachean Ethics*, is health; that of the shipwright's art is a ship, of generalship victory, of household economics wealth (*EN* I.1.1094a8–9). Of course, the proponent of any science will be capable also of achieving the opposite of the end belonging to his science, since "one and the same capacity and science seem to relate to opposite objects" – to use one formulation of a familiar principle (*EN* V.1.1129a13–14). But it will not be his business actually to work for the wrong end, which would be a misuse of his science. (That, at least, I take to be the moral of the discussion in the first chapter of the *Rhetoric*.)[28] And yet this is precisely what the political scientist will be doing, if, as Aristotle suggests, he is to help produce worse constitutions than conditions allow.

One possible escape-route is to suppose that when Aristotle talks about political science "considering" any given constitution, what he has in mind is a purely theoretical, not a practical, concern: just as it is a part of rhetoric to know how to argue on both sides of a question, "not in order that we may in practice employ [our skill] in both ways (for we must not make people believe what is wrong), but in order that we may see clearly what the facts are, and that, if another man argues unfairly, we on our part may be able to confute him" (*Rhet.* I.1.1355a30–33, in the Oxford translation). Aristotle several times suggests that the *Politics* as a whole does have a theoretical as well as a practical aim (I.3.1253b15ff., I.11.1258b9–10, III.8.1279b11ff., IV.15.1299 a28–30). On the other hand, there is nothing to suggest a merely theoretical concern in the present passage; and indeed the analogy with the trainer and the coach suggests just the opposite. A second, and more promising, way out is hinted at by Sabine: "A constitution," he says, "is not only a way of life for the citizens but also an organization of officers to carry on public business, and therefore its political aspects cannot be forthwith identified with its ethical purpose."[29] Thus we might suppose that political science will be involved in setting up, say, an inferior form of democracy, even when this is not the appropriate form of constitution for that city, in so

[27 This might be an unfair way of describing the case : "flabbiness," after all, is a relative concept, and a trainer might well agree to help someone to stay in the condition he is (rather than deteriorating to a still worse one), or to do as well as he can towards his limited aims, if that is not the same thing. Either alternative would give a clear sense to (3) above (compare T. H. Irwin, "Moral Science and Political Theory in Aristotle," in P. A. Cartledge and F. D. Harvey, eds, *Crux* [London, 1985], p. 155), so that the parallel between political scientist and trainer will work here too – but only up to a point: while it is perfectly intelligible, especially from an Aristotelian perspective, why a person should choose not to aim for competition fitness, it is hard to see what grounds a city could have for aiming at less than the best of which it was capable, or a (true) political scientist – who knows both what is absolutely and what is relatively best – for encouraging it to do so.]
28 I.1.1355a28ff.
29 *A History of Political Theory*, p. 105.

far as political arrangements may be judged by their relative efficiency or inefficiency, quite apart from their ethical aspect. But this route seems ruled out by the fact that wherever Aristotle is occupied with the subject of the "organization of officers," the question whether any particular arrangement is efficient or not generally matters less to him than what type of constitution it belongs to.[30]

I confess that I have no solution to offer to this puzzle.[31] But one or two observations may be made: first, that when Aristotle comes formally to announce his programme for Books IV–VI, at the end of chapter 2 of Book IV, there is no item which clearly and unambiguously falls under the heading of "considering any given constitution." The main questions included in the programme are (1) how many varieties of constitution there are; (2) what the most accessible type of constitution is; (3) which of the other types of constitution is choiceworthy for which people; (4) in what way one should set about establishing these constitutions; and (5) what the causes of the destruction and preservation of constitutions are, both generally and with respect to each individual type. It is particularly striking that the question about how constitutions are to be established is brought into connection with the preceding one, about which suit which people; thus here Aristotle does not propose considering how to establish any and every constitution, without regard to the conditions, as he seemed to do in chapter 1: there, Aristotle said that the political scientist "must be able to study any given constitution, both how it might come into existence at the beginning and . . . in what way it might be preserved for the most time."[32] (I differ from Newman[33] in thinking that in this instance the question "how it might come into existence" is the same as that about how one should set about establishing a given constitution.) And as it turns out, Aristotle does indeed discuss the question about how to establish constitutions in connection with

30 See esp. IV.14–16.

[31 Irwin's attempt ("Moral Science and Political Theory in Aristotle," p. 155) to make the puzzle disappear receives a reply in my "Reality and Utopia," in *Elenchos*, 10 (1989), pp. 317–36; the same paper also responds to Irwin's more ambitious claim to be able to connect *Pol.* IV–VI, VII–VIII and *EN* as parts of a single cohesive argument – a claim which would render most of the rest of the present paper redundant.]

[32 In "Reality and Utopia" (see preceding note), I propose to reject this interpretation of 1289b20–22, taking (4) as connecting rather with (1): (1) refers specifically to the varieties of *democracy and oligarchy* whose existence Aristotle has adverted to in IV.1.1289a7ff. ("if indeed there are more than one form both of democracy and of oligarchy," b13–14), and as b21–2 shows ("I mean democracies, according to each form, and again oligarchies"), "these constitutions" in (4) must have the same reference. Since any of these varieties might presumably be established even where conditions allow some better constitutional arrangement (compare IV.12), we could then in principle discover here something comparable to the offending item in IV.1. But if that was Aristotle's intention, it is still scarcely "clear and unambiguous"; and notably the crucial case of tyranny (see below) would be excluded.]

33 W. L. Newman, *The Politics of Aristotle*, vol. IV (Oxford, 1902), on IV (Newman's VI). 1.1288b29.

the question about which suits which people (this mainly in VI). On the other hand, there is much in the discussion of the causes of the destruction and preservation of states in V which plainly *does* belong under the heading in question, "considering any constitution regardless of the conditions" – most notably, of course, the long treatment of tyranny (V.11.1313a34ff.) So far as I know, Aristotle nowhere suggests that any type of population is suited for tyranny – at any rate any population of *Greeks*. M. I. Finley does not think the treatment of tyranny in V is to be taken too seriously: "One can be misled by Aristotle's temperament," he says: "he was a dazzling virtuoso and could not always resist a virtuoso display."[34] But it is difficult to accept this, when the treatment is consistent with Aristotle's formal and official statement of the purposes of political science at the beginning of Book IV. A second point worth mentioning is that there is what looks like a close parallel to Aristotle's apparent misdemeanour in IV. This is in Book I, chapter 11, in the course of the discussion of the science of getting wealth (*chrêmatistikê*). Aristotle has just distinguished between natural and unnatural forms of this science; he then declares: "Since we have adequately discussed the part of our subject that relates to knowledge pure and simple, we must now consider that part of it that relates to practice. In all such things, theoretical speculation is worthy enough of a free man, but practical experience is not" (1258b9–11). He then proceeds to enumerate the parts of both the natural and the unnatural kinds of *chrêmatistikê*, and to give hints about where anyone interested in *chrêmatistikê* of either kind should go to find practical advice. Deplorable, Aristotle's attitude implies; but still a fact of life.

Still, it is unfair to dismiss the whole of IV–VI, as Barker does, as "The Trimmer's Opinion of the Laws of Government."[35] (Sabine's account, too, tends perhaps to imply the same view.) For the most part, IV–VI is concerned – as the programme in IV.2 suggests – with the *reform* of existing states, with reference to some kind of ideal. I therefore propose finally to leave behind the problem of Aristotle's Machiavellian mood, and turn back to the other three functions accorded to political science in IV.1: to consider what the best constitution is absolutely; to consider what constitution fits what people; and to consider what constitution most fits all existing states. Now I suggested that these functions were in principle compatible with one another; in each case, it was the business of political science to establish the highest form of constitution of which the conditions allowed. But this is to assume that the lower forms can be arranged in order according to the standard of the ideal constitution; and it is in fact by no means obvious that this is so.

There are at least two difficulties. Firstly, Aristotle holds that the end of a city is the good life, and this means, ideally, that its end is to provide the conditions for the exercise of virtue by its citizens.[36] But now oligarchy sets

34 "The Ancestral Constitution," in *The Use and Abuse of History*, p. 52.
35 "The Life of Aristotle and the Composition and Structure of the *Politics*," p. 164.
36 I.2.1252b30, III.6.1278b20ff., III.9.1280a31–2, b39; compare IV.4.1291 a16–18.

wealth as its goal (V.10.1311a9–10; compare III.15.1286b15–16), and democracy either wealth (VI.7.1321a41–b1) or freedom (*Rhet* I.8.1366a4),[37]
understood – probably – as the freedom to do as one pleases.[38] This is the
idea that lies behind a passage in Book VII that I have already referred to
once before:

> it happens that some men can partake in happiness, while others can partake in
> it only a little or not at all; and it is clear that this is why more than one kind
> and variety of city and more than one constitution come into being; for each
> type of people hunts after this [i.e. happiness] in a different way, and so brings
> it about that there are different kinds of life and different kinds of constitution
> (VII.8.1328a38–b2).

In so far as political science works within an oligarchic or democratic system,
the goals of oligarchy or democracy will become its own; and since these
goals, in Aristotle's view, are not just lower down on the same scale as the
proper one, but simply *wrong*, it seems to follow that this will be a wrong use
of political science. To some extent, this objection can be blunted. As I have
said, Aristotle's main emphasis in IV–VI is on *reform*; and on the whole, his
suggestions for reform aim at making oligarchies less oligarchical, and
democracies less democratic – the ideal, that is in the context of Books
IV–VI, being the mean between the two. On the other hand, it is quite
obvious that the end or aim of the "mean constitution" is not happiness in
the true Aristotelian sense; there is no suggestion anywhere in the discussion
of this constitution that it is systematically concerned with virtue at all. The
general implication of the discussion is that the mean or middle constitution
has an essentially pragmatic aim, that of ensuring political stability; and it is
an excellent form of constitution precisely because of its excellence at
fulfilling that aim.[39]

The second difficulty is this. Different kinds of constitution, as Aristotle
repeatedly[40] says in the *Politics*, involve different conceptions of justice: under
a democracy, there will be democratic justice, under an oligarchy oligarchic
justice, and under a tyranny – well, perhaps no justice at all (*EN*
VIII.13.1161a32ff.). Only under the correct forms of constitution will we
find justice in an unqualified sense – and this is, indeed, what makes them
correct (III.6.1279a17–21). If it is to function inside the deviant forms of
constitution, as it evidently is, then to that extent political science will be
involved in supporting the appropriate varieties of justice, since it will be
responsible for the laws in which they are embodied. And democratic,
oligarchic, and tyrannical justice are actually *defective* forms; indeed from the

37 In *Rhet.* I.8.1366a5–6, the end or aim of aristocracy is summed up as "what
contributes to education and behaviour in accordance with law and custom (*ta
nomima*)."
38 Compare *Pol.* VI.2.1317b11ff.
39 Note esp. IV.11.1296a7 "That the mean [constitution] is best, is clear; for it alone
is free from faction."
40 E.g. at III.9.1280a7ff., V.1.1301b35ff., V.9.1309a36–9.

standard of unqualified, or "natural" justice, as Aristotle calls it in the *Nicomachean Ethics* (V.10.1134b18ff.), they are actually unjust. Thus the role of political science here will be precisely the opposite of the one it has within the best constitution: under the best constitution it will create just laws; under the deviant forms, it will promote *in*justice.[41]

Once again, it may be replied that this is to ignore Aristotle's preoccupation with reform. What is more, in this case the suggested reforms *will* make the constitution better by the standard of the best; for at least one of their effects will be that it will be more just.[42] The basic tenor of Aristotle's advice is that constitutions generally should be less partisan. He sees oligarchy as the domination of rich over poor, and democracy as the domination of poor over rich (III.7.1279b7ff., etc.); in both cases, one side pursues its own interests at the expense of the other's interests. Each side, he suggests, should be prepared to give more to the other than it does, and should attempt some admixture of the opposite form of constitution (see especially V.9.1309b18ff.). A correct mixture of oligarchy and democracy, such as we would find under a polity, would result in justice being done to both sides (V.7. 1307a5ff.).

On the other hand, in IV–VI as a whole we find Aristotle making very little of this point. The general standpoint of the three books as a whole is that injustice is to be avoided because it leads to stasis; it is a means to an end, rather than being an end in itself. One passage where justice *is* the prime consideration is at IV.13.1297a38ff.:

> So that it is clear that if someone wants to make a just mixture, he must bring together the devices used by both sides: the poor must be paid for attending the assembly and the law-courts, the rich fined for not attending; for in this way everyone will have a share, while in the other way [i.e. if one adopted just one of these devices], the constitution would belong to one side only.

But after this solid sentiment there is a sudden change of tone:

> But [Aristotle goes on] the constitution ought to be only out of those who possess heavy arms; it is not possible to define absolutely what the amount of the property-qualification <should> be, and say that people should have so much, but having considered the highest amount it is possible to require while still leaving those with a share in the constitution in a majority over those without such a share, we ought to fix this amount. For the poor are happy to keep quiet even if they do not possess political privileges, providing no one attacks them or takes away any of their property.

41 Compare III.11.1282b10–13 "This, however, is clear, that the laws must be adapted to the constitutions. But, if so, true forms of government will of necessity have just laws, and perverted forms of government will have unjust laws" (Oxford translation; "unjust" renders *ou dikaious*).
42 I assume here that the best constitution will turn out to possess the highest degree of justice (even though this is not the criterion by which Aristotle calls it best) – higher than "polity," in so far as office is distributed by reference to *virtue*.

One may surely object that it may be *safe* to exclude the poor in this situation; but is it *just*? Here, as in the discussion of the middle constitution, on which the present passage depends, it is stability, not justice, that matters most.

Thus when Aristotle finally sets up his "easier and more accessible" ideal, it turns out to be measured by a different standard from the one it replaces. Political stability and virtue may be perfectly compatible as goals; indeed the achievement of the one may be a necessary condition for the achievement of the other. On the other hand, it patently does not follow from this that a stable constitution will in itself be better in terms of the other standard than an unstable one. But Aristotle nowhere explicitly recognizes that different standards are being used; he talks as if the enterprise of IV–VI were a simple and straightforward extension of that of VII–VIII.

My claim, then, is that Aristotle tacitly attributes at least two quite distinct practical aims to political science: firstly, the creation of a virtuous city, or the closest approximation to such a city; and secondly, the achievement of political stability and order. The first of these aims is implicit in Books VII–VIII, whereas it is the second that predominates in Books IV–VI – although the first never disappears entirely; so, for instance, Aristotle concludes his remarks about the preferability of the less traditional method of preserving tyranny by saying that if he adopts this method, the tyrant "will himself attain a habit of character, if not wholly disposed to goodness, at any rate half-good – half-good and yet half-bad, but at any rate not *wholly* bad" (V.11.1315b8–10 in Barker's translation).

THE USEFULNESS OF THE GENETIC HYPOTHESIS

The last part of this paper will consider the reasons for this uneasy combination of aims in the *Politics*, in a mainly negative way. My chief purpose will be to argue against any chronological explanation, of the type proposed by Jaeger.

According to Jaeger's account, the "purely empirical" part of the *Politics* came later than the "Utopian" part. (Incidentally, it will be clear from what I have said that I regard these tags as misleading: in both cases Utopianism is *combined* with empiricism.)[43] Jaeger refers to the programmatic statement at the end of the *Nicomachean Ethics*, which in the English version of his translation runs as follows:

"First, if anything has been said well in detail by earlier thinkers, let us try to review it; then in the light of the constitutions we have collected let us study what sorts of influence preserve or destroy states, and what sorts preserve or destroy the particular kinds of constitution, and to what cause it is due that some are well and others ill administered. When these have been studied we shall perhaps be most likely to see with a comprehensive view which

43 Compare Ross, "The Development of Aristotle's Thought", p. 70.

constitution is best, and how each must be ordered, and what laws and customs it must use, if it is to be at its best" (X.10.1181b15–22).

This programme [Jaeger says] obviously implies a turning-point in the development of Aristotle's *Politics*. In unambiguous language he here abandons the purely constructive method that Plato and he himself had previously followed, and takes his stand on sober empirical study. What he says is in fact – and nothing but his extreme explicitness has prevented his being understood – : "Up to now I have been using another method. I have made my ideal state by logical construction, without being sufficiently acquainted with the facts of experience. But now I have at my disposal the copious material of the 158 constitutions, and I am going to use it in order to give to the ideal state a positive foundation."[44]

Suitably adapted, this could provide an explanation of sorts of the state of affairs I have attempted to describe in the earlier parts of this paper. Early on in his career, Aristotle satisfies himself with writing a Utopia on the Platonic model; later on, he comes to realize that this approach is useless in terms of practical politics, and proceeds to construct a more accessible ideal. On this account, the difference in aim between the two approaches is of no great importance; there is simply an early and a late Aristotle, and we are absolved from trying to make any consistent sense out of the *Politics* as a whole.

One immediate and crucial objection to this is that Aristotle himself suggests in IV that political science will combine both approaches;[45] for, *pace* Jaeger, there is no reason for supposing that the absolutely best constitution talked about at the beginning of IV is not the one described in VII–VIII. Thus even if it turned out that VII–VIII were written early, it would be wrong to suggest – as Jaeger effectively does – that the approach it embodies is *replaced* by that of IV–VI.

All the same, it could be urged that although Aristotle might still theoretically regard discussion of the absolutely best constitution as a proper part of political science, in practice his real interests were now else-where – namely with the more realistic concerns of IV–VI. In order to answer this suggestion, I want to look in some detail at the last chapter of the *Nicomachean Ethics*.

The argument of the chapter runs, briefly summarized, as follows. In the matter of virtue, Aristotle says, knowledge alone is not enough; what we must do is to try to become good. Argument alone will not suffice for the purpose; the crucial factor is habituation, and we will not achieve this without good *laws*. "But it is difficult to get from youth up a right training for virtue if one has not been brought up under right laws; for to live temperately and hardily is not pleasant to most people, especially when they are young."[46] But the process must go on even when they are grown up, so that laws will be necessary here too. At 1180a5–14, Aristotle appeals to the *Laws* for support

44 Jaeger, *Aristotle*, p. 265.
45 I.e. in IV.1.
46 X.10.1179b31–4, in the Oxford translation (but with "virtue" for *aretē* instead of Ross/Urmson's "excellence," for the sake of consistency).

for his general doctrine. Then he resumes: if a man is to be brought up in the right way, and is to go on to live rightly, and it requires a certain authority to bring this about; if, further, a father's authority is not enough, or indeed that of any single person, unless he is a king, what we will need will be *law*, which does have the necessary compelling force. But only in the Spartan state, or perhaps in a few others as well, does the legislator seem to have paid proper attention to questions of upbringing and people's habits; in most cities, each man lives just as he pleases, Cyclops-fashion. "It is best, therefore, that there should be public care for such matters; but if they are neglected by the community it would seem right for each man to help his children and friends towards virtue. . . . But it would seem from what has been said that he will be better able to do this if he makes himself an expert in legislation."[47] Public control is exercised through laws; a father's injunctions are like laws on the small scale. There may actually be some advantage in private control; but in general what is needed is *expert knowledge*. So how does one gain this knowledge? It will be no good going to the politicians, for none of them either promises to teach the art of legislation, or can teach it. Nor will it be any good going to the sophists; they think that all that is necessary is to collect together the best of existing laws, and that that is a simple matter – but how is one to make the right choice? Collections of laws and constitutions will be useful to those who "are able to study and judge what is good or bad and what enactments suit what circumstances; but those who go through these things without the appropriate disposition [i.e. without the necessary critical faculty] will not have right judgment (unless as a spontaneous gift of nature), although perhaps they may increase their understanding of these matters" (1181b6–12). So far Aristotle has only told us where not to go if we want to learn the art of legislation: don't go to the politicians; don't go to the sophists. Where we should go, as Aristotle proceeds to imply, is to Aristotle; though he has emphasized before that *experience* will be necessary too (1181a9–12). "So," he says, "since our predecessors have left the subject of legislation to us unexamined, it is perhaps best that we should ourselves study it, and in general study the question of the constitution, in order to complete to the best of our ability our philosophy of human nature (1181b12–15)." Finally, there comes the programmatic statement cited earlier in the English version of Jaeger's translation.

There has been considerable discussion about whether this programme does or does not fit our *Politics*. One particularly debated point is the proper interpretation of the last sentence but one: does the question mean, as Jaeger takes it to mean, "what sort of constitution is best absolutely?" Or, as Immisch argues,[48] does it mean, "What is the best out of the types we have collected together?" I do not myself think that this particular issue can be

---

47 1180a29–34. (Here, and in the following two citations from Aristotle, the Ross/Urmson translation is adapted to a rather greater extent.)

48 O. Immisch, "Der Epilog der Nikomachischen Ethik," *Rheinisches Museum für Philologie*, 84 (1935), pp. 54–61.

resolved; and it is therefore not certain whether the programme contains any reference to the description of the absolutely best constitution in Books VII and VIII – although there is a clear reference to Book II, in which Aristotle discusses the opinions of his predecessors. Taken by itself, then, the programme could at least be consistent with the view that IV–VI are essentially independent of, and perhaps a replacement for, the old method embodied in VII and VIII.

But the chapter as a whole – I mean *Nicomachean Ethics* X.10 – is plainly not consistent with such a view. The immediate justification that Aristotle gives for going on to a work on politics – apart from saying that it will complete his study of things human – is that it will help us to acquire the art of legislation; and what we need to acquire the art of legislation for is to help us to produce virtue in others. Now it is Aristotle's complaint that most existing states do not pay attention to the moral health of their citizens at all; only the Spartans do so "and perhaps a few others" – among them, presumably, the Cretans (I.13.1102a10). Moreover, when he actually discusses the subject of Spartan education, he explicitly accepts the criticism of it made by Plato in the *Laws*.[49] It therefore seems inevitable that if we are to learn what Aristotle wants us to learn about the art of legislation, we will be involved in discussing ideal constitutions as well as actual ones; and moreover they will be of the type put forward in VII–VIII, whose central feature is exactly that it educates the citizens for virtue. Quite apart from X.10, it is not too much to say – and it has been said before, for example by Newman[50] – that VII–VIII represent the proper culmination of "the study of things human" as understood by the *Nicomachean Ethics* as a whole. Already in Book I, Aristotle has announced that it is the task – or at least the main task – of political science and its practitioners to make men good (I.10.1099b20–32, 13.1102a7–10). We can also think of Book VI, in which political science is said to be the same disposition as practical wisdom, with the difference that political science is concerned with the city, practical wisdom with the individual (VI.8.1141b23ff.). Since practical wisdom by definition is always aimed towards the best ends, the same is presumably true of political science, and therefore also of the art of legislation, which forms one part of it. And the best end, in the context of the city, is to make men happy, and therefore virtuous.

On the other hand, the programme at the end of the work plainly looks forward to Books IV–VI of the *Politics*. It is fair to say, then, that the *Nicomachean Ethics* leads us to expect a work of more of less exactly the kind we have: one which sets "the constitution of an absolute ideal"[51] side by side with more realistic preoccupations.[52] And this is surely enough to show that

---

49 See n. 17 above.
50 *The Politics of Aristotle*, vol. II, Appendix A.
51 Jaeger, *Aristotle*, p. 269.
52 That is, if we assume that the programme is of a piece with the rest of X.10. This is doubted e.g. by J. A. Stewart (*Notes on the Nicomachean Ethics of Aristotle* [Oxford, 1892], on 1181b12), who regards everything from b12 to the end as an interpolation.

Aristotle is serious when he himself claims at the beginning of *Politics* Book IV that both kinds of enterprise are equally part of political science. We may need the genetic method to explain the peculiarities of the form of the *Politics*; but in the end it will not, I think, seriously affect our interpretation of its contents.[53]

I conclude, then, that the difference between the aims of political science in Books IV–VI and Books VII–VIII of the *Politics* cannot be explained away simply in terms of a change of mind on Aristotle's part. Rather, we should assume the existence of a fundamental ambivalence in Aristotle's attitude, one that is perhaps not difficult to understand. He is firmly committed to the Platonic ideal of the virtuous city; but he is also committed to the idea that political science must have something *useful* to say. In order to do this, he suggests, it must try to do what it can to help existing constitutions, and not satisfy itself with proposing to rub them out and start again (IV.1.

But the chapter plainly cannot end at b12, for this would leave us without any positive answer to the crucial question raised at 1180b28–9. It is possible that Aristotle could have ended with b15; but even supposing this were so, the case for which I am arguing could still be made. At b12–13, Aristotle begins "So since our predecessors have left the subject of legislation to us unexamined." Now if at this point he had been looking forward to a *Politics* without IV–VI, these words would surely be inexplicable, since Plato must be included among "our predecessors" (*pace* K. von Fritz and E. Kapp, in the introduction to their translation of *The Constitution of Athens* [New York, 1950], p. 43), and VII–VIII, which would then form the main positive part of the work, are beyond doubt heavily indebted to the *Laws* (that the *Laws* predates this chapter of the *EN* is established by the unmistakable reference to it at 1180a5ff. G. Morrow's suggestion, in his paper "Aristotle's Comments on Plato's *Laws*" (in I. Düring and G. E. L. Owen, eds, *Aristotle and Plato in the Mid-Fourth Century* [Göteborg, 1960], pp. 145–62), that not all of the *Laws* may have been known to Aristotle at the time when he was writing his criticism of the work, seems to me to be based on insufficient grounds). It is IV–VI that are plainly thought of as going beyond Plato (see especially IV.1.1288b35ff, which may well give at least part of the justification for Aristotle's seemingly extravagant claim in the lines under discussion (i.e. *EN* X.10.1180b12–13)); although the main justification for it seems to lie in the reference that has been made to the collected constitutions – no one else, perhaps Aristotle is saying, has done the necessary ground-work, in the way that I have. Compare R. A. Gauthier and J. Y. Jolif, *Aristote: l'Ethique à Nicomaque* (Louvain, 1970), *ad loc.* X.10 itself is anchored to the rest of the *EN* by what looks like a reference to it at V.2.1130b26–9 – except of course to the extent that Kenny's work (A. Kenny, *The Aristotelian Ethics: A Study of the Relationship between the "Eudemian" and the "Nicomachean Ethics" of Aristotle* [Oxford, 1978]) may have put the position of Book V itself in the *EN* in doubt.

53 Compare the general judgement reached by Augustin Mansion, that even if we accepted Jaeger's hypothesis on the composition of the treatises and the evolution of his philosophical ideas, "still we should have no reason to alter our conception of what we are in the habit of calling 'Aristotle's system' " ("La genèse de l'oeuvre d'Aristote d'après les travaux récents," *Revue néoscolastique de philosophie*, 29 [1927], p. 464; restated by Suzanne Mansion, *Le jugement d'existence chez Aristote*, 2nd edn [Paris 1976], p. 4).

1288b37ff.). But this effectively rules out the possibility of reforming existing oligarchies and democracies by reference to the standard of the best constitution, for even establishing some approximation to the best would involve what amounts to a *change* of constitution, in so far as its end would be changed – from wealth or freedom in the direction of virtue. In that case the reform of existing constitutions must become just a matter of making them *better oligarchies* or *better democracies*; or rather, as Aristotle insists on putting it (IV.2.1289b9–11), less bad oligarchies or democracies. And Aristotle's criterion of superiority and inferiority in this case, the relative orderliness and stability of a constitution, is reasonable enough; at any rate, in an orderly society, an individual might go on to achieve the good life for himself.

3

The Connection between Aristotle's Ethics and Politics

A. W. H. ADKINS

1 THE SITUATION[1]

There are many possible ways of discussing the link between Aristotle's *Ethics* and *Politics*. In the manner of Jaeger and Allan[2] one might attempt to locate each of Aristotle's works on ethics, or individual books of those works, in the light of one's favored theory of the history of Aristotle's intellectual development, do the same for the *Politics*,[3] and try to argue that the *Eudemian Ethics* or the *Nicomachean Ethics*[4] or some part of one or both, is closer to the *Politics* in doctrine than the rest of Aristotle's ethical writings; and a devotee of Kenny's work on the *Ethics*[5] might in addition upgrade or downgrade the *Politics*, or parts of it, according to its resemblances to or differences from the doctrines of the *Eudemian Ethics*.

Questions of this kind will not be discussed here. I shall be concerned with the *Nicomachean Ethics* and its relation to the *Politics*; but so far as I can discern, what I have to say is equally true of the *Eudemian Ethics*.

This article has a different genesis. Several times recently I have endeavored to convince serious students of Aristotle that Aristotle's *Ethics* and *Politics* were intended to be read together, and can be properly understood only if they are so read; but I found difficulty in convincing them.

The situation is rather surprising. After all, Aristotle says at the beginning of the *Ethics* that *politikê* is the art or science of the practical good (*EN*

1 This essay originally appeared in *Political Theory*, 12 (1984), pp. 29–49. My thanks are due to the editor and publishers for permission to reprint it here. I have made a few alterations to the earlier version in the interests of clarity.
2 W. Jaeger, *Aristotle: Fundamentals of the History of his Development*, tr. R. Robinson, 2nd edn (Oxford, 1948); D. J. Allan, *The Philosophy of Aristotle* (London, 1952).
3 Aristotle, *The Politics (Pol.)*. I cite and quote from the versions of Sir Ernest Barker (Oxford, 1946) (Barker); B. Jowett, in *The Works of Aristotle translated into English*, ed. W. D. Ross (Oxford, 1921), (Jowett); and T. A. Sinclair (Harmondsworth, 1962) (Sinclair).
4 Aristotle, *The Nicomachean Ethics* (*EN*) tr. W. D. Ross, in *The Works of Aristotle Translated into English*, ed W. D. Ross, (Oxford, 1921) (Ross).
5 A. J. P. Kenny, *The Aristotelian Ethics* (Oxford, 1978).

I.2.1094a27); and elsewhere that the *eudaimonia* of the individual is the same as the *eudaimonia* of the polis (*Pol.* VII.2.1324a5); that the polis is an association of like people for the sake of the best life, or *eudaimonia* (*Pol.* VII.8.1328a35, see 9.1328b34, 13.1332a7ff.); and he gives the same characterization of *eudaimonia* as in the *Ethics* (*EN* I.7.1098a16); that one needs leisure with a view to the development of *aretê*, human excellence, and with a view to political activities (*Pol.* VII.9.1329a2), with which should be compared "the sphere of activity of the practical *aretai* is the political and the military" (*EN* X.7.1177b6); that the *aretê* of the citizen and ruler is the same as that of the good man (*Pol.* VII.14.1333a11); and that human beings have the same goal individually and in common, so that the definition of the best man and the best constitution must be the same (*Pol.* VII.15.1334a11).

There seems to be a prima facie case for my position. I do not deny that there are differences of emphasis between the *Ethics* and *Politics*, nor that these may create some serious philosophical problems,[6] but for the understanding of Aristotle's ethicopolitical thought, the resemblances and continuities are much more important.

2 ARISTOTLE AND THE FOURTH CENTURY

(a) Values

To throw light on this topic, I shall briefly discuss the relationship of Aristotle's values and presuppositions in ethics and politics to those of his culture. To suggest that Aristotle is not a great moral and political philosopher *simpliciter*, but a great moral and political philosopher who lived in Greece in the fourth century BC, is sometimes held to diminish him. In my view, it diminishes Aristotle solely in comparison with those great moral philosophers who did not live at a particular time and place; not a large group. In fact, Aristotle invites us to consider the values of the culture, saying (*EN* I.4.1095b6) that an adequate member of an audience for lectures on moral and political philosophy must have been well brought up morally; and he had already excluded the young and ethically immature (1095a2). Aristotle will begin from the moral and political values that the well brought-up Greek – the Greek who shares Aristotle's values and attitudes – brings to class. It cannot be irrelevant, and may be illuminating, to consider the relation of Aristotle's values and presuppositions to those of fourth-century, and earlier, Greece.

(b) Words

Ideas are transmitted by words, and Greek ideas are transmitted by Greek words, not all of which are readily translatable into English. Value-terms are

6 See A. W. H. Adkins, *"Theoria* versus *Praxis* in the *Nicomachean Ethics* and the *Republic,"* *Classical Philology,* 73 (1978), pp. 297–312.

the most notorious examples. I shall discuss several here. But any Greek word, by virtue of possessing a different range of usage from any possible English equivalent, may possess different connotations from any English equivalent; and sometimes connotations render a philosophical position more plausible in one language than in another. The Greek word *ergon*, I shall argue, performs important services of this kind for Aristotle.

3   THE DEFINITION OF EUDAIMONIA IN NICOMACHEAN ETHICS 1.7

I begin with Aristotle's definition of *eudaimonia* in the first book of the *Nicomachean Ethics*, for that is generally held to depend entirely on Aristotle's metaphysical biology, and hence to be independent of the values of his, or any, culture. Aristotle remarks that almost everyone agrees that the goal of human life is to attain *eudaimonia* (*EN* I.4.1095a17). (The "almost" is merely a philosopher's caution in the face of an empirical universal generalization: with the earlier near-synonym *olbos*, *eudaimonia* expresses the goal of all the Greeks of whose views we are aware from Homer through Aristotle, and beyond.) Aristotle works towards a definition of *eudaimonia* thus (*EN* I.7.1097b22–1098a18). The translation is that of Ross, with some Greek words added in brackets:

> Presumably, however, to say that happiness [*eudaimonia*] is the chief good [*agathon*] is a platitude, and a clear account of what it is still desired. This might perhaps be given, if we could first ascertain the function [*ergon*] of man. For just as for a flute-player, a sculptor, or any artist, and, in general, for all things that have a function or activity, the good or the "well" is thought to reside in the function, so would it seem to be for man, if he has a function. Have the carpenter, then, and the tanner certain functions or activities, and has man none? Is he born without a function? Or as eye, foot, hand and in general each of the parts evidently has a function, may one lay it down that man similarly has a function apart from all these? What then can this be? Life seems to be common even to plants, but we are seeking what is peculiar to man. Let us exclude, therefore, the life of nutrition and growth. Next there would be a life of perception, but *it* also seems to be common even to the horse, the ox, and every animal. There remains, then, an active life of the element that has a rational principle. . . . Now if the function of man is an activity of soul [*psuchê*] which follows or implies a rational principle, and if we say "a so-and-so" and "a good so-and-so" have a function which is the same in kind, e.g. a lyre-player and a good lyre-player, and so without qualification in all cases, eminence in respect of goodness [*aretê*] being added to the name of the function (for the function of a lyre-player is to play the lyre, and that of a good lyre-player is to do so well); if this is the case, and we state the function of man to be a certain kind of life, and this to be an activity or actions of the soul implying a rational principle, and the function of a good man to be the good and noble performance of these, and if any action is well performed when it is performed in accordance with the appropriate excellence [*aretê*]: if this is the case, human good [*agathon*] turns out to be activity of the soul [*psuchê*] in accordance with virtue [*aretê*], and if there are more than one virtue, in accordance with the best and most complete.

Let me comment on some of the Greek terms. Most of us, when reading translations of Greek philosophy, acknowledge that some English words are being used in rather unusual ways, but we may not always be precise about the nature of what is unusual; and greater precision is needed here.

I begin with Aristotle's conclusion. The human good has been identified with *eudaimonia*, which Ross renders "happiness", but since "human flourishing" seems now to be an uncontroversial rendering of *eudaimonia*,[7] we may restate Aristotle's position thus:

> Human flourishing turns out to be an activity of the soul in accordance with virtue, and if there are more than one virtue, in accordance with the best and most complete virtue.

Next, "soul." Any serious student of Aristotle is aware of Aristotle's meaning, listed as a meaning of "soul" in the *OED*: "5. *Metaph*. The vital, sensitive or rational principle in plants, animals or human beings." Aristotle's argument in the paragraph under discussion makes his meaning clear; but this is not a common usage of "soul" in modern English; it is very difficult to exclude connotations derived from other uses; and connotations cloud the clarity of arguments. It is better to replace "soul" with "the characteristic human life-principle," to produce:

> Human flourishing turns out to be an activity of the characteristic human life-principle in accordance with virtue, and if there are more than one virtue, in accordance with the best and most complete.

Better, but still neither accurate nor entirely plausible as a conclusion to Aristotle's argument: he has not justified the appearance of any word with the meaning of the English "virtue." But *aretê* is not used in Greek in the same way as "virtue" is in modern English. Anything that can be said to be *agathos* ("good," in the sense of "good specimen of") may be said to possess an *aretê*. If we may speak of an *agathos* horse, we may speak of the *aretê* of a horse; if of *agathos* ploughland, then of the *aretê* of ploughland. Now Aristotle has offered an argument, good or bad, for this use of *aretê*: if a lyre-player discharging his function – so to render *ergon* for the moment – well (i.e. efficiently) is performing in accordance with his proper *aretê* (excellence), then a human being performing his function well is performing in accordance with his proper *aretê* (excellence). So we may restate Aristotle's definition yet again:

> Human flourishing turns out to be the activity of the characteristic human life-principle in accordance with human excellence, and if there are more than one excellence, in accordance with the best and most complete.

The conclusion, as now stated, bereft of adventitious connotations, has two advantages over Ross's version:

7 See J. M. Cooper, *Reason and Human Good in Aristotle* (Cambridge, Mass., 1975).

1 It is a more accurate rendering of the Greek.
2 If one grants Aristotle his premises, the conclusion follows from them.

It has, however, two evident disadvantages:

1 It is a purely formal definition, telling the reader nothing about human flourishing or human excellences.
2 *A fortiori*, it has no moral content. Thrasymachus could cheerfully accept it.

4 PROBLEMS WITH ARISTOTLE'S DEFINITION

Yet Aristotle ignores this fact in the *Ethics* and *Politics*. If we term the human *aretê* of the *eudaimonia* definition *aretê** and the "virtues" of *Nicomachean Ethics* II–IX, those accepted as such by Aristotle and his audience, *aretê*, Aristotle simply assumes that *aretê** is identical with *aretê*, though Thrasymachus[8] contended that injustice, not justice, was the *aretê*.

The account of virtue (*aretê*) is of little help. To be informed that an *aretê* is a mean disposition between extremes allows abundant room for interpretation. Misunderstanding of the local interpretation may lead to serious practical and political problems, as anyone who supposed that "moderate" in politics had the same sense in London and in Belfast would rapidly discover. Yet there are extremists, and extremes, acknowledged in Belfast. The Greeks were aware of the problem, as Thucydides shows (III.82):[9]

> What used to be described as a thoughtless act of aggression was now regarded as the courage one would expect to find in a party member; to think of the future and wait was merely another way of saying one was a coward; any idea of moderation was just an attempt to disguise one's unmanly character; ability to understand a question from all sides meant that one was totally unfitted for action.

Thucydides is here describing a change of values under stress, and appeals to a sense of the customary use of words in his readers; but elsewhere he recognizes the possibility of disagreement in the application of value-terms between one group and another, as in the Melian Dialogue (V.105), where the Athenians say: "Of all the people we know the Spartans are most conspicuous for believing that what they like doing is honourable and what suits their interests is just."

These people differ from Plato's Thrasymachus, who is willing to say (*Rep.* I.348c5–10) that injustice is an *aretê*. They commend what is regarded by an observer – Thucydides, or the Athenians generally – as thoughtless aggression or self-interested behavior as being courageous or just, and pursue them

8 Plato, *Republic* I.348c, tr. Allan Bloom (New York, 1968).
9 Thucydides, *The Peloponnesian War*, tr. Rex Warner (Harmondsworth, 1954).

under that evaluation. It is not clear how Aristotle could convince them they were wrong.

But the earlier part of the discussion that led up to Aristotle's definition of *eudaimonia* (*EN* I.7.1097b24ff.) seemed to promise much more; for most translators agree with Ross in rendering *ergon* by "function" here; and "function" has very technical, scientific connotations. (By this I mean that, like many words of Latin or Greek origin, "function" has certain technical uses which the Germanic "work" has not. We have two "dead" languages on whose roots we may draw to produce terms which have originally no connotation in English; the Greeks were constrained to use either words already in use, or coin others from the familiar roots. In the former case, the connotations already possessed by the words are likely to affect it immediately in its new usage; in the second, it may take a little longer. The use of a word of Latin or Greek origin to render into English an everyday word in the language being translated, whether that language be ancient Greek, German or any other, changes the tone and "feel" of what is said.[10] I shall argue that "function" changes Aristotle's argument in the passage under discussion, and that "task", "work" or "job" would convey much better the services performed for Aristotle's argument by the connotations of *ergon*.

I do not deny that the argument by elimination that follows (*EN*. I.7. 1097b33–1098a7) is elliptical and virtually incomprehensible without knowledge of the *De Anima*, on whose teachings it depends. It seems prima facie justifiable to claim, with most interpreters, that the argument to the *ergon* of man depends on Aristotle's "metaphysical biology," particularly as the *Metaphysics* furnishes a very similar, though brief, account of *eudaimonia* (IX.8.1050b1–2).[11] One might have hoped that the definition acquired some factual content from this source.

5　ERGON *IN ARISTOTLE*

The *ergon* argument for *eudaimonia* is certainly linked with discussions in the *De Anima* and *Metaphysics*, and with uses of *ergon* in the biological works. But there is more to be said: the argument may not be derived from these sources alone; its plausibility for a member of Aristotle's audience may be derived from elsewhere; even in the technical works "function" may not adequately represent the Greek *ergon*; and we need to discover not merely why Aristotle supposed human beings to have an *ergon*, but why he characterized the *ergon* as he did, apparently without fear of contradiction from his audience.

Let me begin with a brief discussion of the use of *ergon* and associated words in Aristotle's works. (We may note in passing that, according to

10 Bruno Bettelheim's observations on the difference between Freud's "Es" and "Ich," the ordinary German words for "it" and "I" and the translators' Latin "Id" and "Ego," and its effects on American psycho-analysis, throw light on this question. See B. Bettelheim, *Freud and Man's Soul* (New York, 1982).
11 Aristotle, *Metaphysics*, tr. W. D. Ross, in *The Works of Aristotle Translated into English*, ed W. D. Ross (Oxford, 1921).

Bonitz' *Index*,[12] *ergon* in all its senses is used about twice as frequently in the *Ethics*, *Politics*, and *Rhetoric* as in the *Metaphysics* and the major biological works.) In the biological works, in most cases, the translators render *ergon* by "function" without causing their readers any problems; but an unproblematic translation may not be fully satisfactory. Consider *PA* IV.12.694b12: "Some birds have long legs; the reason is that the life of such birds is spent in marshes; for nature makes the *organa* for the *ergon*, not the *ergon* for the *organa*."[13] "Organs" and "function"? That *we* do not refer to legs as organs is unimportant; that *organa* had meant "tools" since the previous century (Sophocles, *Trachiniae* 905; Euripides, *Bacchae* 1208), and *ergon* "job, task" since Homer, is not. A Greek who had read no other sentence of Aristotle could understand his words here: "Nature makes the tools for the job, not the job for the tools." Compare *GA* II.I.734b28–30. "Just as we should not say that fire alone could make an axe or any other *organon*, similarly fire could not make a foot or a hand" (termed *organa* above): it is evident that "tool" is the sense here, even in a biological context; that, as one would expect, the more recent usage of "organ" is felt as an analogy from the longer-established usage "tool."

Consider now *GA* I.2.716a23. Aristotle is discussing the male and female roles in reproduction: "Since the male and female are distinguished by *dunamis* (ability, power) and some *ergon*, and *organa* (tools) are needed for every work, and the parts of the body are the *organa* for the *dunameis*, both male and female sex organs are required." Note that here the use of *organa* in biological contexts is explained by reference to the sense "tools;" and also that to distinguish male and female by *dunamis* and *ergon*, with no context specified, would readily suggest that men are physically stronger than women, and perform different tasks. At *EN* VIII.12.1162a19 Aristotle says that for other animals the association of male and female extends only as far as reproduction, whereas human beings associate not only for procreation but for the other activities of life: "for immediately the *erga* are distinguished, and those of a man and a woman are different." Ross translates "functions;" but "tasks, work" is appropriate. At all events, a Greek who knew no Aristotelian philosophy at all could assign a meaning to Aristotle's words here; and this suffices for my argument.

Now consider *EN* V.1.1129b19: "The law bids one do [*poiein*] the *erga* of the brave man, for example not to leave one's place in the ranks or run away . . . and the *erga* of the self-controlled man, for example not to commit adultery . . .; the correctly established law does so correctly, the hastily drawn up law does so worse." Ross reasonably renders "do the acts of a brave man:" no metaphysical biology is needed for comprehension, though

12 H. Bonitz, *Index Aristotelicus* (Berlin, 1870 [repr. Berlin, 1955]).
13 Translations are my own where not otherwise indicated. There is an English version of the *Parts of Animals (PA)*, tr. William Ogle and *Generation of Animals (GA)*, tr. Arthur Platt, in *The Works of Aristotle Translated into English*, ed W. D. Ross (Oxford, 1921).

the same phrase in a biological context would be rendered "discharge one's function." At *EN* II.6.1106a15 Aristotle discusses *aretê*, and says (in Ross's translation): "We may remark, then, that every virtue or excellence [*aretê*] both brings into good condition that thing of which it is the excellence and makes the *ergon* of that thing to be done well, e.g. the excellence of the eye makes both the eye and its work [*ergon*] good." The resemblance to *EN* I.7.1097b22ff., with which we began this discussion, is close; but there Ross rendered *ergon* by "function," here by "work."

Next, a few examples from the *Politics*. At I.2.1253a18 Aristotle is arguing that the polis is naturally prior to the household and the individual, since the whole is prior to the part: "for in the absence of the whole body there will be neither foot nor hand, except in an equivocal sense . . . and everything is defined by its *ergon* and *dunamis*." Jowett renders "working and power," Barker "function and capacity," Sinclair "power and function." The disagreement of the translators makes my point. None of these versions is grossly incorrect; but none of them is adequate. *Ergon* is a word with a different range of usage and consequently different connotations from any available English word. In English translation some of the plausibility of Aristotle's Greek vanishes. We may note in passing that here the *ergon* of the individual is necessarily related to the existence of a larger whole, the polis. At *Pol*. IV.15.1299a34 we find, in Jowett's translation:

> For in great states it is possible, and indeed necessary, that every office should have a special function [*ergon*]; where the citizens are numerous, many may hold office . . . and certainly every work [*ergon*] is better done which receives the sole, and not the divided attention of the worker.

Jowett has two different renderings for *ergon* in consecutive lines; but evidently Aristotle means the same thing. (Barker has "function . . . function," Sinclair "tasks . . . assignment.") "Task" seems adequate; at all events, no Aristotelian philosophy is needed to assign a meaning to the Greek.

Lastly, *Pol*. III.4.1276b34ff.:

> It is clear that it is possible to be a good citizen without having the *aretê* which would make one a good man. . . . For if the polis cannot consist entirely of good men, and yet each must do his *ergon* well, and this comes from *aretê*, since the citizens cannot all be alike, the *aretê* of the good citizen and the good man cannot be the same.

This is not Aristotle's last word on the subject; but it is evident that here *ergon* is linked with the different roles of different citizens in the polis, and cannot be the same as the – single – *ergon* of the *eudaimonia* definition, nor yet derived from metaphysical biology, which specifies a single *ergon*. Nevertheless, Aristotle can use the word *ergon* to express this too; and it is evident that the (different) *ergon* of each individual or group of citizens is linked with the *aretê* of each. *Ergon* here denotes the role or task of each citizen qua citizen, whatever the role or task may be. Once again, one needs no Aristotelian philosophy to understand what Aristotle is saying here.

6   ERGON *AND* ARETÊ *BEFORE ARISTOTLE*

To sum up this discussion of *ergon*, a noun, common from the earliest extant – unphilosophical – Greek onwards, which Aristotle nowhere defines. It is evident that the word is not used solely of biological function, or solely in technical senses (indeed, it is doubtful whether an undefined term may be said to possess a technical sense); that the sense of "task, work" is frequently appropriate; and that in the contexts in which the translators render *ergon* as "function," that sense is felt as being derived from the sense that the word has in ordinary Greek. Accordingly, the connotations of "task, work, job" are always present, even in metaphysical and biological contexts, as the versions of the translators inadvertently indicate.[14]

Let me try to clarify what I mean. When I say that the "ordinary Greek" could assign a meaning to an Aristotelian phrase, I do not mean that for those speaking Greek, Aristotle's metaphysics or biology merely expressed what they already knew. I mean that in the case of the kinds of word I am discussing here, Aristotle could use in his works – perhaps especially in the *Ethics* and *Politics* – words and phrases that were entirely familiar to his audience, used in a recognizably similar sense, if the audience has had a good ethical upbringing. That an *agathos* has an *ergon*, the efficient and successful performance of which constitutes his *aretê*, will be an uncontroversial claim, as my citations from earlier Greek will show.

Return now to the definition of *eudaimonia*. There Aristotle begins by considering the *erga* of artists and craftsmen before passing on to the argument that depends on the *De Anima*. Commentators have found it confusing that Aristotle employs both an argument from the *ergon* of a craftsman qua craftsman to the *ergon* of a human being qua human being and an argument from the *ergon* of a biological part of a human being to the *ergon* of a human being as a biological whole.[15] Their complaints are philosophically justified; but Aristotle needs for his argument not merely *ergon* as it appears in metaphysics and biology but *ergon* as it appears in politics and ordinary life, and chooses examples that will keep the full range of *ergon* before the mind. It is the latter part of its range, as will appear, that mediates

---

14 R. G. Mulgan, in *Aristotle's Political Theory* (Oxford, 1977), also doubts whether Aristotle's view of the function of man is derived primarily from metaphysical biology; but he offers no detailed arguments.

15 On function in Aristotelian and other ethics, see P. T. Geach, "Good and Evil," *Analysis*, 17 (1956–7), pp. 33–42; R. M. Hare, "Geach, Good and Evil," *Analysis*, 17 (1956–7), pp. 101–111; A. M. MacIver, "Good and Evil and Mr. Geach," *Analysis*, 18 (1957–8), pp. 7–13; R. Sorabji, "Function," *Philosophical Quarterly*, 14 (1964), pp. 289–302; B. Suits, "Aristotle on the Function of Man," *Canadian Journal of Philosophy*, 4 (1974), pp. 23–40.

the transition from *aretê* as (unspecified) human excellence of the rational aspect of the *psuchê* to *aretê* as the virtues recognized by Aristotle and his audience. There is even some rhetoric in his argument. When Aristotle inquires whether man has no *ergon*, but is *argos*, the translators render "without a function"; but *argos* is the everyday Greek for "lazy," and Liddell-Scott-Jones, *A Greek–English Lexicon*, cites no other example of the sense "without a function."[16] The choice of word is a donnish joke; and it directs the attention to the "task, work" sense of *ergon* even as Aristotle embarks upon his biological argument from the *De Anima*.

Aristotle's choice of the undefined term *ergon* in the argument that leads to a definition of *eudaimonia* gives him a word whose usage ranges from technical biological contexts to completely unphilosophical ones. To throw light on the association between *ergon* or *erga*, *aretê* and *eudaimonia*, I turn next to an early, unphilosophical and indeed prephilosophical poet: Homer, in whose poems *ergon* and *erga* appear frequently in the senses of "work, activity,""product of activity," and "work of art." From the many examples I select a few illuminating ones.

In *Iliad* VI.521ff., Hector tells Paris that no one would find fault with his *ergon* of fighting, for he is warlike.[17] Paris is voluntarily shirking, and Hector hears *aischea*, reproaches at which Paris should feel shame. Paris's failure to perform in the *ergon*, task, of fighting detracts from his *aretê*. Adult warriors are disparaged by being compared with children, "who have no concern with warlike *erga*" (II.337, see XI.719); Polydamas says that the god gives to one man warlike *erga*, to another dancing, to another lyre-playing; and to yet another Zeus gives counsel (i.e., the ability to give counsel), which benefits many (*Iliad* XIII.730). Andromache tells her son Astyanax that when Troy falls he may be compelled to perform unseemly *erga*, toiling for a cruel ruler (*Iliad* XXIV.733–4). Astyanax is a prince, an *agathos*, and it would be the end of his *aretê* were he another's slave.

Like children, women have different *aretai* from men. Hector bids Ajax remember that Hector is neither a child nor a woman, who knows nothing of warlike *erga* (*Iliad* VII.235), and tells Andromache to go home and attend to her own *erga*, the loom and the distaff: "war shall be men's concern" (*Iliad* VI.492). A woman who is chaste and good at household tasks "knows blameless *erga*" (*Iliad* IX.128, 270, etc.), and possesses – female – *aretê*.

This is ordinary language, not philosophy: there is no question of inquiring whether there is *one ergon* for mankind. But since some of the *erga* are related to the *aretê* of men – and women – and *ergon* is related to *aretê* in *EN* I.7.1097b23ff., it is appropriate to inquire about the nature of *aretê* in Homer and later. Male *aretê* is the most relevant, since if contemplation is left out of

16 *A Greek–English Lexicon*, eds H. G. Liddell, R. Scott and H. Stuart Jones, ninth edn (Oxford, 1968).
17 Translations of Homer are legion. Good and readily available versions of the *Iliad* and *Odyssey* are those of Richmond Lattimore, (Chicago, 1951 and New York, 1967, respectively).

account, Aristotle's human *ergon* turns out to be the *ergon* of a limited number of adult male Greeks.

What characteristics, then, has the *agathos*, the man of *aretê* in Homer? He is the head of a large *oikos*, or household. He is wealthy, and his wealth is based on the possession of land and the goods and chattels, animate and inanimate, thereon. The society is moneyless; he and his like possess the significant wealth. Its possession enables them to acquire armor – an expensive and scarce commodity – with which to defend the *oikoi*: their *oikoi* rather than the community in general, for the community has little institutional existence. (It is recorded as a matter of no surprise, and little inconvenience, that there has been no assembly in Ithaca during the twenty years of Odysseus's absence [*Odyssey* II.26–34]. The inconvenience of Odysseus's absence is not to Ithaca, but to Odysseus's household. In his absence, the child Telemachus has been unable to defend the *oikos*, and the suitors have ravaged Odysseus's possessions.) The *agathos* performs the essential function of defending the *oikos*, and in case of a general attack from elsewhere, the wider community, with his superior weapons and, in Homer's phrase, his warlike *erga*. His wealth furnishes the weapons and the leisure to become proficient in their use. He performs the service without which the *oikos* could not continue to exist, and consequently has prestige and authority as well as military power. He it is who gives counsel, takes an active part in such political activity as exists: Nestor reminds Agamemnon and Achilles of the prowess of his youth before attempting to arbitrate their quarrel (in *Iliad* I.260–74), and Thersites is beaten about the head for venturing to give an opinion, though what he says is true (*Iliad* II.212–69).

Agathos and *aretê*, then, commend military effectiveness and the possession of wealth, leisure, and political power and prestige; and the role of the *agathos* in defending his group is understood to be the basis of his claim to be *agathos*. Achilles, "the most *agathos* of the Greeks," is termed by Nestor "a great fence against woeful war for all the Greeks" (*Iliad* I.283–4); and Sarpedon is said to have been the bulwark of the city of Troy, though not a Trojan; for many soldiers followed him, and he was most *agathos* at fighting (*Iliad* XVI.549–51); while Odysseus expects quick reprisals for the killing of the suitors, for he and his companions have killed "the bulwark of the polis, the most *agathoi* of the young men" (*Odyssey* XXIII.121). Similarly, in the first recorded constitution of the Athenians the franchise was given to those who could furnish themselves with military equipment (Aristotle, *Ath. Pol.* 4).[18]

These values continue to prevail. Had one asked the Greek-in-the-street in fifth- or fourth-century Greece what was the most important *ergon* (task) of an *agathos*, the defense of the city and household would have been the almost inevitable answer; and since the cavalryman and the hoplite continued to furnish their own equipment, the association of *aretê* with wealth – more for

---

18 Aristotle, *The Constitution of Athens*, tr. Sir Frederic G. Kenyon, in *The Works of Aristotle Translated into English*, ed. W. D. Ross (Oxford, 1921).

the cavalryman than the hoplite – and leisure continues, together with the political and social prestige. The *agathos* performs certain tasks that are crucial, in the context of a whole way of life.

Even when a writer is trying to include among the *agathoi* those persons and qualities that are not normally included, the same attitudes remain. In Euripides's *Electra* Orestes is praising a poor farmer, not an *agathos*, for his self-control, not until now an *aretê* (367ff.):

> For this man, who neither has a high position among the Argives, nor is puffed up by the fame deriving from noble lineage, has proved to be most *agathos*. Will you not come to your senses, you who wander about full of empty opinions, and in future judge men by their mode of life, and hold those to be noble who lead moral lives? For such men administer well both their cities and their own households, whereas those who are nothing but senseless lumps of muscle are mere ornaments of the market-place, for a strong arm does not even endure a spear-thrust any better than a weak one. No; such ability lies in a man's nature and in his excellence of spirit.

Self-control is being enrolled among the *aretai* here, using the traditional criteria. The self-controlled man is better at performing the essential tasks demanded of the *agathos*, the superior specimen of a man, in ancient Greece: ensuring the well-being of polis and household by military and political means. Whether or not self-control does render one better at these tasks is an empirical question; and Thrasymachus disagrees.

Plato's *Meno* furnishes a fourth-century example of the link between *aretê* and *ergon* in popular thought. The sanguine but unphilosophical Meno gives a number of confident replies to Socrates's question "What is *aretê*?" The first (71d1–72a5) employs the word *ergon*:

> It's not difficult to tell you that, Socrates. First, if you want the *aretê* of a man [*anêr*], it's easy: this is the *aretê* of a man, to be capable of transacting [*prattein*] the affairs of the polis, and in so doing to help his friends and harm his enemies, and to take care to suffer nothing of the kind himself. And if you want the *aretê* of a woman, that's not difficult to tell: she must run her household well, keeping the contents safe and obeying her husband [*anêr*]. And there is another *aretê* for a child, different for male and female children, and for an older man, different for free and slave. And there are many other *aretai*, so that there is no lack of material to supply on the subject of *aretê*; for each of us has *aretê* – and similarly *kakia* too, I think – with respect to each of the activities and times of life, with a view to the performance of each task [*ergon*].

This use of *ergon* is ordinary Greek, and depends on no articulated philosophical position. There are many roles or tasks, which may be well or badly discharged, "well" meaning "efficiently, effectively and/or in a manner pleasing to one's superiors"; and these roles are defined by reference to the culturally-accepted structure of life in household and polis.

Socrates sardonically remarks that Meno has given him not one, but a swarm of *aretai*, and creates his wonted dialectical havoc with Meno's stated views. Meno subsequently offers other definitions of *aretê*: "What else is it than the ability to rule over people [*anthrôpoi*]?" (73c9), and "to desire the kala and be able to get them for oneself," (77b4–5). Socrates immediately induces him to replace *kala* by *agatha* in the latter definition, producing "*aretê* is to desire the things that are beneficial for oneself and to be able to get them for oneself."

Socrates' counter-arguments need not concern us here. What is note-worthy is that Meno, despite the profusion of different *aretai* in his first definition, subsequently offers definitions of *aretê* suitable – as Socrates points out – only for a limited number of free adult males. There are many *erga*; but only a few are really important. Note also that, though he adds the "cooperative" moral excellences[19] to his definitions when Socrates invites him to (73a, d), Meno's immediate thought when *aretê* is mentioned is of *effective* action.

7 ARISTOTLE AGAIN

Consider now Aristotle's similar discussion of the *aretê* of women and slaves (*Pol.* I.12.1259b21ff.): "First we ought to inquire about slaves, whether there is an *aretê* of a slave over and above his tool-like [*organikai*] *aretai* as a menial." (His efficient performance of tasks is of course the *aretê* of his role, reckoned from his master's point of view.) Does the slave (woman, child) need justice, courage, self-control and the other *aretai* discussed in the *Nicomachean Ethics*, or are they necessary only for the adult male ruler? Aristotle replies that all need them, but in different ways, saying (*Pol.* I.13.1260a10ff.) (Barker):

> It is true all these persons possess in common the different parts of the soul; but they possess them in different ways. The slave is entirely without the faculty of deliberation; the female indeed possesses it, but in a form which remains inconclusive, and if children also possess it, it is only in an immature form.

Similarly, with respect to moral *aretê*:

> they must all share in it, but not in the same way – each sharing only to the extent required for the discharge of his or her function [*ergon*]. The ruler, accordingly, must possess moral goodness in its full and perfect form, i.e., the form based on rational deliberation, because his function [*ergon*], regarded absolutely and in its full nature, demands a master artificer; but all other persons need only possess moral goodness to the extent required of them by their particular position.

The discussion invokes the same terms (*aretê, ergon*) as did *Nicomachean Ethics* 1.7, with which we began. There is a temptation to speak of "metaphysical biology"; and Barker renders *ergon* by "function." But in the light of the *Meno*,

19 For the term see A. W. H. Adkins, *Merit and Responsibility: A Study in Greek Values* (Oxford, 1960), p. 7.

which also employs *ergon* and *aretê*, and the earlier Greek discussed, metaphysical biology seems to have little importance; and where, we may ask, did Aristotle get the information that slaves do not have the faculty of deliberation, *to bouleutikon*, while women possess it in a form that remains inconclusive? We may also inquire whence Aristotle derives his account of animal-*psuchê* and plant-*psuchê*, the characteristic life-principles of plants and animals. Evidently by observing what plants and animals are characteristically able to do: plants to nourish and reproduce themselves, animals in addition having perception and motion. Similarly, Aristotle observes what free men, free women, and slaves characteristically do/are able to do in fourth-century – and earlier – Greece. "Metaphysical biology" seems an inappropriate term: the direction of thought is not from a metaphysical biology independently arrived at to an appropriateness of *ergon*-function, but from an observation of *ergon* (behavior) to an explanation in terms of *psuchê*; and only the translation "soul" introduces metaphysical connotations. Not only in the case of plants and animals but also in that of human beings Aristotle *seems* to suppose that actual roles are the only possible ones; but he knew that circumstances had enslaved many free Greeks, and consequently distinguished slaves by nature from slaves by *nomos* (*Pol.* I.6.1255a3–b4). Even in the present passage, note "all other persons *need* only possess moral *aretai* to the extent required of them by their particular position." Earlier, "each needing to share" would be closer to Aristotle's Greek than "each sharing." The implication is not that they are incapable of more, but that they need no more for the performance of their roles. The *ergon* is defined by the society; and though Aristotle sets out to claim that women and slaves have defective *psuchai*, so that the defined role is appropriate "by nature" (*phusê*), his language here betrays him. So far as concerns the *erga* of mankind, their source is common practice; if any biology is involved, it is a normative pseudo-empirical sociobiology.

I now turn to the distinctions drawn by Aristotle between the *erga* of different adult male free Greeks, between the qualities of the *agathos* man (*anêr*) and the *agathos* citizen (*politês*). In most cities they are distinct (*Pol.* III.4.1276b34):

> It is clear that it is possible for a man to be a good [here *spoudaios*] citizen and yet not have the *aretê* in accordance with which one is a good man. . . . For if it is impossible for a city to consist entirely of good men, yet each must do his own *ergon* well, and this derives from some *aretê*; but since it is impossible for all the citizens to be alike, the *aretê* of the *agathos* citizen and that of the *agathos* man must be different.

This passage occurs in *Politics* III.4, a chapter in which, as Barker says (p. 122), Aristotle "shifts his ground." He has previously argued (*Pol.* III.4. 1276b16–34) that the existence of different kinds of constitutions demonstrates that there must be different kinds of good citizen; for being a good citizen is relative to one's task (*ergon*) in the constitution under which one lives. Aristotle does not emphasize the point, but since some kinds of constitution are bad, being a good citizen under some constitutions might require one to be a bad man. Again, he compares the different roles of citizens in the same constitution to those of different sailors on a ship; and the comparison emphasizes skills and aptitudes rather than moral excellence.

This passage, however, refers explicitly to the ideal constitution; and later in the chapter it becomes clear that Aristotle is including all the *aretai* in "performing one's task well" here. Yet even under the ideal constitution the *agathos* man (*anêr*) does not coincide with the *agathos* citizen; a fact that is puzzling, and may – inappropriately – suggest that the definition of the *agathos anêr* is independent of civic role. A brief discussion of the best constitution will show that even here there are tensions in Aristotle's view of the human *ergon*.

To clear the ground for his discussion, Aristotle distinguishes these necessary *erga* of a city's inhabitants (*Pol.* VII.8.1328b5ff.): food, crafts (*technai*), weapons, money, a provision for public worship, and sixth and most necessary, a method of "deciding what is demanded by the public interest and what is just in man's private dealings" (Barker). "*Ergon*" may mean "end-product" as well as "activity"; and Aristotle seems to slide from one sense to the other here. He concludes (Barker): "The polis must therefore contain a body of farmers to produce the necessary food; craftsmen; a military force; a propertied class; and a body for deciding necessary issues and determining what is in the public interest." Each group has its *ergon* in the sense of "activity"; and some have an *ergon* in the sense of "end-product" that can be used by other inhabitants.

The city needs inhabitants to perform all these *erga*; but in the best constitution not all will be citizens; for "being *eudaimôn* necessarily accompanies the possession of *aretê* and we must call a polis *eudaimôn* not with respect to a part of it but with respect to all the citizens" (*Pol.* VII.9.1329a22–4); and "since . . . the most *agathos* man and the most *agathê* constitution must have the same definition, it is clear that the *aretai* which lead to leisure must be present" (*Pol.* VII.14.1334a1–14). We must call a polis *eudaimon* with respect to all its citizens; but since not all the inhabitants can have such *aretê* and such *eudaimonia*, citizenship must be confined to those who are capable of these attainments.

8   THE GOOD CITIZEN IN ARISTOTLE'S BEST CONSTITUTION

What then are the characteristics of the good citizen in Aristotle's best constitution? He may not be a shopkeeper, a craftsman, or a farmer, for *aretê* and political activities need leisure (*Pol.* VII.9.1328b24–1329a22); he may not be a sailor, part of the naval defense of his polis (*Pol.* VII.6.1327b8). His leisure is assured by the possession of a landed estate, to be farmed for him by noncitizens (*Pol.* VII.9.1329a25). He is to employ that leisure in politics and, if need be, war: "the part that engages in warfare and the part that deliberates about what is expedient and gives judgment about what is just are inherent and manifestly especially parts of the polis" (*Pol.*

VII.9.1329a2–5). Each of these roles, the warlike and the deliberative-ruling, should be discharged by the same people; but since each of the *erga* reaches its peak at different periods of life, in a sense they should be discharged by different people: war by the young, deliberation by their elders; for the one needs physical strength, the other, *phronêsis*, practical wisdom. (Note that Aristotle adds a practical consideration: those who have weapons cannot permanently be excluded from power.)

The idea of complete *aretê* is inseparable from that of defending the polis and exercising political power in it. If *theôria* is set on one side, these are the *erga*, or taken together this is the essential *ergon*, of the good man (*anêr*) and – apparently – the good citizen that satisfies the definition of *eudaimonia*, the *ergon* of a man (*anthrôpos*) manifested with appropriate excellence (*aretê*), offered in *Nicomachean Ethics* 1.7.

We may return to *Politics* III.4.1276b34. There, even in the best constitution, Aristotle distinguishes between the *agathos* man and the *agathos* citizen. But surely all the *agathoi* citizens are *agathoi* men, in performing the best *erga*. The discussion of *Politics* III.4 indicates the tensions: "We say that the good ruler must be *agathos* and have practical wisdom, whereas the good citizen need not be *phronimos*" (1277a14–16). Under "political" rule the citizens take it in turns to rule (1277a25ff.). Ruling and being ruled are not equally praiseworthy, however (1277a29): when not ruling, the citizen's *aretê* will be inferior, for *phronêsis* will not be required. The good citizen will strictly be an *agathos anêr* only when ruling; and only so will he satisfy the requirements of the definition of *eudaimonia* in *Nicomachean Ethics* 1.7. His *eudaimonia* is accordingly intermittent, at least when Aristotle insists that actual ruling is necessary for its attainment.

Whether one takes the broader or the narrower definition of the *ergon* of the *agathos* man, it is evident that its nature is derived not from metaphysical biology but from Greek political practice from Homer onwards. It is also evident that Aristotle can be confident that his definition of the *ergon*, thus defined, will not be challenged: that the *agathos* should rule, deliberate and defend his city was agreed by Agamemnon, Socrates and Thrasymachus and every one of Aristotle's Greek predecessors and contemporaries of whose views we are aware. It is not surprising that Aristotle felt able to claim that this *ergon* is related to the nature of the *agathos*.

In the light of the foregoing discussions, some puzzling aspects of the argument for the *eudaimonia*-definition of *Nicomachean Ethics* 1.7 appear a little more comprehensible. The *ergon*-argument is undeniably odd. In the case of other things that have *erga*, not all of them perform those *erga* excellently: not all sculptors are as good as Phidias, not all eyes have 20–20 vision. But all can and must perform the *ergon* to some extent: for Aristotle, a blind eye, which does not perform its *ergon* at all, is not really an eye except homonymously (*GA* I.18.726b24, etc.). However, in the case of the *ergon* of man (*anthrôpos*), the function can be discharged, the task performed, by only a small fraction of mankind: if we take Aristotle seriously, by a limited number of adult male Greeks with a leisured way of life (*Pol.* I.2.1252b7, 5.1254b20, 13.1260a10, 14, VII.7.1327b20ff.). To repeat an earlier quotation: "The ruler, accordingly, must possess *êthikê aretê* in its full and perfect form [i.e., the form based on rational deliberation], because his *ergon* . . . demands a master artificer, and reason is such a master artificer" (*Pol.* I.13. 1260a17ff.). "Perfect" is *teleia*, the same word as is used with *aretê* in the definition of *eudaimonia* with which we began the discussion.

The *ergon* of a human being (*anthrôpos*) has become the *ergon* of some men (*anêr*): there is no *ergon* that human beings as such can all perform, and that is constitutive of human *eudaimonia* attainable by all. Aristotle's change of focus, which occurs even within *Nicomachean Ethics* 1.7, is encouraged by a fact of Greek usage which reflects the cultural attitudes under discussion in this article. One can speak of a good woman, child, or even slave, in the sense of "good of its kind"; but rarely of an *agathos anthrôpos*, since *anthrôpos* is used pejoratively of those who do not possess the prized male *aretê*-qualities: as soon as *agathos* or *spoudaios* is used, the noun tends to change from *anthrôpos* to *anêr*.[20] In *Nicomachean Ethics* 1.7 Aristotle begins by seeking the *ergon* of an *anthrôpos* (*EN* I.7.1097b24), but as soon as the *ergon*, well performed, is characterized as *aretê* and "good" is applied to its possessor, *anthrôpos* becomes *aner* (*EN* I.7.1098a14), and the reference is already to males only.[21]

It may now be easier to understand why Aristotle feels able to assume without argument that the formal *aretê** of *Nicomachean Ethics* 1.7, the efficient performance of the human task, may be identified with the *aretê* or *aretai* accepted as such by Aristotle and his audience. From the time of Homer onwards, *aretê* denoted and commended the efficient performance of tasks, the most important of which were deemed essential for the flourishing, *eudaimonia*, of household and polis. From Homer, through much of the fifth century, the cooperative excellences were not regarded as *aretai*, or as aspects of *aretê*. Those who wished to enroll them among the *aretai* had to demonstrate, or assert, that these excellences constituted an essential means to, or part of, efficient and successful living. In Plato's *Crito* 48b8, Socrates reminds Crito that in the past he has agreed with Socrates that to live *eu*, to live *kalôs*, and to live *dikaiôs* are the same. In an English translation "to live justly is the same as to live honorably, and to live honorably is the same as to live well" is a claim that seems hardly surprising, for the range of usage of the adverbs overlaps, and all are used to commend the cooperative excellences; but in the Greek of the time Socrates' words express a novel attitude. The just life is given a new, more powerful commendation by the use of *kalos*, which belongs – as justice previously did not – to the *aretê*-group: Socrates is claiming that just behavior renders one *agathos*. The use of *eu*, the adverb of *agathos*, emphasizes that the *agathos* lives well in the sense of "efficiently."

20 I do not claim that *agathos* and *anthrôpos* are never used together, merely that the respective ranges and emotive power of *anthrôpos* and *anêr* will be likely to lead quickly to the substitution of *anêr* for *anthrôpos* in any sustained discussion. (In *EN* II.6.1106a23 *anthrôpos* is the subject and *agathos* the predicate.)

21 I believe *EN* I.7.1098a12–16 to be authentic Aristotle. If they are a later gloss, the gloss indicates – what is certainly true – that the tendency continued after the time of Aristotle.

A Greek who acknowledges that any quality is an *aretê* is acknowledging that life is better – more efficient and successful – for those who possess that quality than for those who do not. It is for this reason that Thrasymachus claims that injustice, not justice, is the *aretê*, arguing that injustice, not justice, brings successful living in its train (*Rep.* I.348c).

Since any Greek who accepts a quality as an *aretê* regards it as a means to, or component of, successful living, it is comparatively easy for Aristotle to believe, and carry his audience along with him in believing, that the *aretai* that he and they acknowledge are the qualities that satisfy the definition of *eudaimonia* in *Nicomachean Ethics* 1.7. (Aristotle specified earlier that his audience must accept the same range of *aretai* as he does, *EN* I.4.1095b4ff.) The identification of *aretê** with *aretê* is not argued, much less cogently argued, and Aristotle and his audience might simply be mistaken in identifying their *aretai* as the qualities most conducive to efficient and successful living; but it is evidently easier to claim that Greek *aretê* (in the everyday sense) is true human excellence (in the sense of what makes life most worth living) than to make the claim about virtue in the usual twentieth-century English sense.

Ergon in Aristotle, then, has a wide range of usage; but its uses in ordinary language have a significant effect on its usage in technical contexts, as one might expect in the case of an undefined term. The effect is especially noteworthy in ethics and politics. Even if biology played some part in the argument that human beings have an *ergon*, the identification of that *ergon* is derived from the presuppositions and attitudes of daily life in ancient Greece. (If *metaphysical* biology contributes anything to Aristotle's thought here, it is the debate between the claims of contemplation and the practical life in *Nicomachean Ethics* X, insofar as the claims of the contemplative life are based on the "divine spark" view of *nous*; but those claims could have been stimulated by a quite unmetaphysical excitement over the powers of human reason, with which the Greeks had recently achieved so much.[22] *Ergon* is one of the terms and concepts that bind together Aristotle's ethical and political thought, and link both with the values and attitudes of the culture. If one considers the relationship of *ergon* to *aretê* and *eudaimonia*, and the importance of all three to Aristotle's ethical and political thought, the necessity of reading the *Ethics* and *Politics* together, and both in the context of Greek values and attitudes, seems evident.

Let me conclude with a few remarks on a wider theme. Virtue-ethics has recently been increasing in popularity, after a long period of decline. If the arguments of this essay are acceptable, it seems clear that, though we may learn much from Aristotle's analysis of *aretai*, the psychology of ethics, and similar topics, virtue-ethics and *aretê*-ethics have great differences, some of which pose serious problems for the virtue-ethicist. For it is not nonsense to inquire whether the possession of (a) virtue is conducive to life at its best in

22 See Adkins, "*Theoria* versus *Praxis* in the *Nicomachean Ethics* and the *Republic*," p. 311.

any sense of "best" that renders the virtue indubitably choiceworthy. In the sense of "morally best" the claim is indubitable, for it is tautologous, but it may fail to motivate choice; in the sense of "most flourishing," the virtue becomes choiceworthy but the claim becomes doubtable. In ancient Greece, if a moralist could convince others that a quality was an *aretê*, his problems were over, for *aretai* are choiceworthy; now the problem is rather to demonstrate the choiceworthiness of virtue. Again, there is now no accepted *ergon* (or most important *ergon*). It is evident that even a small nation-state cannot satisfy Aristotle's requirement for the best constitution that all who have the capacity of performing the *ergon* of ruling should do so; and Aristotle has nothing else to say about the *ergon* of the human being. The *aretê* of the good citizen is, for Aristotle, merely relative to the role or task he performs in his particular polis. If *aretê* is based on this conception of *ergon*, it must be relative to a constitution. At least some virtue-ethicists hope for more. It is not my purpose to argue against them, merely to suggest that in some respects Aristotle's *aretê*-ethics is of little use to them in the effective performance of their *ergon*.

4

Man as a Political Animal in Aristotle

WOLFGANG KULLMANN

I

One of the familiar quotations of Aristotle is the statement that man[1] is a *zôon politikon*. It shares the fate of all familiar quotations in that it is used independently of its original occurrence. This does not just happen outside the field of classical scholarship; even within it, the statement is often employed very loosely. In one especially popular usage, it has the sense that man is or ought to be a being who is politically active as a citizen, as if the statement primarily alluded to democracy and referred to a form of life which was confined to a definite historical epoch.[2] This widespread use of the statement has been opposed, particularly by Olof Gigon. He argues that it is quite incorrect to say that the ancient Greek regards being a man, as it were, as coinciding with being a citizen. He sees in the statement the individual thesis of the philosopher who opposes the general disgust with the state with the historical fact that man has never existed without the state.[3] The

1 ["Man" is a rendering of the German "Mensch," being the name of the human species. This article is translated from the German. The original article, "Der Mensch als politisches Lebewesen bei Aristoteles," appeared in *Hermes*, 108 (1980), pp. 419–43. The author has reviewed and corrected the translation and has provided a few additions to the footnotes which are indicated by square brackets.]
2 See for example B. H. Bengtson, *Griechische Geschichte* (Handbuch der Altertums-wissenschaft: 3. Abt., Teil 4) (3rd edn., Munich, 1965), p. 143: "Damals [scil. im Zeitalter der Polis ab 500 v. Chr.] ist der griechische Bürger zum 'politischen Lebewesen' (ζῷον πολιτικόν) geworden." ["At that time (*scil.* in the age of the polis from 500 BC) the Greek citizen became a 'political animal' (*zôon politikon*)"]: V Ehrenberg. *The Greek State* (Oxford, 1960), p. 38: "The fact that slaves, metics and the rest, played such an active and independent part in the state's economic life, made it largely possible for the citizen to devote his life to the state, to be indeed a *zôon politikon*." J. Christes, *Bildung und Gesellschaft* (Darmstadt, 1975), p. 18: "Mit Aristoteles, unserem letzten Zeugen eines ganz auf die Formung des ζῷον πολιτικόν ausgerichteten Paideia–Ideals" ["With Aristotle our final witness for an ideal of *paideia* [education] oriented entirely toward the formation of the *zôon politikon*..."]
3 O. Gigon, *Aristoteles. Politik* (Munich, 1973 [Zurich, 1955, 1st edn., 1971, 2nd edn]), pp. 13ff.

following discussion will not address this general question, and it will not declare a free usage of the statement as illegitimate. But the very "upshot" of the Aristotelian maxim suggests the need to undertake a more precise interpretation of the passages in which it appears. In addition, the statement undoubtedly has an important place within the entire anthropology of Aristotle; it is not merely interesting from the point of view of the participation of man in daily politics. It therefore deserves a detailed treatment. In particular, I shall examine the extent to which this statement has definitional significance (as it is frequently understood), and I shall take up again the much discussed question regarding the precise position of the political element in the framework of Aristotle's concept of man.[4]

The most significant passage – and, as we shall see, the most problematic one of the seven passages in the Aristotelian corpus which contain the statement in question – is *Pol.* I.2.1253a1ff. In order to understand it, it is necessary to consider the preceding train of thought. In chapter 1 Aristotle took exception to the view that between a master (*despotês*), a household manager (*oikonomos*), a statesman (*politikos*), and a king (*basilikos*) there was only a quantitative difference with respect to the number of persons ruled. He explained that he wanted to analyze the compound (*to suntheton*) of the state (the polis) into its "uncompounded" elements (*ta asuntheta*) according to the method which had previously guided him (*kata tên huphêgêmenên methodon*).[5] In chapter 2 a genetic analysis of the polis follows. First, of necessity, there was the community of husband and wife and the community of masters and slaves. From these two relations there arose at first the "house" or the "household" (*oikia, oikos* – the family), which is defined by Aristotle as the community existing for daily needs, established according to nature. The

4 In this context I refer especially to the thesis of Günther Bien's important book, *Die Grundlegung der politischen Philosophie bei Aristoteles*, which is apparently representative of an essential line of interpretation of Aristotle's *Politics* (Freiburg–Munich, 1973). Bien sees in the statement in question "die Bestimmung der Natur des Menschen als einer wesenhaft auf die Stadt und bürgerliche Gesellschaft angewiesenen Vernunftnatur" ["the definition of human nature as a rational nature essentially dependent upon the city and community of citizens"] (p. 70). The object of politics is not man in the sense of his natural conditions as described in the *History of Animals* (p. 121). The sphere of the political is – borrowing from Hegel's formulation – the ethical universe, the ground of the spiritual (*logos*) and the just (*dikaion*). Bien argues that the attributes "human," "political" (in the widest sense), "just" and "having speech" are interchangeable. The sentences which apply these attributes to man are tautologous (p. 72). In a similar way J. Ritter assumed a very close connection between the rational nature of man and the political for Aristotle, in *Metaphysik und Politik. Studien zu Aristoteles und Hegel* (Frankfurt/M., 1969), pp. 76ff.
5 If this translation is correct (see B. Jowett's translation in S. Everson, *Aristotle, The Politics* [Cambridge, 1988]: "according to the method which has hitherto guided us"), Aristotle must have a previous application of the method in view. This could be most plausibly the elucidation of the definition of *eudaimonia* by way of a consideration of its parts, especially the concept of *aretê*, as we find it in the *EE* and *EN*, to which W. L. Newman, *The Politics of Aristotle* (Oxford, 1887–1902), vol. II, p. 101, refers.

first community established from several "houses" or "households" which did not exist solely for the sake of daily needs was the village, which was most in accord with nature if it was a "colony" of the "house" composed of children and grandchildren, and which like the house was itself ruled by the eldest as king. Hence, there was also an ancient kingship in the cities. As evidence that "family kingship" (which is especially exemplified in the rule over children) characterizes ancient kingship, the description of the Cyclopes in the *Odyssey* is cited (IX.114ff.): *themisteuei de hekastos paidôn êd' alochôn* [each one legislates to his children and wives]. It is subsequently argued that the ubiquitous representation of kingship among the gods is an anthropomorphic reflection of the present or original political situation.[6] Then Aristotle turns to the polis. The complete community arising from several villages is the polis, which now largely reaches the limit of complete self-sufficiency. It comes into being for the sake of life, but exists for the sake of the "good life" (*ousa de tou eu zên*). Therefore, every state exists by nature, since the first communities also existed by nature. For the state was the end of these communities, and the nature (the essence) of a thing is its end. What each thing is, when it is completely developed, is called the nature (the essence) of a thing. Further, Aristotle argues, the goal or end is best, and self-sufficiency is the end and the best. Hence, it is clear that the state is among the things which are by nature (*tôn phusei hê polis esti*), and that man is by nature (essentially) a political animal, and that whoever is by nature and not by chance stateless is either a bad man or else higher than a man.

The first question which arises concerns the character of this genetic analysis. There can be no doubt that Aristotle has Plato in mind, who is concerned in both the *Republic* (II.369aff.) and the *Laws* (III.676aff.) with the coming into being of the polis.[7] In the *Republic* Plato intends to have the state come to be in speech (in *logos*) in order to provide a better model than the soul of the individual man for studying the essence of justice and injustice: *ei gignomenên polin theasaimetha logôi* [if we observe the state coming to be by speech]. This phrase is echoed by *Pol.* I.2.1252a24: *ei dê tis ex archês ta pragmata phuomena blepseien* [if one looks at things developing naturally from the beginning]. In both cases we have the same sort of potential optative as is used elsewhere for the characterization of a thought experiment. In both cases the genetic aspect is subordinated to the end of making the structure visible. This is a circumstance which is also characteristic of Plato's myth in the *Statesman*, and the cosmogonical myth in the *Timaeus*. However, Plato and Aristotle differ on the specific manner in which the State comes to be. The starting point may be the same: the state arises out of a lack of self-sufficiency in individuals. But Plato explains this genesis of the state as due to the constraint of the division of labor between members of different professions, whereas Aristotle finds the state originating from the family or, more precisely, the *oikos* [household], hence out of the natural communities of husband and wife and master and slave.

6 On the reasoning of 1252b19–27 compare Gigon, *Aristoteles. Politik*, p. 266.
7 Compare Newman, *The Politics of Aristotle*, vol. I, pp. 36ff.; vol. II, p. 104.

A discussion in Book III of the *Laws* is also germane. There, also, the historical account is not an end in itself but is used to discover the best political institutions. This discussion is especially similar in that the original state of man – in this case, after the great catastrophe of the flood – is modelled after the Homeric society of the Cyclopes in which there were, in the words of the poet, no gatherings for council, no legal statutes, and no communal life; and only the head of the family pronounced law for wives and children (*Laws* III.680b).[8] The more realistic features of the historical process which Plato describes in the *Laws*, among them the catastrophe of the flood, are, however, left out by Aristotle in favor of an abstract exposition of the elements involved in forming the state. Behind Plato's description, especially in the *Republic*, is surely Democritus's theory of the origin of culture, which we can find in another version in the Hippocratean work *On Ancient Medicine*.[9] In contrast to Democritus, the Platonic description in the *Republic* is hardly intended seriously. The obvious goal of the *Republic* is to represent the "essence" of the state, not its genesis.[10] On the other hand, the representation in the *Laws* is not without historical seriousness.

What about the text of the *Politics*? Obviously Aristotle sees no "development" in the formation of the *oikos* [household] out of two original communities, those of husband and wife and of master and slave. He is only analyzing the *oikos* into its constituents. If, however, he conceives of the village as a colony of the "house," which arises in a natural manner through children and grandchildren, he at least has a typical development in mind, even if it is probably not a historical one (i.e., a singular event). One could assume that the same applies to the origin of the polis, if Aristotle did not say – in dependence on Plato's *Laws* – after quoting Homer on the family rule of the Cyclopes, that they lived scattered (*sporades gar*) and that "once in ancient times lived thus." This is clearly an allusion to an historical original state of man. In order to avoid making the historical process leading to the polis appear accidental, Aristotle relies on a comparison from the domain of nature and technology. That which a thing is, after it is fully developed, is its *phusis*, i.e. its nature, its essence, as for example with man, horse, or house. The development of the polis, a development which took many generations, thus appears comparable to a biological or technological process which results in a mature animal or a finished technical product. How far does this comparison extend? How concrete a development is meant?

8 The Cyclopes were the prototypes of "savages" since Homer (compare Plato *Laws* III.680d3 *agriotêta*); see also Euripides, *Cyclops*, lines 118ff. The passage in Homer is one of our most important pieces of evidence for the relatively developed "political" consciousness and the level of political organization, which had been reached by the time of the *Odyssey*.

9 Compare H. Herter, "Die kulturhistorische Theorie der hippokratischen Schrift von der alten Medizin," *Maia*, NS 15 (1963), pp. 464ff., who convincingly and comprehensively treats the research into the sources.

10 Otherwise e.g., more recently, O. Gigon, *Gegenwärtigkeit und Utopie. Eine Interpretation von Platons Staat* (Zurich–Munich, 1976), p. 144.

In any case, it is only in a restricted sense that we can speak of a biological perspective, since apart from his comparison with man and horse Aristotle also mentions an artificial production, the house.[11] The polis as such, therefore, seems to be neither a biological nor a technological product. Hence, we are rather led to think, when the *phusis* of the polis is mentioned, of a metaphorical mode of expression similar to the statement in the *Poetics* (4.1449a14ff.) that tragedy stopped changing after it had attained its *phusis*.[12] Nevertheless, since *phusis* can also signify a substance, we shall inquire separately as to whether Aristotle is thinking of the polis as a substantial entity (see below, section III). We can ask further whether he sees the proof of his thesis more in the natural development of the state, howsoever constituted, or more in its composition out of natural constituents. There is support for the latter interpretation in that he explicitly says that the state comes to be for the sake of life – that is, we may assume, for the sake of survival, without the conscious goal of the *eu zēn* (i.e. living well) being already present from the beginning. This assertion contradicts, in a way, the assumption of a long history preceding the polis, since one wonders how men could have survived when they did not yet have the polis. In Aristotle's view, there must at least have been a provisional polis.

This takes us to an old scholarly controversy. Eduard Meyer saw in Aristotle's thesis the thought that political association was not only conceptually but also historically the primary form of human community.[13] M. Defourny vigorously contradicted him: Aristotle meant that the political culture developed only after humanity had long been content with more primitive forms of community.[14] One should now see that the difficulty lies in the Aristotelian text itself. It is true that Aristotle does *not* speak of the

---

11 Compare below p. 110.
12 Compare W. Fiedler, *Analogiemodelle bei Aristoteles. Untersuchungen zu den Vergleichen zwischen den einzelnen Wissenschaften und Künsten* (Studien zur antiken Philosophie, vol. 9) (Amsterdam, 1978), pp. 162ff.
13 *Geschichte des Altertums* I. 1 (1884, 1st edn; 1907, 2nd edn; Darmstadt, 1953, 6th edn), pp. 11ff.
14 *Aristote. Études sur la "politique"* (Paris, 1932); p. 383. "Quand donc Aristote, ayant montré que l'État est un fait de nature conclut par sa phrase célèbre – ὁ ἄνθρωπος φύσει πολιτικὸν ξῷον ἐστί – il ne veut pas dire que l'humanité se trouve d'emblée et depuis toujours dans la civilisation politique, mais qu'au contraire après avoir vecu pendant un durée indéterminable en dehors de cette civilisation et s'être longtemps contentée de formes plus rudimentaires d'association, elle finit par y arriver et par s'y installer comme dans une terre promise dont la conquête était réclamée par toutes ses forces constitutionelles." ["When, therefore, Aristotle, having shown that the state is a fact of nature, concludes with his celebrated statement – *ho anthrôpos phusei politikon zōon esti* [man is by nature a political animal] – he does not mean that humanity has always been in political civilization from the beginning and throughout all time; on the contrary, he means that, after having lived during an indeterminate extent of time outside this civilization and having been long contented with more primitive forms of association, humanity finally arrives at it and establishes itself in it as a promised land, the conquest of which was demanded by all its constitutional forces."]

historical permanence of the state. Thus far, Defourny is correct. But whether he intended to *emphasize* a *pre-political* stage of the historical existence of man also seems questionable. The assumption of a long pre-political development seems even less compatible with the statement following the political animal thesis – namely, that a man who is stateless by nature is either bad or greater than a man, because such a man is essentially one who loves war and discord. It is hardly conceivable that Aristotle regarded the man of early times as either bad or superhuman.

The following section, 1253a7ff., is decisive, where it is claimed that man is more of a political animal than any bee or herd animal. Aristotle justifies this statement by referring to his statement from his writings on natural science that nature does nothing in vain and that only a man has *logos*, speech, at his disposal. Other animals also possess voice to indicate pain and pleasure. Their nature has developed so far that they possess perception of pain and pleasure and can indicate it to one another. Speech, however, serves the purpose of revealing the advantageous and the harmful, and hence the just and the unjust. Man alone possesses a perception of good and bad, just and unjust. In this passage at least it is clear that Aristotle arrives at the point of characterizing man, insofar as he is a biological being, as political by nature. In this context Aristotle uses the basic proposition of his zoology – that nature does nothing in vain – in order to elucidate the following idea: it is anticipated in the "plan" (*Bauplan*) of the human species that it is by means of the psychosomatic property of *logos* that man carries out his characteristically political works and functions.[15] We learn that there are also other animals which are political, but that man is especially political because of his speech.[16] Since the species of animals are explicitly or implicitly regarded by Aristotle as immutable, the idea that man could have been stateless, without a polis, for a long time in the historically early age is far from his thought. One could thus say that according to this assertion of Aristotle, the political impulse of man is genetically ingrained in him. In retrospect, one will also have to say that this must already be the sense of the sentence of 1253a1ff. For, even there, the expression *zôon* [animal] can only be meant in a biological way. Here and at 1253a2ff. the biological perspective is of course a different one from that in 1252b32ff., where Aristotle speaks of the develop-

15 On the role of this "internal teleology" compare W. Kullmann, *Wissenschaft und Methode. Interpretationen zur aristotelischen Theorie der Naturwissenschaft* (Berlin–New York, 1974), pp. 194ff., 318ff.; "Der platonische Timaios und die Methode der aristotelischen Biologie", in *Studia Platonica*, Festschrift Gundert (Amsterdam, 1974), p. 157 with n. 2; "Die Teleologie in der aristotelischen Biologie. Aristoteles als Zoologe, Embryologe und Genetiker," *Sitzungsberichte der Heidelberger Akademie der Wissenschaften*, Phil.–Hist.Kl. (Heidelberg, 1979), pp. 16ff.; ["Different Concepts of the Final Cause in Aristotle," in *Aristotle on Nature and Living Things*. Philosophical and Historical Studies presented to D. M. Balme, ed. A. Gotthelf (Pittsburgh–Bristol, 1985), pp. 169ff., esp. 173ff.]

16 This implies that the quality of "political" *qua* "political" is not based on man's reason or *logos*, as Bien (*Die Grundlegung der politischen Philosophie bei Aristoteles*, p. 72) paraphrases in what is in other respects a splendid book.

ment of the polis and where this development is only *compared* to a natural (or technical!) development. Here – as the reference to bees and herd animals makes clear – man is indeed understood as a biological species.

Aristotle's thought departs even more strikingly from the idea of a pre-political existence of humanity in his final remarks on this problem (1253a18ff.). He says that the State is, according to nature, prior (*têi phusei proteron*) to the "house" and the individual, just as the whole is always prior to a part. He again uses a biological comparison for this purpose: a foot or a hand detached from the body can only be called foot or hand in a homonymous sense, because when separate they are no longer in a position to carry out their function;[17] the same applies to the isolated individual man in relation to the whole. The isolated individual must consequently be either a wild beast or a god. This is in sharp conflict with the beginning of the chapter, where the isolated men were indeed understood at a natural stage in the development of the polis.

We see, therefore, that Aristotle's argument in the second chapter of his *Politics* arises from two quite different starting points. In the first part it proceeds from the social development of humanity, leading to the polis. This is in the tradition of Plato (*Republic, Laws*), who in turn is likely to have been inspired by Democritus,[18] though in Aristotle's context the theme of development enters into the discussion only in a subsidiary fashion. It is the basic elements of the polis that are here brought into focus. In the second part Aristotle clearly argues from a biological point of view.[19]

But there is still the view that when Aristotle asserts that man is a *zôon politikon*, he may have regarded the genetic aspect as the essentially determining and original aspect and that he may have understood the historical coming-to-be and passing-away of the state as the coming-to-be and passing-away of a concrete substance. In order to conclusively refute this view we must still consider the remaining passages in which it appears.

Nevertheless, the text under consideration already indicates the significance of the political within Aristotle's anthropology. The political is a characteristic which necessarily results from the special biological nature of man. In this connection, Aristotle proceeds as if it is self-evident that this concept is not coextensive with the concept of man, but has a wider scope. It is only when compared with certain other animals that men are political to

17 Compare the parallels *PA* I.1.640b35ff.; *GA* II.1.734b25ff.

18 In *Pol*. VII.4.1326b2ff. Aristotle seems to criticize Plato's exposition in *Rep*. II.369aff., noting that a state exists only if the population is large enough to be self-sufficient for a good life in a political community. In this passage the historical–genetic dimension of *Pol*. I.2 is missing. Compare also Newman, *The Politics of Aristotle*, vol. III, p. 346; E. Schütrumpf, "Kritische Überlegungen zur Ontologie und Terminologie der aristotelischen 'Politik'," *Allgemeine Zeitschrift für Philosophie* (1980), pp. 26ff., p. 41. Due to the kindness of the author I was able to see the unpublished manuscript.

19 This is not the case in the first part; there the biological theme has a purely metaphorical character.

an especially high degree. No matter how much Aristotle contrasts men with certain beasts, he nonetheless presupposes the application of the concept of "political" to animals, a concept which originally derives from the human sphere. It also follows from the description of man as *zôon* that "political" above all describes a biological condition of a group of animals. So the precise connection of this human characteristic with the essence of man, as it is expressed in the definition, becomes clear. The definition of man includes the genus, animal (*zôon*), and differentia, having reason (*logon echon*). Insofar as one follows the preceding text, only the special degree to which the political element is found in man may be traced to this specific differentia of man. *Politikon* is neither a specific differentia of man, as has been thought,[20] nor is it interchangeable with the differentia.[21] According to the text, the greater degree to which man is political is due to the fact that as a being endowed with reason he has a perception of the beneficial and harmful and hence, as Aristotle infers, also of the just and unjust.[22] It is self-evident that he has only the predisposition for justice and is not necessarily always just. Of course, the biological background in this passage raises the question of whether it is appropriate to ascribe to Aristotle the intention to locate man in an autonomous area of the moral and political. The question regarding the precise role of the biological aspect in man as political animal becomes pressing.

II

We now turn to the remaining passages in which the statement in question occurs.

In *Politics* III.6 Aristotle is beginning to work out the distinction between correct and deviant constitutions. As a basis he wants first to establish why the state exists and how many sorts of human rule there are (1278b15ff.). We are here concerned with the first of these problems: *tinos charin sunestêke polis* (i.e., wherefore a polis or state exists). Apropos of this problem, Aristotle refers to the beginning of his work where he has said that man is by nature a political animal, and he adds some further thoughts. First he says that human beings, even if they need no help, nevertheless strive to live together (*tou suzên*). Here he seems consciously to dissent from the atomists' thesis, taken over by Plato in the *Republic*,[23] that it is primarily *chreia* (i.e., need,

---

20 Meyer already speaks (*Geschichte des Altertums*, p. 11) incorrectly of "the well known definition of Aristotle, that man is . . . by nature a being who lives in a state."

21 In this respect Bien's theses (see above note 4) should be formulated in a more differentiated way.

22 *Politikon* and *agathou kai kakou kai dikaiou kai adikou aisthêsin echon* are thus *sumbêbekota kath' hauta* of man in the sense of the theory of science in *An. Post.* I.4 and I.6, i.e. necessary nondefining features, which are derivable from his definition. Compare Kullmann, *Wissenschaft und Methode*, pp. 181ff.

23 In the third book of the *Laws* Plato offers no reason for the emergence of states. There is however no special poverty in their beginning (679b3ff.).

want) which makes men think of establishing the state on the basis of a sort of social contract.[24] At any rate men, according to him, have an innate social instinct, which is the best indication of the naturalness of human social conduct. On the other hand Aristotle would not like to exclude the role of consciously pursued gain, and he adds (1278b21ff.) that the common advantage also brings people together, insofar as a share of the good life (*meros . . . tou zên kalôs*) is attained by the individuals; for this is above all the end for the collective as for the individual.[25] He certainly means by this the pursuit of *eudaimonia* [happiness], which is attainable only by man who has *logos* [speech] at his disposal and possesses *nous* [reason] (see also 1280a31ff., b40ff.[26]). It is thus a conscious, voluntarily chosen[27] end.

As we see, Aristotle explains the existence of the state as due to the mixed effect of two factors. The biological factor is primary, which is expressed in the innate *orexis* [desire] for living together. It probably represents that side of the political which connects man with the gregarious animals (compare 1253a7ff.).[28] The second factor is the conscious, specifically human striving after gain and happiness, which manifests itself in the detailed shaping of the state. This is, in my view, a very significant analysis, which is superior in its balanced approach to many views of the state up to the modern time.

Then Aristotle concludes his reasoning with the following consideration (1278b24ff.): but it is also for the sake of life that men join together and form a political community. Perhaps there is a positive element (*ti tou kalou morion*) also contained in living itself, if it is not marked by any excess of hardships. The mass of men would evidently endure much pain in their longing for life, as if there were contained in it a certain pleasure and natural sweetness. With these statements no third reason for the emergence of the state is named, but Aristotle evidently returns again to the beginning of his reasoning, where he spoke of the primary instinct for communal life. This is also revealed by the parallel I.2.1252b29ff. where in the same way "life" itself is referred to as a primary cause of the state (the state *comes to be* for the sake of life and *is* for the

---

24 Compare Herter ("Die kulturhistorische Theorie der hippokratischen Schrift von der alten Medizin," pp. 472ff.) on *chreia* in Democritus. See further Fritz Steinmetz, "Staatengründung – aus Schwäche oder Geselligkeitsdrang? Zur Geschichte einer Theorie," in *Politeia und Res Publica*, Gedenkschrift R. Stark (Palingenesia vol. 4) (Wiesbaden, 1969), pp. 195ff.
25 Here *suzên* is explicitly excluded as a goal.
26 Compare F. Steinmetz ("Staatengründung – aus Schwäche oder Geselligkeitsdrang?", p. 184) on this passage.
27 Compare, e.g., 1280a34 *tou zên kata prohairesin*.
28 Compare below p. 106. [In modern times the social instinct of man described by Aristotle has often been misunderstood: see W. Kullmann, "Aristoteles' Staatslehre aus heutiger Sicht," *Gymnasium*, 90 (1983), pp. 456 ff.: "L'image de l'homme dans la pensée politique d'Aristote," *Les études philosophiques* (1989), pp. 1ff., esp. pp. 13ff. As to the anthropological foundation of Aristotle's philosophy compare W. Kullmann, "Equality in Aristotle's Political Thought," in *Equality and Inequality of Man in Ancient Thought*, ed. I. Kajanto, *Commentationes Humanarum Litterarum*, 75 (1984), pp. 31ff., esp. pp. 32ff.]

sake of the good life). If one takes *Pol.* I.2 together with III.6, where explicit reference is made back to I.2, it follows that the original instinct for communal life is certainly not aroused by becoming aware of need – it is present, even if no need exists – however, it is still naturally related to the lack of self-sufficiency of the individual man. The natural drive also has a determinate purpose (it is, expressed in an Aristotelian metaphor, not made by nature "in vain"); it is directed to making men self-sufficient and making them capable of life (or survival).[29] An additional factor is the conscious fixing of the aim.[30]

Neither of the factors regarded by Aristotle as decisive in the establishment of the state exactly coincides with the reason which Democritus probably gave for the origin of the state. The original instinct, though it is goal-directed in a certain sense, is unconscious and endowed by nature from the beginning. The second factor aims at the conscious shaping of the state; it is not an alliance made for the goal of survival. The knowledge of both is the presupposition or hypothesis (*hupotheteon*, 1278b15) for the operation of the statesman and of political science.

The statement under examination is also mentioned in the early *Eudemian Ethics*, namely in the treatment of friendship in VII.10.1242a22ff., albeit only incidentally. I read the corrupt text with Fritzsche and Dirlmeier as follows:[31] "Man is not only a political but also a house-holding animal and does not, like the other animals, sometimes couple with any fortuitous partner, whether male or female, and sometimes live in a solitary way." The text evidently refers back to a nonextant passage of the *EE* or another work in which it was stated that man is a *zôon politikon*. In any case, this notion, and perhaps also its justification as well, are presupposed here. The passage states that the institution, defined by *philia* [friendship], of the "household," i.e. of marriage and family (obviously unlike political behavior), is something specifically human.[32] Aristotle adds that there is a community even if there is

---

29 That Aristotle has in mind something very elementary and unconscious when he says that man is directed to *zên* [living] is elucidated by the fact that in the biological treatises he connects mere *zên* with the *threptikê psuchê* [nutritive soul], which is common to men, animals and plants. Compare Kullmann, *Wissenschaft und Methode*, p. 316.

30 When Aristotle explains in *EN* VIII.9.1160a11ff. that the political community originally emerges and survives, according to the general view, for purposes of utility, this abridgment of the problem is explained by the special context of the text, in the treatise on *philia*. Soon afterwards, in *EN* IX.9.1169b18ff., *politikon* is again explained by *suzên pephukos*, i.e., there is an allusion to the original unconscious social drive of man.

31 ὁ γὰρ ἄνθρωπος οὐ μόνον πολιτικὸν, ἀλλὰ καὶ οἰκονομικὸν ζῷον, καὶ οὐχ ὥσπερ τἆλλα ποτὲ συνδυάζεται καὶ τῷ τυχόντι καὶ θήλει καὶ ἄρρενι, ἄλλοτε δ' ἰδιάζει μοναυλικόν. Compare F. Dirlmeier, *Aristoteles. Eudemische Ethik* in Aristoteles, Werke in deutscher Übersetzung, ed. E. Grumach, vol. 7 (Darmstadt, 1962), p. 442.

32 *HA* IX.37.622a4 (i.e., a book which most regard as spurious) even calls the octopus *oikonomikos*, although in another sense: it collects [or hoards] provisions.

no polis (a situation which is evidently presupposed as unreal). So the union of husband and wife possesses a priority which is however not a priority of time (which is still to be discussed). Even if this passage of the *EE* lacks the addition that man is a political animal *by nature*, this is nevertheless intended. Aristotle concludes the chapter with the statement (1242a40ff.): "Therefore in the 'house' primarily lie the origins and sources of friendship and *politeia* [constitution] and the just." This formulation is given again in such a way that it does not assert a *temporal* priority of the "house" to the polis. That is, man is as much a political as an economic animal. A historical development of the polis is not being discussed. At the same time the biological reference is again noteworthy. The special character of the coupling (*sunduasmos*) of the human species is emphasized. As the passage was probably written relatively early, it is particularly important.

We now come to the passages of the *EN*. In *EN* I.7.1097b11 it is asked how far one may extend self-sufficiency in the definition of *eudaimonia*, the complete good and highest end of man. It is said that the concept of happiness cannot be applied to the life of a solitary person but must include life with parents, children, wife and generally friends and fellow citizens, since man is by nature (a) political (animal). It is also here that the political element is a constant anthropological factor.

The following passage, *EN* VIII.12.1162a17ff., is a parallel to the passage from the *EE* which was discussed above. Aristotle speaks of the fact that the union between husband and wife is natural according to universal opinion. He explains this by stating that man is even more a coupling than a political being, and all the more as the "house" is prior to and more necessary than the city, and bearing children is a more universal characteristic of animals. With men this community extends even farther than to childbearing, namely to the satisfaction of the needs of life. We must ask how this passage is related to *Pol.* I.2.1253a19, where it was said that the polis is prior to the "house" according to nature. In fact, there is no contradiction between the two passages if we consider the context. The polis has primacy over the *oikia* [household] because the *oikia* cannot exist without the polis – because of its lack of self-sufficiency. This is an assertion made from the standpoint of political science. The statement that man is *zôon politikon* is, however, as we saw, originally a biological statement (i.e., deriving from natural science), which is adopted in the scientific treatment of politics. The same is true of the statement that man is a (*zôon*) *sunduastikon* [coupling animal]. There is a group of animals which are *politika* and there is a larger group – including most species of animals, even though not all[33] of them – which are *sunduastika*. Insofar as many more species are *sunduastika* than *politika*, man is by nature "coupling" in a more original sense (i.e., *proteron*) than "political." Both are essential characteristics, but the former is more general. Again, it is

---

33 Aristotle regards the following as exceptional: animals which are bisexual, which reproduce by means of division, which are spontaneously generated, and which reproduce unisexually (through the female alone). Compare D. M. Balme, *Aristotle's De Partibus Animalium I and De Generatione Animalium I* (Oxford, 1972), p. 128.

noteworthy how far the statement being examined has a biological background.[34] The reference to sexuality as natural endowment shows that the *philia* between husband and wife is also naturally endowed.[35]

Aristotle subsequently mentions the specific characteristic of *human* coupling, namely, that it extends beyond childbearing and includes the reciprocal support by the division of labor in meeting the necessities of life. The same idea is expressed in *EE* with the concept of *oikonomikon* [householding]. Thus, the inquiry reaches the precision characteristic of political science (*politikê epistême*), which in this case exceeds the precision of biology.

Finally, the statement under examination occurs at *EN* IX.9.1169b16ff. Here the problem of the *EN* I is treated once more: in happy men, who attain the highest stage of human existence, how far does their self-sufficiency, which is an essential character of theirs, extend? Aristotle believes that it would surely be strange to make the happy person a solitary person; for nobody would choose to possess all goods entirely by himself; for man is *politikon* and born for communal life. In substance, nothing new emerges from this passage. It does not go beyond *EN* I.7.

The interpretation of the preceding passages showed that the political aspect is seen as an essential characteristic which man possesses on biological–genetic grounds. Nowhere is there any discussion of a historical development of human social behavior, terminating in the polis, except in *Pol.* I.2.[36] It can by now be said that the historical aspect can have played no part in the conception of this basic statement of the *Politics*. The statement that man is a political animal is used independently of the various historical constitutional forms.

This conclusion is corroborated by *HA* I.1.487b33ff. At the beginning of this work it becomes clear that Aristotle is mainly concerned with giving an account of the morphological and somatic characteristics by means of which the kinds and genera of beasts are distinguished (i.e., the *diaphorai* [differentiae] of the *moria* [parts]). The reason for this is that they have a significance for definition and, therefore, serve to differentiate the species (see *HA* 491a14ff.; *PA* I.4.644b7ff.; I.3.643a35ff.)[37] Moreover, Aristotle intends, as he explicitly states in the beginning of our passage, to examine the differences, in the form of life and in behavior, and he begins with a general survey. His words are:[38]

> There are however also characteristics of the following kind according to the forms of life and the activities. Some are gregarious (herd) animals, others live solitarily – this applies to "land animals" as well as to "birds" and "swimming

34 Compare Aristotle's uses of the words *sunduazein* and *sunduasmos* in H. Bonitz, *Index Aristotelicus* (Berlin, 1870 [repr. 1955]), 725a3ff., a60ff. (The examples are chiefly from the biological writings.)

35 I.e., the situation is – *contra* Dirlmeier, *Eudemische Ethik*, p. 442 – in principle the same as in *EE* VII.10 (see pp. 103–4 above).

36 On *Pol.* VII.4.1326b2ff. compare note 18 above.

37 Compare Kullmann, *Wissenschaft und Methode*, pp. 66, 76.

38 The Greek text of 487b33ff. runs as follows: Εἰσὶ δὲ καὶ αἱ τοιαίδε διαφοραὶ κατὰ τοὺς βίους καὶ τὰς πράξεις. Τὰ μὲν γὰρ αὐτῶν ἐστιν ἀγελαῖα τὰ δὲ [488a] μοναδικά, καὶ

animals" – still others occupy an intermediate place. And of the gregarious animals, some live politically and the others scattered. Examples of the gregarious animals among the birds are: the class of pigeons, cranes and swans (none of the birds with crooked beaks is gregarious), and among the swimmers: many groups of fish, for example the so-called migrants, the tunnies, the pelamyds, and the bonitos.[39] Man however occupies an intermediate position (i.e., between gregarious and solitary animals). Animals that live politically are those that have any kind of activity in common, which is not true of all gregarious animals. Of this sort are: man, bee, wasp, ant and crane. And of these, some are under a leader, the others are anarchical. For example, the crane and the class of bees are under a leader, the ants and countless others are anarchical.

This passage clearly shows that *zôon politikon* is a biological description. Of course, the concept of "political" is in itself no biological concept. The adoption of this concept into biology[40] is accounted for by the explanatory principle of Aristotelian biology, that the differences among the various species of animals are to be measured by the standard of the highest developed species of animal, and this is man (see *PA* II.10.656a7ff.).[41] The explanation given in the *HA* is significant, namely, that the concept of "political" is a mark of animals which as a group have an activity in common. Collective existence as such is insufficient, since it is characteristic of all gregarious animals. As far as beasts are concerned, Aristotle certainly refers to the beehive, the wasp's nest, the ant hill, and the social behavior of

πεζὰ καὶ πτηνὰ καὶ πλωτά, τὰ δ' ἐπαμφοτερίζει. Καὶ τῶν ἀγελαίων [καὶ τῶν μοναδικῶν] τὰ μὲν πολιτικὰ τὰ δὲ σποραδικά ἐστιν. Ἀγελαῖα μὲν οὖν οἷον ἐν τοῖς πτηνοῖς τὸ τῶν περιστερῶν γένος καὶ γέρανος καὶ κύκνος (γαμψώνυχον οὐδὲν ἀγελαῖον), καὶ τῶν πλωτῶν πολλὰ γένη τῶν ἰχθύων, οἷον οὓς καλοῦσι δρομάδας, θύννοι, πηλαμύδες, ἀμίαι· ὁ δ' ἄνθρωπος ἐπαμφοτερίζει. Πολιτικὰ δ' ἐστὶν ὧν ἕν τι καὶ κοινὸν γίνεται πάντων τὸ ἔργον· ὅπερ οὐ πάντα ποιεῖ τὰ ἀγελαῖα. Ἔστι δὲ τοιοῦτον ἄνθρωπος, μέλιττα, σφήξ, μύρμηξ, γέρανος. Καὶ τούτων τὰ μὲν ὑφ' ἡγεμόνα ἐστὶ τὰ δ'ἄναρχα, οἷον γέρανος μὲν καὶ τὸ τῶν μελιττῶν γένος ὑφ' ἡγεμόνα, μύρμηκες δὲ καὶ μυρία ἄλλα ἄναρχα. [488a2 καὶ τῶν μοναδικῶν del. Schneider, Peck].

39 *pelamudes* and *amiai* (bonitos) are species of tunny; compare D'Arcy W. Thompson, *A Glossary of Greek Fishes* (London, 1947), pp. 197, 13ff.

40 Unfortunately nothing certain can be said about the chronological relation between the introduction to the *HA* and the *Politics* and its parts. We should, however, remember that large parts of the *Politics* which were composed before the biological works, reveal a strong relation to biology, so that the question about the date of this passage is not pressing.

41 Therefore, I cannot agree with Bien (*Die Grundlegung der politischen Philosophie bei Aristoteles*, p. 122, note 26), who states in this context that this concept is used equivocally and homonymously. If one considers that the Greeks, in any case Aristotle, do not emphasize the disparity between man and beast as strongly as do the moderns (see below p. 107), the use of the term in different contexts becomes more intelligible. [R. G. Mulgan, *Hermes*, 102 (1974), pp. 438ff. to my mind too strongly emphasizes the slight inconsistency in the use of the word *politikon*. But, however that may be, he comes to the convincing result that Aristotle intended to connect his political theory with his general biological principles.]

the cranes, particularly with respect to their migration to the south.[42] One is reminded of *Pol*. III.6, where the good life is specified as the true purpose of the existence of the state, and the common advantage is also mentioned as a factor. This passage is flatly inconsistent with the assumption of an original solitary state of human beings. One sees how this thought only entered Aristotle's reasoning through the influence of passages from Plato's *Republic* and *Laws*. In the *Politics* it is certainly more important for Aristotle to fight the conception that the state occurred by convention [*nomôi*][43] and is based on a social contract. The biological observations offer good arguments against this thesis, which goes back to Democritus and was probably also advocated by the Sophists.

In view of this passage the question arises how Aristotle basically conceived of the relationship between beast and man.[44] Heidegger once remarked negatively, that when the Greeks understood man as *zôon* [animal], they in principle always thought of man as *homo animalis*, which meant that they had a very low opinion of his nature.[45] However, Heidegger does not really go beyond the modern dichotomy between beast and man, which stems from the Christian tradition and which is also fundamental for more recent social research. Aristotle's conception is more fine-grained. Man is indeed like the beasts a *zôon*, but stands as such in the highest run of the *scala naturae*.[46] He is on the one hand always seen as having a certain connection with the beasts, but, on the other hand, he is clearly elevated above them. Everything supports the view that Aristotle's perspective in his "political science" is basically the same as in his biology. This is especially true for his statement that any one who is not in a position to live in a community or because of his self-sufficiency is not in need of anything, is not part of the state and consequently is either a *thêrion* [wild beast] or a god (*Pol*. I.2.1253a27ff.). This statement sees man as having an essential connection with the beast as much as with the deity.[47]

42 The ancient material is found in D'Arcy W. Thompson, *A Glossary of Greek Birds* (1st edn, Oxford, 1936; Hildesheim, 1966), pp. 70ff.

43 Gigon (*Aristoteles. Politik*, p. 267; cited above n. 3) thinks above all that the opponents are mainly Socratics, especially Aristippus of Cyrene and the Cynics; but one might want to recall older sources in view of what might be conjectured about Democritus and the discussion in Plato's *Protagoras*.

44 Compare U. Dierauer, *Tier und Mensch im Denken der Antike: Studien zur Tierpsychologie, Anthropologie und Ethik*, Studien zur antiken Philosophie, ed H. Flashar, H. Görgemanns, W. Kullmann, vol. 6 (Amsterdam, 1977), pp. 121ff.

45 M. Heidegger, "Über den Humanismus," in *Platons Lehre von der Wahrheit. Mit einem Brief über den 'Humanismus'* (2nd edn, Bern, 1954), p. 66. Bien (*Grundlegung*, p. 123 note 27) already correctly objected that *zôon* does not signify "beast" [*Tier*] (with a pejorative nuance) but "animated being" or "living creature."

46 Besides *PA* II.10.656a7ff. compare also *HA* VIII.1.588b4ff. and *GA* II.1.732b15ff. as well as H. Happ, "Die *scala naturae* und die Schichtung des Seelischen bei Aristoteles," in *Beiträge zur Alten Geschichte und deren Nachleben*, Festschrift für F. Altheim (Berlin, 1969), pp. 220ff.

47 Well stated in Dirlmeier, *Aristoteles. Nikomachische Ethik*, in Aristoteles Werke, ed. E. Grumach, vol. 6 (Berlin, 1956), p. 476 (comment on 141, 3).

The passage in the *HA* is not merely an observation of Aristotle's, but stands in a Platonic tradition as well. Plato says in the *Statesman* (276e10ff.) that the art of free shepherding over free two-footed animals is "politics" and "the art of the king and statesman."[48]

This formulation has certainly something humorous about it. Nonetheless, one ought not to overestimate its irony. The biological component in these divisions is, just as in the *Sophist*, surely meant seriously, if one only thinks of Plato's pupil Speusippus and his zoological work *Homoia*. All of Plato's reasoning proceeds from the statesman and not from man as such, but one sees that for him the political moment emerges as a specification of the gregarious and that there is a first approach to a biological account, which Aristotle then gives.

Let me add a further passage in *HA* VIII.1.589a1ff. Here the concept of "political" is also brought into a zoological context, in a somewhat looser manner. Aristotle says that the animals that are more intelligent and endowed with memory treat their offspring in a more "political" manner, that is, they are concerned more intensely about them. This shows that the concept here has become a general zoological description of the social behavior of animals.

I think it is appropriate to state that, when examining Aristotle's statement, we are dealing with a basic biological/anthropological awareness, which places, from the very beginning, his political investigations on a very firm foundation, one that is firmer than many foundations of more recent times. One now understands the tranquility and open-mindedness with which Aristotle can explain various constitutions as being equally correct and indeed can recommend them as appropriate according to the existing social contexts (see *Pol.* III.7ff.). The classification of constitutions is only a refinement of the differentiations which are made in biology. At the same time it follows that Aristotle did not intend to limit the concept of "political" to the "polis" in the sense of the specifically Greek city-state, just as he did not in fact completely exclude non-Greek examples in the *Politics*.[49] It also becomes clear why Aristotle is far from proclaiming that political involvement is itself a goal of education. One understands why he can suppose that political education has different aims in the individual types of constitution, for example, in democracy and oligarchy, according to specific needs (see V.9.1310a12ff.).

III

The biological origin of the idea that man is a political animal raises the question of the character of the state, of the polis itself. After all, the polis had

---

48 ... τὴν δὲ ἑκούσιον καὶ ἑκουσίων διπόδων ἀγελαιονομικὴν ζῴων προσειπόντες πολιτικήν, τὸν ἔχοντα αὖ τέχνην ταύτην καὶ ἐπιμέλειαν ὄντως ὄντα βασιλέα καὶ πολιτικὸν ἀποφαινώμεθα;

49 Ritter (*Metaphysik und Politik*, p. 71) evidently takes a different view following Jacob Burckhardt.

been compared at the beginning of *Politics* I.2 with the final product of a biological (or technical) process. Does it have for its part any kind of substantial character? It is not easy to answer this question. Nowhere outside of the *Politics* does Aristotle undertake the attempt to categorically classify the "polis." The word is an abstraction, which on one hand designates a community, i.e. a group of citizens, but on the other hand can mean a definite geographical place, a *chôra*. According to Aristotle's account outside of his *Politics*, the state, as a community of citizens, cannot be a species. Man in general is, according to biology, itself an *eschaton eidos* [an ultimate species]; within the framework of the animal kingdom it occupies a position of an isolated species within the blooded animals (i.e., vertebrates) (compare *HA* I.6.490b18, II.15.505b28; *PA* I.4.644a31). According to general Aristotelian doctrine, any individual or group of people, i.e. any unit below the level of the species of "man," cannot be adequately conceived of by theoretical science (compare also *PA* I.4.644a23ff. for biology). Does Aristotle, however, think differently in the *Politics*? The question is not only important for its own sake, but also deserves great attention if we look at it from the point of view of modern political theory. Did Aristotle, like so many modern political theorists, perceive a higher natural being in the polis to which the individual is inferior? This question has been answered affirmatively by some researchers, and at least implicitly so by some others, when they assert the applicability of the theory of the four causes of the *Metaphysics* to the polis. In particular, the most recent attempt of this kind by M. Riedel,[50] who treats this theme from many points of view worth considering, is opposed by E. Schütrumpf[51] with forceful arguments proceeding from linguistic evidence. We shall forego going into the details of the controversy, and begin with following the possible clues in the text, which could be evidence for a substantial character of the polis.

There is no doubt that Aristotle is speaking in *Pol.* I.2.1252b32 of the *phusis* [nature] of the state, which is achieved at the end of a development, and a possible meaning of this word is "substance."[52] He also sees in the state a *holon* [whole], while he sees in the single "house" and the individual

50 "Politik und Metaphysik bei Aristoteles," in *Metaphysik und Metapolitik* (Frankfurt/ M., 1975), pp. 63ff. (*Philosophisches Jahrbuch*, 77 [1970], pp. 1ff.).
51 "Kritische Überlegungen zur Ontologie und Terminologie der aristotelischen 'Politik'," pp. 28ff. (cited above note 18). To the advocates mentioned by Schütrumpf of the application of the theory of the four causes to the *Politics* (W. F. Forchhammer, *Verh. d. Vereins dt. Philologen und Schulmänner* [Cassel, 1844], pp. 81ff.; W. Siegfried, *Untersuchungen zur Staatslehre des Aristoteles* [Zürich, 1942], pp. 4ff. [Schriften zu den Politika des Aristoteles (Hildesheim–New York, 1973) pp. 242ff.]; A. Stigen, *The Structure of Aristotle's Thought* [Oslo, 1966] pp. 392ff.; Ada B. Hentschke, *Politik und Philosophie bei Plato und Aristoteles* [Frankfurter Wiss. Beitr. Kulturwiss. Reihe vol. 13] [Frankfurt, 1971], p. 394; and Riedel, "Politik und Metaphysik", Newman, *The Politics of Aristotle*, vol. I, pp. 44ff. should still be added.
52 In fact, Ada B. Hentschke (*Politik und Philosophie bei Plato und Aristoteles*, p. 394) believes that the meaning of substance, i.e., unity of *hulê* [matter] and form, is evident here.

respectively, a part (1253a20ff.). More striking still is the comparison which he draws in IV.4.1290b21ff. between the possibility of determining the number of existing animal species and the possibility of establishing the number of conceivable constitutions. Just as one could establish the number of animal species by counting the number of various possible combinations of different forms in which the necessary parts of animals appear, one could also reach the number of political constitutions by counting the number of possible combinations among the different types of the parts within the polis. It has been correctly remarked that the method recommended here has nothing to do with the method Aristotle actually uses in his biological writings, and one can attempt to interpret this difference in terms of Aristotle's development.[53] It should nevertheless be emphasized that here the structure of the polis is being compared to the structure of a living animal. This is also true of the reflection in IV.4.1291a24ff., that, if one regards the soul as a more important part of an animal than the body, one must also regard warriors, judges, and advisors as more important than the professional groups producing for life's daily needs, a point Plato did not consider in the *Republic*. A similar instance i; III.4.1277a5ff., where, among other things, the soul–body structure of an animal provides an example of the composition of the polis from dissimilar components. In V.3.1302b34ff. the dependence of the stability of constitutions upon the symmetry of their parts parallels the corresponding dependence of the stability of the body upon the symmetry of its parts. Accordingly, in *Pol.* V.9.1309b23ff. the meaning of the correct proportions in constitutions is compared to their meaning regarding the forms of noses. In VII.4.1326a35ff., too, the structural similarity between state and organism is emphasized. There is a measure for the size of a state, just as "for everything else," whether animal, plant, or tool.

In spite of this, one cannot conclude that Aristotle actually regards the polis as an organism, for apart from the first passage he deals exclusively with comparisons. Even the concept of *phusis* [nature] used in the first passage, in I.2.1252b32, is clearly applied in a very general and vague way. To illustrate that *phusis* designates the condition achieved at the end of a development, not only are (as I have said) man and horse mentioned, but also the house, i.e., a product of *technê* [craft]. Similarly, in VII.4.1326a35ff., tools, i.e., man-made objects, along with animals and plants, are compared to the polis. Thus, the organic quality is not the specific point of the comparison. Moreover, the parallel to I.2 of the *Poetics*, where Aristotle writes about the *phusis* of tragedy,[54] indicates that this term does not necessarily mean something substantial. Aristotle is more careful in his choice of words in VII.8.1328a22, where the polis is counted only among the *kata phusin sunestôta* [things established according to nature] (provided that with *tôn allôn tôn kata phusin sunestôtôn* [the other things established according

53 Compare G. E. R. Lloyd, "The Development of Aristotle's Theory of the Classification of Animals," *Phronesis*, 6 (1961), pp. 69ff., 79ff.; W. Fiedler, *Analogiemodelle bei Aristoteles*, pp. 165ff.
54 See above p. 98.

to nature] the polis is not being contrasted with things existing by nature in general, which would be grammatically possible).[55] That he does not speak of the *eidos* [form] and of the *ousia* [substance] of the state, should at any rate be noted.

There would also be an indication of the substantial character of the polis if Aristotle had written in a strictly terminological manner about the *hulê* [matter] of the polis. But, as Schütrumpf has shown, he clearly does not do that. Only once, in VII.4.1325b40ff. is the idea of *hulê* used in a relevant context. Aristotle compares the statesman and lawgiver with the craftsman, who must have suitable material (*hulê*) at his disposal in order to do his work well. For him this involves men as well as the country. As Schütrumpf has seen, Aristotle is not talking about the polis here at all, but rather about the prerequisites for political action.[56]

So not only the concept of *eidos* but also the concept of *hulê* is to be ruled out as evidence for the assumption of the substantial character of the polis.

Still to be examined is *Pol.* VII.8.1328a21ff. Here there is a distinction between the necessary (indispensable) prerequisites of the polis and the polis itself (*hôn aneu to holon ouk an eiê, toutou heneken – hou heneken*). The direct comparison points to *technê* [craft] again as the probable origin of this distinction. Just as the builder's art and the tools are necessary prerequisites for the house to be built, so, according to Aristotle, polises are in need of possessions, including many living parts (farmers, craftsmen, and laborers), without these being parts of the state, i.e., of the ideal state. Such a teleological relationship between necessary prerequisites and the product is often found in his biological writings (where it is frequently transferred from examples of *technê* to the analysis of animals). Compare, e.g., *PA* I.1.639b19ff., 642a7ff., *Phys.* II.9.199b34ff. (see also *Met.* V.5.1015a20ff.). Nonetheless, it would be rash to conclude from this parallel that Aristotle regarded the polis as an independent substantial being such as a house or animal, for the comparison has only a very limited validity. In *technê* and *phusis* the distinction is normally applied to the relationship of material and product, and then the material is always a part of the whole, whereas the builder is not seen as a necessary prerequisite, but rather is regarded as the efficient cause of the house. Aristotle certainly did not want to claim this regarding the status of the farmer, craftsman or laborer in the ideal state. It is quite remarkable that this teleological terminology is only found in the early Book VII and nowhere else in the *Politics*. In other constitutions there certainly is a hierarchical classification of the population groups, but a direct teleological relationship is missing.

It is revealing that the polis, in the defining statements which are available – although it may also be designated as a *holon*[57] – is always characterized only as "a certain quantity of citizens" (III.1.1274b41: *politôn ti plêthos*; compare VII.4.1325b40, VII.8.1328b16). Aristotle is evidently

55 Compare Newman, *The Politics of Aristotle*, vol. I, p. 39, vol. II, p. 343.
56 "Kritische Überlegungen zur Ontologie und Terminologie der aristotelischen 'Politik'," (cited above note 18), pp. 28ff.
57 Compare Newman, *The Politics of Aristotle*, vol. III, pp. 131ff.

aware, as is shown by this indefinite numerical concept of *ti plêthos*, that with his concept of the polis he is speaking of a group of men below the level of the *eidos* [species]. That agrees most clearly with his theoretical views about the sciences. Politics is a practical science; i.e., Aristotle composes his work to give instruction for actions; he is writing the *pragmateia* not for the sake of contemplation (*ou theôrias heneka*; compare *EE* I.5.1216b16ff.; *EN* I.3.1095a2, II.2.1103b26ff., X.9.1179a35ff.).[58] This is evident not only from the general remarks regarding *politikê* [politics] in both the *Ethics* (ethics being together with *politikê* an integral component of the philosophy of man), but also from the *Politics* itself. So he states in I.10.1258a19ff. that *politikê* does not "make" men, but rather "receives them from nature and uses them." Therefore, the goal of *politikê* is the acting of the statesman. In a further passage, *Pol.* III.8.1279b11ff., Aristotle excuses himself for going a little further afield to look for the essential definition of the various constitutional forms, with the observation that it is characteristic of one who philosophizes about his respective field and does not only consider action, to overlook and omit nothing. It is precisely this limitation of the notion of practical science which shows that the orientation to practice is in principle presupposed. Since *politikê epistêmê* [political science] is a practical science, it does not share the task of the theoretical sciences, to investigate the properties which universally and necessarily belong to a definite substance. Its sphere is *ta hôs epi to polu*, things which are so-and-so "for the most part," and therefore do not possess the character of necessity (compare *EN* I.3.1094b11ff.) like the essence of substances.

What is it that is only "for the most part" such-and-such, in terms of the categories? In *EN* X.9.1181b14ff. Aristotle calls ethics and politics *hê peri ta anthrôpina philosophia*, meaning that the subject to which statements of this discipline refer is first of all man, not the polis, and the topics of this science are certain properties of man (*ta anthrôpina*). It is evidently a feature of the practical *epistêmê* [science], that it is not concerned with substances, but with attributes. To this corresponds the reasoning in the introductory chapter of the *Politics*, which culminates in the characterization of man as a *zôon politikon*. The "political" is the fundamental human characteristic[59] from which the *Politics* proceeds. This is true independently of the fact that the polis is *proteron têi phusei* [prior in nature] if contrasted with the "house" and the individual non-self-sufficient man (1253a19). This is only the anthropological fact that leads to the characterization of man as a *zôon politikon*. Subsequently the political element in man is further specified (*idion* 1253a16) as the possession of a "perception of 'good' and 'bad', 'just' and 'unjust'." From this specific human property the precise theme of politics results (*EN* I.3.1094b14ff.): *ta de kala kai ta dikaia, peri hôn hê politikê skopeitai* [fine and just things, which politics investigates]; i.e., the properties of the ethical good and just are objects for this discipline to study. A related fact is that in the *EN* the

58 Compare above all W. Hennis from the side of political science: *Politik und praktische Philosophie* (2nd edn, Stuttgart, 1977), pp. 1ff. See further Riedel, "Politik und Metaphysik," pp. 64, 85ff.
59 Even if it is not confined to man.

aretai [virtues] and in the *EE* the *dikaion* [just], are cited as examples of the category of quality (*EN* I.6.1096a25, *EE* I.8.1217b31). Properties like these also form the sphere of the *planê* [variable "wandering," irregularity] and of the *hôs epi to polu* [what is for the most part]. This means that the characteristics which man could be said to have, possess degrees of necessity and exact ascertainability. When we look at the zoological writings, only certain morphological and somatic characteristics of the animals have significance for definition (compare *PA* I.4.644b7ff.), not, however, the "psychosomatic" activities such as the mode of locomotion (*PA* I.3.643a35ff.). Therefore, in the collection of facts in the *HA* the distinction of the "parts" of the animals, i.e., their tissues and organs, is most important, while the features concerning their way of life and their activities (I.1.487b33ff. *kata tous bious kai tas praxeis*) are of only secondary importance both because they are not so unambiguously and exactly determinable and because the overlappings of these features with those of other species of animals are particularly numerous.[60] This also applies to "political" (see above p. 106). Nonetheless, it is clear that these features concerning the way of life are *sumbebêkota kath' hauta* [accidents belonging to a subject in itself], i.e., *necessary*, nondefining properties. This is not true for "ethically good" (*kalon*) and just (*dikaion*). Unlike *politikon* and *agathou kai kakou kai dikaiou kai adikou aisthêsin echon* [having perception of good and bad and just and unjust], these do not possess the character of necessity when one looks at them separately. Man in general is not "good" and "just." This partly explains the lack of exactness which the *EN* mentions in reference to these characteristics. It is the fact that these predicates are not necessary which makes a practical science possible. Only where there is room for a choice of behavior, can the attempt be made to influence this behavior. It is only if one combines these characteristics with their opposites, an *aretê* [virtue], for example, with its complementary *kakiai* [vices], that one could perhaps consider interpreting the entire disjunction as necessary. In *An. Post.* I.4 disjunctions such as straight/curved, even/odd, primary/compound, and isosceles/non-isosceles are cited as examples of *kath' hauta* [in itself or *per se*] of the "second type," i.e., of *sumbebêkota kath' hauta* [accidents belonging to a subject in itself or *per se*]. According to *An. Post.* I.8.75b33ff. absolute necessary conclusions can also be drawn in the case of "frequently occurring things," when the objects to be investigated are considered with respect to one side of a disjunction.[61] But nowhere does Aristotle say whether he wants the *aretai* [virtues] and *kakiai* [vices] of the *Ethics* and *Politics* to be taken as disjunctive *sumbebêkota kath' hauta* [accidents belonging to a subject in itself] and not as mere accidents;[62] and even if the first were true, the *aretai* themselves would not be

---

60 Compare Kullmann, *Wissenschaft und Methode*, pp. 256ff.
61 Compare Kullmann, *Wissenschaft und Methode*, pp. 271ff.
62 In an interesting supplementary note to his commentary *Aristotle's De Partibus Animalium I and De Generatione Animalium I,* Balme seems to be inclined to go very far in deriving individual differences of man from the definition of the specific form, which according to him must be expressed as a long disjunction (in: J. Longrigg, *Classical Review*, 27 [1977], p. 39). On the question of ethical properties, however, he is silent.

necessary attributes. In any case, political science is not concerned with substantial beings, but with those characteristics of man which are to be realized (ethically good, just, happy, etc.).

Even when Aristotle speaks of *eudaimonia* [happiness] or *eu zên* [living well] as the *telos* [end] of politics, he is dealing explicitly with the realization of an *anthrôpinon agathon* [good of man] (*EN* I.7.1098a16; *EE* I.7.1217a21ff.), i.e., a feature which applies to man. It is expressly stated in the passage of *EE* just cited that the other animals such as the horse, the bird, or the fish cannot be labeled with the predicate "happy" (*eudaimôn*). This clearly implies that ethical and political investigations are always directed toward the realization of values which apply to man as the subject, and not, as one might have thought, to the polis, which in terms of Aristotelian science is not an entity that can be clearly defined. These investigations are anthropology. Any kind of substantial interpretation of the political is far from Aristotle's mind.[63] Concerning the biological perspective in the *Politics* two points should obviously be sharply distinguished:

1 Man is to a great extent seen as *zôon* [animal]. He is compared with other *zôa* [animals], with a particular emphasis on social behavior.
2 The polis is seen as something natural and in this respect is compared with other *phusei sunestôta* [things established by nature].

The point mentioned first is the essential and most far-reaching one. In the second, biology serves merely as an "analogical model" (Fiedler)[64] for the polis, and the comparisons have a purely heuristic function. *Politikê epistêmê* [political science] is distinguished from biology or zoology, which is a part of natural science (*phusikê*), not by another *genos* (in the sense of *An. Post.* I.10.76b13), i.e., another object, but rather by dealing with a characteristic of man in a more discriminating way than natural science does, insofar as there appear alternative possibilities which can be influenced by the practical measures of the statesman.

Consequently it is clear how the statement (which we should understand primarily in a purely biological sense) that man is by nature a political animal has certain implications, or presents certain possibilities, that open the door to the creative intent of the statesman, and this is the theme of the *Politics*.

In any case we should take into account Aristotle's statements which introduce matter as *principium individuationis*, above all *Met.* VII.8.1034a5ff.; 10.1035b27ff.

63 Compare Riedel, "Politik und Metaphysik," p. 82.

64 See above note 12. See the excellent book by A. Demandt, *Metaphern für Geschichte. Sprachbilder und Gleichnisse im historisch-politischen Denken* (Munich, 1978), which also contains a section "Organische Metaphern im antiken und christlichen Geschichtsdenken," which is, pardonably in a first collection of the material, not yet detailed enough to be informative about our problem.

IV

The previous considerations indicate that the characteristic of "political" is not the feature which constitutes the essential nature of man. We hereby arrive at the often discussed problem, how the *bios theôrêtikos* [contemplative life], which Aristotle sets out as the ideal (especially in *EN* X.6–8) is related to the political character of man. Flashar, for example, rightly insisted that Aristotle recognized the primacy of the contemplative form of life as opposed to the political form of life.[65] Pure *theôria* [contemplation] is exactly where man finds himself at a boundary and approaches the divine, which is according to *Pol.* I.2.1253a29 totally self-sufficient in virtue of having no needs. Thus, the real human *telos* [end] – even if it finally transcends mere human existence, in the sense of biological existence – supersedes the characteristic of the political. This idea of Aristotelian ethics, which cannot be pursued in detail here, will in any case be much more understandable, if one takes fully into account that the political side of man is closely linked to the area of biology. We can hereby understand why Aristotle in the *EN*, although he emphasizes the analogy between the *eudaimonia* of the polis and of the individual,[66] sees ethics merely as "a sort of political treatise" (1094b10ff.: *politikê tis methodos*), which constitutes "the philosophy concerning the sphere of human existence" (1181b15: *hê peri ta anthrôpina philosophia*) only when it is combined with political science in the restricted sense.[67] From an historical point of view the connection between ethics and politics in Aristotle is probably to be explained by the Platonic tradition, while the distinction between these spheres was first seen clearly by Aristotle himself. Inasmuch as there is an element present in the human soul which is missing from the soul of other *zôa* [animals], man has the capacity to leave behind the sphere of the political *koinônia* [community].

V

One question remains to be decided. How does the statement under discussion cohere with the concept of a development of human culture which

65 H. Flashar, "Ethik und Politik in der Philosophie des Aristoteles," *Gymnasium*, 78 (1971), p. 287 against G. Bien, "Das Theorie–Praxis–Problem und die politische Philosophie bei Platon und Aristoteles," *Philosophisches Jahrbuch*, 76 (1968–9), pp. 264ff. Further literature is cited in Flashar, "Ethik und Politik."
66 On this point compare P. Weber–Schäfer, *Einführung in die antike politische Theorie II* (Darmstadt, 1967), pp. 37ff.
67 For an excellent example of the differentiation of the two as carried out by modern political scientists, see A. Schwan, "Die Staatsphilosophie im Verhältnis zur Politik als Wissenschaft," in D. Oberndörfer, *Wissenschaftliche Politik. Eine Einführung in Grundfragen ihrer Tradition und Theorie* (Freiburg, 1962), pp. 153ff., especially the reference to the task of politics, namely, to recognize and protect the autonomy of the *bios theôrêtikos*.

includes the growth of the state? It has already been noted that this concept of a development derives from Plato. In Plato it was connected in part with a theory of periodic catastrophes and cyclic historical development (compare *Laws* III.677aff.; *Timaeus* 22c),[68] It is clear that not only the assumption of a linear, unique teleological development of man from a stateless existence to a state, but also the thesis of a repeated cyclical development of this kind would baldly contradict the interpretation I have offered of the statement discussed, which presupposes a biologically constant political factor in man. But Aristotle did not support this concept in a strict sense.[69] In *Pol.* II.8.1269a4ff., he argues on one occasion that the age of laws does not necessarily imply their goodness, because primitive men (*prôtoi*) were presumably rather unintelligent, "because they were earth-born, or because they had saved themselves from a catastrophe." Here both theories are reported from a distance.[70] The "catastrophe" is certainly reminiscent of Plato's cyclical theory, but from passages such as *Pol.* VII.10.1329b25ff., *Met.* XII.8.1074b10ff. it is clear that Aristotle is taking into account irregular, even if frequently occurring, catastrophes rather than recurring cycles. This corresponds with his own historical knowledge as well as with his conviction, expressed, e.g., in *De Int.* 9, that historical events occur indeterminately. If states reappear immediately after such catastrophes, that

68 H. J. Krämer, *Arete bei Platon and Aristoteles* (Abh. Heid., 1959), p. 221.
69 Compare this to R. Zoepffel, *Historia und Geschichte bei Aristoteles* (Abh. Heid., 1975), pp. 51ff.
70 The assumption that men are earth-born is not Aristotle's in any sense. He characterizes it himself as a "legend" (1269a7), and the eternity of the species and their characteristics is a central point of his philosophy. According to him, this constancy results (as e.g. can be seen from his critique of Empedocles's theory of evolution) from his doctrine that form is primary, ungenerated, and immutable. One may compare from the biological works in the first place *GA* II.1.731b35ff. where "eternity" is affirmed for men, animals and plants. The common catchphrase for this is the statement, "A man generates a man" (*anthrôpos anthrôpon gennai*). On this compare K. Oehler, *Antike Philosophie und byzantinisches Mittelalter* (Munich, 1969), pp. 131ff. Against this interpretation of Aristotle the occasionally misunderstood passage in *GA* III.11.762b28ff. should not be admitted as evidence, where Aristotle poses the problem as a thought-experiment, whether men, if they were earth-born, would emerge from larvae or from eggs. That the presupposition made here is not Aristotle's own view has been correctly argued by J. Bernays, *Theophrastos' Schrift über Frömmigkeit* (Berlin, 1866), pp. 44ff.; E. Zeller, *Die Philosophie der Griechen* II 2 (Darmstadt, 5th edn, 1963), p. 508 n. 1; and L. Edelstein, "Aristotle and the Concept of Evolution," *Classical Weekly*, 37 (1943–4), pp. 148ff. See also Reimar Müller, "Aristoteles und die Evolutionslehre," *Deutsche Zeitschrift für Philosophie*, 17 (1969), pp. 148ff.
Apart from this it is evidently true that the modern theory of the constancy of species, as it appears in Linnaeus and others, as D. M. Balme remarks ("Aristotle and the Beginnings of Zoology," *Journal of the Society for the Bibliography of Natural Science*, 5 [1968–71], p. 281), derives from the much more dogmatic ancient doctrine that the species are ideas in the mind of God (which is perhaps already in Xenocrates; compare H. J. Krämer, *Der Ursprung der Geistmetaphysik* [Amsterdam, 1964], pp. 22ff.).

is only a confirmation of the biological constancy of the political character of man. There remains a certain contradiction, however, because Aristotle in *Pol.* I.2 thinks of an organic development of the polis comparable with the development of an animal. One could take this to mean that the political is latent in man, but is only realized after a cultural awakening. But Aristotle does not say how we can conceive of man who is not self-sufficient existing without a state for many generations. The contradiction cannot be completely explained. One may claim this much, that for Aristotle man *sub specie aeternitatis* is only conceivable as a constant (i.e., natural) political biological being.

5

Three Basic Theorems in Aristotle's Politics

DAVID KEYT

1 INTRODUCTION

One of the basic issues between Aristotle and Thomas Hobbes in political philosophy concerns the nature of the political community. Aristotle argues that the political community, or the polis, is a natural entity like an animal or a man.[1] Hobbes maintains in opposition to Aristotle that the political community is entirely a product of art. Now, I claim that Aristotle ought to agree with Hobbes, that according to Aristotle's own principles the political community is an artifact of practical reason, not a product of nature, and that, consequently, there is a blunder at the very root of Aristotle's political philosophy.

Consider, for example, Aristotle's idea that a statesman and a lawgiver is a sort of craftsman, the idea of the following passage from *Politics* VII:[2]

---

1 In Aristotle's view a polis, though an animal only figuratively, is literally a natural object. Thus in the *Politics* Aristotle says that the polis exists "by nature" (*phusei*) (I.2.1252b30, 1253a25), that it is "one of the things that exist by nature" (*tôn phusei*) (1253a2), and that it is "one of the things that are composed according to nature (*tôn kata phusin sunestôtôn*) (VII.8.1328a21–2); and he goes on to liken a polis to an animal (IV.4.1291a24–8). In other parts of the corpus he likens an animal or a man to a polis (*MA* 703a29–b2; *EN* IX.8.1168b31–3). The likeness, it should be noted, is not, as in Plato's *Republic*, between a polis and a soul but between a polis and a compound of soul and body.

2 Unless otherwise indicated, all references are to the *Politics* – in particular, to W. D. Ross's Oxford Classical Text edition (Oxford, 1957). Other editions referred to are: Alois Dreizehnter, *Aristoteles' Politik* (Munich, 1970); W. L. Newman, *The Politics of Aristotle*, 4 vols (Oxford, 1887–1902), and Franz Susemihl and R. D. Hicks, *The Politics of Aristotle* – Books I–V [I–III, VII–VIII] (London, 1894). All translations of Aristotle are my own.

For just as other craftsmen, such as a weaver or a shipbuilder, must have matter that is suitable for their work (for the better prepared this happens to be, the finer must be that which comes into being by their art), so also must the statesman and the lawgiver have proper matter in a suitable condition (VII.4.1325b40–1326a5).

This idea occurs in at least three other places in the *Politics*. At the end of Book II Aristotle twice calls lawgivers craftsmen of laws and constitutions (12.1273b32–3, 1274b18–19); and even in the second chapter of Book I, whose standpoint is quite distant from that of the passage just quoted, Aristotle remarks that "he who first framed the political community was a cause of the greatest goods" (1253a30–31). The analogy developed in the passage above is, indeed, simply an elaboration of a basic idea of the *Nicomachean Ethics* and the *Politics*, namely, that there is an art or science of politics (*hê politikê* [*sc. technê* or *epistême*]) just as there is an art or craft of weaving or shipbuilding.[3] By this analogy as a shipbuilder constructs a vessel by imposing a form upon lumber, nails, canvas, and so forth, a statesman or a lawgiver creates a polis by imposing a form – a constitution (III.3.1276b1– 11) – upon a population of citizens and a territory[4] (VII.4.1326a5–8). By the analogy, then, a polis is an artifact of practical reason just as a ship or a cloak or a sandal is an artifact of productive reason.[5] But throughout his philosophy Aristotle carefully distinguishes the products of reason from those of nature.[6] To the extent that an object is a product of reason it is not a product of nature. Consequently, if the polis is an artifact of practical reason, it cannot be a natural entity. Is the *Politics*, then, fatally flawed? Is there a contradiction at its very root?

The general consensus among scholars is that there is not. Andrew Cecil Bradley, in his important though little known study of the *Politics*, remarks that "[w]hen Aristotle said that the State was by nature, he was not denying that it is due to human thoughts and resolutions."[7] (But what, then, *was* he denying?) And Ernest Barker, in a note to I.2.1253a30–31 (quoted above), says that

Aristotle here concedes, and indeed argues, that in saying that the state is natural he does not mean that it "grows" naturally, without human volition and action. There is art as well as nature, and art co-operates with nature: the

3 *EN* I.2, VI.8, 13.1145a10–11, X.9.1180b23–1181b12; *Pol.* I.10.1258a21–3, II.8. 1268b34–8, III.12.1282b14–16, 22–3, VII.2.1324a19–20.
4 Since a constitution is defined as "a certain arrangement of those who inhabit the polis" (III.1.1274b38; see also III.6.1278b8–10 and IV.1.1289a15–18), territory should be counted, strictly speaking, not as part of the matter of a polis but only as something without which a polis could not exist.
5 For the distinction between practical and productive reason see *Met.* VI.1. 1025b25; *EN* VI.4, 5, and 8; and *Pol.* I.4.1254a5.
6 See *Phys.* II.6.198a9–10; *Met.* VII.7.1032a12–13, XI.8.1065b3–4, XII.3.1070a6–9; *EN* III.3.1112a31–3, VI.4.1140a14–16; *Pol.* VII.14.1333a22–3; *Rhet.* I.4.1359a30– b2.
7 "Aristotle's Conception of the State," Essay 1 in this volume, p. 26.

volition and action of human agents "construct" the state in co-operation with a natural immanent impulse.[8]

Now, clearly on Aristotelian principles natural objects and natural conditions often come into being with the aid of art. The art of medicine assists nature when a physician restores a sick man to health (see I.9.1257b25–6) and when a midwife helps a woman to give birth (*HA* VII.10). The problem is that conversely no artifact comes into being without the aid of nature. The bricks and lumber that compose a house come from clay, straw, and trees; and the products of the mimetic arts such as painting, sculpture, poetry, and dance owe their origin to a natural human tendency to imitate (*Poet.* 4.1448b4–24). The difference between the two types of case, between art aiding nature and nature aiding art, is that natural conditions and natural events such as health and parturition are ends that nature can, and indeed usually does, attain unaided (see *Phys.* II.8.199b15–18, 24–6) whereas objects of art such as paintings, statues, and poems are never produced by nature alone. The thrust of much of the *Nicomachean Ethics* and the *Politics*, it might be argued, is toward the view that the polis comes into being in the same way as poetry: it originates in a natural immanent impulse of people to live together but is brought to completion by the art of politics. By this line of argument the polis must be just as much an artifact as a poem. Thus the scholarly consensus concerning the consistency of Aristotle's political philosophy may well be wrong.

The idea that the polis is a natural entity cannot be fruitfully discussed in isolation from two other ideas to which it is closely tied – that man is by nature a political animal (I.2.1253a2–3, 7–9) and that the polis is prior in nature to the individual (1253a18–19, 25–6). These three ideas together may fairly be said to characterize Aristotle's standpoint in political philosophy and to distinguish it from rival views such as that of Hobbes. In the second chapter of Book I, the longest stretch of continuous argumentation in the *Politics*, Aristotle advances a series of arguments in support of these three ideas. Clearly these arguments must be examined before Aristotle can be charged with inconsistency. How good are these arguments within the context of Aristotle's general philosophy? Do they proceed from and are they consistent with the general principles of Aristotle's philosophy? But before examining these arguments we need to understand the three theses themselves, which requires in turn an understanding of the technical vocabulary in which they are couched.

2   *NATURAL GENESIS*

In Aristotle's philosophy of nature an object or a state of affairs can come into being in four different ways: by nature, by art, by luck (*tuchêi*), or by

8 *The Politics of Aristotle* (Oxford, 1946), p. 7, n. 1.

spontaneity (*tôi automatôi*) (*Met.* VII.7.1032a25–32, XII.3.1070a6–7; *Phys.* II.4–6). When an object is produced by nature or by art, the efficient cause of its existence is the form of the object in another object (*Phys.* II.7.198a22–7; *Met.* XII.4.1070b30–34). In natural genesis product and producer have the very same form. In artificial production the producer has the form of the product only in his mind. Thus man generates man, and house (that is, the form of house in the mind of the builder) generates house (*Met.* VII.9. 1034a21–6). Objects produced by luck, which simulates art, or by spontaneity, which simulates nature, have no such efficient cause. If a nonphysician, in vigorously shaking hands with someone, relocates the person's dislocated shoulder, this is due to luck, not to the medical art. And Aristotle thought that certain plants and animals such as mistletoe, lice, intestinal worms, and eels[9] were spontaneously rather than naturally generated (*HA* V.1.539b7–14, 19.550b32–551a13, VI.15.569a24–b9, VI.16; *GA* I.1.715b25–30).

As an explanation of the origin of the political community, each of these causes has had its champion (though luck and spontaneity are usually lumped together). Hobbes is the prime exponent of the view that the state is created by art. The *Leviathan* opens with the declaration that the state exists by art just as the *Politics* opens with the contrary declaration that the polis exists by nature: "For by Art is created that great LEVIATHAN called a COMMON-WEALTH, or STATE . . . which is but an Artificiall Man" (Intro.). This view, like most philosophical ideas, has its roots in the ancient period. It appears, for example, in *Laws* X as part of the world view of the atheists, whom Plato is intent on refuting (888d7–890b2). Nature and chance (*tuchê*),[10] according to this world view, antedate art. The cosmos was produced, not by mind or god or art, but by nature and chance. Art is entirely a human phenomenon, and among its products are political institutions and law (888d6–e1) as well as the gods themselves.

The idea that the political community comes to be neither by nature nor by art but by luck or spontaneity has only recently come to have its champions, though this idea too is foreshadowed in the *Laws*. Two such champions are F. A. Hayek and Robert Nozick. For Hayek society is a "spontaneous order,"[11] and the "invisible hand" to which Nozick attributes the origin of the state[12] is simply Aristotelian luck.[13] This idea flickers for a

9 Revealing once more the acuteness of his observation. The reproductive organs of the European eel do not develop until it is about to spawn, and it spawns in the deep sea southwest of Bermuda. After spawning it promptly dies.

10 I translate this word as "chance" since in Plato it includes what Aristotle calls "spontaneity" as well as what he calls "luck."

11 See *Laws, Legislation and Liberty*, vol. I: *Rules and Order* (London, 1973), ch. 2.

12 *Anarchy, State, and Utopia* (New York, 1974), pp. 18–22, 52, 118–19.

13 Invisible-hand explanations, according to Nozick, "show how some overall pattern or design, which one would have thought had to be produced by an individual's or group's successful attempt to realize the pattern, instead was produced and maintained by a process that in no way had the overall pattern or design 'in mind' " (ibid. p. 18). Compare this with Aristotle's characterization of luck as the

moment on the pages of the *Laws* when the Athenian Stranger considers the possibility that the real maker of laws is not man with his art but chance in the guise of war, poverty, and disease (IV.709a1–b2).

Although Aristotle maintains that the polis exists by nature (φύσει ἐστιν)[14] (I.2.1252b30), he never explictly asserts that the polis comes to be by nature (*phusei gignetai*). As I explain in the next section, it is possible on Aristotelian principles for a thing to exist by nature without coming to be by nature. But such a thing is an anomaly. Consequently, if Aristotle wished to convey the idea that the polis is such a thing, he would need to say so explicitly. In the absence of an assertion to this effect Aristotle's claim that the polis exists by nature implies a belief that it also comes to be by nature.

One reason for separating the two claims is that Aristotle's account of the origin of the polis in *Politics* I.2 is inconsistent with his theory of natural genesis. By this theory, as noted above, a thing that comes to be by nature comes to be through the agency of a distinct object that is the same in species as itself (*Met.* VII.7.1032a15–25, 8.1032b29–32). But according to I.2 the polis evolves from the village and the household, both of which differ in species (though not in genus)[15] from the polis. The only occasions when the generation of a polis fits Aristotle's theory of natural genesis are when one polis founds another (as Corinth, for example, founded Syracuse).

The one community whose generation does fit Aristotle's theory is the family or household (*oikia*). As Aristotle describes it in I.2, the household arises from two relations (*koinôniai*) (1252b9–10), that of male and female and that of master and slave. Each relation is grounded in a powerful natural instinct: the one, in the instinct to procreate; the other, in the instinct for self-preservation (1252a26–34). Aristotle's description of the origin of the household might seem to imply that the male–female and master–slave relations antedate the household. But it is difficult to see how they could. For if the master of the master–slave relation is to have offspring, he must have a wife; and if he has a wife as well as slaves, he is *ipso facto* the head of a household. Not only is there no first man in Aristotle's temporally infinite universe, there is no first family either. But if this is so, household generates household just as man generates man.

3 NATURAL EXISTENCE

In Aristotle's philosophy of nature natural existence and natural genesis are distinct concepts. The two concepts apply on the whole to the same objects, but there are exceptions.

accidental cause of an outcome that directly affects adult human beings and that could have been (but was not) due to thought (*Phys.* II.5–6 especially 197a5–8, b1–8, 20–22).

14 Ross's accentuation. Susemihl, Newman, and Dreizehnter all prefer the non-existential ἐστίν.

15 All three are communities (*koinôniai*) (I.2.1252b12–16, 27–30).

The difference Aristotle finds between an object that exists by nature, such as a stone or a fish, and one that exists by art, such as a bed or a sandal, is that the one "has in itself a source of motion and of rest in respect of place or of increase and diminution or of alteration" whereas the other, at least *qua* artifact, does not (*Phys.* II.1.192b13–19). An animal such as a fish has an internal source of all three sorts of motion: it can swim (change of place), grow (change of quantity), and perceive (change of quality) (*DA* II.4.415b21–8). A bed, on the other hand, though it has an internal source of motion *qua* composed of wood, has no internal source of motion *qua* bed.

The polis, interestingly enough, satisfies this definition of natural existence. For a polis *qua* polis can move from one site to another (as Athens evacuated Attica during the Persian invasion); it can adopt a population policy that controls its size (II.6.1265b6–16, 7.1266b8–14; VII.16.1335b19–26); and through its officials it can in a way perceive and think (IV.4.1291a24–8). Thus it is curious that Aristotle, in attempting to prove the naturalness of the polis, never appeals to his definition of natural existence.

On Aristotelian principles not everything that exists by nature comes to be by nature. In Aristotle's cosmos the celestial bodies exist by nature (*DC* III.1.298a27–31); but, being eternal (*Met.* XII.8.1073a30–35 and elsewhere), do not come to be (*DC* I.12.281b25–7, 282a21–3) and *a fortiori* do not come to be by nature. At the opposite end of Aristotle's *scala naturae* plants and animals that are spontaneously rather than naturally generated satisfy his definition of natural existence. A spontaneously generated eel, like a naturally generated fish, swims, grows, and perceives.

The view that the polis is a product of spontaneity or luck would provide one way to reconcile Aristotle's idea that the polis is a natural entity that evolves from the household and the village with the principles of his natural philosophy. The reason he never even considers this possibility may be that he found it difficult to associate the polis with lice and intestinal worms.

4 NATURALLY POLITICAL

The second of the three theses of *Politics* I.2, that man is by nature a political animal, raises two interpretive questions. Firstly, what is a political animal? And, secondly, what is it for a man to be a political animal by nature?

"Political animals," Aristotle says, "are those whose joint work (*ergon*) is some one common thing" (*HA* I.1.488a7–8). By this definition other species of animal besides man such as the bee, wasp, ant, and crane are political animals (*HA* I.1.487b33–488a10). Although the concept of a polis does not enter into this definition of *politikon zôon* from the *History of Animals*, in the *Politics* Aristotle argues that man is a political animal to a greater degree than any other animal since man is the only animal to form a polis (I.2.1252a7–18; see also III.9.1280a32–4). Consonant with this, in six of the eight passages in the Aristotelian corpus where Aristotle uses the expression *politikon zôon* it is linked either to *polis* (I.2.1253a1–4, 7–18; *EN* VIII.12.1162a17–19; *EE*

VII.10.1242a22–7) or to *politikê koinônia* ("political community") (III.6.
1278b19–25) or to *politês*("citizen") (*EN* I.7.1097b8–11).[16] It seems apparent that Aristotle takes the cooperation found in a polis as his standard in
applying the word *politikon* to other animals besides man.

A more complex issue is the nature of the joint work of a polis. Since "the
work of each thing is its end" (*EE* II.1.1219a8; see also *Met.* IX.8.1050a21),
the work of a polis[17] is its end. Thus the members of a polis work together to
realize the end of their polis. But the end of a polis varies with its
constitution. An aristocracy pursues virtue; an oligarchy, wealth; and a
democracy, freedom (IV.8.1294a10–11; *EN* V.3.1131a27–9; *Rhet.* I.8.1366a2–
8; and elsewhere). In Aristotle's view these ends are not equally legitimate
(III.9, 12.1283a16–22). Since Aristotle holds that the polis is a natural
entity, we can follow his principle that "that which is by nature should be
investigated preferably in things that are according to nature, and not in
things that are corrupted" (I.5.1254a36–7) and restrict our attention to those
constitutions that are according to nature (see III.17.1287b37–41). Aristotle
says that "one [sc. constitution] alone is in all places according to nature – the best" (*EN* V.7.1135a5), and the best constitution in his judgment
(apart from absolute kingship) is true aristocracy (IV.2.1289a30–33,
8.1293b23–6, 1294a22–5). The reason it is best is that it realizes the true end
of the polis – good life and happiness – for its citizens (I.2.1252b29–30, III.9,
VII.9.1329a22–4, 13.1331b24–1332a7). (For present purposes noncitizens
can be ignored.) In the *Politics* good life and happiness are defined as "an
actualization and a sort of perfect use of virtue" (VII.8.1328a35–8,
13.1332a7–27). Thus the joint work of the citizens of Aristotle's best polis is
to maintain a community in which each of them can lead a life of moral and
intellectual virtue. Their joint work, in short, is to form and to maintain an
ethical community (see *EN* I.9.1099b29–32, 13.1102a7–10).

This brings us to the second question: what is it for a man to be a political
animal by nature? Does Aristotle mean to claim that men form political
communities by nature as bees form colonies by nature? Does he, in
particular, think that men belong to his best polis by nature? Clearly not. For
if men were citizens of his best polis by nature, they would possess the moral
and intellectual virtues by nature, which Aristotle denies: "neither by nature
nor contrary to nature do the [moral] virtues arise in us; but we are fitted by
nature to receive them, and brought to completion through habit" (*EN*
II.1.1103a23–6). This is Aristotle's doctrine of natural virtue (*phusikê aretê*).[18]
A natural virtue is an innate capability of acquiring a particular virtue and a

16 The two other passages are *HA* I.1.488a7–10, cited above, and *EN*
IX.9.1169b18–19. All eight passages are discussed in R. G. Mulgan, "Aristotle's
Doctrine that Man is a Political Animal," *Hermes*, 102 (1974), pp. 438–45, and in W.
Kullmann, "Man as a Political Animal in Aristotle," Essay 4 in this volume.
17 For the expression *poleôs ergon* see VII.4.1326a13.
18 *HA* VIII.1.588a18–b3; *EN* II.5.1106a6–10, VI.13, X.8.1178a14–16, 9.1179b20–
1180a24; *EE* III.7.1234a23–33; [*MM*] I.34.1197b36–1198a22.

natural, arational impulse (*hormê*) to act in accordance with the virtue. Thus the man who possesses the natural virtue of temperance is capable of becoming temperate (*sôphronikos*) (*EN* VI.13.1144b5) and has a natural impulse toward temperate acts (*ta sôphrona*). Full virtue (*kuria aretê*) is acquired through habituation guided by practical wisdom and law. It would seem, then, that when Aristotle claims that man is a political animal by nature, the most he can mean is that nature endows man with a latent capacity[19] for civic virtue (*politikê aretê*)[20] and an impulse to live in a polis. And, indeed, this does seem to be the message of I.2: "Accordingly the impulse for such a community [*viz.* a polis] is in everyone by nature" (1253a29–30). For to have such an impulse is to have a foundation for civic virtue; it is not to possess the virtue itself (see [*MM*] I.34.1197b36–1198a22). This point was clearly seen by J. A. Stewart:

> When man is said to be φύσει πολιτικὸν ζῷον, it is not meant that he is produced by Nature in ready-made correspondence with a complex social environment. His correspondence is only the final result of prolonged contact with society; but he has a *natural tendency* to correspond. In other words, the uncivilized man is not civilized already, but *has it in him* to become civilized.[21]

In understanding Aristotle's idea about man's natural endowment, it is helpful to consider the view of someone who denies what Aristotle affirms. Although Aristotle's idea was challenged almost immediately by Epicurus,[22] his leading adversary is Hobbes. As *Leviathan* opens with a denial of the naturalness of the state, *De Cive* opens with a denial of the complementary idea that man is by nature a political animal.[23] For Hobbes civil society runs, not with, but against the grain of man's nature. Hobbes's men are asocial or antisocial beings who have no impulse toward civil society. "In the first place," Hobbes writes, "I set down for a Principle by experience known to all men, and denied by none, to wit, that the dispositions of men are naturally such, that except they be restrained through feare of some coercive power, every man will distrust and dread each other" (*De Cive*, Preface, 10). And also: "I hope no body will doubt but that men would much more greedily be

19 For Aristotle's distinction between a latent and a developed capacity, between a first and a second potentiality, see *Phys.* VIII.4.255a30–b5; *DA* II.5.417a21–b2, III.4.429b5–9; and *GA* II.1.735a9–11.
20 For the expression see III.9.1280b5, 1281a7, and VIII.6.1340b42–1341a1.
21 *Notes on the Nicomachean Ethics of Aristotle*, 2 vols (Oxford, 1892), note to 1103a19.
22 See the report in *Arrian's Discourses of Epictetus* II.20.6–14.
23 "Since we now see actually a constituted Society among men, and none living out of it, since we discern all desirous of congresse, and mutuall correspondence, it may seeme a wonderfull kind of stupidity, to lay in the very threshold of this Doctrine, such a stumbling block before the Readers, as to deny *Man to be born fit for Society*" (roman and italic typefaces reversed), note to I.2. All quotations from *De Cive* are from the Howard Warrender edition (Oxford, 1983), which is volume III of *The Clarendon Edition of the Philosophical Works of Thomas Hobbes*.

carryed by Nature, if all fear were removed, to obtain Dominion, then to gaine Society" (*De Cive*, I.2). Men enter civil society, according to Hobbes, only because they fear a violent death at the hands of other men and calculate that their lives are more secure within civil society than outside it. They make a covenant with one another to institute a common-wealth and to back its government with their wealth and strength against any foreign enemy and against any fellow citizen who would abrogate his covenant. Civic virtue, or justice, which for Hobbes is the settled disposition to obey the laws of one's common-wealth (*De Homine*, XIII.8–9), is not widely shared among one's fellow citizens: "Many also (perhaps most men) either through defect of minde, or want of education remain unfit [*sc.* for society] during the whole course of their lives" (*De Cive*, note to I.2). As David Gauthier remarks, "Hobbes's men never acquire any genuine regard for one another; they remain always potential enemies, held in harness by the power of the sovereign."[24]

Aristotle does not discuss the question whether man's natural impulse to live in a polis entails the naturalness of the polis, but it should be noted that it does not. The product of a natural impulse need not itself exist by nature. Both poetry and full virtue originate in natural impulses, but neither exists by nature.

5   FOUR TYPES OF PRIORITY

Aristotle distinguishes a number of respects in which one thing is prior or posterior to another, of which the following are relevant to the ideas and arguments of *Politics* I.2: in generation (*genesei*), in substance (*ousiai*), in formula (*logôi*), and in nature (*phusei*).

One thing is *prior in substance* to another if, and only if, the one is more fully developed or more fully realized (*teleioteros*) than the other (*GA* II.6.742a19–22; *Met.* IX.8.1050a4–b6; *Rhet.* II.19.1392a20–23).[25] It is an Aristotelian principle that what is posterior in generation is prior in substance (*Met.* IX.8.1050a4–7). Consequently, just as a man is posterior in generation but prior in substance to a boy (ibid.) so is a polis posterior in generation but prior in substance to a village, a household, and an individual. Aristotle's main argument for the naturalness of the polis turns on this fact.

One thing is *prior in formula* to another if, and only if, the one is mentioned in the formula of the other but not the other in the formula of the one (*Met.* VII.10.1035b4–6, IX.8.1049b12–17, XIII.2.1077b3–4). Thus right angle is prior in formula to acute angle since an acute angle is an angle that is less than a right angle (*Met.* VII.10.1035b4–8). By Aristotle's definition of man

---

24 *The Logic of Leviathan* (Oxford, 1969), p. 211.
25 This sort of priority is sometimes called "priority in nature." See *Phys.* VIII.7. 261a13–14, 9.265a22–4; *PA* II.1.646a25–6; *Met.* I.8.989a15–18; and perhaps *Cat.* 12.14b4–8.

and of polis neither is prior in formula to the other. Since man is a *political* animal, the formula of man mentions the polis; and since a polis is a community of free *men* (III.6.1279a21), the formula of polis mentions man. Similarly a soldier (*stratiôtês*) is a member of an army (*stratia*), and an army is an organized body of soldiers.

One thing is *prior in nature* to another if, and only if, the one can exist without the other but not the other without the one (*Met.* V.11.1019a2–4; and see *Cat.* 12.14a29–35, *Phys.* VIII.7.260b17–19).[26] Thus the sun is prior by nature to any plant, for the sun can exist without the plant but not the plant without the sun. And a colony of honey bees is prior in nature to each of its members, for the colony can exist minus any given bee – even the queen[27] can be replaced – but the bee cannot exist apart from the colony. When Aristotle says that "a polis is prior in nature to a household and to each of us" (I.2.1253a19), he presumably does not mean to deny that an individual or a family can exist apart from a polis. By his own account in I.2 the household exists before and hence independently of the polis. But further discussion of the content of the organic thesis must await the argument Aristotle offers in its support.

Neither priority in substance nor priority in formula entails priority in nature. A house is prior in substance to the bricks and stones of which it is composed (*PA* II.1.646a24–9) but posterior in nature since bricks and stones can exist without there being a house but a house cannot exist without bricks and stones. And the musical is prior in formula to the musical man but posterior in nature, for a man can exist without being musical but not musicalness without a man (*Met.* V.11.1018b34–7, XIII.2.1077a36–b11). Thus, that the polis is prior in substance to the individual does not entail that it is also prior in nature. Nor does the (false) proposition that the polis is prior in formula to the individual.

It should also be noted that neither priority in substance nor priority in nature entails natural existence. A house is prior in substance to the bricks and stones of which it is composed but exists by art, not by nature. Similarly, each sandal of a pair of sandals is prior in nature to the pair itself; for each sandal can exist without the other and hence without the pair, but the pair cannot exist unless both sandals exist (compare *Cat.* 12.14a29–35). And a sandal exists by art, not by nature. Consequently, that the polis exists by nature is entailed neither by the proposition that it is prior in substance to the individual[28] nor by the proposition that it is prior by nature to the individual.[29]

---

26 This sort of priority is sometimes called "priority in substance." See *Met.* IX.8.1050b6–19 along with W. D. Ross, *Aristotle's Metaphysics*, (Oxford, 1924), 2 vols, *ad loc.*, and *Met.* XIII.2.1077a36–b11.

27 In spite of her generative function, of which he was aware (*GA* III.10), Aristotle calls her "the king" (ibid.).

28 Ernest Barker makes this mistake in the third sentence of the following passage: "The state is natural because it develops from natural associations. But it would be wrong to think it is only natural because *they* are natural and because it grows from

6 THE GENETIC ARGUMENT

The arguments that Aristotle advances in *Politics* I.2 for his three theorems suffer from all the shortcomings characteristic of informal arguments. It is not always clear where in the text a particular argument begins or ends. Nor is it always clear what a particular argument is meant to establish. Important premisses are presupposed. Those that are furnished are at crucial spots loosely expressed. The order of steps is often unclear. In this situation it is unlikely that our understanding of I.2 can be much advanced by a summary of its contents. What is needed is expansion rather than contraction. We need a formal statement of each of Aristotle's arguments where all tacit premisses are supplied and all steps displayed. But any such formal reconstruction is certain to be underdetermined by the text of I.2. There are bound to be plausible alternative reconstructions. Consequently, any formal reconstruction of one of Aristotle's informal arguments must be regarded as simply an interpretive hypothesis – one that may fail to capture Aristotle's thought. One aim of such formal reconstruction, however, is to make an error of interpretation easier to spot.

Aristotle argues first for the naturalness of the polis:

> The community composed of several villages, when complete, is a polis, attaining forthwith the limit of complete self-sufficiency so to speak, coming into existence for the sake of life, but existing for the sake of good life. Therefore, every polis exists by nature, since the first communities so exist. For it is the end of these, and nature is an end; for what each thing is when its coming-into-being is completed, this we call the nature of each thing, whether of a man, a horse, or a house [?household?]. (I.2.1252b27–34)

This argument is not self-contained. One of its premisses is that "the first communities," that is to say, the household (*oikia*) and the village (*kômê*), exist by nature. So the first question the passage raises is why Aristotle thinks the household and the village exist by nature.

The household in Aristotle's view exists by nature because the relations (*koinôniai*) (I.2.1252b10) of which it is composed are grounded in natural instincts:

1.1   The household consists of the relations of husband and wife and of master and slave (as well as of parent and child) (I.2.1252a26–31, 3.1253b3–7, 12.1259a37–9). Premiss.

1.2   The relation of master and slave is grounded on the natural instinct for self-preservation; and the relation of husband and wife, on the natural instinct to procreate (I.2.1252a26–34; see also *EN* VIII.12.1162a16–19). Premiss.

them. It is natural *in itself*, as the completion, end, or consummation of man and man's development – the essentially natural condition of anything being its final, or complete, or perfect condition" (*The Politics of Aristotle*, p. 5, n. 2).
29 Newman makes this mistake: "if [the polis] is prior by nature to the individual, it exists by nature itself" (vol. II, p. 125).

1.3   [If the relations in a community are all grounded on natural instincts, the community exists by nature.] Tacit premiss.

1.4   Hence the household exists by nature (I.2.1252b12–14). From 1.1–1.3.

The train of thought by which Aristotle infers that the village exists by nature is more obscure. Almost everything he has to say about the village is contained in one sentence: "The first community formed from several households for the sake of nondaily services is the village" (I.2.1252b15–16). His idea is that the village ministers to a wider range of needs than the household, which exists to meet everyday needs (b12–14), but to a narrower range than the polis, which aims "at what is advantageous for all of life" (*EN* VIII.9.1160a21–3). The interpretive problem is to find a set of Aristotelian principles that connect this idea with the idea that the village exists by nature. Rummaging through the *Politics* and the *Physics*, one can, I think, find all but one of the tacit premisses that Aristotle is relying on:

1.5   The village comes to be from (is posterior in generation to) the household (I.2.1252b15–16). Premiss.

1.6   The village ministers to a wider range of needs than the household (1252b12–16). Premiss.

1.7   [If one community ministers to a wider range of needs than another, the one is more self-sufficient[30] than the other (VII.5.1326b29–30).] Tacit premiss.

1.8   [If one community is more self-sufficient than another, the one is a greater good and more choiceworthy than the other (II.2.1261b14; *Rhet.* I.7.1364a5–9).] Tacit premiss.

1.9   [If one thing comes to be from another and if the one is a greater good and more choiceworthy than the other, the one is prior in substance to the other (*Phys.* II.2.194a28–33).] Tacit premiss.

1.10   Therefore, the village is prior is substance to the household. From 1.5–1.9.

1.11   [If one thing is prior in substance to another and if the other exists by nature, then the one exists by nature.] Tacit premiss. (The transitivity of naturalness principle.)[31]

1.12   Therefore, the village exists by nature. From 1.4, 1.10, and 1.11.

If this interpretation of Aristotle's train of thought is along the right lines, his conclusion, that the polis exists by nature, follows with the addition of two more premisses:

---

30   What a man needs to stay alive (*to zên*) is much less than what he needs to live well (*to eu zên*). Thus a community that is "self-sufficient for good life" (*autarkês pros to eu zên*) (VII.4.1326b8–9; I.8.1256b32) is more self-sufficient than one that is merely "self-sufficient in necessaries" (*autarkês en tois anagkaiois*) (VII.4.1326b4).

31   This principle lies just below the surface of Newman's interpretation of the genetic argument: "The household cannot be natural and the State other than natural: what holds of the former must hold of the latter: if the household is natural, *a fortiori* the State is so, for it is the completion of the household" (vol. I, pp. 29–30). It is implicit also in the interpretation of Susemihl and Hicks: "[The 'city'] is the outcome and realization, the final cause, of the previous societies: they are natural, so also is the 'city' " (note to 1252b30).

1.13 The polis comes to be from the village (I.2.1252b27–8). Premiss.
1.14 The polis ministers to a wider range of needs than the village b28–30). Premiss.
1.15 Therefore, the polis is prior in substance to the village (b31). From 1.7–1.9, 1.13, and 1.14.
1.16 Hence, the polis exists by nature (b30). From 1.11, 1.12, and 1.15.

This reading of Aristotle's first argument for the naturalness of the polis makes no use of the third and final sentence of the primary text: "For it is the end of these, and nature is an end; for what each thing is when its coming-into-being is completed [literally, has reached its end], this we call the nature of each thing, whether of a man, a horse, or a house [?household?]" (I.2.1252b31–4). This sentence, as far as I can see, adds nothing, or at any rate nothing coherent, to the foregoing argument. The concept of nature defined in the second half of the sentence is that of nature as shape or form as distinct from that of nature as matter (*Phys.* II.1.193a9–b18; *Met.* V.4.1014b26–1015a11). In the *Physics* this concept is explained as follows: "So in another way nature would be the shape or form of things that have in themselves a source of motion. . . . (That which consists of these [*viz.*, form and matter] – for example, a man – is not a nature, but exists by nature.—)" (II.1.193b3–6). Things that have in themselves a source of motion are natural objects (*Phys.* II.1.192b13–15). Thus by Aristotle's account in the *Physics* the only objects that have a nature in the sense of shape or form are natural objects. Consequently, this concept of nature can be applied to the polis only if the polis is a natural object. Hence it cannot enter an argument for the naturalness of the polis without begging the question. Aristotle remarks in *Metaphysics* V that in an extended sense *every* essence is a nature (4.1015a11– 13).[32] In this extended sense every object, natural and artificial, has a nature. But now there is no connection between having a nature and existing by nature. Consequently, it seems that this extended concept could contribute to Aristotle's argument for the naturalness of the polis only by virtue of an equivocation. Thus whichever concept is being defined in 1252b31–4, the strict sense of nature as form or the extended sense,[33] the passage can be of no help in proving the naturalness of the polis.

The main difficulty with the genetic argument is that the principle on which it tacitly relies, the principle of the transitivity of naturalness, is false within the context of Aristotle's own philosophy. A house is prior in

32 At any rate this is one interpretation of the passage. See Christopher Kirwan, *Aristotle's Metaphysics Books* Γ, Δ, *and* E (Oxford, 1971), *ad loc.* In the *Nicomachean Ethics* and *Politics* Aristotle often speaks of the nature of nonnatural objects. See *EN* I.3.1094b25, V.10.1137b18, 26, IX.9.1170a21; *Pol.* VIII.5.1340a1, 7.1341b35, 1342b16; and *Poet.* 4.1449a15.

33 If the strict sense is being defined, *oikia* in line 34 *must* mean "household"; if the extended sense is being defined, the word *may* mean "house." One reason for thinking that Aristotle is referring to houses is that a house, like a man and a horse, comes into being and reaches its end through a series of stages whereas a household is the *first* stage in the coming-into-being of a polis.

substance to the materials of which it is composed (*PA* II.1.646a24–9); and all of these materials are ultimately provided by nature – lumber comes from trees, bricks from clay and straw, and so forth – but houses exist by art, not by nature.

It will be replied, no doubt, that this criticism reveals, not a flaw in Aristotle's argument, but a flaw in its interpretation. The counterexample to the principle of the transitivity of naturalness shows that the principle is not sensitive to the fundamental difference between a house and a polis. The lumber in a house comes from *dead* trees, from trees whose nature as living things has been destroyed, whereas, according to Aristotle, it is only in a polis that the nature of man is fully realized. A. C. Bradley takes this to be the nub of the argument:

> As a child [a man] is only potentially what he should be or is destined to be; and therefore he grows. And so, as a master, a husband, a father, a member of a village, his possibilities are still in various degrees latent, only partially brought into life. It is only in the state that they come into full play, and therefore the State is "natural" to him.[34]

This reply does not, I think, save Aristotle's argument. An object or an institution that aids a man in fulfilling his nature does not necessarily exist by nature. A man's ambulatory capacity is more fully realized if he wears sandals or shoes than if he goes around barefoot. So in a sense wearing sandals or shoes is natural to man. Nevertheless, sandals and shoes exist by art, not by nature. Man's latent capacity for theoretical knowledge is brought to life by education. So in a sense it is natural for man to be educated. But educational institutions such as the Academy and the Lyceum do not exist by nature. Aristotle remarks that "no one is a philosopher by nature" (*EN* VI.11.1143b6–7). Generalizing from this remark, one can say that in Aristotle's view man does not realize his nature by nature.

Thus it seems that the genetic argument does not succeed within the context of Aristotle's own philosophy.

7 THE TELIC ARGUMENT

Aristotle's second argument is compressed and elliptic almost to the point of unintelligibility. That it *is* a second argument and not a continuation of the generic argument is signaled by Aristotle's favorite word for marking divisions between arguments – *eti* ("moreover"):

> Moreover, that for the sake of which [a thing exists], the end, is best; and self-sufficiency is both an end and best. From these considerations, then, it is evident [a] that the polis is one of the things that exist by nature and [b] that man is by nature a political animal and [c] he who is polisless by nature and

---

34 "Aristotle's Conception of the State," p. 25.

not by chance is either a low sort or superior to man, like the "clanless, lawless, hearthless" man reviled by Homer. For no sooner is he such [that is, polisless] by nature than he is a lover of war, in as much as he is isolated as in checkers. (I.2.1252b34–1253a7)

In the first sentence Aristotle says that self-sufficiency is an end without saying what it is an end of. Presumably he is still speaking about the polis, which he has just said attains the limit of self-sufficiency (1252b27–30; see also III.9.1280b33–1281a1, VI.8.1321b14–18, VII.4.1326b7–9, 8.1328b16–17). If so, the first sentence is an argument in support of conjunct (a) of the second sentence, that the polis exists by nature. Conjunct (b), that man is by nature a political animal, would seem then to be offered as a corollary of (a); and (c), as an elaboration or explanation of (b). By this interpretation the argument of the passage runs as follows:

2.1   The polis exists for the sake of self-sufficiency. Premiss.
2.2   That for the sake of which something exists is best. Premiss.
2.3   Hence the polis exists for the sake of the best. From 2.1 and 2.2.
2.4   [That which is natural exists for the sake of the best.] Tacit premiss.
2.5   Therefore, the polis is natural. From 2.3 and 2.4.
2.6   Consequently, man is by nature a political animal. From 2.5.

If this expansion of Aristotle's cryptic argument is along the right lines, his argument is defective on two scores. First of all, since the propositions composing the argument are implicitly universal, (2.5) is inferred from (2.3) and (2.4) by means of a second-figure syllogism (*An. Pr.* I.5.26b34–6) but one that happens unfortunately to be invalid (*An. Pr.* I.5.27a18–20).[35] To restore validity one must replace (2.4) by its converse:

2.4′   That which exists for the sake of the best is natural.

The reason interpreters supply (2.4) rather than its converse is that (2.4) is an Aristotelian principle (*DC* II.5.288a2–3; *PA* IV.10.687a15–16; *IA* 12.711a18–19) whereas its converse is not.[36] Reason, as well as nature, aims at the best (*EN* I.9.1099b20–25, IX.8.1169a17; *EE* II.3.1220b27–9). Both

---

35 Aristotle's counterexample is "All animals are entities; all numbers are entities; therefore, all numbers are animals."

36 Newman (*ad loc.*) supplies (2.4). He is followed by Barker in his translation of the *Politics* (*ad loc.*). In interpreting the telic argument in his earlier work *The Political Thought of Plato and Aristotle* (London, 1906), Barker tries to have it both ways and writes: "Again, 'Nature always works for the best'; and one may convert the proposition, and say, that what is best is the product of Nature" (p. 270). R. G. Mulgan attempts a similar rescue of Aristotle's argument: "According to Aristotle's view of nature the natural is best and the best natural. It is therefore open to him to prove the conclusion that the *polis* is natural from the premiss that the *polis* is best for man" (*Aristotle's Political Theory* [Oxford, 1977], p. 23).

the craftsman and the man of practical wisdom aim at, and sometimes attain, the best. Consequently, there seems to be no way of rescuing the syllogistic step from (2.3) and (2.4) to (2.5). The syllogism will either be invalid or contain a premiss that Aristotle cannot accept.

The second problem concerns the step from (2.5) to (2.6). It is clear from conjunct (c) of the second sentence that when Aristotle asserts that man is by nature a political animal he means to assert that *every* man is by nature a political animal – "he who is polisless by nature . . . is either a low sort or superior to man," that is, "either a beast or a god" (I.2.1253a29). As I have already remarked, that man is by nature a political animal does not entail that the polis is a natural entity. It is time to point out that the entailment does not run in the opposite direction either. A colony of bees is just as much a natural entity as a polis. But this fact does not entail that the bee, that is, that every kind of bee, is a political animal. Some bees, as Aristotle was aware (*HA* IX.40.623b5–13), are solitary (*monadika*) and do not form colonies – for example, the carpenter, plasterer, and mason bees. Similarly, that the polis is a natural entity does not exclude the possibility that some men are by nature asocial.

8   THE LINGUISTIC ARGUMENT

In a passage that looks like an elaboration of a Socratic remark,[37] Aristotle argues next, by appeal to the fact that man is the only animal to possess language, that man is a political creature to a greater degree than any other animal:

> That man is a political animal more than any bee or any gregarious animal is evident. For nature, as we say, makes nothing in vain; and man alone of animals possesses language. The mere voice, it is true, is a sign of pain and pleasure, and hence belongs also to the other animals (for their nature has come this far, to have perception of pain and pleasure and to signify them to each other); but language is designed to declare the advantageous and the harmful, and so also the just and the unjust; for this is peculiar to men in comparison with the other animals, to alone have perception of good and bad and just and unjust and the like; and community in these things makes a household and a polis. (I.2.1253a7–18).

Aristotle's argument is straightforward, and there is no serious problem in interpreting it. The only question of interpretation is what the possession of language implies. In my formal rendition of the argument, I have taken Aristotle's thought to be that the possession of language implies a capacity to perceive the things that language is designed to express. I have also supposed

37 "And do not the gods give the power of speech, through which we give a share of all the good things to one another by teaching and form communities and make laws and engage in politics?" (Xenophon, *Mem.* IV.3.12).

that Aristotle would identify the capacity to perceive and to express the just and the unjust with the capacity to form communities based on justice. This identification is not essential to the argument, but a weaker relation would lengthen its formal expression.

3.1   Nature makes nothing in vain. Premiss.

3.2   [An endowment that is useless to its possessor is given it in vain.] Tacit premiss.

3.3   Man possesses language; the lower animals, only voice. Premiss.

3.4   Language is designed to express the just and the unjust whereas voice without language can express no more than pleasure and pain. Premiss.

3.5   [If man did not have the capacity to *perceive* the just and the unjust, he could not use language to *express* the just and the unjust.] Tacit premiss.

3.6   If man could not use language to express the just and the unjust, language would have been given him in vain. From 3.2–3.4.

3.7   But language was not given to man in vain. From 3.1.

3.8   Therefore, man has the capacity both to perceive and to express the just and the unjust. From 3.5–3.7.

3.9   The capacity to perceive and to express the just and the unjust is the same as (though perhaps differing in essence from) the capacity to form communities based on justice such as the household and the polis. Premiss.

3.10 Hence man alone of animals has the capacity to form communities based on justice. From 3.3, 3.4, 3.8, and 3.9.

3.11 [Animals that are capable of forming communities based on justice are more political that those that are not.] Tacit premiss.

3.12 Therefore, man is more a political animal than any bee or any gregarious animal. From 3.10 and 3.11.

Although this argument appears innocuous, one of the ideas behind it, when developed further, is at variance with the naturalness of the polis. The idea, of which (3.9) is an interpretation, is that what man alone of animals posseses that allows him alone to form political communities is the "perception (*aisthêsis*) of good and bad and just and unjust and the like" since "community in these things [presumably, the good and the just][38] makes a household and a polis" (1253a15–18). This moral perception,[39] which Aristotle regards as at least a necessary condition of the existence of a polis, is not an inborn capacity like sight.[40] For in order to be able to perceive the just and the unjust and the good and the bad, a person must to some extent be just and good. He need not be fully virtuous, for even the morally weak man (*ho akratês*) can perceive the just and the unjust and the good and the bad (*EN* VII.1.1145b12–13, 8.1151a20–24). But he cannot be totally lacking in virtue,

---

38 "... every community is held together by what is just" (*EE* VII.9.1241b14–15).

39 For this sort of perception see III.11.1281b34–5 and *EN* II.9.1109b20–23, IV.5,1126a31–b4, IX.9.1170b8–10.

40 The capability of *acquiring* moral perception, on the other hand, is innate; for it is part of the capability of acquiring the moral virtues.

for the evil man is morally blind (*EN* III.1.1110b28–30, VI.12.1144a34–6, VII.8.1150b36). Now, it is a central tenet of Aristotle's ethical philosophy than men become good, not by nature, but by habituation guided by law and practical wisdom (*EN* II.1.1103a18–b6, X.9.1179b20–24). This means that the bonds of justice that unite the members of a polis, unlike the bonds of instinct that unite the bees in a colony, are the bonds of (practical) reason, not the bonds of nature, and that the polis is an artificial rather than a natural entity. Thus the distinction Aristotle draws between a polis and a colony of bees provides a basis for denying the naturalness of the polis. Instead of buttressing the genetic and the telic arguments, the linguistic argument actually undermines them.

Hobbes reaches a similar conclusion from a different direction. Aristotle's linguistic argument is one of his favorite targets. For Hobbes men and bees do not have much in common: first, bees, unlike men, are not competitive and do not hate and envy each other; secondly, bees do not distinguish their private good from the common good; thirdly, bees do not find fault in the administration of their common business; fourthly, bees do not use language to create dissension – "the tongue of man is a trumpet of warre, and sedition" – fifthly, bees do not distinguish between injury (breach of covenant) and harm; and, finally, "the agreement of these creatures is Naturall; that of men, is by Covenant only, which is Artificiall."[41] The first five items attribute to men and deny to bees those qualities that foster insurrection and civil war. The final difference between men and bees, the crux of the matter for Hobbes, is a consequence of the first five. The point that Hobbes apparently did not see is that Aristotle's own principles entail that bee colonies are natural and political communities artificial.

9   THE ORGANIC ARGUMENT

The fourth and final argument in the series is the most elaborate argument in the entire treatise. The great care with which it is presented is a measure of the importance Aristotle attaches to it:

> And a polis is prior in nature to a household and to each of us. For the whole is necessarily prior to the part; because when the whole [body] is destroyed, there will be neither foot nor hand, except homonymously, just as [would be the case] if one were to call a stone hand [a hand] (for a hand, when destroyed [by the destruction of the body] will be of such a nature [as a stone hand]); and all things are defined by their function and by their capacity, so that when they are no longer of such a nature [as to perform their function] one must not say they are the same things [as before] but [only] bearers of the same name (*homônuma*).

41 *De Cive* V.5; *Leviathan* XVII.5. The first direct quotation is from the former work; the second, from the latter.

Therefore, that the polis both exists by nature and is prior (*kai phusei kai proteron*) to each person, is clear, for if each person when separated [from the polis] is not self-sufficient, he will be related [to the polis] as other parts are to their whole, whereas he who is unable to share in a community or has no need since he is self-sufficient is no part of a polis, so that he is either a beast or a god. Hence the impulse for such a community is in everyone by nature; nevertheless, he who first constituted [such a community] is a cause of the greatest goods. For just as man when perfected is the best of animals, so also is he when separated from law and adjudication the worst of all. (I.2.1253a18–33)

The first problem in interpreting the organic argument is to identify its conclusion. Aristotle sets out in the first sentence of the passage to prove the organic thesis, that the polis is prior in nature to the individual; but the conclusion he seems to reach later on (a25–6) is the conjunction of this thesis and the proposition that the polis exists by nature. Does Aristotle think that the argument in this passage establishes both conjuncts? Is the organic argument, among other things, a further argument for the naturalness of the polis? The solution of this problem depends upon the solution of a second: how universal is the priority principle introduced in the second sentence, that "the whole is necessarily prior [*sc.* in nature] to the part?" (That the priority in question is priority in nature is clear from the first sentence of the passage and from the argument Aristotle offers in support of the principle.) Does it apply to every whole, natural and artificial,[42] or only to natural wholes? If the latter, the principle can be applied to the polis only on the assumption that the polis is a natural entity. But if the principle cannot be applied to the polis without making this assumption, it cannot be used to prove that the polis exists by nature without begging the question. Hence, if the priority principle applies only to natural wholes, the conclusion of the organic argument (unless Aristotle is nodding) must be the organic thesis alone.

Aristotle's argument in support of the priority principle, which occupies the first half of the passage, though it has a bearing on the question whether the principle applies only to natural wholes, does not settle the matter:

4.1   [Two things differ both numerically and specifically if their definitions[43] differ (*Top.* I.7; *Met.* V.6.1016b31–1017a3, 9.1018a9–11).] Tacit premiss.

4.2   Each thing is defined by its capacity to perform a particular function (I.2.1253a23). Premiss.

4.3   Consequently, when a thing loses its defining capacity, it becomes a different thing (and if the new thing continues to bear the same name as the old, the name is defined differently when borne by the new thing than when borne by the old) (a23–5). From 4.1 and 4.2. (The principle of homonymy.)

42 For the distinction between natural wholes (*ta phusei hola*) and artificial wholes (*ta technêi hola*) see *Met.* V.26.1023b34–6.

43 Where the definition of a thing is the formula of its being (*ho logos tês ousias*) (*Met.* V.9.1018a10–11).

4.4   [A hand or a foot possesses its defining capacity only as a part of a living body.] Tacit premiss.

4.5   Thus a hand or a foot cannot exist apart from a living body (a20–23; see also *Met.* VII.10.1035b23–5). From 4.3 and 4.4.

4.6   [On the other hand, a living body can exist minus a hand or foot.] Tacit premiss.

4.7   [One thing is prior in nature to another when the one can exist without the other but not the other without the one (*Met.* V.11.1019a2–4).] Tacit premiss.

4.8   [Therefore, a living body is prior in nature to a hand or a foot.] From 4.5, 4.6, and 4.7.

4.9   Therefore, every [?natural?] whole is prior in nature to its parts (1253a20). From 4.8. (The priority principle.)

This argument is partly deductive and partly inductive. The first eight lines are a valid deductive argument, but then the last line is an inductive generalization from the line before. Since the basis of this induction is a fact about a kind of animal, it is reasonable to generalize to natural wholes but not so reasonable to generalize to wholes in general. This should make one cautious about attributing an unrestricted priority principle to Aristotle.

Another reason for caution is a dialectical precept in the *Topics*: "Again, [see] if the parts are destroyed along with the whole; for although it is necessary for the reverse to happen, for the whole to be destroyed when the parts are destroyed, it is not necessary also for the parts to have been destroyed when the whole was destroyed" (VI.13.150a33–6). A comment earlier in the same chapter (a18–21) indicates that what Aristotle has in mind is the dissassembling of an artifact. When a cart is disassembled, its wheels do not lose their capacity to roll and to support weight and hence do not become wheels in name only.[44] A completely broken wheel would be a wheel in name only, not one that is merely unattached to an axle. (Similarly, the nature of a saw does not change when a carpenter lays it down. If it has the capacity to cut wood, it is a saw strictly speaking whether in his hand or lying on his workbench.) But if the parts of a whole can survive the destruction of the whole, the whole is not prior in nature to its parts. Thus by this precept not every whole is prior in nature to its parts.

---

44 In discussing the homonymy principle in his article "Aristotle's Definitions of *psuchê*,' John Ackrill asks, "Is a newly-made rudder not yet a rudder (strictly) because not yet installed in a boat?" and complains about finding no answer in Aristotle. After remarking that Aristotle "signally fails to make plain which of the circumstances and conditions that are necessary conditions of a thing's exercising a power are also necessary conditions of its simply having the power," he presses upon Aristotle the suggestion that the homonymy principle should be maintained in a form that would allow an uninstalled rudder to count as a rudder (strictly speaking). (See *Proceedings of the Aristotelian Society*, n.s. 73 [1973], p. 128. Reprinted in *Articles on Aristotle*, vol. 4, edited by Jonathan Barnes, Malcolm Schofield, and Richard Sorabji [London, 1979].) Ackrill's suggestion seems, however, to be no more than a reasonable interpretation of Aristotle's concept of potentiality, or *dunamis*.

A cautious interpreter, then, has two reasons for taking Aristotle's statement that "the whole is necessarily prior to the part" (1253a20) to apply only to natural wholes. As we have seen, if the priority principle applies only to natural wholes, the conclusion of the organic argument (unless Aristotle is arguing in a circle) must be the organic thesis alone. So, on a cautious reading, Aristotle's argument continues as follows:

4.10 The individual when separated from the polis is not self-sufficient (1253a26). Premiss.

4.11 [If one thing when separated from another is not self-sufficient, then the one is a part of the other.] Tacit premiss.

4.12 So the individual is a part of the polis (1253a26–7). From 4.10 and 4.11.

4.13 The polis is a natural whole (1253a25). From 1.16 and 2.5.

4.14 Therefore, the polis is prior in nature to the individual (1253a18–19, 25–6). From 4.9, 4.12, and 4.13. (The organic thesis.)

That the polis exists by nature is, by this interpretation, a premiss rather than a conclusion of the organic argument. This seems to be contrary to Aristotle's explicit words, for he says, "*Therefore (oun)*, that the polis both exists by nature and is prior (*kai phusei kai proteron*) to each person, is clear" (1253a25–6). This is disconcerting but not fatal. First of all, Aristotle may not have written what is printed in our modern texts. There are variant readings of 1253a25, and by one of them the first conjunct disappears. Although *kai phusei kai proteron* is well attested and is the reading adopted by Newman, Ross, and Dreizehnter, there are manuscripts that omit the first *kai* and others that omit the second.[45] If the second *kai* is omitted, Aristotle's conclusion is the organic thesis alone: "Therefore, that the polis is prior in nature also to each person, is clear." But, secondly and more importantly, the reading adopted by our modern editors is not, strictly speaking, inconsistent with the above interpretation. For the word *oun* may simply signal that the naturalness of the polis is the conclusion of *some* preceding argument. Since this proposition is needed as a premiss of the organic argument and since it has already been established to Aristotle's satisfaction by the genetic and telic arguments, there is some point in coupling it with the organic thesis.

The organic argument does not end with the derivation of the organic thesis but continues on to a proposition that amounts to the claim that man is by nature a political animal: "Hence (*oun*) the impulse for such a community [*viz.*, a political community] is in everyone by nature" (1253a29–30). Until this point in the argument the only thing that has been said to be due to nature is the existence of the polis. So presumably Aristotle intends, as before in the telic argument, to infer that man is a political animal by nature from the proposition that the polis exists by nature. This time, though, it is possible to see a plausible connection between the two propositions:

---

45 See the critical apparatus in Dreizehnter's edition *ad loc*. Dreizehnter's report of the manuscripts is fuller than Ross's.

4.15 [The parts of a natural whole belong to it by nature.] Tacit premiss.
4.16 Hence the individual belongs to the polis by nature). From 4.12, 4.13, and
   4.15.

By this interpretation of the organic argument the organic thesis and the proposition that man is by nature a political animal are both corollaries of the naturalness of the polis.

The organic thesis is undoubtedly the most provocative assertion in the *Politics*. For consider what it entails in the following situation. Suppose that a person – call him "Philoctetes" – is forced to live in isolation because he is suffering from a snake bite that will not heal and which gives off a stench that no one can stand. Suppose, further, that Philoctetes is less than a god and, consequently, is not the sort of person who "has no need [to share in a polis] since he is self-sufficient" (1253a28). Now, the organic thesis entails that any given polis can exist without Philoctetes but not Philoctetes without a polis. To say that Philoctetes cannot exist without a polis is not to say that, like a honey bee separated from its colony, he would perish without a polis but rather that he would cease being a human being and sink to the level of a lower animal. "[H]e who is unable to share in a [political] community (*ho . . . mê dunamenos koinônein*)," Aristotle says, is a beast (*thêrion*) (1253a27–9). Thus in respect of the species to which he belongs Philoctetes would be, like a eunuch in respect of his sex, a man in name only.

This consequence of the organic thesis is not only provocative; it is also false by Aristotle's own principles. For Philoctetes' inability to share in a polis is not the sort of inability that destroys humanness. There are two ways in which *A* may be unable to do *B*: *A* may lack the capacity or skill to do *B* or *A* may have the capacity or skill but lack the opportunity (see *Phys.* VIII.4.255a30–b5; *DA* II.5.417a21–418a6, III.4.429b5–9). The man untrained in carpentry and the carpenter without tools and material are both unable to build a house but in different senses. A person untrained in carpentry is no carpenter, but a carpenter out of work still is. Philoctetes living in isolation is like a carpenter out of work. Since he is polisless through misfortune rather than through lack of capacity to live with others, he remains a human being just as a carpenter out of work remains a carpenter. Aristotle concedes as much in the course of the telic argument, for he says that "he who is polisless by nature (*dia phusin*) and *not by chance* (*dia tuchên*) is either a low sort or superior to man" (1253a3–4). Thus by Aristotle's own principles Philoctetes while living in isolation remains a human being. Since the organic thesis entails the contrary, it must be false.

This argument that the organic thesis is false is also an argument that the polis does *not* exist by nature. The organic thesis is validly derived from three propositions: (4.9), (4.12), and (4.13). The first of these is the priority principle, the second is the idea that the individual is a part of the polis, and the third is the proposition that the polis exists by nature. Now, if the organic thesis is false, at least one of the three propositions from which it is derived must be false. The priority principle, when restricted to natural wholes, is firmly grounded and difficult to give up. Thus the proposition that the polis exists by nature can be saved only by sacrificing the idea that the individual is a part of the polis. But it seems impossible to maintain that the polis is a natural whole while denying that its simple parts[46] are individuals. For what could the simple parts of a polis be except individual human beings? Thus if the organic thesis is false, it must also be false that the polis is a natural entity.

10   CONCLUSION

One of the basic ideas of the *Politics* is that the polis is a natural entity like an animal or a man. Two subsidiary ideas are that man is by nature a political animal and that the polis is prior in nature to the individual. Aristotle offers four arguments in support of these three ideas. The genetic and telic arguments, which are meant to establish the naturalness of the polis, are both flawed. Although the genetic argument is valid, one of its tacit premisses, the principle of the transitivity of naturalness, is false. The telic argument, on the other hand, is invalid under its most plausible interpretation. The linguistic argument is a good argument; but, contrary to Aristotle's intentions, it is actually an argument against the naturalness of the polis. For what emerges from the argument is that a polis is held together by the artificial bonds of justice rather than by the natural bonds of instinct. The organic argument, by my interpretation, validly derives the natural priority of the polis to the individual from the naturalness of the polis. However, if the organic thesis means what it seems to mean, that an individual when separated from a polis loses his humanness, the organic thesis must be false. And if the organic thesis is false, it must also be false that the polis is a natural entity. Finally, Aristotle's idea that there is an art or science of politics implies that the polis is an artifact of practical reason. Thus not only is Aristotle unable to establish that the polis exists by nature but there are three good reasons within the context of his own philosophy for denying it. On this one issue at least, whether the political community is a natural or an artificial entity, Hobbes is better than Aristotle.[47]

46 In the *Politics* (see I.1.1252a18–20), as in his biological works (*HA* I.1.486a5–8), Aristotle distinguishes two types of part: simple and composite. On the atomic level of simple parts (*elachista moria, asuntheta*), the parts of a polis are individual human beings in one guise or another; on the molecular level of composite parts (*suntheta*), they are groups or classes of individuals.

47 This paper is the latest version in a series of attempts at a correct analysis of the arguments in *Politics* I.2. The original version was written during the 1983–4 academic year at the Institute for Advanced Study and presented to the Classical Philosophy Colloquium at Princeton in December of 1984, where it drew heavy fire. A second version, which tried to answer this fire, was presented at a conference sponsored by the Society for Ancient Greek Philosophy and hosted by Baruch College in October of 1986. The second version was revised and published under the title

---

"Three Fundamental Theorems in Aristotle's *Politics*" in *Phronesis*, 32 (1987), pp. 54–79. The current version is a slight revision of the *Phronesis* article.

I am indebted to the participants at the colloquia where the earlier versions were presented – especially William W. Fortenbaugh, who was the commentator on my paper at Princeton, and David Depew, who performed the same role at Baruch College – for forcing me to think harder about the issues and for giving me a number of valuable suggestions. I am also indebted to Jonathan Barnes, Fred Miller, and Martin Tweedale. I am grateful, finally, to the Institute for Advanced Study, the National Endowment for the Humanities, and the University of Washington for their support during my sabbatical leave.

6

Aristotle's Theory of Natural Slavery

NICHOLAS D. SMITH

In Book I of the *Politics*, Aristotle develops a theory of natural slavery that is intended to serve two purposes: to secure the morality of enslaving certain human beings and to provide the foundation for the uses of slaves that he advocates in later books. But modern commentators have been nearly unanimous in finding that Aristotle's proffered theory does neither of these things.[1] Specifically, critics have argued that the theory he offers is itself incoherent and that many of the uses to which he proposes putting slaves in subsequent books of the *Politics* are unwarranted, or even proscribed, by the theory in Book I.

None of Aristotle's critics, however, has given Aristotle sufficient credit for basing his theory upon two models of authority each of which is both coherent and well defended in Aristotle's work. In this discussion, I shall show how Aristotle's theory is developed according to the dictates of these two models for the relation of natural master and natural slave: one provided by the relationship of reason to emotion, and one provided by that of soul to body or (equivalently for these purposes) man to beast. I shall provide as complete a synthesis of these models' effects on the theory as I think can be given, but then conclude by showing precisely how and why such a synthesis still fails to make a success of Aristotle's defense of slavery.

1 THE PROBLEM

From the beginning of the *Politics*, Aristotle treats the state as if it were an organic entity. Book I of the *Politics* thus attempts to trace the development of this "organism" through its more primitive components and stages, beginning with individuals of different natures, developing through the emergence of the household, and reaching an immature state in the village and its

---

1 The sole exception – to which I shall pay detailed attention below – is W. W. Fortenbaugh, "Aristotle on Slaves and Women," in *Articles on Aristotle 2: Ethics and Politics*, ed. J. Barnes, M. Schofield, and R. Sorabji (London 1977), pp. 135–9.

primitive economic arrangements. That biology provides the model for the political analysis Aristotle hopes to complete is soon clear: at I.2.1253a18–29 he claims that the household and individual are part of the state in the same way that a hand is a part of the body. Later, he makes this model explicit (IV.4.1290b25–38). Thus, political prescriptions, like medical ones, will be made properly only if they are in accord with nature.

But as Aristotle develops his civic "organism," he makes a commitment that repels modern readers: among the relationships that contribute to the formation of the household from mere individuals, he lists that of natural master to natural slave (I.2.1252a30–34). Though he considers the view that slavery is simply a matter of convention (I.6.1255a3–b4), he rejects it, holding that there are human beings who are marked out by nature from birth as slaves (I.5.1254a21–4). In defense of this view, Aristotle offers a number of characterizations of a natural slave. Some of these are psychological: we are told, for example, that the natural slave lacks deliberation and foresight (I.13.1260a12, III.9.1280a33–4; compare also I.2.1252a31–4, I.5.1254b20–23). At other times, the natural slave is identified by his aptitude for bodily labor (I.2.1252a32–4, I.5.1254b17–19, I.5.1254b25–6, I.11.1258b38, I.13.1259b25–6). Aristotle even claims that the natural slave is rightly considered a part of his master's body (I.6.1255b11–12).

In addition to the obvious and unanswerable point that slavery is beyond moral defense, critics have charged that this aspect of Aristotle's philosophy is logically problematic. Typically, such commentators argue that the theory of slavery Aristotle presents in Book I frequently conflicts with the practical proposals of other books of the *Politics*. For example, though he explicitly characterizes the natural slave as a tool of action and not of production (I.4), he elsewhere advocates the use of slaves for agriculture (VII.10.1330a25–6), a productive enterprise.[2] Similarly, it seems at least odd to learn first that only natural masters can use forethought (I.2.1252a31–2) and that all barbarians are natural slaves (I.2.1252b9), but to discover later that Asians are intelligent in a way that, in context, seems to imply no lack of forethought. Rather, they are inferior to Greeks only in their lack of spirit (VII.7.1327b23–38).[3] It is also puzzling that Aristotle would defend the morality of slavery by citing its accord with nature, but subsequently advocate using emancipation as a reward (VII.10.1330a32– 3).[4] If Aristotle

2 This criticism is expressed, for example, by R. O. Schlaifer on p. 192, n. 2 of his article, "Greek Theories of Slavery from Homer to Aristotle," *Harvard Studies in Classical Philology*, 47 (1936), pp. 165–204; reprinted in *Slavery in Classical Antiquity*, ed. M. I. Finley (Cambridge, 1960), pp. 93–132.
3 The argument seems merely to put the Greeks between the extremes of the Asians, who have intelligence without spirit, and the Europeans, who have spirit but appear to lack intelligence. No stronger entailments about the Asians can be drawn from this argument (e.g., that they have only technical intellect, as Schlaifer suggests in an attempt to avoid the problem; see "Greek Theories of Slavery from Homer to Aristotle" p. 193, n.7).

is not thinking of natural slaves when he says this, then enslaving them in the first place would not be morally defensible according to his own theory (I.6.1255a3–26). But if they are natural slaves, and nature provides sufficient moral grounds for enslaving them, then to free them would be wrong. Worse, if Aristotle is right in Book I, the natural slave is benefited by being the slave of a proper master (I.5.1254b19–20, I.6.1255b6–7, I.6.1255b12–14). In this case, freeing him would be to deny him such benefits as well. Perhaps the morality of slavery in Aristotle's own thought erodes as rapidly as the alleged benefits to the slave: we soon learn that any advantage to the slave is merely accidental (III.6.1278b32–7).[5] Indeed, it would seem that even Aristotle was ultimately uneasy with his own theory, for he provided in his will that his own slaves be freed.[6]

Because the *Politics* is almost certainly not a single, finished treatise, however, but rather a composite of several incomplete drafts dealing with several related issues,[7] it may be somewhat unrealistic to expect consistency among its various parts; Aristotle may have made no particular effort to preserve the formulations of Book I elsewhere. But Aristotle's critics also argue that, in defending slavery, Aristotle must resort to an account of the psychology of the natural slave that effectively ensures that no living human being (or, at the very most, extremely few of them) would actually qualify for slavery.[8] Though man, on Aristotle's view, is a rational animal, the natural

4 This criticism is suggested by a number of people. See, e.g., Ernest Barker, *The Political Thought of Plato and Aristotle* (London, 1906), pp. 365–6; W. L. Newman, *The Politics of Aristotle* (Oxford, 1887), vol. I, p. 152, n.1.
5 This accords, however, with the view of slaves as parts of their masters in Book I, because on Aristotle's view any advantage to the whole is also an advantage to the part, but then only accidentally.
6 In the introduction to Edward Walford's translation of the *Politics* and *Economics* (London, 1853), John Gillies celebrates Aristotle's act as one practical illustration of the "liberal maxims of his philosophy" (p. xxvii), calling this provision of Aristotle's will "an injunction conformable to the maxims inculcated in his *Politics*, that slaves of all descriptions ought to be set free, whenever they merited freedom, and are qualified for enjoying it" (p. xxviii). Though he makes no reference to the text, one must suppose that Gillies has VII.10.1330a32–3 in mind, though such a generous reading seems an overstatement of Aristotle's claim. The less "liberal" temper of Book I goes without comment in Gillies's short essay. Others are less inclined to see Aristotle's will in such a charitable light. For example, Ernest Barker dryly observes, "These dispositions serve as a commentary on the general view of slavery propounded in the first book of the *Politics*," in *The Politics of Aristotle* (Oxford, 1946), p. xxiv.
7 For a detailed argument as to the extent of this, see J. L. Stocks, "The Composition of Aristotle's *Politics*," *Classical Quarterly*, 21 (1927), pp. 177–87; for a quite different view, however, see Barker, *Politics*, pp. xxxvii–xlvi. For other discussions of this point, see J. Aubonnet in *Aristote Politique* (Budé, 1960), vol. I, pp. xcv–cxx, and C. J. Rowe, "Aims and Methods in Aristotle's *Politics*" (Essay 2 above).
8 For examples of this criticism, see Barker, *The Political Thought of Plato and Aristotle*, p. 365, and Franz Susemihl and R. D. Hicks in *The Politics of Aristotle*, Books I–V [I–III, VII–VIII] (London, 1894), p. 160, note on I.5.1254b16.

slave can only share in reason received from his master (I.5.1254b20–23). As he constructs his state, however, Aristotle feels he must resort to the use of slavery. Thus his earlier attempts to justify slavery are characterized by modern critics as a precarious attempt to use psychology to justify an assumption that springs from a residue of a cultural bias.[9] And this bias blinds Aristotle even to arguments of his own that would seem to undermine the practice he undertakes to defend; he admits, for example, that the same social functions could be performed by nonslaves (e.g., at VII.10.1330a25–30),[10] but does not feel compelled because of this to reconsider the justice of slavery.

Some critics have even argued that Aristotle's theory is internally incoherent, quite apart from any abandonment of it in later books. For example, it is in Book I that Aristotle advocates the use of stewards to execute the (however modest) "science" of properly employing slaves (I.7.1255b35–6), the same book as that in which Aristotle advances his theory that slavery is natural only when those enslaved are lacking in reason and without forethought. Yet stewards are themselves slaves.[11] Others question how it can be that the slave can have a share in virtue (I.13.1259b21–1260b7), a characteristic requiring at least some reason (*EN* II.6.1106b36–1107a2).[12] Still others have written that there is an inconsistency in holding both that slaves are themselves alive (I.4.1253b32) and that they are no more than parts of their masters' bodies (I.6.1255b11–12).[13] Aristotle's assertion that

---

9 Thus, Newman says Aristotle's "bias was in favor of accepting and amending the institutions to which the collective experience of his race had given birth, rather than sweeping them away" (*The Politics of Aristotle*, vol. I, p. 151). Also, Schlaifer concludes that Aristotle's only real argument in favor of slavery is "the simple assertion that all barbarians are natural slaves," citing I.2.1252b5ff. and I.6.1255a28ff. Schlaifer goes on to say that "this assertion, however, in view of its general acceptance by the Greeks, might be called an argument *ek tôn ginomenôn* valid for his age" ("Greek Theories of Slavery from Homer to Aristotle," p. 198). Against this view, Fortenbaugh explicitly denies that Aristotle's view is "the sophistry of a prejudiced Greek male enjoying a privileged position" ("Aristotle on Slaves and Women," p. 135).

10 See also the reading of VII.14.1333a6–11 in Barker, *Politics*, p. 316, which, if correct, would further support this point. That the same labors were often performed by slave and free alike is evident from Xenophon's remarks in *Memorabilia* II.3.3. See also Philochorus in Macrobius, *Saturnalia* I.10.22.

11 See the *Economics* (I.5.1344a25–6), attributed by some to Aristotle. It was in any case typical for stewards to be slaves. This criticism was suggested to me by David Keyt.

12 For example, Newman says, "How any form of moral virtue can subsist in the absence of the deliberative faculty, Aristotle does not explain, nor how the use of the body is the best that comes of the slave . . . if virtuous action is not beyond him" (*The Politics of Aristotle*, vol. I, p. 149).

13 For example, Schlaifer proclaims flatly that Aristotle "simultaneously grants to the slave a participation in reason and denies it to him utterly, making him a mere body. His entire thought on this point is hopelessly confused: the slave was *ktêma ti empsuchon* [an ensouled possession] now he is only *sôma* [body]." ("Greek Theories of Slavery from Homer to Aristotle," pp. 193–4).

masters and slaves can be friends, provided that the relationship is according to nature (I.6.1255b13–14), has puzzled those who have noticed that he is very explicit in other works in saying that no such friendship can exist (*EN* VIII.11.1161a32–4; *EE* VII.10.1242a28–9).[14] Finally, some have noted that whereas the relationship of master to slave is despotical, and thus modeled on that of soul to body (I.5.1254b4–5), the fact that the slave can receive reason from his master (I.5.1254b20–23, I.13.1260b5–7; compare also I.13.1259b27–8) is better modeled by the relationship between the rational and emotional parts of the soul; Aristotle stipulates the relationship between those two parts of the soul as being a political, regal rule (I.5.1254b5–6), in contrast to the despotical rule of the master.[15] The disparity between these forms of rule is critical: the regal ruler rules in a fatherly way (I.12.1259b1, 10–11), acting in the interest of those ruled (III.6.1278b37–40); the despot acts solely in his own interest (III.6.1278b32–7, 1279a17–21; see also *EN* VIII.10.1160b29–31).

In the remainder of this paper, I shall reconsider this last criticism in some detail. I will argue that although the apparent inconsistency of the models can be somewhat diminished by considering the slave apart from his master, this alone, of all the above criticisms, locates a major and irreparable flaw in the theory of slavery Aristotle proposes. In order to develop this argument, however, let us look more carefully at the two models to which it refers and the attempt to defend Aristotle through the use of one of them.

2   REASON AND EMOTION

Despite the near unanimity, variety, and occasional vehemence of Aristotle's critics,[16] a more charitable assessment of Aristotle's theory can also be found: W. W. Fortenbaugh urges that careful consideration of the psychology of the

14 For an example of such a criticism, see Barker, *The Political Thought of Plato and Aristotle*, p. 366.

15 Examples of this criticism can be found in Barker, ibid., p. 365, and Schlaifer, "Greek Theories of Slavery from Homer to Aristotle," pp. 197–8.

16 See, for example, Eric A. Havelock, *The Liberal Temper in Greek Politics* (New Haven and London, 1957), pp. 343–52, whose discussion of Aristotle's view of slavery is one of unambiguous disdain. Havelock dismisses the whole matter as Aristotle's attempt to make a "crude concrete application of his authoritarian philosophy" (p. 352). Most critics at least give Aristotle credit for espousing a view that was relatively liberal for its day (see, for example, Newman, *The Politics of Aristotle*, vol. I, p. 151). But until Fortenbaugh's article, the only commentator inclined to defend Aristotle was Gillies (see note 6 above), of whose motives we might be especially wary; Gillies concludes his discussion of Aristotle's theory with the following rather chilling remarks: "Those rights, and those only, are inalienable, which it is impossible for one person to exercise for another: and to maintain those to be natural and inalienable rights, which the persons supposed to be invested with them can never possibly exercise, consistently either with their own safety, or with the good of the community, is to confound all notions of things, and to invert the whole order of nature" [p. xxxix].

slave will show that Aristotle's theory is at least coherent, if only "theoretical."[17] In essence, Fortenbaugh's argument relies upon Aristotle's theory of the relation between reason and emotion. According to this approach, when Aristotle says that slaves lack the ability to deliberate, this does not thereby remove them from our species:

> In more technical language, Aristotle denies them [slaves] the logical or reasoning half of the bipartite soul but not the alogical or emotional half. This means that slaves can make the judgments involved in emotional responses and therefore have at least a minimum share in the cognitive capacity peculiar to men in relation to other animals (compare I.2.1253a16).[18]

Fortenbaugh concludes by saying that "in denying slaves the capacity to deliberate (I.13.1260a12) Aristotle is not robbing them of their humanity."[19]

According to Fortenbaugh, this view allows us to see that "there is nothing inconsistent or precarious"[20] in the thesis that slaves do not have, but can apprehend, reason. Moreover, Fortenbaugh is inclined to applaud Aristotle's moderation in avoiding the excesses of Plato, whom Aristotle understands as saying that slaves ought only to be given commands (*Laws*, VI.777e5–778a1).[21] This moderation can be seen in Aristotle's remark that slaves ought to receive reasoned admonition (I.13.1260b5–7). Based upon his understanding of *Rhetoric* II.19.1392b10–11, Fortenbaugh sees in this a commitment to:

> giving the slave his due. For offering a reason involves acknowledging that slaves can follow reasoned admonition and judge for themselves whether or not a particular course of action is appropriate.[22] In other words, to offer slaves reasoned admonition is to invite them to make the sort of decision they are capable of making. Slaves cannot put together reasoned arguments and cannot offer their master reasoned advice. But they can perceive their masters' reasons and can decide to follow them. To this extent they can partake of reason, so that Aristotle is on firm moral as well as psychological ground when he protests against refusing slaves reasoned admonition. To offer reasoned explanation is to respect a slave's cognitive capacity and to allow him to partake of reason as best he can.[23]

17 Fortenbaugh, "Aristotle on Slaves and Women," p. 137.
18 Ibid., 136.
19 Ibid.
20 Ibid.
21 That Aristotle is incorrect in his conception of Plato's view is compellingly argued by Glenn Morrow in *Plato's Law of Slavery* (Urbana, Illinois, 1939), pp. 44–5.
22 Fortenbaugh's note 6 appears here, the text of which reads, "when we admonish (*nouthetein*) a man, he decides whether he should obey. Compare *Rhet.* II.19.1392b10–11, where the admonished man is described as a judge (*kritês*)." In the context of Aristotle's remarks here in the *Politics*, Fortenbaugh's understanding would appear to overstate rather implausibly the extent of the slave's prerogatives.
23 Fortenbaugh, "Aristotle on Slaves and Women," p. 137.

It is on these grounds that Fortenbaugh believes that "we may conclude that Aristotle's view of slavery is neither psychologically foolish nor morally repulsive."[24]

If only it were true. It would now follow that there can be such human beings as Aristotle's natural slaves. In fact, accounting for the slave's psychic lack as Fortenbaugh does would also explain much of what Aristotle allows slaves to do in other books. For example, so long as the slave can comprehend the reasoned explanations of his master, there is no reason to suppose that he cannot engage in modestly responsible activities, such as stewardship and agriculture. Moreover, it would now be clear that the slave could have a share in virtue, so long as he stood in a relationship with a natural master such that the appropriate reason was provided. In this way, the virtue of a slave would be exactly as Aristotle says it is: dependent upon and caused by the reason of the master (I.13.1260b3–7). And as a human being with at least some virtue, there is no reason to suppose that the slave could not enjoy friendship with his master.[25] We might even speculate that Aristotle's view, so interpreted, allows the natural slave to develop the right moral habits – habits not of the deliberative part of the soul, but of the emotional – given a sufficiently ample exposure to his master's reason. In such a case, it would remain true that all virtue (in the strict sense)[26] is gained from the master, and that the individual is a natural slave because of his initial and substantial need for his master's reason, but his relationship to the master ultimately might not need to be the same as it had initially been. Through sufficient exposure to his master's reason, the natural slave – however naturally a slave – might conceivably be able to earn his freedom, thus resolving another apparent contradiction between the first and later books.[27] And that the same social functions could be performed by free men would in no way modify the fact that natural slaves exist and stand to

24 Ibid.

25 This is admittedly only a partial answer to the criticism that Aristotle elsewhere rules out such friendships. For more detailed expressions of the way this argument would work, as well as cautions as to its ultimate incompleteness, see Schlaifer, "Greek Theories of Slavery from Homer to Aristotle," pp. 194–6 and Newman, *The Politics of Aristotle*, vol. I, p. 150.

26 Aristotle allows that there can be natural virtues, which are not virtues in the strict sense and which may be had by children and nonhuman animals. It is noteworthy that these may be transformed into virtue in the strict sense by the acquisition of reason. (See *EN* VI.13.1144b1–17; also *EE* III.7.1234a27–30.)

27 Note, however, that Greeks distinguished between freed slaves and free men. Manumission did not give the former slave citizen status but made him a "resident alien," with, at Athens, a significant special disability. All "resident aliens" required citizen patrons. Unlike free foreigners, the free slave had no choice of patron, but had to be represented by his former master. Certainly, for anything like the status of a citizen, the deliberative faculty would be required, which is something presumably still lacked by the slave. In any case, Aristotle does not address this issue in any detail, so this argument remains highly speculative at best.

benefit through slavery. Finally, that the slave has no share of the happy life or purposive life remains always true: considered on his own, he lacks the requisite psychic capacities for the purposive life and thus the happy life. Having received the appropriate reason from his master, however, he might be freed to engage in what he could never have achieved alone; for he has been provided with the right habits and reasons for action.

There is a curiosity in this, however, that leads us to its inadequacy. Critics have argued that Aristotle's account of the natural slave ensures that few, if any, human beings would qualify. On this conception, however, it would seem that *too many* qualify: namely, all those that gain their good moral habits and reasons for action from others. There is ample reason to suppose that this is the case for each and every one of us, for we all receive moral training of the requisite sort. Moreover, left initially and utterly to ourselves, we would be unlikely to generate these habits and reasons on our own. Of course, free children, on Aristotle's account, ultimately have the potential to come to engage creatively in the development of these habits and reasons, whereas slaves are condemned by their psychic lack always to depend upon their master's guidance. But until the child's potential is realized, both child and slave stand in similar need of guidance. (This similarity is perhaps reflected in the Greek practice of calling both child and slave *pais*.)

But Aristotle clearly states that the rule of free father over free child is not the same as that of master over slave, for the former is regal in nature (I.12.1259b1, 10–11) and the latter is despotic (I.5.1254b4–20). No doubt this distinction reflects the fact that the parent-child relationship is one of flesh and blood, whereas slaves are not kin to their masters. There is thus a natural relation of affection and emotional concern between a father and child that is no part of the master-slave relationship. Hence, a father rules the child like a king, with real concern for the welfare of the ruled. Similar considerations plainly apply as well to the "regal" rule of intelligence over emotion, for these are also related in such a way as to involve mutual concern.

But though such consideration may plausibly be supposed to have moved Aristotle to assign different forms of being ruled to children and to slaves, they are neither part of nor entailed by the theoretical warrant he offers for slavery. Aristotle does not attempt to defend the despotism of slavery on the grounds that the slave is not kin – nor could he, for such a defense would provide no ground for distinguishing conventional from natural slavery. Neither sort of slave is kin. Aristotle's defense of natural slavery, rather, is only that the proper slave is psychically deficient.

It might be replied in Aristotle's defense that it is the child's potential for independent rationality that earns him a regal rule by his father. If true, this would preserve the theoretical basis Aristotle offers, for now the distinction in modes of rule over child and slave would again be based on their distinct psychologies. Unfortunately, however, the potentiality of the thing ruled does not seem to be an important ingredient in Aristotle's distinctions between the proper sorts of rule. An obvious example of this can be found in the model Fortenbaugh appears to have in mind in the development of his interpretation: the relationship between intelligence and emotion. As with master and slave, intelligence rules emotion. As with master and slave, intelligence supplies reason to emotion, which the latter itself lacks, but can perceive and be guided by. As with slave and master (but *unlike* child and father), emotion is not even potentially intelligence, nor does it have the potential ever to have reason in any other way than by being given it by intelligence. Yet intelligence rules emotion in a regal fashion, or in the same way as a father rules his son. The potential of the child is plainly not essential to the analogous relation of ruler to ruled within the parts of the soul. This part of Aristotle's analogy, therefore, must derive from some other feature, as I proposed above.

Since, then, intelligence rules emotion in a regal way, this relationship cannot provide the proper model for the relationship of master to slave, a despotical rule. Hence, despite the numerous apparent advantages in interpreting Aristotle's defense of natural slavery according to the psychological model, such an interpretation cannot account for what is perhaps the most noteworthy ingredient of the master–slave relationship. The despotism of slavery requires another explanation.

3   SOUL AND BODY, MAN AND BEAST

One natural relation of despotism is that of soul to body (I.5.1254b4–5). Another is presumably that of man to beast (I.8.1256b16–26).[28] And Aristotle does not fail to apply these relations as models for the slavery he seeks to defend:

> We may thus conclude that all men who differ from others as much as the body differs from the soul, or an animal from a man (and this is the case with all those whose function is bodily service, and who produce their best when they supply such service) – all such are by nature slaves. (I.5.1254b16–19)[29]

Looking at the slave in this manner, it is not surprising to see that the only way in which he differs from a beast is that he can perceive reason and thus be subservient to it, whereas beasts "simply obey their instincts" (I.5.1254b23–4).

But this ability to serve reason is apparently not an important distinction for the quality of rule or consideration slaves are to receive, for Aristotle repeatedly compares them to tame animals (I.2.1252b12, I.5.1254b24–6). In this way, slaves are so much more beast-like than man-like that it is Nature's design that slaves would actually be distinguishable *physically* from masters, a design that, unfortunately, she too often fails to satisfy in fact (I.5.1254b27–34).

28 One mark of a despotical rule is that the relationship exists for the advantage of the ruler (III.6.1279a17–21).
29 This is Barker's translation, as is the next short quotation.

Because the natural slave can be characterized in this way, a number of inferences can be drawn, all of which contribute neatly to Aristotle's theory. First, it is clear that Aristotle would not expect anyone to argue that nonhuman animals are anything more than goods to be used by, and for the sake of, men. To the extent that Aristotle has given us a theory that identifies some biologically human beings as the moral equivalent of nonhuman animals, therefore, he has given us a defense not only of using such creatures, but of using them despotically. This is an important point, and one not sufficiently shown simply by his identification of slaves as living tools (I.4.1253b32). As Aristotle allows, the look-out man is a living tool for the pilot (I.4.1253b29–30), but there is no need to suppose that look-out men are or should always be slaves. If, however, it can be shown that there is a class of beings that are human but no more deserving of consideration in their own right than nonhuman animals, it will have been shown that owning such beings is morally appropriate.

The obvious way to proceed in this proof is to explore the comparison between nonhuman animals and those human beings who are to be identified as natural slaves. But the argument here is tricky, for Aristotle explicitly says that the essential characteristic of a slave is psychic and not physiological in nature (I.5.1254b34–1255a2). It is also clear that the natural slave lacks reason, though he can apprehend it. On the face of it, this would not make the slave sufficiently distinct from the freeman to warrant enslaving him; as was shown above, the appropriate model for this would appear to be that provided by the relationship of intelligence to emotion, a regal rule.

How, then, can Aristotle turn what would apparently require a regal rule into despotism? We can only speculate on the actual nature of such an argument, for Aristotle never makes it more explicit. It is interesting in this regard, however, that Aristotle's defense of slavery against those who would claim it to be merely conventional concludes with a stipulation of the difference between Greeks and barbarians, for elsewhere he says that barbarians have no natural rulers and thus all live as slaves (I.2.1252b5–9).

It is tempting to infer from this remark that Aristotle thinks that barbarians lack the capacity for deliberation, for this is the quality by which he distinguishes the natural ruler. There is obviously reason to resist making such an inference, however, for Aristotle could not plausibly suppose that *all* barbarians were so sorely deficient, especially given the heights to which he well knows the civilization (for example) of the Egyptians had risen (see VII.10.1329a40ff.). Aristotle, then, may well mean only that those barbarians who were not deficient in the relevant way did not end up being the rulers, or at least that the ones who did in fact become rulers among the barbarians did not rule as natural rulers should rule.

It is clear at any rate that Aristotle thought natural slaves were best (or perhaps only) to be sought from among non-Greek cultures, which means that he was committed at least to believing that a significant number of barbarians were deficient in the relevant way. And though these barbarians (unlike nonhuman animals) would still have the potential to perceive reason, without a masterly Greek to supply it (since their own rulers could or would not do so), this potential would be wholly unactualized. Thus, when living among their own kind, such barbarians would not be different from nonhuman animals in any actual way. This, perhaps, is Aristotle's reason for saying that capturing slaves through just wars is no different in genus than hunting (both are arts of acquisition – I.8.1256b23–6).

Similarly, just as the nonhuman animals that are owned and tamed benefit from this relation, despite the fact that the relation exists properly for the advantage of their owners, so Aristotle could argue that a barbarian is benefited by being the slave of a masterly Greek, despite the fact that the advantage of the master is the only essential concern of the relationship.[30] Such an assertion, however likely to be readily accepted by his Greek audience, is certainly unacceptable according to modern moral principles and has been roundly criticized as a mere appeal to cultural bias. But if we take seriously two principles assumed from the beginning by Aristotle, we might find more uniquely Aristotelian reasons for this.

What distinguishes men from nonhuman animals is that only the former have *logos* (I.2.1253a9–10). In context, it seems so clear that Aristotle means language (for he contrasts it with nonhuman animals' capacity merely to make noise) that no translators have even attempted to render it in a way that shows a relation to later passages where he denies *logos* to the natural slave. Yet Aristotle says that the purpose of *logos* is the identification of the advantageous from its opposite, and thus the just from the unjust (I.2. 1253a14–15). It is difficult to see how this could be achieved by those who lack the capacity for deliberation. Thus, even if Aristotle would allow that languages other than Greek counted as real languages,[31] it would remain true that (at least many of) their native users were incapable of using such languages (or, for that matter, Greek if they ever learned it) in such a way as to satisfy fully the distinction between man and nonhuman animal. Hence, when the barbarian/natural slave is captured and enslaved, he finally has the opportunity to come into contact with the proper use of *logos* – reasoned arguments designed to identify right from wrong. It is in (presumably Greek) language, after all, that the master gives reasoned admonition to the slave. Lacking such a master, however, the barbarian would lack at least the full actualization of the thing that distinguishes him from nonhuman animals. So in this way, too, in lacking the capacity to deliberate, the barbarian/natural slave, when left among his own kind, fails to be in any actual way distinct from the beasts that all would allow are rightly owned as property.

Secondly, Aristotle says that the natural slave is a part of his master – specifically, a part of his master's body (I.6.1255b11–12). From this

---

30 See note 5 above.

31 It is worth remembering in this regard that the etymology of *barbaros* is probably onomatopoeic, coming from the sounds such people made, as if we called the speaker of a foreign language a "blah-blah." Ironically, according to Herodotus (II.158.2), this was the determining factor employed by the Egyptians, who called anyone who used a foreign language a barbarian.

claim, we can conclude even more securely that the model for the master–slave relation that Aristotle uses is that of soul to body. Considered in this way, there is a sense in which the slave is to the master as the master is to the state; at I.2.1253a18–29, it is clear that the individual is related to the state as a part is to the whole. The dissimilarity, however, is more striking: being a part of a state requires freedom and deliberative capacity, whereas this is plainly not required to be a part of the body. In addition, Aristotle seems disinclined to make the slave a real part of the state, as opposed to a mere condition of it (III.5.1278a1–3). Similarly, the hand of a citizen would not be considered a proper part of a state, even though the citizen himself is. But Aristotle says that the man who is not part of a state is either a beast or a god (I.2.1253a3–7, 27–9; compare also 35–7). The slave, we may be assured, is not a god.

Thus, Aristotle can rightly characterize the slave as properly deserving a relationship like that of the body's to the soul or a beast's to a man. And rather than conflicting with this characterization, the slave's psychology in no way elevates him (in actuality) from the beasts. Indeed, without guidance, he can have no virtue and thus is the worst of beasts (cf. I.2.1253a35–7). In these ways, the slave is sufficiently beast-like to require a comparable analysis.

But the heart of this defense lies in conceiving of the slave in two importantly different circumstances: (1) outside of slavery, where he is, for the above reasons, effectively a beast; and (2) enslaved, where he has the benefits of his master's reason. This is crucial, for if we look at the two states, we find that different models apply. It is not enough to defend slavery by saying that the slave would be no different from beasts (in actuality, if not in potentiality) were he apart from his master, even if Aristotle can offer a reason for thinking that is the case. The same man, when guided by another with reason, is no longer beast-like: he can have some share of virtue; he can at least enjoy (or suffer) reason. Thus, the model of body to soul may provide a useful picture of the natural slave when living out of natural slavery – and may theoretically justify treating him in ways similar to the ways we treat nonhuman animals – so long as he is in that state. But once he is brought into the household of a natural master, this model can no longer accurately apply, for now the slave's psychological potential can be actualized.

We thus come to a paradox: however Aristotle might be able to justify owning such creatures as natural slaves apart from their masters,[32] we

---

32 I do not mean to suggest that the above account is clearly adequate in this regard, but only that it may have been what led Aristotle to his view. It might well be argued that this is still not sufficient, for even among his own people, the barbarian/natural slave has the capacity to receive reason, however unactualized, and that this alone is sufficient to require no less than a kingly rule. However Aristotle would argue this, the above observations are suggested only as possible motives for his arguments, motives that would show at least a superficial plausibility in making such arguments from his point of view. Validity, of course, is another matter. An example of an interpretation of Aristotle that provides him with such a view can also be found in A. E. Taylor, *Aristotle*, rev. edn (New York, 1955), pp. 102–3.

cannot justify owning them at the time they are actually *owned*, for then the model must be that of reason to emotion, for it is a feature of the slave *qua* slave that he receives his master's reason. The only way the slave might be kept in a state where he is no different in actuality from the beasts would be for the master to *fail* to give him reason. But then we would have come no further than the view for which Aristotle rebukes Plato.[33] The defense for the actual practice of continued slavery can now only be that unless such creatures are *owned*, they would not enjoy the actualization of their (however limited) humanity. It would not be surprising if Aristotle thought that slaves ought to be owned only for a time (while they are being "tamed," for example) and then emancipated. But an argument is still needed as to why they must be owned at all, especially during the time that they enjoy their master's reason; again, this stage of the relationship appears to require a nondespotical relationship. I do not see how such an argument can be made on theoretical grounds, though it is easy enough to imagine a practical argument to that effect. Still, a defense of slavery solely on pragmatic grounds was not all that Aristotle sought to achieve, for such an argument could have been offered without most of the moral and metaphysical considerations Aristotle imports to assist him in this theory; indeed, it could, no doubt, be offered for conventional slavery as well. In any case, Aristotle attempts no such argument.

4 SUMMARY AND CONCLUSION

I have argued that two important models are employed in Aristotle's theory of natural slavery, both of which allow some application of his conception of the natural slave: (1) that cited by Fortenbaugh, where the slave is to his master as the emotions are to reason; and (2) that criticized by most critics, where the slave is to his master as bodies are to souls or nonhuman animals are to humans. The former explains many of the uses to which slaves would be put, allows there to be such human beings (at least in theory), and, *qua* human, even allows them to enjoy some friendship with their masters. But the model of emotion to reason does not warrant the despotism of slavery. The second model, of body to soul or beast to man, would entail such despotism, and can be defended by taking the natural slave in a context where he does not have the natural master's guidance and direction. But this model cannot accurately apply to the relationship of natural slave to natural master, for it is in relation to the master that the slave is made in actuality more than beast, more than mere body. Hence, once exposed to his master, the slave no longer deserves the despotism he receives, for now the proper model is again reason to emotion.

Aristotle has told us why we can hunt some human beings as we do nonhuman animals (though not, presumably, for meat) and why some

---

33 Unfairly, as noted above – see note 21.

human beings are only actualized as human beings through the guidance of others. But he has never explained why some human beings deserve to suffer continuing despotical rule. Fortenbaugh's insights notwithstanding, Aristotle's theory fails.[34]

34 This article has been revised from the version that first appeared in *Phoenix*, 37 (1983), pp. 109–22. I am indebted to David Keyt, Fred D. Miller, Jr, Daniel Devereux, Allen Gotthelf, David Depew, Lawrence Nannery, Kent Anderson, and the anonymous referees of *Phoenix* for many suggestions and constructive criticisms. All errors are my own.

7

Aristotle and Exchange Value

S. MEIKLE[1]

Those parts of the Aristotelian corpus which deal with "economic" matters
are *EN* V.5 and *Pol.* I.8–10. In recent decades the interpretation of *EN* V.5 in
particular has become chaotic. There hasn't been agreement even about
whether it is ethics or economic analysis. This contentiousness is new. Over
centuries of commentary the chapter did not prove so troublesome; the
ancient commentaries do not make such heavy weather of it, and neither do
the medieval ones. The chaos has arisen only in the last hundred years or so.
The substance of the chapter is not obscure, nor is the logic of Aristotle's
argument difficult. The order of his remarks is jumbled, and we may have the
transmission to thank for that, but worse textual problems are overcome as a
matter of routine, and it is difficult to believe that the cause of the chaos can
lie there. Perhaps it is to be found in some weakness in modern thought
which is absent from the thought of earlier times; if so, the obvious suspicion
is that it will have something to do with the modern subject of economics
which has loomed so large in recent interpretation.

Athens had significantly developed the production and circulation of
commodities by the fourth century BC and we shall see that Aristotle has a
body of thought directed specifically at analyzing that development. In the
past century, the most ferocious dispute has centred on the analysis of the
commodity, and I shall argue that this is the cause of the chaotic comprehension of Aristotle.

EN V.5 and *Pol.* I.8–10 are not commonly regarded today as being among
Aristotle's outstanding successes, and *EN* V.5 has attracted some especially
unflattering appreciations. I think it can be shown that Aristotle's work has
been absurdly undervalued, and that the main reason for this is to be found
in the predilections in modern social science which scholars have brought to
the study of Aristotle. The thought of the two passages will be examined in
sections 1 and 2; the conclusion will be that the passages contain a coherent
analysis of economic value which has been overlooked partly because it
embodies a metaphysics which has been little understood and greatly

1 This is a revised version of a paper that originally appeared in *The Journal of Hellenic
Studies*, 99 (1979), under the title "Aristotle and the Political Economy of the Polis."

despised for part of the present century. Section 3 will draw out the contrasting objectives of Aristotle's two discussions, and will consider some arguments for the view that *EN* V.5 is ethics rather than economic analysis. Sections 4, 5 and 6 will try to explain how Aristotle's problems in the *Ethics* arose out of the changing social relations in classical Athens, and how little his thought is understood if it is approached from the perspective of recent orthodoxies in economics and the Humean metaphysics they usually embody. Finally, section 7 deals with some of the "primitivist" exaggerations that have arisen in attempts to correct the anachronism of modern economic interpretations of Aristotle.

1 EN *V.5*

It is necessary to examine the thought of Aristotle's chapters in detail for two reasons. The first is that the nature of Aristotle's problems, and the treatment he gives them, have so consistently been misconstrued on the basis of selective and impressionistic accounts of what the chapters contain, and the principles governing the selections and impressions have had such potent ideological motivation, that a review of Aristotle's argument is indispensable. The second reason is that conclusions I shall draw later can be substantiated only on the basis of a review of the texts. I shall argue that Aristotle's discussion in the *Ethics* is a theoretical effort of such a nature that its outcome would have been, had his efforts been successful (which they were not), an understanding of the *commodity*, i.e., the historical social form acquired by the product of labour in a society whose social relations are those of private labour and private exchange. Athens in the fourth century was in considerable part already a society of such a kind, but, obvious though that may be, the idea that Aristotle was trying to penetrate the secrets of the commodity might, nonetheless, seem to be as anachronistic as the interpretations of Kauder, Soudek, Spengler, Lowry and others who have sought to portray Aristotle's thought as a prototype of modern economic thinking.[2] However, this is not a thesis arrived at by speciously coaxing out of the text the principles required. It rests simply on what Aristotle says, and on the structure of his argument. Accordingly, the task of this section and the next is one of retrieval.

2 J. Soudek, "Aristotle's Theory of Exchange: an Enquiry into the Origin of Economic Analysis," *Proceedings of the American Philosophical Society*, 96 (1952), pp. 45–75; W. F. R. Hardie, *Aristotle's Ethical Theory* (Oxford, 1968), pp. 191–201; J. Schumpeter, *History of Economic Analysis* (Oxford, 1954), pp. 60–62; Joseph J. Spengler, "Aristotle on Economic Imputation and Related Matters," *Southern Economic Journal*, 21 (1955), pp. 371–89; E. Kauder, "Genesis of the Marginal Utility Theory," *Economic Journal*, 63 (1953), pp. 638–50; Barry J. Gordon, "Aristotle and the Development of Value Theory," *Quarterly Journal of Economics*, 78 (1964), pp. 115–28; "Aristotle and Hesiod: the Economic Problem in Greek Thought," *Review of Social Economy*, 21 (1963), pp. 147–56; S. Todd Lowry, *The Archaeology of Economic Ideas* (Durham, 1987).

The uniting theme of *EN* V.5 and *Pol*. I.8–10 is exchange-value, and it will be useful to say a little about this. The distinction between use-value and exchange-value is one of the foundations of economic thought, and Aristotle was the first to draw it. The artifacts of human labour are intended to serve particular purposes. They are designed and made so as to have just those qualities which make them useful for particular purposes, and they are said to have value in use, or to be use-values. If social arrangements are such that these artifacts are subjects of systematic exchange in a market, then they have a second sort of value too in virtue of the capacity of exchangeability which the market confers on them: they have value in exchange or exchange-value. Aristotle makes the distinction in these terms: "with every article of property there is a double way of using it; both uses are related to the article itself, but not related to it in the same manner – one is peculiar to the thing and the other is not peculiar to it. Take for example a shoe – there is its wear as a shoe and there is its use as an article of exchange; for both are ways of using a shoe, inasmuch as even he that exchanges a shoe for money or food with the customer that wants a shoe uses it as a shoe, though not for the use peculiar to a shoe, since shoes have not come into existence for the purpose of exchange" (*Pol*. I.9.1257a6–13).[3] Use-value is straightforwardly a matter of the natural properties of the artifact. Exchange-value, however, is not so straightforward. A given sum of money represents certain amounts of every kind of thing that is made. In Aristotle's examples, 5 *minae* = 1 house = 5 beds = so much food = so many shoes. The problem is to explain how, when the things themselves are by nature incommensurable with one another, they may be brought into equations at all. This becomes Aristotle's main problem in the chapter.

Book V of the *Ethics* deals with justice. Various requisite distinctions are made in the first two chapters, and the third and fourth deal with distributive and corrective justice respectively. The fifth, with which we are concerned, opens with a brief criticism of the Pythagorean view that justice in general is reciprocity. Aristotle rejects this view as fitting neither corrective nor distributive justice. The purpose of this polemical preamble is made clear immediately: the notion of reciprocity (*antipeponthos*) may be inadequate in accounting for corrective and distributive justice, "but in associations for exchange justice in the form of reciprocity is the bond that maintains the association" (1132b31ff.); in other words, in the subject of the new chapter, voluntary transactions of exchange of goods, the appropriate form of justice is precisely a form of reciprocity. At this point Aristotle takes the first step in defining the particular form of this reciprocity; it is, he says, "reciprocity . . . on the basis of proportion, not on the basis of equality" (*to antipeponthos kat' analogian kai mê kat' isotêta*, 1132b32–3). The idea is that "simple reciprocity" would enjoin that builder and shoemaker exchange one house

---

3 The translations of the *Ethics* used in citations are those of Rackham, Ross and Irwin, and of the *Politics* those of Jowett, Rackham and Barker.

for one shoe, but a house is too great (*kreitton*), or too much to give, for a shoe (1133a13), so they exchange in proportions, so many shoes to a house.[4]

Aristotle resumes after a brief digression (which will be discussed in the final section) by asking how reciprocity of proportion is to be effected. His answer is that it is done by establishing "equality of proportion" (*to kata tên analogian ison*, 1133a10–11); that is, the proportions of shoes and houses should be equalized (*isasthênai*, 1133a18, 1133b15–16). If that is done first, he says, and the exchange transacted on that basis, then the previous requirement of "reciprocity of proportion" will have been achieved (1133a10–12). So the development of his argument has put him in this position: further progress in explaining what fair exchange as "*reciprocity* of proportion" means, now depends on explaining the meaning of "*equality* of proportion" between products.

This problem is soon seen to rest on another which is logically prior to it: if a certain quantity of one product is to have the relation of equality to a certain quantity of another, then the two kinds of product must be "comparable in a way" (*sumblêta pôs*, 1133a19). His point is that a relation of equality can exist between things only if there is a dimension in which they are commensurable; two things of different kinds cannot be equal *sans phrase*; they can be equal *in length*, for example, and that is because they are commensurable in both being extended in space. The vague relation of being "comparable in a way" is more closely defined in due course as "commensurability" (*summetria*, 1133b16, 18, 19, 22). Two-thirds of the chapter still remain, and they are devoted entirely to the problem of explaining how this commensurability can be possible when products are so various. Nothing further is said about fair exchange.

Aristotle knew that his theory of fair exchange is only as good as the solution he produces to this problem of commensurability. If he cannot say exactly how products can be commensurable, then he cannot say that a relation of equality can hold between proportions of them, and his theory of justice in exchange collapses, and he recognized the fact: "If there were no exchange there would be no association, and there can be no exchange without equality, and no equality without commensurability" (1133b17–18).

Aristotle is clear about how the problem arises. It arises because "one man is a carpenter, another a farmer, another a shoemaker, and so on" (*Pol.* III.9.1280b20ff.). He suggests that if like were exchanged with like, medical services with medical services for instance, there would be no problem. But the things exchanged are, of course, always different things: "For it is not two doctors that associate for exchange, but a doctor and a farmer, or in general people who are different and unequal; but these must be

---

4 *Kreitton* usually means "better than" or "superior to." If it is translated in that way here, however, this could be misleading if it suggests, as it has to some commentators, that Aristotle might, at least in part, be concerned with the quality of products, or even with the position of their producers in a hierarchy. His problem throughout the chapter is exclusively to do with quantities. He assumes that goods are of exchangeable quality.

equated. This is why all things that are exchanged must be somehow comparable" (*EN* V.5.1133a16–19).

The problem presents itself sharply for Aristotle because of his doctrine of substance. Each thing has its own nature, and it has certain qualities in virtue of that nature. He holds that in respect of their qualities things may be said to be like or unlike (*Cat.* 8.11a15–16). But the relation he has established between proportions of products like shoes, houses and food, is not one of likeness or unlikeness, and commensurability, therefore, is not to do with qualities. The relation he has established is one of *equality*. He also holds that "what is really peculiar to quantities is that they can be called equal and unequal" (*Cat.* 6.6a26). Consequently, proportions of shoes, houses and food stand together in these equations, not as qualitatively different things, but as different quantities of something qualitatively the same. His problem is to discover what they are quantities of; this is what the problem of commensurability amounts to.[5] On Aristotle's metaphysics, the import of the argument is that exchange-value is a substance or nature of quite a different kind from use-value. Use-value is in its nature qualitative, but the nature of exchange-value is purely quantitative (see section 5). The product bears two natures which are joined, as it were, in a hypostatic union. Aristotle's problem is to identify the essence of exchange-value.

The development of Aristotle's thought from this point (1133a19) is fertile yet contradictory. He repeatedly changes direction as he tries, now in one way and now in another, to explain commensurability, and in the end he gives up the task as epistemically impossible. In this development, Aristotle introduces two attempts at a solution which appear and reappear, interweaving with each other and with observations that contradict them. The first of these is the idea that money, just because it is a common measure of everything, *makes* products commensurable and thus makes it possible to equalize them. The second is the idea that it is need (*chreia*) which makes things commensurable.

His first thought is that money was introduced in the first place precisely because "all things exchanged must be able to be compared in some way." He says that "it is to meet this requirement that men have introduced money . . . for it is a measure of all things . . . how many shoes are equal to a house or to a given quantity of food" (1133a19–22). The idea is that the existence of a common standard of measurement itself constitutes commensurability and makes equalization of goods possible; the same thought reappears later at 1133b16: "Money, then, acting as a measure, makes goods commensurate and equates them"; and a third time a few lines later: "There must, then, be a unit . . . for it is this that makes all things commensurate, since all things are measured by money." This idea is inadequate, and Aristotle drops it. It is inadequate because there can be no common measure where things are incommensurable. The possibility of a measure *presupposes*

---

5. This was Marx's reading of *EN* V.5; see *Capital* I (London, 1976), p. 151, and *A Contribution to the Critique of Political Economy* (Chicago, 1913), pp. 78–9, 153–4, 184.

commensurability, and presupposes it in the dimension where measurement is to be possible. In any case, exchanging x silver for y shoes raises the same problem.

Aristotle's second idea runs alongside the first in the text as we have it, but it is easily extracted, and it is clearly intended as a further attempt at a solution following the failure of the first. Repeating the need for a common standard or measure of things, he now separates the standard (*chreia*) from the measure (money), and makes money a conventional representation of *chreia*. We now appear to have not just a means of measurement (money), but a dimension of commensurability (need) for things to be measurable in; or to put it another way, we appear to have a commensurable dimension (need) which, though capable of variable magnitude, lacks a unit of measure until money provides it. "This standard is in reality *chreia*, which is what holds everything together . . . but *chreia* has come to be conventionally represented as money" (1133a25–31).[6] He goes on a little later to provide argument for giving this role to *chreia*: "That *chreia* holds everything together in a single unit is shown by the fact that when men do not need one another . . . they do not exchange . . . This equation must therefore be established" (1133b6–10). Something which "holds things together" (*sunechei*) is not quite the same thing as a dimension in which things are commensurable (*summetra*), but it is perhaps more like it than his first idea of a common measure.

There are reasons for doubting that *chreia* can be the solution to Aristotle's problem, however, and for doubting that he thought it was. Firstly, Aristotle always frames his problem as having to do with the things exchanged (how can 1 house = 5 beds?), and *chreia*, though it may take those things as its objects, is a condition of the people exchanging them, not a property of the things. There is nothing in the chapter that would lead us to suppose that Aristotle would be prepared to accept a solution in these terms, and there is one passage, which we shall come to shortly, that rules out even the possibility that at a stretch he might. Secondly, he never links *chreia* with commensurability (*summetria*). He has two other problems with which he connects it. He wants to know what is the one thing by which all things are measured (*dei ara heni tini panta metreisthai*), and suggests that this is in truth *chreia* (1133a25–6). He also wants to know what it is that holds everything together (*panta sunechei; sunechei hôsper hen ti on*), by which he means what it is that brings and holds people together in associations for exchange, and he twice suggests that it is *chreia* that does this (1133a27–8, 1133b6–7). But he

6 Here, and in subsequent citations from Rackham and others, I have left *chreia* (need) in place of the translation "demand" which, together with "supply," is now a theory-laden term carrying a weight of suggestion that cannot be attributed to a Greek author. The use of "demand" might also suggest that ways might be found for attributing to Aristotle a modern subjective theory of value. He held nothing of the kind, since, as will be argued shortly in this section, he considered and rejected such a theory (see also footnote 7). M. I. Finley's criticism of the kind of anachronism exemplified in this use of "demand" is cited below, and the nature of the anachronism is discussed in sections 5 and 6.

never says of *chreia* (as he does of money) that it creates commensurability (*summetria*), and, since he frames the problem as having to do with the products rather than their owners, it would have been wrong if he had. These considerations do not decisively rule out *chreia* as Aristotle's solution to the problem, but they are strengthened in their tendency to do so by a third, which must be seen as decisive even on its own.

At 1133b19–20 he says that "really and in truth (*têi men oun alêtheiai*) it is impossible for things so very different to become commensurate (*summetra*), but in respect of *chreia* they admit of being so sufficiently (*hikanôs*)." Sufficiently for what? Rackham suggests that he means sufficiently "for practical purposes," which seems reasonable since the implied contrast is with "really and in truth"; or perhaps he means sufficiently for "holding together" (*sunechei*) the association, which he says twice is something that *chreia* does (1133a27–8, 1133b6–7). Anyway, Aristotle's final thought is that for purposes of *epistêmê*, houses, beds, shoes and food cannot really be commensurable at all. He had obviously been looking for an answer that would be satisfactory for *epistêmê* or scientific knowledge, and he is now admitting that he has not found one. *Chreia*, therefore, in Aristotle's view, provides no basis for an answer, any more than money did. (This admission, and Aristotle's reasons for making it, constitute a serious obstacle for those interpretations which seek, on the basis of *chreia*, mistranslated as "demand," to read into Aristotle some version of modern subjective value theory.)[7]

In the ordering of the chapter as we have it, Aristotle now once again says of money that "such a standard makes all things commensurable, since all things can be measured by money." He follows this with the argument that really eliminates money as the solution: money does not create commensurability because proportionate exchange existed before money did, and in any case the exchange-value of a house is expressed *indifferently* by the five beds for which it exchanges, or by the money value (five *minae*) of five beds (1133b27–8). The analysis ends at this point, and Aristotle returns to the question of justice as a mean between too much and too little, political justice and so forth.

At the end of it all, he has succeeded in formulating a problem to which he can find no acceptable solution. We are still in the dark about what to do to be fair in exchange, because fairness is achieved by exchanging equal proportions, and he cannot explain the logical possibility of the equation of things that are incommensurable by nature. Nonetheless, the achievement of

7 Van Johnson, who explicitly sets out to overturn Marx's view that Aristotle formulates but does not solve the problem of value, fails to mention the passage in arguing that Aristotle held that "'demand' (χρεία) . . . is at bottom the real unit of value," and that "χρεία is as much a 'concept of value' for Aristotle as labor is for Marx," "Aristotle's Theory of Value," *American Journal of Philology*, 60 (1939), p. 450. Sir Ernest Barker, among others, took a similar view: "As Aristotle himself tells us, value depends on demand, on felt utility," *The Political Thought of Plato and Aristotle* (London, 1906)," pp. 379n2, 384.

the chapter is formidable. He has suceeded in formulating the problem which lies at the heart of the theory of value in economics. The achievement was appreciated by Marx who, at a difficult stage in his own argument about the equivalent form of value, suggests that matters will become clearer "if we go back to the great thinker who was the first to analyse so many forms, whether of thought, society, or nature, and amongst them also the form of value. I mean Aristotle." After examining chapter 5, Marx concludes that "the brilliancy of Aristotle's genius is shown by this alone, that he discovered, in the expression of the value of commodities, a relation of equality."[8]

2   POLITICS *I.8–10*

In *Pol.* I.9 we find Aristotle looking at exchange in quite a different way. The discussion here of exchange, barter, retail-trade and usury, is sometimes treated as a series of discrete discussions; or, if it is seen to have any unity, it is thought to be a unity brought to it by Aristotle's moral concerns. In fact the discussion has a theoretical unity. Aristotle is analysing the evolution of exchange-value through its successive forms, subjecting each to an analysis which reveals the aim or *telos* inherent in its form, and evaluating where necessary the compatibility of that aim with the aim of the *koinônia* or community of the polis.

The general outline of Aristotle's discussion is well known. The bedrock of the discussion is the natural process by which people cooperate to satisfy their needs by the use of their common human capacities, which Aristotle calls *oikonomikê* or the art of household management. (The naturalness of this process is particularly important to him, so it is a little awkward that he should incorporate an institution, the *oikos* or household, into its designation.) *Oikonomikê* requires a supply of the means by which it is conducted, and if these are not found ready to hand they must be acquired. Acquiring them is itself an art, the art of acquisition or *chrêmatistikê*, and this art is a part of *oikonomikê* (1256b27ff.). Aristotle thinks, however, that there is a second and quite different art of acquisition which, because of its affinity to natural acquisition, is supposed by many people to be identical with it, but which is in fact unnatural: the art of trade or commerce, which he calls *kapêlikê* or *chrêmatistikê* in the bad sense (1256b40–1257a5). *Kapêlikê* is not by nature a part of the art of acquiring true wealth (*ho alêthinos ploutos*, 1256b30ff.), for true wealth is a stock of instruments that are useful to the household or the polis (1256b36ff.), and *kapêlikê* aims at wealth considered as a quantity of money, and is rightly discredited because it is not in accordance with nature, but involves men taking things from one another (1258a39ff.).

Within this overall argument there is embedded an account of the development of exchange-value. Exchange is, first of all, agreed to be natural because it arises out of the natural fact that some have more and others less

8 Marx, *Capital*, vol. I, p. 60.

than suffices for their needs (1257a15ff.). Aristotle then introduces the first form of exchange, the form that is primitive both historically and logically, that is, barter, or the direct non-monetary exchange of one commodity against another, which we shall represent as C–C, to indicate the unmediated exchange of two commodities.[9] In the household, the first form of association where all things were held in common, there was no purpose for exchange to serve. That purpose arose with the increased scope of association of the village, whose members, he says, were more separated and had things to exchange. They did so in a direct manner, one useful thing for another (i.e., without money). Such exchange is natural because it serves to satisfy the natural requirement of sufficiency (1257a17–30).

When Aristotle introduces the second form of exchange relations he presents it explicitly as a development out of the primitive one: the other more complex form of exchange grew, as might have been inferred, out of the simpler (1257a30ff.). This form is the exchange of goods mediated by money. One commodity is exchanged for money, i.e. a sale (C–M), and money in turn for another commodity, i.e. a purchase (M–C). This form of exchange or circulation will be represented as C–M–C.

Aristotle explains the appearance of the new form of circulation of goods, and the appearance of money, as a response to, and an integral part of, a developing social reality which over time leads to the displacement of the less developed form of exchange relations by the more developed (1257a32–41). Such a form of explanation is entirely Aristotelian; it is an application of his metaphysics of substance, form and change.[10] In the *Ethics* he explains the advantage of the new form. In C–C the acts of sale and purchase are fused into a single act, with consequent difficulty in using what you have in order to get what you need. Money separates them into C–M and M–C which is much more flexible: "money serves us as a guarantee of exchange in the future: supposing we need nothing at the moment, it ensures that exchange shall be possible when a need arises, for it meets the requirement of something we can produce in payment so as to obtain the thing we need" (V.5.1133b10–13).

Aristotle is somewhat inclined to take as lenient a view of C–M–C as he does of C–C. What is wrong with *chrêmatistikê*, in the bad sense of *kapêlikê*, is its aim: that the trader seeks to gain by another's loss. Barter is acceptable because of its aim: the satisfaction of natural needs. Since the aim of the

9 The notation using C and M to denote the circuits of commodities and money is Marx's; see *Capital*, vol. I, chs 3 and 4.
10 Ross misses the point. Instead of understanding Aristotle to be thinking of the passage of exchange relations from an early form to a more mature one, Ross's evaluation is that "this notion of money as facilitating barter, instead of (practically) driving it out of the field, is a curious one." He adds in mitigation that "it must be remembered that in economics. . . . Aristotle was almost the earliest worker," *Aristotle*, 5th edn (London, 1949), p. 213. Susemihl–Hicks, however, had suggested that Aristotle recognizes the process as a "necessary development"; F. Susemihl and R. D. Hicks, *The Politics of Aristotle* (London, 1894; [repr. 1976]), p. 29.

circuit C–M–C is the same as that of C–C, Aristotle at times regards it too as natural. This is confirmed by his recognition of the ethically acceptable use of money in C–M–C as a "means of exchange," which he terms "the necessary process of exchange," and describes as "necessary and laudable" (1258b4).

But things are not quite so simple. There are indications of a rather different attitude to C–M–C in Aristotle's mind. For example, at 1257a6ff., he says that the use made of a shoe in selling it "is not its proper and peculiar use," and the reason he gives is that "the shoe has not been made for the purpose of being exchanged."[11] He does not go so far as to say that the use of a thing in exchange is unnatural, but this only glosses over, and does not remove, the suggestion of an irreconcilability between "necessary and laudable" exchange and the use of an article in exchange not being its "proper and peculiar use." There seems no obvious way of resolving the matter by reference to Aristotle's text. Rather the reverse: if the text suggests anything, it suggests an ambivalence in Aristotle's mind towards exchange of the C–M–C form. On the one hand he sees it as sharing the same natural aim as C–C; but on the other, because he recognizes it as a stage in the development of exchange relations, he also sees it as leading naturally into M–C–M or *kapêlikê*. He cannot make up his mind whether it is a good thing or a bad one. Aristotle has got himself into, or rather, historical development has put him in, a difficult position. His scientific method is to comprehend a whole in terms of its *ergon* or typical behaviour, and its *telos* or point, and to do that it is sometimes necessary to enquire into its origins and development. ("He who considers things in their first growth and origin, whether a state or anything else, will obtain the clearest view of them," I.2.1252a24.) The application of that method here to the polis in the material aspect of acquisition is producing results that are antagonistic to his idea of the *ergon* and *telos* of man within the polis. However, this must be left on one side. What is important here is Aristotle's achievement in thinking through the development of exchange-value and the social relations that embody it. It is precisely this that is the source of his difficulties.

Things are more straightforward with *kapêlikê*, where people come to market, not to sell what they have grown or made in order to buy what they need to consume, but rather to buy in order to sell, M–C–M. Aristotle introduces this form too as a necessary development out of the preceding form C–M–C, and he understands it to have a development of its own. He writes:

11 Aristotle did not think much of the Delphian knife. The nature of this knife is not entirely certain, but Oresme (following Aquinas) suggests that it was a crude implement that could serve as a knife, a file and a hammer, and its advantage was that it was cheap (see Susemihl–Hicks, *The Politics of Aristotle*, pp. 141–2). In that case it will have been an implement whose use-value was compromised by exchange-value considerations – something of which Aristotle could hardly be expected to have approved. Aristotle's criticism of it is that it is not a proper tool; a proper tool being one that is made to serve one purpose properly, not many purposes imperfectly (1252b1–4).

When, in this way, a currency had once been instituted, there next arose, from the necessary process of exchange [i.e. exchange between commodities, with money merely serving as a measure], the other form of the art of acquisition, which consists in retail trade [conducted for profit]. At first, we may allow, it was perhaps practised in a simple way [that is to say, money was still regarded as a measure, and not treated as a source of profit]; but in the process of time, and as a result of experience, it was practised with a more studied technique, which sought to discover the sources from which, and the methods by which, the greatest profit could be made. (1257b1–5; the interpolations are Barker's.[12])

The C–M–C circuit begins and ends with use-values. Its aim is to acquire something that is needed, and once it is acquired, that thing leaves the sphere of circulation for good and enters the sphere of consumption. Exchange here is an instrument falling within the first of Aristotle's two arts of acquisition, namely that "kind which is by nature part of the management of the household" (1256b27, 1257b20ff.). This is so because its aim is the acquisition of wealth as use-value not as exchange-value; its object is wealth "defined as a number of instruments to be used in a household or in a state" (1256b37–8). This form of exchange, however, makes possible another, *kapêlikê* (*chrêmatistikê* in the bad sense), "and it is concerned only with getting a fund of money, and that only by the method of conducting the exchange of commodities" (1257b21ff.). The owner comes to market, not with goods, but with money which he advances against commodities, M–C, and he resells these for a greater sum, C–M′. He does not stop there, however, because once he has finished one circuit he still has as much reason for advancing the increased sum M′ as he had for advancing the original sum M in the first place. This is the main contrast Aristotle draws between the circuits M–C–M and C–M–C. He is clear that the aim or point of C–M–C has to do with the fact that the first C and the second C are different use-values. The aim is to acquire the specific utility of the second which is needed, and the sale of the first is simply a means to that end. The M–C–M circuit, however, has no natural terminus or *telos*. It begins with money and ends with money, and since there is no difference of quality between one sum of money and another, the only possible difference being one of quantity, this quantitative growth of exchange-value in the form of money is the only conceivable aim that M–C–M′ can have. But if M can be advanced to become M′, so can M′ be advanced to become M″, and so on. Aristotle saw this, and he writes: "money is the beginning and the end of this kind of exchange" (1257b22ff.): "there is no limit to the end it seeks; and the end it seeks is wealth of the sort we have mentioned . . . the mere acquisition of currency" (1257b28ff.): "all who are engaged in acquisition increase their fund of money without any limit or pause" (1257b33ff.). The two forms of exchange or acquisition, C–M–C and M–C–M, "overlap because they are both handling the same objects and acting in the same field of acquisition; but they move along different

12 E. Barker, *The Politics of Aristotle* (Oxford, 1946).

lines – the object of the one being simply accumulation, and that of the other something quite different" (1257b34ff.).

The fourth form in the development of exchange-value, and the final one in Aristotle's account, is "the breeding of money from money" (1258b5), that is, usurer's interest or M–M', which, he says, is the most unnatural of all and is most reasonably hated. His brief treatment of this confirms his decision to permit C–M–C, and the function of money specific to it as distinguished from its function specific to M–C–M' and M–M' (1258b2–8).

Aristotle's dislike of *kapêlikê* is no doubt connected with the traditional distaste for trade, and with the values of the aristocratic *oikos*. But the criticism he makes of it goes beyond anything that can be attributed to taste and tradition. Certainly, he does not refrain from observing that *kapêlikê* involves people taking things from each other, and one can argue, as commentators have, about whether the *kapêlos* just grubs for money or performs a service. But none of that should obscure Aristotle's deeper criticism, which is not primarily of *kapêlikê* at all, but of its aim, the getting of wealth as exchange-value, and this is a more general thing (1257b40–1258a14). People may pursue that aim by means of *kapêlikê*, and then they are not living well for the familiar reasons; but they may pursue it by other means too. Aristotle instances the military and the medical arts, but he means that almost anything people do, and every faculty they have, can be put to the pursuit of exchange-value (1258a8–10). All these human activities, medicine, philosophy or sport, have a point for the sake of which they are pursued, and they can all be pursued for the sake of exchange-value as well or instead. When that happens, their own real point becomes a means to the end of exchange-value, which, being something quite different, transforms the activity and can threaten the real point and even destroy it. Aristotle is concerned, not only about the invasion by exchange-value of *chrêmatistikê*, but about its invasion of ethical and political life as a whole. So it will hardly do to suggest that his hostility to *kapêlikê* is simply a piece of reactionary primitivism ("Back to the simple and the primitive"), based on political preference and snobbish prejudice against money-makers.[13]

3   CONTRASTS BETWEEN THE ETHICS AND POLITICS

Attempts to show *EN* V.5 to be economic analysis have usually been so unconvincing and anachronistic that their effect has been to strengthen the view that the chapter is ethical, rather than weaken it. The ethical interpretation stands on two struts. The first is the claim that inequality and status pervade the chapter, and the main evidence for this is thought to be provided by the ratio of producers which Aristotle introduces twice as a specification of fair exchange: "as builder to shoemaker, so many shoes to a house" (1133a23–5 and a32–3). This is an intractable problem and it will not

---

13 See, for instance, E. Barker, *The Political Thought of Plato and Aristotle*, p. 376.

be dealt with here.[14] The second strut is the contrast between the *Ethics* and the *Politics* passages.

The salient difference between them is that the *Ethics* contains no discussion of *kapêlikê* or trade. The *Politics* goes through four forms, C–C, C–M–C, M–C–M and M–M, but the *Ethics* is confined to exchange between two producers without the intervention of a middleman C–M–C. Furthermore, Aristotle never uses any of the usual Greek terms for "trade" and "trader," as he does systematically in the *Politics*, but uses the neutral word for "exchange" (*metadosis*). These features might be thought odd if the discussion really had been intended as economic analysis. Trade, both *kapêlikê* and *emporikê* or mercantile trade, were commonplace in his world, and he knew perfectly well that a large volume of goods circulated in this manner and not in the C–M–C manner. This might appear to be a deliberate lack of realism on Aristotle's part, and if that is what it is, then, firstly, it would be difficult to explain on the supposition that he had been trying to do economic analysis, and, secondly, it might be more readily explained on the supposition that he had been doing ethics.[15]

The first of these suggestions is that if Aristotle had been attempting economic analysis, then he would have discussed such a familiar thing as trade. The tacit premise here is that economic analysis deals only with familiar things like trade. This is, indeed, a view commonly taken of their subject by economists. Schumpeter, for instance, defines economic analysis as "intellectual efforts made to *understand* economic phenomena," and he identifies that with "analysing actual market mechanisms."[16] Aristotle is plainly not doing that in *EN* V.5, so it follows, given a definition of this kind, that his analysis of the commensurability of products as exchange-values is not economic analysis. It is difficult to see what other name to give it, and equally difficult to see how the problem might be solved by attending to actual market mechanisms. Such definitions have caused mischief in the interpretation of Aristotle. Finley, for instance, arrived at the view that *EN* V.5 is ethics rather than economic analysis with the help of Schumpeter's definition.

The second suggestion is that Aristotle deliberately excluded trade because the subject of the chapter being, according to the ethical view, the justice of each having "his own" in the *koinônia*, Aristotle cannot introduce the *kapêlos*, or trader, since justice in exchange is achieved when "each has his own," when, in other words, there is no gain from anyone else's loss.

14 In fact inequality has no place in the chapter, and Aristotle intends builder and shoemaker to be considered as equals in his theory of fair exchange; see my "Aristotle on Equality and Market Exchange," *Journal of Hellenic Studies*, 111 (1991).

15 The arguments are given by M. I. Finley, "Aristotle and Economic Analysis," *Past and Present*, 48 (1970); republished in *Studies in Ancient Society* ed. M. I. Finley (London 1974). All page references to this article will be to the latter publication.

16 J. Schumpeter, *History of Economic Analysis*, pp. 1 and 60; cited by Finley, ibid., pp. 26 and 44.

Aristotle's insistence on the unnaturalness of commercial gain is thought to rule out the possibility of a discussion of profit-making exchange M–C–M.

The *Ethics* chapter, however, is not simply about the justice of each having his own. It is mostly about how goods can possibly be commensurable, or, how it can be possible that a proportion of one good might be *equal* to some proportion of any other you care to choose, however different: 5 beds = 1 house = so much money (1133b27–8). Naturally, since Aristotle was aware of the successive forms of exchange relations, he studied his problem against the setting of the form of exchange in which that relation of equality is expressed, C–M–C, and not a form in which an inequality is expressed, M–C–M'. That is why Aristotle is talking exclusively of an exchange between two producers without the intervention of a middleman. What would a consideration of M–C–M' have done to advance the solution of this problem? The objective nature of this circuit, which becomes the subjective aim of the *kapêlos* engaging in it, lies, as Aristotle himself explains, in the fact that unequals are exchanged; the sum advanced, M, is exceeded by the sum extracted, M'. This is a subordinate species of exchange; Aristotle is aware of that and makes the point explicitly in the *Politics*. In the *Ethics* he has uncovered a more general problem to do with the possibility of exchange of any kind. That being so, he has no need to discuss subordinate species, so he does not discuss them. To put the point in another way, it is impossible to come to understand the later and derivative form of the exchange of unequals, until one has understood what equality in exchange means; and it is impossible to come to understand that until one has solved the underlying problem of commensurability, which is the presupposition of systematic exchange relations existing at all. He is not concerned with the forms through which they pass in the development of exchange-value. That matter is gone into in the *Politics*. That is why trade (M–C–M') is discussed there and not in the *Ethics*. Indeed, this very disposition of material between the two works reveals his awareness of the different levels of generality.

Aristotle consistently uses the neutral word "exchange" in the *Ethics*, and avoids using any of the normal Greek words for "trade" and "trader" which he uses all the time in the *Politics*. It is hardly convincing to suggest that the reason for this is that Aristotle cannot introduce the *kapêlos* because justice in exchange is achieved when "each has his own" and there is no gain from anyone else's loss. Even if the fairness of each having "his own" really had been the main subject of the chapter, this need not be thought to have given Aristotle reason to *avoid* the use of *kapêlos* and *kapêlikê*. It might be thought to have given him better reason for using them ruthlessly, since the *kapêlos* is a prime example of unfairness, and Aristotle is usually cool but unsparing about unfair men. Whatever one's preferred intuition in the matter, Aristotle's silence about trade in the *Ethics* cannot be explained by supposing his concern to have been ethical, because that supposition, even if it were correct, would explain the presence as well as the absence of a discussion of trade. If the *Ethics* had contained such a discussion, the explanation would explain this too.

4   ARISTOTLE AND THE COMMODITY

It is clear that *EN* V.5 contains a body of thought which is analytical in substance and intention. Its nature, however, does not conform to any recent orthodoxy in economics. Identifying its nature is a large question, but if it is shirked altogether it will remain unclear what the analytical significance of the problem of commensurability is, what the historical significance is of the fact that this problem should have arisen for a thinker of the fourth century, and why twentieth-century commentators on Aristotle should without exception have read through it as if it wasn't there. These matters will be looked at in this section and the two that follow.

What kind of analytical endeavour is Aristotle engaged in which is so imperspicuous to modern economists and those influenced by them? This can be put in another way: within which modern school of analysis, if any, do Aristotle's efforts, as we have seen them to be, become comprehensible? The answer, to cut a long story short, is the Marxian school of value theory. The essence of Aristotle's problem is to explain the capacity products have to exchange in non-arbitrary proportions; to discover the dimension in which products that are incommensurable by nature can become commensurable, and to determine what sort of relation it can be that comes to exist between products when they are equated as subjects of systematic exchange. It is also the problem which Marx intended his theory of value to solve. Aristotle saw that the dimension can have nothing to do with the natural or physical constitution of products. Marx drew the same conclusion, and concluded further that the commensurability goods acquire when they become subjects of systematic exchange, or exchange-values, is a social character which they acquire historically with the appearance of a certain manner of dividing labour socially; products acquire the social form of "commodities" (products bearing both use-value and exchange-value) and become commensurable in virtue of new social relations that come to exist between people. Products had, in considerable part, acquired this social form in Aristotle's Athens, just because the appropriate conditions of divided labour had made their appearance.

Something further must be said about these social relations, and about their existence, alongside others, in the historical complexity of fourth-century Athens. Among the conditions of socially divided labour, two are especially important. Firstly, there was a certain level of specialization in production, between agriculture and the crafts and among the crafts themselves. (This had also been true, to a lesser degree, of the palace-based cultures of the earlier period.) Secondly, each producer produced privately and on his own account, had private property in the product and marketed it. (This had not been true of the palace-based cultures.) Where each producer produces his own good or narrow range of goods privately, each is more or less in a situation where he has more than he can use of the product of his own specialized labour, and none of all the other goods produced by the specialized labours of others, which, since his needs are manifold, he must acquire. Thus, along with the development of specialization on the one hand, and of privacy in production on the other, there goes a complementary development of exchange between the private specialists. A point is reached in this development where producers are producing partly or exclusively with a view to exchange, and acquire through exchange all the other useful things they need but do not themselves produce. Under these social relations of privately conducted labour and systematic exchange, the product of labour acquires a particular historical form. The product is still a use-value, something directly useful, but it is no longer made or grown by the producer only or predominantly because of its use-value to him, for he produces far more of his item than he can consume. His product is of interest as a use-value only to others. To him it is of interest because as a potential subject of exchange it represents exchange-value, and he makes it in order to realize this value in exchange with others who need its use-value, and who produce and purvey all the other things he needs. The product of labour has now taken on an independent social identity of its own as an exchange-value, and it enters into social relations with other products which are expressed in relations of equality (1 house = 5 beds, or = so much money) which Marx terms "the elementary form of value."[17] The existence of systematic market exchange is the complement of the private form in which social labour is supplied; the *private* nature of the producers is complemented by the *social* relations that come to exist between their products. The form in which the members of the society pass around their various contributory efforts to the common production does not appear in direct relations of cooperation between them as contributors to the common stock, for they are private and produce on their own account; it appears as a social relation between their products, amount x of product A = amount y of product B. If our knowledge of the historical development of Athens down to Aristotle's time did not tell us that the social relations of commodity production had made significant strides, we could in any case infer that they had from the very fact that it had become possible for Aristotle to be brought to the point of investigating the commodity form.

To be sure, the social relations of commodity production had developed within the integument of a society of subsistence agriculture in which the surplus was extracted, not through commodity relations, but through dependent labour. Those relations had not developed in the higher form of capitalist commodity production, as some have argued, most notably Eduard Meyer.[18] They had developed in the form of petty commodity production.

17 See Marx, *Capital*, vol. I, pt I, ch.1, section 3A.
18 "Athens in the 5th and 4th centuries stands as much under the sign (*unter dem Zeichen*) of capitalism as England has stood since the 18th and Germany since the 19th century," E. Meyer, *Kleine Schriften* (1st edn 1910), vol. I, pp. 79ff.; cited by H. Bolkestein, *Economic Life in Greece's Golden Age*, ed. E. J. Jonkers (Leiden, 1958), pp. 148–9. When Meyer was writing, Europe's first big working-class party with a programme opposed to exchange-value, the SPD led by Kautsky, Bernstein and Liebknecht, was growing vigorously and causing alarm. Bolkestein noted that

The essence of the distinction between the two forms can be made in practical terms with reference to Athens: it was emergent petty, not capitalist, commodity production because there was virtually no market in labour-power, that is, no significant class of people working for wages;[19] with the possible exception of bottomry, money did not function as capital; there was no credit system advancing loans for the establishment of firms, and so on.[20]

5   ECONOMICS, HISTORY AND METAPHYSICS

In forming a view of what *EN* V.5 is about, it is necessary to have some notion of what economics is, and commentators have usually adopted orthodox notions. What orthodox economics does is study the workings of market economy, or as Schumpeter put it, "actual market mechanisms." But this is not always how it thinks of itself. Robbins enshrined a common view in his definition of it as the study of the "relationships between men and economic goods."[21] These two positions are often held simultaneously, though they are incompatible, as Marxian economists have tirelessly pointed out to little effect.[22] Market economy is a fairly recent historical arrival, and so, since the study of a thing can hardly precede the existence of the thing to be studied, its study is a fairly recent arrival too. Robbins's definition of that study, however, gives it a timeless reference rather than a historical one. Economics, on that definition, deals with "relationships between men and economic goods," as if these were as general and unchanging as the relationships studied in chemistry or mathematics, rather than with the particular form of those relationships peculiar to market economy. Such a view is a standing invitation to anachronism, and a sizeable part of the literature on the economic history of the ancient world, of which Finley has been such a rewarding critic, is testimony to the fact. This confusion may not matter much so long as the object of study is some aspect of a society based on market economy, for in that case an accompanying false belief that the relationships involved are timeless might be irrelevant. The position is quite

Meyer's opinion, and its pretty clear underlying message that civilization is to be identified with the system of capitalism, was endorsed by many scholars, especially in Germany.

19 Hired labourers (*misthotoi* or *thêtes*) were not very numerous or mobile, and many were slaves hired out by their masters. The propertied class extracted the surplus mainly through dependent (or unfree) labour, and only to a limited extent through hired labour. See G. E. M. de Ste Croix, *The Class Struggle in the Ancient Greek World* (London, [1981] 1983), pp. 179–204.

20 See G. E. M. de Ste Croix, "Ancient Greek and Roman Maritime Loans," in *Debits, Credits, Finance and Profits*, eds H. Edey and B. S. Yamey (London, 1974), pp. 41–59.

21 L. Robbins, *The Nature and Significance of Economic Science* (London, 1932), p. 69.

22 See, for example, Paul M. Sweezy, *The Theory of Capitalist Development* (Oxford, 1942), pp. 5–6.

different, however, when the object of study is itself historical. In the literature on *EN* V.5 there is much that is unsatisfactory, and most of it is due to this confusion. If there were not this confusion to explain the fact, it might otherwise beggar the imagination how anyone could have read Aristotle's chapter and got the idea that he was looking for a theory of price-formation, or laying down markers in mathematical economics.

Schumpeter took the view, as Roll and many others have, that in economics, Aristotle, unlike Plato, had a genuinely analytical intention for which he deserves to be recognized as the father of economic science as they understand it.[23] Yet in the accounts given of what is supposed to be Aristotle's contribution, its substance often appears slight for something thought to deserve such an accreditation, and the evaluations of Aristotle's success in fulfilling his analytical intention are sometimes rather low. Schumpeter's judgment, for instance, is that Aristotle offers no more than "decorous, pedestrian, slightly mediocre, and more than slightly pompous common-sense."[24] Finley rightly sees paradox here. Why, after all, when Aristotle was capable of "monumental contributions to physics, metaphysics, logic, meteorology, biology, political science, rhetoric, aesthetics and ethics," should he have been so dismal at economics once he had set his mind to it?[25] Finley's conclusion is, of course, that he did not do dismally because he never set his mind to it in the first place; he was doing ethics and not attempting any sort of economic analysis. But Schumpeter sees no paradox. Aristotle was simply rotten at economics, and has to be given poor marks, because his analysis is restricted to the artisan alone, ignores the "chiefly agrarian income of the gentleman," disposes perfunctorily of the free labourer, judges the trader, shipowner, shopkeeper and money-lender only in moral and political terms, and does not subject their gains to an explanatory analysis.[26] Finley concurs. His opinion is that, had Aristotle been attempting economic analysis, Schumpeter's low marks would have been perfectly justified because "an analysis that focuses so exclusively on a minor sector of the economy (*sc.* artisans) deserves no more complimentary evaluation."[27] Schumpeter uses a definition of economics which makes it impossible that anyone of Aristotle's period, or for two thousand years after it, might have done any such thing, and then criticizes him for not doing it properly. Finley, accepting the same definition, recognizes that Aristotle was not doing economics as defined, but takes this to mean that he was not doing economic analysis on any conceivable definition.

Aristotle, however, is not *discussing* artisans, he is using them as examples. The problem of commensurability is at a high level of generality, and in going about it, Aristotle needs as an example only the simplest case. He does

23 E. Roll, *A History of Economic Thought* (London, 1961), p. 31.
24 J. Schumpeter, *History of Economic Analysis*, p. 57.
25 Finley, "Aristotle and Economic Analysis," p. 28.
26 Schumpeter, *History of Economic Analysis*, pp. 64–5.
27 Finley, "Aristotle and Economic Analysis," pp. 37–8.

not need to catalogue every manifestation in sight, every derivative form of exchange, every occupation and form of revenue and so forth. That would not have got him any nearer solving his problem. To say that Aristotle was discussing only artisans is to mistake the examples he uses for the subject under discussion. Schumpeter's listing all the items Aristotle does not discuss, and his propaedeutic admonition of Aristotle's lack of professional accomplishment in not discussing them, reveals less about Aristotle than it does about Schumpeter. Humean metaphysics, which pervades modern economics, constitutionally favours assemblages of appearances and repudiates the idea of Aristotelian natures or essences lying behind appearances.

The primary tradition of metaphysics in European philosophy has, since antiquity, been the Aristotelian tradition. Modern fashion has tended to favour Humean metaphysics, and whatever may be thought to be the benefits of the shift, an advance in the understanding of the commodity has not been among them. Aristotle's partial analysis of it, and particularly his problem of commensurability, seem to have become opaque to modern commentators, and Marx's completion of that analysis has largely suffered the same fate.

Neither Smith nor Ricardo showed any philosophical sensitivity to the problem of commensurability, and neither cites Aristotle's discussion of it. In their versions of the labour theory of value, it is assumed that products are commensurable with one another simply because they are all alike products of labour. Neither of them reflected that, as natural activities, weaving and mining are no more commensurable with each other than, as natural entities, their products, cloth and coal, are.[28]

Marx considered this oversight to be the principal weakness in classical political economy. Following Aristotle, he noted the incommensurability of products as natural objects or use-values, and following out the logic of Aristotle's argument, he also noted the incommensurability of the natural labours that produce them. So natural labours logically could not be the substance of value as Smith and Ricardo had supposed. He concluded that only as exchange-values could products be commensurable, and only as productive of exchange-value could labours be commensurable. Just as products (as subjects of systematic exchange) bore two distinct and quite different natures, use-value and exchange-value (see section 1), so the labours that produced them bore the same two natures, which Marx

28 Ricardo seems to be raising the problem in the first sentence of chapter I, section II, of the *Principles*: "In speaking, however, of labour, as being the foundation of all value . . . I must not be supposed to be inattentive to the different qualities of labour, and the difficulty of comparing an hour's or a day's labour, in one employment, with the same duration in another," (*The Principles of Political Economy and Taxation*, ed. P. Sraffa [Cambridge, 1986], p. 20). But Ricardo goes on in the second sentence to discuss intensity and skill, which are modifications (relating to productivity or quantity) of particular kinds of natural labour, neither of which has any bearing on the problem of how those distinct kinds can be commensurable.

distinguished as "useful labour" and "abstract, simple and homogeneous labour."[29]

Ricardo had elided the two natures and their divergent aims, and so, lacking the distinction between them that would allow the reflection that production under market economy might aim at something other than providing use-values to meet needs, he supposed it aimed at that. Marx, having distinguished the two natures and their different aims, faced a choice of alternatives. He concluded that use-value was not the end, but the means to the end of exchange-value, namely, its quantitative expansion. In his view, all the defects of capitalism were owing to that fact, and were derivable from it theoretically.[30]

Marx's conception of "the twofold nature of the labour embodied in commodities" constitutes a deep and fundamental divergence from Ricardo, and it is among the two or three things that Marx claimed as original in his own work.[31] It is all the more remarkable, therefore, that the divergence should have been so commonly overlooked, and that it should have become almost the conventional view that Marx adopted Ricardo's version of the labour theory of value, lock, stock and barrel, and was novel only in the use he made of it. This view goes back at least to G. D. H. Cole, and it informs Samuelson's much-cited quip that Marx was no more than a minor post-Ricardean.[32] Perhaps one of the more interesting reasons for the persistence of this view is a utilitarian insensitivity to the distinctness of different kinds of thing, deriving from Humean metaphysical convictions about substance, and skepticism about Aristotelian natures.

Schumpeter considered that Marx "was under the same delusion as Aristotle, viz., that value, though a factor in the determination of relative prices, is yet something that is different from, and exists independently of, relative prices or exchange-relations."[33] Humean metaphysics lies at the root of this traditional criticism too. Aristotle and Marx are trying to explain a power or capacity: the capacity products have as commodities to exchange in non-arbitrary proportions in the way that they do. They take the fact that commodities do this to be the exercise of a capacity, and Marx's theory of value is an attempt to explain that capacity. In the Aristotelian tradition in metaphysics, Marx recognizes a distinction between a capacity and its

29 Curiously, this proposed solution to the problem of the commensurability of different labours has usually been understood in such a way, that it has come to be a standard objection to Marx that he postulates, but cannot prove, a reduction of all labours to a single labour. See, for example, J. Schumpeter, *Capitalism, Socialism and Democracy* (London, 1952), p. 23 n. 2. The objection is less interesting than it may appear, because the "reduction" meant is not that of different labours, but that of different degrees of skill and intensity.

30 See K. Marx, *Theories of Surplus Value*, vol. II (Moscow, 1968), pp. 495–501.

31 *Capital*, vol. I, ch. 1, section 2.

32 G. D. H. Cole's introduction to the Everyman edition of Marx's *Capital* (London, 1930), p. xxi.

33 Schumpeter, *Capitalism, Socialism and Democracy* (London, 1952), p. 23 n. 2.

exercise; a distinction we all acknowledge when we allow that people with a capacity to speak French have that capacity even when they are asleep, speaking English, just keeping quiet, or otherwise not exercising it. According to Humean metaphysics, no distinction is to be drawn between a capacity and its exercise.[34] Schumpeter, implicitly espousing the Humean view, denies the need for any commensurating nature (value) in the exchange relation of products, and condemns it as a "delusion."[35] On Humean metaphysics, all Aristotelian capacities, including Marx's value, are to be dismissed as "metaphysical" in the opprobrious sense of the word once favoured by empiricists.[36]

6   THE ATHENIAN "ECONOMY"

Fourth-century Athens did not have a market economy and was not regulated by exchange-value. Nonetheless, a thinker of the fourth century, even Aristotle, could not have formulated the problems we find in *EN* V.5 unless exchange-value had already developed considerably. Much has been made of the fact that artisans were a minor sector of the economy, and that Aristotle, in supposedly restricting his discussion to artisans, greatly weakens that discussion. Artisans were not minor in the sense of being unimportant, however, even if they were minor in terms of the percentage of total production that they accounted for and the percentage of producers they represented. But whatever the truth of the matter, it is beside the point. Aristotle is not discussing artisans alone; even his examples make this clear, since they include farmers and physicians, and not just shoemakers and builders. He is discussing the entire sector of commodity production and distribution, and this included not only the products of artisans, but those of slaves and peasants too, where they were sold rather than directly consumed.

33 David Hume, *A Treatise of Human Nature* (Oxford, 1960), pp. 160, 166, 172. The Humean view has not fared well in recent thought about capacities; see M. R. Ayers, *The Refutation of Determinism* (London, 1968), pp. 55–75, 80–95; and A. J. P. Kenny, *Will, Freedom and Power* (Oxford, 1975), pp. 122–44.
35 The objection is traditional and was made by Bailey in 1825: "value is the exchange relation of commodities and consequently is not anything different from this relation. . . . Value denotes nothing positive or intrinsic, but merely the relation in which two objects stand to each other as exchangeable commodities." This is cited and replied to by Marx in *Theories of Surplus Value*, vol. III (Moscow, 1971), p. 140.
36 Schumpeter, always a shrewd critic, took issue with Tausig who thought there was no difference between Ricardo and Marx on value and exchange-value. Schumpeter observed that "there *is* a difference between Ricardo and Marx, since Ricardo's values are simply exchange-values or relative prices," and Marx's are not. He draws the interesting conclusion that "if we could accept this view of value, much of his [Marx's] theory that seems to us untenable or even meaningless would cease to be so," (*Capitalism, Socialism and Democracy*, p. 23 n. 2). If we are to take Schumpeter at his word, then much of what stood between Marx and himself rested on his adoption of a Humean analysis of capacities and Marx's adoption of an Aristotelian one.

This was a dominant part of the economy of the polis, because production for direct consumption rather than for exchange, though it existed in agriculture and textiles for example, was not very important. The true index of the importance of the commodity sector is not the percentage of total production that it accounted for, or the percentage of total labour engaged in it. However much one may try to minimize its proportions, to maximize the degree of household self-sufficiency, to emphasize the small scale of workshops and so on, it is all in the end beside the point. For the polis in Aristotle's time rested in large part on the separation of the crafts from agriculture, and conse-quently on the relations of exchange that existed between the producers in the countryside and those in the workshops, and between the suppliers of goods and services in the town itself. Aristotle knew it, and knew the importance of it, and that is why he says in the *Ethics* that fairness in exchange is "the salvation of states," as Jowett put it, and holds the polis together (V.5.1132b34), – a judgment which Aristotle quotes subsequently in the *Politics*: "Hence reciprocal equality (*to ison to antipeponthos*), as already remarked in the *Ethics*, is the salvation of states" (II.2.161a30–31).[37]

The persistence of pro-market anachronism in the interpretation of the literature and economic history of antiquity, in the work of the "modernists," has produced its own counter-anachronism in the work of the "primitivists." In order to deal with the confusion of the former, the latter have emphasized the low level of economic development in antiquity. They have also rightly drawn attention to the absence from ancient literature of anything remotely resembling what is called "economics" today, and the absence from Greek and Latin of words for modern economic ideas like "labour," "profitability," "productivity," "the economy" and so forth. This case, however, has been pushed beyond the point of exaggeration.

Schumpeter's excuse for Aristotle's bad showing in economics is that "in the beginning of scientific analysis, the mass of phenomena is left undi-sturbed in the compound of commonsense knowledge." Finley retorts: "the mass of what phenomena?"[38] – invoking the low level of economic develop-ment in antiquity. He cites Roll: "If, then, we regard the economic system as an enormous conglomeration of interdependent markets, the central problem of economic enquiry becomes. . . ."[39] Finley justly replies again that antiquity knew no such enormous conglomerations of markets. How, then, so the logic of the argument runs, can we expect to find in Aristotle a scientific study of such "masses" and "conglomerations" when none existed? Without them it would "not be possible to discover or formulate laws . . . of economic behaviour, without which a concept of 'the economy' is unlikely to develop, economic analysis impossible."[40] Here Finley finds the reason why Aristotle,

37 See D. G. Ritchie's perceptive evaluation of the implications of this in his "Aristotle's Subdivisions of Particular Justice," *Classical Review*, 8 (1894), p. 192.
38 Finley, "Aristotle and Economic Analysis", pp. 44–5.
39 M. I. Finley, *The Ancient Economy* (Berkeley, 1973), p. 22.
40 Ibid., p. 22.

whose programme was to codify the branches of knowledge, wrote no *Economics*. He readily concedes that in spite of the low level of the Greek "economy," nevertheless "non-capitalist or pre-capitalist societies have economies, with rules and regularities . . . whether they can conceptualize them or not," and that these can be studied. But their study can, in his view, be a matter only for us in the present, not for the contemporaries of those "economies" who could not conceptualize them.[41] The picture is confusing. On the one hand, the Greeks did not have an economy with masses of phenomena and associated laws such as our science of economics studies, and that is why they had no economics. On the other hand, they did have an economy with laws and regularities which they could not study though we can. Did they have laws or didn't they? And if they did why couldn't they make some attempt to study them? Are these, perhaps, laws of different kinds? There is a related contradiction over whether or not they wrote anything resembling economics: on the one hand, they did not; on the other, they did, but it was banal.[42] So what was Aristotle doing in *EN* V.5 – banal economic analysis or nothing that could be called economic analysis at all? There is evidently a confusion somewhere.

The confusion was already present in the earlier work of Polanyi. He had found that the source of the persistent modern anachronism in interpreting ancient economic life lay in an ignorance of the vast difference between modern capitalist market economy and all pre-capitalist "economies." He sought to correct this by distinguishing between the "embedded economy," one which is integral to the whole social fabric and does not stand above it, and the "disembedded economy," one which is torn out of the social fabric to become an independent entity.[43] The difference was real enough, but the distinction was ambiguous: was "the economy" a single sort of thing that could be present in two different ways which the distinction distinguished, or was the distinction really between two things of quite different kinds which are misleadingly called by the same name, "the economy"? To mark the real difference, the distinction should be used in the second way, but it has usually been used in the first, and this usage has provided occasion for puns on the word "economy" which defeat the intended purpose of the distinction.

In order to capture the difference between capitalist economy and pre-capitalist "economy" the distinction required is that between use-value and exchange-value. The most fundamental question to be asked about a society is which of these predominates in it. A capitalist society is predominantly a system of exchange-value; economics is the study of the developed forms of exchange-value and of the regularities in its movement, or "actual market mechanisms," and it can come into being only with the appearance of full-blown market economy, that is, with markets in labour and capital.

---

41 Ibid., p. 23.
42 Finley, "Aristotle and Economic Analysis," *passim*, and *The Ancient Economy*, p. 22, for the first view. and *The Ancient Economy*, p. 20, for the second.
43 See K. Polanyi, "Aristotle Discovers the Economy," in *Primitive, Archaic and Modern Economies*, ed. G. Dalton (New York, 1968), p. 81.

Antiquity was predominantly a system of use-value, partially administered, and if it had regularities, these were nothing like the cycles, laws, and trends which characterize a system of exchange-value.

Polanyi's distinction is a blunt instrument, and it does not help in drawing the finer discriminations needed to avoid the pitfalls of the "modernist–primitivist" debate; indeed, it contributed to the development of that unilluminating debate. Antiquity was not a system of exchange-value, and its production, distribution, and consumption were not regulated by it. But exchange-value, markets and money did exist in early forms of their development, and they were what Aristotle was trying to come to understand. Polanyi's distinction, together with orthodox definitions of economics, have not helped in appreciating what is to be found in Aristotle, and have done something to obscure it. Aristotle did not conceptualize capitalism, and he did not develop anything like Robbins's conception of "the economic system" as something divorced from history and reduced to a series of tenseless "relationships between men and economic good." These points were worth making, but they are negative and tell us nothing about what Aristotle *did* do. Indeed, both Polanyi and Finley were led to conclude that Aristotle achieved very little. It is a bizarre judgment to pass on an author who first distinguished between use-value and exchange-value, perhaps the most fundamental distinction in economics; first analyzed the development of forms of exchange; and first formulated the problem of value.

7 RECIPROCITY AND COMMUNITY

The spirit of the Graces and of reciprocity is introduced by Aristotle near to the beginning of *EN* V.5: "That is why we set up a shrine to the Charites in a public place, since it is a duty not only to return a service done one, but another time to take the initiative in doing a service oneself" (1133a3–5). What significance should be given to this passage?

The passage, according to one view, should influence the reading of the entire chapter, because it is to be understood as announcing that the ensuing discussion is to be exclusively ethical, that exchange is to be seen in the context of the *koinônia*, and that *koinônia* is to be as integral to the chapter as the act of exchange itself. The notion of *koinônia* carries elements of fairness, mutuality and common purpose, and these elements are thought to pervade the chapter. Consequently, on this view, Aristotle's chapter can have little to do with economic matters except under the strict aegis of ethics.[44]

This seems an exaggerated view. Maybe Aristotle is saying that exchanges should be seen somewhat in the spirit of the Charites, of gift and counter-gift, and not as occasions for assembling in a public place to "cheat each other with oaths" which, as Herodotus makes clear, the Greeks had a long-standing reputation for doing.[45] That he intends something of the sort is

44 The case is made by Finley, "Aristotle and Economic Analysis," p. 32.
45 Herodotus I.152–3.

more than likely since he thinks there must be *philia* or friendliness in any sort of relationship. Can we conclude, however, that *koinônia* is as integral to the chapter as the act of exchange? It is obviously integral to Aristotle's conception of fairness in exchange, and we know, because he says it twice, that Aristotle was convinced that fairness in exchange is the most important single thing for holding together a polis many of whose citizens were private producers and exchangers. But, as we have seen, the substance of the chapter is not about any of that. Its greater part is an attempt to analyze a quite distinct problem. The chapter begins with the problem of how to be fair in exchanges, and that passes into the problem of how to bring proportions of different things into the relation of equality required for fairness so that each "has his own" after the exchange as well as before it. But it then develops as its major theme the problem of how such a relation could conceivably be possible when the things themselves are incommensurable by nature. To this problem, *koinônia* and the Spirit of the Graces of gift and counter-gift, have no application. The conclusion must be that *koinônia* is not such an important element in the chapter after all.

Polanyi pursues the *koinônia* line of thought to its final conclusion, and arrives at the view of Aristotle as simply a defender of archaic institutions, "the philosopher of *Gemeinschaft*."[46] Polanyi sees Aristotle as living "on the borderline of economic ages," and thus finds "every reason to see in his work far more massive and significant formulations on economic matters than Aristotle has been credited with."[47] These massive formulations turn out to be small beer, however, for Polanyi goes on to interpret Aristotle as a defender of the archaic institutions of *Gemeinschaft* in awkward historical circumstances. Aristotle's concern with the relation of equality in exchange, he interprets as an expression of those institutions of archaic societies or kinship groups where ritual gift and counter-gift are made in order to cement group bonds, and are reckoned on a traditional and non-quantitative basis of status.[48] This interpretation is introduced with information about the Arapesh people of Papua New Guinea, the reciprocity institutions of the Trobriand Islanders, and so forth. Aristotle's strictures about *koinônia*, *philia*, and *autarkeia* or self-sufficiency, are all interpreted in this way, and their importance is attributed to the fact that "the regulation of mutual services is good since it is required for the continuance of the group."[49] Polanyi observes that in the *Ethics* Aristotle is looking for the form of *philia* appropriate to exchanges, but he fails to see that in the search, the prevailing conditions in Athens ("on the borderline of economic ages") led Aristotle into uncovering "equality of proportion" between goods themselves, and thence into the problems of the commodity. Having missed that, his own account of the "massive and significant formulations on economic matters" which he

46 Polanyi, "Aristotle Discovers the Economy," p. 107.
47 Ibid., p. 95.
48 Ibid., p. 109.
49 Ibid., p. 96.

expected from Aristotle amounts to this: Aristotle was concerned to find ways of determining at what level prices should be *set*, legally promulgated and enforced, in order to preserve the social relations of which archaic reciprocal gift-giving on the basis of status was a part.[50] This reading can be sustained only at great cost, and Polanyi is driven to the ridiculous observation that "surprisingly enough, Aristotle seemed to see no other difference between set price and bargained price than a point of time, the former being there before the transaction took place, while the latter emerged only afterward."[51]

Aristotle's concern with holding together the bonds of the polis does not, in the end, take the form of a defense of reciprocity in gift-giving. It takes the form of an attempt to specify reciprocity (*to antipeponthos*) as a relation of equality between proportions of products being exchanged. This means that the problem of holding the polis together in Aristotle's period is no longer a matter of preserving mutual gift-giving on the basis of status; it has become a matter of regulating, or finding some form of *philia* for, buying and selling. Whatever Aristotle may begin with, and he does begin with the spirit of the Charites, he ends with the problem of the commodity. The co-presence of these things in itself suggests that Aristotle's thought is reflecting a process of historical change. If mutual cheating and general lack of *philia* in the agora had been a joke two centuries earlier in the court of Cyrus the Great, then archaic gift-giving was well on the way out even then. So it is scarcely possible to read Aristotle, after two centuries of further development, as nothing more than an apologist for archaic institutions. If one is determined to see him either in that way, or as no more than a moralist of *koinônia*, then one has either to ignore the analytical content of his thought, or distort it in some way, as Polanyi does in portraying it as prophetic rather than as reflection on (and of) existing reality.[52]

---

50 Ibid., pp. 97, 106–7, 109. See the review by G. E. M. de Ste Croix, *Economic History Review*, 12 (1959–60), pp. 510–11.
51 Polanyi, ibid., p. 108.
52 Ibid., p. 53.

8

Aristotle's Criticism of Plato's Republic

R. F. STALLEY

The chapters in *Politics* II where Aristotle discusses Plato's *Republic* have elicited a mixed, though generally critical, response from scholars.[1] The main difficulty is the apparent absence of any serious attempt to discuss the *Republic* as a whole. Aristotle concentrates largely on the proposals for the abolition of the family and of property. He treats these proposals in almost complete abstraction from their context, and gives the impression that they apply to all citizens in the ideal state, not just to the guardians. He says nothing about such important matters as the education of the guardians and the requirement that philosophers should rule. The picture he offers of the *Republic* is thus incomplete and misleading. Moreover, many of his objections have been thought unfair. Some look like sophistical quibbles, while others seem to be based on the assumption that the *Republic's* proposals are intended for implementation among human beings as they now are, not as they ideally might be. For reasons such as these, E. Bornemann, the author of the most detailed study so far published of these chapters, concludes that Aristotle is incapable of understanding Plato's thought and shows only the most cursory acquaintance with the *Republic*.[2]

---

1 A typically ambivalent treatment is that of Susemihl and Hicks, *The Politics of Aristotle*, Books I–V (London, 1894), pp. 32–3. Susemihl begins by counting the criticism of the *Republic* among the most successful parts of the *Politics* but qualifies this by adding that "its author had not the power, if indeed he ever had the will, to transfer himself to the innermost groove of Plato's thought."

E. Bornemann, "Aristoteles' Urteil über Platons politische Theorie," *Philologus*, 79 (1923), pp. 70–111, 113–58, 234–57, treats the section in an immensely detailed but almost wholly negative way. Some of Bornemann's arguments are reflected (in a more moderate form) by T. J. Saunders in his notes on the Penguin translation of the *Politics*, revised edn (London, 1982), though he concedes that more than one view is possible.

A neoplatonic criticism of these chapters is to be found among the works of Proclus. It is printed in vol. II of the Teubner edition of Proclus' Commentary on the *Republic*, ed. Kroll (Leipzig, 1899–1901), pp. 360–68.

2 See note 1 above.

I hope to defend Aristotle against such criticism, but I shall not pretend that he offers a full and fair assessment of the *Republic* as a whole. I shall argue, instead, that his critics have failed to understand what he is really trying to do. There is a way of reading these chapters which not only shows them to make sense but also reveals that they offer a valuable contribution to political philosophy.

1   THE IDEAL OF POLITICAL COMMUNITY

Our first question is "What was Aristotle's purpose in writing these chapters?" The answer to this looks fairly easy. In the opening sentences of Book II (1.1260b27–36),[3] Aristotle tells us that he is going to examine constitutions actually in force in cities that are regarded as having good laws as well as those constitutions proposed by earlier writers which seem to have merit. He regards this as an essential preliminary to the task he is about to undertake: describing "the best form of political community (*koinônia politikê*) for human beings able, so far as possible, to follow their ideal way of life." Presumably, he has the ideal constitution of *Politics* VII and VIII in mind. He needs to preface this account of the ideal constitution with an examination of existing and imaginary constitutions – partly to discover their good features, and partly to show that, since none of them is adequate, he has good grounds for presenting an alternative ideal. In practice, the negative aim predominates. Aristotle's main concern in considering these constitutions is to demonstrate their deficiencies.

This introduction implies that Aristotle's interest is not primarily in the *Republic's* political philosophy, but rather in its constitutional proposals. It is therefore somewhat surprising that instead of proceeding forthwith to describe the merits and defects of the constitution, he begins his discussion by exploring in a quite abstract way the implications of the phrase *koinônia politikê*: political community.[4] Since *koinônia* means literally "having in common," these words seem to imply that a city necessarily involves sharing. Aristotle distinguishes three possibilities here. The citizens might share (1) in nothing, or (2) in everything that can be shared, or (3) in some things but not others. The first possibility is quickly eliminated. The citizens must share in something, if only the locality. Aristotle then considers the second possibility – that the citizens should share in everything that can be shared. It is possible, he thinks, for them to share children, wives, and property. This, he claims, is what happens in Plato's *Republic*, for there Socrates[5]

---

3 Except where otherwise indicated all references to Aristotle are to *Politics* Book II.
4 Those commentators I have consulted seem not to have noticed the abrupt change of approach. Saunders, *Aristotle's Politics*, pp. 101, brings out the connection between *koinônia politikê* and sharing but does not comment on the odd way in which Aristotle pursues this issue instead of approaching the *Republic* directly.
5 Throughout these chapters Aristotle directs his criticisms at "Socrates," meaning thereby the Socrates of the *Republic*, not the Socrates of history. This need not mean

maintains that children, wives, and property should all be common. Aristotle accordingly asks whether the existing arrangement is better, or whether the rule proposed in the *Republic* would be preferable (1.1260b36–1261a9). He first argues against the idea that women and children should be common on the grounds that (1) it is based on the incorrect assumption that the state should be as unified as possible (2.1261a10–b16) and (2) the measures proposed would, in any case, not promote that goal (3.1261b16–1262b36). He then brings similar arguments, though in reversed order, against the idea that property should be held in common (5.1262b37–1264a1).

The question of how much the citizens should hold in common dominates the section on the *Republic* in *Politics* II, though Aristotle manages a few other comments – mostly on the class system. Thus he offers not so much a critique of the *Republic* or its ideal constitution as a discussion of political community. His interest in this idea is easy to understand. Since he starts the *Politics* with the claim that the city is essentially a community or partnership – one which aims at the supreme end, the good life (I.1.1252a1–6), he has every reason to analyze the notion of a political community. An obvious way to approach that topic is by use of the idea that, in an ideal community, as much as possible would be shared. Since Socrates advocates this extreme kind of sharing in the *Republic*, it is natural for Aristotle to base the discussion on his arguments. The difficulty, of course, is that in the *Republic* it is only the guardians who share wives, children and property. One may therefore complain that Aristotle gives a thoroughly misleading impression of Plato's views.

Several commentators have recognized that much of Aristotle's argument is based on a short passage in *Republic* V.[6] At 461e, Socrates, having described the guardians' way of life (which, of course, involves the abolition of families and private property), sets out to demonstrate that community (*koinônia*) of this kind brings the greatest possible benefit to the city. He argues that whatever binds the city together and makes it one is its greatest good. Conversely, its greatest evil is to be pulled apart and made into many rather than one (462a–b). What binds the city together is a community or sharing of feelings (*koinônia* again) which comes about when all citizens (as far as possible) feel pleasure or pain at the same events. A sign of this is that the greatest possible number within the city use the words "mine" and "not mine" with reference to the same things. The ideal for the city is, in fact, to

that Aristotle intends to distance Plato from the "Socrates" he criticizes. In the concluding section of Book II he attributes some of the main proposals in the *Republic* explicitly to Plato (12.1274b9–11).

6 The notes of both Susemihl–Hicks, *The Politics of Aristotle*, pp. 214ff., especially p. 219, and Saunders, *Aristotle: the Politics*, pp. 104, 107, 116 indicate the relevance of this passage. Bornemann ("Aristoteles' Urteil," p. 115) regards it as the "Hauptgrundlage" of Aristotle's criticism and discusses it at length (pp. 123–7), but does not, so far as I can see, consider the possibility that Aristotle may mean to discuss the concept of *koinônia* as it is found there rather than to deal with the doctrine of the *Republic* as a whole.

resemble as closely as possible an individual person. Just as the community (*koinônia*) of soul and body means that the whole man feels pain when one part of him suffers, so it is best that the whole city should feel pleased or pained when one of its members experiences good or evil.

At 462e, Socrates applies these general points to his own ideal city. He argues *inter alia* that the guardians will look on each other as members of the same family. This will not be just a verbal matter. They will genuinely regard each other as brothers, sons, or fathers and act accordingly. Because they have so much in common and share the same feelings, they will be free from the evils that beset other cities – assaults and violence and the other disgraceful practices resulting from the possession of property and money. They will thus be even more blessed than Olympic victors. Here Socrates recalls the earlier complaint (IV.419a–421c) that the guardians will not be particularly happy. His reply is that by making them into *guardians* he has secured happiness for the city as a whole, not just for one class.

The constant use of *koinônia* and its cognates demonstrates that the central theme of this passage is community. It is thus an obvious basis for Aristotle's discussion of that topic. Socrates' insistence that the citizens ideally should share in as much as possible suggests that the more they share, the more genuine their community. Notice, too, that Socrates' remarks are not confined to the benefits of *koinônia* within his ideal state. He first offers a completely general argument to the effect that since unity is a city's greatest good, all citizens should ideally share in as much as possible (462a–e). Only when he has established this as a general thesis does he apply it to his own ideal state, arguing that the community of wives and children and the abolition of private property among the guardians will bring about its greatest good.

There is clearly a tension between this general thesis about the benefits of sharing and Socrates' account of the ideal state. He claims that it is good for the state to be as unified as possible and that this requires a community of feeling among *all* citizens which is to be induced by the abolition of families and private property. But this surely implies that all citizens (not just the guardians and auxiliaries) ideally should have wives, children and property, in common.[7] Although Socrates glosses over this point, his language betrays the difficulty. At 464a, he speaks of the *citizens* (not just the guardians) using the word "mine" when referring to the same things and thus sharing their feelings of pleasure and plain. This may be a verbal slip, but it shows what Socrates' principles really entail. His failure to extend the community of family and property to all citizens marks an outright inconsistency in his approach.[8]

---

7 *Laws* V.739b–e suggests that complete community of wives, children and property is the ideal but could only be realized among gods or the sons of gods.

8 Bornemann ("Aristoteles' Urteil," pp. 124–7) regards this as simply a verbal point, but it cannot be so easily explained away. Even if Plato does mean his comments about unity to refer only to the guardian class, such reasons as he gives are purely general. Bornemann is remarkably willing to overlook problems in Plato's arguments while treating possible failings on Aristotle's part with severity.

This may explain Aristotle's puzzling comment towards the end of his discussion of the *Republic* (II.5.1264a14–17) that it is "not determined" whether the arrangements concerning the community of wives, children, and property are to apply to the third class.[9] This, though a gross inaccuracy in the context of the *Republic* as a whole, is a reasonable comment in relation to the passage we have just considered; after all, the logic of Socrates' argument is that *all* citizens should share in as much as possible. Moreover, Aristotle is right to point out that there is a real problem here. If the lowest class does not partake in the communal arrangements, how can the city as a whole be a unity? If, on the other hand, they are permitted to share in these arrangements, much of the distinction between the classes would disappear. The inconsistency between the discussion of *koinônia* in *Republic* 461ff. and the account of the ideal state is therefore no mere superficiality. It reaches to the heart of Plato's proposals.[10]

If my reading is correct, Aristotle is justified in attributing to the Platonic Socrates the thesis that the members of a community should ideally hold as much as possible – including wives, children and property – in common. At the very least, Socrates implies that families and private property are not good things in themselves. Of course, by our standards, Aristotle behaves unfairly in abstracting this passage from its context and in failing to distinguish his comments on it from his criticisms of the ideal constitution. But, as we all know, Aristotle did not feel bound by the standards to which modern scholars, at least in theory, adhere.

A more puzzling question is why the discussion of political community dominates Aristotle's treatment of the *Republic* to the exclusion of almost everything else. It may well be that this is the area in which Aristotle felt his disagreements with Plato to be strongest, but we must also take into account the manner of composition of *Politics* II. It does not look like a finished work. If what we have is, in effect, a set of notes, it is not surprising that they should appear incomplete and unbalanced.

9 Even Susemihl–Hicks (*The Politics of Aristotle*, p. 241) regards this as "very culpable carelessness." Bornemann ("Aristoteles' Urteil," pp. 147–8) sees it as evidence of Aristotle's complete failure to understand Plato.

10 Several commentators have noticed this difficulty in the *Republic* and have tried to explain it away. Thus J. Adam (*The Republic of Plato* [Cambridge, 1920], vol. I, p. 305) suggests that Plato's aim is to keep the whole city one by preventing one of its constituent factors from becoming many. Bornemann ("Aristoteles' Urteil," p. 124) believes that Socrates concedes that full unity is the ideal for the whole state but restricts it to the guardian class in the *Republic* for practical reasons. I can find no textual warrant for either of these views, but in any case they both concede that the argument of V.461–6 logically implies that the measures designed to achieve unity should apply to all classes. Aristotle can hardly be blamed for taking this implication at its face value.

2   *THE UNITY OF THE STATE*

According to Aristotle, Socrates' fundamental mistake was to assume that the whole city ideally should be as much of a unity as possible.[11] Thus, in Aristotle's view, he denies the essential plurality of the city. The city, Aristotle claims, is by nature less of a unity than the household and that, in turn, is less of a unity than the individual man. Thus, to make the city one would be to destroy it (2.1261a20–22).

Bornemann, using an argument ultimately (though perhaps misleadingly) derived from Proclus, complains that Aristotle here confuses two senses of "one."[12] When Socrates says that the city should be one, he means that it should enjoy inner harmony and agreement. Aristotle, on the other hand, takes the word in a purely numerical sense, as though Socrates somehow denied that the city is necessarily composed of a number of distinct individuals. Of course Aristotle can hardly have supposed that Plato or anyone else thought that the state could literally be turned into a single individual. Elsewhere Aristotle apparently sees that a central aim is to create agreement among the citizens (3.1261b31–2). Thus, in Bornemann's view, the argument is sheer sophistry.

Before attributing so dishonest an argument to Aristotle, we should at least consider whether there is an alternative interpretation. It may be helpful to bear in mind the passages in the *Metaphysics* (XIV.4.1091b16ff.) and *Eudemian Ethics* (I.8.1218a6ff.) where Aristotle criticizes those Platonists who identify the good with the one and see plurality as the source of evil. From that doctrine it would follow that the more a city is a unity, the better it is. In the *Politics*, the rather vague reference to "certain people" who say that the city should be one (2.1261b7), implies that the *Republic* is not Aristotle's only target. I suggest, therefore, that we should see the present passage as part of a wider assault on the Platonist metaphysic that identifies unity with goodness. Aristotle's view is that, far from being an imperfection, the plurality of a city is part of what makes it valuable.

Aristotle is well aware that the world as we know it is not neatly divided into distinct units, and that we use different criteria in different contexts for determining what is or is not to count as one.[13] A man, for example, may be

---

11 Aristotle may be referring to *Republic* V.462a–b where Socrates explicitly treats unity as the greatest good of the city and designates it as the object at which the legislator should aim in establishing his laws. But he could also have in mind IV.422e–423d where it is certainly implied that unity should be a major goal of legislation.

12 Bornemann, "Aristoteles' Urteil," p. 128; see also Saunders, *Aristotle: the Politics*, pp. 106–7. Although Proclus (*Commentary on the Republic*, ed. Kroll, pp. 362–3) does indeed criticize Aristotle for confusing two senses of unity, the general tendency of his argument is in the opposite direction from that of modern critics. He believes that the state should be a unity and admires Plato for having seen this.

13 *Met.* IV.2.1003b23–1004a2, V.6, X.1–3.1052a15–1054a32.

thought of as a single human being, or as comprising many bodily parts. He is unlikely, therefore, to have made the crude assumption that to unify the state is to turn it into an individual. This is confirmed by his claim that the man is more of a unity than the household, which in turn is more of a unity than the city (1261a20–2, b10–11), as well as by his talk of making the city "too much of a unity" – claims which would not make sense if he meant to contrast the human being as a kind of atomic individual with the household and the city as collections of such individuals. From that point of view, the household – even if it contained only two members – would be as much of a plurality as would the city. There would be no room for more or less. The same point emerges at 5.1263b31–2, where he says that the city, like the household, should be one in some respects, though not in all. The implication is that different kinds of unity are appropriate to different kinds of things. A city for example, cannot be a unity in the same sense as a plant or animal. To show that a social arrangement makes for unity, therefore, is not necessarily to show that it is a good thing. An excess of unity could destroy the essential characteristics which make the city what it is. This, I take it, is the implication of the passage (4.1262b11–13) in which Aristotle refers to the speech of Aristophanes in the *Symposium*. If two things become one by growing into a single organism (*sumphunai*), then one or both must be destroyed. Thus if the city were to become a unity in that sense, the citizens would lose their individual identities.

In the *Metaphysics*, Aristotle distinguishes a number of different senses of "one" and "many" (X.1.1052a15–b1). He starts from the idea that something is one if it is continuous: that is, if its parts are joined together in such a way that one of them cannot move without the others. He then claims that a thing is one in a fuller sense if it has a definite shape or form – especially if it is so by nature, rather than as the result of some sort of constraint. Something which has the cause of its continuity within itself is more of a unity than something held together by glue or string. In this sense, he contrasts a *sumphuton* – something with a single nature – and a *sôros* – a mere pile (*GA* I.8.722b). He uses this idea in at least two different ways. One paradigm of a single being is clearly an organism which has a nature – a *phusis* – that is, an inner principle of movement and growth (*Met.* V.4.1014b16ff.). Another paradigm is the fusion of two quantities of the same material into a single mass. Water and air can be juxtaposed; when water is brought into contact with water, however, the two quantities become one (*Phys.* IV.5.213a9). I suspect both paradigms exert some influence on the present passage.

The point of Aristotle's claim that the man is more of a unity than the household – which itself is more of a unity than the city – is presumably that the man is more closely knit together by nature than the household, and the household more so than the city. This is precisely what we would expect from the contrast he draws elsewhere between the city and the household. Although the city normally has more members than a household, the essential difference between the two lies not in numbers but in the kinds of authority they each involve (I.1.1252a8ff.). The king or the statesman rules over free men while the master of a household rules over the slave: a living tool who lacks a deliberative faculty and belongs to the master in much the same sense that a part belongs to the whole (I.4.1254a8ff., I.5.1254b16ff., I.6.1255b9ff.). Just as there can be no partnership between a part of my body and myself or between a tool and its user, there can be no real partnership between master and slave or between a father and a non-adult son.[14] Where there is no partnership, there is no room for the forms of justice and of friendship that characterize the relationships of fellow-citizens.[15] The household is, therefore, essentially different from the city. It has, as we might say, a single centre of choice and is thus more of a unity – more like a single organism.

At II.2.1261a22, Aristotle argues that the city must not merely consist of a number of people but must also include different kinds of individuals. It is not like an alliance whose components resemble one another in kind, for things that are to become one differ in kind (II.2.1261a29–30). He develops this point with reference to his own doctrine that reciprocal equality holds the state together. The citizens must be able to exchange goods or services with one another, which presupposes some differentiation of roles (*EN* V.6.1134a24ff.; *EE* VII.10.1242b33ff.). Thus even those who belong to a community of free and equal citizens must occupy the roles of ruler and the ruled in turn. Aristotle concludes that "it is not in the nature of a city to be one in the way in which some people say it is and what is said to be the greatest good for cities actually destroys them" (II.2.1261b7–9).

The remark that "things which are to become one differ in kind" (II.2.1261a29–30) shows that Aristotle cannot be using "one" in a purely numerical, atomistic sense, for he acknowledges that the city can be one while having many members of different kinds. The difficulty is to see how this could be an objection to the political proposals of the *Republic*, based as they are on the premise that citizens should be allotted different roles according to their natural aptitudes. Bornemann[16] argues that the passage must be interpreted either as a digression or as a criticism of the claim in *Republic* V.462b–e that citizens ideally should share the same feelings and aspirations. There may be something to both these points. Aristotle's language shows that his argument is not directed primarily at the *Republic* but against any thinker who says that the unity of the state requires the citizens to be alike. On the other hand, he could be arguing that Socrates in the *Republic* commits himself to this view by his claim that the state will be unified when all citizens share the same feelings.

Aristotle has good grounds for opposing such views. As he sees it the friendship (*philia*) that holds the city together (*EN* VIII.1.1155a22–3)

14 *EE* VII.10.1242a10ff.; *MM* I.33.1194b6; see M. Nussbaum, "Shame, Separateness and Political Unity: Aristotle's Criticism of Plato," in *Essays on Aristotle's Ethics*, ed. A. O. Rorty (Berkeley, 1980), pp. 395–435.

15 Aristotle's main discussion of political friendship is in *EN* VIII.9.1159b25ff. See also *EE* VII.10.1242b22ff. Political friendship is based on utility and as such requires that the parties be dissimilar to one another (*EE* VII.2.1235b34).

16 Bornemann, "Aristoteles' Urteil," pp. 119–20.

depends on the citizens having different characteristics, so that they can usefully enter into relationships of exchange with one another. He must therefore object to any understanding of the ideal of unity which would discourage or prevent such relationships by requiring that the characters or personalities of the citizens be assimilated to one another.

Aristotle's final argument against those who seek too much unity in the city rests on the idea of self-sufficiency (II.2.1261b10–15). The household is more self-sufficient than the individual; the city more self-sufficient than the household. Indeed, the city comes into being at the point when the *koinônia tou plêthous* (literally, the community of the multitude or of the plurality) becomes self-sufficient (II.2.1261b13). Thus, if what is more self-sufficient is to be preferred, one should prefer greater plurality.

It is natural here to assume that Aristotle is making a point about numbers. The city must contain a fair number of people to be self-sufficient. But that, of course, is quite irrelevant to the idea that the city should be a unity, for it would be absurd to say that the city should comprise only one human being. On this interpretation, then, Aristotle is either confused or dishonest. But is another reading possible?

The word *plêthos*, which I have just translated as meaning "multitude," is commonly opposed, as it is here, to the one. Aristotle himself defines this contrast not in terms of numbers, but in terms of divisibility (*Met.* X.3.1054a20ff.). The *plêthos* is divisible while the one is indivisible. We should also notice that the present passage recalls *Politics* I.2 which expounds Aristotle's view of the city as the self-sufficient community or association subsuming within itself the lesser associations of the family and the village. Self-sufficiency is partly economic – we need to exchange our products with one another – but this kind of self-sufficiency seems to be secured at the level of the village. The city exists for the good life. It requires its members to share a conception of law and justice and to enter into more complex, non-economic relationships.

For these reasons, I would suggest that when Aristotle argues that the city must be a plurality if it is to be self-sufficient, he does not mean simply that it must contain a number of people, but rather that these people must be distinct from one another. They need to be distinct in order to have the different kinds of relationships with one another that make life worth living. Those who "seek too much unity in the city" (i.e., those who would obliterate the distinctness of the individual citizens) neglect this point. The plurality of the city is precisely what makes it valuable.

There is strong evidence for this interpretation in the later passage (II.5.1263b30ff.) where Aristotle, after discussing the community of property, returns to the idea of unity as an aim of legislation. He argues that the city, like the household, must be one in some respects but not in all. If it becomes too much of a unity, it will be like a harmony that is destroyed by being turned into a unison, or a rhythm that is turned into a single foot. The city is a plurality which should be formed into a single community by education. Obviously Aristotle is not objecting to attempts to unify the city as such, but only to attempts to unify it in the wrong kind of way. The city is like music or poetry: its beauty depends on the existence of diversity within the unity of the work as a whole. The right kind of unity can be achieved by education and other forms of legislation, such as the common meals of the Cretans and Spartans, but the measures proposed by Socrates in the *Republic* would wreck the city by obliterating all differentiation within it.[17]

I would not claim that Aristotle's arguments on unity are easy to follow. The main problem is the lack of clarity about what he is attacking. His sights seem to be set on anyone who argues that the state should be a unity in a way which would play down or deny the distinctness of individual citizens. This is what one would expect, given Aristotle's ethical views as a whole. Human good consists in virtuous activity (*EN* I.7.1098a16–17). Activity involves choice, and one's choices must be founded on one's own conception of the good.[18] In the *Republic*, Plato suggests that the majority of citizens lack the reasoning powers to make such choices. They are dependent on the reason of the guardians. The dialogue, as a whole, may thus be taken to play down or even deny the importance of individual choice.[19] This aspect of Plato's thought is expressed most clearly when Socrates, in the passage at V.462ff. cited above, argues that the city's greatest good is unity and this will be achieved, he argues, when the citizenry resembles a single man as closely as possible and shares the same feelings and attitudes. There is a clear implication here that the distinctness of the citizens should be eroded. Aristotle has good reason for objecting to this; on his view the community that constitutes the city is valuable precisely because it is a community of distinct individuals.

3   THE COMMUNITY OF WOMEN AND CHILDREN

Between 3.1261b16 and 4.1262b36, Aristotle argues that the kind of community envisaged in the *Republic* would not in fact make for the unity of the city and would involve other practical difficulties. He begins by suggesting that there is an ambiguity in Socrates' claim that the city will have achieved unity when all its members use the terms "mine" and "not mine" for the

17 See W. L. Newman, *The Politics of Aristotle* (Oxford, 1887–92), vol. II, p. 230.
18 See *EN* II.6.1106b36, III.2.1111b26–9, III.4.1113a22–4. These passages imply that to live well an agent must exercise choice and that choice must be directed to something the agent conceives to be good. It is a matter of controversy whether Aristotle thinks each person must have an overall conception of the good. On this point see *EN* I.2.1094a18–22; W. F. R. Hardie, *Aristotle's Ethical Theory* (Oxford, 1968), ch. 2; J. Ackrill, "Aristotle on Eudaimonia," in Rorty, *Essays on Aristotle's Ethics*, pp. 15–34. I take *EE* I.1.1214b7–11 to imply that a rational human being should form a coherent overall conception of the good. Some such view seems to be implicit in the view adopted in the *Politics* of the state as an association for the sake of the good (I.1.1252a1–6).
19 This point is made most clearly at IX.590c; see Nussbaum, "Shame, Separateness and Political Unity," pp. 407–10.

same things. The point here seems to be that, in most circumstances, someone who calls a thing "mine" implies that it belongs to him and no one else. The word has, one might say, an exclusive sense. But if everyone calls the same thing "mine," they must be using the term in a collective sense so that "mine" means not "belonging to me alone" but "belonging to me along with many others." This verbal point is by no means trivial. Aristotle believes that the attitudes and feelings we attach to things seen as uniquely ours are different from our attitudes and feelings to things we share with others. Thus, the fact that members of a community call the same things "mine" is not a sign of any special unity among them.

This point is reinforced by some of Aristotle's other arguments. He claims (3.1261b33–1262a14) that people pay less attention to things held in common than to things private to them. Thus if a citizen has a thousand sons, each of whom belongs equally to him and to every other citizen, he will not care particularly for any of them. We do better, Aristotle claims, with the present system where one person will be son to one man, brother to another, and nephew to someone else. Other members of the community will look on him as a kinsman or fellow tribesman. It is preferable to be a nephew under this system rather than a "son" under that of the *Republic*. In practice, then, Socrates' proposals will have the opposite effect from those intended. They will weaken the bonds of friendship and create disunity. They would be more appropriate for a class kept in subjection than for rulers. *Philia* (friendship or mutual affection) not only prevents revolution but also, as Socrates fully recognizes, makes for unity. But the proposals of the *Republic* would dilute this feeling and produce merely a "watery" friendship. In such a community, there would be little incentive to care for someone as a son or a father since the motives which lead people to care for one another – the sense that something is one's own and the corresponding feeling of pleasure in it – will be lacking.

Aristotle also introduces a number of more practical objections to the abolition of the family. People will inevitably suppose that individuals who display similarities with one another are closely related (3.1262a14–24). There will be a danger of assaults on parents as well as of incestuous relationships (4.1262a25–40). Such problems will become more serious when we take into account the fact that some individuals will be transferred from one class to the other (4.1262b29–35).

Aristotle's arguments have been praised as a definitive refutation of utopian communism, but they have also found their detractors.[20] Their basic complaint is that Aristotle counters Plato's idealism with purely empirical objections. It is irrelevant, they say, to point out that men as they now are would not be better disposed to one another were the family abolished; after all they have not had the education and environment of Plato's guardians.

One could defend Aristotle here by pointing out that, at least in *Republic* V.461–6, there is no indication that the benefits of the abolition of the family

20 Contrast Susemihl–Hicks, *The Politics of Aristotle*, pp. 31–2, and Bornemann, "Aristoteles' Urteil," pp. 132–41.

depend on the satisfaction of other conditions. The implication is that it will in itself promote unity by making the citizens feel as one. But a more fundamental point emerges when this section is read in conjunction with the discussions of *philia* – friendship – to be found in both versions of the *Ethics*. As Aristotle sees it, friendship is an essential ingredient in the good life, not just because it is useful but because it is the source of some of our greatest satisfactions.[21] The friend may even be called "another self" (*EN* IX.9. 1170b6–7; *EE* VII.12.1245a30–31). Friendship also has a political dimension. It is both what holds the city together and a main reason for its existence. The city is formed for the good life, which – as we have seen – requires relations with one's fellows. It involves "parents, children, wife and in general one's friends and fellow-citizens" (*EN* I.7.1097b8–11). Thus the city is to be valued as providing the context for friendship.

Plato would, of course, acknowledge the importance of friendship – that is indeed the whole purpose of the abolition of the family – but, at least in the *Republic*, he differs from Aristotle on two quite essential points. (1) He treats friendship as a means of preserving the state rather than the state as a means of preserving friendship. (2) He pays little attention to the fact that, since friendship is essentially a relationship between individuals, the number of one's friends is necessarily limited. Aristotle, by contrast, explicitly recognizes this point. He argues that in the truest sense of friendship (friendship for the sake of the good), one cannot have a great many friends. The reason for this is that friends must spend time in each other's company, must have strong feeling towards each other, and must be aware of each other. One cannot be in this state with respect to a large number of people.[22] The impossibility here could not be rectified by education or social change. As finite beings, we can be in the company of and attend to only a limited number of our fellow men. It follows that only in a secondary sense can we enjoy friendship with a large number of people.[23] For this reason, Aristotle attaches importance not only to the family but also to other forms of social organization within the state. These enhance rather than diminish the unity of the whole – a point Plato himself accepts in the *Laws*.[24]

---

21 *EN* VIII.1.1155a1–9; IX.9.1169b3–1170b19; *EE* VII.12.1244b1–1245b19.
22 *EN* VIII.6.1158a10; *EE* VII.12.1245b19; see also *EN* VIII.3.1156b25ff.; IX.10. 1170b20ff.; *EE* VII.2.1236a14–15, 1237a30–2, b35, 1238a9.
23 This is I think the weak point in Saunders' attempt (*Aristotle: the Politics*, pp. 106–7) to defend Plato by pointing out that Christians (and others) have supported the ideal that all men should regard each other as brothers. They have not, in general, taken this to require the abolition of the family or other social groups. (If anything they have taken the opposite view.) They have thus recognized that the idea that we are all one family cannot be taken literally.
24 See my *Introduction to Plato's Laws* (Oxford, 1983), pp. 103–4.

4   COMMUNITY OF PROPERTY

Much of what has been said about Aristotle's comments on the proposals for the abolition of the family would apply equally to the comments in 5.1262b37–1263b29 on the abolition of private property, though the order of exposition is reversed. Aristotle first argues that the community of possessions would not make for unity and would have other disadvantages, and then that, here too, Socrates has gone wrong through an ill-considered emphasis on unity as the goal of legislation.

The first part of this section (5.1262b37–1263a39) is concerned with the ownership and use of agricultural land. Aristotle distinguishes three possibilities: (1) ownership and use may both be common, (2) ownership may be common but the produce may be distributed for private use, or (3) ownership may be private but the produce pooled for common use. He argues that common ownership will create particular problems if the proprietors work the land themselves, since there will then be disputes between those who take a lot but have worked little and those who take little but have worked a lot. He recognizes that this problem will not arise when the land is not actually worked by those who share the ownership. Aristotle's own preference is for a modification of the present system (i.e., of a system of private property) by good customs and legislation. If property is private, there will be fewer disputes and people will apply themselves more to its care. But they should put their possessions at their friends' disposal and should use it as though it were common. Aristotle thinks that this is pretty well what happens in Sparta.

Most of the points made in this discussion have no direct bearing on the *Republic*. In Socrates' ideal state, the guardians and auxiliaries do not own land whereas the members of the third class seem to have their own farms paying a contribution from the proceeds to support the guardians and auxiliaries. Thus the *Republic* cannot be said to advocate common ownership as Aristotle understands it in this passage. Indeed, the passage has so little to do with the *Republic* that it seems unlikely to have been written with that dialogue in mind. It is difficult to resist the impression that a piece originally intended as part of a general discussion of property in land has been incorporated into the criticisms of the *Republic* without much regard to its relevance in that context.[25]

The lines that follow (5.1263a40–b29) contain a number of points about the desirability of private property which could have some application to the

---

25 Several commentators have noted that this passage seems to have little relevance to the *Republic*. See, for example, Bornemann, "Aristoteles' Urteil," p. 142. It is notable, too, that the opening sentences of the chapter (5.1262b37–9) suggest that Aristotle is embarking on an entirely general discussion of the question how property ought to be held in an ideal state. On the manner in which this part of the *Politics* is composed see the last paragraph of section 1 above. Chapter 5 is particularly disjointed.

Republic, though there is no direct reference to any of that dialogue's specific proposals.[26] Aristotle argues that we are by nature so constituted as to feel great pleasure in thinking of something as our own. Self-love is part of our nature and cannot therefore have been given us in vain. It is to be distinguished from selfishness which is an excess of self-love. Thus Aristotle implies, not merely that we do as a matter of fact love ourselves, but that we cannot flourish unless self-love is given some scope. We also derive great satisfaction from bestowing favours on friends, guests or associates and from helping them. This would be impossible without private property. Aristotle argues in addition that "those who seek too much unity in the state" would necessarily abolish two virtues – self-restraint with regard to women and liberality. In general "this kind of legislation" (presumably Aristotle means legislation designed to produce a community of property) seems attractive in that it purports to promote a marvellous friendship among all members of the community. This attractiveness seems all the greater if someone attacks present evils such as lawsuits about contracts, trials for false witness, sycophancy and the like; but Aristotle denies that these evils stem from private property. Common ownership, he thinks, gives rise to more disputes. And it is important to remember the good things which such a system would take from us as well as the bad.

Aristotle's objections to common ownership rest partly on experience. He believes that living together and sharing with one another is in general difficult. This is shown by the disputes that arise over trivial matters among fellow travellers and by the tendency people have to get most annoyed at servants with whom they are in continual contact during their daily lives (1263a17–21). But this is not the only kind of argument Aristotle employs. He suggests that self-love and the joy of possession are part of human nature. From this it follows that we cannot flourish unless some scope is given for these tendencies. Active friendship also requires some personal property so that we may do good to our friends. In the *Ethics* he argues that there is a particular pleasure in being a benefactor and that benefactors love those they have helped in much the same way that we love what we have ourselves produced (*EN* IX.7.1167b16ff., *EE* VII.8.1241a35ff.). In helping our friends we, as it were, extend our own personalities. This helps us to understand Aristotle's complaint that those who abolish private property would thereby abolish the virtue of liberality. Bornemann (following Schlosser) claims that

26 At 5.1263b7–8 Aristotle refers to "those who seek too much unity in the state"; at 1263b15 he talks about "this kind of legislation." Both references suggest he has other targets in mind besides the *Republic*. At 5.1263b18–22 Aristotle describes various evils which it is claimed would be prevented if property was common. There may be a reference here to *Rep.* 5.464c–465d but the differences between the evils Aristotle mentions and those described by the Platonic Socrates are such that this is by no means certain. The explanation of Socrates' "mistake" (*parakrousis*) in 5.1263b29 seems to refer to something discussed in the immediately preceding lines but Aristotle does not say precisely what this is. His arguments thus seem to be directed, not so much against the *Republic*, as against the general idea that it would be good for property to be held in common.

one can show liberality as much in voluntarily renouncing property as in its use.[27] Even if we leave on one side the question whether a Platonic guardian could be said voluntarily to have renounced property, this still misses the point. For Aristotle active friendship is part of human well-being. We therefore need private property, in order that we may bestow benefits on our friends. Although both Plato and Aristotle cite more than once the maxim that "the possessions of friends are common property" they understand it in diametrically opposed senses.[28] Plato seems to think that having property in common makes us friends and therefore wishes to abolish private property. Aristotle's view is that friendship consists in part in the free bestowal of one's goods upon another. Private property is thus a prerequisite of friendship rather than an obstacle to it.

Aristotle's remarks about temperance in relation to women seem, on the surface at least, more difficult to defend. Plato expects his guardians to exercise a high degree of self-restraint, so the passage not only looks odd in a discussion of property but also, assuming that it is really directed at Plato, seems to miss the point. There is, however, a way in which one can make good sense of this comment. Aristotle is here arguing that we derive great satisfaction from helping friends, guests and associates. In this context he emphasizes the value of liberality and self-restraint with respect for women, because, he says, "it is a fine thing to abstain from a woman, through temperance, because she belongs to someone else" (5.1263b10–11). The belonging to someone else seems to be the important point here. Aristotle sees abstinence from adultery with a woman as a way of showing respect presumably to her husband. To our way of thinking this sounds odd, but it reinforces Aristotle's general point that a sense of the self is important and that friendship requires recognition of others as selves in this sense. This, in turn, requires that we have the scope for exercise of our selfhood which is given us by marriage and property.

5   HAPPINESS AND COMMUNITY

From 5.1264a1 or thereabouts the focus of Aristotle's argument becomes less clear. He first asserts that, given the immense length of human history, the institutions of the *Republic* would already have been known if they were really any good (1264a1ff.) and then claims that if an attempt was made to introduce the Platonic state it would have to be divided into common messes, brotherhoods, and tribes, so that the only principle to be enacted would be that the guardians should abstain from agriculture. He next argues at some length that, since Socrates has not dealt adequately with the farmer class, he has left the workings of his state unclear. It is dangerous, too, that the same

27 Bornemann, "Aristoteles' Urteil," pp. 143–4, citing J. G. Schlosser, *Aristoteles Politik* (Leipzig, 1798), p. 109.
28 *Rep.* IV.424a; *Laws* V.739b; *EN* VIII.9.1159b31, IX.8.1168b7–8.

people should rule all the time. These arguments have little, if any, bearing on the concept of community which has dominated Aristotle's discussion up to this point. In so far as they have any common theme it is that Plato has not thought through the practical implications of his proposals.

Aristotle's final argument is in many ways more interesting. At 5.1264b16 he accuses Socrates of depriving the guardians of happiness while insisting on the happiness of the city as a whole. This he takes to be absurd since the city cannot be happy unless each of its parts is happy. Being happy is not a characteristic like that of being an even number – it cannot belong to a whole without belonging to its parts.

Presumably Aristotle is here referring to *Republic* IV.419a–421c where Socrates considers the objection that he has not made his guardians particularly happy, but he could also be thinking of V.465e–466a where Socrates recalls the earlier point. Either way Aristotle seems to have misinterpreted the *Republic*. Socrates' answer to the objection is that he has sought the happiness of the whole city, not just of one class. He does not say that a city could be happy without the majority of its citizens being happy or that the happiness of the city is distinct from that of its members.[29] Aristotle's misreading is, nevertheless, understandable. Socrates' main concern has been to assure the strength and cohesion of the city. Since a strong and peaceful city need not necessarily have happy citizens, it might seem that he distinguishes its happiness from theirs. The simile he uses to illustrate his argument adds to the confusion. He claims that when painting a statue we would not necessarily put the most beautiful colour (purple) on the most beautiful part (the eyes). His point is that the guardians must not be given a form of happiness which would prevent them fulfilling their role, just as we do not give the eyes a colour which prevents them being eyes. But since the parts of a beautiful statue need not be individually beautiful, the simile could suggest that a happy city need not have happy citizens.

If the arguments of my last paragraph are correct, both Aristotle and Plato could agree that a city is happy if and only if its citizens are happy, but they would understand this claim in quite different senses. According to Aristotle the object of the partnership which is a city is the good life, that is, a life of virtuous activity. Thus, as is clear from the early chapters of *Politics* VII, Aristotle's ideal state is one that gives scope for this kind of activity. Activity

29 Aristotle's view, or something like it, has been accepted by many commentators on the *Republic*. See, for example, G. Grote, *Plato and the Other Companions of Socrates* (London, 1888), vol. IV, p. 139. Surprisingly Sir Karl Popper does not discuss *Rep.* IV.419a–421c, though he seems to endorse the view that Plato saw the happiness of the state as something over and above the happiness of the citizens – see *The Open Society and its Enemies*, 5th edn (London, 1966), pp. 76, 79, 169. This view has been powerfully criticized by G. Vlastos, "The Theory of Social Justice in the Polis in Plato's *Republic*," in *Interpretations of Plato*, ed. H. North (Leiden, 1977), pp. 1–40 (especially pp. 15–19). See also J. Neu "Plato's Analogy of State and Individual," *Philosophy*, 46 (1971), pp. 238–54; C. C. W. Taylor, "Plato's Totalitarianism," *Polis*, 2 (1986), pp. 4–29, especially pp. 15–16.

involves choice, so the citizens must be able to make their own decisions. This, it can plausibly be argued, requires private property and relations with others as individuals. Plato, of course, also believes that happiness requires virtue but emphasizes *being* virtuous – that is, having a harmonious soul – rather than *acting* virtuously.[30] Moreover he assumes too easily that virtue in this sense is identical with the qualities required for the good of the city – that is, for its survival in peace and security.[31] His theory thus lacks the Aristotelian emphasis on individual activity.[32]

These different conceptions of human good underlie the two philosophers' accounts of political community. Both Aristotle and the Plato of the *Republic* would agree that a city cannot exist unless the citizens have something in common. Since Plato lays little stress on individual activity, he can entertain the idea that everything should ideally be common. Aristotle's position is quite different. We need the city not just to provide the means of survival but also because our relations with others are essential to the good life. This is why the ideas of justice and of friendship are so prominent in the *Ethics*. Because our well-being depends on our relations with others we are political animals, that is, we need to live in a community. This means that we have to share conceptions of law and virtue and to partake in common political institutions. These require some public property. But if private property were to be abolished altogether, and if the family and other narrower social groups went with it, then the very kinds of activity which constitute the raison d'etre of the city would be abolished with them. In this way Aristotle's conception of the good life dictates his account of *koinônia politikê*.

It is, or used to be, commonplace to contrast the empirical and practically minded philosophy of Aristotle with the idealism of Plato. Bornemann goes so far as to speak of an enormous gulf separating the thought of Plato, which in its idealism reaches for the heavens, and the Aristotelian ethic which clings tenaciously to earthly things.[33] This mundane approach prevents Aristotle from ever coming to grips with Plato's ways of thought.[34] Without putting the point so strongly or so tendentiously we can concede that Aristotle is more interested than Plato in the empirical and practical side of political theory. Ostensibly, at least, in *Politics* II he draws on the experience of different cities and on the theories of earlier thinkers in order to find ideas

30 See especially *Rep.* IV.443c–444a, IX.588b–591d. In these passages Plato depicts justice as concerned with the inner self, not with external actions. He sees a just act as one which tends to create the right condition of the soul.

31 This is, I think, most apparent in the *Republic* at 519e–520a, where Socrates seems to assume that binding the city together will make the whole happy. The same tendency is evident in the *Laws*. See Stalley, *An Introduction to Plato's Laws*, pp. 37–40.

32 Nussbaum argues that the different attitudes to the individual which underlie the political philosophies of Plato and Aristotle are, in their turn, based on deeper differences about human nature and its needs ("Shame, Separateness and Political Unity," pp. 422–3). See also Newman, *The Politics of Aristotle*, p. 263.

33 "Aristoteles' Urteil," p. 143.

34 Ibid., p. 158.

which could be adopted in his own best city. In following this plan one of his major concerns is that the institutions proposed should actually work. Thus, as we have seen, his criticisms of the *Republic* are sometimes of a purely practical nature. I have said little about these points, though I find most of Aristotle's practical arguments plausible. The real question, of course, is whether this kind of criticism is appropriate. Whatever Plato's purpose in writing the *Republic* it cannot be regarded as a set of proposals for application in the short term. Thus to treat it as a textbook for constitution makers is surely to miss its point.

This argument is, I think, correct; but it does not follow that Aristotle's discussion of the *Republic* is valueless or irrelevant. Although some of his objections are purely empirical or practical, the main line of his argument works at a more abstract and theoretical level. He uses the *Republic* section of *Politics* II as an excuse to discuss the suggestion that in the ideal political community everything possible would be held in common. In arguing against this idea he does appeal to experience, but his claim is not simply that a system which has not been tried or has not worked in the past cannot be expected to work in future. Experience is valuable because it is a guide to human nature; and an understanding of human nature, in turn, enables us to see what kind of a life is truly good. Aristotle's fundamental objection to the ideal of political community he finds in the *Republic* is that it is contrary to nature. Thus even if it could be realized in ideal conditions, it would frustrate, rather than promote, the well-being of the citizens.

9

Aristotle's Defense of Private Property

T. H. IRWIN

1 ARISTOTLE'S OBJECTIONS TO PLATO[1]

In the course of discussing Plato's legislation about private property in the *Republic*, Aristotle recognizes that this legislation may well appeal to our moral sentiments:

> This sort of legislation admittedly looks attractive,[2] and might seem to display love of humanity (*philanthrôpos an einai doxeien*). For the hearer accepts it gladly, supposing that there will be some wonderful sort of friendship of all towards all, especially when someone condemns the present evils in political systems, claiming that they come about because property is not held in common – I mean legal actions about contracts, convictions for giving false evidence, and flattery of rich people. (*Politics* II.5.1263b15–22)

Aristotle believes, however, that we should not be deceived by the attractive appearance of this legislation. First, he argues that the abolition of private property is a more drastic means than is necessary.[3] Commenting on the evils that Plato seeks to remove, he says:

> In fact these come about not because people do not hold property in common, but because they are vicious. For in fact we see that those who have acquired

---

1 This paper is derived from "Generosity and Property in Aristotle's *Politics*," *Social Philosophy and Policy*, 4 (1987), pp. 37–54. It includes material from a paper delivered to the XIth Symposium Aristotelicum in August 1987; part of that paper will appear as "The Good of Political Activity" in the Proceedings of the Symposium (ed. G. Patzig). In some places it also overlaps with *Aristotle's First Principles* (Oxford, 1988). I have especially benefited from criticisms by Gisela Striker and Richard Kraut, and by the editors of this volume. Unless otherwise indicated, references to Aristotle are to the *Politics* and references to Plato are to the *Republic*. Translations from the Greek are by the author.

2 I understand *esti* with *euprosôpos* and take *an einai doxeien* only with *philanthrôpos*. Alternatively, it might be taken with both adjectives.

3 Plato actually abolishes private property and the nuclear family only for the guardian class. I will not keep mentioning this restriction.

and hold possessions in common actually have far more disputes with each other than those with separate property have. . . . Further, it is only fair to mention not only the evils that they will be rid of by common property, but also the goods they will be deprived of. And in fact their life appears to be altogether impossible. (II.5.1263b22–9)

Aristotle argues that the bad results of private property can be removed without removing private property, whereas its good results cannot be secured without private property. Hence Plato offers us a bad bargain. In his own ideal state Aristotle retains private property, but prescribes the common use that allows the benefits of common ownership without abolishing private property (VII.10.1329b41–1330a2).

A major benefit of private property is the opportunity it provides for generosity; for Aristotle claims that generosity has its function (*ergon*) in the use of possessions (II.5.1263b13–14). Without private property citizens have no private resources they can use in generous actions; they are deprived of any initiative that is independent of the coercive authority of the state. The arrangement Aristotle prefers is private ownership and common use, relying on the generosity of individual owners. He defends his preference against Plato as follows:

Indeed such arrangements are already present in sketchy form in some cities, on the assumption that they are not impossible, and especially in the cities that are finely governed some of them exist and some might easily exist; a person has his own private possessions of which he makes some available for his friends' use and keeps some for his private use. In Sparta, for instance, they have practically common use of each other's slaves, and also of dogs and horses and of the fields in the country, if they need provisions on a journey. Evidently, then, it is better for the possessions to be private but to make them common by the way they are used; and it is the special task of the legislator to see that people of the right sort to do this develop. (1) Further, counting something as our private property enormously increases our pleasure. For one's love towards oneself is certainly not pointless, but is a natural tendency. Certainly, selfishness is justifiably criticized; but selfishness is not loving oneself, but loving oneself more than is right – just as greed [is not love of money, but love of it more than is right], since practically everyone has some love of such things. (2) Moreover, doing favours or giving aid to one's friends or guests (*xenoi*) or companions is most pleasant; and one can do this if possession is private. None of these things, then, results for those who make the city excessively unified. (3) And besides they evidently abolish any function for two of the virtues – for temperance (since it is a fine action to leave a woman alone because of temperance when she belongs to someone else), and for generosity with possessions; for no one's generosity will be evident and no one will do any generous action, since the function of generosity is in the use of possessions. (II.5.1263a30–b14)[4]

4 In II.5.1263a35–6 I follow H. Richards in reversing the ms. order of *koinois* and *idiois*. His suggestion is mentioned, but not endorsed, in the apparatus of the Oxford Classical Text.

The argument about generosity shows that Aristotle is not merely raising a practical objection to Plato's arrangements. Since Plato makes the exercise of the moral virtues impossible, the arrangements he proposes are morally worse than private property would be.

I would like to examine the merits of Aristotle's criticisms of Plato's abolition of private property. Before I do that, however, I want to show how these criticisms illustrate one of Aristotle's broader objections to Plato; for the broader objection may be sound, or at least worth attention, even if we find some particular examples unconvincing. In claiming that Plato makes the exercise of generosity impossible, Aristotle cites one instance of what he takes to be a general failure in the *Republic* – that it fails to consider the kinds of activities that are appropriately pursued for their own sake in an ideal political community.

2   A BASIC DISAGREEMENT

Aristotle's broad objection to Plato is most easily seen in his comments on the first city described in the *Republic*, the "city of pigs." Aristotle thinks that the description reflects Plato's failure to ask the right questions:

> For the city is self-sufficient, and lack of self-sufficiency is characteristic of a slave. Hence the account in the *Republic* of these matters is inadequate, though ingenious. For Socrates says that the city is composed of the four most necessary people, whom he takes to be a weaver, a farmer, a cobbler, and a builder; but later, assuming that these are not self-sufficient, he adds a smith, herdsmen for the necessary herds, and in addition a wholesale and a retail trader. And these turn out to complete the first city, since it is assumed that every city is constituted for the sake of necessities, and not for the sake of the fine more than them, and that it has no less need of cobblers than of farmers. (IV.4.1291a10–19)

In Aristotle's view, Plato does not include all the parts that belong to a proper city; and the basis of this criticism is quite instructive.

Plato and he begin from quite similar questions. In the context Aristotle discusses the components of a self-sufficient city. Similarly, Plato argues that we need a city because individuals are not self-sufficient (*autarkês*) by themselves (*Rep*. II.369b5–7). Aristotle of course agrees that we have reason to form cities in pursuit of a complete and self-sufficient life (III.1.1275b20–21); but he includes more in self-sufficiency than Plato evidently includes in his rather casual reference to it. In Aristotle's view – derived from a different Platonic context (*Phlb*. 20d–22b) – happiness must be complete and self-sufficient, so that "by itself it makes life choiceworthy and lacking in nothing" (*EN* I.7.1097b14–15). The polis counts as the complete community only in so far as it achieves the complete and self-sufficient life. This "eudaimonic" self-sufficiency demands more than the economic self-sufficiency that makes the state independent of imports of goods or services from elsewhere. Aristotle approves of economic self-sufficiency (VII.4. 1326b26–30); and no doubt Plato has it in mind in the construction of the city of pigs. But for Aristotle it is strictly secondary to, and derivative from, eudaimonic self-sufficiency; and planning for a complete and self-sufficient polis has to take eudaimonic self-sufficiency into account.

If the two types of self-sufficiency conflict – so that a polis cannot supply all the goods and services needed for happiness without importing some of them – then economic self-sufficiency would have to be abandoned in favour of the prior demands of eudaimonic self-sufficiency. This is Aristotle's argument about the happiness of the individual in the *Ethics*; because individuals cannot ensure their own happiness from their own resources, they have to become more dependent on other people to secure a more self-sufficient life for themselves. Aristotle does not point out clearly that a state may face the same choice; but his theory obliges him to resolve it in the same way. Indeed, he effectively abandons economic self-sufficiency for the ideal state of the *Politics*; for the external goods required for happiness (allegedly) make it necessary for citizens to rely on the labour of non-citizens for the supply of these goods.

We could state Aristotle's criticism of the city of pigs by saying that Plato considers only the secondary, economic, aspects of self-sufficiency, to the exclusion of the primary, eudaimonic, aspects. The criticism would be relatively uninteresting if Aristotle simply meant that Plato had not included the right economic functions to secure economic self-sufficiency. But he plainly also rejects Plato's view of the functions that are sufficient for the "most necessary city" (II.369d11–12). Plato takes the ground for the city to be our need (*chreia*, 369c10); and the most necessary city contains the minimum that is sufficient for satisfying our needs. But Plato construes the relevant needs as those that must be satisfied for us to stay alive in barely tolerable conditions (compare *tou einai te kai zên heneka*, 369d2). In this construal of relevant needs he wrongly, in Aristotle's view, supposes that the city is for the sake of merely staying alive rather than of living well; or, as Aristotle puts it, he confuses an end for which the city comes into being with the end for which it remains in being (I.2.1252b27–30, III.6.1278b17–30, III.9.1280a31–6).

Aristotle argues that Plato neglects "the fine," which is the proper end of the city (IV.4.1291a17–18); and he sees this neglect in the omission of any military, judicial, or deliberative elements in the original city (IV.4.1291a19–24). We might suppose that these are just further necessary services besides those that Plato includes. But this is not Aristotle's point; he thinks they are more than merely necessary. Just as an animal's soul is part of it more than its body is, so these further elements are parts of a city more then the elements providing necessities are (IV.4.1291a24–8). Aristotle implies that these functions do not simply provide necessities for the state; they must be parts of the end for the sake of which the state remains in being, and they must include the different types of fine action that the city pursues.

3   THE FIRST CITY IN THE REPUBLIC

It might well seem unfair of Aristotle to examine the city of pigs apart from its place in the developing argument of the *Republic*. For Plato does not in the end neglect those aspects of the city that are absent from the city of pigs. Indeed, he introduces them quite soon, in the account of the "swollen and luxurious" city. But his treatment of the swollen city does not really meet Aristotle's criticisms.

Plato's intentions are quite puzzling. Socrates insists that the city of pigs is the "genuine" and "healthy" city (II.372e6), and describes the rustic pleasures of the members of this city with apparent satisfaction (372a5–d3). Still, he does not protest vigorously when Glaucon suggests that this life is fit for pigs rather than human beings (372d4–5). He notes that Glaucon's protest requires them to consider a swollen and luxurious city for which the resources provided by the first city will no longer be adequate; and he acknowledges that this is the city they should look at if they want to see how justice and injustice arise in cities (372e2–6). The people in the swollen city want more than the necessities of mere life, and on this point Aristotle agrees with them. It is not clear what Socrates thinks; he refrains from saying that the swollen city is worse than the first city, or that the people in it are worse off, less happy; on the other hand, he does say that the first city is the genuine and healthy city.

The most important point for Aristotle's purposes is the role of justice and injustice in the swollen city. Socrates does not actually say that only a swollen city displays justice; he might mean that we can see both justice and injustice in a swollen city, but only justice in the first city. Nor, however, does he claim that the members of the first city are just; and he has a good reason for not claiming this, since their placidly rustic life does not seem likely to give much exercise to the rational part of the soul at all. At any rate, the active and deliberate exercise of the virtues seems to require a swollen state. If Plato means this, he ascribes a remedial function to justice. When we demand more than the conditions of mere life, we demand some degree of luxury; this demand produces a higher and more insistent demand for goods and services that are in limited supply – the "contested" goods (see IX.586a–c); the demand for these contested goods results in greedy and grasping attitudes (*pleonexia*), and justice corrects these. A city needs a political life, and needs the moral virtues to go with it, because otherwise its non-political life will go badly wrong.

To this extent Socrates seems to endorse something fairly close to Hume's view that when goods are in plentiful supply there is no place for justice.[5] In the city of pigs people are not exactly more just than in the swollen city; but they are less unjust, since their modest desires are easily satisfied from the

5 See Hume, *Inquiry concerning the Principles of Morals*, III, pp. 183ff., ed. L. A. Selby–Bigge (Oxford, 1902).

available goods and they have no motive for aggression on their neighbours. Justice and political life have a point once we have some strong temptation to injustice, and therefore need something to correct and restrain it.

Perhaps it is not clear how seriously Plato actually intends these suggestions about the role and point of justice and political life. But for one crucial move in the *Republic* they have to be taken very seriously. In the first city specialization and division of labour are advocated on instrumental grounds, as the most efficient way to satisfy the basic needs that explain the formation of the first city. In the swollen city Socrates takes it for granted that the same principle of specialization works for the defense of the city, and therefore justifies a specialized military class (II.374a–d). It takes quite some time before it is clear that a subclass of this military class is also the ruling class; and we are still supposed to take it for granted that the principle of specialization applies (III.412b–d).

As the *Republic* proceeds, Plato adds further arguments to show that there is such a thing as specialized moral and political knowledge, and that it is hard to acquire, so that a specially selected group is needed to acquire it. But the conclusion that the people with the moral and political knowledge should be absolute rulers relies on the same old principle of specialization that was introduced in the city of pigs; and since that was a principle defended on grounds of efficiency, the rest of the argument assumes that questions about the distribution of political power are also simply questions of efficiency. The education of the guardian class, and later of the philosopher-rulers, is designed to make sure that they apply their specialized knowledge, without the distorting influence of selfish or ignorant desires, for the benefit of the whole state; and such a defense assumes that this is all we can reasonably ask.

Plato, therefore, relies on an assumption he never defends, that questions about who should rule and how they should rule are strictly questions of instrumental efficiency in reaching some independently identified end. It is clear how these considerations are meant to support specialization in the first city, and he relies on them throughout the argument. In postponing the introduction of justice, he suggests that its role is strictly instrumental.

4   LATER DEVELOPMENTS IN THE REPUBLIC

On the other hand, it is hard to believe that Plato entirely accepts his initial assumption. In suggesting that the first city is a city of pigs, Glaucon implies that it does not include the activities that are central parts of a human being's good. Nor does the swollen city add these parts of the human good simply by assuming expanded appetites and the conflicts that make justice necessary. Plato even focusses our attention on this defect in his argument. For Adeimantus interrupts to complain that the guardians do not seem especially happy, on a common conception that identifies happiness with material resources and the sensual pleasure that they secure (IV.419a); and Socrates admits that this is so. The conception of happiness is the same as the one that is assumed in the swollen city, which is simply an elaborate version of the conception in the city of pigs.

Plainly Plato rejects this conception. Socrates warns Adeimantus that the common conception of happiness may not be a reliable measure of a guardian's happiness (IV.420b), and later he argues that the guardians are in fact the happiest of all the citizens (V.465d–466c). Between Socrates' initial doubt about the common conception of happiness and his later claim that the guardians are happiest we have read the account of the virtues. This account claims that the virtues are to be valued for their own sakes, as health is (IV.445ab), not simply as the best policy for securing other goods. The guardians, being just people, do not regard their just actions as means to securing the goods pursued by the other citizens; they regard them as a higher order of goods altogether. Plato thinks we can see why they are right, even before we see the benefits of philosophy; and his account of the virtues suggests the sort of argument that he has in mind.

It is perhaps strange that this aspect of Plato's moral argument is very imperfectly applied to his political argument. For he never retracts the suggestion that questions about who should rule are simply questions about efficiency; but he ought at least to reconsider that suggestion. For if Plato wants to revise the common conception of happiness, he ought also to reconsider the assumption that the only goods to be considered in deciding who should rule are the goods recognized in the city of pigs and the swollen city. If it turns out, in the light of Plato's revised conception of happiness, that ruling and deliberating are themselves intrinsic goods, then questions about ruling involve the distribution of intrinsic goods, not simply of instrumental goods. But Plato never acknowledges that this further question arises; and he never reconsiders the contribution of the city to happiness in the light of his revised conception of happiness.

Why does Plato not mention any of this? Two aspects of the *Republic* may make the issue less clear to him.

First, Socrates argues that though philosophers must be rulers, they will find ruling rather a burden, and will approach it as something necessary, rather than something fine (VII.519d4–7, 520e1–3, 540b2–5). Plato's exact point here is a matter of controversy, and we might well suppose that he actually denies that ruling is an intrinsic good for the philosopher rulers. I do not think we should suppose this. Though the actual task of administration may involve necessary but burdensome activities, it might still be true that political activity itself is to be valued for its own sake. It is not unusual to find that an intrinsically good activity can be carried on only through a disagreeable and burdensome task (compare *EN* X.7.1177b6–20). Plato's remark, then, is consistent with belief in the intrinsic value of political activity. Still, it is possible that his emphasis on the purely instrumental aspects of ruling obscures his awareness of his commitment to its intrinsic value.

A more important feature of the development of the *Republic* is the changing role of Plato's principle of specialization. When he initially introduces the division of labour, it is not suggested that some of us are smiths rather than weavers because we could not be competent weavers if we tried and the weavers could not be competent smiths. We specialize so that we can all benefit from the better performance by the specialists. This argument suggests that similar considerations of efficiency should determine whether or not we decide to have specialized rulers; and I have argued that Plato is wrong to assume that efficiency is all that matters.

Later, however, the principle of specialization is derived not from considerations of efficiency, but from the good of each person, which is determined by a person's nature.[6] Most of us, in Plato's view, are incorrigibly dominated by our appetitive part,[7] and will simply ruin ourselves if we try to rule ourselves. The point is not just that specialist rulers will do somewhat better for us, but that we will suffer catastrophically unless we are ruled by the people who are ruled by their rational part (IX.590c–591a).

This second aspect of the *Republic* is important because it shows how Plato might reply to a criticism of his appeal to efficiency. We might suggest that a share in government and political life is good in itself, because it allows me to share in deliberation about what affects my life. Plato might reply (plausibly, though not conclusively) that a share in deliberation is no benefit to me if I am the sort of person who is dominated by appetite rather than rational deliberation; on this view, I need the right sort of soul if ruling is to be an intrinsic good for me. Even if we persuaded Plato that he had to restate his argument for philosopher rulers in the light of his revised conception of happiness, he might argue that he would reach the same conclusion as the one he reaches by his actual argument. The extensional equivalence of the conclusions of the two arguments might obscure the difference between their underlying principles.

Still, the second line of argument (from the different intrinsic goods of different souls) throws some light on Plato's conception of the philosopher rulers. Officially, they are simply a subset of the citizens, the ones assigned the task of ruling on behalf of the others. If, however, they are the only ones for whom the traditional political activities of the citizen are really good, then from another point of view they are the only genuine citizens of the ideal state, and the productive class are mere appendages to the city of philosophers. This impression is easiest to form from *Republic* V, and from Aristotle's criticism of it. Plato advocates social and psychological unity for

6 The division of labour, as it is explained in Book II, takes account of natural differences in ability (370a7–b5, 374b6–c2), but Socrates does not suggest either (1) that this is the main reason for the division of labour, or (2) that this division is required for the good of each person. Efficiency is the primary consideration; and since efficiency requires division of labour, it is sensible to pay attention to natural differences in ability. This is a different sort of argument from the one that relies on deep differences in people's psychic structure.

7 I am assuming – though the question is certainly controversial – that Plato thinks this is true even in people who have had the sort of moral education (whatever exactly that is) that is appropriate for the producing class in the ideal state. They are ruled by other people's rational parts, but not by their own.

the state (V.462ab), and he claims to achieve this through the social and psychological unity of the guardians (V.462c–e). It is easy to see how he does this if the guardians constitute the whole city. Otherwise his argument faces severe difficulties; for the guardians' way of life separates them so sharply from the productive class that social and psychological disunity within the whole state seems bound to increase.

Plato does not simply assume that the unity of the guardians increases the unity of the whole city. He tries to connect the two kinds of unity. But he introduces a quite different sort of consideration from the social and psychological unity considered so far. He argues that the unity of the guardian class will make them more devoted to the interests of the whole city, and that the producers, seeing this, will be grateful to the guardians for ruling them so well (V.463a–c).

But this argument does not show that the guardians and the producers will embody the sort of social and psychological unity that is present in the guardian class. A rich producer will care about his investments, his yacht, his children and wife, and his other private possessions. He may (if we concede several points to Plato) realize that the guardians protect these for him; but guardians cannot possibly feel social and psychological unity with his acquisitive goals, any more than he can feel such unity with their communitarian goals. Since this social and psychological division has to be counted against the unifying effects of the guardians' incorruptibility, Plato has not argued conclusively for his claim that unity within the guardian class implies unity in the whole city. His argument would be far more plausible if the guardians constituted the whole city.

Both aspects of Plato's argument are reflected in Aristotle's criticisms. Aristotle both challenges Plato's ideal of unification for a city (II.2.1261a12–b15), and rejects his account of how the guardians are good for the non-guardians (II.5.1264a22–9). It might seem inconsistent of Aristotle to criticize Plato first for making the city too unified and then for making it too divided. But his criticisms are quite appropriate; they focus on two distinct, indeed conflicting, tendencies in Plato's argument.

At any rate, it is useful to consider Plato's account of the guardians, not as an account of a ruling class within a state, but as an alternative picture of an ideal state. If they are the citizens, they are united by friendship and by common concern for the common good; and for them their activities on behalf of the common good will be part of their own good. For this "city of the guardians," as opposed to the city of pigs and the swollen city, the benefits of ruling are not purely instrumental; and it shows what was wrong with the initial claim that the city of pigs was a city at all.

I have certainly not considered all that might be said on Plato's behalf. For I have not examined the development of his moral and political ideas in the course of the *Republic*; nor have I considered possible developments in the later dialogues. But I hope I have shown that Aristotle's main line of criticism both focusses on an important issue and raises some serious and reasonable questions about Plato's arguments.

5 PHILANTHRÔPIA *VERSUS PHILANTHROPY*

This wider context allows us to see what is important to Aristotle in his defense of private property against Plato. In Aristotle's view, Plato's arrangements for securing friendship among the guardians reflect the sort of error that underlies the political argument of the *Republic* as a whole. Plato focusses on the bad results of private property, and devises legislation to avoid these bad results. He thinks (according to Aristotle) of legislation as a remedial device for removing evils; but he does not think carefully about the kind of intrinsically valuable activities that are made possible or impossible, or easier or more difficult, by different kinds of laws and political systems. In particular Plato does not see that his legislation undermines the conditions for the exercise of some of the virtues that are constituents of a good life.

Why should Plato's legislation appeal to our love of humanity, *philanthrôpia*? The interesting, and unfortunately not too surprising, history of this word actually throws some light on his case against private property.

It would clearly be wrong to translate *philanthrôpos* and *philanthrôpia* by "philanthropic" and "philanthropy," in the contemporary senses of these words. *Philanthrôpia* is seldom mentioned in Aristotle's ethical works; it is explicitly connected with generosity and justice only in the spurious work *On Virtues and Vices* (5.1250b33, 7.1251b3). But he says enough to show that he takes *philanthrôpia* to be a general sympathy and concern for other people (*Rhet.* II.13.1390a18–23). He mentions our feeling of kinship with other human beings to explain our approval of the *philanthrôpos* person (*EN* VIII.1.1155a16–21).

For our present purposes it is important to notice that *philanthrôpia* is (1) relatively independent of other moral judgments or attitudes towards the person who is the object of our sympathy, and (2) relatively easily impressed by the immediate and (in some cases) superficial aspect of situations. In particular, it is not restricted to sympathy with virtuous people or victims of undeserved misfortune. Even the dramatic presentation of a vicious persons's fall from good fortune to bad fortune appeals to our *philanthrôpia*, even though it does not excite our pity or fear. Pity is directed towards someone who does not deserve ill-fortune, and fear towards someone like ourselves, but *philanthrôpia* is subject to neither of these restrictions (*Poet.* 13.1452b36–1453a7).[8] Aristotle suggests that young people are especially prone to pity

8 I will not discuss the interesting dispute about the remarks on *philanthrôpia* at 13.1452b36–1453a7 and 18.1456a18–20. I follow the view that (1) *philanthrôpia* refers to one's sympathy for the victim of misfortune. The alternative view holds that (2) it refers to our sense of satisfaction that vicious people get what they deserve. For support of (1) see R. Stark, *Aristotelesstudien* (Munich, 1972), ch. 7; R. D. Lamberton, "*Philanthrôpia* and the Evolution of Dramatic Taste", *Phoenix*, 37 (1983), pp. 95–103; S. Halliwell, *Aristotle's Poetics* (London, 1986), p. 219, n. 25. For support of (2) see D. W. Lucas, *Aristotle's Poetics* (Oxford, 1968) comment on 1452b36; J. L. Moles, "*Philanthrôpia* in the *Poetics*", *Phoenix*, 38 (1984), pp. 325–35; R. Janko, *Aristotle's Poetics* (Indianapolis, 1987), comment on 1452b36.

because of *philanthrôpia*, without identifying themselves with the person they pity (*Rhet.* II.13.1390a18–23), because their optimistic attitude to others leads them to overlook any question about whether the victim of misfortune has deserved it (12.1389b8–10).

Aristotle's use of *philanthrôpia* corresponds to the normal use in Classical Greek, referring to a generalized attitude of kindness and consideration for a human being. The gods accuse Prometheus of being a "human-lovei," intending the term in an unfavourable sense, when he confers on human beings the benefits that should have been confined to the gods.[9] *Philanthrôpia* is the attitude of a kind and considerate person, even if she lacks material resources, and it can be displayed without the transfer of material resources.

In later Greek, however, *philanthrôpia* and its cognates sometimes tend to suggest some definite favour done by a superior to an inferior.[10] Philanthropy is the attitude that God displayed towards human beings in the Incarnatioi (Titus 3.4); and it became a standard virtue of kings, especially of the Roman Emperor. Papyri record addresses to the Emperor as "Your Philanthropy," and Julian is referred to as "the most divine, greatest, and most philanthropic king."[11] Any exercise of royal favour, including relief from taxation or some other concession, was recognized as a *philanthrôpon*; and eventually the term simply refers to a cash payment, suffering the fate that "gratuity" and "honorarium" have suffered in English.[12] The use of the term for the Emperor's exercise of his arbitrary power suggests that his subjects became used to regarding as an act of kindness and charity what they might properly have regarded as a right.[13]

The English term "philanthropy" seems initially to have been a conscious borrowing of the Greek to express a concept for which (Dryden claimed) there was no exact English term. Bacon speaks appropriately of "The affecting of the Weale of Man: which is that the Graecians call Philanthropie."[14] This very general sense persists in the *OED*'s definition: "Love to mankind; practical benevolence towards men in general; the disposition or active effort to promote the happiness and well-being of one's fellow-men."

9 See Aeschylus, *Promentheus Vinctus*, lines 11 and 28. Prometheus' attitude to human beings is not condescending; he displays solidarity with his human friends. See M. Griffith, *Aeschylus, Prometheus Vinctus* (Cambridge, 1983), p. 201.

10 In saying "sometimes" I mean to indicate that these examples do not constitute a representative selection to indicate the full range of the term in later Greek.

11 See *Sylloge Inscriptionum Graecarum*, ed. W. Dittenberger, 3rd edn, vol. 2 (Leipzig, 1917), no. 906b. For other references see B. Snell, *The Discovery of the Mind* (Oxford, 1953), pp. 246–52. This is in turn largely based on S. Tromp de Ruiter, "De vocis quae est *philanthrôpia* significatione atque usu," *Mnemosyne*, 59 (1931–2), pp. 271–306. For "Your Philanthropy" see Tromp de Ruiter, p. 301.

12 See Tromp de Ruiter, p. 293: "Deinde verbum *philanthrôpia* vel *philanthrôpon* exarescit, ut ita dicam, in sententiam 'salarii' vel 'mercedis annuae'".

13 See Snell, *Discovery*, p. 252: "'love of man' retained a strong admixture of condescension" (referring to the use of *to philanthrôpon* for a tip).

14 These references are taken from *OED*, s.vv.

But probably this definition has not quite caught up with the more restricted modern use of the term for organized "good works" undertaken by private societies. For this sense the *OED* quotes two interesting nineteenth-century passages. A magazine in 1830 mentions "a convention met for the purpose of philanthropizing the blacks"; and a newspaper expresses some reservations: "Till they get them [votes] we look jealously at these attempts to philanthropize woman *malgré lui*."

On the difference between philanthropy and other forms of benevolence Webster is more definite than the *OED*. To a definition similar to that in the *OED* it adds a second definition of "philanthropist": "a generous giver to education, charity, social work, &c; a liberal benefactor." In comparing philanthropy with charity it comments:

> Philanthropy, the broader term, is the spirit of active good will toward one's fellow men, especially as shown in efforts to promote their welfare; charity (cf. mercy) is benevolence as manifested in provision, whether public or private, for the relief of the poor; as, "In benevolence, they excel in *charity*, which alleviates individual suffering, rather than in *philanthropy*, which deals in large masses and is more frequently employed in preventing than in allaying calamity" (Lecky).[15]

In these passages we probably recognize something closer to our most frequent use of "philanthropy" than is evident in the *OED*'s very general sense.

The fortunes of the cognate Greek and English terms seem quite strikingly similar in some ways, and significantly different in others. Both terms initially refer to a general attitude of goodwill that could be expressed in many different ways by people in quite different material positions, and later come to refer to a more definite material transaction, frequently (in Greek) or normally (in English) involving a benefit by a superior to an inferior. But whereas the Greek term easily and frequently refers to favours conferred by the state, the English term does not. We normally think, for instance, of the welfare state not as an exercise in philanthropy, but as a replacement of it.

This digression into lexicography allows us to define one of the issues raised by Plato's and Aristotle's views on private property. Plato's legislation appeals to *philanthrôpia* in the broad sense. Aristotle's criticisms argue for the value of philanthropy in the narrow sense, in so far as they claim to defend the sort of generosity that presupposes inequality of private property. Moreover, the fact that Aristotle seems to be defending philanthropy may give us some reason for being doubtful about his arguments. It is striking that in both Greek and English a term initially referring to an uncontroversially desirable attitude to human beings comes to be used to put a good face on the largesse of the better-off to the worse-off. It is easy to suppose that we leave room for philanthropy only by slighting the claims of justice. Philan-

15 Quoted from Webster's *New World Dictionary* (New York, 1934).

thropy requires the philanthropic person (or institution) to have some surplus beyond his or her needs, and requires a beneficiary who is in some way significantly worse off than the benefactor. It is natural to ask whether the inequality between benefactor and beneficiary could not have been removed by some other means, and whether the interests of the beneficiary could not be better served by making him less dependent on the charitable impulses of the benefactor. This is the sort of suspicion that Kant expresses in his rather pointed "casuistical questions" about beneficence:

> The ability to practice beneficence, which depends on property, follows largely from the injustice of the government, which favours certain men and so introduces an inequality of wealth that makes others need help. This being the case, does the rich man's help to the needy, on which he so readily prides himself as something meritorious, really deserve to be called beneficence at all?[16]

Kant points out that private property and inequality leave room for philanthropy; if they must be assumed, then philanthropy is better than no philanthropy, but we might wonder if it would not be better to remove the conditions that make philanthropy desirable.

A natural reply to Kant's suspicion is to defend the system of private property and the inequalities that it may permit. One familiar defense is historical and deontological, appealing to the right of acquisition, and the resulting justice of property-holdings that are licensed by this right. If we accept such a defense, and we believe that the right of acquisition overrides other moral principles, we can freely admit that everyone would be better off under a more redistributive system. We will simply argue that such consequences cannot outweigh the claims of justice, even if justice has regrettable consequences.

A different and equally familiar line of defense might argue for private property on utilitarian grounds, claiming that it promotes the relevant good consequences better than any alternative system would, and that these good consequences outweigh any bad side-effects of the sort that Kant alludes to. This consequentialist defense leaves us with two possible attitudes to private philanthropy and beneficence. We might admit that on the whole its existence is regrettable, but unavoidable, as an unfortunate side-effect of desirable arrangements of property. Alternatively, we might argue that in fact it is more efficient than any other system, and in fact is one of the arrangements that positively promote the good consequences of private property.

It is worth sketching these different and familiar strategies so that we can see what is distinctive about Aristotle's view of beneficence and private generosity. He does not offer a deontological defense, appealing simply to a

16 Kant, *Doctrine of Virtue*, tr. M. J. Gregor (New York, 1964), p. 122 (= Akad. p.453).

basic principle about the justice of private property.[17] Nor, however, does he exactly offer either of the consequentialist defenses we mentioned. He certainly does not think the opportunity for private beneficence is a regrettable side-effect of the beneficial arrangement of private property. Nor does he think its value is merely instrumental, lying in any contribution to the further consequences resulting from private property. Indeed, he practically reverses this order of argument; he actually defends private property because it provides the resources for the exercise of beneficence, and regards the exercise of beneficence as valuable in itself. He does not have to prove that beneficence is more efficient in distributing goods than any alternative method would be; indeed, he can readily allow some inefficiency as a fair price to pay for the good of exercising beneficence.

Beneficent activity needs to be very good if it is to play the role Aristotle intends for it.[18] If we are to examine his defense of generosity, we need to see first what is so good about it, and then why it requires private property.

6   PRIVATE PROPERTY AND GENEROSITY

We can now understand more exactly why Aristotle remarks that Plato's arrangements might appeal to our *philanthrôpia*. He implicitly warns us that they may appeal to our sympathetic and humane feelings, before we consider more carefully all the moral questions that they raise. If, like Plato, we focus on the evils that are removed by the abolition of private property, and do not think more broadly about the sorts of actions and virtues that Plato makes impossible, our sympathetic feelings may be mistakenly aroused. To counteract this first impression, we need to consider the relevant virtue that Plato inadvertently abolishes.

The Aristotelian virtue that encourages beneficent and (in the modern sense) philanthropic activity is generosity, *eleutheriotês* (discussed fully in *EN* IV.1). This plainly involves the transfer of material resources in circumstances where no principle of justice requires it. Without this transfer there is

17 "Simply" and "basic" are important here. Aristotle certainly believes the holding of private property is just. On some issues that I treat very briefly here I have benefited from reading Fred Miller's paper, "Aristotle on Property Rights" (read to the Society for Ancient Greek Philosophy, March 1986, and in *Essays in Ancient Greek Philosophy*, vol. IV, ed. by J. Anton and A. Preus [Albany, 1990].)

18 Aristotle's argument from generosity arouses scepticism in L. C. Becker, *Property Rights* (London, 1977), p. 86: "But turning remarks like these into a sound argument for property rights is a difficult task. It is difficult because the argument will depend on contestable premises about what counts as an element of virtuous character, as well as contestable premises about human behavior." It is hard to find any argument for property, however, that does not rest on some contestable premises; this fact about Aristotle's argument is hardly a reason for dismissing it. Becker's more specific criticisms are much more reasonable; they are similar (though presented without much argument) to those I offer later.

no generous action; and to this extent Aristotle is clearly right to say that generosity has its function in the use of possessions. But Aristotle needs a stronger claim. For in defending private property as a means to generosity, he evidently needs to appeal to a virtue that essentially involves the use of *private* possessions, which are not mentioned in his claim about the function of generosity.

He can show what he needs in either of two ways. First, he might argue that generosity itself requires private property to be generous with. Alternatively, he might concede that generosity is possible without private property, but argue that there is a type of generosity (which we may call "private generosity") that does require private property, and that something of distinctive value is lost if we cannot exercise this virtue. If we are to focus on the most controversial aspects of Aristotle's position, we must see if either of these lines of argument is at all promising. If generosity is possible without private property, one of Aristotle's main arguments for private property collapses. If, however, we confine ourselves to the sort of generosity which is essentially generosity with one's own private property, we can ask Aristotle why this particular sort of generosity is important enough to deserve to be protected by the existence of private property. My discussion of Aristotle's views does not sharply separate his views about property from his views about generosity. I hope this fusing of the two questions will not matter; in the end it should be fairly clear what we have found about each issue.

7   THE VALUE OF GENEROSITY

For reasons that Aristotle himself makes clear, it will not be enough if he simply shows that the virtue of generosity requires private property, or is most valuable in a society that recognizes private property. For some virtues seem to be needed precisely because they make bad circumstances better; and the fact that we value them as virtues, and so cultivate them for their own sakes, does not show that we ought to want to preserve the circumstances that make them possible or desirable. The argument that we need private property because we value generosity is by itself no more persuasive than the argument that we need wars because we value bravery, or that we need temptations to injustice because we value justice, or that we need beggars because we value charity. As Aristotle says:

> Now the activity of the virtues concerned with action is in politics or war, and actions in these areas seem to be unleisured. This seems entirely true of actions in war. For no one chooses to fight a war, and no one makes war for the sake of fighting the war; for someone would seem an utter murderer if he made enemies of his friends, so that there could be battles and killings. (*EN* 1177b6–12)

Aristotle answers this difficulty by distinguishing virtues that are desirable in undesirable circumstances from those that are desirable even in desirable circumstances (*Pol.* VII.13.1332a7–25, 15.1334a16–34). He mentions just punishments as examples of actions that are fine, but in circumstances that we would prefer to get rid of (13.1332a12–15); and he remarks that bravery and endurance (*karteria*) have their appropriate area of operation in circumstances where we lack leisure (15.1334a22–3). These virtues (or these exercises of the virtues) are contrasted with those that retain their value in good circumstances; among these Aristotle mentions justice and temperance.

Several further questions arise about the distinction or distinctions that Aristotle draws or ought to draw in these passages. But I have perhaps said enough to expose one issue about generosity and private property. It is important for Aristotle's argument to convince us that generosity is not related to private property in the way that bravery (he may be taken to suggest) is related to war and danger – as being the best response to circumstances that it would be better to be rid of. It must be so desirable that we ought, if we have the choice, to create the conditions that make it possible.

Aristotle's defense of private property reflects one essential aspect of justice in the ideal state. Justice is intended to promote the common interest of members of a community (*EN* V.1.1129b17–19), and the branch of it called "special" justice (2.1130a14–b5) is meant especially to protect their self-confined interests – those interests that essentially involve the satisfaction of desires for states of oneself rather than states of other people.[19]

Aristotle uses these points about self-confined interests to criticize Plato for going to self-defeating extremes in his efforts to make the whole city promote its common interest. Aristotle supposes (most dubiously) that Plato has deprived the guardians of happiness to secure the happiness of the whole city, and argues against Plato that the happiness of the whole cannot be secured by forcing one large part to renounce its own self-confined interest for the sake of the other parts (II.5.1264b15–25).

The treatment of the guardians is one sign of Plato's neglect of the self-confined aspects of a person's interest. Aristotle sees the same neglect in his arrangements for property in the ideal city. After alleging inconsistencies in Plato's arrangements he explains, in the passage I quoted earlier, how Plato's abolition of private property also abolishes the valuable activities for which private property is a prerequisite. Plato hopes to strengthen friendship and cooperation in the ideal state; but he has abolished one of the conditions that make friendship valuable. Friendship essentially involves individuals, each of whom is aware of himself as a bearer of distinct self-confined interests, which he freely and willingly adapts to those of the others. With no self-confined interests we have nothing to adapt and nothing to adapt to; and private property strengthens the proper sense of self-confined interest. We do not make friendship and cooperation easier by removing each person's self-confined interest; we deprive friendship and cooperation of their point. The friendship that is supposed to exist in Plato's ideal city will in fact be "watery" (II.4.1262b15) because it is supposed to rest on some generalized concern for the common good among people who will lack a sufficiently lively sense of their own self-confined good (1262b7–24).

19 On special justice see *Aristotle's First Principles* § 232, 250.

Aristotle presents a related general criticism of Plato's ideal, in attacking what he takes to be the excessively unifying tendencies of Plato's city. Plato recognizes the dangers resulting from different individuals with different conceptions of their self-confined interests; seeing that these conceptions may result in conflict, he thinks it better to remove the difference between people's different conceptions, and to concentrate everyone's individual conception on goals that are shared with everyone else and aim at the common welfare. In Plato's preferred order no one has any conception of a self-confined interest, but everyone devotes her effort to some common good. This is the arrangement that Aristotle rejects as excessive unification. He suggests that Plato treats the individuals as part of a single organism (compare II.2.1261a10–22); in failing to recognize their distinct self-contained interest Plato ignores an essential condition for the achievement of their good.[20]

The criticism of Plato's ideal, from the point of view of special justice, assumes that a person's self-confined interest is an important, even an indispensable, part of her good. In advocating private generosity, Aristotle affirms the importance of one's own choice and decision in determining what happens to the goods that one associates with one's self-confined interest.[21]

If I have my own supply of external goods under my own control, it is my choice and decision that determines what happens to it. If I do not control it, I must depend on someone else; nothing is under my control to use in generous actions. Even if the result of private generosity is the very same as the result that the wise legislator would prescribe, the fact that it results from the private generosity of many is a further good feature of it that is lost if the result is produced by legislation. The importance of external goods for individual initiative explains why special justice is needed. It is needed not simply, as Plato assumed, to supply us with the external goods needed for survival or for other "necessary" (in Aristotle's sense) purposes, but also to secure external goods needed for the exercise of our individual initiative. Aristotle criticizes Plato for making private generosity impossible, because he thinks Plato's arrangement betrays failure to recognize the importance and value of individual initiative in a person's good. Aristotle values private generosity, and therefore the private property that allows it, because it expresses the virtuous person's desire to benefit others through his own choice and the exercise of his own initiative.

These arguments support Aristotle's general claim that Plato has neglected "the fine" in favour of "the necessary" in his design for the ideal

---

20 Aristotle's views on distinctness and unity in political contexts are favourably regarded by M. C. Nussbaum, "Shame, Separateness, and Political Unity," in *Essays on Aristotle's Ethics*, ed. A. O. Rorty (Berkeley, 1980), ch. 21. I do not discuss Aristotle's own use of the organic analogy in I.2.1253a15–29, VIII.1.1337a27–30; there is an apparent prima facie difficulty in making it consistent with his criticism of Plato's use of the analogy.

21 For further discussion of control and initiative in Aristotle's conception of leisure (*scholê*) see *Aristotle's First Principles* § 220–2.

state. Plato's provisions overlook the preconditions of virtuous actions, and especially of generous actions. If Aristotle's argument is sound, he has also explained why *private* generosity, and hence private property, should be protected. He believes that if virtuous activity is to express my initiative (as opposed to my conformity to the law), it must use resources that are entirely up to me to use; they must be wholly at my disposal, and hence they must be my private property.

8   RESTRICTIONS ON PRIVATE PROPERTY?

We noticed earlier that Aristotle's argument might arouse suspicion if it involves the imposition of serious harm on the worse-off in order to make room for the generosity of the better-off. Before we examine the cogency of his argument, we should notice that he tries to answer this objection on behalf of the worse-off. For his defense of private property has a significantly restricted scope. Private property is meant for a state in which all the citizens are in a position to live a life of leisure and virtue, so that each has a sufficient supply of externals to free him from concern with them. Aristotle is not arguing for private charity to the destitute and desperately poor; indeed he argues against this in stressing the evil of letting the lower classes be impoverished and dependent (e.g. V.8.1309a20–26). In describing land tenure in the ideal city Aristotle first reaffirms the principle of private property with friendly provision for sharing (VII.10.1329b41–1330a2). But he at once makes a crucial exception to the general rule of private property, seeing that "none of the citizens must lack sustenance" (VII.10.1330a3); the ideal city subordinates the protection of private property to the avoidance of great inequalities of wealth and poverty. It follows the Spartan custom of common meals (*sussitia*), but rejects the Spartan method of administering them. A Spartiate who became too poor to pay his contribution to the common meals had to relinquish his status as a full citizen (II.9.1271a26–37, 10.1272a12–21). Instead of allowing this increasing inequality Aristotle prefers the Cretan system that requires public provision for the common meals, and he designates publicly-owned land for this purpose (VII.10.1330a3–13).

This provision for collective ownership of land in the ideal state should be an important corrective to a one-sided view of Aristotle's criticism of Plato on private property, since it shows very clearly which principles Aristotle takes to be prior to which. All the disadvantages of public ownership that he urges against Plato are no less present for Aristotle's own arrangement. We could imagine him arguing that the collective farms will be worked with less enthusiasm, and so less productively, than the private land will be, and that in any case we should leave it to the generosity of the richer citizens to make sure that the "truly needy" do not sink into destitution. We might even expect him to challenge the admittedly democratic institution of the common meals, as a restriction on the individual's use of his own resources. For he recognizes that the system of common meals is a democratic feature of the Spartan system (II.6.1265b40–41). In commending the common meals, he promises to explain later why he favours them (VII.10.1330a4–6). Unfortunately he does not keep his promise anywhere in the extant *Politics*; but presumably he suggests at least part of his reason when he argues that they prevent destitution and severe inequality (VII.10.1330a2).[22]

In fact he considers none of these objections; and if he had considered them, he could fairly argue that they are subordinate to the overriding demand of securing the necessary means of a good life to all the citizens. Though Aristotle does not say much about the reasons for this subordination, he clearly accepts some restriction on the opportunities to acquire and use property, in order to assure the provision of an important good for the worse-off. Since these are Aristotle's assumed background conditions for private property, he lays himself open, as he should, to the argument that in conditions where private property encourages poverty, pauperism, clientship, dependence and social conflict, its advantages may be overridden by the greater importance of avoiding these other evils.

It is not clear that Aristotle himself sees the importance of the restriction he imposes on the extent of private property. His restrictions imply that in states that do not provide the appropriate background conditions through public ownership, private property may not be justifiable. And yet he never suggests that the acceptance of private property in non-ideal states is open to criticism. The principles that he implicitly appeals to are important, but he may not see how important they are.

For this reason, it becomes difficult to say how far Aristotle means to defend private philanthropy, in so far as that requires significant inequality of private property. He seems to assume that in the ideal state the welfare of the poorer citizens is not to depend entirely on the generosity of the richer citizens. On the other hand, his remarks about private property (and especially his acceptance of it in non-ideal states that include significant inequalities) suggest that he means to defend it even in conditions where it involves significant inequality. We should therefore consider how many of the benefits he sees in private property could actually be secured without large inequalities.

9   PRIVATE PROPERTY AND MORAL EDUCATION

We may be initially sympathetic to Aristotle's defence of private property because it appeals to one highly plausible principle. Aristotle recognizes something important that Plato never clearly recognizes about the relation of an individual to political authority. He sees that my having some initiative

---

22 Newman notices that Aristotle has quite a bit to explain: "Aristotle, we note, though he is strongly in favour of the household, is also strongly in favour of syssitia or public meal-tables, perhaps a somewhat antagonistic institution" (W. L. Newman, *The Politics of Aristotle* [Oxford, 1887–1902], vol. I, p. 333). The same could be said about the public provision for common meals in relation to private property.

and control over what happens to me is a good in itself; he therefore sees that mere efficiency in achieving my other interests is not the only proper standard for the criticism of a political system.

On the other hand, Aristotle acknowledges Plato's charge that private property is to be avoided because it encourages the natural tendency to greed, cupidity and competitiveness (II.5.1263b15–22); for Plato the abolition of private property is a small price to pay for the removal of these tendencies. Aristotle argues that the blame for these bad results should be placed on vice, not on private property. He thinks it naive to suppose that social conflicts can be removed by altering the distribution of property. He is no less scathing about equalization of property than about the more radical Platonic solution (II.7.1266b38–1267a2). His criticism does not always distinguish necessary from sufficient conditions. He agrees that equality of property is somewhat useful, though not very significant, in preventing conflicts (1267a37–9), and we might agree that it is insufficient without agreeing that it is unnecessary. He evidently believes, however, that private property may be harmless, and that its potential harm can be avoided by the proper sort of moral education.[23]

Aristotle believes, then, that the best political system need not forego the benefits of private property in order to avoid the evils that it may produce in non-ideal states. For the right sort of moral education will produce concern for the genuine virtues and for the common good; a citizen will not prize the accumulation of external goods over the good of his friends or the community, and so he will avoid dangerous competition, flattery and greed. The institutions of the ideal state and the practices it encourages should support each other, and should not create the sorts of conflicts that undermine the structure of the state. These conflicts would result if moral education encouraged altruism but we were taught to value private property for its advantages to us in competition with others. However, Aristotle intends moral education to teach us the proper use of private property; it is regulated by friendship and justice, and in turn supports the activities appropriate to these virtues. In these conditions private property will actually promote concern for the common interest; it will provide resources for the virtue of generosity without creating serious temptations to vice.

In his support Aristotle might fairly point out that Plato expects profound effects from moral education in his ideal state; it might well seem arbitrary of Plato to suppose that moral education could not produce the right attitude to private property.

If, however, we are inclined to support Aristotle's appeal to moral education in reply to Plato's attack on private property, it is only fair to notice that a similar argument will support a Platonic rejoinder. For Aristotle argues that the abolition of private property goes against the grain of human nature, violating the natural human pleasure in our own possessions (II.5.1263a40–b7), and that the sort of friendship Plato wants to create will

23 On moral education see further *Aristotle's First Principles*, § 223.

be watery, compared with what we are used to in smaller associations. Why not reverse the direction of Aristotle's argument? Plato seems to be free to claim that Aristotle underestimates the difficulty of removing the evils resulting from private property, and exaggerates the difficulty of educating people to be less indifferent to common possessions.

Aristotle might argue that Plato overestimates the power of moral education if he thinks it can alter such basic tendencies in human nature. But this is a dangerous line for him to take, since it seems to work equally well against his own appeal to moral education in support of private property. To see how serious an objection this might be, it is worth exploring its implications a little further.

If we are sceptical about Aristotle's appeal to moral education, our reason may be that we think he puts too little weight on the effects of actual concern with private property. Aristotle would think it was silly to expect moral education to train us to copulate without sexual desire. Is it not equally silly to expect that it will train us to handle private property without the greed, competitiveness and hostility to others that are normally associated with it? Perhaps these attitudes must be cultivated for the successful accumulation and protection of private property; and once we acquire and cultivate them, Aristotle himself will tell us that it is folly to pretend we can talk ourselves out of deeply ingrained habits. He seems to recognize some aspects of this tension when he allows that generous people may be worse than others at managing their assets (IV.1.1120b4–6, 14–20), and that the process of acquisition tends to make people more acquisitive and less generous (1120b11–14). Surely he allows too little for the motives that are encouraged by the objective nature of accumulation and possession.

Aristotle might be unmoved by this sort of objection. For the property-owners he has in mind simply possess goods and use them; they need not be concerned with accumulation. But this is an inadequate reply to the objection. While some individuals may inherit enough property for their private generosity, the system as a whole cannot work unless enough individuals are acquisitive enough to accumulate possessions for themselves in competition with others. Even individuals who inherit enough property have to think about managing and maintaining it; and Aristotle expects them to acquire some strong attachment to what they have (II.5.1263a40–b5). Just as Plato has to consider the psychological and moral effects of the abolition of private property, Aristotle has to consider the psychological and moral effects of retaining it.

We can strengthen this objection by appeal to one of Aristotle's own arguments. He prohibits the citizens of his ideal state from menial work, because such work is inconsistent with the virtue that is required for a happy life (VII.9.1328b39–1329a2).[24] In his view, someone who must spend most of

24 On menial occupations see I.11.1258b37–9, VIII.2.1337b8–11, III.5.1278a12, 17, 21, IV.12.1296b29, VI.1.1317a25, VI.4.1319a27, VIII.6.1341b13, VIII.7.1342a20, 22.

his time and effort working for a precarious living, or in dependence on the favour of another, will never develop the right virtues of character for a citizen. If Aristotle is right about this, he has a good prima facie reason for excluding menial workers from citizenship.

This argument seems to assume, however, that the menial occupation itself ruins a person's character, and that it is futile to expect moral education to have any countervailing effect.[25] Aristotle might correctly warn us that moral character cannot simply be imposed on occupations and circumstances. We cannot reasonably exhort someone to care about virtue and force him to spend all his time in occupations where success requires the subordination of virtue to other aims. To expect such results from moral education is to expect too much from it; it is not a magical protection against the influence of other objective circumstances.

If we absorb this salutary reminder, we might be tempted to agree with Aristotle that Plato expects too much in expecting to avoid the bad effects of common ownership by moral education. But how can we then also agree with Aristotle in discounting the bad effects of private property and hoping to avoid them by moral education? It is hard to see what would justify different conclusions in the two cases.

So far, we might decide that the dispute between Aristotle and Plato is a draw, if they rely on the sorts of arguments that I have discussed. But a further point needs to be added on Plato's side, if we notice the restrictions on Aristotle's argument for private property. I stressed earlier that Aristotle must himself advocate a considerable degree of public ownership in the ideal state, to avoid serious inequality and deprivation. In that case, he must agree that moral education can prevent the indifferent and negligent attitude that he thinks people will take to common resources in Plato's ideal state. If this "watery" attitude to common resources is inevitable, then Aristotle should not advocate the degree of public ownership that he advocates; but if it is not inevitable, then it does not constitute a decisive objection to Plato. The fact that Aristotle allows a significant extent of both public and private ownership may not be an advantage; if people are required to cultivate the attitudes appropriate to both types of property, the attitudes may be weaker and less stable than they would be in more single-minded people. Aristotle recognizes the danger in cities in which people are educated to take one sort of attitude but the political system itself requires them to take another; it is not clear that he does not expose himself to the same sort of objection. It is difficult to settle this issue between Plato and Aristotle about the possible effects of human nature and moral education; but we should not assume that Aristotle clearly has the better of the argument.

---

25 It is not clear that Aristotle always takes this view. See III.4.1277b3–7, VII.14. 1333a6–16, VIII.2.1337b17–21, VIII.6.1341b10–17; *Rhet.* III.18.1419b7–9.

10   GENEROSITY WITHOUT PRIVATE PROPERTY?

I have still not examined Aristotle's argument from the unique value of private generosity. To see what it really proves, we should notice first that its most evidently plausible part is not sufficient for Aristotle's purposes. Aristotle makes a good case to show that Plato ought not simply to think of private property as a mechanism for distributing external goods, and therefore ought not to suppose that common property is just as good if it delivers the same external goods. If Aristotle is right to emphasize the importance of individual initiative and private generosity, then it would be a mistake to abolish private property, as Plato does, without considering its effects on private generosity.

If, however, we consider these effects, must we agree with Aristotle in insisting that nothing but private property allows private generosity? Could we not, for instance, secure to individuals the resources and opportunities needed for private generosity without private property? Aristotle does not raise this question; but unless he can show that no alternative arrangement allows private generosity, his justified criticisms of Plato do not really constitute a defense of private property.

Aristotle values freedom and individual initiative. But he does not accept the democratic conception of freedom as "living as one wishes."[26] He thinks the democratic conception of freedom is unworthy, because a life that is guided by the political system should not be regarded as slavery, but as safety (V.9.1310a36–8). Aristotle concedes that it is slavish to live for another, so that one's actions are determined by the other's will independently of one's own. But he recognizes a crucial exception. The magnanimous person will refuse to live for another, except for a friend (*EN* IV.3.1124b31–1125a2); and actions that would otherwise be menial are not menial if I do them for myself or for a friend (III.4.1277b5–7, VIII.2. 1337b17–21). Similarly, the virtuous person's relation to his city is not slavish. If he regards his fellow-citizens as his friends, he is concerned about the common good of all of them as a part of his own good. In so far as his actions are regulated by the common good he is not being made to live for another as the slave is; for the slave's interests have no non-instrumental weight, but this is not true of the citizen.

It seems possible, then, for a citizen in an ideal state to exercise generosity without exclusive ownership. My own generosity may be properly expressed through my role in collective actions; it does not seem to need resources under my exclusive control. Even if we think the practice of generosity requires me to be free to dispose of some resources on my own initiative, it does not follow that the resources must be under my exclusive control. The

26 See VI.2.1317a40–b17; compare I.12.1259a39, V.7.1307a34, V.9.1310a28–36, VI.4.1318b39, 1319b30; *Rhet.* I.8.1366a4.

state might assign them to me, and allow me to dispose of them as I please within certain limits and in certain circumstances; such an arrangement would leave ample room for the exercise of generosity.

We might argue that this provision for individual initiative really includes the most important aspects of private property, and therefore does not refute Aristotle's claim that generosity requires private property. The mere fact that goods are not entirely at my disposal is consistent with my owning them – Greek states, for instance, sometimes limited the alienability of land. Aristotle's argument, we might suggest, does not require property that is completely at the owner's disposal.[27]

This defence of Aristotle forces us to ask which features of private property are crucial for his argument. If we are right to say that individual control and initiative are important for generosity, then these are the crucial aspects. And while it is fair to concede that property and ownership do not require completely unrestricted possession, nonetheless it still seems possible for a system to allow individual control and initiative without anything readily recognizable as private property.

If, for instance, the state assigned resources to me for only ten years, and at the end of that time reallocated resources for private use by considering how well different people had used their previous allotment,[28] it would not be tempting to describe the resources as the private property of the individuals who use them. For we are not tempted to say that allotments to individual gardeners are private property, even if they are free of rent. If I am free to grow what I like on my patch, but the local authority retains the right to reclaim it if I do not use it, or if it wants to build a house on the ground, then I am left some control over my patch, but within limits that would not apply to my private property. Again, my property rights in the produce would be restricted if I were not free to let it rot or to give it away foolishly. Why should a similar system of allotments not supply the resources needed for private generosity?

My point in mentioning this alternative arrangement is not to defend it over the one Aristotle prefers, but simply to display the gap between the requirements of private generosity and the conditions for private property. If several systems of distribution and ownership would allow generosity, then an argument from the value of generosity cannot by itself justify private property in particular.

We might argue that this is not real generosity, if the virtuous person's action does not cost *him* anything, and that it does not cost him anything

27 Different aspects of ownership are discussed by A. M. Honoré, "Ownership," in *Oxford Essays in Jurisprudence*, ed. A. G. Guest (Oxford, 1961), ch. 5, esp. pp. 112–28; and by J. Waldron, *The Right to Private Property* (Oxford, 1988), ch. 2, pp. 48–53. Though Aristotle does not offer any comparable list of components of ownership, what he advocates against Plato still seems to be a more extensive degree of ownership than his arguments actually support.
28 A somewhat similar situation is envisaged in the Parable of the Talents (Matthew 25.14–20).

unless he gives from his exclusive possessions. But this objection seems to overlook the virtuous person's attachment to the common good. He will regard the distribution of his friend's resources as a cost to himself, because he regards his friend's resources as his own; and he will take the same view of the community's resources. We might object that such identification of one's own interest with the interests of others is impossible or undesirable; but Aristotle should not be easily persuaded by any such objection, since it would undermine his whole account of friendship. Perfectly genuine generosity seems to be quite possible without private property; and to this extent private property seems unnecessary for anything of distinctive value.

Aristotle might perhaps reply that private generosity does express some distinctive value that is overlooked in the account of generosity that we have given. He suggests that self-love naturally attaches itself to something that is exclusively my own, and that without ownership the desirable aspects of self-love will be lost. Once again we may wonder if he is not being pessimistic about the powers of moral education when it suits him.

It may well be important that an individual should have a strongly developed conception of himself as an individual, a source of desires, interests, and claims, distinct from those of other individuals. Exclusive ownership may be one way to develop and strengthen such a conception. But it is hard to see why it should be the only way, in Aristotle's ideal state. In a political system where the citizen's interests, views and advice count in the collective actions of the community, self-love will be appropriately encouraged; it does not seem to need the extra encouragement derived from exclusive ownership. Aristotle has not shown that private property contributes uniquely or distinctively to the exercise of any virtue that we legitimately value; and he has not shown that the sort of generosity that requires private property at my exclusive disposal is a genuine virtue in its own right.

I conclude that Aristotle has not succeeded in the task we imposed on him, of defending essentially private generosity, and therefore the private property that makes it possible. He charges that Plato's system has only the appearance of *philanthrôpia*; but I do not think he has shown that proper *philanthrôpia* clearly requires private philanthropy.

11   CONCLUSION

Aristotle advocates private property and private generosity as an ideal. It is therefore legitimate to compare them with his other ideals, and especially with some other aspects of his ideal state; for present purposes it is irrelevant to object that the other features of the ideal state are impractical. On Aristotle's own terms we have reason to conclude that his defense of private property is seriously defective. It rests on legitimate demands for individual freedom and initiative; but other aspects of the ideal state show that these legitimate demands can be satisfied without private property. Moreover, the rest of Aristotle's theory should warn us of certain dangers in the acceptance of private property, to be measured against its advantages.

Once we see that the ideals safeguarded by private property can be safeguarded in other ways, the advantages secured by private property are fairly small, and we can fairly doubt if they compensate for the dangers. I have not been criticizing Aristotle by appeal to principles foreign to him. I have challenged his defense of private property by appeal to the more general principles of his own political theory.

If I am right, then we had better not look to Aristotle's political theory as a whole for a defense of private property and the private philanthropy that involves the use of private property. I don't want to say that we must at once be sceptical about the defense of private property; before we draw that conclusion we would need to be sure that Aristotle has exhausted all the possible ideals and principles that might be invoked. Still, I think we might reasonably draw some tentative conclusions that go beyond the evaluation of Aristotle's argument.

Though Aristotle does not anticipate the variety of arguments for private property and philanthropy that later theorists have devised, his failure to defend private property successfully casts some significant doubt on whether a successful defense can be found. It remains possible that we could defend private property and generosity as the best expedient in certain empirical circumstances; but in that case we would of course have to weigh its benefits against the costs that Plato emphasizes and Aristotle illegitimately discounts. Many defenders of private property think it is more than a practical expedient; and they ought to be worried by the failure of Aristotle's arguments.

Some defenders of private property may not be worried by Aristotle's failure because they rely on a deontological argument for a right to private property, and Aristotle does not rely on any such argument. If someone is prepared to argue that we have a right to private property, he will be well advised to appeal to some further principle about the value of individual freedom and initiative as the basis of this right. Such an appeal takes us straight back to one of the Aristotelian ideals. If my objections to Aristotle are right, an appeal to these ideals is unlikely to show precisely that we have a right to private property. Though Aristotle himself does not explicitly appeal to rights, the weaknesses in his argument allow us to predict weaknesses in arguments appealing to rights.

10

Aristotle on Prior and Posterior, Correct and Mistaken Constitutions

WILLIAM W. FORTENBAUGH

In *Politics* III.1 Aristotle offers a first, tentative definition of citizen (1275a22–34) and then considers the relationship of citizen to constitution. His remarks are brief, but the general point is clear enough. The notion of citizen depends upon that of constitution. Since constitutions differ not only in kind but also in priority and posteriority (correct constitutions are prior and mistaken or deviant constitutions are posterior), there is no single, common notion of citizen (1275a35–b5). With this conclusion I do not wish to quarrel. What I want to do is to focus on the priority and posteriority which Aristotle attributes to correct and mistaken constitutions. For scholars have not always understood this priority and posteriority and in any case they have left unsaid certain things which seem to me of philosophic interest and importance.

In Section 1, I shall argue briefly against a temporal interpretation of the priority and posteriority of constitutions and then in Section 2, I shall point out that the familiar comparison of constitutions with numbers, figures and psychic faculties may be more misleading than helpful. In Section 3, I shall refer to Plato's *Laws* and suggest that Aristotle's analysis can be more fully appreciated, when it is seen as a rejection of persuasive definition. Finally in Section 4, I shall focus on passages which not only bring out the normative aspect of Aristotle's analysis but also manifest considerable insight into the logic of grading.

1 THE TEMPORAL INTERPRETATION

We may begin by rejecting an interpretation recently advanced in the literature.[1] This is the view that the priority and posteriority mentioned in *Politics* III.1 is to be construed temporally. At first glance such an interpretation seems attractive. For Aristotle not only describes the temporal use of

---

1 E. Braun, *Das dritte Buch der aristotelischen "Politik"* (Vienna, 1965), pp. 20–22, 54–60.

"prior" as primary and most proper (*Cat.* 12.14a26–8)[2] but also speaks of the city in a way which encourages a chronological interpretation of political purpose and constitutional arrangement (I.2.1252a24–1253a39, III.6. 1278b15–30). Common advantage is said to bring men together (1278b21–2) and common advantage is declared the goal of correct constitutions (1279a17–20). It is tempting to conclude that correct constitutions are temporally prior, being due to some sort of natural, primitive instinct for association and common advantage. Deviant constitutions are a later phenomenon arising only when the motive of common advantage has been lost.[3]

This interpretation enjoys an initial plausibility, but ultimately it must be rejected. The introduction of priority and posteriority in *Politics* III.1 is not based upon a genetic theory of the polis whose historicity is open to question and whose relevance to the larger discussion in III.1 is not at all obvious. For Aristotle wants to argue from the priority and posteriority of constitutions to the absence of a single, common genus. Toward this end the details of history are irrelevant. Tyranny, for example, may be a historically later phenomenon than kingship (compare III.15.1286b16–17 with V.10.1310b18–20 and Thucydides 1.13.1), but this piece of history does not in itself rule out treating kingship and tyranny as coordinate species under the common genus of monarchy. Moreover, temporal sequence is hardly touched upon in *Politics* III; and when it is, the ordering is not always from correct to deviant constitution (III.15.1286b8–22; compare IV.11.1296a1–5, 13.1297b16–28; V.1.1301b6–10, 12.1316a29–34). Even in the *Ethics* where passage from correct to deviant constitution is emphasized (*EN* VIII.10.1160b10–17), Aristotle is careful not to say that such a sequence is invariable. It is only especially common, because the change involved is least and easiest (1160b21–2). We must conclude that temporal order is not central to Aristotle's thinking and that a different interpretation is to be preferred.

2   THE COMPARISON WITH NUMBERS, FIGURES AND PSYCHIC FACULTIES

In *Politics* III.1 Aristotle is consciously applying the general principle that whenever things form a series such that one comes first and another second

2 Strictly speaking, Aristotle describes the temporal use of *proteron* as primary and most proper. Nevertheless, here and frequently in this paper, I substitute an English equivalent for the Greek word occurring in the Aristotelian text. Two considerations stand behind this practice. First, I want to make the argument of the paper readily intelligible to the Greekless reader. Second, the issues under discussion are for the most part independent of the Greek language. They can be discussed using English equivalents and indeed are no less relevant to us today than to the ancient Greeks of the fourth century BC.

3 Braun, *Das dritte Buch*, pp. 59–60. Compare E. Barker, *The Political Thought of Plato and Aristotle* (London, 1906), pp. 310–11, whose remarks concerning chronological order are properly kept apart from an analysis of priority and posteriority.

and so on, there is nothing or hardly anything common to such things (1275a35–8).[4] Hence scholars have been quick to group constitutions with numbers, figures and psychic faculties, for Aristotle holds that the members of these classes form such a series and lack a proper genus.[5] In the *Metaphysics* Aristotle argues that there is no number and figure apart from the specific numbers and figures, for whenever things form an ordered series, that which is predicated of the things cannot be something apart from them (III.3.999a6–10). Similarly in the *De Anima* Aristotle holds that there is no figure apart from the triangle, the quadrilateral, etc. and no soul apart from the faculties of nutrition, sensation and intellect (II.3.414b20–32).[6] What interests me here is that Aristotle does not mention constitutions in connection with numbers, figures and psychic faculties. I do not want to suggest that Aristotle fails to mention constitutions because he thinks they cannot be grouped together with numbers, figures and psychic faculties conceived of as ordered series lacking a proper genus. But I do want to suggest that the priority and posteriority of constitutions is in some respects different. In the *Politics* Aristotle is well advised not to illustrate the priority and posteriority of constitutions by reference to numbers, figures and psychic faculties, for such a move might have the unfortunate effect of diverting attention from features which are not shared and which are important for appreciating fully Aristotle's remarks on correct and mistaken constitutions.

A comparatively superficial difference is that while numbers, figures and psychic faculties form single series in which every member is in some relationship of priority or posteriority to every other member, constitutions as presented in *Politics* III.1 do not form such a single series.[7] Instead they divide into three groups: kingship and tyranny, aristocracy and oligarchy, polity and democracy. Each group involves priority and posteriority, because each group is composed of a correct and a mistaken form of constitution. But across groups there is no priority and posteriority, so that the correct forms of

4 The addition of *glischrôs* in III.1.1275a38 is probably not significant. It seems to have been added to affect a tentative manner and may be compared with similar additions at *Phys*. V.3.226b27–8 and *DA* III.3.428b19. See my *Aristotle on Emotion* (London, 1975), p. 47, note 2.

5 The grouping takes various forms in different authors. See, for example, W. L. Newman, *The Politics of Aristotle* (Oxford, 1887–1902), vol. I, p. 242; J. Cook Wilson, "On the Platonist Doctrine of the *asymblêtoi arithmoi*," *Classical Review*, 18 (1904), p. 256; H. H. Joachim, *Aristotle, The Nicomachean Ethics*, ed. D. Rees (Oxford, 1955), p. 38; W. D. Ross, *Aristotle's Metaphysics* (Oxford, 1924), vol. I, p. 237; D. W. Hamlyn, *Aristotle's De Anima* (Oxford, 1968), p. 94. In what follows I shall not discuss these scholars individually. I am only concerned with the cumulative impression that the priority and posteriority of constitutions can be usefully elucidated by reference to numbers, figures and psychic faculties.

6 In another context it might be important to focus on differences between *Met*. III.3.999a6–10 and *DA* II.3.414b20–32. See the interesting remarks of A. C. Lloyd, "Genus, Species and Ordered Series in Aristotle," *Phronesis*, 7 (1962), pp. 67–90.

7 To *Politics* III.1 might be added III.6–8, but either way I am expressing myself cautiously, for later and from a different perspective Aristotle will order the correct and incorrect constitutions in a single series. See below, Section 4.

kingship, aristocracy and polity can be coordinate species of correct constitution – that is to say, species of political arrangement aiming at the common interest (1279a17–18).[8]

Later on we must complicate our account and recognize that in a different context Aristotle will rate and order the correct constitutions, so that finally all six take their place in a single series. But at this moment we should go below what I have called a comparatively superficial difference and notice that this difference is based on Aristotle's teleology. For Aristotle constitutions are by nature purposeful and properly directed toward a specific end, or *telos* (IV.1.1289a17; compare III.6.1278b23, 9.1280b39). This is not true of numbers and figures. In the case of psychic faculties teleology is important; and it is of some interest that when Aristotle names the primary faculty, he does so with an appeal to the principle that everything is properly named from its end (*DA* II.4.416b23–5). But in psychology teleology serves to specify rather than to unite the faculties which are ordered along the *scala naturae*. This is different from the sphere of politics where the end of common advantage serves to unite three different constitutions under the label "correct constitution."

A further difference between constitutions and numbers, figures and psychic faculties concerns the priority of greater value. In the *Categories* Aristotle recognizes that "prior" is often used in an evaluative sense (12.14b4–8) and in the *Metaphysics* he says that the better is always prior to the worse and that a genus is lacking (III.3.999a13–14). The application to constitutions is clear enough. Correct constitutions are valued higher than mistaken ones, because they have a proper goal and conform to simple justice (III.6.1279a17–19). Mistaken constitutions are deviations which may be called despotic in that they disregard the interests of free men (1279a19–21). They are bad, not good, and therefore are posterior in an evaluative sense. This is not true of numbers and figures, and while Aristotle would want to rate intellect higher than sensation and both of more worth than nutritive and reproductive capacity, he would not want to say that the lower faculties are in any way deviations and violations of simple justice. Deviant constitutions are positively bad. Lower psychic faculties are not in themselves bad, though they can be troublesome and in any case lack the value of intellect.

A final difference is conceptual. The mistaken constitutions are posterior not only because they are of negative value but also because they are

---

8 It might be objected that the species of both the correct and incorrect constitutions form ordered series in that they differ in number: kingship and tyranny are the rule of one man, aristocracy and oligarchy are the rule of the few and polity and democracy are the rule of the many. But this objection seems to forget that in certain cases Aristotle does not think number an essential feature. At least he goes out of his way to argue that oligarchy and democracy are only incidentally the rule of the few and the many (III.8), and when he comes to discuss polity his focus is upon the middle class in contrast with the very rich and the very poor (IV.11.1295b1–3). See Barker, *The Political Thought of Plato and Aristotle*, p. 312.

conceived of in terms of the correct constitutions. We may compare the *Eudemian Ethics* where primacy is related to definition. "Surgeon" is said to be prior to "surgical instrument," because the *logos*, or definition, of the former is mentioned or implied in the *logos* of the latter and not *vice versa* (VII.2.1236a17–22). Viewed this way, a correct constitution is prior, because it is conceptually independent, while a mistaken constitution is posterior, because it is conceptually dependent upon a correct constitution: tyranny is (essentially) a deviation from kingship, oligarchy is a deviation from aristocracy and democracy is a deviation from polity (III.7.1279b4–6, IV.2.1289a28–30; compare *EE* VII.9.1241b32). This kind of logical analysis – often called focal analysis – is well known to readers of the *Metaphysics*.[9] Aristotle applies it to being and uses it to explain the priority of substance (IV.2.1003a33–b10, VII.1.1028a34–6). But he does not use it to establish priority and posteriority among numbers, figures and psychic faculties. Two is prior not because it is conceptually independent of other numbers but rather because it is first among the numbers (*Met.* III.3.999a8) – i.e., comes first in the series of natural numbers. This series is a developing, open-ended series whose principle of continuation is understood as soon as any member of the series is understood. This is not required in the case of a focal series. We can understand and define "surgeon" without understanding "surgical instrument" (*EE* VII.2.1236a22), and we can define both "surgeon" and "surgical instrument" without being certain how this particular focal series is to be extended.

Aristotle's comparison between figures and psychic faculties (*DA* II.3. 414b20–32) is of considerable independent interest, but in this context we may confine our remarks to the fact that Aristotle does not introduce focal analysis to explain the serial order which marks kinds of figures and psychic faculties. Rather he speaks of the prior always being present potentially in the posterior (414b29–30) and in so speaking passes over an important difference. For while it is a demonstrable truth that any given quadrilateral can be divided into two triangles, it is a matter of empirical observation that sensation does not occur apart from nutritive capacity.[10] Of course, we might

9 On focal analysis see G. E. L. Owen, "Logic and Metaphysics in Some Earlier Works of Aristotle," in *Aristotle and Plato in the Mid-Fourth Century*, eds Düring and Owen (Göteborg, 1960), pp. 163–90.

10 See Sir David Ross, *Aristotle, De Anima* (Oxford, 1961), p. 224. Here two caveats should at least be mentioned. First, Aristotle might concede that psychological research involves observation and still claim that all developed sciences including psychology can and should be conveyed in a demonstrative manner; see J. Barnes, "Aristotle's Theory of Demonstration," *Phronesis*, 14 (1969), pp. 123–52, reprinted in *Articles on Aristotle*, ed. Barnes et al., (London, 1975), pp. 65–87. Second, the comparison of psychic faculties with rectilinear figures may be quite helpful in pointing up the way in which a higher psychic faculty tends to inform the activity of a lower psychic faculty. Much as the triangle is not actually present in the quadrilateral, so simple manifestations of nutritive and sensitive capacity are rare in the case of human beings. Man's intelligence seems to affect almost everything he does, so that

develop a conception of soul such that higher faculties logically imply the presence of lower ones, but Aristotle does not do this, not only because empirical issues are properly settled by observation (see II.2.413a31–b1), but also because he accepts the possibility of a separable intellect (413b24–7, 3.415a11–12). This is not to say that Aristotle's analysis of psychic faculties makes no use of logical ties. When he comes to consider the psychic faculties individually, he tells us that activities are logically prior to capacities and in the same way objects are prior to activities (II.4.415a16–22). In other words, objects are prior in the focal series object–activity–faculty and therefore are properly investigated first (416a20, 6.418a7–8).[11] But between the faculties Aristotle does not try to establish a focal series. He treats nutritive capacity first, because it is most common (II.4.415a24) and not because its definition will be mentioned in the definition of any higher faculty.

3   PLATO'S LAWS

It turns out that Aristotle's analysis of constitutions differs from his analysis of numbers, figures and psychic faculties. This in itself is of some interest, but if we want to appreciate fully Aristotle's remarks concerning the priority of correct constitutions and the posteriority of mistaken ones, we should get away from numbers, figures and psychic faculties and consider Plato's *Laws* IV.712b8–715e2. For here we find the Athenian Stranger anticipating much of Aristotle's argument.[12] The Stranger recognizes a distinction between constitutions which benefit the entire population and those which are despotic and enslave a portion of the city (*Laws* IV.713a1–2; compare *Pol.*

only in special (often breakdown) cases can we describe the behavior of a human being as a simple manifestation of nutritive and appetitive capacity. See Joachim, *Aristotle, the Nicomachean Ethics*, pp. 38–9, who perhaps overstates the way in which lower faculties are "essentially modified" in creatures endowed with higher faculties. For while human beings often manifest intelligence in taking nutrition, their nutritive faculty is said not only to be common (to all living things) and vegetative in nature but also to be especially active during periods of sleep (*EN* I.13.1102a32–b5).

11 I understand *trophê* to have the same sense in 416a20 as in 416a22, and I interpret the former passage with reference to 415a21 and 6.418a7–8. Hence I prefer the translation of W. S. Hett, *Aristotle: On the Soul*, Loeb edn (London, 1957), p. 91, to that of Ross, *Aristotle, De Anima*, p. 226, and Hamlyn, *Aristotle's De Anima*, p. 20.

12 See Newman, *The Politics of Aristotle*, vol. I, pp. 215–16. That Aristotle was much impressed by *Laws* IV.712b8–715e2 should be obvious from the passage I am about to cite. Here I would add only that (1) when Aristotle mentions guardians and servants of law (III.16.1287a21–2) his words seem to echo *Laws* 714a2, 715c7; (2) when he mentions a connection between law and reason (III.16.1287a29–30) he seems to be recalling *Laws* 714a2 and (3) when he is concerned with constitutional mixture and mentions Sparta approvingly (IV.7.1293b16, 9.1294b19, compare II.6.1265b35) he seems to be influenced in part by *Laws* 712d2–e9.

III.6.1279a20–1). He also connects correctness with the common interest (*Laws* IV.715b3–4; compare *Pol.* III.6.1279a17–20, 13.1283b36–42) and even argues in such a way as to suggest that the notion of citizen is dependent upon that of constitution. For the Stranger first decides to withhold the label "constitution" from political arrangements which do not consider the good of the entire community (IV.712e10, 715b3) and then makes a similar decision concerning the use of "citizen" (715b5). To be sure, the Stranger does not formulate a notion of conceptual dependence in the way that Aristotle does (III.1.1275a35–6), but he does argue in a way that agrees with Aristotelian method. At the very least he seems to recognize the principle that coordinates (*sustoicha*) follow coordinates (*Top.* II.9.114a38–b1, III.3.118a35–6, VII.3. 153b25–6, VIII.1.156a27–30) – that a decision concerning the use of *politeia* ("constitution") affects the use of *politês* ("citizen").[133]

There is, however, one important respect in which the Stranger cannot be said to anticipate Aristotle. This is in withholding the label "constitution" from associations which are not directed toward the common good. The Stranger is not ignorant of the fact that Kleinias and other Greek-speakers use "constitution" quite generally to refer to various arrangements including democracy, oligarchy, aristocracy, kingship and tyranny (IV.712b8–c5). Nevertheless, he decides to restrict the use of "constitution" and thereby to give special dignity to a particular kind of constitution – namely, the kind which considers the interest of all citizens. This is what Stevenson and other modern philosophers have discussed under the rubric "persuasive definition."[14] To introduce as a defining mark something which is absent for many arrangements generally spoken of as constitutions is not so much to analyze usage as to recommend a particular kind of constitution, presumably because this kind of constitution is thought to have desirable features lacking in other forms of constitution. What is troubling and perhaps a fault is that in recommending arrangements which consider everyone's interest, the Stranger begins in a way that does not distinguish clearly between making a recommendation concerning how we might beneficially use words and giving a report concerning how we actually do use words: "Those (arrangements) which we just now named are not constitutions but settlements" (712e9–10).[15] It is only toward the end of the discussion that the Stranger speaks in a

13 The conceptual dependence in question is perhaps more obvious to the Greek speaker than to the English speaker. For *politeia* and *politês* are coordinates sharing a common stem, which is not true of "constitution" and "citizen." But the argument itself does not depend upon the Greek language and can be discussed using standard English equivalents. See above, note 2.

14 C. L. Stevenson, *Ethics and Language* (New Haven, 1944), pp. 206–26. Compare R. Robinson, *Definition* (Oxford, 1950), pp. 165–70, who has discussed persuasive definition under the heading "Real Definition as the Adoption and Recommendation of Ideals."

15 Here and at the end of the paragraph, the translation is my own.

way which seems to indicate that he is recommending something new: "These we *now* say not to be constitutions" (715b2–3).[16]

With this restricted usage Aristotle is unsympathetic. He is prepared to speak of correct and mistaken forms of constitution, but he is adverse to violating everyday language by withholding the label "constitution" from democracies, oligarchies and tyrannies. Accordingly he offers an analysis which makes room for correct and mistaken forms of constitution and at the same time actually wards off arbitrary linguistic decisions. For Aristotle's analysis not only makes evident the goal of political associations; it also provides a clear explanation of why democracies, oligarchies and tyrannies are called constitutions. They are essentially deviations from polity, aristocracy and kingship and therefore are called constitutions by reference to these correct and primary forms. Ambiguity is mitigated, so that we are disinclined to follow the Stranger. Whatever the practical political gains his restricted usage may promise, we are tempted to follow Aristotle in respecting everyday language.[17]

4   NORMATIVE ASPECTS AND THE LOGIC OF GRADING

Aristotle's interest in the priority of correct constitutions does not blind him to alternative ways of classifying constitutions, and in *Politics* IV he reports that men recognize two basic constitutions – oligarchy and democracy. They are said to classify aristocracy as a kind of oligarchy and polity as a kind of democracy in much the same way that they treat the west wind as a kind of north wind and the east wind as a kind of south wind (IV.3.1290a13–19). In this particular passage Aristotle does not state explicitly the reasons why men pick oligarchy and democracy as basic constitutions, but two reasons come readily to mind. The first is suggested by a later passage in the *Politics*, where Aristotle reports that since the rich and the poor are mutually exclusive classes which normally coincide with the few and the many, constitutions seem to divide into oligarchies and democracies (IV.4.1291b7–13). In other words, a consideration of groups within the city encourages a

16 The use of *nun* ("now") at 712e10 seems to differ from the use at 715b3. In the earlier passage *nun* is used to refer back half a page to 712c3–4. (The *OCT* is correctly punctuated at 712e10.) In the later passage *nun* does not seem to pick up something just said but rather to emphasize a present decision concerning the usage of *politeia* ("constitution").

17 Aristotle's interest in everyday language is well known, but perhaps it may be noted in this context that Aristotle not only preserves ordinary language in using "constitution" widely to cover deviant as well as correct forms but also appeals to ordinary language in order to explain using "constitution" narrowly to refer to the specific form of polity (1293a40; compare 1297b24). This is not to suggest that Aristotle was rigidly bound by a devotion to everyday language. In the *Ethics* he acknowledges that men are accustomed to use "constitution" to refer to polity and yet he offers "timocratic" as an appropriate label (*EN* VIII.10.1160a33–5).

division into oligarchies and democracies. The second reason is suggested by the analogy with winds. In the *Meteorologica* we are told that north and south winds are most frequent (II.4.361a6). They are the prevailing winds and this fact seems to explain why certain people treat these two winds as standard winds from which other winds are deviations.[18] Similarly with constitutions frequency might be used to select oligarchy and democracy as basic forms (IV.11.1296a22–3, compare V.1.1301b39–1302a2). Certainly on the criterion of frequency none of the correct forms could qualify. Kingship and aristocracy are beyond most cities and polity is a regrettably rare occurrence (see IV.11.1295a25–34, 1296a37–40).

Aristotle acknowledges that a division into oligarchies and democracies is especially widespread (IV.3.1290a22–4), but he is equally explicit in declaring it truer and better to divide constitutions according to his own framework and so to regard oligarchy and democracy as deviations from one or two well established forms (1290a23–9). In speaking of one or two forms Aristotle is thinking of kingship and aristocracy (see IV.2.1289a30–3) and in speaking of a truer and better division Aristotle is thinking of a normative division. We have already touched upon this point in Section 2, where we observed that correct constitutions are prior not only in a conceptual but also in an evaluative sense. Here we may add that a concern with grading leads Aristotle to reject an alternative framework built around two frequent but mistaken constitutions. This is not to overlook the fact that when Aristotle turns his attention from grading to the causes of revolution, he is quite prepared to speak of aristocracy being in some way an oligarchy (V.7. 1306b24–7). But when Aristotle is interested in grading he prefers a normative framework and not one built around oligarchy and democracy.

This interest in grading also prompts Aristotle to criticize an unnamed predecessor for speaking of good oligarchy and calling democracy best among bad constitutions (IV.2.1289b5–9). What is interesting here is not so much the identity of Aristotle's opponent as the logic of his criticism.[19] He considers the normative aspect of his division so important that he not only objects to speaking of, say, good oligarchy (1289b7–8) but also favours a mode of expression which suggests his fundamental normative distinction. He does not call it an outright error to speak of one oligarchy being better than another (1289b10–11), but he does not like this mode of speech, for it leaves open whether oligarchy is essentially bad. "Better" is a comparative word which is quite indifferent to the actual value of things graded. Two items may be both very bad and yet one may be properly spoken of as better than the other. Hence Aristotle recommends "less bad" (1289b11), for this expression is commonly used to grade items of negative value. To call one

18 See H. Rackham, *Aristotle, Politics*, Loeb edn (London, 1950), pp. 288–9, note a.
19 Aristotle may be thinking of Plato's *Statesman* 302–3; but if this is the case, Aristotle is not only misremembering the Platonic text but also misremembering it to his own advantage (Robinson, *Definition*, p. 72). I prefer to leave the matter undecided.

oligarchy less bad than another is to imply that all are bad – that they are all mis-directed and therefore all belong to the class of mistaken constitutions.

Aristotle's remarks concerning "better" and "less bad" make clear his interest in maintaining a fundamental distinction between correct and deviant constitutions. However, we should not ignore the fact that these remarks are immediately preceded by an ordering of the correct constitutions. Aristotle recognizes the superior value of kingship and aristocracy (IV.2.1289a30–3) and then goes on to create a single series running from best to worst political arrangement (1289a38–b5; compare *EN* VIII.10.1160a35–b22). What we need to be clear about is that such a single series is quite compatible with holding that there are three correct constitutions from which three other constitutions deviate. The important point is that grading requires some standard, so that a complication of the standard is likely to complicate the graded series. When Aristotle first introduces correctness in *Politics* III, he seems to have Plato's *Laws* in mind and in any event is concerned solely with correctness of goal. Correct constitutions are those which consider the common good and mistaken constitutions are those which consider the ruler's good (6.1279a17–20). This analysis in no way precludes the introduction of a second criterion and therefore a more complicated ranking of constitutions. At the very end of *Politics* III, Aristotle reaffirms the existence of three correct constitutions and then adds that the best of these correct constitutions must be that which is managed by the best men (18.1288a32–4). We have here an additional standard – namely, that of virtue (1288a36, or virtue accompanied by resources IV.2.1289a33).[20] This standard is not intended to replace the standard of proper orientation. But it can supplement it and in particular can be used to help grade correctly oriented constitutions. Kingship may be deemed best (*EN* VIII.10.1160a35), for the (true, absolute) monarch is a man of quasi-divine qualities (III.13.1284a10, IV.2.1289a40). Alternatively kingship and (ideal) aristocracy may be grouped together and rated best (IV.2.1289a30–3; compare V.10.1310b3, 32–4), or possibly aristocracy is to be preferred (III.15. 1286b3–7). But whatever the decision concerning these two constitutions, polity ranks third, for a large number of citizens cannot (or at least not easily) possess virtue fully (III.7. 1279a40). When virtue is the standard,

---

20 The possibility of making virtue an additional standard is perhaps implicit in III.7, for here Aristotle associates aristocracy with excellence and polity with military virtue (1279a34–b4). But in this context, Aristotle does not go on to complicate the standard against which he grades constitutions. Instead, he maintains a simple division between correct and deviant constitutions and uses the presence and absence of full virtue to explain the names of two forms of correct constitution. Excellence is introduced to explain the label "aristocracy" (*aristokratia* is the rule of the *aristoi* or a rule oriented towards *to ariston*) and lack of excellence is cited to explain why the rule of the many needs its own name. (This is not to claim that Aristotle's remarks concerning polity are entirely perspicuous. See R. Robinson, *Aristotle's Politics Books III and IV* [Oxford 1962], pp. 24–5.).

polity falls short of perfection and therefore may be counted among deviant forms, though from the standpoint of proper orientation, polity is a correct form from which democracy deviates (IV.8.1293b23–7).

These last remarks concerning polity have been said to reflect a fundamental mistake in Aristotle's division of constitutions.[21] But this criticism is itself mistaken, for properly understood Aristotle's remarks on polity exhibit considerable understanding of what may be called "asymmetrical pairs" – opposites of which one member is a limit that does not admit comparison.[22] When Aristotle calls properly oriented constitutions correct and then goes on to speak of mistaken deviations, he is recognizing at least implicitly that correctness is not a matter of degree but rather a limit from which it is only possible to fall away. And when Aristotle uses parekbasis (literally, "a going out aside from") to refer to deviant forms, he is not choosing a poor word.[23] In fact his choice of label is just right. We may compare correctness with straightness – a comparison which is encouraged in Greek by the ambiguity of orthos.[24] Being straight is the opposite of being crooked, but while a line can be more or less crooked, a line is either straight or not straight. Similarly with noses straightness is an all or nothing proposition. Hooked and snub noses may vary in their contour, but they do not approach the Classical ideal by becoming more and more straight. Rather they become less and less crooked until they are straight. At this point they have reached a limit and become paradigms from which hooked and snub noses are properly said to deviate (see V.9.1309b23).

In the same way constitutions are either correct or incorrect, and Aristotle tacitly recognizes this when he groups polity together with certain (non-ideal) aristocracies, states that these constitutions are not deviations and then goes on to call them deviations of which there are deviations (IV.8. 1293b23–7). The point is that when the virtue of rulers becomes a (part of the) standard, then polity and certain aristocracies are properly spoken of as deviations, though deviations in lesser degree than democracy, oligarchy and tyranny. But when goal-direction is the criterion in play, then polity and the several aristocracies in question meet the standard and are properly spoken of as correct constitutions from which other forms deviate to greater or less degree. In other words, Aristotle recognizes both that correctness requires a standard which may be varied and also that correctness is not a matter of degree. When the standard is complicated by the addition of virtue, then

---

21 E. Zeller, *Aristotle and the Earlier Peripatetics*, tr. Costelloe and Muirhead (New York, 1962), pp. 243–4.
22 I have taken the phrase "asymmetrical pairs" from N. Cooper, "Pleasure and Goodness in Plato's *Philebus*," *The Philosophical Quarterly*, 18 (1968), p. 12. See also E. Sapir, "Grading, a Study in Semantics," *Philosophy of Science*, 11 (1944), pp. 115–17.
23 Barker, *The Political Thought of Plato and Aristotle*, p. 308, note 2, suggests that *elleipsis* would be better label than *parekbasis*.
24 In labeling the correct constitutions Aristotle uses the adjective *orthos* (1279a18) which can mean not only correct but also straight. Compare *LSJ* 1249 s.v.

polity becomes not less correct but rather a deviant form.[25] All this may be rather complex,[26] but it is not mistaken confusion. On the contrary, it is the mark of a philosopher who understands the logic of grading.[27]

25 Of course, Aristotle may slip into everyday language and speak of "the most correct" constitution (1293b25). But if this is a slip or perhaps a concession to ordinary language (compare Sapir, "Grading, a Study in Semantics," p. 116), it is far more important that Aristotle speaks of polity and certain aristocracies as deviations, for in so doing he is tacitly recognizing the idea of grading downwards from some standard of perfection.

26 The matter can be made even more complex by considering the deviant constitutions. For in discussing them Aristotle seems to introduce still another criterion – namely, durability. Democracies are likely to endure longest, then oligarchies and finally tyrannies (V.1.1302a8–15; 12.1315b11–39). This means that democracy may be rated highest (i.e., least bad) among the deviant constitutions on three different criteria: (1) in considering the interests of a large number of people, it departs least from the proper goal of seeking the common interest; (2) while a large group of people will never excel in virtue, it is least likely to be marked by extreme vice; (3) it is least likely to experience revolution and collapse in a short period of time (compare V.1.1302a8–9). Tyranny gets the lowest rating on these criteria and oligarchy takes the middle position. Of course, the characterization of any actual constitution is an empirical matter. The tyranny at Sicyon lasted a considerable time, and (because) its rulers exhibited certain marks of good character (V.12.1315b12–21). Moreover, when several criteria are used to establish a hierarchy, there is no principle requiring that each criterion, taken independently, would produce the same ordered series as they all do taken together. Durability may be a case in point. For while the reign of a fully virtuous king would seem to be extremely stable, finding a successor who has all the qualities required for kingship is no easy matter (compare III.15.1286b22–7).

27 In conclusion I want to thank the editors of this volume for helpful suggestions which are reflected in certain changes to the original version published some 13 years ago.

11

Aristotle's Theory of Distributive Justice

DAVID KEYT

1 INTRODUCTION

Aristotle's political philosophy, like his zoology, has two phases. In the analytic phase Aristotle divides the object of his investigation, the polis, into its parts (*Pol.* I.1.1252a18–23; IV.3.1289b27–1290a5, 4.1290b38–1291b8; VII.8[1]). In the synthetic phase he describes the various ways these parts can be put together to form a polis (*Pol.* IV.4.1290b21–39; and see *Top.* VI.13.150b23–6). The way the parts of a polis are put together is its form;[2] its form is its constitution (*Pol.* III.2.1276a17–b13); and a constitution in turn is a kind of justice. "All constitutions," Aristotle says, "are a kind of justice; for they are communities, and every community is held together by what is just" (*EE* VII.9.1241b13–15). Aristotle distinguishes two kinds of (particular) justice: distributive (*dianemêtikon*) and corrective (*diorthôtikon*) (*EN* V.2.1130b30–1131a1, 4.1131b25–9). Although a polis is held together to some extent by corrective or judicial justice, the justice of the dikast or juror (*Pol.* I.2.1253a37–9), a constitution is primarily a kind of distributive justice. Aristotle defines a constitution as "an ordering of the offices[3] in a polis *in respect of the way they are distributed*, and of the questions what is the supreme element of the constitition and what is the end (*telos*) of each community" (*Pol.* IV.1.1289a15–18; see also III.1.1274b38, 6.1278b8–11). Thus the large part of Aristotle's political philosophy that is concerned with the description, classification, and evaluation of constitutions is essentially a theory of distributive justice. The basic principle of this theory is introduced and given mathematical expression in Aristotle's essay on justice, one of the common books of the *Nicomachean* and *Eudemian Ethics* (*EN* V = *EE* IV); but it is only in the *Politics* that the theory is fully developed and applied.

In his theory of distributive justice Aristotle tries to steer a middle course between Protagorean relativism according to which "whatever things *appear*

---

1 References to the *Politics* and the *Nicomachean Ethics* are to the editions of W. D. Ross and I. Bywater respectively in the series of Oxford Classical Texts. All translations of Aristotle are my own.
2 See especially *eidos tês suntheseôs* ("form of the compound") at 1276b7–8.
3 For the sort of offices Aristotle has in mind see *Pol.* IV.14–16 and VI.8.

just and fine to each polis *are* so for it as long as it holds by them" (Plato, *Theat*. 167c4–5) and Platonic absolutism with its appeal to transcendent standards (*EN* 1.6.1096b31–1097a3; Plato, *Rep*. V.472a8–e6, IX.592a10–b4). This is a project with obvious attractions. How is it carried out? One aim of this paper is to answer this question by tracing Aristotle's theory of distributive justice to its foundations.

A second aim is to show how three divergent and seemingly incompatible elements in the *Politics* are connected. The first element is the description in Books VI and VIII of the best constitution. What Aristotle describes is a form of constitution under which a polis is ruled by its older citizens, all of whom are men of complete virtue – the sort of constitution that elsewhere in the *Politics* he calls a "true" aristocracy (IV.7.1293b1–19, 8.1294a24–5). The second element is the defense of democracy against Platonic criticisms in Book III, chapter 11. "That the many ought to be supreme rather than the few best men would seem to be held," Aristotle says, "and to present some difficulty *but probably to be true*" (1281a40–42). The third element is the justification of absolute kingship in Book III, chapter 17 (see also III.13. 1284a3–17, b22–34; 14.1285b29–33; VII.14.1332b16–23). Under this "first and most divine" constitution (IV.2.1289a40) an individual who is "like a god among men" (III.13.1284a10–11) rules according to his own wish unrestricted by law.

It is tempting to seek an explanation of these divergent elements of the *Politics* in Aristotle's complex personal situation as a former member of Plato's Academy, a resident alien in democratic Athens, and a client of the Macedonian monarchy.[4] One who succumbs to this temptation will find in the close similarity of the best polis of Books VII and VIII to the Cretan polis of Magnesia described in the *Laws*[5] an offset to Aristotle's earlier criticism of the *Republic* and the *Laws* in Book II and a proclamation of Aristotle's fealty to Platonic ideals.[6] He will see Aristotle's defense of democracy as a sop thrown by a resident alien, aware of the fate of Socrates, to the Athenian populace. And he will believe that the justification of absolute kingship is addressed to Aristotle's Macedonian patrons.[7] One who seeks such extraphilosophical motivation for these divergent elements of the

4 For a recent account of Aristotle's life see W. K. C. Guthrie, *A History of Greek Philosophy*, vol. VI (Cambridge, 1981), pp. 18–45. Passages from ancient and medieval writers bearing on Aristotle's relations with Philip and Alexander are collected in Ingemar Düring, *Aristotle in the Ancient Biographical Tradition* (Göteborg, 1957), pp. 284–99.

5 For Aristotle's debt to the *Laws* in *Politics* VII and VIII see Ernest Barker, *Greek Political Theory*, 3rd edn (London, 1947), pp. 380–2; and Ellen Meiksins Wood and Neal Wood, *Class Ideology and Ancient Political Theory* (Oxford, 1978), pp. 245–8.

6 Wood and Wood claim that a comparison of the two descriptions reveals "the common aristocratic, authoritarian, and anti-democratic pattern of the political thought of the two philosophers" (ibid., p. 248).

7 Hans Kelsen holds that Aristotle's "apology for royalty was intended to be the ideology of one definite hereditary monarchy" – namely, the Macedonian. See "The Philosophy of Aristotle and the Hellenic–Macedonian Policy," *The International Journal of Ethics*, 48 (1937), p. 37.

Politics may also be blind to the underlying unity of Aristotle's political philosophy and to the fact that all three elements have their origin in a single conception of distributive justice.

2 THE PRINCIPLE OF DISTRIBUTIVE JUSTICE

Distributive justice for Aristotle is concerned primarily with the distribution of political authority (*politikê archê*) and only secondarily with the distribution of wealth.[8] It is the virtue of both the *nomothetês*, or lawgiver, and the ekklesiast,[9] or assemblyman; and there are occasions for its exercise when the lawgiver is called upon to establish a constitution, "an ordering of the offices in a polis" (*Pol.* IV.1.1289a15–16), and when the ekklesiast is called upon to select particular men to fill these offices. Its principle, a refinement of an idea of Plato's (see *Gorgias* 507e6–508a8 and *Laws* VI.765e9–758a2), is a political application of the mathematical idea of geometric proportion, whose formula is:

$$\frac{A}{B} = \frac{C}{D}$$

Geometric proportion (*geômetrikê analogia*) (*EN* V.3.1131b12–13) is so called on account of the large role it plays in geometry: for example, in the definition of the similarity of rectilinear figures.[10] It is contrasted with arithmetic proportion, the mathematical idea underlying Aristotle's principle of corrective justice. Geometric proportion is an equally of ratios (*isotês logôn*) (V.3.1131a31); arithmetic proportion, of differences.

The just, Aristotle says, "requires at least four terms: for those for whom it is just are two, and that in which it resides, the things, are two" (*EN* V.3.1131a18–20). This statement suggests that Aristotle intends the following application of the formula of geometric proportion:

(1) $$\frac{\text{Callias}}{\text{Coriscus}} = \frac{\text{Parcel } a \text{ of land}}{\text{Parcel } b \text{ of land}}$$

This is often the way he is taken by his commentators.[11] But, as his

---

8 For the items distributed see the relevant occurrences in the *Politics* of the verbs for distributing and apportioning: *nemein*, *aponemein*, and *dianemein*. *nemein*: II.6.1265b25, III.12.1282b24, IV.1.1289a16, 8.1294a10, 12.1297a9, V.8.1309a28, VI.5.1320a30, VII.9.1329a16, 10.1330a16. *aponemein*: IV.8.1293b41, V.8.1309a21–2, 11.1315a6–7. *dianemein*: III.10.1281a15, a18, 17.1288a14, IV.3.1290a8, 4.1290b4, VI.5.1320a37, b2, VII.4.1326b15.

9 The *nomothetês* is distinguished from the ekklesiast and the dikast at *Rhet* I.1. 1354b5–8. See also *EN* VI.8.1141b24–33.

10 See Aristotle's definition of such similarity at *An. Post.* II.17.99a12–14, which corresponds exactly to Definition VII.1 of Euclid's *Elements*.

11 See, for example, J. A. Stewart, *Notes on the Nicomachean Ethics of Aristotle* (Oxford, 1892), vol. I, pp. 427–8, and H. H. Joachim, *Aristotle – The Nicomachean Ethics* (Oxford, 1955), p. 142.

commentators are well aware, this proportion does not have any meaning until the respect in which the men, on the one hand, and the parcels of land, on the other, are being compared is specified. The parcels of land might be compared in size, location, productivity, and so forth; and the men, in age, height, physique, wealth, lineage, moral virtue, and so forth. What Aristotle is weighing is, in general, the *axia*, or worth, of the persons (1131a24–6) and the positive or negative value of the things (1131b19–23). The application of the formula is thus more complex:

(2) $$\frac{\text{The worth of Callias}}{\text{The worth of Coriscus}} = \frac{\text{The value of parcel } a \text{ of land}}{\text{The value of parcel } b \text{ of land}}$$

Now, "the worth of Callias" expresses the application of the function *worth of* to Callias, and "the value of parcel *a* of land" expresses the application of the function *value of* to parcel *a* of land. The notation for functional application is $\varphi(\alpha)$. $\varphi(\alpha)$ is the value[12] of the function φ for the argument α. If "Q" signifies the function *worth of* and "V", *value of*, (2) can be written:

(3) $$\frac{Q(\text{Callias})}{Q(\text{Coriscus})} = \frac{V(\text{parcel } a \text{ of land})}{V(\text{parcel } b \text{ of land})}$$

Thus in the notation of modern mathematics the general formula is:

(4) $$\frac{Q(x)}{Q(y)} = \frac{V(s)}{X(t)}$$

A simple manipulation of (4) yields:[13]

(5) $$\frac{Q(x) + V(s)}{Q(y) + V(t)} = \frac{Q(x)}{Q(y)}$$

This is a modern rendition of Aristotle's principle of distributive justice (1131b9–10). The reason Aristotle prefers (5) to (4) is that he wants his formula to display the yoking together (*hê suzeuxis*) of *s* and *x* and *t* and *y*. He wants his formula to show that *s* is the thing assigned to *x* and that *t* is the thing assigned to *y*. But (5) can be improved upon by a further exploitation of modern functional notation. For "the thing assigned to *x*" expresses the application of the function *thing assigned to*[14] to *x*. Thus if "T" signifies the function *thing assigned to*, $T(x) = s$ and $T(y) = t$. By substitution (4) becomes:

(6) $$\frac{Q(x)}{Q(y)} = \frac{V(T(x))}{V(T(y))}$$

This formula combines simplicity with the proper logical multiplicity. In ordinary language, a distribution is just to the extent that the value of the

12 The mathematical use of this word is not to be confused with its axiological use elsewhere in this paragraph.

thing it assigns to one person stands to the value of the thing it assigns to another as the worth of the one person stands to the worth of the other.

Aristotle believes that everyone shares this general principle (*EN* V.3. 1131a10–14, *Pol.* III.12.1282b18–21) and that people agree in their evaluation of the things being distributed (*Pol.* III.9.1280a18–19). Where they disagree is over worth. "All agree," Aristotle says, "that the just in distribution must be according to worth of some sort (*kat' axian tina*[15]), though all do not recognize the same sort of worth; but democrats say it is freedom, oligarchs wealth or birth, and aristocrats virtue" (*EN* V.3.1131a25–8). People disagree over *axia*, or worth, because they evaluate it according to different standards. Adopting an idea of John Rawls', we can distinguish the *concept* of distributive justice from the various *conceptions* of it.[16] If the letter "*Q*" in formula (6) is regarded as a variable ranging over the various standards of worth, the formula expresses Aristotle's concept of distributive

13

$$(1) \quad \frac{Q(x)}{Q(y)} = \frac{V(s)}{V(t)}$$

$$(2) \quad \frac{Q(x)}{V(s)} = \frac{Q(y)}{V(t)} \quad (1131b5\text{–}7) \qquad \text{Euclid, Proposition V.16}$$

$$(3) \quad \frac{Q(x) + V(s)}{V(s)} = \frac{Q(y) + V(t)}{V(t)} \quad \text{Euclid, Proposition V.18}$$

$$(4) \quad \frac{Q(x) + V(s)}{Q(y) + V(t)} = \frac{V(s)}{V(t)} \qquad \text{Euclid, Proposition V.16}$$

$$(5) \quad \frac{Q(x) + V(s)}{Q(y) + V(t)} = \frac{Q(x)}{Q(y)} \qquad \text{Euclid, Proposition V.11}$$

It is presupposed of course that all denominators differ from zero.

14 To ensure that this relation *is* a function the items assigned to each person are treated as a single thing. Thus if a person is assigned both an estate and a political office, the estate and the office are treated as one thing, his portion according to the given assignment.

15 This is the broadest use of *kat' axian*. Aristotle uses the expression in two narrower ways. Sometimes *kat' axian* is contrasted with *kat' arithmon* and distinguishes *virtue and wealth* from freedom (*Pol.* V.1.1301b30–1302a8, VI.2.1317b3–4). Other times *kat' axian* is associated with *kat' aretên* and marks *virtue* off from wealth and freedom (*Pol.* III.5.1278a19–20, V.10.1310b33). See W. L. Newman, *The Politics of Aristotle* (Oxford, 1887–1902), vol. III, p. 177.

16 In drawing the distinction between the concept of justice and various conceptions of justice Rawls refers to the section of H. L. A. Hart's *The Concept of Law* (Oxford, 1961) entitled "Principles of Justice." From the notes to this section it is clear that Hart wrote it with *EN* V before him. Thus it is not surprising that Rawls' distinction fits Aristotle so well, for it derives from Aristotle. Only the terms marking it are new.

justice. When the letter is replaced by an expression for one of these standards, the formula that results expresses one of the various conceptions of distributive justice that fall under the general concept. Thus if "Q" is replaced by "the wealth of," the resulting formula expresses the oligarchic interpretation of Aristotle's principle of distributive justice or, in short, the oligarchic conception of justice.

Do the various interpretations of Aristotle's principle of distributive justice have any content? Do they determine definite distributions of the apportionable goods. In particular do they determine definite distributions of political authority? Suppose one were an ancient Greek lawgiver given the task of devising a democratic constitution for an Athenian colony – a Protagoras charged with writing a constitution for a Thurii. Would the democratic conception of distributive justice provide a helpful guide?

The first step in applying the formula for democratic justice is to understand its standard of worth, *eleutheria*, or freedom. As the standard that in a democracy determines citizenship, freedom is contrasted not only with slavery but also with foreignness. To be free in this narrow sense is to be a freeman as opposed to a slave (an *eleutheros* as opposed to a *doulos*) and a native as opposed to a foreigner (an *astos* as opposed to a *xenos*).[17] Freedom in this narrow sense is a matter of citizen birth, not simply of free status; and in the *Politics* Aristotle indicates the scale by which Greek democracies graded a person's extraction (III.5.1278a28–34, VI.4.1319b6–11):

   (a) Both parents citizens
   (b) Citizen father, alien mother
   (c) Citizen mother, alien father
   (d) Citizen father or mother, other parent a slave

As Aristotle's remarks in the passages just cited make plain, freedom was an elastic standard in Greek political history that could be stretched or shrunk depending upon the needs of a given democracy at a particular time or the political aims of its leaders. In good times a democracy would count as free and admit as citizens only those of grade (a); as times got harder and the stock of citizens became depleted, it would gradually relax its standard until even those of grade (d) were admitted.

Two other restrictions, those of sex and age, narrow the application of the formula still further. Every historical (but not every imagined) Greek polis excluded women from full citizenship. And of course only an adult could be a full citizen. (In Athens a male who was free in the narrow sense was enrolled as a full citizen upon reaching eighteen [*Ath. Pol.* 41.1].)

17 For the word *astos* see *Pol.* III.5.1278a34, IV.16.1300b31–2; and Plato, *Gorgias* 515a7. Aristotle never explicitly opposes *eleutheros* and *xenos*, but *eleutheros* clearly has this narrow sense at *Pol.* IV.4.1290b9–14 where Aristotle remarks that at one time in Apollonia and in Thera the only people counted as *hoi eleutheroi* were the descendants of the original settlers.

Even though the standard that an adult male had to satisfy to be counted as free and registered as a citizen of a Greek democracy was elastic, there were no degrees of freedom among those who met the standard: one man's freedom was equal to any other's. "Democracy arose," Aristotle says, "from those who are equal in any respect whatever thinking they are absolutely equal (because they are all alike *free*, they claim to be absolutely *equal*) . . . " (*Pol.* V.1.1301a28–31; see also III.9.1280a24–5). The democratic argument, then, is that since the freedom of one man is the same as that of any other, the value of the things assigned to one free man should, by the democratic conception of justice, equal the value of the things assigned to any other (V.1.1301a34–5). This is easily symbolized. (Let "*F*" signify the function *freedom of*; let "$\forall$" abbreviate "for each," and let the variables "*x*" and "*y*" range over the free men of a given polis.)

$$(1) \quad (\forall x)(\forall y) \left(\frac{F(x)}{F(y)} = \frac{V(T(x))}{V(T(y))} \right) \quad \text{(The democratic conception of justice)}$$

$$(2) \quad (\forall x)(\forall y)(F(x) = F(y)) \qquad \text{(Equal freedom)}$$

$$(3) \quad \therefore (\forall x)(\forall y)(V(T(x)) = V(T(y))) \quad \text{(Equal awards)}$$

Aristotle distinguishes a constitutional principle (*axiôma, hupothesis*) (*Pol.* VI.1.1317a39, 2.1317a40) such as (3) from "all the things . . . appropriate to the principle" (VI.1.1317a36–7). In the case of democracy he distinguishes the principle of democratic justice (*to dêmotikon dikaion*) (VI.3. 1318a18) from the institutions designed to realize the principle (*ta dêmotika*) (VI.1–2. 1317a19, b18). Political egalitarianism, which follows from (3) when the thing being distributed is taken to be political authority, is the primary expression of democratic justice.[18] The Greek institutions that were designed to realize it are sketched in *Politics* VI.2. It is democratic for "the ekklesia [to which all free men are admitted] to be supreme over all things or the most important" (1317b28–9) and for the dikasteries, or law courts, to be selected from among all free men and to deal with all matters "or with most and the greatest and most important, such as the scrutiny of the conduct of officials and constitutional matters and private contracts" (b25–8). It is democratic for administrative, executive, and military offices to be open to all free men (b18–19) and thus to require no property qualification or at most a minimal one (b22–3), to be filled by lot wherever no special experience or skill is required (b20–21), and to have short terms (b24–5) and minimal power (b29–30). It is democratic, furthermore, for repeated tenure of the same executive or administrative office to be restricted or prohibited (b23–4) and, so far as funds allow, for all who exercise political functions to be paid – ekklesiasts, dikasts, and officers (b35–8).

18 But not the only expression. Other forms of egalitarianism mentioned by Aristotle as characteristic of democracy are parity of rearing and education and of food and dress (*Pol.* IV.9.1294b19–29; compare III.16.1287a12–16).

All of these institutions are devices for maximizing political equality within the bounds of the practicable. The ideal situation according to political egalitarianism would seem to be one in which no free man *at any time* has more political authority than any other. But this is not practicable since not everyone can be a dikast or city treasurer or general at the same time (see *Pol.* II.2.1261a32–4). The political egalitarian, when forced by practical considerations to depart from his ideal, always gives up as little as possible. Each of the democratic institutions that Aristotle lists in *Politics* VI.2 can be brought under one or another of four successively weaker egalitarian maxims. (1) No free man *at any time* should have more political authority than any other. In conformity with this ideal maxim all free men are members of the ekklesia; and, along with this, the power of the ekklesia is maximized and that of individual officials minimized. (2) No free man *during an average lifetime* should have more political authority than any other. Although it is not practicable for every free man to sit on every dikastery, it is practicable in a Greek polis for every free man during an average lifetime to sit on as many as every other. This second maxim is one expression of the democratic motto "to rule and be ruled in turn" (1317b2–3). (3) The *probability* of being selected to fill a particular position of authority *sometime during one's life* should be the same for all free men and should be as high as practicable. The use of the lot makes the probability the same for all; short terms and restrictions on the repeated tenure of the same office increase the probability of selection.[19] (4) If an office requires experience or skill, it should be filled by election; but every free man should be eligible to stand for election and every free man should have exactly one vote. The point of providing pay for ekklesiasts, dikasts, and officers is to ensure that no free man is forced to forego his share of political authority by the daily pressure to grind out a living. It seems, then, that the democratic conception of justice, charitably interpreted, does have content.

The institutions designed to realize oligarchic justice (*ta oligarchika*) (*Pol.* V.9.1309b21, 37) are the opposite of those designed to realize democratic justice (see VI.6.1320b18–21). It is oligarchic, first of all, for the governing class to be determined by wealth rather than freedom (VI.6.1320b20–33). Thus it is oligarchic to select the dikasteries from the rich (IV.16.1301a12–13), to restrict membership in the ekklesia[20] to those who satisfy a high

---

19 Aristotle remarks several times that a boule is a democratic institution whereas a committee of probuloi ("precouncilors") is oligarchic (*Pol.* IV.15.1299b30–32, 37–8, VI.2.1317b30–31, 8.1322b16–17, 1323a6–9). This is sufficiently explained by the one difference that Aristotle mentions: a committee of probuloi is much smaller than a boule (IV.15.1299b34–6). (The one appointed in Athens in 413 BC in the wake of the Sicilian disaster consisted of only ten members.) For the larger the body, the greater the probability that any given citizen will be appointed to it. In Athens, where the boule had 500 members who served for one year and were eligible after an interval to repeat only once, the probability that a citizen would be a *bouleutês* at least once in his life was quite high – almost one-half. Thus it is not surprising that Socrates should have been a member of the boule on a notable occasion (Plato, *Apol.* 32a–c).
20 If one exists. Not every oligarchy had an ekklesia. See *Pol.* III.1.1275b7–8.

property-qualification (IV.9.1294b3–4), and to set a still higher property-qualification for the higher administrative, executive, and military offices (VI.6.1320b22–5). Secondly, it is oligarchic to appoint officers by election rather than by lot (IV.9.1294b7–9, 31–3). Thirdly, it is oligarchic, if the ekklesia and the dikasteries are composed of rich and poor, not to pay the poor for attending but to fine the rich for nonattendance (IV.9.1294a37–9, 13.1297a17–19, 21–4, 14.1298b16–18). Fourthly, it is oligarchic, in vivid contrast to democratic practice, for offices to be few in number, to be held for long periods by the same individuals, and to have maximal power (II.11. 1273a15–17; IV.9.1294b31–4; V.1.1301b25–6, 6.1306a12–19; and *EN* VIII. 10.1160b12–16). It is oligarchic, finally, not to equalize political power among citizens but to proportion it to wealth (VI.3.1318a18–21).

As devices for realizing oligarchic justice the institutions that Aristotle describes are not comparable in ingenuity to those invented by Greek democrats for realizing democratic justice. Comparisons of wealth can be given precise numerical values; for, as Aristotle remarks, "by wealth we mean everything whose worth is measured by money" (*EN* IV.1.1119b26–7). Let "*W*" signify the function *wealth of*, let m and n be nonnegative integers, and let $n \neq 0$. then:

$$(1) \qquad \frac{W(x)}{W(y)} = \frac{m}{n}$$

The oligarchic conception of justice is:

$$(2) \qquad \frac{W(x)}{W(y)} = \frac{V(T(x))}{V(T(y))}$$

Consequently

$$(3) \qquad \frac{V(T(x))}{V(T(y))} = \frac{m}{n}$$

The institutional problem is to discover devices for realizing (3) – in particular, to find ways of exactly proportioning political authority to wealth. Although the oligarchic institutions that Aristotle describes have the general effect of giving the very wealthy most of the political authority in a polis, they do not proportion political authority to wealth very exactly. This is due to a failure of imagination or of conviction on the part of Greek oligarchs, for it is not difficult to think of ways of approaching the oligarchic ideal more closely. One device that comes immediately to mind, of which the last item on Aristotle's list of oligarchic institutions may be a glimmer, is to think of a polis as a joint-stock company and to propotion votes to wealth (III.9. 1280a25–31; see also *EN* V.4.1131b29–31). If Callias is twice as wealthy as Coriscus, he is given twice as many votes as Coriscus. By adopting this device an oligarchy would not need to restrict membership in the ekklesia to those who satisfy a given property-qualification. Every free man could be a member and have exactly as much weight in its actions as he has wealth. A second device that comes to mind is to proportion terms of office to wealth, to allow Callias, if he is twice as wealthy as Coriscus, to hold a given executive, administrative, or military office twice as long as Coriscus. Consequently, there are institutions through which the oligarchic conception of justice, as well as the democratic, can be realized.

The application of the aristocratic conception of justice, on the other hand, faces a formidable obstacle. If one person is more virtuous than another, by the aristocratic conception of justice he should be allotted more political authority than the other. But how much more? To this question the aristocratic conception of justice can give no answer. For virtue, unlike wealth, is an intensive rather than an extensive quality. One person can be more virtuous than another, but it has no clear sense to say that he is x times as virtuous as the other. Consequently, there is no basis for inferring that the one person should have x times as much political authority as the other. Although Aristotle does not discuss this problem in the *Politics*, he was probably aware of its existence; for he neatly evades it in his best polis, which is a kind of aristocracy, by means of some special assumptions.

3   THE CORRECT STANDARD OF WORTH

In the middle section of the third book of the *Politics*, the philosophical core of the entire treatise, Aristotle attempts to mediate the claims of the various rivals for the supreme political authority (*to kurion*) in a polis (III.9–13). Should the many have supreme authority, or the rich, or the good, or the one best man, or a tyrant (III.10.1281a11–13)? In answering this question Aristotle begins where he left off in *EN* V.3. The view of the *Ethics* that distributive justice is a matter of geometric proportionality is generally accepted, he says; what remains to be determined is the standard of worth to combine with it (III.12.1282b18–23; see also III.9.1280a7–25). The problem Aristotle tackles in this section of the *Politics* is thus that of evaluating and ranking the various standards of worth advanced by the various rivals for political authority and of ascertaining, if he can, which is the absolutely correct standard (*ho orthos horos*) (see III.13.1283b28).

Aristotle begins by considering the idea that, other things being equal, "superiority in any good" is a legitimate ground for distributing political offices unequally (III.12.1282b23–7) and offers two arguments against it (1282b27–1283a9),[21] both of which are of the form *modus tollens*. The first, the "fitness and contribution" argument, divides into three segments. In the first segment Aristotle points out that if the idea under consideration is true, then any personal attribute whatever even height or complexion[22] will be part of a

21 The general structure of this passage was clarified for me by Charles Young.
22 *chrôma*. Since Aristotle is considering how political authority should be distributed among the free men of a Greek polis, all of whom will be Greek, he is presumably referring to light and dark complexion rather than to white and dark races as Franz Susemihl and R. D. Hicks suggest in their note on this passage in *The Politics of Aristotle*, Books I–V [I–III, VII–VIII] (London, 1894).

correct standard of worth. The consequent of this conditional strikes
Aristotle as transparently false (1282b30), and so he infers (implicitly) that
the antecedent is false. (Aristotle does not mean to deny that such irrelevant
properties as height or complexion are never used as standards of worth.
Remembering his Herodotus [3.20], he notes in another context that in
Ethiopia offices are distributed according to height [IV.4.1290b4–5].) In the
second and third segments of the argument Aristotle explains the transparent
falsity of the consequent by reference to "the other sciences and abilities"
(1282b30–31) – by reference, in particular, to the art of flute-playing. In
staging a performance of flute music, it would be proper, he observes, to
distribute the better flutes to the better flutists. In this situation skill in
flute-playing is the only standard of worth that is relevant. Generalizing from
this case we get the "fitness-for-the-job" criterion: "The one who is superior
at the work (*ergon*) should be given the superiority also in instruments"
(1282b33–4; compare *PA* IV.10.687a7–15).[23] Pressing the point still further,
Aristotle goes on to say in the third segment of the argument that even if the
person who excels as a flutist falls short in birth and beauty and if the value of
each of these exceeds the value of skill in flute-playing more than his skill
exceeds the skill of one who is wellborn and beautiful,[24] he should still,
nevertheless, get the better flute. For birth and beauty do not contribute to a
musical performance; skill in flute-playing does. This suggests a second,
distinct criterion: contribution to the task (1283a1; see also III.9. 1281a4–8).

In the second argument,[25] the "incommensurability" argument, Aristotle
points out that if every personal attribute were part of a correct standard of
worth, all goods would have to be commensurable.[26] It would have to be
possible to weigh the height of one man against the virtue of another. And if
height can be weighed against virtue, then a good height must be equal in
worth to some fraction of virtue. (Similarly if the goodness of a man is
commensurable with the goodness of a dinner, then some number of good
dinners – a million, say – must be equal in worth to a good man.) But this is
absurd. Virtue and height are goods in different categories: the one is a good
in the category of quality; the other, in the category of quantity (compare *EN*
I.6.1096a19–29). In addition, one is a good of the soul; the other, of the body.
They are no more commensurable in worth than a pen, a taste of wine, and
a musical note are commensurable in sharpness (*Top.* I.15.107b13–18, *Phys.*
VII.4.248b7–10). Consequently, not every personal attribute can be part of a
correct standard of worth.

23 The comparison between skill in flute-playing and political excellence goes back
at least as far as Protagoras's Great Speech in Plato's *Protagoras* 327a–c.
24 $B(y) > B(x)$ and $V(B)/V(S) > S(x)/S(y) > 1$ where "V," "B," and "S" signify *value
of, beauty (of)*, and *skill in flute-playing (of)* respectively.
25 Although the text of this argument is very uncertain, Aristotle's point is clear
enough.
26 The concept of commensurability is discussed in section 5 below.

Aristotle concludes from these two arguments that "it is on the ground of the elements of which a polis is composed that the claim [to political office] must be based" (1283a14–15). The elements he enumerates – the free, the wealthy, the wellborn (who drop out as redundant[27]), and justice and military[28] virtue (a16–20) – make a heterogeneous list. Justice and military virtue are qualities; the other items are groups. Since each group consists of individuals who possess a given attribute, we have the following progression:

1 an attribute (e.g., *aretê*, virtue)
2 its possessor (e.g., *ho agathos*, the good man)
3 the group of its possessors (e.g., *hoi agathoi*, the good)

Although Aristotle moves carelessly from one sort of item to another, the first and third members of this progression find their home in separate stages of Aristotle's overall argument. A group taken as a whole can possess an attribute that its individual members lack. Thus although every worker in a polis may be poor, the wealth of the whole group of workers may be enormous. This point is the nub of Aristotle's summation argument[29] and is important in adjudicating the claims of the wealthy, the free, and the good to political authority. But the summation argument, which weighs the attributes of various groups taken as wholes, is separate from and posterior to the search for a correct standard of worth, which is a search for an attribute or a conjunction of attributes.

To determine which attributes enter into the correct standard of worth Aristotle appeals, as we have seen, to two second-order attributes: contribution and fitness. Aristotle does not explain how contribution differs from fitness; indeed he gives no indication that he even regards the two as distinct. Consequently, in interpreting this crucial part of Aristotle's theory of distributive justice one is forced to develop Aristotle's rather meager suggestions. One attractive line of interpretation, which preserves both plausibility and consistency, takes contribution as the primary criterion and fitness as a secondary and supplementary criterion. By this interpretation, for an attribute to be part of the correct standard of worth of the principle of distributive justice it must either enable or have enabled its possessor to make a contribution of some sort to the enterprise whose goods are being apportioned by means of the principle. Furthermore, if the good being apportioned is a function (*ergon*) of some sort, the attribute in question must fit its possessor to fulfil the function.

27 As Newman remarks in his note to 1283a33, "the [wellborn] are in a superlative degree what the [free] are in a positive degree" (see 1283b19–20). Freedom and good birth are both matters of ancestry. A man is free (in the narrow sense) if his ancestors are neither slaves nor aliens. A man is wellborn if in addition his ancestors are virtuous and rich (*Pol.* IV.8.1294a21–2, V.1.1301b3–4).
28 Reading *polemikês* with the majority of manuscripts rather than *politikês* with a small minority and Ross.
29 See section 5 below.

Suppose, for example, that the enterprise whose benefits and functions are being apportioned is a performance of flute music. Skill in flute-making and skill in flute-playing, but not height or good birth, contribute to such a performance. So by the contribution criterion both attributes are relevant when the roles, the proceeds, and the honors connected with the performance are being distributed. However, skill in flute-making fits its possessor to manufacture flutes whereas skill in flute-playing fits its possessor to play a flute. Therefore, by the fitness criterion the flute maker should be assigned the role of manufacturing flutes; and the flute player, the role of playing the flute. Both should share, though perhaps not equally, in the profits and honors of the performance.

Suppose the enterprise is a polis. In this case the application of the two criteria is not so straightforward. For what sort of enterprise is a polis? Neither criterion can be applied until this question is answered. Defenders of oligarchy think of the polis as a joint-stock company whose end is to enrich its shareholders (*Pol.* III.9.1280a25–31, IV.9.1294a11; *Rhet.* I.8.1366a4–5). Champions of democracy regard it as a free society where one is able "to live as one wishes" (*Pol.* VI.2.1317b11–12). Advocates of aristocracy regard it as an ethical community directed to education and virtue (*Pol.* IV.8.1294a9–11; *Rhet.* I.8.1366a5–6). Now, a contribution to one of these enterprises may not be a contribution to another. Virtue, for example, may lead its possessor – think of Plato's *Republic* – to fear freedom and to scorn wealth. Thus the contribution criterion yields different results given different conceptions of the polis. So too does the fitness criterion. The job of the ekklesiast, for example, is to deliberate about things to come (*Rhet.* I.3.1358b4–5). Shrewdness may fit a person for this job when the aim is the preservation or the increase of wealth; but practical wisdom, or *phronêsis*, will be required when the cultivation of virtue is the goal (see *Rhet.* I.8.1366a2–8).

Aristotle's theory of distributive justice thus comes to hinge on a fundamental question, What is a polis?[30] The fullest discussion of this question is in *Politics* III.9, Aristotle naturally, seeks, not a nominal (*An. Post.* II.10. 93b30), but a real definition of "polis" (*Pol.* III.9.1280b6–8), a definition that expresses the essence of a polis (*Top.* VII.3.153a15–16; *Met.* VII.5. 1031a12). A standard Aristotelian definition defines a species by its genus and differentia (*Top.* I.8.103b15–16, VII.3.153b14–15, and elsewhere); and if the species (unlike, say, triangle and square) has an end, or *telos*, the differentia will be its end (see *DA* I.1.403a25–b7). In genus a polis is a *koinonia*, a community or association (*Pol.* I.1.1252a1, III.3.1276b1, and elsewhere). To find its end and differentia Aristotle considers six candidates and tries to show that all except the sixth yield defective definitions. The six are:

1 Property (*Pol.* III.9.1280a25–6)
2 Self-preservation (a31)

---

30 For the question see *Pol.* III.1.1274b32–4.

3 Mutual defense against outsiders (a34–5, 40, b26–7)
4 Trade and mutual intercourse (a35–6)
5 Prevention of injustice to each other (a39, b4–5, 30–31)
6 Good life (a31–2, b33–5, 39)

One way to rebut a definition is to show that it is too wide, that the feature it picks out is not peculiar (*idios*) to the species being defined (*Top*. I.4.101b19–23, VI.1.139a31–2). And this is the strategy Aristotle uses. Taken severally or jointly the first five candidates, Aristotle claims, differentiate at most a *summachia*,[31] or alliance, not a polis (*Pol*.III.9.1280b8–33; see also II.2. 1261a24–5).[32] So he infers that the sixth candidate is the right one and defines a polis as "a community of households and clans in living well, for the sake of a perfect and self-sufficient life" (1280b33–5; see also VII.8.1328 a35–7). Then, combining this definition with the contribution criterion, he concludes that "those who contribute most to such a community have a larger share in the polis than those who are equal or superior in freedom and birth but unequal in political virtue, or those who exceed in wealth but are exceeded in virtue" (1281a4–8).

This is an elimination argument: its major premiss consists of an allegedly exhaustive list of alternative conceptions of the end of a polis, and the argument proceeds by eliminating all of the candidates except one. The first objection to Aristotle's argument is that his list is not exhaustive. One end (among others) that he notices elsewhere but omits from his list here is the end of the constitutions of Sparta and the polises[33] of Crete: conquest and war (*Pol*. II.9.1271b2–3, VII.2.1324b3–9, 14.1333b12–14; see also VII.2. 1325a3–4).

Aristotle can, I think, meet this objection by shifting his ground slightly and bringing all the possible ends of a polis under one or another of three general heads that seem more plausibly to exhaust the field, namely, bare life, shared life, and good life – *to zên*, *to suzên*, and *to eu zên*. The difference between bare life and shared life is explained in the *Eudemian Ethics*: "It is

---

31 In war, a *summachia* is an offensive and defensive alliance in contrast to an *epimachia*, which is an alliance for defense only.
32 An Aristotelian polis is thus neither a Hobbesian commonwealth, whose end is the protection of life (*Leviathan*, ch. XVII), nor a Lockian commonwealth, whose end is the preservation of life, liberty, and estate (*The Second Treatise of Civil Government*, ch. IX).
33 The word "polis" has now even invaded English poetry:

> We can at least serve other ends,
> Can love the polis of our friends.
>
> W. H. Auden, *New Year Letter* III.51

It ought, therefore, to be regarded as a fully naturalized word of English and no longer as a transliterated Greek word. Acting on this conviction, I write it unitalicized and use the English rather than the Greek inflection ("polises" rather than "poleis"). The Greek plurals of third-declension nouns never establish themselves in English as the fate of "metropoleis" bears witness.

clear that just as life [*sc*. for man] is perception and knowledge, so also shared life is shared perception and shared knowledge" (VII.12.1244b24–6; see also *EN* IX.9.1170b10–14). Good life in turn, to reduce Aristotle's moral philosophy to a simple motto, is life in accordance with reason (*kata logon zên*) (*EN* I.7.1098a7–20, II.6.1106b36–1107a2, *EE* III.1.1229a1–2, 7, and elsewhere). Shared life is a part of a good life: "No one would choose to have all good things all by himself; for man is a political being and formed by nature to share his life (*suzên*)" (*EN* IX.9.1169b17–19). But not all shared life is good life, for example, that of a band of thieves. In *Politics* III.6 these three general ends are presented as a hierarchy. Thus Aristotle says (1) that "men come together . . . and maintain the political community for the sake of life itself (*tou zên heneken autou*)" (1278b24–5), (2) that "even when they need no help from each other, they none the less desire to live together (*oregontai tou suzên*)" (b20–21), and (3) that the end of the polis is good life (*to zên kalôs*[34]) (b21–4). This three-step progression is only slightly less prominent in III.9. Bare life and good life are items (2) and (6) on Aristotle's list of possible ends, and good life and shared life are sharply distinguished at the end of the chapter. Aristotle says that the various ways of sharing life such as marriage connections, brotherhoods, and religious sacrifices "are the work of friendship; for the pursuit of shared life is friendship.[35] The end of the polis is good life, whereas these things are for the sake of the end" (1280b36–40). He goes on to say that "it must be laid down that the political community exists for the sake of good actions but not for the sake of shared life" (1281a2–4). Aristotle's idea seems to be that to associate for the sake of property, or freedom, or conquest, or mutual defense, or trade, or the prevention of injustice is to enter a friendship for utility or for pleasure, not a friendship of good men.[36] Consequently, such an association is a mode of shared life but not of good life. This interpretation is borne out by a passage from the *Nicomachean Ethics* where all alliances are characterized as friendships for utility: "men call friends those who associate for utility, just as polises are called friends (for alliances seem to arise among polises for the sake of expediency)" (VIII.4.1157a25–9).

A second objection to Aristotle's argument is that in eliminating rival candidates it relies on a controversial (and indeed a false) premiss – namely, that a polis is more than an alliance and hence must have a higher end than an alliance. According to this objection a polis *is* simply a kind of an alliance alongside commercial and military alliances: as a military alliance is an alliance of polises a polis is an alliance of households. When Aristotle eliminates shared life as the end of a polis on the ground that shared life differentiates at most an alliance, he reasons, it is claimed, like the man who eliminates sentient life as the end of a horse on the ground that sentient life differentiates at most an animal.

---

34 *to eu zên* = *to zên kalôs* = *to eudaimonein* (*EN* I.4.1095a19–20; *EE* I.1.1214a30–31).
35 For the connection between friendship and shared life see also *EN* VIII.5. 1157b19, IX.9.1170b10–14, 10.1171a2, 12.1171b32.
36 For these three types of friendship see *EN* VIII.2–3 and *EE* VII.2.

One would anticipate this sort of objection from those early political theorists who held that a polis is nothing more than a mutual protection society. The sophist Lycophron, as Aristotle points out in *Politics* III.9 itself, maintained that "the law is an agreement and . . . a guarantee to one another of what is just, but not something able to make the citizens good and just" (1280b10–12). Glaucon in the *Republic* (II.359a1–2) mentions the same view in almost identical words. And Hippodamus, the city-planner and political theorist, limited law to the negative functions of protecting person and property. According to Aristotle's report, he thought that law should be confined to three matters only: insult, harm (to person or property), and homicide[37] (II.8.1267b37–9).

Aristotle's answer to this second objection, that, contrary to his claim, the polis *is* only an alliance, can be gleaned from an analysis of the argument that opens the *Politics*:

> Since we see that every polis is a kind of community and that every community is formed for the sake of some good (for all men do all their actions for the sake of what seems good), it is evident that whereas all communities aim at some good, the one that is most supreme (*kuriôtatê*) of all and includes (*periechousa*) all the others aims especially at the good that is most supreme of all. This is the so-called polis and the political community. (I.1.1252a1–7)

The argument of this passage runs as follows:

1 Every community aims at some good. Premiss.
2 [And every good – life, shared life, and good life – is aimed at by some community.] Tacit premiss.
3 [If one community is supreme over another and includes the other, the good aimed at by the one includes that aimed at by the other.] Tacit premiss.
4 Therefore, the community that (a) is most supreme of all and (b) includes all others aims at the most supreme good. From (1)–(3).
5 The polis is the community that is most supreme of all and includes all others. Premiss.
6 Hence, the polis aims at the most supreme good. From (4) and (5).

Adding a premiss that describes the supreme good, we reach the conclusion that the end of the polis is good life:

7 The most supreme good is good life and happiness (*EN* I.4.1095a14–20). Premiss.
8 Therefore, the polis aims at good life and happiness. From (6) and (7).

---

37 *hubris*, *blabê*, and *thanatos*.

This is a second and more direct argument for the view that the end of the polis is good life, and it suggests that Aristotle thinks that a polis is more than simply an alliance because he thinks that a polis is in some sense more inclusive than an alliance.

In this argument the polis is given a twofold characterization. First of all, it is called the most supreme community (*hê kuriôtatê koinonia*). *Kuriôtatê* is the superlative of the adjective *kuria*, which means "having authority over." By this characterization, then, the polis is a community with a system of authority. As Aristotle says elsewhere, "every political community is composed of rulers and ruled" (*Pol.* VII.14.1332b12–13). The superlative is used to express the idea that the authority of the polis in a given territory is ultimate, that its rulers can, for example, overrule the authority of a father within his family. The polis is characterized, secondly, as the community of which all other communities are parts. Aristotle presumably does not mean by this that the polis is the widest community, for in Greece there were panhellenic festivals such as the Olympian and Pythian Games which while they lasted were communities of wider extent than the polis. He seems to mean rather that the end of the polis embraces the ends of all other communities:

> The other communities aim at what is advantageous in fragments; for example, sailors at what is advantageous on a voyage with a view to making money or something of that sort, fellow-soldiers at what is advantageous in war, desiring either money or victory or a polis. . . . All of these seem to be under the political community, for the political community aims, not at what is advantageous for the moment, but at what is advantageous for all of life. . . . Thus all the communities seem to be parts of the political community (*EN* VIII.9. 1160a14–29).

This is Aristotle's idea again that only in the polis does man attain complete self-sufficiency. It also seems to be Aristotle's reason for holding that the polis is more than an alliance. The end of an alliance, unlike that of a polis, encompasses only a part of a man's life.

Aristotle's twofold characterization of the polis has led some scholars to claim that his argument that the polis aims at good life and happiness, the crux of his theory of distributive justice, plays upon an ambiguity in the word "polis." Aristotle uses the word, so it is maintained, in an "exclusive" and an "inclusive" sense. In the exclusive sense the word "polis" refers to "the institutions [of a city-state] concerned with control over the rest of society"; in the inclusive sense it refers to "the whole of [city-state] society, including both the controlling, 'political' institutions and the other communities which they control."[38] The distinction between these two senses is similar to that

38 R. G. Mulgan, *Aristotle's Political Theory* (Oxford, 1977), pp. 16–17.

between "state" and "society" in modern political philosophy. All that Aristotle's argument establishes, so that criticism goes,[39] is:

8′ The polis (understood as city-state society as a whole) aims at good life and happiness.

But Aristotle believes he has established:

8″ The polis (understood as the city-state institutions concerned with control over the rest of society) aims at good life and happiness.

Consequently, he favors using the coercive power of the state in pursuit of the end: "He believes that the statesman, through the law and other institutions of government, should exercise general control over the citizens in order to make them achieve the good life."[40] Aristotle has thus invalidly derived a kind of "authoritarianism"[41] or "paternalism."[42]

There is another, more charitable, way of analyzing Aristotle's argument that rescues it from the fallacy of equivocation. Since the polis is the subject of Aristotle's political philosophy, it would be unfortunate if the *Politics* were infected with a hidden ambiguity in the word "polis," for this would mean that throughout the work Aristotle was discussing two distinct subjects without being aware of their difference. The way to rescue Aristotle from the charge of equivocation is to note that the two expressions "the most supreme community" and "the community that includes all others" are different descriptions, not different definitions, of the polis. Aristotle believes that both expressions refer to the polis:

The polis = the most supreme community = the community that includes all others.

39 "It may be unexceptionable," Mulgan writes, "to say that the *polis* aims at total human good if the *polis* is thought to include all aspects of human society. It does not follow from this that the exclusively 'political' institutions of the *polis* should be directly concerned with the achievement of all facets of the good life, many of which may be left completely in the control of other institutions, groups or individuals" (ibid., p. 17).

Fred Miller writes: "The end of the *community*, which is the fundamental justification for its existence, is the good and happy life, in the sense that the fundamental reason *individuals* have for living in communities and for engaging in a wide variety of community relations is to lead good and happy lives, i.e., to realize themselves and be virtuous. But it does not follow at all that the function of the *state* is to use coercive force against its citizens so as to *make* them virtuous and happy. Aristotle, in making such an inference, is confusing the two senses of 'polis,' and is assigning to the *polis*, in the sense of 'state,' a function which belongs properly to the *polis*, in the sense of 'community'" ("The State and the Community in Aristotle's *Politics*," *Reason Papers* 1 [1974], p. 67).

40 Mulgan, *Aristotle's Political Theory*, p. 17.

41 Ibid.

42 Miller, "The State and the Community in Aristotle's *Politics*," p. 67.

Indeed, this assertion is a premiss of his argument – line (5). But given this identity premiss, there is no equivocation: (8″) follows from (8′) together with (5). The Homeric scholar who believes that "the author of the *Iliad*" and "the author of the *Odyssey*" both refer to the same man and who draws inferences about this man from both poems indifferently may be making a mistake, but he is not commiting the fallacy of equivocation. He is different from the student who confuses Thucydides, son of Olorus, (the historian) and Thucydides, son of Melesias, (the Athenian statesman). Aristotle is like the Homeric scholar, not the student. He is acutely aware that there are many different conceptions of the polis and even that the word "polis" is ambiguous (*Pol.* III. 3.1276a23–4). He is aware in particular of the views of those who hold a protectionist conception of the polis and deny his identity premiss. Aristotle may be mistaken in this premiss, but he is aware that it is a premiss.

Furthermore, it is not an ultimate premiss of Aristotle's political philosophy; for it seems to be a consequence of his organic theory of the polis (*Pol.* I.2.1252b27–1253a1, 18–29, VII.8.1328a21ff.). When a natural object has an end, it always has a part whose job it is to realize that end. For example, one end of every plant and animal is to generate another like itself, and to realize this end every plant and animal has a reproductive soul (*DA* II.4.416b23–5, *GA* II.1.735a17–19). Since the all-embracing community is a natural entity and since it aims at good life and happiness, there must be a part of this community whose job it is to realize this end. And there seems to be no other candidate in sight for the job except the governing class. This sort of defense of the identity premiss is suggested by the following passage:

> If one would count the soul more a part of an animal than the body, one should also count the corresponding elements of polises – the military and the part engaged in judicial justice, and in addition to these the part that deliberates, which is the work of political intelligence – more truly parts than those directed to necessary use. (*Pol.* IV.4.1291a24–8; see also *EN* IX.8.1168b31–3.)

A determined critic of the argument of *Politics* III.9 might reply to the above defense of its premisses by shifting attention to its conclusion, which seems patently false. Since the argument is a disjunctive syllogism and hence valid, something must be wrong with its premisses if its conclusion is false. The reason for thinking its conclusion is false is that few, if any, polises have good life and happiness as their end. (One way to defeat a definition, as Aristotle points out in the *Topics*, is to show that it is not true of every member of the species being defined: "for the definition of 'man' must be true of every man" [VI.1.139a25–7].) The only constitutions that aim at good life and happiness are the two best: absolute kingship and true aristocracy (*Pol.* IV.2.1289a30–33, VII.2.1324a23–5). But Aristotle is unable to cite an example of either. When he considers the polises that are reputed to be well-governed in *Politics* II.9–11, he mentions only Sparta, Carthage, and the polises of Crete. These are so-called, or secondary, as distinguished from true, aristocracies (*Pol.* IV.7.1293b1–19) and do not have good life and happiness as their end.

Sparta and the polises of Crete aim at power (*to kratein*) (*Pol.* II.9.1271b2–3, VII.2.1324b5–9, 14.1333b12–14), and Carthaginian law honors wealth more than virtue (*Pol.* II.11.1273a37–9). Furthermore, Aristotle says that even this inferior sort of aristocracy is beyond the reach of most polises (*Pol.* IV.11.1295a25–34). Thus Aristotle concedes himself that most polises do not pursue the end that he claims differentiates a polis from other communities. He does not in fact know of a single polis that satisfies his definition. This is the reason no doubt that in attempting to establish his definition Aristotle appeals, not to the many, but to those who "give thought to good government" (*Pol.* III.9.1280b6) or "inquire accurately" (b28).

How, then, is Aristotle's definition of "polis" and his theory of distributive justice, which hinges on it, to be saved? Aristotle's strategy is to distinguish constitutions that are according to nature (*kata phusin*) from those that are contrary to nature (*para phusin*). The correct (*orthai*) constitutions are according to nature; the deviations (*parekbaseis*) from these are contrary to nature. Thus Aristotle says:

> There is that which is by nature (*phusei*) fitted for rule by a master, and another for rule by a king, and another for rule under a polity, and this is just and expedient; but rule by a tyrant is not according to nature (*kata phusin*), nor are any of the constitutions that are deviations; for these come about contrary to nature (*para phusin*) (*Pol.* III.17.1287b37–41).

The correct constitutions are the three general types that "look to the common advantage": kingship, aristocracy, and polity. The deviations from these – tyranny, oligarchy, and democracy – "look only to the rulers' own advantage" (*Pol.* III.6.1279a17–20). Once these general types are divided into subtypes, Aristotle distinguishes degrees of correctness. The *most* correct (*orthotatê*) constitution is the best constitution, the one that aims at good life and happiness, of which there are two species: absolute kingship and true aristocracy (*Pol.* IV.2.1289a31–3, 8.1293b23–7, VII.2.1324a23–5). So-called or secondary aristocracies and polities are deviations from the best constitution; and tyranny, oligarchy, and democracy are deviations from these first deviations. Strictly speaking, the only constitution that is according to nature is the best or most correct. Aristotle says this explicitly in the *Nicomachean Ethics*: "one [*sc.* constitution] alone is in all places according to nature – the best" (V.7.1135a5).[43]

---

43 In a long note on this one line of text J. J. Mulhern considers whether it means (1) "There is only one constitution that is best by nature for every place" or (2) "For every place, there is only one constitution that is best by nature for it." In other words, does the universal quantifier follow or precede the uniqueness quantifier? The first alternative, which is the traditional rendering, seems incompatible with Aristotle's view that absolute kingship is best in some places whereas true aristocracy is best in others; and so Mulhern concludes that (2) must be the correct interpretation. See Mulhern, "ΜΙΑ ΜΟΝΟΝ ΠΑΝΤΑΧΟΥ ΚΑΤΑ ΦΥΣΙΝ Η ΑΡΙΣΤΗ (*EN* 1135a5)," *Phronesis*, 17 (1972), pp. 260–68. However, the alleged incompatibility vanishes once one notices that "the one constitution that is best" is a genus whose species are absolute kingship and true aristocracy (*Pol.* IV.2.1289a31–3).

With this distinction in hand Aristotle can draw upon his theory of freaks of nature (*terata*).[44] "Freaks of nature are failures of that for the sake of which" (*Phys.* II.8.199b4) and are contrary to nature (*GA* IV.4.770b9–10). They inherit the generic form of their parents but not the specific form. Aristotle says, for example, of a freak of nature born of human parents that it is "not even a human being but only a sort of animal" (*GA* IV.3.769b8–10).[45] Now, a polis that does not aim at good life and happiness is a failure of that for the sake of which and is contrary to nature. So it would seem to be a kind of freak of nature and not to deserve the name "polis" at all. And there are passages in the *Politics* that say just that. In one place Aristotle says that "the polis truly so called" must be concerned about virtue (III.9.1280b6–8). In another he describes city-states with deviant constitutions as despotisms (*despotikai*) whereas "the *polis* is a community of the free" (III.6.1279a20–21). By this strict doctrine the word "polis" can be applied to a city-state with a deviant constitution only in virtue of an equivocation. In the strict sense, the word only applies to communities that aim at good life and happiness although in a loose sense it also applies to city-states that deviate in one degree or another from this end.[46] The word "polis" thus turns out to be ambiguous in the *Politics* after all. The ambiguity is not, however, that generally alleged between city-state society as a whole and those institutions of a city-state concerned with control over the rest of society, between society and state, but rather between a community whose rulers seek good life and happiness for all those within the community capable of attaining it and an alliance of families whose rulers seek only their own advantage or at any rate some end inferior to good life and happiness.

A polis with a deviant constitution differs from a freak of nature in the animal kingdom in one important respect. A freak of nature in the animal kingdom is an anomaly, a deviation from what happens for the most part (*epi to polu*) (*GA* IV.4.770b9–13). That which is contrary to nature is the complement of that which is according to nature; and that which is according to nature, Aristotle holds, is that which happens always or for the most part (*Phy.* II.8.198b35–6, *GC* II.6.333b4–7, and elsewhere). Hence that which is contrary to nature is that which happens on those rare occasions when what happens for the most part does not happen (*Phy.* II.6.197b34–5, 8.198b36; and see *Met.* VI.2.1026b27–1027a17). In Aristotle's political philosophy this situation is reversed. The best polis, the only one that strictly speaking is

---

44 For which see *GA* IV.3–4 especially 767a36–b15 and 770b9–17.

45 Similarly in the *Politics* the claim that "man is by nature a political animal" (*politikon zôon*) (I.2.1253a2–3) is followed by the assertion that he who is unable or has no need to live in a polis "is either a beast or a god" (not a man) (a27–9).

46 A helpful analogy here is Aristotle's account of friendship: "There are several kinds of friendship," Aristotle says, "firstly and strictly that of good men *qua* good, the others [i.e. friendships of utility and of pleasure] by resemblance [to true friendship]" (*EN* VIII.4.1157a30–32). Similarly first and strictly there is the polis of good men; all others are polises by resemblance to this one.

according to nature, occurs rarely, if ever, whereas polises that deviate from this norm and are contrary to nature are the rule.

So Aristotle has a problem. His theory of distributive justice requires a true standard of worth; this standard is tied to his definition of "polis," and his definition is anchored to his concept of nature. But rather than supporting his definition his philosophy of nature seems to undermine it. A crucial question for Aristotle is why the best polis is according to nature even though it rarely, if ever, occurs. This question will be considered in the next section.

But let us pause for a moment and consider the nature of the end that Aristotle attributes to the polis – good life and happiness. By Aristotle's account happiness is "an actualization and a sort of perfect use of virtue" (*Pol.* VII.8.1328a37–8; see also VII.13.1332a7–10; *EN* I.7.1098a7–20; *EE* II.1.1219a38–9, and elsewhere). The virtue of which happiness is an actualization is intellectual as well as moral, and the intellectual virtues include those of the theoretical as well as of the practical intellect. A good life for Aristotle includes both politics and philosophy (*Pol.* I.7.1255b35–7, VII. 2.1324a23–32, 3.1325b14–21, 14.1333a16–b3, 15.1334a11–40). But *sophia*, or philosophical wisdom, the virtue of the theoretical intellect, does not *fit* a person for political office or other civic duties even though theoretical activity by being a part of good life and happiness does *contribute* to the end of the polis. The difference between the two criteria, fitness and contribution, makes itself felt at just this point. The relevant virtue in distributing political authority is political virtue (*politikē aretē*) (*Pol.* III.9.1280b5, 1281a7, VIII.6. 1340b42–1341a1), the virtue exercised in the political life (*ho politikos bios*) (*Pol.* I.5.1254b30–31; VII.2.1324a32, 40, 3.1325a20; and elsewhere). This virtue is a combination of the virtues of character and the virtue of the practical intellect – of the *ēthikai aretai* and *phronēsis* (see *Pol.* III.4. 1277b25–7).

Although political virtue is for Aristotle the most important part of the correct standard of worth, it is not the only part. For the exercise of political virtue requires an ample supply of material goods (*EN* I.8.1099a31–b8; X.8.1178a23–b3, 1178b33–1179a13; *Pol.* VII.1.1323b40–1324a2; VII.13. 1331b41–1332a1). Small sums of money are required, for example, for the exercise of liberality (*eleutheriotēs*); and large sums, for the exercise of munificence (*megaloprepeia*) (*EN* II.7.1107b8–21, IV.1–2). (Munificence, like bravery, is an important part of political virtue; for it is munificence that ensures that the various liturgies such as equipping a trireme are properly discharged.) A good man who is impoverished will find it difficult to lead a political life. Consequently, the standard of worth that Aristotle ultimately endorses is "virtue fully furnished with external means" (*aretē kechorēgēmenē*) (*Pol.* IV.2.1289a31–3; see also VII.1.1323b41–1324a1). Since Aristotle clearly does not mean to admit slaves or aliens to office, his standard tacitly includes freedom. Thus his correct standard of worth embraces all of the original candidates: virtue, wealth, and freedom. I shall call this the *Aristotelian* standard of worth and the conception of distributive justice resulting from it the *Aristotelian* conception of distributive justice.

4 TRUE ARISTOCRACY

Aristotle's theory of distributive justice rests in the end on his description of the best polis (*hê aristê polis*) (*Pol.* VII.1.1323b29–31) in Books VII and VIII of the *Politics*. The best polis, a true aristocracy (IV.8.1294a24–5), embodies the Aristotelian conception of distributive justice. Consequently if the best polis is absolutely just, the Aristotelian conception of distributive justice is absolutely just. But, Aristotle argues, the best polis *is* absolutely just. For it is according to nature, and everything (within the field of human conduct[47]) that is according to nature is absolutely just.[48] Therefore, the Aristotelian conception of distributive justice is absolutely just. Aristotle's argument raises two fundamental questions. First, why does Aristotle regard true aristocracy as natural even though it seldom, if ever, occurs? And, secondly, why does he believe that everything (within the field of human conduct) that is natural is absolutely just?

The social and political structure of the best polis is laid out in three stages in *Politics* VII.8–10. Aristotle first lists the occupations and offices that every polis needs; he then introduces groups representing the various occupations and offices; and, finally, he divides these groups into a higher and a lower order.

The occupations and offices, the *erga*, that every polis needs are (8.1328b4–15):

1 food
2 arts
3 arms
4 "a certain abundance of wealth"
5 "the superintendence of religion, which they call a priesthood"
6 "judgment of what is advantageous and what is just toward one another"

---

47 This qualification is necessary since many things that are according to nature lie outside the sphere of justice altogether. For a plant to send down roots is according to nature, but it is neither just nor unjust. Even the field of human conduct is broader than the sphere of justice since justice and injustice, for Aristotle, always involve at least two persons (see *EN* V.1.1129b25–7, 1130a10–13, and 11.1138a19–20).
48 For this principle see *Pol.* I.5.1255a1–3, III.17.1287b37–9, and VII.9.1329a13–17. For the negative principle linking the unnatural and the unjust see I.10.1258a40–b2, VII.3.1325b7–10, and (without endorsement) I.3.1253b20–23. For both principles together see I.5.1254a17–20 and III.16.1287a8–18. The negative principle is not the converse of the positive transposed. If it were, then it would be Aristotle's view that within the sphere of human conduct the concepts of the just and the natural are coextensive. But this is not his view. As he deploys the two principles, they leave open the possibility that some things that are just are neither according to nature nor contrary to nature (for examples see *EN* V.7.1134b18–24).

This is a typical Aristotelian list, a jumble of items of different types. Food is a product (of agriculture); arts are states (*hexeis*) (*EN* VI.4.1140a9–10, 20–21); arms are implements (of war); wealth is a possession; and superintendence and judgment are actions (*praxeis*). The list is held together, to some extent at least, by the different senses of *ergon*, which can mean (1) a capacity (*dunamis*),[49] (2) the exercise (*chrêsis, energeia*) of a capacity, or (3) the product of the exercise of a capacity (see *EE* II.1.1219a13–18, *Pol.* II.11.1273b10, III.4.1277b3, IV.15.1299a39). The English word "work" has the same three senses. By the "work" of a cobbler one can mean (1) his occupation, (2) his toil, or (3) the shoes his toil produces.

The groups, or *genê* (VII.9.1329a20, 27, 10.1329a41, b23), of the inhabitants engaged in these various endeavors are (VII.8.1328b20–23):

1 farmers
2 artisans
3 the fighting class
4 the wealthy
5 priests
6 "judges of the necessary and advantageous"

This cannot be regarded as a complete list of the occupational groups in Aristotle's best polis. Other remarks in Book VII make it plain that the best polis will contain at least three additional groups:

7 day-laborers
8 traders
9 seamen

The group of day-laborers (*to thêtikon*) is added to the list at the end of chapter 9 (1329a36; see also VIII.7.1342a20). Since Aristotle's best polis will, to some extent at least, import and export commodities (VII.6.1327 a11–40), merchants (*emporoi*) will be necessary; and since both foreign and domestic commodities will need to be distributed shopkeepers (*kapâloi*) are implied.[50] Aristotle, in fact, provides his best polis with a commercial agora distinct from the free agora where the citizens spend their leisure (VII.12. 1331a30–b13). Merchants and shopkeepers together compose the group of traders (*to agoraion*) (*Pol.* IV.4.1291a4–6, 16). Aristotle also thinks that for security a polis ought to have a navy (VII.6.1327a40–b15), which means that his best polis will contain seamen.

These nine groups, or *genê*, are "things without which a polis would not exist" (*Pol.* III.5.1278a3, VII.8.1328b2–3). But not all things that are

49 What in *Pol.* VII.8 Aristotle calls an *ergon* in *Pol.* IV.4 he calls a *dunamis* (1291b2). In one place he conjoins *ergon* and *dunamis* (I.2.1253a23); in other places he conjoins *ergon* and *technê* (III.11.1282a10–11, VIII.5.1339a37).

50 For the distinction between *emporoi* and *kapêloi* see Plato, *Rep.* II.371d5–7 and *Soph.* 223d5–10.

indispensable for the existence of a polis are parts[51] (*moria, merê*) of a polis (1328a21–5); some are only accessories. The distinction between a part and an accessory, which is crucial to Aristotle's account of the best polis, is illustrated but never explained. In the *Eudemian Ethics* Aristotle says that eating meat and taking a walk after dinner are for some people indispensable for health but are not parts of health (I.2.1214b11–27). And in *Politics* VII.8 he says that a craftsman and his tools are indispensable for the existence of a house but are not parts of a house (1328a30–33). The explanation that these illustrations suggest is that one thing is an accessory of another if, and only if, the one is indispensable for the existence of the other but does not enter into the essence of the other. Thus a particular group is an accessory of a polis if, and only if, the group is indispensable for the existence of the polis but does not enter into the essence of the polis. A polis is defined, it will be recalled, as "a community of households and clans in living well for the sake of a perfect and self-sufficient life" (*Pol.* III.9.1280b33–5). It would seem, then, that a particular group would not enter into the essence of a polis if the life characteristic of that group is incompatible with the sort of life that defines a polis, namely, a life of moral and intellectual virtue. And this is the way Aristotle argues. The group of craftsmen and the group of traders are not parts but mere accessories of a polis since the life of an artisan or a trader "is sordid and opposed to virtue" (VII.9.1328b39–41; see also 1329a19–21 and III.5.1278a17–21). The group of farmers is an accessory since the life of a farmer lacks the leisure necessary "for the growth of virtue and for political activities" (1328b41–1329a2). The groups in Aristotle's best polis thus divide into two orders, a higher order of parts and a lower order of accessories (a34–9):

The Higher Order

1 hoplites[52]
2 officeholders[53]
3 priests
4 the wealthy

---

51 Parts in the strict sense (*oikeia moria*) (VII.4.1326a21). In a loose sense every group on the list is a *morion* or *meros* of a polis (see *Pol.* IV.4.1290b24, b39, 1291a32–3; but notice also 1291a24–8).

52 And (presumably) cavalrymen. Cavalry is not mentioned in Book VII. But elsewhere in the *Politics* cavalry and hoplites are linked (VI.7.1321a5–21). Only the well-to-do (*hoi euporoi*) could afford heavy armor; only "those who possess large property" (*hoi makras ousias kektêmenoi*) could afford to keep a horse.

53 Ekklesiasts, dikasts, and officials. In VII.8–9 Aristotle mentions only the first two (1328b13–15, 1329a3–4, a31) though a number of officials make an appearance later in the book (VII.12.1331b4–18). See *Pol.* IV.15 and VI.8 for a detailed account of the various executive and administrative offices in a polis.

The Lower Order

5 farmers
6 traders
7 artisans
8 seamen (VII.6.1327b7–9)
9 day-laborers

The division between the two orders also divides citizen from noncitizen. The higher order alone has citizen status (*Pol.* VII.9.1328b33–1329a2, 17–19).

The noncitizen population in a normal Greek polis fell into three juristic categories: metics (*metoikoi*), foreign visitors[54] (*xenoi*), and slaves (*douloi*) (see *Pol.* III.1.1275a7–8, 5.1277b38–9, VII.4.1326a18–20, b20–21). Metics were resident aliens. They were excluded from all political offices; could not own land; had to have a citizen as a patron (*prostatês*) (see III.1.1275a8–14); were subject, unlike citizens, to a head tax (in Athens 12 drachmas a year for adult males, 6 for women living on their own); and were liable, if male, for military service in the army or navy.[55] Aristotle does not discuss the legal status of the traders and artisans in his best polis; but presumably, as in Plato's *Laws* (VIII.846d1–847b6, XI.920a3–4), they will be metics or foreign visitors. The main occupation of the lower order, farming, is assigned to slaves or barbarian serfs (VII.9.1329a25–6, 10.1330a25–33).

This system of slaves or serfs is Aristotle's solution to a basic political problem – how to secure leisure for the citizens of a polis. The problem is posed early in the *Politics* in the course of Aristotle's examination of the institutions of the two historical polises that deviate least from his ideal, Sparta and Carthage:

> The arrangement of the Carthaginians deviates from aristocracy toward oligarchy chiefly in respect of a certain idea that commends itself [not only to the Carthaginians but also] to the many; for they think that the rulers ought to be chosen not only on the basis of virtue but also on the basis of wealth, since it is impossible for the poor man to rule well and to occupy leisure well (II.11.1273a21–5).

That poverty is a bar to a political life Aristotle agrees; but he thinks that the Carthaginian practice of filling the highest offices, those of king and general, on the basis of wealth alone is wrong (a35–b5). The proper solution is not to make wealthy men rulers, but to make the best men well-off:

---

54 In the *Laws* Plato distinguishes four types of foreign visitor: merchants, tourists, ambassadors, and intellectuals (XII.952d5–953d7).
55 See Douglas M. MacDowell, *The Law in Classical Athens* (Ithaca, 1978), pp. 76–8; M. M. Austin and P. Vidal–Naquet, *Economic and Social History of Greece: An Introduction* (Berkeley, 1977), pp. 99–101; and David Whitehead, *The Ideology of the Athenian Metic, The Cambridge Philological Society*, supp. vol. no. 4 (1977).

For from the outset one of the greatest necessities [*sc.* for the lawgiver] is to see that the best men may be able to have leisure and to avoid unworthy occupations not only while in office but also while living a private life (a32–5; see also b5–7).

Aristotle prefaces his discussion of the Spartan helot system with a similar remark: "That a polis that intends to be well-governed must have leisure from necessary work is something agreed; but how this is to be realized is not easy to ascertain" (II.9.1269a34–6). The difficulty is that this leisure from necessary work is likely to be purchased, as it was in Sparta and Thessaly, at the price of a constant threat of insurrection from those performing the work (II.5.1264a34–6, 9.1269a36–b7). To avoid such a threat in his best polis Aristotle wants its slaves to be "neither all of the same stock (*homophulôn*)[56] nor of high spirit" (VII.10.1330a26–7).

Aristotle's best polis is ruled by members of the higher order in the interest of the higher order. The welfare of the lower order is of concern to the rulers only in so far as it contributes to the welfare of the higher order. This is the point of the distinction between parts and accessories. Since the lower order is not a part but only an indispensable condition of the existence of the best polis, the rulers will have exactly the same concern for it as they would have for a foreign city they were dependent on for their grain supply.[57]

Aristotle offers no justification for the subservient position of the lower order of his best polis beyond that which is implicit in his theory of natural slavery, which is not mentioned in Book VII. In this book itself Aristotle is more interested in justifying the distribution in his polis of those occupations fit for citizens: arms, politics, and religion. Each (male) citizen, during successive periods of his life, is to engage in all three occupations. As a young adult he is to be a hoplite; during middle age, an ekklesiast, dikast, and official; and in old age, a priest (9.1329a2–34).

This scheme harmonizes with Aristotle's earlier account of the four types of citizen. First of all, a man who "is entitled to share in deliberative or[58] judicial office" is a *full* citizen, a *politês haplôs* (III.1.1275a19–23, b17–19). Secondly, a boy or a young man who will in the future be entitled to be enrolled as a full citizen is an *immature* citizen, a *politês atelês* (1275a14–19, 5.1278a4–6). Thirdly, an old man who was a full citizen but is now exempt from political duties is a *superannuated* citizen, a *politês parêkmakôs* (1275a15–17). Fourthly, a woman or a girl of the proper descent is a *female* citizen, a *politis* (III.2.1275b33, 5.1278a28). The hoplites in Aristotle's polis are immature citizens; its officeholders are full citizens; and its priests are superannuated citizens. (Women are ignored in *Politics* VII.1–15 except for one disparaging remark at 3.1325b3–5.)

The distribution of arms and politics is justified as follows:

---

56 For examples of what Aristotle regards as difference of stock (*to mê homophulon*) see *Pol.* V.3.1303a25–b3.
57 See Newman, vol. 1, p. 119.
58 Retaining in 1275b19 the *ê* of all manuscripts.

It remains then for the [best] constitution to assign both of these [occupations] to the same men, not however at the same time, but in the way that strength occurs naturally in younger men, practical wisdom in older; therefore it is advantageous and just for the distribution to be made to both [age-groups] in this way; for this division is according to worth[59] (*Pol.* VII.9.1329a13–17; see also 14.1332b35–41).

This is an important passage for understanding Aristotle's theory of distributive justice. It contains all of its key concepts: justice, distribution (*nenemêsthai*, a16), worth (*kat' axian*, a17), and nature (*pephuken*, a14). Furthermore, the argument of the passage proceeds through just the stages that his theory requires. The content of the principle of distributive justice depends upon a standard of worth, which in turn is determined by a second-order attribute – in this case, fitness-for-the-job:

1 Strength (*dunamis*[60]) fits a man to be a hoplite; practical wisdom (*phronêsis*) fits him for political office.
2 Hence, it is just according to the principle of distributive justice for service as a hoplite to be distributed on the basis of strength and for political office to be distributed on the basis of practical wisdom.
3 Younger men are strong [but not practically wise].
4 Older men are practically wise [but no longer strong].
5 Therefore, it is just for political offices to be assigned to older men and service as a hoplite to younger men.

We are now in a position to derive the political structure of Aristotle's best polis from the Aristotelian conception of justice. The standard of worth of this conception, it will be recalled, is "[political] virtue fully furnished with external means" (*Pol.* IV.2.1289a31–3, VII.1.1323b41–1324a1). Thus according to the Aristotelian conception of justice a distribution of political authority is just to the extent that the value of the authority assigned to one person stands to the value of the authority assigned to another as the political virtue and wealth of the one stands to the political virtue and wealth of the other:

$$(1) \qquad\qquad (\forall x)(\forall y) \left(\frac{P(x) \cdot W(x)}{P(y) \cdot W(y)} = \frac{V(T(x))}{V(T(y))} \right)$$

In this formula "P" signifies the function *political virtue of*, and "$\cdot$" signifies multiplication. The other symbols are the same as before. The variables "x" and "y" in this and the following formulas range over the adult male inhabitants of Aristotle's best polis who are free in the narrow sense, that is,

59 This is a translation of Ross's text, which is heavily emended. For the emendations see both Susemihl–Hicks and Newman *ad loc*. The sense of the passage is not affected.
60 For *dunamis* = *ischus* see *Pol.* VII.17.1336a4 and VIII.4.1339a4.

are neither aliens nor slaves. This last device is a symbolic representation of the fact that Aristotle, reflecting contemporary opinion, takes it for granted that the widest conceivable distribution of political authority in a polis would be to its free native adult males. Multiplication (when the factors are neither greater than one nor less than zero) is a convenient analogue for conjunction. Among other things the two operations give the same result for a null component. Just as political virtue and wealth have no weight by themselves under the Aristotelian conception of justice, so a product is zero if either of its factors is zero.

All the free men in Aristotle's best polis are endowed by nature with intelligence and high spirit (*Pol.* VII.7) and through learning and habituation acquire political virtue, whose chief component is practical wisdom, by the time they reach middle age:

$$(2) \qquad (\forall x)(Mx \to P(x) \neq 0)$$

In this formula "M" signifies the property of being middle-aged, and the arrow stands for material implication. Thus the formula asserts that every free middle-aged man in Aristotle's polis possesses political virtue. Conversely, only those men who have reached middle age possess political virtue:

$$(3) \qquad (\forall x)(P(x) \neq 0 \to Mx)$$

Although Aristotle envisions that some of the men in his polis who have had the full course of moral habituation and instruction will occasionally stumble (see *Pol.* VII.16.1335b38–1336a2, 17.1336b3–12), he supposes that in general they will possess and act in accordance with all of the virtues including *megalopsuchia*, or greatness of soul (VII.7.1328a9–10, VIII.3. 1338b2–4). Being superlatively virtuous, they are equally virtuous. Thus any two men in his polis who possess political virtue possess it to the same degree:

$$(4) \qquad (\forall x)(\forall y)[(P(x) \neq 0 \ \& \ P(y) \neq 0) \to (P(x) = P(y))]$$

Superlative as their virtue is, it remains *human* virtue. Aristotle's moral philosophy allows for a still higher moral state, "a certain heroic and divine virtue" (*EN* VII.1.1145a19–20), which excels human virtue by as much as gods and heroes excel ordinary Greeks (a15–30). The implications of this higher state for Aristotle's political philosophy are considered in Section 5 below.

The distribution of political authority in Aristotle's best polis is unaffected by the inequalities of wealth that Aristotle is apparently prepared to tolerate among its households (see *Pol.* VII.10.1330a5–8) even though wealth is a part of the Aristotelian standard of worth. Since the wealth a man needs for the exercise of the moral and intellectual virtues, the wealth he needs to be a good warrior, officeholder, and head of a family, has a limit (*Pol.* I.8.1256b26–39) and since the wealth available to every free man from his family estate or the public lands equals or exceeds this limit, every free man has all the wealth that is relevant to the Aristotelian standard of worth:

$$(5) \qquad (\forall x)(W(x) = 1)$$

(where "1" represents the limit of "true wealth" [b30–31]).

From (1) through (5) it follows that only the older free men in Aristotle's polis should have political authority and that they should all have equal shares:

(6) $(\forall x)(\forall y)[(Mx \ \& \ My) \leftrightarrow (V(T(x)) = V(T(y))) \neq 0)]$

Aristotle sums up this entire argument in two sentences:

> it is clear that for many reasons it is necessary for all [the citizens of the best polis] to share alike in ruling and being ruled in turn. For equality requires the same [shares] for those who are alike. (*Pol.* VII.14.1332b25–7)

The Aristotelian conception of justice does not entail the other three conceptions even though its standard of worth includes freedom, wealth, and virtue. A polis can exemplify the Aristotelian conception without exemplifying any of the others. To see this, imagine that the population of Aristotle's best polis is increased by two free men of whom one is poor but good and the other wealthy but worthless. If political authority continues to be distributed in accordance with Aristotelian justice, neither of these men will receive a share even though the first man deserves a share by the aristocratic conception of justice, the second man by the oligarchic conception, and both men by the democratic conception.

This is worth noting because it highlights the fact that Aristotle's best polis, due to the special provisions expressed in premisses (2) through (5) above by which all of its free middle-aged male inhabitants are both wealthy and good, exemplifies (in a fashion at least) the aristocratic, oligarchic, and democratic conceptions of justice as well as the Aristotelian. The aristocratic conception, whose standard of worth is political virtue alone, is fully realized. The democratic conception is realized in the sense that every free man who does not die prematurely eventually becomes a full citizen. And the oligarchic conception is realized to the extent that those, and only those, who own land are full citizens. Thus no free man in Aristotle's polis, be he aristocrat, democrat, or oligarch, can reasonably object to the way it distributes political authority. Hence Aristotle's best polis is in a strong sense perfectly just.

But only from the perspective of its free men. Other members of its population might harbor some doubts. The full citizens of Aristotle's best polis are just those members of its population who exemplify in their persons or in their lives the popular Greek values of the fourth century. These may be tabulated in an Hellenic Table of Opposites where the first item of each pair is the one taken to be the more valuable:[61]

1 good/base
2 dignified/sordid

61 If evidence be needed that this table does reflect popular Greek values of the fourth century see K. J. Dover, *Greek Popular Morality in the Time of Plato and Aristotle* (Berkeley, 1974): item (2): pp. 32–3; item (4): pp. 102–3; item (5): pp. 95–102; items (6) and (7): p. 83; item (8): pp. 114–16.

3 leisure/work
4 mature/immature
5 male/female
6 native/foreigner
7 Greek/barbarian
8 free/slave

The more dubious items in this table – free/slave, male/female, dignified/
sordid, and Greek/barbarian – were already questioned in the fourth century, as the *Politics* itself makes plain. Aristotle's theory of natural slavery is
an answer to those who maintain that all slavery is unjust. "Some hold,"
Aristotle reports,

> that slavery is contrary to nature (for it is by law [*nomôi*] that one man is a
> slave, another free, by nature [*phusei*] there is no difference); therefore it is not
> just; for it is based on force (I.3.1253b20–23).

In Book II he comments on Plato's idea in the *Republic* that "women must
follow the same pursuits as men" (5.1264b5–6; see *Rep*. V.451d–457c). Plato
was intent in particular that the occupations Aristotle assigns to male
citizens, those of warrior and ruler, be open to women (*Rep*. V.457a,
VII.540c). In chapter 5 of Book III Aristotle considers the question whether
artisans can be full citizens. Athenian democracy, by answering this question in the affirmative, denies the political relevance of the distinction
between dignified and sordid occupations. Finally, the respect Aristotle
accords the institutions of Carthage and Egypt implies that he himself
did not regard all barbarians as inferior to Greeks. He ranks the Carthaginian constitution above even the Spartan and just below the best constitution (IV.7.1293b14 –19) and appeals to the example of Egypt in support
of his separation of farmers and warriors in his best polis (VII.10.1329a
40–b5, 23–5).

The Table of Opposites expresses some of the common opinions, or *endoxa*,
with which political philosophy begins and with which to a large extent it is
supposed to be in accord (see *EN* I.8.1098b9–12, VII.1.1145b2–7). Common
opinions cover a broad spectrum. According to the *Topics* common opinions
are those subscribed to "by everyone or by the majority or by the wise, that
is, by all of the wise or by the majority or by the most notable and
distinguished of them" (I.1.100b21–3). When Aristotle appeals to common
opinion at crucial points in the *Politics*, he appeals invariably to the opinions
of the wise rather than of the many. Thus in attempting to arrive at a
definition of "polis," he appeals, as we have seen, to the opinions of those
who "give thought to good government" (*Pol*. III.9.1280b6) or "inquire
accurately" (b28). Still, Aristotle's goal in *Politics* VII is not to describe the
sort of polis that the best opinion of his day would favor but to discover the
natural state of a political community. Although common opinion can be a
guide in the discovery of the natural, it often needs to be corrected and
refined. The most notable instance of this in the *Politics* is Aristotle's attempt
to maintain along with law and common opinion that there is a distinction

between free and slave while shifting the demarcation line between the two (I.4–7). In political philosophy we must begin with common opinions because they are better known to us; but our goal, in Aristotle's view, is to discover what is natural and hence better known in the order of nature (*EN* I.4.1095a30–b13; for the distinction see *An. Post.* I.2.71b33–72a5 and *Top.* VI.4.141b3–14).

The naturalism of the *Politics* has two layers. The first is the basic idea that a political community is a natural entity like an animal or a man (I.2.1252b30, 1253a2, 25; IV.4.1291a24–8; VII.8.1328a20–25) and has a nature of its own separate from the natures of the individuals that compose it (I.2.1252b31–43 together with *Phys.* II.1.192b33–193a2). The second layer, which follows upon this, is the idea that, as a natural entity, a polis can be in either a natural or an unnatural condition. (A man, for example, is in a natural condition when his soul rules his body but in an unnatural condition otherwise [I.5.1254a34–b21].) In describing the best polis Aristotle is concerned with this second layer. He takes it for granted in *Politics* VII that the polis is a natural entity and attempts to describe its natural condition. Now, Aristotle has a variety of reasons for claiming that the social and political structure described in *Politics* VII.8–10 is the natural condition of a polis. First and most importantly, the structure is designed to realize the true end of human nature. Secondly, it distributes military, political, and religious offices to its adult male citizens in a manner that corresponds to the natural stages of life. Thirdly, it distributes these offices only to the naturally superior sex (*Pol.* I.5.1254b13–14, 12.1259b1–3). And, finally, it assigns natural slaves to natural masters. These considerations are apparently strong enough in Aristotle's mind to outweigh the fact that the best polis does not satisfy his main criterion of the natural, namely, happening always or for the most part.

Thus we reach the foundation of the Aristotelian conception of justice. But is the foundation rock or sand? In inferring that the best polis is absolutely just because it exists by nature Aristotle is alleged to have committed the fallacy of deriving an "ought" from an "is." R. G. Mulgan writes:

> Assuming that certain characteristics can be identified as natural or innate does it follow that these characteristics ought to be developed rather than restricted? Is this not an unjustifiable inference from what is to what ought to be? We must accept that Aristotle's assumption that the natural is necessarily best and the best necessarily natural is not logically sound. Of anything natural one may always ask whether it is good or bad and either answer is logically possible.

This raises the second of the two fundamental questions about the argument from nature that grounds Aristotle's theory of distributive justice.[62] Although it is a large and difficult question, the general explanation of Aristotle's linkage of nature and justice is clear enough. Aristotle subscribes to a teleological view of nature according to which "nature makes everything for

62 See the first paragraph of this section.

the sake of something" (*PA* I.1.641b12, 5.645a23–6; *Phys*. II.8; *Pol*. I.2. 1252b32) where this something, the end or *telos* of the making, is something good (*Phys*. II.2.194a32–3, 3.195a23–5; *Met*. I.3.983a31–2; *Pol*. I.2.1252b34–1253a1).[63] Thus, according to Aristotle's teleology, whatever is natural is good. Adding a plausible assumption connecting goodness in the realm of human activities and justice, we have the following quasi syllogism:[64]

1 Everything natural is good.
2 Everything (within the field of human conduct) that is good is just.
3 Therefore, everything (within the field of human conduct) that is natural is just.

The principle linking nature and justice in Aristotle's argument from nature is thus a corollary of his natural teleology. Aristotle's theory of distributive justice is a late chapter of his philosophy of nature. Whether this philosophy of nature is satisfactory is another matter, but not, as the quotation from Mulgan implies, a matter of logic.

5   THE SUMMATION ARGUMENT

Aristotle usually regards democracy as a deviant constitution (*Pol*. III.7. 1279b4–10, IV.2.1289a26–30, 38–b11), but he considers one justification of democracy, the famous "summation" argument, according to which democracy would seem to be absolutely just in some circumstances and not a deviant constitution at all (*Pol*. III.11). This argument is interesting for its clever application of Aristotle's principle of distributive justice, an application which, if valid, would seem in other circumstances to justify absolute kingship. The strategy of the argument is to apply the principle of distributive justice to men taken collectively as well as individually. In terms of our formulation of the principle in modern functional notation the strategy is to allow the individual variables "x" and "y" to range not only over individual free men but also over groups or bodies of free men.

Aristotle envisions a situation, which he thinks may sometimes occur (*Pol*. III.11.1281b15–21), where the worth of the free men in a polis, though individually quite negligible, is nevertheless collectively greater than that of the few best men (1281a42–b2; and compare VII.13.1332a36–8). The collection envisioned is not a random collection, an unordered set of the free men in the polis, but an organized body of them – the many meeting together (*hoi polloi sunelthontes*, 1281b1, 5,35, 1282a17), as in the ekklesia. The worth of such an organized body may be greater or less than or equal to the worth of the corresponding unordered set, which is simply the worth of each of its

63 In one passage these two points are combined: "we say that nature makes for the sake of something, and that this is some good" (*Somn*. 2.455b17–18).
64 It is not a syllogism strictly speaking since the parenthetical expression counts as a fourth term. The argument is of course valid.

members added to that of the others. (Similarly, the value of a complete collection of coins of a certain kind has a value for a collector that is greater than the sum of the values of the individual coins.) To call Aristotle's argument a "summation" argument is thus a misnomer.

Aristotle infers that in the circumstances envisioned, where the worth of the many meeting together is greater than that of the few best men, the many ought to be supreme (1281a40–42). This inference rests upon an unstated major premiss that links greater authority to greater worth. The only such principle of linkage that Aristotle ever appeals to is his principle of distributive justice. So it seems reasonable to find this principle in this argument.

The argument in favor of the many is intended to overthrow the exclusive claims to political authority of the few best men.[65] Strictly speaking, it does not justify making the many supreme over *every* other group of free men. For the circumstances envisioned leave open the possibility that there might be some group consisting of more than the few best men but less than all the free men whose worth is greater than that of the many. (We might get such a body by excluding from the ekklesia all those who are especially stupid or cowardly.) To reach the conclusion that the many should be supreme over every other group of free men a stronger minor premiss is required to the effect that the worth of the free men in the polis meeting together is greater than the worth of any individual among them or of any other (actual or possible, large or small) body of them.

A remarkable feature of this justification of democracy is that it employs the Aristotelian standard of worth – virtue fully furnished with external means. Attention is focused first on character and thought (*ta êthê kai hê dianoia*) (1281b7), and the many are compared with the few best men in respect of virtue and practical wisdom (*aretê kai phronêsis*) (b4–5).[66] But later in the chapter wealth also enters the picture. Aristotle remarks in regard to the members of the ekklesia, the boule, and the dikasteries in a democracy that "the assessed property of all of these together is greater than that of those who hold great offices individually or in small groups" (1282a39–41). When the argument is repeated twice in a later chapter, the two factors of virtue and wealth are conjoined (III.13.1283a40–42, b30–35). Thus Aristotle's argument in favor of democracy is not simply aporetic. If the free men in a polis meeting together have the sort of superiority that Aristotle describes, then by the Aristotelian conception of justice they should be supreme. And Aristotle does indeed indicate that the view under consideration is "probably true" (1281a42).[67]

---

65 See Newman's note to 1281a40.
66 Compare *Pol.* VIII.2.1337a38–9; for the distinction between the moral and intellectual virtues see *EN* I.13.1103a3–10.
67 Two subsidiary arguments in favor of democracy also make an appearance in III.11: the safety-valve argument and the shoe-pinching argument. To totally exclude those who are poor and of little merit from political power, since there are so many of them, Aristotle warns, creates a situation that is frightening (*phoberos*) (1281b21–31).

In the circumstances Aristotle envisions, the worth of the many meeting together is greater, but not incommensurably greater, than that of the few best men. So the principle of distributive justice would not justify completely excluding the few best men from office. Furthermore, the summation argument provides no rationale for opening executive and administrative offices, even minor ones,[68] where the duties are discharged by single individuals or small bodies, to free men in general. The argument only justifies giving authority to the many when they meet together and act as a body. Thus Aristotle recommends that the many be admitted to the ekklesia, the boule, and the dikasteries (1281b31, 1282a24–b1) but not to the highest offices (1281b25–8) such as those of war and finance (1282a31–2; see also VI.8.1322a29–b12), which by implication will fall to the few best men.

If the many do not hold the highest offices, in what sense are they supreme? The only political functions that Aristotle assigns to the many in *Politics* III.11 are the election of officers and the scrutiny of their conduct (1281b33, 1282a13–14, 26–7). But he regards these functions as higher than those discharged by the individual officers themselves (1282a24–38; see also Plato, *Laws* 945b3–e3). Furthermore, he may have intended[69] for the ekklesia of free men to have all of its usual powers, which by his own account were quite extensive: "The deliberative part is supreme about war and peace, and alliance and disalliance, and about laws, and about death and exile and confiscation, and about the election of officers and their scrutiny" (*Pol.* IV.14.1298a3–7).

Aristotle's principle of distributive justice yields different results in different cases. In one situation it justifies democracy; in an opposite situation it justifies kingship. And in one passage Aristotle explicitly connects the two justifications:

> Therefore if [1] the many also really ought to be supreme because they are superior (*kreittous*) to the few, then too [by parity of reasoning], [2] if one person, or more than one but fewer than the many, were superior (*kreittous*) to the rest, they ought to be supreme rather than the many. (*Pol.* III.13. 1283b23–7)

The first question this passage raises concerns the meaning of *kreittôn*. Does it mean "stronger" (as at *Pol.* II.8.1268a25, III.10.1281a23, 15.1286b36,

---

Thus to avoid a political explosion the many must be given a modicum of political power. Furthermore, Aristotle argues (using houses, rudders, and feasts as his examples rather than shoes), as the man who wears the shoes is the best judge of how they fit and where they pinch, so those who are ruled are the best judges of their rulers and thus should be the ones who elect them to office and scrutinize their conduct when their term is over (1282a17–23).

68 Elsewhere Aristotle suggests that under certain circumstances free men in general might be admitted to minor administrative offices. See *Pol.* V.8.1309a27–32, VI.5.1320b9–14, and Newman's note to 1281b31.

69 Contrary to Susemihl and Hicks, p. 39.

IV.12.1296b15, and elsewhere) or "better" (as at II.3.1262a7, 9.1271b9) or "superior (in any respect)."[70] In interpreting and translating the passage scholars have generally overlooked the third, or generic, sense;[71] but clearly it is the correct choice. For in *Politics* III.13.1283b13–b35 Aristotle sets forth a puzzle, or *aporia*, that arises for any conception of justice (see b13–14). The puzzle consists of an argument that the many can make against the few (given already at 1283a40–42) and a reverse argument that one man can make against the many (b13–23) on any standard of worth. Since the passage above is meant to connect the two arguments, it must maintain their neutral perspective. The second question concerns the object of the superiority of the one or the few in clause (2), the consequent of the conditional. Are the one or the few superior to everyone collectively or individually? The argument of the one man against the many is vague about this, but not the argument of the many against the few: they make their claim because they are superior to the few collectively (b33–5). Thus if the antecedent is to support rather than conflict with the consequent, the claim of the one or the few must rest on the opposite assumption that the one or the few are superior to all the others put together. Consequently, both the antecedent and the consequent, both (1) and (2), express versions of the summation argument.[72] The second version regarded as an instance of Aristotle's principle of distributive justice is as follows: if the worth (by a given standard) of one person or of a small body of persons in a polis is greater than the worth of all the other free men in it put together, then the value of the things assigned to the one person or to the body of persons should be greater than the value of the things assigned to all the others put together.

The argument favoring absolute kingship[73] is more than merely the reverse of that favoring democracy. The conclusion of the one is much stronger than that of the other and, consequently, is derived from a stronger premiss. Unlike the many in a just democracy, the absolute king has a monopoly on the political authority in a polis. He is supreme over everything and rules according to his own wish untrammeled by law (*Pol.* III.13. 1284a13–14, 14.1285b29–30, 16.1287a1–3, 8–10). Like a tyrant, he has all the authority and his subjects none, though he differs from a tyrant in ruling

---

70 To signify one of the specific senses without risk of ambiguity, a Greek writer could conjoin *kreittôn* in the generic sense with a prepositional phrase indicating the appropriate respect. Thus on occasion Aristotle uses the phrases *kreittôn kata dunamis* ("superior in respect of strength") and *kreittôn kata aretên* ("superior in respect of goodness") for "stronger" and "better" respectively (*Pol.* I.6.1255a10, VII.3. 1325b10–11).

71 Newman in his note on 1283b23 takes it to mean "stronger." The majority of translators (Welldon, Jowett, Barker, and Robinson) render it as "stronger." Rackham chooses "better." Only Lord adopts the neutral translation "superior."

72 Strictly speaking, (1) is an argument ("*q* because *p*") whereas (2) is a conditional proposition ("if *r*, then *s*").

73 *pambasileia*, which means "kingship over everything" (Newman's note to 1285b36).

over willing subjects for their benefit rather than his own and in pursuing the fine (*to kalon*) rather than pleasure (*Pol.* III.7.1279a32–4, b6–7, IV.10. 1295a17–23, V.10.1310b40–1311a8; *EN* VIII.10.1160a35–b12). To say that the king pursues the fine is presumably to say that he pursues the true end of the polis, namely, a life of moral and intellectual virtue for everyone of his subjects capable of leading such a life.

The standard of worth of absolute kingship is a bit more complex than that of true aristocracy. In addition to the aristocratic factors of virtue and wealth (*Pol.* IV.2.1289a30–33) it comprises political ability (*politikê dunamis*) (*Pol.* III.13.1284a3–10; see also V.9.1309a33–7 and VII.3.1325b10–14) and possibly even bodily superiority (*Pol.* VII.14.1332b16–23; compare I.5. 1254b34–1255a1). (Bodily superiority is helpful to silence doubts about moral, political, and intellectual ability.) Thus a list of the factors constituting the standard of absolute kingship consists of five items: moral and intellectual virtue, wealth, political ability, bodily excellence, and freedom.[74] Aristotle's justification of absolute kingship, however, appeals to only two of these: virtue and political ability.

In a labyrinthine sentence Aristotle explains the circumstances under which absolute kingship is justified:

> If there is some one man who differs so much in excess of virtue, or more than one but not enough to be able to make up the complement of a polis, that the virtue and the political ability of all the others is not commensurable with theirs, if they are more than one, or if one, with his alone, then these men must no longer be reckoned a part of the polis; for they will be treated unjustly if deemed worthy of equal things, being so unequal in virtue and political ability; since such a man is in all likelihood like a god among men (*Pol.* III.13.1284a3–11; see also a11–17, III.17.1288a15–19, and VII.14.1332b16–27).

Aristotle in effect distinguishes three cases: (1) where there is one man whose virtue and political ability are outstanding, (2) where there are several but not enough to make up the complement of a polis (*plêrôma poleôs*),[75] and (3) where there are enough.[76] In case (3) true aristocracy is presumably the appropriate constitution with the exceptional individuals ruling and being ruled in turn. Case (2) is a plural kingship (as in Sparta). To say that the godlike man of case (1) should not be reckoned a part of the polis is to say that he should not share authority with others in the polis – that he should rule as an absolute monarch (compare *Pol.* III.17.1288a26–9). Such rule is justified according to Aristotle when "the virtue and the political ability of all the others (*tôn allôn . . . pantôn*) is not commensurable (*mê sumblêtên*) . . . with his . . . ". Both Greek expressions require comment.

---

74 See Newman, vol. I, p. 275, n. 1
75 For the expression see *Pol.* II.7.1267b16 and IV.4.1291a17.
76 The three cases correspond to those mentioned at *Pol.* III.18.1288a35. See Susemihl and Hicks *ad loc.*

First, what does *sumblêtos* mean? Two things are *sumblêta* in respect of a given attribute if, and only if, the attribute can in both cases be measured by the same standard (*GC* II.6.333a20–27; *EN* V.5.1133a19–26). Thus two musical notes are commensurable in sharpness; but a pen, a taste of wine, and a musical note are not (*Top.* I.15.107b13–18; *Phys.* VII.4.248b7–10). Incommensurability need not preclude all comparisons. Although knowledge and wealth are measured in respect of goodness by different standards (*EE* VII.10.1243b22), still knowledge is better than wealth (*Pol.* VII.1.1323b16–18). We might say in this case that the one standard is higher than the other. The virtue and political ability of the absolute king must be both superior to and incommensurable with that of all the others in the polis. It must be superior to justify giving political authority to him rather than to the others, and it must be incommensurable to justify giving him all of it. If his virtue and political ability were commensurable with theirs, then it would seem that in justice they should have a share of authority, though perhaps a small one.

The second expression requiring comment is *hoi alloi pantes*. As Aristotle points out in the course of his criticism of the communism of Plato's *Republic*, *pantes* is ambiguous: it can mean everyone individually or everyone put together (*Pol.* II.3.1261b20–30). It might seem that in the passage under discussion it must be taken in both ways. For the virtue and political ability of an absolute king, if his rule is justified, must be incommensurably superior to that of all the others individually and collectively. However, on the basis of a plausible assumption – that the worth of a body of men (all of whom are commensurable in worth) is commensurable with the worth of its individual members – the one is equivalent to the other. For if two things are commensurable in respect of a given attribute, whatever is incommensurable with the one in respect of the given attribute is also incommensurable with the other. Thus it is a matter of indifference which way *pantes* is taken in the above passage.

As I have mentioned, Aristotle's justification of absolute kingship is not the mirror image of his justification of democracy. For one thing, the concept of incommensurable superiority figures in the one justification but not in the other. For another, in his justification of democracy Aristotle compares the worth of the whole body of free men in a polis with that of the few best men *among them* whereas in his justification of absolute kingship he compares the worth of the godlike man with the worth of all *the others* – not with the worth of a group of which the godlike man is himself a member. Strictly speaking, for absolute kingship to be justified by the Aristotelian conception of justice the candidate must be incommensurably superior in worth, not only to all others in the polis both individually and collectively, but also to every (actual or possible) group that contains the candidate himself. But might not an ekklesia with the godlike man as its leader be at least commensurable in worth with the godlike man himself? Aristotle thinks not. If a godlike man were to arise in a polis, there are three ways of dealing with him: he can be removed (killed, exiled, or ostracized); he can, like an ordinary citizen, be asked to rule and be ruled in turn; or he can be obeyed as an absolute king

(*Pol.* III.13.1284b25–34, 17.1288a24–9). Aristotle dismisses the second alternative as unnatural (1288a26–8): to ask such a man to submit to being ruled would be like claiming "to rule over Zeus" (1284b30–31).

6   CONCLUSION

The symbolism introduced earlier provides a convenient vehicle for examining the status and consistency of Aristotle's three diverse justifications and for explaining how he means to avoid Protagorean relativism without embracing Platonic absolutism.

When the variables "x" and "y" are allowed to range over the groups of free men in a given polis as well as over individual free men, the formula for the Aristotelian conception of justice expresses the major premiss of Aristotle's three justifications:

$$(1) \qquad (\forall x)(\forall y)\left(\frac{P(x) \cdot W(x)}{P(y) \cdot W(y)} = \frac{V(T(x))}{V(T(y))} \right)$$

Democracy is justified by adding a minor premiss to the effect that as a group the many (m) are superior ($>$) in virtue and wealth to the few best men (b):

$$(2_d) \qquad (P(m) \cdot W(m)) > (P(b) \cdot W(b))$$

$$(3_d) \qquad \therefore V(T(m)) > V(T(b))$$

Absolute kingship is justified when a godlike man (g) appears in a polis who is incommensurably superior ($>>$) in political virtue and wealth to all the remaining free men (r):

$$(2_k) \qquad (P(g) \cdot W(g)) >> (P(r) \cdot W(r))$$

$$(3_k) \qquad \therefore V(T(g)) >> V(T(r))$$

True aristocracy requires a more complex justification, which was symbolized in Section 4.

These justifications are compatible with each other since they apply to different situations. The polises where democracy and true aristocracy are justified contain no godlike men, and the polis in which democracy is justified differs from that in which true aristocracy is justified in containing a large group of free men who individually have little virtue (*Pol.* III.11. 1281b23–4, 1282a25–6).

Each of the justifications is a valid deductive argument. Aristotle affirms the major premiss they share on the basis of a twofold appeal to nature. The principle of distributive justice, the *concept* as distinguished from the various *conceptions* of distributive justice, is itself according to nature (*Pol.* VII.3. 1325b7–10) and so too is one particular standard of worth, the standard of the best polis. Consequently, the question of the status of these three justifications, whether they are purely hypothetical or not, is a question about the minor premiss or premisses of each.

In the case of the democratic premiss Aristotle's answer is straightforward: it is sometimes but not always true (*Pol.* III.11.1281b15–21). Hence the justification of democracy is not purely hypothetical. Nor is the justification of absolute kingship.[77] The man who is "like a god among men" (*Pol.* III.13.1284a10–11) would be a man of heroic virtue (see VII.14.1332b16–27); and such a man, Aristotle says, is "rare" (*spanios*) (not nonexistent) (*EN* VII.1.1145a27–8).[78]

The minor premisses of the aristocratic argument describe a situation where all of the free men in a given polis have sufficient wealth for the exercise of the moral and intellectual virtues and where all of the older free men of the polis are men of practical wisdom. In the *Politics* Aristotle makes only the modest claim that such a situation is possible:

> It is not possible for the best constitution to come into being without appropriate equipment [that is, the appropriate quality and quantity of territory and of citizens and noncitizens]. Hence one must presuppose many things as one would wish them to be, though none of them must be impossible (*Pol.* VII.4.1325b37–8; see also II.6.1265a17–18).

But Aristotle appears to subscribe to the principle that every possibility is realized at some moment of time (*DC* I.12, *Top.* II.11.115b17–18; *Met.* IX.4.1047b3–6).[79] This principle together with the claim that the situation described is possible entails that the situation sometimes occurs. There are hints in this direction in the *Politics* itself (II.5.1264a1–5, VII.10.1329b25–35). An additional point is that true aristocracy is the natural condition of a natural entity; and it would be an anomaly in Aristotle's philosophy of nature if there were a kind of natural entity that was never in a natural condition. Thus even Aristotle's justification of true aristocracy is not purely hypothetical.

The final question is Aristotle's way of avoiding Protagorean relativism without embracing Platonic absolutism. The relativist, along with everyone else (*EN* V.3.1131a13–14; *Pol.* III.12.1282b18), can accept the principle of distributive justice:

$$\frac{Q(x)}{Q(y)} = \frac{V(T(x))}{V(T(y))}$$

---

77 Contrary to Mulgan, who writes that "[a] god among men would . . . be an anomaly of nature which Aristotle the biologist would not happily countenance. . . . The discussion [of absolute kingship] in Book Three is purely hypothetical" (*Aristotle's Political Theory*, p. 87).

78 Notice, too, that when the justification of absolute kingship is summed up in a complex sentence at *Pol.* III.17.1288a15–19, the subordinate clause, which contains the minor premiss, begins with "when" (*hotan*) rather than "if."

79 See Jaakko Hintakka, *Time and Necessity* (Oxford, 1973) especially chapter V, and Sarah Waterlow, *Passage and Possibility* (Oxford, 1982).

And he can concede that particular instances of this principle, particular conceptions of justice, accurately describe the modes of distributing political authority that appear just to particular polises and to particular philosophers. What he denies is that there is any basis for ranking these various conceptions of justice or for singling one out as the best (Plato, *Theat.* 172a–b). Aristotle, following in Plato's track (*Laws* X.888d7–890d8), maintains against the relativist that nature provides such a basis. But he departs from Plato in his conception of nature. For Plato "the just by nature" (*to phusei dikaion*) (*Rep.* VI.501b2) is the Form of justice, an incorporeal entity (*Phdo.* 65d4–5, *Soph.* 246b8) that exists beyond time and space (*Tim.* 37c6–38c3, 51e6–52b2),[80] whereas for Aristotle the sensible world is the realm of nature (*Met.* XII.1.1069a30–b2). Thus in appealing to nature Aristotle does not appeal to a transcendent standard. Nor does he appeal to his main criterion of the natural, namely, happening always or for the most part. Aristotle's theory of justice is anchored to nature by means of the polis described in *Politics* VII and VIII, and he regards this polis as natural because it fosters the true end of human life and because its social and political structure reflects the natural hierarchy of human beings and the natural stages of life. Thus the nature that Aristotle's theory of justice is ultimately founded on is human nature.[81]

80 For the identification of the realm of nature with the world of Forms see *Phdo.* 103b5, *Rep.* X.597b5–7, c2, 598a1–3, and *Parm.* 132d2.
81 This paper is an extensively revised version of an article entitled "Distributive Justice in Aristotle's *Ethics* and *Politics*" that appeared in *Topoi*, 4 (1985), pp. 23–45. This latter paper was in its turn a revision of a still earlier paper presented at a conference in the History of Ethics at the University of California, Irvine, in January of 1984. I am grateful to the participants at this conference – especially Charles Young, who was the commentator on my paper – and to Thomas Hurka, Rex Martin, and Nicholas Smith for many helpful comments, criticisms, and suggestions.

   The work leading up to the *Topoi* paper was accomplished during a sabbatical year spent at that modern Lyceum, the Institute for Advanced Study at Princeton. I am grateful to the Institute, the National Endowment for the Humanities, and the University of Washington for making this year of study possible.

12

Aristotle on Natural Law and Justice

FRED D. MILLER, JR.

1 INTRODUCTION

Aristotle has been hailed as "the father of natural law."[1] Nevertheless, many modern commentators deny the concept of natural law a legitimate place in his philosophical thought. This denial generally rests on three sorts of arguments: that it is impossible to construct a natural-law interpretation of Aristotle which is consistent with all of the texts, that the particular natural-law claims which he mentions are too inconsistent with other well attested Aristotelian doctrines for it to be credible to attribute them to him, and that, in any case, the concept of natural law as such does not play an important role in his ethical or political writings.

A satisfactory interpretation of Aristotle's views on natural law must take into account the following difficult facts: Aristotle refers with apparent agreement to the distinction between natural law and conventional law in *Rhetoric* I.10, 13, 15. But the way in which he relates this distinction to the distinction between unwritten and written law in these chapters is not entirely consistent. Nor does he make explicit use of the notion of natural law in his other writings. On the other hand, in the *Rhetoric* he does link natural law to natural justice, which he discusses in *Magna Moralia* I.33 and *Nicomachean Ethics* V.7. However, the latter discussions seem to conflict with the *Rhetoric*, for they agree with each other that natural justice is in some

---

1 M. S. Shellens, "Aristotle on Natural Law," *Natural Law Forum*, 4 (1959), p. 72. Compare W. von Leyden, *Aristotle on Equality and Justice* (New York, 1985), pp. 87–90; E. Barker, *The Politics of Aristotle* (Oxford, 1946), p. 366; and L. Strauss, *Natural Right and History* (Chicago, 1953), chs 3–4, who emphasizes Aristotle's connections with Socrates and Plato. Strauss's article "Natural Law" in the *International Encyclopedia of the Social Sciences* (New York, 1968), is a clear and concise statement of his interpretation.

sense compatible with change, but this seems to contradict the claim of the
Rhetoric that natural law is immutable. In addition, many commentators
have found the discussions of justice and change in the *Magna Moralia* and
Nicomachean Ethics to be obscure. Moreover, the discussions of natural justice
in the *Magna Moralia* and *Nicomachean Ethics* disagree with each other on
important issues, such as the relation of natural justice to political justice.
Finally, the relevance of the ideas of natural law and natural justice for
Aristotle's ethics and politics is controversial.[2]

Several interpretations have been offered. First and least charitably,
Aristotle's treatment is sometimes dismissed as "neither clear nor consistent."[3] Second, at the other extreme is the attempt to read and interpret
the text with a view to supporting a consistent, unitarian account of natural
law and natural justice running throughout the Aristotelian corpus.[4] Third,
a number of commentators try to cut through the Gordian knot by simply
rejecting the *Rhetoric* as a source for Aristotle's considered views. This work,
it is argued, is intended for an audience lacking philosophical training and is
merely "reporting the stock phrases of current oratory" and the opinions
widely accepted by his contemporaries which will prove persuasive in a legal
or political arena.[5] This case is presented most emphatically by Ritchie who
finds Aristotle's recommendations concerning natural law to be rather
cynical: "'No case: talk about the law of nature,' is a more lofty suggestion
than 'No case: abuse plaintiff's attorney,' but is equally a *rhetorical* device."[6]
A fourth approach is to explain the discrepancies between the main
discussions as due to Aristotle's own philosophical development. If one
adopts some version of the Jaeger thesis,[7] one can view the claims about
natural law in the *Rhetoric* as part of an earlier and more Platonic stage of
Aristotle's thought, whereas the discussion of natural justice in the common

2 R. G. Mulgan, *Aristotle's Political Theory* (Oxford, 1977), p. 141: "the idea of natural
law as such does not play an important role in his political theory." H. Kelsen,
"Aristotle's Doctrine of Justice," in *What is Justice?* (Berkeley, 1957), p. 384 n. 15: "this
concept [i.e. natural justice] does not play an essential part in his *Ethics*."
3 J. W. Jones, *The Law and Legal Theory of the Greeks* (Oxford, 1956), p. 64.
4 Regarding the consistency of the *Rhetoric* account, see W. M. A. Grimaldi, *Aristotle,
Rhetoric I: A Commentary* (New York, 1980), for example, pp. 317–18.
5 F. Wormuth, "Aristotle on Law," in *Essays in Political Theory Presented to George H.
Sabine*, eds M. Konvitz and A. E. Murphy (Ithaca, 1948), p. 58, and compare
Shellens, "Aristotle on Natural Law," p. 81.
6 D. G. Ritchie, *Natural Rights* (London, 1894), pp. 30–31. Discerning in Aristotle his
own reservations about the natural law doctrine, Ritchie suggests Aristotle may have
had a "prophetic vision on the vast turgid river of rhetoric flowing through long ages
from its source in the upspringing protest against the rocky barrier of mere external
authority – a river destined to sweep away in its course some things that were evil and
some things that were good."
7 W. Jaeger, *Aristotle: Fundamentals of the History of His Development*, tr. R. Robinson,
(Oxford, 1948 [1934]).

books of the *Nicomachean Ethics* and *Eudemian Ethics* represents a significantly later stage.[8] In addition, the dating of the *Magna Moralia* and even its Aristotelian authorship are controversial.[9] Finally, it may be suggested that the doctrines of natural law and natural justice are not relevant to the practical concerns of Aristotle's ethics or politics.[10]

Although there is something to be said for each of these interpretations, each also leaves something to be desired. The first underemphasizes the substantial overlap of doctrine in these various passages, whereas the second must disregard the inconsistencies mentioned above. The third interpretation tends to underestimate the philosophical importance of the *Rhetoric* and to exaggerate the eristic and cynical qualities of the work, ignoring Aristotle's statement, "Rhetoric is useful because true and just things are stronger by nature than their opposites, so that if decisions are not what is proper, the defeat must be due to the speakers themselves,[11] and this is deserving of blame." Further, "generally speaking, true and better things are by nature always easier to prove and more persuasive" (I.1.1355a20–24; 37–8). The fourth interpretation, even if correct, is not very informative about the logical relations among the different discussions or about the relations of these to Aristotle's other writings. Indeed, critical discussions of these passages neglect to a surprising extent the connections between Aristotle's statements about natural law and justice and his account of what is "natural" in his physical and biological writings. The fifth interpretation, although correct to emphasize the practical character of Aristotle's ethics and politics, is mistaken to deny natural law and justice an important place in them, as I argue in sections 5 and 6.

I shall take a different approach to the problem here. Although Aristotle does not himself describe this problem in these terms, the various claims concerning nature, law and justice which are contained in his different discussions present typical Aristotelian *aporiai* or puzzles. As such, they require treatment along lines similar to that accorded to the puzzles associated with moral weakness or incontinence (*akrasia*):

8 The relatively early date for the bulk of *Rhetoric* I–II is supported by the references to Isocrates and the absence of references to Demosthenes, by the mention of historical dates prior to 355 BC, and by the sharing of the philosophical interests of the Academy. I. Düring accordingly proposes a date of composition toward the end of the period 360–355. Some argue for a later date, ca. 330, in view of events of 339–336 referred to in II.23–34. Düring, however, views these as a later interpolation written after Aristotle's return to Athens in 334 BC; see *Aristoteles* (Heidelberg, 1966), pp. 118–125. Max Hamburger takes the opposed idiosyncratic view that "the *Rhetoric* contains the consummation of Aristotle's legal philosophy and theory," in *Morals and Law: The growth of Aristotle's Legal Theory* new ed. (New York, 1971), p. 65.

9 Düring provides again a judicious treatment of the linguistic and chronological evidence in *Aristoteles*, pp. 441–4. He conjectures that our *MM* is a reworking by a Peripatetic, perhaps Theophrastus, of lectures which Aristotle orginally wrote around his Academy years. See note 20 below.

10 See note 2 above.

11 I read *di' hautôn* at 1355a23. All translations are mine.

As in the other cases we must set out the appearances (*tithentas ta phainomena*), and first discuss the puzzles (*aporiai*); in this way we must prove, preferably, all the common beliefs (*endoxa*) about these affections, but if not all [the common beliefs], then most of them, and the most authoritative. For if the objections are solved and the common beliefs are left, it will have been proved sufficiently. (*EN* VII.1.1145b2–7)

According to this approach the appearances include the claims about natural law and justice contained in Aristotle's different discussions. These claims present puzzles because they seem to be inconsistent with each other. Aristotle is seeking in his different discussions to accommodate the common beliefs as far as possible, but he is not merely taking these beliefs to be given and putting them, as far as possible, into a coherent system. He is also seeking a deeper normative theory which tries to draw upon "things that seem to be the case" in order to justify common ethical beliefs and correct them if necessary. As part of this method, he argues that the principles of ethics depend upon principles of his natural and metaphysical works which are themselves defended by reference to nonethical *endoxa* and *phainomena*.[12] Accordingly I shall be concerned not only with the manner in which Aristotle endeavors to accommodate most common ethical beliefs about natural law and justice but also with how these are related to nonethical principles in his physical and biological sciences. After developing this interpretation of Aristotle's theory of natural law and justice in sections 2–4, I shall consider in sections 5–6 very generally the relation of the theory of natural law and justice to his politics.

2   *NATURAL LAW AND* RHETORIC *I*

There is substantial agreement among the three discussions in *Rhet.* I.10, 13 and 15[13] concerning the doctrine of natural law. On each of the following claims there seems to be agreement:

R1   The law (*nomos*) is both particular (*idios*) and common (*koinos*) (compare 10.1368b7 and 13.1373b4).

R2   The common law consists of things agreed upon by all persons (compare 10.1368b7–9 and 13.1373b6–9).

---

12 Compare the approach in T. H. Irwin, "Aristotle's Methods of Ethics," in D. J. O'Meara, *Studies in Aristotle* (Washington, 1981), p. 222. Irwin characterizes the method, so understood, as "strong dialectic" in *Aristotle's First Principles* (Oxford, 1988). See also J. Barnes, who notes that the aporetic method "actually governs a large part of Aristotle's philosophical researches," in "Aristotle and the Methods of Ethics," *Revue Internationale de la Philosophie*, 34 (1981), p. 494. On the meaning of *ta phainomena* see G. E. L. Owen, "*Tithenai ta phainomena*," in *Logic, Science and Dialectic* (Cornell, 1986).
13 All references in this section are to these chapters unless otherwise indicated.

R3   The common law is law according to nature (*kata phusin, phusei*) (compare 13.1373b6–7, 10 and 15.1375a32).

R4   It is tacitly assumed that the common law is equivalent to common or natural justice (compare 13.1373b6–9 and 15.1375a27–9, b3–5).

R5   The common law is eternal and never changing, because it is natural (compare 13.1373b9–13 and 15.1375a31–b2).

R6   The common law can come into conflict with the particular law in the sense that the same act can be in accord with the one but against the other (as in Sophocles' *Antigone*) (compare 13.1373b9–13 and 15.1375a27–9, a33–b2, 7–8).

The three discussions of the *Rhetoric* make a number of other points which seem to contribute to a coherent account of natural law and justice. Each contains a claim which shows particular law to be contractual or conventional:

R7   Particular law is the law according to which people govern themselves (10.1368b7–8).

R8   Particular law is the law which is defined by each group in reference to themselves (13.1373b4–5).

R9   Particular law is a sort of contract or covenant (*sunthêkê*) (15.1376b7–11).

Hence, in contrast to the common law,

R10   [Particular] written laws change often (15.1375a32–3).

On the other hand,

R11   Natural or common law does not presuppose a community (*koinônia*) or contract (13.1373b6–9).

The citations from Sophocles and the reference to Alcidamus also suggest that natural or common law has a divine origin (13.1373b9–18 and 15.1375a33–b2), but it should be emphasized that this claim is not explicitly made in the *Rhetoric*. (The examples from Alcidamus, Empedocles, and Sophocles seem intended to illustrate the notion of natural law from familiar sources, rather than to single out specific precepts which Aristotle himself endorses.[14]) Nevertheless, Aristotle does state an important implication of the preceding claims:

R12   Natural law is the law of all in the sense that if an act is just for some persons it is just for all (13.1373b14–17).

14 See R. Hirzel, *Agraphos Nomos* (Leipzig, 1900), pp. 28–9, 65–8; and L. Arnhart, *Aristotle on Political Reasoning* (Dekalb, Ill. 1981), pp. 102–3.

That is, common or natural law differs from particular law in that it is absolute whereas particular laws are relative to the communities which agree upon their enactment. This account of natural law or justice contradicts the sort of view which is advanced by Glaucon in Plato's *Republic* II.358e3–359b5: that justice originates only when people make laws and contracts and when they call the injunction of the law "lawful" and "just." (See also *Laws* X.889e3–890a2.)

So far, these three discussions provide an account of natural law which is on the whole coherent. The main difficulties involve the notions of unwritten law and equity. Particular law is described as a kind of written law at 10.1368b7–8, whereas particular law is either unwritten or written at 13.1373b56. This inconsistency has been discussed by Martin Ostwald,[15] who argues that "unwritten law" (*agraphos nomos*) for Aristotle and other Greek authors does not have a single fixed meaning but varies from context to context depending upon what it is contrasted with. In I.10 "the unwritten law" is used for the common or natural law, comprised of rules holding for mankind at large, in contrast to the particular or "written law."[16] In I.13 "the unwritten law" is used for the portion of the particular law of a community which consists of unwritten customs rather than codified statutes, which might vary between communities, such as burial customs.[17]

The second inconsistency concerns the term "equity" (*epieikes*). The equitable is identified at 15.1375a31–2 with the common, natural law which is eternal and unchanging. It is also described in 13.1374a26–8 as a sort of justice which goes beyond (*para*) the written law, but it is described in the passage 1374a28–b22 very much along the lines of *EN* V.10, which emphasizes the role that equity plays in supplementing[18] the law by adapting to complex and unpredictable circumstances (compare 1137b26–32 and

15 M. Ostwald, "Was There a concept of *Agraphos Nomos* in Classical Greece?," in E. N. Lee, *Exegesis and Argument* (Assen, 1973). In some contexts "unwritten" is contrasted with "legal." See, for example, the distinction between unwritten (*agraphon*) and legal (*kata nomon*) justice, and the suggested parallel with the distinction between ethical (*êthikê*) and legal (*nomikê*) justice in *EN* VIII.13.1162b21–3.

16 There seems to be a similar contrast in Pseudo-Aristotle, *Rhet. Al.* 2.1421b35–1422a4: "[The] just is the unwritten custom (*ethos agraphon*) of all or the majority of men which distinguishes between noble and base acts. Examples are the honoring of parents, doing good to one's friends, and returning good to one's benefactors; for these and similar things are not commanded to human beings by written laws, but they are observed by unwritten and common law. These things then are just, but law is the common agreement (*homologêma*) of the polis, which commands in writing how the citizens ought to act under every kind of circumstance." Note that some of these examples occur also at *Rhet.* I.13.1374a23–5.

17 Compare *Pol.* III.16.1287b5–8 and VI.5.1319b40–1320a1. On the appeal to unwritten laws in Greek legal practice, see D. M. Macdowell, *The Law in Classical Athens* (Ithaca, 1978), p. 46.

18 See Shellens, "Aristotle on Natural Law," p. 77, on *para ton gegrammenon logon* at 1374a27.

1374a28–33).[19] Rather than attempting to reconcile these two references to equity, it is probably best to take the use in I.15 to reflect a more popular sense in which "equity" is synonymous with "justice" generally, and to understand I.13 as concerned with equity in Aristotle's technical sense as a specific form of justice.

In conclusion, then, apart from these two difficulties, which involve subordinate issues, the *Rhetoric* offers a coherent account of natural law and justice with recognizable similarities to subsequent natural-law theories. A central feature of this account is (R5) the claim that natural law is eternal and immutable. But Aristotle finds it hard to square this claim with the appearances (*phainomena*) as we shall see in the next section.

3 *NATURAL JUSTICE IN* MAGNA MORALIA *I.33 AND* NICOMACHEAN ETHICS *V.7*

Except for one important contradiction, the discussions of *MM* I.33[20] and *EN* V.7 are on the whole consistent and in fact complement each other in illuminating ways.[21] The major parallels between the two discussions are found in the following claims:

MN1   The just (*MM*) or political just (*EN*) is part natural and part legal (compare *MM* 1194b30–31 and *EN* 1134b18–19).

MN2   The just by nature is changeable (compare *MM* 1194b31–2 and *EN* 1134b29–30).

MN3   Other things which are by nature undergo change (compare *MM* 1194b32–3, 37 and *EN* 1134b29–30).

MN4   For example, the right hand is by nature superior to (*MM*) or stronger than (*EN*) the left, although anyone can become ambidextrous through practice (compare *MM* 1194b33–7 and *EN* 1134b33–5).

MN5   There is an analogy between things which are by nature and the just by nature (compare *MM* 1195a1–3 and *EN* 1134b33).

MN6   The just according to law (*kata nomon*) is that which is established or enacted (*thôntai*) and complied with (compare *MM* 1195a4–5 and *EN* 1134b20–21, 35–1135a1).

19 The relation of equity to law and justice in Aristotle is discussed further in section 6 below.

20 The authorship of *MM*, as noted above, is controversial. Rather than ignoring this work, however, I shall follow J. M. Cooper in using it "with the necessary circumspection," as indicative of Aristotle's views. See Cooper, *Reason and Human Good in Aristotle* (Cambridge, Mass, 1975), p. xi, and "The *Magna Moralia* and Aristotle's Moral Philosophy," *American Journal of Philology* 94, (1973), pp. 327–49.

21 All references in this section are to these two chapters unless otherwise indicated.

In general, the *Nicomachean Ethics* discussion appears more expansive than the *Magna Moralia* discussion. For example, the *Nicomachean Ethics* gives a fuller account of the character of legal justice. It, like the *Magna Moralia*, characterizes legal justice as something which is "established" (MN 6), but further describes it as contractual or conventional, that is, arising from contract or convention (*kata sunthêkên, sunthêkêi*) (1134b30–33, b35–1135a1).[22] Legal justice is also described as due to people's believing something or not (1134b19–20), and as a human product (1135a3–4). These descriptions reinforce the general parallel between contractual justice and particular law as described in the *Rhetoric* (compare R7–9). The *Nicomachean Ethics* characterizes legal or conventional justice as initially indifferent:

N7   The legal [just] is that which is such that at first it does not make a difference whether or not it is the case, but when it has been established it does make a difference (1134b20–21).

It also provides examples of legally just rules: that a prisoner's ransom shall be a mina, that a goat and not two sheep shall be sacrificed; also laws for particular cases, e.g. to make sacrifice in honor of Brasidas; and special decrees (1134b21–4).

The *Nicomachean Ethics* sets out more fully the objection which (MN2–5) are used to answer.

> That which is by nature is unchangeable and everywhere has the same power (*dunamin*) as fire burns here and in Persia (1134b25–6).
> Just things undergo change (1134b27).
> Therefore, there is no just by nature but all just things are just by law (1134b24–25).

The *Nicomachean Ethics* makes a tentative distinction between justice among the gods where there is no change, and among humans, where there is change (1134b27–30; but contrast X.8.1178b10–12). But, according to the *Nicomachean Ethics*, the fact that *human* just things are capable of being otherwise does not exclude them from being by nature (1134b30–35).

However, there is an important point in the *Magma Moralia* which is missing from the *Nicomachean Ethics*:

M8   That which is for the most part and the greater time (*epi to polu kai ton pleiô chronon*) is by nature (1194b37–9).

---

22 The word *nomos* is often translated "convention," when it is contrasted with *phusis* (nature). It is true that *nomos* admits of this translation in some contexts. However, in this essay I translate *nomikon* and *nomôi* as "legal" and "by law" in order to indicate their connection with *nomos*, "law." See W. K. C. Guthrie, *A History of Greek Philosophy*, vol. 3 (Cambridge, 1969) ch. 4, and G. B. Kerferd, *The Sophistic Movement* (Cambridge, 1981), ch. 10. I render *sunthêkê* as "contract," and *kata sunthêthên* and *sunthêkêi* as "contractual" to avoid confusion, although some translators use "convention" and "conventional." On *sunthêkê* see Guthrie, p. 136.

Relying upon the analogy of (MN5) Aristotle uses the same account for the just by nature:

M9   That which continues for the most part (*hôs epi to polu*) is manifestly just by nature (1195a3–4).

This enables him to assert natural justice in spite of change:

M10   Even if things change due to our usage, there is still a just by nature (1195a1–3).

Whatever may be one's general evaluation of the *Magna Moralia* as a source for Aristotle's ethics, there is good reason to take this contribution seriously. For the connection between what is natural and what holds always or for the most part is found often in Aristotle's nonethical treatises.[23] It appears elsewhere in the *Nicomachean Ethics* itself, in Aristotle's response to the argument that the noble and the just are by convention rather than by nature because they are subject to difference and variation. Aristotle concedes this but proceeds:

> We must be content, then, in speaking of such subjects and with such premisses to indicate the truth roughly and in outline, and in speaking about things which are only for the most part (*tôn hôs epi to polu*) and with premisses of the same kind to reach conclusions that are no better (I.3.1094b19–22).

This contribution of the *Magna Moralia* sheds light on the example of right-handedness and ambidextrousness which is common to the two discussions: even though people may become ambidextrous through training, the right hand is still superior for the most part and the greater time. Moreover, it also makes clear the main difference between the notion of natural law or justice in the *Rhetoric* and the notion of natural justice in the two ethical discussions: while the *Rhetoric* regards the natural as eternal and immutable, the *Magna Moralia* suggests that nature may be understood in terms of "the most part," as in the biological works.

There is one important contradiction between the two ethical discussions, regarding the relationship between political justice and natural justice. The *Magna Moralia* concludes that natural justice is superior (*beltion*) to legal justice, and then states, "But what we are seeking is political justice; but the political just is by law, not by nature" (1195a6–8). This is to oppose natural justice to political justice or to confine it to relations between persons who do not share the same polis. Either way the relation of natural justice to just political practice remains problematic. The *Nicomachean Ethics* takes a different and more promising tack: having defined political justice as the justice found among men who share their life with a view to self-sufficiency,

23 See *An. Pr.* I.3.25b14, 13.32b5–6; *Phys.* II.8.198b35–6; *PA* III.2.663b28–9; *GA* I.19.727b29–30, IV.4.770b11–13, 8.777a19–21; and even *Rhet.* I.10.1369a35–b2 (compare *Met.* VI.2.1027a8–11).

and who are free and either proportionately or arithmetically equal (V.6. 1134a26–8), it distinguishes the legal and natural as parts of political justice, so that the natural is included in rather than opposed to the political just. Natural justice is viewed as in some way "permeating" political justice.[24] This suggests that if one were to examine the constitution, laws, and customs of a polis which possessed political justice, one would find that certain features could be deemed to be naturally just, whereas others such as the example of the prisoner's ransom would be indifferent until they were instituted. When the *Nicomachean Ethics* states that "constitutions are not [the same], though everywhere only one is the best according to nature" (1135a4–5), it is implied that constitutions can be evaluated and compared as better or worse on the basis of the extent to which they possess naturally just features. (This implication is considered in section 6.)

Unfortunately, the two ethical discussions are tantalizingly unclear about the alleged status of natural justice. The *Magna Moralia* says that "the right is none the less by nature superior (*beltiô*) to the left, even if we do everything with the left just as with the right" (1194b35–37) and, as we have noted, describes natural justice as superior (*beltion*) to legal justice (1195a6). The *Nicomachean Ethics* says that "the right is stronger (*kreittôn*) by nature, but it is possible that everybody become ambidextrous" (1134b33–5). The *Nicomachean Ethics* also characterizes natural justice as having "everywhere the same power (*dunamin*) and not by [people's] believing or not" (1134b19–20). This is subsequently qualified, as noted above, so as not to assert that natural justice is immutable (compare 1134b25–6).[25] But the right-handed analogy clearly implies that the natural is "superior" or "stronger" in some sense. On the other hand, the above-cited claim that everywhere only one constitution is the best according to nature (1135a4–5) indicates that the natural is "better" in some sense.

These claims raise some hard questions: what is the analogy between natural justice and right-handedness supposed to consist in? In what sense could Aristotle claim that natural justice is "superior" or "stronger," by analogy to right-handedness? And even if an analogy could be found, why suppose that it would support normative conclusions? Does the fact that the right hand is generally stronger than the left imply that it is better?

Commentators have found such questions extremely difficult to answer.[26] Nevertheless, I think that the example of right-handedness provides us with

---

24 On this point and others I am indebted to R. Polansky for permitting me to read his unpublished notes on *EN* V.7. See J. Finnis, *Natural Law and Natural Rights* (Oxford, 1980), pp. 281–90.

25 J.J. Mulhern points out that for Aristotle a thing with the *dunamis* to F may be capable of doing the opposite of F-ing, citing *DI* 13.22b36–23a4, in "ΜΙΑ ΜΟΝΟΝ ΠΑΝΤΑΧΟΥ ΚΑΤΑ ΦΥΣΙΝ Η ΑΡΙΣΤΗ (*EN* 1135a5)," *Phronesis*, 17 (1972), 260–8.

26 Shellens ("Aristotle on Natural Law," p. 82) contends that "the distinction between 'being in force' and 'being valid' is one between two different spheres of spiritual being," and complains that discussions of right-handedness "fail to shed any light on the real meaning of natural law in the *EN*" (p. 84). I seek to rebut both of these points in what follows.

a valuable clue, in that it suggests a biological perspective on natural justice. Aristotle finds it necessary to adopt this biological perspective because he has repudiated the metaphysical foundations of Plato's theory of natural law and justice. Plato's *Laws* represents justice and law as "natural" in the sense of having a divine origin (see IV.715e7–716a3, 716c4–6; X.888d7–890d8). Nature in Plato's *Republic* is a transcendent, eternal and immutable principle involving the theory of Forms.[27] Aristotle has replaced this with a notion of nature as a principle of change which is inherent in substances and which, in the sublunary realm at least, holds always or for the most part.[28] Aristotle has much to say about the difference between the right and the left in his biological writings, and these discussions provide both clarification and justification for the discussions of the *Magna Moralia* and the *Nicomachean Ethics*.

4   AN ANALOGUE TO NATURAL JUSTICE IN ARISTOTLE'S BIOLOGY

Right-handedness, the nonethical analogue to natural justice, is discussed in various biological writings, as well as in *De Caelo*.[29] In *De Incessu Animalium* Aristotle claims that the right is the same in all animals (4.706a9–10) and that all animals alike are necessarily right-handed (a17–18). This is coupled with the judgment that the right is by nature better (*beltion*) than the left (a20), a claim which, as we have seen, figures importantly in the discussion of natural justice in the *Magna Moralia*. Further, he argues in *De Incessu* that the right is superior to the left in human beings to a greater extent than other animals: "Human beings have their left limbs detached most of all the animals because they are according to nature (*kata phusin*) most of all the animals; now the right is by nature (*phusei*) better than the left, being separate from it, and so in human beings the right is most right [among all the animals]" (a18–22).

The claim that the right is superior to and better than the left has a teleological justification in *De Incessu*. Teleology is advanced as a basic principle of this treatise:

27 The guardians are supposed to establish, guard, and preserve legal rules (*nomima*) by looking to the Forms, and especially, the Form of the Good (see *Rep.* VI.484c6–d3, 500c2–5, VII.540a7–b1). The Form of justice is called "the just by nature" (*to phusei dikaion*) (V.501b2, compare X.597c2, 598a1; also *Phaedo* 103b5). See J. P. Maguire, "Plato's Theory of Natural Law," *Yale Classical Studies*, 10 (1947), pp. 151–178.
28 On the grounding of natural law in Aristotle's teleogical theory of nature, compare H. B. Veatch, *Human Rights* (Baton Rouge, 1985), ch. II. However, some scholars deny that Aristotle's use of "natural" is based upon his metaphysics. J. Finnis, for example, argues that "references to what is (humanly) natural need not be regarded as an appeal to, or expression of, some independent, 'value-free' investigation of the sort that [H. B.] Veatch would call (Aristotelian) physics, and that we might call general anthropology" in *Fundamentals of Ethics* (Oxford, 1983), p. 20. The following sections indicate my agreement with Veatch.
29 I am indebted to A. Preus for very helpful suggestions regarding Aristotle's treatment of right-handedness.

> At the beginning of the inquiry we must make the hypotheses which we are accustomed often to use for our investigation of nature, that is, we must assume this manner of hypothesis in all the works of nature. Of these one is that nature does nothing in vain, but always the best possible concerning each kind of animal with respect to its substance. Therefore, if one way is better (*beltion*) than another, that is also according to nature (*kata phusin*). (2.704b12–18)

The teleological theory which explains the superiority of the right is that "the nature of the right is to initiate movement, that of the left is to be moved" (4.705b33–706a1). Aristotle supports this with the observation that people carry burdens on the left shoulder: they thereby release the side which initiates movement and enable the side which bears the weight to be moved. The theory also explains why people hop more easily on the left leg: "The burden must rest on the side which is to be moved, not on that which is to do the moving, but if it be set on the moving side and the source of movement, it will either not be moved at all or it will be more difficult" (706a1–4). Perhaps most importantly, the theory explains why humans tend to lead with their left feet; namely, they push off from their right. The argument for the universality of the right is as follows (a9–13):

> The origin of motion is the same for all animals and has its position in the same place according to nature.
> The right is the origin of motion.
> Therefore, the right is the same for all animals.

For Aristotle this teleological account has normative implications. "Generally, as regards above and below, front and back, right and left, the better (*beltion*) and more honorable (*timiôteron*) is always found above, in front, and on the right, unless some greater thing prevents it" (*PA* III.3.665a22–6). In *IA* 5.706b12–16 Aristotle supports this normative claim with the following argument:[30]

> The starting point is honorable (*timion*).
> The above, right and front contain the starting points.
> Therefore, the above, right and front are more honorable than their opposing parts.

According to this argument, the right side is more honorable and nobler *because* it contains the origin of movement.[31] This argument belongs to a more

---

30 Aristotle offers an alternative argument in this same passage: The starting point is honorable. The above is more honorable than the below, the front than the back, and the right than the left. Therefore, the above, right and front contain the starting points. This version of the argument evidently commits the fallacy of the undistributed middle.

31 See J. G. Lennox, "Theophrastus on the Limits of Teleology," in *Theophrastus of Eresus*, eds W. W. Fortenbaugh, P. M. Huby, and A. A. Long (New Brunswick, 1985).

general pattern of reasoning which is used elsewhere in Aristotle's biological writings, notably in *De Somno* 2.455b17–28 in his explanation of sleep:[32]

> since we say that nature acts for the sake of something and that this is a good; and that to everything which by nature (*pephukoti*) moves, but cannot with pleasure to itself move always and continuously, rest is necessary and beneficial; and since, taught by truth itself, men apply to sleep this metaphorical term, calling it a rest: we conclude that it occurs for the sake of the preservation of animals.

The reasoning is that nature operates for the sake of the end, which is good, so that what is needed for the end is beneficial, and nature provides what is beneficial. The general form of the explanation runs:

> What is good for the organism is present by nature.
> Rest is good for the organism.
> Therefore, rest is present by nature.

The presence of an attribute is explained by the fact that it is beneficial or needed for the end or good of the organism, which in this instance is its continued existence. Self-movement is an essential characteristic of all animals, and the part by which the animals originates movement is consequently of preeminent value. It is a distinctive feature of Aristotle's biology that the presence, structure and interrelationships of the parts and processes of living things are explained in terms of their value for these living things understood as teleological systems. Thus, the claim that the right side is better and more honorable than the left is supported by Aristotle's teleology.[33]

As with his other teleological explanations, Aristotle couples his final-cause account of the superiority of the right with a material-cause account. As with sexual generation, the material cause of the superiority of the right

---

32 Compare the discussion of D. Keyt, "Aristotle's Theory of Distributive Justice," Essay 11 of this volume, pp. 269–70.

33 Aristotle's teleology has been criticized on the grounds that he unconsciously adopts an anthropocentric or culturally determined view which compels him to see nature in a certain way, even when the facts are clearly otherwise. Aristotle's appeal to norms in science is simply a matter of imposing the human realm on nature. The criticism is advanced especially by G. E. R. Lloyd in "Right and Left in Greek Philosophy," *Journal of Hellenic Studies*, 82 (1962), pp. 67–90; *Polarity and Analogy* (Cambridge, 1966); and *Science, Folklore and Ideology* (Cambridge, 1983). J. G. Lennox makes detailed objections against Lloyd's view, and in support of an interpretation like the one I offer here: namely that Aristotle uses normative principles regarding biological functions, the locations of these functions, and the manner in which nature selects among possibilities in order to *explain* observed phenomena. This is not of course to say that his observations or explanations are satisfactory by our lights. See also Lennox's review of *Science, Folklore and Ideology* in *Oxford Studies in Ancient Philosophy*, 3 (1985), pp. 307–24.

involves vital heat. That is, just as concocted semen is hotter than uncon-
cocted semen, the right side of the body is hotter than the left (*GA*
IV.1.765a34–b4). This alleged difference in temperature is explained in
terms of the blood which possesses vital heat. Heat as opposed to cold is one
of the three measures of the quality of blood, along with clearness or turbidity
and thinness or thickness. Heat is a material requirement for strength and
courage, and thinness for intelligence. Hence, the best animals are those
which have blood that is hot and at the same time thin and clear. "For such
are at the same time finely suited for courage and of practical rationality
(*phronêsis*)" (*PA* II.2.648a9–11). In general, animals are right-handed
because they possess more or better vital heat on their right side, and they
need that sort of heat in order to function as moving beings.[34]

Aristotle also recognizes that there are exceptions to the general superiority of right handedness among the lower animals (see *HA* II.17.507a19–24;
PA IV.8.684a32–b1; *IA* 19.714b8–14). But the most striking exception is
found in human beings, for "of all animals a human alone can learn to make
equal use of both hands" (*HA* II.1.497b31–2) In the *Politics* he mentions
Plato's proposal that all humans be taught to be ambidextrous
(II.12.1274b12–15), and does not make any indication that he regarded this
as infeasible.[35] Aristotle does not, as far as I have been able to determine,
address the phenomenon of dominant left-handedness among humans. It is
possible that he would have regarded it as a congenital, unnatural (*para
phusin*) condition. Or he may have thought that although every human being
is by nature right handed, anyone can develop his left side to equality with
the right through habituation.

In conclusion, Aristotle's discussions of right-handedness in his various
biological treatises include the following important points. The fact that the
right side is generally dominant is ultimately explained in terms of its final
cause and function; namely, the right is by nature the source of motion for all
animals. This theory also offers an explanation in terms of necessary material
conditions, i.e. vital heat, blood and organs. The superiority of the right is
natural; as such, it holds always or for the most part. Yet exceptions are
admitted; it is possible for human beings to become ambidextrous through
habituation. Nevertheless, the right remains superior by nature in virtue of
final and material causes operative in human nature. Moreover, as we have
seen, the superiority of the right has normative implications. The right is
better and more honorable than the left. This is consistent, as we have noted,
with Aristotle's general method of explanation in biology. Biology is not a
value-free science for Aristotle. On the contrary, it explains the presence,
structures, and interrelationships of organs in terms of their value for living,
teleological systems. In this case, the right is better because, as the source of
movement, it is beneficial and necessary for the life or animals.

34 Compare the discussion of uprightness in A. Preus, "Man and Cosmos in
Aristotle: *Metaphysics* Lambda and the Biological Works" (unpublished).
35 Aristotle would, however, reject the claim of the Athenian stranger that human
beings are naturally ambidextrous (*Laws* VII.794d5–795d5).

5 NATURE, JUSTICE AND LAW IN POLITICS I[36]

The specific implications of the theory of natural justice for the practical science of politics are not developed in *MM* I.33 and *EN* V.7. Indeed, the latter contains only the very general pronouncement that "constitutions are not [the same], though everywhere only one is the best according to nature" (1135a4–5). However, a study of the *Politics* sheds light on both the theoretical basis and the practical applications of this theory.

Politics I.2 lays the foundations for the remainder of the work in the form of a theory of political naturalism. This theory contains, centrally, the claim that:

P1   Humans are by nature political animals (1253a2–3).

which is closely connected with two other claims:

P2   The polis exists by nature (1252b30).
P3   The polis is by nature prior to the individual (1253a25–6).[37]

In the arguments for these claims the notions of nature, justice, and law play an important role.

The claim (P1), that human beings are by nature political animals[38] – that is, that humans have an innate potential for the political life – rests upon the arguments that they are naturally adapted for the political life (1253a1–18) and that they have a natural impulse for political communities (1253a29–30 and III.6.1278b19–30). The former argument proceeds from Aristotle's teleology: Nature makes nothing in vain, and human beings are the only animals endowed by nature with *logos* or speech. Human speech serves to reveal the advantageous and the harmful, and hence also the just (i.e. common advantage) and the unjust. Humans alone have a perception of

---

36 All references in this and the following section are to the *Politics* unless otherwise indicated.

37 For a fuller treatment of these claims, see W. Kullmann, "Man as a Political Animal in Aristotle" (Essay 4 of this volume); D. Keyt, "Three Basic Theorems in Aristotle's *Politics*" (Essay 5 of this volume); and my "Aristotle's Political Naturalism," Apeiron, 22 (1989).

38 An apparent difficulty for this thesis is the statement at *HA* I.1.488a7 that a human being "dualizes" (*epamphoterizei*) between being political and dispersed. However, John Cooper argues persuasively that Aristotle's meaning is that "human beings dualize between living in large groups and solitarily, but the latter is an exception and a departure from the norm." (The gregarious animals include the political and the dispersed.) See "Political Animals and Civic Friendship," n.5, in *XI. Symposium Aristotelicum: Studien zur Politik des Aristoteles* ed. G. Patzig (Göttingen, 1989). This is, again, in agreement with the "for the most part" reading of "natural" of *MM* I.33.

good and bad and just and unjust; and the community in these things makes a household and polis. The invocation of teleology at the beginning of this argument presupposes that humans have natural ends and innate potentials necessary for attaining these ends. In this context humans have the innate capacity to perceive and express justice and injustice because this is necessary in order for them to attain their natural ends. For humans must engage in cooperative forms of social and political organization in order to fulfill their nature and these forms of cooperation require a conception of justice. The claim that humans have a natural impulse for the political community presupposes this same teleological viewpoint. Nature endows humans with the desire to live together because life in political communities is necessary for their common advantage (compare III.6.1278b17–30).

The claim (P1), that human beings are by nature political serves as a premiss for the claim (P2), that the polis exists by nature.[39] For the polis serves to promote human natural ends and, in accordance with Aristotelian teleology, arises from the natural human potential for life in the polis. The polis arises out of more basic forms of community (the household and the village) which are themselves grounded in the natural impulse of individuals for self-preservation and reproduction. But the polis represents a complete community because it attains the level of self-sufficiency necessary for full realization of the natural ends of individuals. Hence, although the polis comes to be for the sake of life it exists for the sake of the good life (I.2.1252a24–1253a1).

This provides in turn the basis for the claim (P3), that the polis is prior by nature to the individual. The point of (P3), is that human beings need the polis in order to realize their natural ends, and hence are incomplete apart from the polis. Anyone who is unable to join a community or who is self-sufficient on his own "is no part of the polis, and thus is either a beast or a god" (see 1253a18–29). This claim is defended more fully at 1253a31–9:

> For just as a human being is the best of the animals when completed (or perfected, *teleôthen*), so also when he is separated from law and justice (*dikê*) he is the worst of all. For injustice (*adikia*) is harshest when it possesses arms; but a human being is born (*phuetai*) possessing arms for the use of practical rationality and virtue, which are especially [apt] for the use of their opposites. Therefore, when he is without virtue he is the most unholy and savage [animal], and the worst concerning sex and food. But justice (*dikaiosunê*) is political; for justice (*dikê*) is [the] order (*taxis*) of the political community; but justice (*dikê*) is a judgment regarding the just (*dikaiou*).

This argument maintains that:

---

39 For a contrasting view see Keyt, "Three Basic Theorems in Aristotle's *Politics*," pp. 138–9. Keyt treats (P1) as a corollary of (P2). However, as I have just noted Aristotle defends (P1) independently of (P2), and the argument for (P2) proceeds from the claim that individual beings have natural impulses for communal life (I.2.1252a24–34).

P4   Law and political justice are necessary for human beings to realize their natural human ends.

If human beings were unable to cooperate in accordance with justice, virtue and practical rationality, they would sink into a state worse than the Hobbesian state of nature: not only would "the life of man" be "solitary, poore, nasty, brutish, and short," but human beings also would be unable to fulfill their nature as human beings. This argument also sheds light on (MN5) the analogy between natural right-handedness and natural justice discussed in sections 3 and 4: just as animals are by nature right-handed in order for them to fulfill their nature as moving beings, so also human beings are by nature political and adapted to justice in order for them to fulfill their nature as human beings.

This argument asserts that justice, law and order[40] are necessary if human beings are to attain their natural ends. In the *Nicomachean Ethics* Aristotle argues that human beings generally need the laws in order to develop their natural capacity for moral virtue. Although human beings have a natural potential for virtue this potential must be developed through habituation: "the virtues arise in us neither by nature (*phusei*) nor against nature, but we are naturally (*pephukosi*) able to acquire them, and reach our completeness (perfection, *teleioumenois*) through habit" (*EN* II.1.1103a23–6). The soul of the student of moral virtue must have been prepared by habituation for noble joy and hatred like earth that is to nourish seed (X.9. 1179b24–6). Further, the laws can best provide the habits needed to inculcate and sustain moral virtue (1179b31–1180a5). Although individual households can make an important contribution, the law has a compelling power (*anagkastikên dunamin*) which an individual such as a father lacks, and the law does not meet with the same resentment as interference by individuals (1180a21–4, compare a30–b13).[41]

However, it has been objected[42] that Aristotle's political theory cannot accommodate a theory of natural justice. For if the polis with its constitution

---

40 The notions of justice and law are closely linked, explicitly at 1253a32–3 and implicitly at a37–9. For the order or structure (*taxis*) of the polis is elsewhere identified with the law (III.16.1287a18, VII.4.1326a29–31). Plato also makes this connection: see *Gorgias* 504d1–3; *Laws* III.688a2, IX.875d4; *Phlb.* 26b7–10.

41 Aristotle cautions against changing the laws except when necessary, for the polis will not be benefited as much from change as it will be harmed due to the citizens being habituated to disobey the laws (*Pol.* II.8.1269a12–24; compare Plato *Laws* VI.772a4–d4). Indeed, around 400 BC the Athenians made it more difficult for the assembly (*ekklêsia*) to change the laws. Every proposed change had to be approved by a special body called the lawgivers (*nomothetai*). See MacDowell, *The Law in Classical Athens*, p. 48. The function of guarding the laws belonged in earlier years to the Areopagus (see *Ath. Pol.* 3.6). In Plato's *Laws*, of course, this is the primary task of the lawguardians (*nomophulakes*) (VI.754d6). Aristotle indicates that "lawguardians" was an official title in some city-states (*Pol.* IV.14.1298b29).

42 Wormuth, "Aristotle on Law," pp. 56–7.

and legal structure are the creation of the lawgiver exercising practical wisdom and moral virtue, then justice and law are more like the products of craft (*technê*) than like the products of nature. And, indeed, Aristotle does compare the lawgiver (*nomothetês*) and politician (*politikos*) to a craftsman (*dêmiourgos*) (VII.4.1325b40–1326a5; compare Plato *Republic* IV.421c2 and *Laws* IX.858a7–c1).[43]

However, this objection overlooks the full complexity of Aristotle's theory which is evident in the claim:

P5   There is by nature an impulse for such a [i.e. political] community in everyone; but the one who first established [the polis] was the cause (*aitios*) of the greatest of goods (1253a29–31).

On Aristotle's theory the causal explanation for the existence of the polis includes two cooperating factors:[44] the natural potential of a given population for the political life, and lawgivers and politicians applying the science of politics. Although the two conditions are not jointly sufficient (because the formation of the polis also requires favorable resources, the absence of overwhelming enemies, etc.), each is a necessary condition for the creation of any polis. Aristotle also regards the existence of the polis and its laws as a precondition for the development of justice and virtue generally. Therefore, the development of justice and virtue generally also requires a population with a natural potential for justice and law (1253a1–18, compare *EN* V.6.1134b13–15) and a lawgiver who fashions the legal structure (1253a30–39).

Claim (P5), that human nature and the lawgiver (and politician) are cooperative causes of the polis and laws, provides a theoretical basis for claim (MN1) in *EN* V.7: political justice is partly natural and partly legal or contractual. The fact that political justice is in part natural is due to the fact that the polis is itself in part due to nature, and the fact that political justice is in part legal or contractual is due to the fact that the polis is in part due to the inventiveness of the lawgiver. In exercising his practical rationality the lawgiver should fashion the laws so that they are in accord with the nature of the members of the polis. Thus, the work of the lawgiver is constrained by human nature: they should follow nature as a guide and proceed in accord with the natural ends of the members of the polis (see, e.g., *Pol.* VII.17.1337a1).

An example of how the lawgiver might be constrained by nature is suggested by Aristotle's discussion of slavery. For Aristotle takes very

43 He distinguishes between those who are craftsmen of laws only and those who are craftsmen of both laws and constitutions (II.12.1273b32–3, 1274b18–19). For Aristotle the primary task of the lawgiver is the fashioning of the constitution, and the framing of the laws is secondary. For purposes of simplicity in this section, however, I assume that the task of lawmaking involves that of constitution making. I turn to the relation of the constitution and the laws in the following section.

44 I defend this interpretation more fully in "Aristotle's Political Naturalism," cited above.

seriously the objection that slavery is against nature: "by law (*nomôi*) one person is a slave and another free, but by nature (*phusei*) they do not differ; therefore slavery is not just, for it is due to force" (I.3.1253b20–23). Aristotle's reply to this objection involves many qualifications and difficulties.[45] However, it is relevant here only to note that Aristotle tries to distinguish two sorts of cases: in one case the master and slave differ by nature (due to a natural inferiority of the slave), so that it is advantageous and just for the one to be enslaved and the other to be master; but in the other case slavery is based upon law rather than upon nature. The sense in which one is a slave "by law" is based upon a supposed agreement (*homologia*) by which people have the right to possess whatever they have seized by force in war, even if it is another human being. But Aristotle notes that many jurists criticize this right, just as they indict anyone making a political proposal that is "against the laws" (*graphontai paranomôn*) of the polis (I.6.1255a5–9). Aristotle ends up agreeing with these critics when a naturally free person is enslaved by law and by force: in this case slavery is not advantageous or just (I.6.1225b4–15). This is perhaps the closest Aristotle comes in the *Politics* to an explicit recognition of a "law of nature" reminiscent of claim (R6) in the *Rhetoric*.[46]

The principal work of the lawgiver involves exercising his practical rationality to make numerous particular decisions suitable to particular circumstances. In many of these cases nature does not provide any specific guidance. Hence, the particular laws of the polis will exemplify a great deal of inventiveness, arbitrariness and variability. This helps to account for Aristotle's remarks (MN6) and (N7) about legal justice in *EN* V.7: at first it does not make a difference (i.e. from the point of view of nature) whether or not a particular law is set forth, but when it has been established it does make a difference. For human beings must cooperate in accordance with a legal structure established by the lawgiver in order to realize their natures fully. In addition to the ransom and religious rules mentioned in *EN* V.7, many of the particular political institutions Aristotle describes in the *Politics* would be of this sort: particular offices and their particular functions, terms of office, numbers of persons on councils, juries, and other bodies, precise methods of selecting officials, and so forth. Further, on Aristotle's political theory the citizens must be habituated and educated to accept and obey the laws set forth by the lawgiver (see V.9.1310a14–17). This explains why legal justice involves general belief and is contractual (*kata sunthêkên*, 1134b19–20, 30–33, b35–1135a1). Aristotle can thus accept as partially true the common belief (R9), that law is a sort of contract (*sunthêkê*) or agreement (*homologia*), (*Rhet.* I.15.1376b9–10; compare *Pol.* I.6.1255a6, III.9.1280b10). Hence, Aristotle's

---

45 N. D. Smith, "Aristotle's Theory of Natural Slavery," Essay 4 in this volume, discusses the inconsistencies in Aristotle's argument.
46 Compare F. Susemihl and R. D. Hicks, *The Politics of Aristotle* (London, 1894 [repr. 1976]), p. 164. On prosecution for proposals against the law (*graphê paranomôn*), see MacDowell, *The Law in Classical Athens*, p. 50.

political theory can account for the claim (MN1) of *EN* V.7, that political justice contains both a natural and a legal (conventional) component.

6   *NATURAL JUSTICE IN* POLITICS *III*

Particular laws define the rights and duties of the citizens.[47] For example, they determine who has the right to serve in which offices and what authority each office has, who has the duty to possess arms and perform military service, who has the right to acquire or transfer property under what circumstances, what compensation or punishment is appropriate for unjust acts, and who is to be educated and in what manner. Particular laws are able to perform their function because they possess two distinctive properties:

L 1   The laws are universal or general rules (*EN* V.7.1135a5–8, 10.1137b13; compare *Pol.* III.11.1282b4–6, 15.1286a9–11, II.8.1269a9–12, and *Rhet.* I.13.1374a28–b1).

In this respect a law (*nomos*) differs from a decree (*psêphisma*), which is concerned with a particular circumstance or action, such as the decree to sacrifice to Brasidas (V.7.1134b23–4, 10.1137b27–32, VI.8.1141b24–8; compare *Pol.* IV.4.1292a36–7).[48] Further, it is suggested that:

L2   The written laws are (or should be) as clear, unambiguous, and definite as possible (compare *EN* VIII.13.1162b21–1163a1 and *Rhet.* I.13. 1374a29–30, 34).

The law should offer a precise and definite statement of the acts which are expressly prohibited or permitted and of approximate sanctions. For example, a law might state that all citizens are at liberty to attend the assembly, but impose a specified fine upon citizens who are wealthy enough to meet a certain property assessment (*Pol.* IV.13.1297a17–19).

L3   The laws have a compelling power (*anagkastikên dunamin*, *EN* X.9. 1180a22).

That is, the laws involve sanctions and are enforceable by the appropriate officials in the polis. In the most favourable circumstances, the laws will also exhibit rationality (III.15.1286a17–20), impartiality (III.16.1287a41–b5), and stability over time (II.8.1269a9–27). Because of all these features, the laws are able to perform the function of organizing or structuring the polis

---

47 M. Gagarin, *Early Greek Laws* (Berkeley, 1986), pp. 53–5, offers an illuminating general description of Greek written laws. On the historical emergence of law see also M. Ostwald, *Nomos and the Beginnings of the Athenian Democracy* (Oxford, 1969).
48 See MacDowell, *The Law in Classical Athens*, p. 45, on the difference between *psêphisma* and *nomos*.

(III.16.1287a18, compare II.10.1271b32) and of instructing and habituating the citizens (*Pol.* III.16.1287b25–6; *EN* V.1.1129b19–25, X.9.1179b34–5)

Aristotle recognizes that the laws of the polis may be correctly framed or badly framed (*Pol.* IV.8.1294a5–7, *EN* V.1.1129b19–25). A particular law may be mistaken, so that it may have to be changed (II.8.1269a12–13). But in general, the laws which belong to a correct constitution are just, whereas those which belong to a deviant constitution are unjust (III.11.1282b6–13). Similarly in Book IV he says:

C1   The laws should be framed relative to the constitutions and all are so framed, but the constitutions should not be framed relative to the laws (1.1289a13–15).

Hence, throughout most of the *Politics* the central focus is on the constitution rather than on the laws.[49]

C2   The constitution (*politeia*) is a structure (*taxis*) of polises concerning the manner in which offices are distributed, what the authority (*to kurion*) of the polis is, and what the end is of each community. But the laws are separate from the things that indicate the constitution, and it is according to the laws that the officials should rule and guard against those who violate them. (IV.1.1289a15–20).

Here it is the constitution which is the order or organization (*taxis*) of the polis. It is, in effect, the form which the lawgiver has provided for the polis (see III.3.1276b7–8). It will be recalled that justice is this *taxis* in I.2.1253a37–8. This suggests that the constitution is in some manner identical with justice (in the sense of being the embodiment of justice), and this is affirmed at *EE* VII.9.1241b13–15. The relation between justice and the constitution is a central theme in Book III and indeed throughout the remainder of the *Politics*.

As the above definition indicates (compare IV.3.1290a7–11), the constitution organizes the polis by assigning political authority or rule within it. In III.6 Aristotle distinguishes constitutions accordingly: "those constitutions which look to the common advantage (*to koinêi sumpheron*) are correct according to what is just without qualification, and those which look only to the advantage of the rulers are all mistaken and deviations from the correct constitutions; for they are despotic but the polis is a community of free persons" (1279a17–21). By "seeking the common advantage" Aristotle understands "producing and safeguarding happiness and its parts for the political community" (*EN* V.1.1129b14–19). Accordingly:

C3   A constitution is correct or unqualifiedly just if it aims at the common advantage or the happiness of the entire polis; a constitution is deviant

49 Plato is criticized for talking about the laws and neglecting the constitution in the *Laws* (II.6.1265a1–2).

and unjust in the unqualified sense if it aims at the advantage of the rulers rather than of all the citizens.

Pol. III.7 proceeds with the distinction among constitutions in terms of how many rule (one, few, or many) and how they are ruled (correct, deviant), resulting in six constitutions. They may also be ranked from best to worse (see IV.2.1289a39–b5): kingship (one, correct), aristocracy (few, correct), polity (many, correct), democracy (many, deviant), oligarchy (few, deviant), and tyranny (one, deviant).

The conception of nature underlies Aristotle's account of the correctness and justice of constitutions. He remarks that different groups are suited by nature (*phusei*) for different types of rule, for example, despotic rule for natural slaves and kingly or political rule for others, and that each of these is just and advantageous. But there is not a group which is suited according to nature (*kata phusin*) for tyranny or any of the other deviant constitutions, because these come to be against nature (*para phusin*). (III.17.1287b37–41) Hence:

C4　The polis is in a natural condition (*kata phusin*) when it has a correct or just constitution and in an unnatural condition (*para phusin*) when it has a deviant or unjust constitution.

Aristotle thus explicitly extends to his theory of constitutions the teleological account of justice discussed in sections 3–5. What is good for an organism is natural on Aristotle's view, and when a community of human beings have what is their common good, i.e. they are in a condition of justice, they are also in a natural condition.

As (C3) indicates, the constitution is the basis for political justice. In the book on justice (*EN* V) universal justice is identified with being lawful (*nomimos*). In this sense "we call just the things that produce and safeguard happiness and its parts for the political community" (1.1129b17–19). Being just in this sense is opposed to being lawless (*paranomos*). Universal justice is distinguished from particular justice, which is identified with fairness or equality (*isotês*) and opposed to overreachingness (*pleonexia*). Aristotle distinguishes forms of particular justice, namely distributive justice, corrective justice, and perhaps also commutative justice.[50] Distributive justice (*EN* V.3) is concerned with distribution of goods, including political offices and

---

50 The place of commutative justice or "the reciprocal" (*to antipeponthos*) in Aristotle's theory is obscure. At *EN* V.2.1130b30–1131a9 he expressly distinguishes between two types of particular justice: distributive justice and corrective justice (compare *to loipon hen*, "the remaining one," at 1131b25). But at 5.1132b31–4 he recognizes reciprocal justice as a distinct type involved in communities of exchange and emphasizes that it holds the polis together (compare *Pol.* II.2.1261a30–31). See A. R. W. Harrison, "Aristotle's *Nicomachean Ethics*, Book V, and the Law of Athens," *Journal of Hellenic Studies*, 77 (1957), pp. 44–5. Finnis suggests that Thomas Aquinas uses the term "commutative justice" for both Aristotle's corrective justice and his reciprocal justice (*Natural Law and Natural Rights*, pp. 178–9).

property, among the members of the community according to some principle of merit or desert (*axia*). Corrective justice (*EN* V.4) protects individuals from involuntary losses due to aggrandizement (*pleonexia*) or insolence (*hubris*). The law prescribes appropriate compensation and restitution from wrongdoers to victims. Commutative or reciprocal justice (*EN* V.5) ensures that parties to a voluntary exchange receive a fair or equal outcome. This equality is measured in terms of need (*chreia*), Aristotle says rather obscurely. Money is introduced as a representative of need by contract (*kata sunthêkên*). It exists by law (*nomôi*) rather than by nature (*phusei*), which is why it is called *nomisma*, "money" (*EN* V.5.1133a25–31; compare *Pol.* I.9.1257b10–11). Each of the particular forms of justice contributes to the aim of universal justice, namely the common advantage of the community. Commutative justice enables individuals to engage in voluntary cooperation rather than remaining isolated individuals and corrective justice prevents the polis from degenerating into a Hobbesian war of all against all. But distributive justice is of particular interest in Aristotle's constitutional theory.

As (C2) indicates, the constitution determines the distribution of political offices; hence, it provides a particular interpretation of distributive justice. Aristotle remarks in *EN* V.3.1131a25–9: "Everyone agrees that the just in distributions should be according to some sort of worth, but they do not all say that worth is the same thing; partisans of democracy say it is freedom, those of oligarchy wealt[1], others good birth, and those of aristocracy virtue." Aristotle is describing a dispute over the distribution of political authority involving partisans of the poor free citizens, of the wealthy citizens, of the old noble families, and of those who have been educated to possess the moral virtues. All of them may be said to share a general concept of distributive justice, namely that individuals should receive shares according to their worth, but they disagree as to the standard of worth and thus each group has a different conception of distributive justice. This dispute concerning the just distribution of political authority is the central topic of *Politics* III and is an important theme in the later books. Aristotle's own view is, briefly, that constitutions such as oligarchy and democracy are deviant because they are based upon conceptions of distributive justice which fall short of justice in the unqualified sense, because they have a mistaken standard of worth. The correct conception of justice for Aristotle is one which makes moral virtue, along with freedom and sufficient equipment or property, the criterion of worth.[51] For only this enables the possessor of authority to promote the natural end of the polis (III.9.1280b39–1281a8).[52] This conception of justice

51 For an elegant interpretation of this analysis see Keyt, "Aristotle's Theory of Distributive Justice." Keyt also offers an ingenious explanation of how to reconcile the claim of *EN* V.7.1135a4–5 that only one constitution is everywhere by nature the best according to nature with Aristotle's recognition of more than one type of constitution.

52 H. Kelsen argues that for Aristotle the correct conception of distributive justice can only be defined by positive law: "Only if it is supposed that the positive law decides the question which rights shall be conferred upon citizens, and which

provides the theoretical basis for the best constitution (see *Politics* III.17–18 and VII–VIII).[53]

The correct conception of distributive justice provides the basis not only for the assignment of political authority to deserving individuals, but also in most cases provides a justification for the rule of law. Aristotle sums up the case for the rule of law as it is presented by "some persons":[54]

> Concerning what is called absolute kingship, i.e. where the king rules in all things according to his own wish, some people think that it is not according to nature (*kata phusin*) for one person to be in authority over all the citizens, where the polis is established out of similar persons; for persons who are similar by nature (*phusei*) necessarily have the same right (*to dikaion*) and the same worth according to nature (*kata phusin*). So if it is harmful with respect to their bodies for unequal persons to have equal food and clothing, so also are matters regarding honors, and similarly therefore if equal persons have what is unequal. Consequently, it is no more just to rule than to be ruled, and it is just [to rule and be ruled] by turns. But this is already law; for law is the structure (*taxis*) [of the polis]. Hence the rule of law is preferable to that of a single citizen, by this same argument, and if it is better that some [citizens] rule, these are appointed as guardians of the law or servants of the laws; for it is necessary that there be some offices, but it is not just for this individual [to rule] when everyone is similar. (III.16.1287a8–23)

differences between them are relevant, [is] Aristotle's mathematical formula of distributive justice applicable" ("Aristotle's Doctrine of Justice," p. 128). This is based upon the claim that for Aristotle the content of moral virtue can only be determined by the positive law (p. 125), which is based in turn on the claim that Aristotle separates his ethics from his metaphysics "by emphasizing that it is 'the good for man,' and not the transcendent good of the unmoved mover, which his *Ethics* intends to determine" (p. 113). Kelsen's interpretation of Aristotle fails to take into account the place of human ends in Aristotle's ethics and politics, discussed in sections 4 and 5 above. Kelsen's interpretation of Aristotle's philosophy of law, like that of Wormuth in "Aristotle on Law," correctly emphasizes the importance of legal justice, but incorrectly discounts the role of nature in guiding and constraining legislation.

53 There remains the difficult question of whether the lawgiver and politician should be guided by the concept of natural justice in framing or reforming the inferior constitutions. Some commentators hold that when Aristotle deals with this matter in *Politics* IV–VI, he sacrifices virtue and justice to expediency. (Wormuth, "Aristotle on Law," p. 61. Compare Christopher Rowe, "Aims and Methods in Aristotle's *Politics*," Essay 2 above.) Space does not permit me to address this difficult question here. The issue is whether Aristotle regards the deviant constitutions as wrong or unjust *simpliciter* or whether he sees them as better or worse approximations to the best constitution. If he takes the latter view then natural justice might play a role even for inferior constitutions. I am inclined to think that the latter is in fact his view, and I argue for this interpretation in a forthcoming book *Nature, Justice and Rights in Aristotle's Politics*.

54 It should be noted that the statements about the laws and about the rule of law in *Pol*. III.15–16, although important, occur in a context involving interchanges between proponents of the absolute kingship and of the rule of law, and thus need to be treated in a careful manner.

Aristotle subsequently indicates that he finds this line of argument convincing in cases in which the citizens are in fact similar and equal (17.1287b41–1288a5; compare *EN* V.6.1134a26–30, b13–15). This passage mentions some of the key elements of the rule of law:

1 It is contrasted with rule of an individual (or select group of individuals), and with rule according to that individual's wish or will (*kata boulêsin*). The rule of individuals according to their own wish is exemplified by monarchs who rule by injunction (*epitagma*) and the extreme democracy which rules by decree (*psêphisma*) (IV.4.1292a6–7, 18–21).
2 The rule of law is characteristically found in cases where the citizens share in ruling, alternating or taking turns in ruling and being ruled. For each person must be willing to rule with a view to the advantage of others and to yield up authority when it is another persons's turn to rule (compare III.6.1279a8–13).
3 The rule of law is justified on the basis of distributive justice: if all the citizens are supposed to be naturally equal in the relevant respects, then according to distributive justice they all have an equal right to share in political authority. In such a case the laws define the structure (*taxis*) within which the citizens exercise their equal political rights.
4 The rule of law is consistent with individuals holding high offices, including the offices concerned with maintaining the authority of law. Here the point seems to be that such officials as the guardians of the laws are assigned the special role of preventing other officials from overturning the constitution. The rule of law is maintained through a separation of powers (see IV.14.1298b26–1299a1).[55]

The argument from justice for the rule of law is supplemented by additional arguments drawn from Plato and others: the law, in contrast to individual rulers, is impartial (III.16.1287a41–b5). If all political activity were left up to decisions by individuals on a case-by-case basis, there is a danger that they would be influenced by particular factors such as friendship or animosity, and self-interest rather than by justice. The process of framing the laws involves considerable deliberation and the lawgiver and politician can take a broader view of the issues (see *Rhet.* I.1.1354a34–b11; compare *Pol.* III.9.1280a14–16). Moreover, the law is the embodiment of "reason (*nous*) without desire" (III.16.1287a32).[56] Aristotle would presumably accept the equation of law with reason if it meant that the lawgiver or politician uses the science of politics and his practical rationality (*phronêsis*) to identify the best constitution and to fashion the laws best suited to this constitution

---

55 Plato makes similar points at *Laws* IV.714b3–715d6. Compare also III.690cl–3 where the rule of law is characterized as natural. See G. R. Morrow, "Plato and the Rule of Law," *Philosophical Review*, 50 (1941), pp. 105–26.
56 Plato connects law (*nomos*) with reason (*logos*) at *Laws* IV.714a1–2; compare I.644d1–3, 645a1–2, VIII.835e4–5.

(compare *EN* X.9.1180a21–22; *Pol.* IV.1.1289a11–13. Impartiality and the rule of reason are connected at *EN* V.6.1134a35–b2).

These arguments in support of the rule of law have continued to be advanced by proponents of constitutionalism.[57] But they have also been criticized by other legal theorists on the grounds that they overlook the ways in which clear and consistently administered laws can serve the most evil political ends.[58] Aristotle's own view is of course that the citizens must not only have good laws and institutions but must also be morally habituated (*Pol.* V.9.1310a14–17). This is necessary if they are to be committed to their constitution and if it is to become their "way of life" (IV.11.1295a40).

Aristotle states that "where the laws do not rule, there is no constitution" (IV.4.1292a32). However, he seems in *Politics* III to recognize one important exception to this claim, namely, the case of absolute kingship. For by his own principle of distributive justice Aristotle must admit as a theoretical possibility that if one person or a small number so exceeds the other citizens in moral virtue and political ability that the others are not even commensurable with them, then the superior person should have complete authority over all. To deny them complete authority would therefore be unjust and unnatural (III.13. 1284a3–11, 17.1288a24–9). Aristotle tries to relieve the problem by remarking that the absolute kings are themselves a law (13.1284a13–14, 17.1288a3). Perhaps he means to suggest that the absolute king rules over the polis in a manner which is consistently virtuous, practically rational, and impartial to the same degree and as consistently as the rule of law. Nevertheless, absolute kingship does not qualify as the rule of law in Aristotle's sense.[59] When he consider the best constitution in *Politics* VII, it turns out that there are no persons who qualify as an absolute king, so that this candidate remains a merely theoretical possibility; and "it is evident due to many causes that everyone must share in ruling and being ruled in turn" (14.1332b23–7) and that the best constitution will be characterized by the rule of law.[60] But it should be noted that the rule of law is a corollary of the principle of distributive justice only if it is correct to assume that the citizens

57 See, for example, L. L. Fuller, *The Morality of Law* (New Haven, 1964), who sets forth what he calls "eight demands of the law's inner morality," namely, the laws should be general, be publicly promulgated, be prospective (not retroactive), be clear, not be contradictory, not require the impossible, not be changed too frequently, and be congruent with official action.

58 Fuller's theory has been widely criticized, most notably by H. L. A. Hart in *Harvard Law Review*, 78 (1965), pp. 1281–96, reprinted as Essay 16 in Hart, *Essays in Jurisprudence and Philosophy* (Oxford, 1983). Fuller replies to Hart and other critics in the revised edition of *The Morality of Law* (New Haven, 1969).

59 See E. F. Miller, "Prudence and the Rule of Law," *American Journal of Jurisprudence*, 24 (1979), pp. 181–206.

60 The Eleatic Stranger in Plato's *Statesman* argues that absolute kingship exercised by the enlightened individual is superior in principle to the rule of law (294a7–8, 297b7–c4, 300c9–d2) but remarks that such individuals do not commonly arise (301d8–e4). Compare the Athenian Stranger in *Laws* IX.875c3–d5, who advocates the rule of law as the second-best solution.

are equal or at least commensurable in virtue. And even in the best constitution of Book VII only a minority of the population will qualify as naturally equal citizens, since the laboring classes are excluded as inferior and incapable of virtue (VII.9.1328b33–13289a2).

One final qualification on the rule of law concerns Aristotle's theory of equity (*epieikeia*). Although, as we have seen, the universality of the laws is a source of their strength, it can sometimes be a cause of weakness. The lawgiver tries to frame laws which are almost always correct but recognizes that in some cases they may yield unjust results. Equity is the correction of a law insofar as it is defective due to its universality. In such a case the equitable decision is just, because it is what the lawgiver would have decided in these particular circumstances if he had been present. Not all things can be decided according to the laws; in some cases a decree is needed. There is an indefiniteness in particulars which can sometimes only be handled in an *ad hoc* way. Aristotle compares the use of decrees to the use of a Lesbian rule made of soft lead: just as the rule is not rigid but adapts itself to the shape of the stone, the decree is adapted to particular circumstances (*EN* V.10. 1137b26–32; compare *Pol.* III.11.1282b1–6, and *Rhet.* I.13.1374a25–b22, which is mentioned in section 2 above).

The lawgiver uses his practical rationality to frame a constitution and to fashion laws which bring the polis into a just or natural condition: that is, which will promote the common advantage of the citizens in the sense of enabling them to realize their natural ends and attain the good life. Although nature constrains the lawgiver in that he must cooperate with the nature of the citizens, he nevertheless has considerable room for inventiveness and discretion in crafting the conventional component of political justice. Although the laws are very important in providing the structure in which the citizens can share authority and seek the good life, they are nevertheless subordinate to the lawgiver's ultimate goal and should be corrected when they conflict with this goal.

7 CONCLUSION

There is considerable agreement among Aristotle's different discussions of natural law and justice. They all recognize a distinction between, on the one hand, common (natural) law or natural justice which has an objective basis and applies to all persons and, on the other hand, particular law or political justice which depends upon local agreement and consequently differs for different localities. Moreover, natural law or justice serves as a standard by which the laws of different localities may be compared and evaluated. His different discussions give rise to puzzles (*aporiai*), particularly as to whether natural justice is immutable and whether it is external to political justice. These are ultimately resolved by connecting natural justice with Aristotle's teleological account of nature, which involves regularities holding "for the most part." The teleological account of justice rests upon his political naturalism, which treats the political community as arising in part from human nature. Since the lawgiver must cooperate with nature in order to create the polis with its constitution and laws, political justice has both a natural and a legal (conventional) component. The concept of nature imposes constraints upon the activities of framing the constitution and legislating, but it also permits considerable latitude for the lawgiver's practical wisdom. The principle of natural justice provides the theoretical foundation for the best constitution and its legal structure, and also a rationale for the rule of law. At the same time because natural justice is based upon natural teleology and thus implies generalities holding "for the most part," it can also justify exceptions to the law in exceptional circumstances. For example, Aristotle believes that a system of private property with a provision for common use (in contrast to the communism of Plato's *Republic*) is generally best suited to promote the natural ends of the citizens (see *Politics* II.5). But the particular laws governing private property would depend on particular circumstances and would admit of exceptions.

Aristotle's account of natural law and justice differs in important respects from the view of Cicero, Aquinas and later natural-law theorists.[61] Nevertheless, Aristotle does offer a distinctive theory of natural law and justice which has important implications for his political philosophy. This account, as I have interpreted it, stands or falls with his teleological view of human nature and the polis, which has of course been the object of many criticisms. But given this teleological view, his account of natural law and justice is coherent and plausible.[62]

---

61 See G. Striker, "Origins of the Concept of Natural Law," in J. J. Clear, *Proceedings of the Boston Area Colloquium in Ancient Philosophy*, vol. II; H. Jaffa, *Thomism and Aristotelianism* (Chicago, 1952), pp. 168–9; and D. N. Schroeder, "Aristotle on Law," *Polis*, 4 (1981), pp. 17–30.

62 In revising this paper I benefited from the written criticisms of Anthony J. Lisska, James Lennox and Anthony Preus and from the editorial suggestions of David Keyt. I also gratefully acknowledge the support of my research by the Earhart Foundation.

13

Aristotle's Analysis of Oligarchy and Democracy

RICHARD MULGAN

1 THE "REALISTIC" BOOKS

Though few would still subscribe to Jaeger's sharp distinction between an early theoretical and a later empirical Aristotle, the middle books of the *Politics*, Books IV–VI, are still commonly seen as more empirical and "realistic" than the rest of the work. To a certain extent this characterization is accurate and uncontentious. In contrast to other books, particularly the discussion of utopias in Book II and the ideal state in Books VII–VIII, Books IV–VI deal with constitutions and political remedies which are more within the reach of the average Greek city and statesman. This is part of Aristotle's express aim, announced at the beginning of Book IV: "political writers, although they have excellent ideas, are often unpractical. We should consider, not only what form of government is best, but also what is possible and what is easily attainable by all" (IV.1.1288b35–8).[1] To this extent, the books are undoubtedly more "realistic."

Moreover, it is also certainly true that these books contain the most frequent references to specific examples of actual constitutions and historical events. This is particularly true of the analysis of political change and revolution in Book V. In quoting individual examples, Aristotle may be making use of the detailed research into individual constitutions which he is said to have conducted or at least directed (Diogenes Laertius [V.27] includes 158 constitutions in his list of Aristotle's works); or he may simply be drawing on his own accumulated experience and knowledge. Whatever the source of his information, Books IV–VI clearly deserve to be described as more empirical, at least in contrast to the other books.

However, if we were to approach these books on their own, completely disregarding the rest of the *Politics*, and were to treat them as an independent exercise in empirical political science, other characteristics might be equally,

---

1 Translations of Aristotle are from *The Complete Works of Aristotle*, the revised Oxford Translation, edited by Jonathan Barnes (Princeton, 1984) occasionally amended. Unless otherwise indicated all references are to the *Politics*.

if not more, striking. We would notice, for instance, the overwhelmingly practical purpose of the inquiry. Knowledge is being sought not for disinterested academic reasons but because it will help the statesman improve the government of his city. Political science, like ethics, poetics, economics and rhetoric, is a practical, not a theoretical, science, aimed not just at knowledge but at action (*EN* 1.3.1095a5–6). Thus, the reason why revolution is chosen as a topic for study is not that it is an interesting political phenomenon; that is incidental. Revolution threatens the stability of constitutions and therefore the security and values of the community and its citizens. It is a dangerous disease, whose causes must be understood with a view to preventing its occurrence (IV.1.1288b28–30, V.1.1301a20–5). Thus, the analysis of the causes of revolution leads straight on to practical remedies for its avoidance. In comparison, modern political science, particularly if it has empirical pretensions, will usually avoid any explicit recommendations for action and will confine itself to disinterested description and analysis.

Apart from the overtly practical orientation, the modern political scientist would notice, though not necessarily with disapproval, the theoretical and abstract method with which much of the subject matter is treated. Far from being a mass of discrete empirical material, more or less randomly collected, which some of the descriptions of these books might lead one to expect, Aristotle's account of actual constitutions is based on categories and typologies which are highly generalized and often a priori. The use of abstract and general categories is valuable, indeed unavoidable, in the social sciences as a means of making sense of what would otherwise be an infinite mass of undifferentiated phenomena. But if their purpose is scientific, the abstract categories must be tested against empirical evidence. The measure of how successful a particular schema or theory is will be the extent to which it captures what is empirically significant and thereby enhances our understanding of the social world.

From this point of view, the verdict on Books IV–VI may be a mixed one. The account of change and revolution itself in Book V, as I have argued elsewhere,[2] can be seen as a highly successful piece of political science – its categories are helpful, its theoretical hypotheses plausible and its recommendations therefore worthy of close attention. Aristotle's approach is undogmatic and open-ended; he is ready to amend and supplement his analysis if new evidence suggests itself even if this means disrupting the structure of his argument.

But he is not always so successful. This chapter deals with another topic or set of topics covered in the middle books, namely the nature of oligarchy and democracy, in particular the principles on which oligarchy and democracy are based, their different species and their relative merits. Aristotle's account of oligarchy and democracy is in many respects perceptive and carries political analysis considerably further forward than the level which had been achieved by his predecessors. Nonetheless, when compared with the high

2 *Aristotle's Political Theory* (Oxford, 1977), ch. 7.

standards that he set himself, it can sometimes be seen as excessively schematic and distorted by a priori preconceptions.

2 OLIGARCHY AND DEMOCRACY AS CONTRASTING POLES

Aristotle's analysis of oligarchy and democracy begins in Book III as part of the general account of constitutions and their classification. He distinguishes different constitutions in terms of their institutional structure of political authority, in particular the size of their supreme or "sovereign" body, and the aim pursued by those who belong to this supreme body (III.6.1278b9–10, IV.1.1289a15–18). In these terms, he can accommodate what had become a well-established six-fold classification of constitutions, depending on the size of the supreme body – one, few or many – and whether the members of this body pursued the common interest or their own self-interest. Those constitutions in which the members rule for the common interest are described as "correct" forms; those in which the rulers rule in their own interests are "perverted" forms. In these terms, oligarchy and democracy are classified as the perverted forms of rule by the few and the many, corresponding to the correct forms, aristocracy and "polity" respectively (III.7.1279b4–6).

Of the six main types of constitution, oligarchy and democracy were much the most common in the Greece of Aristotle's day. Not surprisingly, therefore, when Aristotle turns to describe actual constitutions oligarchy and democracy figure most prominently. The other forms are not overlooked entirely – for instance, monarchy, in its two forms of kingship and tyranny, is treated quite extensively in the analysis of revolution (V.10–12). Occasional reference is also made to "so-called aristocracy." This is not the true, ideal aristocracy, the government of the men of true virtue, but an inferior form in which noble birth and a reputation for virtue are one of the criteria for office. This emphasis on birth as distinct from wealth is sufficient to distinguish it from oligarchy and Aristotle treats "so-called aristocracy" as a form of mixed constitution (IV.7.1293b2–21). He also devotes some chapters to describing the "polity" and recommending it as the best constitution for most circumstances (IV.8, 9, 11). But oligarchy and democracy are mentioned most frequently and are the subject of most detailed discussion.

Oligarchy and democracy also provide, to a considerable extent, the analytical framework for the middle books, being often seen as contrasting poles or opposites. Aristotle's usage of what constitutions are "opposite" to what other constitutions varies according to the context.[3] Sometimes the contrast is between correct and perverted constitutions in terms of the six-fold classification; thus kingship and tyranny are opposites as are aristocracy and oligarchy, polity and democracy (*EN* VIII.10.1160b21). On other occasions, however, opposite constitutions may be constitutions sup-

---

3 See W. L. Newman, *The Politics of Aristotle* (Oxford, 1887–1902), vol. IV, pp. 483–4.

ported by sets of political opponents, e.g. tyranny and democracy or democracy and aristocracy (V.10.1312b1–7). The main opposition in Books IV–VI is between oligarchy and democracy and therefore they are the key pair of opposites (VI.1.1317a17, VI.6.1320b19–20).

That oligarchy and democracy are a pair of contrasting opposites is already indicated in Book III. As soon as he has sketched in the six-fold classification in III.7, Aristotle moves immediately in the next chapter to consider an issue which arises only in the case of oligarchy and democracy and only when they are seen in their most contrasting mode as rule of the rich and poor respectively. "Oligarchy is when men of property have the government in their hands; democracy, *the opposite*, when the indigent, and not the men of property, are the rulers" (III.8.1279b17–19). The problem raised is whether both the degree of wealth in the ruling group, that is, whether they are rich or poor, and the size of the ruling group, whether they are few or many, can be considered differentia of oligarchy and democracy. This question will be discussed further below. For the moment, we need simply note that democracy and oligarchy are contrasted as opposites.

In the following chapter, oligarchy and democracy are again contrasted, this time in relation to their competing conceptions of distributive justice (III.9). These are analyzed in terms of a pair of contrary views. Democrats think that because they are equal in some respects they should be equal in all; oligarchs, on the other hand, think that because they are *un*equal in some respect they should be *un*equal in all. This is an important part of Aristotle's constitutional analysis. Different constitutions embody different conceptions of justice with differing criteria of how honours and other public goods should be distributed. Oligarchs think that the wealthy should benefit exclusively, ahead of the poor. Democrats hold that all citizens should benefit equally. In this chapter the contrast is expressed in terms of a clash between supporters of inequality and supporters of equality. This is not the only way in which it can be expressed. Sometimes Aristotle uses the theory of the two types of equality, arithmetic (strict or absolute equality) and geometric (proportionate equality); democrats believe in arithmetic equality, that everyone should be treated the same; oligarchs believe in geometric equality, that everyone should be treated in proportion to their worth, i.e. in proportion to their wealth (V.1.1301b29, VI.2.1317b4). At other times, Aristotle makes the same point in yet another way by saying that all agree that justice is distribution according to merit (*axia*) but people differ about what is to count as merit – democrats identify it with the status of the freeman, oligarchs with wealth (*EN* V.3.1131a27–9).

All three formulations of the contrast between democratic and oligarchic conceptions of justice make the same point – that different people are thought worthy of receiving or not receiving certain goods on the basis of their relevant characteristics and that what characteristics are seen as relevant to the distribution varies with different conceptions of justice. The last formulation in terms of competing views of merit is perhaps the most sophisticated. It emphasizes that all conceptions have a view of individual worth and that all subscribe to a principle of equality in relation to that view.

It also reveals that even democrats draw the line somewhere, at the status of freeman. However, when comparing the oligarchic and democratic formulations alone, Aristotle prefers the less subtle formulation in terms of equality and inequality (V.1.1301b37–9). The reason, presumably, is that it emphasizes the contrasting nature of two opposite constitutions by giving them apparently opposite conceptions of justice. This is one instance, then, though a relatively insignificant one, where a desire for logical symmetry may have deflected Aristotle from a more perceptive analysis.

The analytical prominence of oligarchy and democracy in Books IV–VI is evident in the treatment of polity. In Book III, polity was defined as the correct form of rule of the many. It thus held its own independent position within the six-fold classification. In Book IV, however, a polity is described in terms of oligarchy and demoracy, as a mixture of them (IV.8.1293b33–4) or as a mean between them (IV.11.1295b3). Analytically, its nature is therefore dependent on that of oligarchy and democracy; so too is the nature of so-called aristocracy which is defined as another mixed constitution, different from the polity. Oligarchy and democracy thus operate as the analytical poles, the two contrasting types of contemporary political reality in terms of which all other constitutions, with the exception of the monarchical forms of kingship and tyranny, are identified. Aristotle indeed mentions the view that there are only two principal forms, oligarchy and democracy: "as men say of the winds, that there are but two, north and south, and that the rest of them are only variations of these, so of governments there are said to be only two forms – democracy and oligarchy" (IV.3.1290a13–6).

Plato in *Laws* III had adopted a similar approach to constitutional analysis, describing two tendencies in government in which different individual constitutions shared to different extents. His two types were not oligarchy and democracy but monarchy and democracy, with monarchy represented in its extreme form by Persia and democracy in its extreme form by Athens. Such an approach, essentially one of contrasting ideal types, is analytically flexible, allowing particular constitutions to be analyzed in terms of the extent to which they share the characteristics of each type. Moreover, given that each extreme type is morally objectionable, such a schema also naturally leads to an argument in favour of a constitution which is a mixture of both tendencies, as Plato's recommended constitution in the *Laws* is a mixture of the monarchic and democratic tendencies.

Aristotle is also arguing for the merits of a mixed constitution, the polity, which is a mean between two extremes; it would have been similarly natural for him in this context to adopt a typology of constitutions in which the two extremes, oligarchy and democracy, were the two dominant types or tendencies. He is not, however, happy with officially adopting such a scheme. The reason is that oligarchy and democracy are defective constitutions. Aristotle prefers to take as his archetype of any class the best instance of that class; this preference is part of his teleological view of nature according to which the essential character of any object is revealed in its best stage of development. Thus the best, not the worst, types of constitution must be the logically fundamental types of constitution. Soon after stating the view that oligarchy and democracy are the two main types like the north and south wind, he rejects it in these terms: "the better or more exact way is to distinguish, as I have done, the one or two which are true forms, and to regard the others as perversions, whether of the well-tempered or of the best form of government" (IV.3.1290a23–6). Thus oligarchy and democracy are to be seen as perversions of the polity (the well-tempered constitution); that is, logically and analytically, the polity must be prior to oligarchy and democracy, even if, when analyzing it, we have to use the previously identified characteristics of oligarchy and democracy as the elements of the mixture. This seems an unnecessary complication which, indeed, Aristotle does not follow in the rest of his discussion of oligarchy, democracy and polity. Polity continues as the derivative mixture and oligarchy and democracy function effectively as the two logically prior poles, even if Aristotle is unwilling to admit it openly.

3   THE TYPES OF OLIGARCHY AND DEMOCRACY

The polarity between oligarchy and democracy is continued and fleshed out in the enumeration of the sub-types of each main type (IV.4–6, VI.4–6). Aristotle embarks on his account of the different varieties of constitution with an analogy from biological classification (IV.4.1290b25–38). The essential elements of the polis are like the essential organs of an animal. There will be as many different constitutions as there are possible combinations of these elements, which suggests a very large number of different species. In the event, Aristotle describes only a few species for each main type. In the case of oligarchy and democracy, the treatment is extremely schematic and is dictated by the underlying analytical structure.

Each main type has a number of species or sub-types, usually given as four. (In the first account of the types of democracy [IV.4], there are five rather than four types; the additional one, described first, is an anomalous type of "pure" democracy, giving equality to rich and poor alike, and is omitted from subsequent typologies [IV.6, VI.4]. The reasons for this omission are discussed below. The last and briefest account of oligarchies [VI.6] mentions only three types specifically, rather than the four mentioned in IV.4, 6.)

The first type in each case is very moderate and only just distinguishable from the polity. Thus the first, moderate democracy has a property qualification and does not allow citizen rights to all free men. The mass of citizens take little interest in politics – for this reason an agricultural populace is suited to this type – and government, which is conducted under law, is left very much in the hands of officials elected from the well-to-do. On the other hand, the fourth extreme type is a democracy in which all power resides with the assembly which is dominated by an urban populace paid to attend meetings. The rule of law is abandoned and government is by decree, as in a tyranny. The second and third types are intermediate between the

most moderate and the extreme types, as the citizen body becomes progressively less exclusive, more urban and takes on more power.

Similarly, in the case of oligarchy, the first, most moderate oligarchy has
its property qualification for office set comparatively low, though still
sufficient to exclude the poor majority, and there are no other conditions set
for entry to the ruling class; government is carried on in accordance with law.
The fourth type is extreme or pure oligarchy; power is in the hands of a very
few rich men, a closed, hereditary ruling family or group of families, a
dynasteia (IV.5.1292b10) and there is no rule of law. Again, the second and
third types are intermediate between the most moderate and the extreme
types.

That the demands of the abstract scheme and the need to get theoretical
symmetry is the main rationale of the typologies is openly admitted
by Aristotle. Introducing the account of the types of oligarchy in Book
VI, after the parallel account of the types of democracy, he says; "From
these considerations, there will be no difficulty in seeing what should
be the constitution of oligarchies. We have only *to reason from opposites*
and compare each form of oligarchy with the corresponding form of
democracy" (VI.6.1320b17–20). After a brief description of the most
moderate form, he continues, "the principle [of qualification for office],
narrowed a little, gives another form of oligarchy; until at length we reach
the most cliquish and tyrannical of them all, answering to the extreme
democracy" (VI.6.1320b29–31).

As a result of these typologies, the contrasting poles between oligarchy and
democracy become joined by a more or less continuous spectrum with
extremes at each end shading off into increasingly more moderate versions
until both merge into the perfect mixture, polity. Interestingly, Aristotle
makes little attempt to fit these typologies to instances of individual
constitutions. The typology of democracy may reflect a perception of the
course of Athenian history – it was commonplace among conservative critics
of Athenian democracy that Athens had developed, or rather degenerated,
from a moderate democracy, usually in the time of Solon, to an extreme
democracy in the later fifth century. But the parallels are by no means
precise. For instance, the Solonian constitution, unlike Aristotle's moderate
democracy, did not provide for appointment of minor officials by lot
(III.9.1280b30). Periclean democracy was restrictive in its citizenship
criteria while Aristotle's extreme democracy is not.[4]

Apart from these implicit echoes of Athens, there is little direct reference to
actual cities which might be thought to exemplify any of the sub-types. In his

4 For further details see Newman, *The Politics of Aristotle*, vol. IV, pp. xl–xli. The
question whether the account of Athenian history in the Aristotelian *Constitution of
Athens* was influenced by Aristotle's categories in the *Politics* is a separate question. See
J. Day and M. Chambers, *Aristotle's History of Athenian Democracy* (Berkeley, 1962);
P. J. Rhodes, *A Commentary on the Aristotelian Athenaion Politeia* (Oxford, 1981) pp.
10–13.

accounts of the different types of democracy in Book IV (IV.4, 6), Aristotle makes no mention at all of individual examples. In the Book VI account (VI.4), he mentions five different cities (Mantinea, Elis, Aphytis, Cyrene and Athens). However, even here the density of individual examples is not nearly as great as in the analysis of revolution, for instance in the account of the causes of revolution in democracy (V.5). Moreover, the cities are referred to in connection with particular laws or particular measures which are said to be characteristic of one of the sub-types. The cities as a whole are not directly mentioned as possible instances of one of the sub-types.

There is even less historical reference in the case of oligarchy. There was no well-known Greek oligarchy whose constitutional history, even in broad outline, mirrored Athens by following a progression from moderate to extreme. Nor, in either of the accounts of the types of oligarchy, does Aristotle make reference to any individual cities at all. The whole treatment is very perfunctory.

In this respect, there is a contrast between Aristotle's lists of species of the other main constitutional types. For instance, he lists five types of kingship (III.14). One of these, the Spartan kingship, is an actual historical institution. Two others, the *aesymnetia* and the heroic kingship, are derived closely and explicitly from well-known historical species; another (the second) type is described more abstractly, as a mixture of kingship and tyranny, though it is explicitly intended to refer to the kingships of Asia. Only the fifth type, the absolute kingship (*pambasileia*), is a totally theoretical construct in the same way as the types of oligarchy, and to a lesser extent those of democracy. The species of so-called aristocracy (IV.7.1293b14–21) and of tyranny (IV.10) similarly include historical examples as well as abstract categories.

It can be argued that the plethora of actual instances of oligarchy and democracy made it impossible to base the specification of sub-types on actual examples. A certain degree of abstraction and generalization is inevitable in constructing categories into which large numbers of individual instances are to be classed. However, as we have said, the effectiveness of categories is to be tested in their use, whether they aggregate and distinguish data in enlightening ways. In this respect, it is significant that Aristotle makes little or no attempt to test his typologies by applying them to actual instances. In spite of the apparent richness of historical material available to him, he does not begin to provide us with an informative analysis of the types of democracy and oligarchy that actually existed in classical Greece.

W. L. Newman, in his great commentary on the *Politics*, provides an indication of what we are missing.[5] For instance, taking the general category of oligarchy, and using only examples mentioned elsewhere in the *Politics*, he provides a list of twelve different types which reflect actual differences in institutional and social structure among Greek oligarchies. Similarly, in the case of democracy, he lists a number of sub-types, additional to Aristotle's four, again based on Aristotle's own evidence. The large number of Greek

---

5 Newman, *The Politics of Aristotle*, vol. IV, pp. xxiv–xxlii.

cities, each with its unique constitutional structure and yet each sharing a common culture, provided an extraordinary opportunity for comparative political analysis. Aristotle was aware of this opportunity and of the need to describe and compare the different laws and constitutions as part of a comprehensive political science. However, at least in respect of the task of classifying the different types of oligarchy and democracy, he cannot be said to have progressed as far as he might have.

A number of reasons for Aristotle's failure to capture and make sense of the variety of constitutions in his day may be suggested. One may be just a lack of time or interest – the structure was sketched in and details could follow. We should never forget, in our absorption in one of Aristotle's works, the prodigious extent and breadth of his output. Omissions may simply be due to the existence of more pressing inquiries elsewhere. Another, more funda-mental, reason is his approach to classifying constitutions. He explicitly wants a classification which not only classifies constitutions but also ranks them in terms of their value; hence the range of sub-types from the most moderate to the most extreme. This produces typologies which are logically and ethically straightforward and simple. But they may not have been as easy to apply to real instances as ones derived more directly from a consideration of actual constitutions, having regard for the most common characteristics and major differences among them. At any rate, whatever the reason, his failure must be noted and set against the undoubted advances he made in the empirical study of politics.

4   OLIGARCHIC AND DEMOCRATIC PRINCIPLES

Another respect in which Aristotle's emphasis on abstract simplicity and symmetry may have hindered as well as helped our understanding of Greek oligarchy and democracy is in his treatment of the dominant values and principles of each constitution. He rightly sees a constitution as more than just institutions and laws; it is also based on, and pursues, certain social goals and values. Each constitution, as we have seen, has a dominant principle or value. This principle provides both the basis on which the ruling group is selected and the aim which the members of the group pursue in their role. In the case of ideal aristocracy, for instance, the principle is virtue: rule is confined to men of virtue and the city as a whole aims at the good life or life of virtue (III.17.1288a9–12, 32–41). Similarly, the principle of oligarchy is wealth. Wealth is the criterion for office (III.8.1280a1–6) and those in power aim at increasing their wealth (V.10.1311a10).

On the whole, this fits reasonably well with the facts of oligarchy. Oligarchies restricted power to men of property; men of property tended to use their political power to maintain and enhance their wealth. It could be argued that Aristotle should have given more recognition to the close association of many oligarchies with traditions of hereditary nobility. Few were strict "plutocracies" which treated all the rich equally. The conscious aim at least of many of those in power in oligarchies was as much honour and fame as the accumulation of wealth. Sometimes, indeed, Aristotle does identify good birth and culture (*paideia*) as characteristics of oligarchy (IV.8.1293b36–8, V.8.1309a2–3). On other occasions, these are more the characteristics of "so-called aristocracy," the form of mixed constitution which places emphasis on noble birth. In general, Aristotle follows Plato in seeing the fundamental aim of oligarchs as their own enrichment, a judgment which, though severe and open to some counter-examples, is by no means implausible.

More difficulties surround Aristotle's account of the principle of democracy. This is identified as freedom. Freedom, in the sense of the status of a free man, is the qualification for office; freedom, in the sense of living as one likes, is the aim of democracy. In Aristotle's fullest and most careful account of democratic freedom (VI.2.1317a40–b17), the aspect of freedom which provides the criterion for office is linked to numerical or arithmetic equality:

> One principle of liberty is for all to rule and be ruled in turn, and indeed democratic justice is the application of numerical not proportionate equality; whence it follows that the majority must be supreme, and that whatever the majority approve must be the end and the just. Every citizen, it is said, must have equality, and therefore in a democracy the poor have more power than the rich, because there are more of them, and the will of the majority is supreme. This, then, is one note of liberty which all democrats affirm to be the principle of their state. (VI.2.1317b2–11)

The status of the free man does not directly define the ruling group in the same way as a certain level of wealth identifies the members of an oligarchy or virtue singles out the members of an aristocracy. Aristotle's whole political analysis of democracy, and its contrast with oligarchy, is based on the assumption that the ruling group in a democracy is the poor, just as the ruling group in an oligarchy is the rich. However, the status of free man includes all citizens, rich as well as poor, and not just the poor. The same applies when the qualifying principle of democracy is expressed in terms of equality. Whereas the oligarchs' use of inequality (or geometric equality) singles out those wealthy "unequals" who are members of the oligarchic civic body, the democrats' equality (or arithmetic equality) includes everyone, rich as well as poor, oligarchs as well as democrats.

Thus, if democracy is to be equated with rule by the poor, while its criterion for office is free status or arithmetic equality, the poor will need to be in a majority. In Book III, when discussing whether economic class (rich or poor) or numerical size (few or many) is the more important criterion for distinguishing oligarchy and democracy, Aristotle concludes that economic class is the essential criterion. Thus if a rich majority were in power the constitution would be an oligarchy and not a democracy; conversely, if a poor minority ruled, this would be a democracy (III.8.1280a1–3). However, if the qualifying characteristic for democracy is the status of a free man or arithmetic equality, government by the poor will emerge only if the poor are in a majority. If the poor were a minority and the rich a majority, political rights of equal freedom would produce rule by the rich, i.e. oligarchy and not democracy.

By recognizing freedom as the principle of democracy, Aristotle has therefore admitted that size is an essential, not an accidental, characteristic of democracy. In fact, he does not stick to his strict position that only economic class is essential; when he raises the issue again in Book IV both class and number are made to be defining characteristics of oligarchy and democracy (IV.4.1290b17–20). This means that the anomalous cases of rich majorities or poor minorities would be mixtures, neither clearly oligarchy or democracy. Including number has the advantage of bringing both democracy and oligarchy closer to their usual connotations. Oligarchy, after all, was rule by the "oligoi," the few; democracy was rule by the "demos," the people, commonly associated with the *plêthos* or mass.[6]

The majority principle itself is not unique to democracy; it applies in any group in which members are treated equally, as Aristotle recognizes (IV.8.1294a11–14, VI.3.1318a28–30). A group of oligarchs or aristocrats may well treat themselves as equals, while excluding the mass of citizens, and apply the majority principle to the settling of disputes within their group. It is, however, particularly associated with democracy, partly because the group from whom the majority in question is taken is the group of all free men; partly because the majority principle is needed to explain how the procedures which in theory should give power equally to all free citizens, rich and poor, can, in actual practice, give power to the poor only. The majority principle is thus essential to the understanding of democracy as rule by the poor mass. Aristotle's inclusion of number as an essential criterion, additional to economic class, is therefore an improvement on the classification in terms of class alone and not, as sometimes claimed,[7] a less satisfactory version.

The fact that the distributive principle of democracy does not directly single out the ruling group in democracy has another consequence: it allows the possibility, in theory at least, that the principle could be implemented at face value, and that the power could be shared equally among all free citizens, rich and poor alike. Arithmetic equality, after all, requires equal shares for all; though it implies the majority principle as a means of resolving disputes by counting every voice equally, it does not necessarily imply majority *rule*, in which the same people are always in the prevailing majority. More equal would be a regime in which everyone had a fair chance of being in the majority. Modern democratic thinking is often critical of majority domination, where one group is a permanently entrenched majority and another group a permanently oppressed minority as in Ulster or Sri Lanka. This is often equated with "majority tyranny" and contrasted with true democracy in which everyone has an equal chance of being in a majority and influencing decisions.

6 See Newman, *The Politics of Aristotle*, vol. IV, pp. 158–9.

7 E. g. by Ernest Barker, *The Politics of Aristotle*, (Oxford, 1946), p. 163, following Newman, *The Politics of Aristotle*, vol. IV, pp. 158–9.

Aristotle recognizes this possibility; in the first list of the types of democracy, as we have seen, he mentions such a democracy as the first and best type:

Of forms of democracy first comes that which is said to be based strictly on equality. In such a democracy the law says that it is just for the poor to have no more advantage than the rich; and that neither should be masters, but both equal. For if liberty and equality, as is thought by some, are chiefly to be found in democracy, they will be best attained when all persons alike share in the government to the utmost. (IV.4.1291b30–7)

In the chapter which analyzes the principles and procedures of democracy (VI.2), he adds the possibility as an after-thought:

But democracy and demos in their truest form are based upon the recognized principle of democratic justice, that all should count equally; for equality implies that the poor should have no more share in the government than the rich, and should not be the only rulers, but that all should rule equally according to their numbers. (VI.2.1318a4–10)

The Greek word *dêmos* in "democracy" was ambivalent in meaning; it could mean "the mass," i.e. the majority, or it could mean the whole people, all who had the right to attend the assembly. While the critics of democracy saw it as rule by the poor mass, its supporters could claim it, in principle at least, as rule by all the people. Though Aristotle normally defines democracy as rule by the poor majority, he does allow that its principles could generate a much fairer type of government and society from which no one was excluded. Democracy could also mean, as it does in the modern democratic tradition, political equality for all. He recognizes too that such a regime would have a claim to be called "true" democracy based on a "true" demos.

This type of regime, though it would truly implement equality, would still be open to objection from Aristotle on the ground that the principle of strict or arithmetic equality was itself mistaken and took no account of relevant differences between free men in their legitimate claims to a share in government. In this respect, the "true" democracy must be clearly distinguished from Aristotle's ideal constitution of Books VII and VIII. The latter is an aristocracy in which the citizen body is restricted to men of virtue and excludes the artisans and laborers who would count as free citizens in a democracy.

Nonetheless, "true" democracy would not be open to the standard criticism against all the perverted forms of government, that they were unjustifiable rule by one section of the community in their own interests to the complete exclusion of the others. It is for this reason, presumably, that Aristotle does not make much of this "ideal" democracy. It is dropped from the later classifications of democracy and is mentioned only as an after-thought to the discussion of democratic principles. To give it more prominence, to feature it as the prime instance of democracy from which the other types diverge, would be, again, to disturb the symmetry of his classification of constitutions. If democracy is a perverted form, its extreme or pure type must be the worst instance not the best, in just the same way as the extreme forms of oligarchy or tyranny are the worst instances of their respective types.

For similar reasons, perhaps, Aristotle does not attempt to link "true" democracy with polity. Though they are not strictly speaking identical – polity is a mixture of oligarchic and democratic principles and is based on the middle class – there are close affinities between them. A "true" democracy, which gave equal power to both rich and poor, could be said to be providing a balance between the exclusive rule of either the rich or the poor. Such a constitution could also be amenable to the emergence of a large and potentially dominant middle class. When Aristotle includes "pure" demo-cracy in the typology of democracies, he puts it first, ahead of the otherwise most moderate version and therefore by implication closest to polity. However, to draw these connections would have upset the logical symmetry. If democracy is a perverted constitution, its purest form must be furthest from polity, the correct constitution from which it deviates, not closest to it.

These issues arise from the use of freedom, in the sense of free status implying strict equality, as a qualification for office in democracy. The other aspect of freedom is as an end or goal for democracy. Aristotle analyzes it in these terms:

> Another [note of liberty] is that a man should live as he likes. This, they say, is the mark of liberty since, on the other hand, not to live as a man likes is the mark of a slave. This is the second characteristic of democracy, whence has arisen the claim of men to be ruled, by none, if possible, or, if this is impossible, to rule and be ruled in turns; and so it contributes to the freedom based upon equality. (VI.2.1317b11–17)

"Living as one likes," it should be remembered, is not Aristotle's own definition of freedom. He himself regards the essence of freedom as being one's own person and as having independent value rather than being, like the slave, merely an instrument for the purposes of others. Such freedom is consistent with restraint and obedience and does not, like the democrat's version, imply an absence of such impediments.[8] Aristotle criticizes the democratic conception of freedom on the same grounds as the oligarch's life of luxury – it works against the security of the constitution and is therefore not in the democrats' own interest (V.9.1310a19–36).

However, even this democratic view of freedom does not adequately cover Aristotle's own view of the interests pursued by the poor majority in a democracy. Elsewhere in the *Politics*, Aristotle refers to the economic motives of those who support democracy and is aware that they seek their own economic advantage as much as oligarchs do. Indeed, in contrast to the

---

8 See the author's "Liberty in Ancient Greece" in *Conceptions of Liberty in Political Philosophy*, ed. Z. Pelczynski and J. Gray (London, 1984), pp. 18–19.

nobility, the many are said to be more interested in gain than in honor (VI.4. 1318b16–7). In the discussion of revolution, one of the aims of democrats is to confiscate the wealth of the rich (V.5.1304b35), and democracies, if they wish to survive, are advised to spare the property of the rich (V.8.1309a15–20).

Aristotle was not mistaken to identify personal freedom as one of the characteristics of democracy; the tolerance and variety of democratic Athens are well-attested. Yet, by singling out freedom as the aim of democracy, he omits much that is important in the dynamics of democracy and much which is indeed suggested by his own political analysis and the considerable emphasis he lays on economic motives. Indeed, he might have been better to begin with his initial characterization of the perverted constitutions as being conducted not in the common interest but in the self-interest of the rulers: oligarchy in the interests of the wealthy, democracy in the interests of the poor (III.7.1279b9–10). If he had then proceeded dispassionately to identify the interests of the poor, he might have included the desire for personal freedom; but he would also have referred to their desire for the material means to enjoy this freedom and their use of political power to secure these means.

On closer inspection, the actual differences between the motives of oligarchs and democrats are less than the similarities. Both oligarchs and democrats aim for material economic advantage; both do so in order to gratify their desires, in the case of oligarchs living a life of luxury and license (IV.11.1295b15–18, V.9.1310a22–4), in the case of democrats "living as they like." The personal license of democracy is not unique to that form of government; it is found among all self-interested ruling groups, among the rich in oligarchies and in the tyrant in tyrannies. What makes democracy unusually liberal is that the desire to live as one likes is there extended widely through the community, because the ruling group includes most of the ordinary citizens, and is not, as in oligarchy, confined to a small section of the community. The extent to which the law and the courts seek to control the ordinary citizen will therefore need to be restricted. In oligarchy, on the other hand, the ruling group is small and its members can live freely among themselves while still applying the law strictly to the rest of the population.

Aristotle's comments on liberty as the characteristic aim and vice of democracy no doubt owe much to Plato's well-known views on democracy (e.g. *Rep*. VIII.555–6). In Plato's case, however, criticisms of the personal license of democracy were linked to his political analysis. Plato considered that democracy was an especially lax and ineffectual form of government, a factor which led him in the *Statesman* to describe democracy as the best of the perverted forms of constitution because least capable of action (*Statesman* 303a). Aristotle, however, does not wholly share this view of democratic government; if anything, democracy, by being less prone to internal dissension than oligarchy, is a more consistent and secure form of government (V.1.1302a8–13). His concentration on liberty is therefore less justified. The main explanation, we may surmise, is again the urge for conceptual simplicity and symmetry, the need to provide a single value which would do the same work for democracy as wealth and virtue do, respectively, for oligarchy and aristocracy.

However, even given this concern to find a single value it might still be questioned whether freedom, rather than equality, was the correct value to choose. In his analysis of the two aspects of democratic freedom (VI.2), Aristotle traces a connection between them through the principle of arithmetic equality. The first aspect, the criterion for office, is identified with numerical or arithmetic equality and thus with alternation of ruling and being ruled. Alternation is also linked to the second aspect of freedom, the goal of living as one likes. The best condition is not to be ruled at all. But, failing that, ruling and being ruled is the preferred alternative and "contributes to the freedom based on equality."

Equality was the value the democrats themselves emphasized and incorporated in their original catchword and slogan, *isonomia* (roughly "equality of rights"). It is equality, as Aristotle himself admits, which underpins the first aspect of democratic "freedom," equal sharing in power. As far as the second aspect, the goal of democracy, is concerned, equality may not highlight the libertarian aspects of democracy as well as freedom does. But it has the advantage of pointing to the redistributive aim in democracy, the desire to make the wealth of society available to all, to take from the haves and give to the have-nots.

Equality, however, was a more contested value than freedom and Aristotle may have been reluctant to concede it to the democrats. He followed Plato,[9] Isocrates[10] and, presumably, other members of the intellectual opposition to democracy, in arguing that democratic equality was only one version of equality, and inferior to proportionate or geometric equality. In contrast, Plato had been content to leave freedom to the democrats and to argue against having too much of it. Aristotle does not go that far but contests the democrats' conception of freedom (V.9.1310a32–6). Nonetheless, within the aristocratic tradition, Aristotle may have felt more at ease with attributing freedom rather than equality to democrats as their single dominant value.

Aristotle's own analysis, however, shows that neither value is sufficient on its own. Both egalitarianism and libertarianism are essential to democracy. In this respect, Aristotle's account of democracy is similar to many modern versions of democratic theory in which both liberty and equality are seen as basic democratic values. (For the Greeks, however, without a clear commitment to individual rights, these values were less likely to be in tension than they are in the modern liberal democratic tradition.) Indeed, Aristotle does on occasion mention equality and freedom together as the principles of democracy (e.g. IV.4.1291b34–6, V.9.1310a28–31). But to have incorporated both formally into his analysis of democracy would again have jeopardized the symmetry of his constitutional analysis.

9 *Gorg.* 508a; *Rep.* VIII.558c; *Laws* VI.757c.
10 *Areopagiticus*, 21–2.

5   RELATIVE RANKING OF OLIGARCHY AND DEMOCRACY

Finally, brief mention should be made of Aristotle's relative ranking of oligarchy and democracy.

In Book III, though he criticizes both oligarchs and democrats for having partial conceptions of justice, he nevertheless sees some merit in the arguments of the democrats. The two arguments for the rule of the many, the summation argument in favor of the greater collective wisdom of the many (III.11.1281a42–b38), and the "customer knows best" argument against the supposed wisdom of experts (III.11.1282a17–23), have become part of the stock-in-trade of democratic justification. Even if Aristotle is not prepared to endorse them wholeheartedly, he certainly presents them with clarity and a degree of sympathy he never shows for oligarchic arguments on behalf of wealth. In the later books, where political stability becomes the dominant value, democracy is clearly preferred over oligarchy because it is more likely to have the stabilizing influence of a large middle class (IV.11.1296a13–18) and because oligarchies are particularly prone to internal dissension (V.1.1302a8–13).

Early in Book IV (IV.2.1289b2–5) Aristotle endorses Plato's ranking in the *Statesman* (303a–b) of tyranny as the worst of the perverted forms of government, and democracy as the most moderate. This is based on the six-fold classification of constitutions in which oligarchy and democracy are perversions of the good forms of rule of the few and rule of the many respectively. As we have seen, this schema is then superseded by one in which both oligarchy and democracy are perversions of the same constitution, the polity. Using a musical metaphor, Aristotle compares the polity to a well-tempered harmony and the others to departures from this harmony. The degree of deficiency of any particular constitution will depend on the distance from the mean. A moderate constitution, whether an oligarchy or democracy, will therefore be better than either of the extremes.

The most that Aristotle will admit is that the democratic deviations from the well-tempered harmony of the polity are "more slack and soft" while the oligarchic deviations are more "taut and despotic" (IV.3.1290a27–9). His determination to preserve the logical symmetry of his analysis, with oligarchy and democracy the two polar extremes and polity the well-mixed mean, militated against a general preference for democracy as such, however much his own values and the evidence of political experience would have suggested otherwise.

14

Aristotle on Political Change

RONALD POLANSKY

Revolutions and other forms of political change pervade modern life. Understanding them is therefore vital. This was true in the past, however, as well as the present. Those ancient Greeks who bequeathed us most of our important political notions also concerned themselves with political change because it figured prominently in their time. A lengthy treatment of political change potentially of great interest to us occupies Aristotle's *Politics* V. Rather surprisingly, this section of the *Politics* has not received the attention it would seem to deserve.[1]

When we begin to study this book, we surely find fascinating points, but our overall reaction is likely to be bewilderment in the face of a confusion of topics and a mass of detail. It might be useful then to highlight its design.[2] Concentrating upon how Aristotle's investigation of political change may be both scientific and practical, I attempt to enhance access to his illuminating analyses. There is first some basic reflection upon the concepts connected with political change. Of special concern is the relation of political changes with the sorts of change discussed in the *Physics*. Part 2 reveals the structure in Aristotle's dense examination of the causes of political change. Part 3 outlines the modes of prevention of change. The next part inquires why Aristotle devotes so much attention to monarchy (a full third of Book V) and

1 The well-known commentaries upon the entire *Politics* devote some attention to this book, of course, but there is remarkably little beyond this in the secondary literature.
2 Even the basic structure of *Politics* V has eluded some of its prominent students. For example, Benjamin Jowett's analytic table of contents in the complete Oxford translation (ed. by J. A. Smith and W. D. Ross) breaks the book into only two parts: the first several chapters he entitles "Of Revolutions, and Their Causes in General" while the rest is "Revolutions in Particular States, and How Revolutions May be Avoided." This understates the extent to which Aristotle gives special treatment to causes of change and preservation of monarchies. Moreover, Jowett's table makes it appear that the discussion of the means of preserving constitutions (chapters 8 and 9) pertains just to aristocracies and polities, whereas it applies to all but monarchy. Ernest Barker also divides the book into the same two parts (*The Politics of Aristotle* [Oxford, 1946]). He, however, considers chapters 8 and 9, which treat means of preserving constitutions, merely a digression (p. 203, n. 1).

its relation to what preceded. The concluding section reviews main points and considers the place of change in political life.

1   CONSIDERATION OF POLITICAL CHANGE AS A TYPE OF CHANGE

Political investigations belong in what Aristotle calls "practical science." Practical science, the very name *praktikê* indicates, pertains to human *praxis* (action). In several important contexts Aristotle distinguishes *praxis* from making (*poiêsis*) and from change (*metabolê*) or motion (*kinêsis*) (see *EN* VI.4, VII.12.1153a7–17, X.4.1174a13ff., and *Pol.* I.4.1254a1–7). In its narrow, technical sense, *praxis* differs from production or motion because unlike these it is not a process of transition toward some external end.[3] *Praxis* is the exercise of individual or collective character or moral habits; instances are brave, cowardly, just, or unjust acts. Consequently, political change will not generally be *praxis* in the most proper sense and, in fact, not even the normal result of it. Political change follows from disruption of a previous pattern of life and action in a community whereas *praxis* is the actualization of some form of moral or political life.[4] Since practical science aims ultimately at engendering good action rather than change, change is not its main topic. Nevertheless, political change is a major concern because changes crucially affect the conditions for action. A statesman understanding the causes of political change will be more capable through his own action of warding off undesirable changes or effecting necessary ones.

The term Aristotle uses to name his main topic in Book V, *metabolê*,[5] is his general word for change in the *Physics*, and we shall find it quite useful to apply his basic analyses of change to the case of political change. In *Physics* V.1 there are four main kinds of change: in substance (genesis or destruction), in quality (alteration), in quantity (growth or diminution), and in place (locomotion). Similarly in the *Politics* there are several kinds of change. The most striking kinds of political changes are those in which the

---

3 For discussion and defense of the basis of this distinction, see my article "*Energeia* in Aristotle's *Metaphysics* IX," *Ancient Philosophy*, 3 (1983), pp. 160–70.

4 Though political change is not the aim of normal political action, some segment of the population may be in action to modify the conditions for or the form of action predominate in the community, and so be seeking political change. The action of that *part* of the population is the effort to actualize its sense of justice. See my conclusion and note 38 below.

5 Aristotle also uses the term *kinêsis* in *Politics* V, but he tends to insert *metabolê* or the corresponding verb forms into passages in which he indicates his main subject (e.g., 1.1301a20 and 2.1302a16–17). We also note that *metabolê* is often linked with sedition or faction (*stasis*). This is likely the case because the sort of change of most concern to the statesman is that which arises as a result of the conscious conflict of various segments of the political community. Aristotle, however, recognizes the possibility of change without sedition (see 3.1303a13–14). Ernest Barker goes so far as to claim that sedition rather than change is the main topic of Book V since he believes Aristotle more concerned with disturbances than with change (*The Political Thought of Plato and Aristotle* [London, 1906], p. 487). I shall have more to say about *stasis* below.

community shifts completely from one sort of constitution to another. This radical change resembles genesis or destruction, rather than, say, alteration.[6] But not all political changes are so fundamental. Aristotle has to consider the possibility of changes in which merely some part of a constitution is altered, or a group of men take for themselves the offices of an existing constitution without otherwise changing it, or a constitution becomes relaxed or tightened so that it is a more or less extreme instance of the sort of constitution it was (see 1.1301b5ff.). Any of these less fundamental changes might be likened to the species of motion other than genesis or destruction.[7]

Political change clearly covers many possibilities. Moreover, changes may occur purely unintentionally, such as when a good harvest effectively lowers the property qualification for office. For reasons such as these the modern term "revolution" is an inappropriate translation for Aristotle's "change." We tend to restrict "revolution" to cases of rebellion which succeed in fundamentally changing the constitution. Aristotle evidently speaks too broadly of possible kinds of change to call them all revolutions.

The other main term in *Politics* V, *stasis* or sedition, which might seem even more promising, will also not do so well for "revolution." *Stasis* refers to a dispute or firm disposition to dispute that may or may not end in political change (see n. 24 below). We would restrict "revolution" to just those cases of sedition that result in major constitutional changes. Also, Aristotle uses *stasis* or the corresponding verb forms for conflicts between individuals as well as for class antagonisms (see 1.1302a9–13; 4.1303b21–2, 28, and 31–2). We should hardly apply "revolution" to disputes between individuals. Thus it does not appear that Aristotle has any specific term for what we call revolution. His concern is for the broadest treatment of the possible types of

6 From the very start of Book V Aristotle conjoins the word for destruction (*phthora*) with *metabolê* (1.1301a22). It is evident from III.3.1276b1ff. that some changes change the polis completely.

7 By distinguishing these different kinds of political changes through likening them to the various species of physical change, we hold open the possibility of questioning Wheeler's contention that because the Greeks lacked "political parties" of the modern sort that they had no way to change policy except by sedition, i.e., by employing unlawful means to capture power (Marcus Wheeler, "Aristotle's Analysis of the Nature of Political Struggle" *American Journal of Philology*, 72 [1951], p. 147: rep. in *Articles on Aristotle*, vol. 2, eds J. Barnes, M. Schofield, and R. Sorabji [London, 1977]). Aristotle may allow for many kinds of changes besides those involving sedition in this sense (see V.3.1303a13ff. and 7.1307a40ff.), though these are of primary interest in *Politics* V. Also, attention to all the possibilities of change takes us some way toward addressing a difficulty R. G. Mulgan finds in this book, that is, that Aristotle advocates measures that change the constitution he is ostensibly trying to preserve (*Aristotle's Political Theory* [Oxford, 1977], see pp. 134 and 137). When, for example, a democracy or oligarchy is moved toward moderation in order to preserve it, it undergoes one of the lesser sorts of change to avoid radical, substantial change. This is logically quite plausible. Mulgan goes on, however, to make the more serious complaint that Aristotle's suggestions are not too realistic since the extreme constitutions are unlikely to accept those measures that would moderate them (p. 134). We return to this below.

political changes, with particular attention to those troublesome cases involving sedition.[8]

The analysis of change in the *Physics* has more to offer us than the analogy so far employed of diverse forms of change. Aristotle there discloses the main principles of all change as such, and we shall see how helpful this analysis can be for political reflection. *Physics* I.6–7 develops three principles of change: form, matter, and privation of form. Change occurs when some underlying matter takes on a new form. For example, wood may be shaped into a chair, where wood is matter and the configuration of the chair the form. Or, a chair might be painted a new color or moved to a different location, in which cases the chair is the matter which undergoes changes in color or place. To the extent political change is genuine change, the standard factors and account of change must apply to it, though Aristotle himself does not bother to state this explicitly.[9]

It is promising to conceive the *politeia* (constitution or regime) as the form that is received by the matter of the polis (city-state).[10] This matter is primarily the available classes of persons – the poor, rich, well-born, virtuous, etc. – and secondarily the physical setting, level of technical development, and so on of the community (see esp. VII.4 on population as matter and VII.5 for territory). In constituting the particular polis, the constitution, given the physical and technical possibilities, arranges the classes of citizens in a distribution of political power enjoining definite patterns of life in the community. Each class can make a claim to merit a position of dominance – the rich due to their wealth, the poor due to their free status, the virtuous due to their goodness. The constitution fixes the role each class will play, thus ordering the community and comprising its form. Since distributive justice for Aristotle is allocation according to merit (*EN* V.3.1131a25–9; and *Pol.* III.9.1280a16–18, V.1.1301a25–7), the constitution serves as the primary establishment of justice.

8 For a discussion of the meaning of the term *stasis*, see Wheeler, "Aristotle's Analysis of the Nature of Political Struggle." My comments have given reason to doubt, however, that he is correct that the "essential feature" of *stasis* is the use of violence and that it must always involve groups (pp. 149 and 159–60). Wheeler reluctantly endorses "sedition" as the best, though imperfect, translation of *stasis*. I shall also use "sedition." But Wheeler's comment that "the class of situations which constitute the meaning of the word [*stasis*] is one with which in our public life there is nothing strictly comparable" (p. 159) may be questioned. If he means that this Greek term covers matters for which we do not have a single comparable term, he is probably correct. Yet if he means that the phenomena of factional disputes are nowadays totally different, he may surely be wrong.

My translations from the *Politics*, unless otherwise indicated, are those of Jowett in the Oxford *The Works of Aristotle Translated into English* eds J. A. Smith and W. D. Ross.

9 Since politics, like ethics, is a practical science (see *EN* I.2–3 and *Met.* VI.1), Aristotle may well be leery of introducing too explicitly his notions from theoretical science into practical contexts.

10 This seems to be clear from the discussion opening *Politics* III. See, also, the employment of *eidos* at III.3.1276b1–9 and *hulê* at VII.4.1325b40–1326a5.

Though only implicit in Aristotle's thought, this analysis of the polis into form and matter is enlightening. It should hardly surprise us that Aristotle, as Newman points out, was aware of the role of "social conditions" that are the background for the constitution.[11] Social conditions fall under the "matter" of the community. This matter presents constraints to the sort of constitution that may inform it. If, for instance, the wealthy class of men were politically indifferent or very weak, there would be little chance for a coherent oligarchical constitution. But though the matter thus offers constraints to the form, once the constitution is in place there is reciprocally a great impact upon the classes of citizens of the ways of life it has ordained. The sort of constitution tends to habituate the citizens to certain modes of life.

Where form and matter are compatible, there should be, we might suppose, a happy union and a large degree of stability. Yet political changes occurred rather frequently in the Greek cities, and the general explanation should evidently be incompatibility of the form with the matter. In spite of the initial constraint of the matter on the formation of the constitution and the impact of the constitution in turn to shape the matter, the matter may be recalcitrant to the form. This seems even likelier because humans comprise the matter rather than some inorganic or unintelligent organic material.[12] Humans make judgments about the appropriateness of the constitution. Not only when the constitution is, in fact, unjust to its various classes of citizens, but also when it is merely perceived as unjust, people hanker for change.[13]

The different constitutions arise because of the different, typically erroneous, determinations of what is just (V.1.1301a25–8). Opposing views of

11 Newman states, "In tracing the constitution to social conditions, Aristotle gives explicit recognition to an important truth, which Plato had certainly not recognized with equal clearness, though the facts which pointed to it were familiar enough" (W. L. Newman, *The Politics of Aristotle* [Oxford, 1887–1902], vol. I, p. 223). Newman's supposition that Plato is less clear than Aristotle is certainly disputable – note the stress in the *Republic* on the proper territory and so on and even more centrally the proper education to prepare the citizens for the constitution – but surely Aristotle is quite alive to the importance of "social conditions."

The use of quotation marks around "social" follows Hannah Arendt's discussion in chapter 2 of *The Human Condition* (Chicago, 1958). She there contends that the Greeks recognized the private sphere and the public sphere, but that the realm of the social is a much later development. Arendt's remarks may be interestingly related with those of Karl Polanyi in "Aristotle Discovers the Economy" (reprinted in *Primitive, Archaic and Modern Economies*, ed. George Dalton [New York, 1968], pp. 78–115. Polanyi believes the social, economic sphere of life only becomes disembedded from other spheres in recent times. Nevertheless, he argues that Aristotle had a clear grasp of economic essentials. See also Moses I. Finley "Aristotle and Economic Analysis" reprinted in *Articles on Aristotle*, vol. 2, pp. 140–58.

12 Aristotle's awareness of the peculiar recalcitrance of humans is surely fostered by Plato. See, e.g., *Theaet.* 174d–e.

13 Aristotle says, "both parties [democrats and oligarchs], whenever their share in the government does not accord with their preconceived ideas, stir up revolution." (V.1.1301a37–9). Mulgan stresses the importance of the "subjective" sense of injustice (*Aristotle's Political Theory*, p. 121).

justice mean there is nearly always justification for sedition and political change. The classes not favored in the existing set up – and, as Aristotle asserts, the virtuous especially – have justification for seeking to overthrow the given order.

Democrats and oligarchs demand justice though they fail to hit upon what is absolutely just (1.1301a35–6). The democrats, basically the poor free population, appeal to their free status and contend that being all equally free each should have an equal share in the rulership of the community (1301a28–31). But the oligarchs contend that since they are wealthier superiority in this respect entitles them to an unequal share in the rulership (1301a31–3). Sedition arises when these classes become discontent with their respective share in the community (1301a37–9). Yet Aristotle insists that the class of citizens which would most justly enter into sedition is that which alone has rightful claim to inequality, namely, those superior in virtue (1301a39–b1).

Mention of the virtuous attacks the somewhat mistaken views of rich and poor alike with regard to justice. Since there are superior men, the argument of democrats that all are equal because all are equally free loses some of its force and the argument of the oligarchs that they deserve more because they have more wealth withers in confrontation with the truth that only superiority in virtue is true inequality. By pointing to the virtuous and their rightful claims, Aristotle corrects the common reasoning about justice and provides statesmen with arguments to pose against the various classes in the community.

These arguments have more than academic interest, for democracy and oligarchy occupy central positions in Aristotle's analysis. In spite of Aristotle's awareness of the several possible types of constitution and their numerous subspecies – the variety being due to the great diversity in the matter that the constitution must organize (see IV.3.1289b27–8) and the correspondingly diverse conceptions of justice (in Book VI Aristotle identifies many kinds of democracy and oligarchy based on different sorts of populations) – he can keep the discussion of change manageable by focussing upon democracy and oligarchy. The other constitutions may generally be conceived as some sort of blend of democracy and oligarchy (see V.10.1310b2–7 and 7.1307a5–16).[14] Hence these two constitutions are para-

---

14 To the ready objection that along with numbers and wealth Aristotle recognizes virtue as a crucial third factor in the composition of the constitutions, I might point out that virtue only belongs to the few so Aristotle is prepared to speak of aristocracies as "oligarchical" and as vulnerable to similar sources of perturbance as oligarchies (see 7.1306b22–7). The virtuous, being so few, are not generally significant sources of change (4.1304b4–5). Moreover, what most people usually refer to as "aristocracy" is in fact just a mixture of democracy and oligarchy that leans more toward the latter (7.1307a5–16). Though Aristotle never loses sight of the place of virtue in constitutions, he also has occasion to emphasize the other principles of wealth and numbers. He seems, as we shall see, to appreciate one of the great ironies of political life, much later fastened upon by Rousseau in his *First Discourse*, that as a people becomes more sophisticated the role of virtue in its constitution tends to become smaller.

digmatic for all the changes that arise in any of the constitutions. Those factors explaining changes in these two constitutions will also be applicable elsewhere.

Not only are democracy and oligarchy somehow components of the other constitutions, but also these two constitutions are dominant in Aristotle's time. He states, "Hence [since equals in freedom seek general equality and superiors in wealth think themselves worthy of superiority] there are two principal forms of government, democracy and oligarchy; for good birth and virtue are rare, but wealth and free status are more common" (1.1301b39–1302a1, Jowett trans. slightly altered). The aspirations of the social classes move toward but two kinds of constitution. Aristotle's awareness of social conditions contributes to his cognizance of historical shifts. Though Aristotle lacks our "historical consciousness" and is notorious for maligning the worth of history – he asserts in *Poetics* 9.1451b5–6 that "poetry is more philosophical and serious than history"[15] – he does have some sense of Greek history. Aristotle can see a direction in the change in social conditions, or matter, with which statesmen have to contend.

Throughout the *Politics* Aristotle has occasion to note changes in warfare, manners of acquiring the essentials of life, the size of cities, and sophistication of individuals (see, e.g., III.6.1279a10–16, 15.1286b8–22, IV.2.1289 b36–8, 6.1293a1–10, 11.1296a22–b2, 13.1297b16–28, V.5.1305a18–34, VI.4. 1318b6–1319b32, 7.1321a5–21). Such changes mean a changed social situation. We may clarify Aristotle's sense of history, if we recur to the analysis of change in terms of form and matter.

Matter as such cannot undergo change, as neither can form (see *Met.* VII.8). It is rather the composite of form and matter that actually comes to be. However, "matter" is a relative term. Matter, for Aristotle, is always relative to form or to a process toward form. So while wood is matter for making a chair, the chair in turn is matter for changes such as moving or painting. There is thus higher- and lower-level matter. Blood, bone, and such

---

15 Aristotle must deride history when that is understood as the chronicle of individual events (see 9.1451b6–7), for these could only be viewed by him as individual happenings resulting from numerous accidental conjunctions and so not subject to scientific study (see *Met.* VI.2 about the inappropriateness of accidents for scientific study). Hence, even events that actually occurred in the past, which we suppose fitting matters for eternally true statements and so knowledge (e.g., Socrates' death from poison in Athens in 399 BC), Aristotle would consider singular, accidental occurrences and therefore not proper subjects of knowledge. Not everything about which true statements can be made is a proper subject of knowledge, Aristotle would assert. Not individuals but kinds are genuinely subjects for knowledge for only these have non-accidental causes. My comments, which contrast things due to accidental with those due to non-accidental causes, give an alternative explanation of Aristotle's insistence upon unchanging objects of knowledge to that given by Jaakko Hintikka in his essay, "Time, Truth, and Knowledge in Aristotle and Other Greek Philosophers" reprinted in *Knowledge and the Known* (Dordrecht, 1974), pp. 50–79, esp. pp. 58–62. Raymond Well, in "Aristotle's View of History" in *Articles on Aristotle* (1977), vol. 2, pp. 202–3, similarly stresses the importance of generalizability.

homogeneous tissues are lower-level matter than the organs and body they compose (see *PA* II.1). Matter itself can then change if it is in fact composite, i.e., there is some matter below it which permits the taking on of a new form. This is how we may understand changes in the social conditions that are the background for the polis. While the available classes of citizens are matter for the form that is the constitution, this matter itself, being composite, may be in process of change.

The matter of a city is especially liable to change for the reason indicated before, that humans principally comprise the matter of the city. Indeed, much more than inorganic matter and even more than organic material which lacks man's intellectual and emotional life, the matter of political communities permits change. Whereas living things undergo patterns of material change, e.g., reptiles or insects proceed through their stages of development and mammals gain tusks or antlers, the human material of the political community undergoes changes of more varied sorts which need not have a definite natural trajectory.

The most important changes in the human material of a community take place when the goals and desires of its parts or of the whole population are transformed. Aristotle saw this occurring in the cities of his day (see, e.g., III.15.1286b8–22). The social scene was changing through the shift in people's desires.[16] These shifts created conditions such that democracy and oligarchy, rather than the older political forms, prevailed. What is more, these democracies and oligarchies tended toward extremes and at the extreme democracy and oligarchy are types of tyrannies: tyrannies of the poor or rich (see, e.g., V.10.1312b5–6, 6.1306b17–21, IV.4.1292a17–18). Due then to changes in the social background of the constitutions, Aristotle recognized the constitutions were changing toward forms that were destructive to the constitutions themselves.[17]

Aristotle is not, as some have supposed, oblivious to the dangers to the Greek polis in his time. Careful reading of the *Politics* shows him acutely aware of the danger to its continued existence. Aristotle needs to be concerned with two levels of change: changes in the matter or social conditions of the constitution and the parallel changes in the form or

16 An awareness of "history" in this sense, that is, an awareness of certain directions of change in communities though without the view that such history leads to safe predictions or rules, is hardly unique to Aristotle. Compare, for example, 325d–e in the Platonic *Seventh Letter* and Thucydides *Hist.* III. 82–3.

17 Some good support for these comments occurs in V.9.1309b31–5: "Oligarchy and democracy, although a departure from the most perfect form, may yet be a good enough government, but if any one attempts to push the principles of either to an extreme, he will begin by spoiling the government and end by having none at all." Weil ("Aristotle's View of History," pp. 213–15) also emphasizes the material shifts as crucial motors in Aristotle's view of Greek history, though Weil seems to limit the material factors too exclusively to economics. In addition Weil thinks Aristotle much more optimistic than I suppose him about the political situation of his day and the role of technological progress.

constitution. Both levels of change are toward extremes. Thus much of the treatment of political change is really a consideration of how to deal with the social changes that have altered the background for the polis and threaten its very existence. For tyranny, as we learn in Book V (11.1313a34–8), is the basic situation in Persia and the life of the nations outside the polis.

But Aristotle does not suppose there is a single determined pattern of historical change. Surely no constitution of any type inevitably changes into another particular sort of constitution, and the matter, in spite of its tendency to change in some direction, is not determinative of but only influential upon the form that will arise. So it cannot suffice to assume a single historical line of political change. Moreover, given that there are so many Greek cities and so many possibilities that may confront the statesman, a truly practical political science must prepare for every eventuality. Hence Aristotle discusses political changes of all the conceivable types whether more or less likely in his own day. Even the less likely changes are instructive to consider; for, as has been indicated, many of the constitutions can be viewed as mixtures of the others so that analogues of remote changes still take place.

How optimistic is Aristotle about statesmen succeeding in reforming the Greek cities? Mulgan suggests that Aristotle is rather naive in supposing he could get extreme democrats or oligarchs to accept moderating reforms.[18] But this seems to presume, I think erroneously, that the book is written for democrats and oligarchs themselves rather than for statesmen. I believe Aristotle is writing for statesmen fairly far along in virtue. If this is so, Aristotle's repeated emphasis upon the justice of virtuous men bringing about change takes on considerable importance (see, e.g., 1.1301a39–b1, 3.1303b15, 4.1304b4–5). The virtuous, we learn, are those most justified in engaging in sedition but those least capable of doing so because of limited numbers and power. When this is combined with the passage indicating that the basic means to effect changes in constitutions are force and persuasion (even more bluntly named "fraud": 4.1304b7–18), we are left to suppose that only were the virtuous, the true statesmen, able to persuade the bulk of the population might they manage large-scale change.[19] This seems a dismal prospect for the large, sophisticated cities of Aristotle's day. Aside from this remote possibility, there is the chance that a knowledgeable statesman might

18 Mulgan, *Aristotle's Political Theory*, p. 134.
19 The virtuous statesman can hardly be encouraged to engage in fraud or force to change a constitution in the light of Aristotle's later comment that the resort to deceit and compulsion seems to be the approach of the tyrant (10.1313a9–10). Moreover, though Aristotle allows it is just possible that the many might be persuaded permanently (4.1304b15–17), he also suggests it is unlikely (8.1307b40–1308a3). Thus, we might suppose Aristotle to acknowledge the rightness of sedition by the virtuous but to discourage it as fruitless. He gives a sobering portrait of political possibilities. There is here a subtle argument for the superiority of the contemplative to the political life, since there are quite limited prospects for significant success in politics. However, preservation of the polis seems crucial to the continuing possibility of the contemplative life.

be well-situated at some point in the course of a political change so that he can direct it promisingly. Aristotle, while hardly sanguine about the prospects for preserving the Greek polis by effecting the modifications which could safeguard it, nevertheless does what he can to equip the statesman to do what is possible. (See further part 3 below.)

2   THE CAUSES OF POLITICAL CHANGE

We have already seen some of the complication of Aristotle's subject: that changes may be total or merely like lesser movements in the political constitution and that humans as matter pose extra difficulty. We have also noted some foundation of simplification: that democracy and oligarchy are in a sense the models of the other constitutions. Let us now trace Aristotle's attempt at a scientific account of political change.

Scientific treatment of political change, just as of any topic, requires that there be attention to causes and principles, for Aristotle thinks we only know when we grasp the causes of what is to be known. In addition, science, as opposed to experience, requires that the causes grasped be universal rather than particular (see, e.g., *Met.* I.1). Combining these points, we ascertain that for there to be genuine causal knowledge of political change it must secure a set of universal causes that is manageable; an infinite or too numerous set either eliminates the possibility of knowledge or proves too unwieldy for use. Neither, however, must the set of causes be too few or it misses the phenomena of interest, and the statesman trying to understand and deal with the world will be ill-equipped to do so. Too few principles tend to be too general and consequently poorly adapted for application to concrete cases. Such concerns are not, of course, peculiar to the study of political change, but they are pressing here due to the complexity of the subject.

The announced organization of Aristotle's treatment of the principles of political change is into causes that apply universally and then causes that apply more particularly (V.2.1302a16–18, 4.1304b5–7, and 5.1304b19–20). This division should permit a treatment that is comprehensive yet applicable to concrete cases. But what Aristotle means by the general and particular causes of change is possibly ambiguous. A cause might be universal in at least three senses: (1) it applies to all types of *change*, (2) it applies to every type of *constitution*, and (3) it applies primarily to *types* of changes or constitutions rather than to instances of these. Sense (3) is not specially relevant since even the particular causes of change will probably apply to the change or constitution as a type. In regard to senses (1) and (2), some commentators have too quickly assumed Aristotle means (1) and so found a mistake in Aristotle's analysis because the supposed causes of all change do not apply to every case of change. For example, Newman complains about part of Aristotle's set of general causes:

> The list of causes of *stasis* and constitutional change here given seems incomplete. Other causes besides the seven or eleven here mentioned appear to

disclose themselves when Aristotle proceeds in cc. 5–7 to deal with each constitution separately. The overthrow of oligarchies, for instance, by the demagogy of some of the oligarchs (1305b22ff.) or by spendthrift and ruined oligarchs (1305b39ff.) cannot easily be brought under any of the eleven heads.[20]

But the mistake Newman thinks he finds, were Aristotle to suppose a universal cause or set of causes for all political changes, would be even greater than Newman recognizes. Near the end of the whole discussion of the causes of change (7.1307b19–25, and compare 10.1312a40–b9), Aristotle announces that political changes may be due either to internal or external causes. He means that political changes may be precipitated by situations internal to constitutions – and the cause would be principally internal even when an external affair such as a war occasioned a depletion of citizens and so contributed to a movement for change – or by some external compulsion (such as when the Athenians are imposing democracies and the Spartans oligarchies upon conquered cities). This distinction into internal and external causes of change reveals that almost all Aristotle's attention is devoted to the internal causes. These alone are actually the general causes he is considering. Since this is so, it is clear that there can be no completely universal cause of all political change. No matter how comprehensive a principle we locate of internal political changes, there will always be the uncovered possibility of some totally external source of change. Moreover, we shall see that Aristotle cannot really even come up with a comprehensive general cause for all internal political change. Rather, he arrives at most at a single cause for all instances of sedition (see 1.1301b26–9).[21]

Rather than saddling Aristotle with the mistake of supposing he has a universal cause or set of causes of all political changes, and to fit with his actual project, it seems most appropriate to view the universal causes of change as applying universally to the constitutions, i.e., our sense (2) above. "Universal" causes are such because they operate in several of, if not all, the kinds of constitutions, whereas the particular kinds of constitutions may each also have causes of change peculiar to the kind.[22] Even more accurately stated, I suggest the universal causes of change operate *both* in democracies and oligarchies. Hence, given that the other constitutions are largely blends of these, they may operate in each of the other kinds of constitutions. Some other causes of change are, however, more especially important either in democracies (and the closely related constitutions, e.g., polity) or in oli-

20 Newman, *The Politics of Aristotle*, vol. IV, p. 296.

21 In addition it should be noted that the lengthy discussion of universal and individual causes of change is not immediately directed at monarchical forms of constitutions, which are saved for the end of the book. So it seems even more unlikely Aristotle supposed himself to have causes universal in the sense that they applied to every case of change.

22 Compare Mulgan, *Aristotle's Political Theory*, pp. 119ff.

garchies (or closely related kinds, e.g., aristocracy: 7.1306b22–7). Evidence for my suggestion may be found in Aristotle's frequent use, in his account of the general causes, of illustrations with instances from both democracy and oligarchy (e.g., 3.1302b18–19 [ostracism used in both oligarchy and democracy], b25–9, b40–1303a11).

Though I have argued that Aristotle primarily means by universal or general causes of change, causes that apply generally to the various sorts of constitutions, it is nonetheless the case that his order of treatment of the causes is from those that apply to almost all cases of change and every case of sedition to causes that apply to fewer cases. This should be so since causes that operate in more types of constitution are likely to apply to more cases of change. When we examine Aristotle's universal causes of change, they are divided into three groups, the first having but one cause within it, the second two, and the third several. The one cause in the first division should apply most widely to all sorts of change. The two in the second group, since two, probably apply alternatively to very many cases. The third class of causes is more numerous, so each perhaps figures only in some cases. It seems plausible that Aristotle deliberately develops his discussion with these various levels of generality in mind so that he can combine comprehensiveness (in the sense of touching on nearly every conceivable source of change) while retaining applicability (by the grading of the generality of the causes).

The three sorts of general causes operative in political changes and seditions Aristotle describes as: the disposition of those persons who seek change, their objectives, and factors prompting changes. He states this thus: "For we must ascertain what state of affairs (*pôs echontes*) gives rise to sedition, and for what objects it is waged, and thirdly what are the origins of political disorders and seditions among the citizens" (2.1302a20–22, Rackham trans. slightly altered). Such principles as these are found in several contexts outside natural science where Aristotle seeks to organize the factors involved in changes. The most striking of these is *Rhetoric* II.1.1378a22–6 (compare I.10.1368b27).[23] The analysis of what engenders emotional responses has some interesting parallel to that we find here in the *Politics*. Aristotle suggests we must consider the frame of mind of those who feel the emotion, the sort of persons to whom it is directed, and the things that occasion it. Emotions in the individual seem analogous to sedition in the city. Sedition may be likened to an intense collective passion. Much as passions serve as motivations or moving causes of actions, so sedition may effect a collective enterprise that results in political change. Aristotle may shift easily between sedition and change because sedition is often, if not always, involved in and the moving cause of change. And just as emotions may be fought off, restrained, or

23 Newman notes the kinship of the *Politics'* analysis to the latter passage of the *Rhetoric*, as well as *EN* VII.3.1146b15ff. (*The Politics of Aristotle*, vol. I, p. 593 n. 1 and vol. IV, pp. 293–4).

redirected, so that the deeds they might cause are resisted or improved, so sedition might be controlled to prevent an unsatisfactory political change.[24]

Since change produced through sedition is the kind of most concern, Aristotle's presentation of the causes contributing to change pertains mainly, though not exclusively, to sedition. In the passage quoted right above, it is evident that sedition is a principal concern. The disposition readying men for or propelling them toward sedition is the sense of incompatibility in the constitution of matter and form. That is, some individuals or groups perceive distributive injustice in the community. They believe the arrangement of the constitution does not fit those arranged by it. In this disposition people are ripe for change. Since those that potentially become involved in change seem, according to Aristotle, to have a claim that the current state of affairs is somehow unjust, they have a pretext or justification for change. Aristotle is therefore likely to expect that even those whom others in the community label renegades and tyrants can justify their seditious activity. When, for example, out of contempt for the ability of the present constitution to resist an attack or due to loss of estate on account of profligate spending a group of men attempts an illegal takeover, it will seem a just move to its instigators. While only the virtuous may have the finally compelling ground for sedition, others are unlikely to consider themselves so lacking in virtue that they ought not engage in sedition. Since the disposition fostering change or sedition is ultimately the sense of injustice in distribution in the community, this must be the most general of all the causes operative in change. Wherever men consciously set out to change their own constitution, this is the underlying motivating source. Hence it is most essential for the statesman to grasp this most pervasive cause.

The next sort of cause Aristotle considers is not singular, but an alternate or possibly combined pair. Hence this pair cannot have the generality of the cause we just considered. That for the sake of which men initiate or pursue political change Aristotle names as gain or honor, either for themselves or others close to them and either to obtain the gain or honor or to resist their loss (2.1302a31–4). Aristotle does not name as the end the change the seditious party aims to bring about, such as a new kind of constitution, but that about which citizens or the disenfranchised feel disgruntled and what they hope to obtain for themselves or avoid. The matters about which men develop the sense of injustice thus appear to reduce to but two, gain or honor. Why these two?

24 Aristotle considers all actions that result from passions to be voluntary. Similarly sedition occasions deliberate political changes. There are also, however, unintentional political changes (6.1306b6–16). That not all sedition leads to the attempt to overthrow the constitution seems to explain Aristotle's distinction of attack (*to epitithesthai*) from sedition (*stasis*) (3.1302b25 and see Newman's comments in *The Politics of Aristotle*, vol. IV, p. 284). Observe in addition the distinction between *stasis* and resort to arms (*machê*) in 3.1303a28–b2.

What can be distributed in the community by the existing constitution is property or honors of various sorts.[25] Virtue, however, and other such goods are not similarly matters which the community distributes, even if it attempts to make provision for them. Therefore, when men determine that the present constitution is unjust, it is about the distribution of properties and honor that they conclude this. Were even virtuous men to undertake sedition, they would do so because they determine that there is a faulty distribution of honors (such as offices) or dishonors (such as punishments). Aristotle is surely hardly romanticizing the objectives of those seeking political change. Since the ends Aristotle lists are those that enter into men's reflections about justice, it should be evident that these are conscious objectives leading to *sedition*, and Aristotle himself says that these are the ends for the sake of which men engage in sedition (3.1302b32 and 34).

The third and final group of general causes of internal political changes or sedition are more specific precipitating causes. Aristotle lists seven causes which have some tie to the previous two groups of causes because they frequently lead to the perception of injustice and sometimes the pursuit of the objectives of gain or honor. But there are also some other causes (bringing the total in this third group up to at least eleven) which may lead to change without sedition (see 3.1303a13–14) or without the perception of injustice (about enmity rather than injustice leading to change, see below). Aristotle thus considers causes which may apply to political changes brought about either deliberately or accidentally.

The eleven named causes provoke changes in various ways. What should be of particular interest to us is the resistance this discussion of so many causes shows to any reductionistic account of change and sedition. Aristotle will not attribute them to any single ubiquitous cause, and certainly not a low cause, but the closest he gets to a single explanation is the remarkable emphasis on the role of virtue or justice in sedition. While alive to the importance of what we would call economic factors, Aristotle locates other causes that he believes figure as prominently, such as virtue and honor. And even in discussing gain he recognizes diverse ways in which it operates. Gain is included in both the second and third classes of causes. As a member of the second group, gain is the very objective sought by men involved in sedition, whereas as a cause in the third group it occasions sedition not so much in order that men may gain for themselves or avoid loss but because they are annoyed at the spectacle of other men gaining unfairly. They seek not so

25 Wheeler ("Aristotle's Analysis of the Nature of Political Struggle," p. 149) supposes that the objective of gain can refer to gain only as remuneration from holding political office. There is no really good reason to limit this objective so narrowly, however, for it is likely that some prospective tyrants and oligarchs expect to gain monetarily from a political change beyond what they will legally receive for serving in office.

much to improve their own standing in the scale of wealth as to put an end to a situation in which individuals or groups gain unfairly.[26]

A further striking indication of Aristotle's appreciation of the array of causes of change is his discussion of how differences among the residents of a city may cause them to fall out among themselves.[27] In his final formulation of the point, Aristotle asserts:

> For just as in war the impediment of a ditch, though ever so small, may break a regiment, so every cause of difference, however slight, makes a breach in the city. The greatest opposition is confessedly that of virtue and vice; next comes that of wealth and poverty; and there are other antagonistic elements, greater or less, of which one is this difference of place. (3.1303b12–17)

Aristotle could not make plainer his conviction that there are political conflicts that can receive little explanation beyond the tendency of humans to be antagonistic toward those differing from them. Hatred and anger suffice to produce political mayhem. Racial and other differences he coolly announces to be fundamental sources of conflict. This sober vision prevents any easy optimism about overcoming political conflict through improvements in certain spheres of life such as the economic, or even, unfortunately, through achieving justice.

Aristotle also discusses causes of change especially important to each of the several constitutions (V.5–7). Some of these causes are among the general causes, though others may be peculiar to one sort of constitution. What Aristotle concentrates upon are the special causes prominent in changes in each of the constitutions. This focus on the constitutions individually gives another form of practicality to his treatment of causes. One thing to observe is that none of the constitutions changes simply in one direction, but each may change in several possible directions.

Demagogues are the primary source of change in democracy. By setting the wealthy against the democrats they cause change into oligarchy or even into tyranny, if one of them can take over (as used to happen more commonly in the days when cities were smaller and the demagogues military men rather than rhetoricians – 5.1305a7–28). In Aristotle's time the traditional democracies were tending to change to more extreme democracies in which

---

26 As I read 3.1302b10–14, Aristotle is making a distinction regarding honor similar to that which he makes for gain as a cause of *stasis*. When he refers in b11–12 to themselves and others being honored or dishonored, I suppose that attention to themselves causes them to seek honor for themselves (the second kind of cause of *stasis*), whereas when they are more concerned with the honor others receive it is the third class of causes of *stasis* or change that is at issue.

27 Aristotle notes that even the different regions within a polis may engender different interests and sedition (3.1303b7–12). In a series of publications Raphael Sealey has emphasized the geographical foundation of much of the political conflict in Greek cities. See, e.g., "Regionalism in Archaic Athens," *Historia*, 9 (1960), pp. 155–80.

the people operated above the law due in part to faulty procedures for filling offices (5.1305a28–32). Oligarchy has several primary sources of change. The main ones are conflict of oligarchs with the poor or of the oligarchs among themselves.[28] Such conflicts arise in quite varied ways and may result in changes of many varieties. Oligarchies like democracies can remain the same type of constitution while becoming more extreme and lawless (6.1306b17–21). Aristocracy and polity, at least the conventional instances, being kinds of mixtures of democracy and oligarchy, change in all sorts of ways due to causes similar to those operative in their components (7.1307a5–27).

In developing his account of the general causes and particular causes of change and sedition, Aristotle appeals often to historical examples for illustration. These frequently clarify what Aristotle means by the cause he mentions. They also get the statesman to think beyond the narrow confines of his own community and of his own day by bringing in the experience of many cities and many times. Thereby too the basic direction of movement of social conditions and the resulting drift of constitutions from the past into the present is indicated. Moreover, the possibility of the causal efficacy of the cause under consideration is shown by instantiating its past actuality. In some cases the illustrations, by referring to more than one kind of constitution or focussing on just one kind, support the conception of the cause as a general or particular cause. Thus Aristotle's illustrations serve as evidence of the scientific standing of his analysis and enhance the practical usefulness of his presentation.

3 PREVENTION OF POLITICAL CHANGE

Having investigated Aristotle's presentation of the causes of political change, I follow his order and turn to the preservation of constitutions from change. Aristotle indicates that his organization will parallel that of the treatment of causes because he takes up the safeguarding of constitutions in general and for each constitution separately (8.1307b26–7). Moreover, he announces that the causes of destruction of constitutions are contraries of the safeguards, so to know the one is to know the other, just as arts are productive of contraries (1307b27–30). We might then expect that this section which considers the contraries of the causes of change will follow the first part very closely. In fact, however, Aristotle does not repeat his previous analysis.

Aristotle respects the distinction of the safeguards that apply to all the kinds of constitutions from those pertaining especially to one sort, but does not keep things so clearly demarcated. He has a different organizing

---

28 Aristotle mentions demagogues in connection with change in oligarchies as well as democracies, but they act differently in the two. Demagogues in oligarchy are members of the ruling group who seek to divide it or stir up the many against it (6.1305b22–39 and 8.1308a16–18).

principle at play in this section from those preceding. Whereas in considering the causes of change, Aristotle basically proceeded from the more to the less general causes, now he seems to be more directly practical. The reason for this may be that the statesman usually only needs to *know* the causes of change, but he often has to *employ* the safeguards.[29] It was therefore practically helpful for learning the cause of change to go by Aristotle's order there, yet for effectively safeguarding constitutions it would hardly be a good order. Here he seems to be guided by the thought of ease of implementation for the astute statesman. That is probably why he begins with the point about preventing small transgressions of the law, which the astute statesman will readily discern and fairly easily counter,[30] and moves eventually to more difficult matters such as strengthening the middle class and implementing a system of education suited to the constitution. Characteristic of his latter proposals is that they typically escape the notice or concern of the cities of Aristotle's time (see 9.1309b18–19 and 1310a12–14). The order thus also reflects Aristotle's sense, as discussed previously, of the direction of Greek social history.

Noteworthy in this section is the absence of particular illustrations. Perhaps the easier preventative measures are quite intelligible without instantiation while the more difficult safeguards are so rare and involved with subtle policies they can hardly be conveniently illustrated. Instead we hear about them at some length in other sections of the *Politics*. Also, since the preventative measures are so much closer to practice than to universal knowledge as sought in the case of the causes of change, Aristotle has less need for inductive justification of them.[31]

4 MONARCHY AND POLITICAL CHANGE

The discussion of the causes of change and how to prevent their working has occupied much of Book V, but a very substantial portion – well over a third of the book – remains devoted to a similar treatment of monarchical forms of constitution. It is a matter of considerable interest why Aristotle takes up questions concerning monarchy, government by a single ruler, with such care and apart from the rest. After all, of the two key forms of monarchy, kingship was a type of constitution basically outmoded in Aristotle's day (see

29 Though Aristotle says the safeguards of constitutions are contraries to the causes of change, it must be appreciated that the causes of *change* usually occur apart from the statesman's contrivance, while the safeguards are the statesman's implementation of modes of *action* that secure a pattern of action in the community.
30 This first safeguard seems to correspond to one of the third group of causes of change.
31 Could it be too that the absence of illustrations shows the small fame which accrues to those who have engaged in politics to save constitutions as opposed to overthrowing them? This would again indicate a problem with the political life.

10.1313a3–4) and tyranny hardly seems the sort of government that Aristotle would wish to preserve. Nevertheless, there is an extended analysis of monarchy and its preservation, and we ought to consider why.

An initially plausible, but I think basically incorrect approach to the answer, is found impressively presented by Charles Howard McIlwain. He believes that Greek revolutions were such shocking affairs that it was felt anything should be done to avoid them. He says:

> This fundamental and far-reaching character of most actual revolutions in Greece, in so many cases touching everything in the state, social, economic, and intellectual, as well as governmental . . . changes usually carried out by violence, proscription, ostracism, and even death, in ways very similar to the proceedings so familiar to us in parts of Europe today and with much the same underlying causes – it is this wholesale character of so many contemporary revolutions that accounts for the Greek fear of *stasis*, and the nervous desire to risk almost anything that might prevent it. . . . Nothing less than such revolution and the constant dread of its results could have led Aristotle, for example, to advise tyrants how to prolong a type of government which he admits to be the most oppressive in the world as well as the shortest-lived.[32]

A great difficulty with this view is that it misses the extent to which Aristotle sets out to reform monarchy rather than to preserve it in its worst varieties. Newman seems closer to Aristotle's intention in his observation, "[Aristotle] probably wished to do what could be done to amend the worst of Greek institutions, and he may also have desired to keep the Macedonian kingship in the right track."[33]

I believe that Aristotle's extended attention to monarchy has several compelling motivations. One is that the *Politics* seems directed to men who are or aspire to be statesmen, and such men are often quite gifted. We may recall how earlier in the book it was emphasized that the virtuous have a justification for sedition, and we note in these latter sections that tyrants and kings are usually credited with fairly great abilities. A purpose, therefore, for a discussion of tyranny which puts it in an unattractive light is to keep it from having much appeal to the kinds of men who would be statesmen and capable of assuming tyrannical power. This gives these sections a task akin to that of parts of Plato's *Republic* which aim to turn gifted young men from the meretricious appeal of the life of supreme injustice, especially tyranny.

32 Charles Howard McIlwain, *Constitutionalism Ancient and Modern* (New York, 1947), pp. 38–9. Interestingly enough, whereas McIlwain, writing in the 1930s and 1940s, observes the kinship of ancient and modern revolutions, Newman, writing near the start of the present century, says, "Perhaps what Aristotle says here of constitutional change [that constitutions change frequently into their contraries] is less true of modern Europe than it was of ancient Greece, where constitutional change was usually sweeping and sudden" (*The Politics of Aristotle*, vol. IV, p. 484).

33 The prospective philosopher cannot be indifferent to the emergence of tyranny, however, for leisure and philosophical discussion are generally very out of place in tyrannical constitutions (see 1313a39–b6).

Another purpose is to awaken the realization in the aspiring statesman, if he is not already sufficiently aware from what preceded, that politics is not all sweet persuasion and reasonableness. The sober sketch of the destruction of monarchies and the means of preserving tyranny may shock the student of politics into an appreciation of reality and loss of illusions. As a beneficial by-product, some may come to a preference for the philosophical life over the political life.[34]

The purposes so far mentioned pertain to the *student* of political philosophy, but there is surely a more directly political purpose for the attention to monarchy. This is connected with the peculiar status of monarchy. Of all the forms of constitution, monarchy is the least political (when we keep in mind that "political" is connected with the Greek form of polis and the Greek for citizen [*politês*]). By this I mean that if the naturalness of the polis is due to its being that arena in which men are most able to engage in common, public action, i.e. be full-fledged citizens, then kingship and tyranny interfere with this desideratum. Where rulership tends to be monopolized by an individual or small group, the rest of the community is left to occupy itself with private rather than public matters. This constitutes a severe shrinking of the field for virtuous action. We should note that the metaphors most frequently used for monarchy, such as a father ruling over children, a shepherd over sheep, or, in the case of tyranny, the master dominating his slaves, point out just what I have stated about the limitations of these constitutions as conducive for virtuous action. I suggest that even when Plato and Aristotle seem to favor kingship, that is only where the king is understood to be so surpassingly wise that he can direct all his subjects to more virtuous action than they could find on their own. Thus, kingship and tyranny are at the fringes of properly political life. More than once Aristotle directly contrasts monarchy and the other constitutions (10.1310a40–b2 and 1311a22–5), so that it might seem that monarchy is not even a form of polis. But Aristotle recognizes that most of the barbarian nations have some sort of monarchical governance, and, as I explained earlier, that the Greek cities seemed to be heading toward a similar fate. Consequently, the discussion of monarchy has the role of giving the statesman some insight into the forms of organization of many non-Greek peoples and into the means that must be taken to preserve the city-state.[35]

The best evidence for these claims is Aristotle's insistence, followed up by argument, that the monarchical forms are like hybrids of some of the other constitutions. Kingship is much like aristocracy, while tyranny is a combination of extreme oligarchy and democracy (10.1310a40–b7). (We recall that conventional aristocracies and polities were also mixtures [see

34 Newman, *The Politics of Aristotle*, vol. IV, p. 413.
35 I am in fundamental disagreement with Hans Kelsen's position in "Aristotle and Hellenic–Macedonian Policy" (reprinted in *Articles on Aristotle*, vol. 2) that Aristotle in the chronologically latest stratum of the *Politics* greatly favors the Macedonian monarchy and believes kingship the best form of constitution. Kelsen supposes he does not say this outright to "avoid hurting democratic sensibilities" (p. 179). It seems to me that this view discounts Aristotle's concern for virtuous action.

7.1307a7–16].) Tyranny, Aristotle contends, having as its end the pleasure and private advantage of the tyrant and requiring a guard of foreign mercenaries, combines the end and means of extreme oligarchy – i.e., pursuit of money to pay the troops and abuses of the many – with the tactics of extreme democracy, the destruction of the notables (10.1311a2–22). Moreover, Aristotle can readily illustrate tyranny and kingship by appealing to barbarian nations, especially Persia (see, e.g., 10.1310b37–8, 1311b38, 1312a12, 11.1313a38, 1313b9–10). Thus the analysis of these forms of organization is taking us to the edge of what Aristotle would consider politics. As the Greek city-states plunge into extreme democracy or oligarchy, they tend toward tyranny and the situation of the barbarian nations. Such seems to Aristotle a desperate plight for the polis, and he seeks its salvation.

While it is literally true that he presents the means to save even the most egregious tyranny, it can hardly be supposed that he favors this route. He indicates his preference for the other approach, and he shows that extreme tyrannies have had quite brief existences. I suggest that he does nothing to advocate the extreme strategy for saving tyranny, but rather presents this loathsome approach as essential for the edification of the statesman. His reduction of the varied maneuvers of tyrants to the three basic heads – humble the population, put individuals in mistrust of each other, and keep men powerless – is quite a demystification, much as he earlier had demystified the secret of amassing a large fortune.[36] If tyranny is somehow a mixture of democracy and oligarchy, then means used in its preservation may well be analogues of those applicable to democracy or oligarchy, and so it suits the statesmen to know them.

I do not suppose Aristotle embraces tyranny in any enthusiastic way. Yet some of his comments might permit us to see him finding some good use for it. The "benign" strategy for securing a tyranny seems to remove most of the evil of tyranny. While the tyrant during his life would hold on to the reins of power, it is likely that such a constitution could make a favorable change to an even more desirable situation following the tyrant's death. This moderate monarchy might even be preferable in some instance to more extreme types of democracy or oligarchy.

There might also be a further application of tyranny. If we examine the causes Aristotle gives for changes in monarchy, we find that all those listed earlier for the other sorts of constitutions appear except the last four kinds within the third group, i.e., election intrigue, carelessness, neglect of trifles, and dissimilarity in the population. I suppose that the first three do not come

36 Polanyi emphasizes Aristotle's intention of demystifying the technique of acquisition of wealth by exposing it as simply the development of a position of monopoly, see "Aristotle Discovers the Economy," p. 113. Newman points out (*The Politics of Aristotle*, vol. IV, p. 449) that all Aristotle's mentioned techniques for wicked application by tyrants were well known to earlier authorities and that Aristotle takes them over from them. I would suggest, however, that the reduction of these techniques to the three heads is Aristotle's contribution.

up because they have little place in monarchy. The last cause, however, which seemed so hopelessly explosive in the other types of constitution might well call for monarchy, even tyranny, as the only constitution that could displace it from the attention of the citizens. I admit Aristotle never states this, but he might see tyranny as sometimes necessary to handle extreme social divisions. (Recall his remark in 5.1304b23–4 that the greatest enemies may be brought together by a common fear with his recommendation in 8.1308a24–30 to make men care more for the constitution by confronting them with something fearful near at hand.)

We should note that Aristotle's insistence that the monarchical constitutions are hybrids of the other constitutions and that the same causes of change are operative in them suggests that he supposes his analysis of political change and sedition applies well beyond the Greek city-state. To the extent that communities can be conceived as involving elements of the kinds of constitutions Aristotle thinks basic, his treatment should prove pertinent. This appears especially likely because Aristotle finds no unusual causes of change of monarchies – his discussion of their causes of change turns up no new ones and none peculiar to them – and if these most uncharacteristic constitutions present no new causes, there is probability that there are no further types of causes. Aristotle does not seem, then, to acknowledge history as some sort of power likely to disqualify his analyses. Thus the question of the extent to which Aristotle's political philosophy is truly scientific and has relevance outside his own time must draw special attention to this section on monarchy.

5 CONCLUSION

The final portion of *Politics* V contains criticism of Plato's treatment of the changes of constitutions in *Republic* VIII and IX. Aristotle elsewhere often begins his analyses by reviewing what his predecessors have stated; here instead he saves it for the end. This occurs presumably because no one previously had attempted so general an account of political change. The attack on Plato is really a defense of the scientific standing of Aristotle's work. Aristotle merely uses Plato's text as a foil (even straw man) for defending his own approach. He knows Plato's intention in the *Republic* was not a comprehensive analysis of political change, but avails himself of this entertaining way to secure his own position.

Aristotle targets principally three things: (1) that Plato fails to give specifically *political* causes for changes or causes specific to particular constitutions, (2) that he suggests a single historical pattern in change, (3) that there is too reductionistic an account of causes.

Regarding (1), Aristotle observes that the reason Plato gives for change from the best constitution is not peculiar to it (12.1316a3–4). Aristotle means that Plato in fastening upon the "nuptial number" assumes a sort of cause not necessarily directed at political change, and applies it as if it pertains specially to the best constitution though it might just as well apply to any of the others. This puts us in mind of our attention to political change in relation to change generally and our efforts to sort out the articulations of Aristotle's account of the factors in political change.

As for (2), Aristotle attacks Plato's scheme because of its single direction of change (12.1316a17–39). In Plato it seems the best constitution must change into something like the Spartan constitution, that into oligarchy, that into democracy, and that into tyranny. Tyranny would presumably have to change back again into the best constitution. Aristotle wishes to hold open the possibility for changes among any of the constitutions because these can be instanced in actual experience. Nonetheless, I showed in section 1 Aristotle's acceptance of a pattern of social and political history. It is really the case that Plato and Aristotle share the same fundamental conception, that is, that there is a degeneration of the city-states due to a progressively decadent unleashing of desires.[37] Plato for his purposes abandons the variegated phenomena of actual experience to accentuate the pattern. Aristotle, while basically agreeing, rejects any suggestion of a single line of history. There are two many constitutions and too varied a social scene to limit change too definitively. And it is a logical error to suppose that matter determines form.

. (3) gets to the heart of Aristotle's intention in the treatment of political change, to be comprehensive (see 12.1316a39ff. esp. 1316b14–15). Plato seems to suggest there is only one possible cause for each kind of change. Such a reductionistic account of the causes falls short of the aspiration of true science for it fails to divide the phenomena into their right kinds. We have seen repeatedly Aristotle's effort to make his treatment adequately detailed and complex so that he remains true to the phenomena under investigation.

In the course of the discussion, I have several times mentioned the relationship of political change (*metabolê*) with action (*praxis*). Aristotle's analysis of political change may be said to be a reflection upon the limits of political action. Not only has the investigation of monarchy taken us to the extremes of political life and opened a view of life outside the polis, but also the inquiry into the factors involved in change have exposed the material side of things. The place of history has emerged. Aristotle has indicated how hard it is to prevent changes or even to direct them. There are many factors at play, several of them very hard to control. The statesman must understand what the possibilities of retaining or improving a constitution are and the prospect of deterioration.

It should have been established that Aristotle seeks comprehensiveness in his treatment of political change. It should also be evident that he aims to give virtue as full a place as he practically can in political life. A large part of the task of enhancing the role of virtue is to reveal to the prospective statesman, hopefully well along in virtue, the small chance virtue has in dominating the scene. Exaggerated expectations may easily lead to perver-

37 See also Thucydides *Hist*. III. 82–4 and Nietzsche, *Twilight of the Idols*, the section entitled "The Problem of Socrates."

sion of virtue. The virtuous must assess their chances as low due to their limited numbers and power, to their natural reluctance to resort to force or fraud, and to the historical tendencies for the cities in Aristotle's time to expand in size and to head for political extremes. Appreciating the small prospect complete virtue has for taking over the constitution, the statesman must limit himself to moderating the classes in their competing claims for justice and blending the classes together better in the constitution. Thereby he may secure for the constitution the contribution that each class may rightly make toward a just order.

The polis is natural to man as offering that sphere in which men's powers for action, for exercising moral virtue, best come into play. Some constitutions, such as tyranny, terribly constrict the opportunities for action, while the better constitutions foster it. Now since action does not usually have an end outside itself, political action in the better constitutions does not bring about any change in the constitution but just realizes the proper capacities of the community. Where there is change or sedition there has been or may be a breakdown in the normal mode of action of the community. The actions of some section or sections of the polis have caused or may cause a fundamental or lesser change in the form of the constitution.[38]

The statesman must have an understanding of the political objective of virtuous political action and how changes which enhance or diminish its prospects come about. Aristotle has been seen to offer the statesman as scientific and yet as practical an account of political change as he could.[39]

38 Aristotle speaks of the activity of individuals or groups endeavoring to overthrow a tyrant as *praxis* (see 10.1312b25ff.). Such sectional *praxis* is not the fully public action that is the objective of the polis. Those intentionally endeavoring to engender a political change are themselves engaged in action (*praxis*), though this is not fully public action since it is not that of the polis or constitution but of some segment trying to change it and so bring about the possibility for a new sort of public action.

39 I wish to thank the editors of this volume for helpful comments on an earlier version of this essay.

15

Politics, Music, and Contemplation in Aristotle's Ideal State

DAVID J. DEPEW

Politics VII–VIII contains Aristotle's portrait of a best or aristocratic (*aristos* = best) state. The treatise begins with a preface (*Pol.* VII.1–3) in which Aristotle sets forth certain normative principles for an ideal constitution. He says that the best state must be a happy state; that if a state is to be happy, its citizens must lead an active life (*bios praktikos*) (for happiness is activity of the soul in accord with virtue); and that contemplation (*theôria*) is an activity. The first section of this essay is an interpretation of this prefatory argument. I take Aristotle to mean that only when contemplation is regarded by the citizens as the highest of all activities can the entire range of *other* intrinsically good pursuits, such as political engagement, be clearly distinguished from activities having merely instrumental worth, and so be pursued *as* intrinsic goods. This implies that Aristotle is envisioning what has come to be called an "inclusive ends" conception of happiness, in which the good life consists in engaging in a range of excellent activities.[1] But the kind of inclusivism I see in *Pol.* VII.1–3 differs in important respects from most versions of that doctrine, especially in the role it assigns to contemplation.

In the second section I argue that Aristotle's sketch of a best constitution, which occupies the extant remainder of *Pol.* VII–VIII, embodies the

---

1 Proponents of an "inclusive ends conception of happiness," or "inclusivists," include J. L. Ackrill, "Aristotle on *Eudaimonia*," *Proceedings of the British Academy*, 60 (1974), pp. 339–59; John M. Cooper, *Reason and Human Good in Aristotle* (Cambridge Mass., 1975); David Keyt, "Intellectualism in Aristotle," in *Essays in Ancient Greek Philosophy*, eds John P. Anton and Anthony H. Preus, vol. 2 (Albany, 1983), pp. 364–87; T. Irwin, *Aristotle's First Principles* (Oxford, 1988), pp. 608, n. 40, pp. 616–17, n. 24; Martha C. Nussbaum, *The Fragility of Goodness* (Cambridge, Mass., 1986), p. 375; Timothy D. Roche, "*Ergon* and *Eudaimonia* in *Nicomachean Ethics* I: Reconsidering the Intellectualist Interpretation," *Journal of the History of Philosophy*, 26 (1988), pp. 175–94. When Aristotle claims that "happiness is activity in accord with complete virtue (*teleia aretê*)" (*EE* 1219a35–9; *EN* 1100a4–5), inclusivists interpret "complete" to mean "including all virtues, moral as well as intellectual, in the flourishing or happy life (*eudaimonia*)." Not all proponents of attributing this view to Aristotle think he does so consistently. See notes 12–15 below.

principles of this prefatory argument. Aristotle's main contentions in these portions of *Pol.* VII–VIII are the following. Laborers, craftsmen and merchants are merely necessary conditions, rather than proper parts, of a best polis. Citizenship is restricted to landowning males, who serve as soldiers when they are young, hold political offices in rotation when they mature further (ages 35–70), and eventually retire to civic priesthood. Exclusion of the producing and distributing classes allows the citizens to dissociate their activities – and the very concept of activity itself (*praxis*, *eupraxia*) – from the pursuit of instrumental goods, enabling them to conceive a life devoted to intrinsically good leisure pursuits (*diagôgê en têi scholêi*) as an active life (*bios praktikos*). The educational system, with which Aristotle is particularly concerned, is designed to foster virtues that enable citizens to use their leisure well. Chief among these virtues is love of wisdom (*philosophia*). Because this education seems to be focused on music (*mousikê*) – the whole range of imaginative literature and performance attended by music in the literal sense – rather than on more abstract studies, some interpreters have been led to take "*philosophia*" broadly and to ascribe to Aristotle an intention to offer music as a political analogue of, and substitute for, contemplation proper, which they presume to be politically inaccessible even in a best regime.[2] I agree that "*philosophia*" should be taken broadly. But I do not think that music *substitutes* for contemplation in the political sphere. I argue that contemplation is conceived as an intensification of the learning (*mathêsis*) that goes on in music; that in the best regime theoretical pursuits will be continuous with, and to some extent will emerge naturally from, musical pursuits; and that contemplation will be regarded as the highest pursuit even by those citizens who are themselves incapable of engaging in it, by virtue of the practical wisdom (*phronêsis*) they can all be expected to have.

Aristotle's portrait of an ideal aristocracy differs markedly from Plato's ideal regimes. Seen in this light, *Pol.* VII–VIII is intended to avoid the mistakes in the *Republic* and the *Laws* that Aristotle identifies in *Pol.* II. At the heart of Aristotle's objections to Plato is his contention that the latter thinks of good politics as something like "applied contemplation" (*theôria*). For Aristotle, on the contrary, practical reason (together with practice-oriented reflection on practical matters) is entirely adequate for politics; and the value of purely contemplative wisdom does not depend on or increase with any instrumental or practical purposes it might serve. Practical reason itself recognizes this. If contemplation is valued instrumentally, as Aristotle thinks it is in Plato's ideal states, citizens will be unable to discriminate adequately

---

2 Friedrich Solmsen, "Leisure and Play in Aristotle's Ideal State," *Rheinisches Museum*, 107 (1964), pp. 193–220, reprinted in Solmsen, *Kleine Schriften II* (Hildesheim, 1968), pp. 1–28 (all references are to the latter text); Carnes Lord, "Politics and Philosophy in Aristotle's *Politics*," *Hermes*, 106 (1978), pp. 336–57, and *Education and Culture in the Political Thought of Aristotle* (Ithaca, 1982); P. A. Vander Waerdt, "Kingship and Philosophy in Aristotle's Best Regime," *Phronesis*, 30 (1985), pp. 249–73.

between intrinsic and instrumental goods. Such a state cannot be ideal. In the third part of the essay I show why Aristotle thinks that this is Plato's crucial mistake, and why misinterpretations of *Pol.* VII–VIII commonly rest on tacit regression to Platonic assumptions about the relation between theory and practice.

1   AN INCLUSIVE ENDS INTERPRETATION OF POLITICS VII.1-3

Aristotle clearly intends the first three chapters of *Pol.* VII to set out principles in accord with which he can lay down specifications for a best state (VII.4.1325b33–4). His strategy is to apply what has been learned elsewhere, especially in the *Ethics*,[3] about individual happiness to the parallel question of the happiness of states (VII.1.1323a14–23, 1323b37–1324a5; 13.1332a7–10). Accordingly, Aristotle brings over from the *Ethics* the following threefold conceptual analysis of the components of happiness (*eudaimonia*):

The virtue component: A choiceworthy life – a life that, barring great misfortune, can be expected to be happy – must be focused on cultivating virtue for its own sake. (VII.1.1323a27–b12,b40–1324a1,13.1332a9–19; see *EE* II.1.1219 a26–8; *EN* I.7.1097b17–18, 8.1098b30–32)

The activity component: Happiness requires activity (in accord with virtue) over a lifetime. (VII.1.1323b22–33, b40–1324a2; see *EE* II.1.11219b1–12; *EN* I.7. 1097b18–20, 8.1098b32–1099a7)

The instrumental goods component: In a happy life, goods of the body [e.g. health and beauty] as well as external goods [e.g. wealth, property, power, reputation and friends] are necessary conditions, but not constituents. These goods are to be acquired and used pursuant to the purposes of, and in amounts required by, activity in accord with virtue. (VII.1.1323a24–7, 1323a39–b21, 13.1332 a19–34; see *EE* II.1.1219b2–4, VIII.3.1248b26–38, 1249a22–b25; *EN* I.8.1099 a31–b8)

The argument of *Pol.* VII.1–3 is centered on the fact that two ways of life (*bioi*) seem sufficiently conformable to this analysis to be candidates for the

---

3 Aristotle's references in *Pol.* VII–VIII to the *Ethics* probably are to the *Eudemian Ethics*, for reasons first suggested by J. Bendixon, *Philologus*, 10 (1856), p. 575, and developed in detail by Werner Jaeger, *Aristotle: Fundamentals of the History of His Development*, 2nd edn, tr. R. Robinson (Oxford, 1948), pp. 282, 284, n. 2. Jaeger's work is outdated in numerous respects, but not in this (even though he is quite wrong to assimilate the *EE* to the earlier, Platonizing *Protrepticus*). For this reason, I refer as often as possible in the text to *EE* rather than to *EN*. Nonetheless, I provide many references to *EN* as well, particularly to the so-called "common books" (IV–VI) shared by both *EE* and *EN*. The reader should, however, continuously bear in mind the greater distance from *Pol.* VII–VIII of references taken from *EN*.

way of life of a happy state. These are the overtly "political and practical life"
of the statesman (the political life, *bios politikos*) and the "free" life devoted to
"speculations and thoughts" (the contemplative life, *bios theorêtikos*) (VII.2.
1324a25–34). Which should be the focus of an ideal state?

To resolve this question, Aristotle constructs a dialectical debate between
two extreme types – the conventionally political man, who is suspicious of
intellectuals, and the exclusively contemplative man, who is in turn contemptuous of the self-styled "man of action" (and whom I shall sometimes
call an "apolitical intellectual"). In adjudicating their dispute Aristotle
assures us that both sides have got hold of something relevant to the project
of reading individual into civic happiness. Defenders of the conventionally
political life are right to insist that a good life is an active one
(VII.3.1325a31–4; b12–15). But they are wrong in taking political life, and
hence activity and happiness, to be tied ineluctably to exercising power over
others (VII.3.1325a26–30, 37–b6). Defenders of the exclusively contemplative life are right in thinking of a happy life as free from debilitating
dependence on external goods, and on the wearisome task of securing and
deploying them, which the pursuit of power involves (VII.3.1325a24–7). In
what way, then, are these apolitical intellectuals wrong? They are wrong,
Aristotle says, in assuming that all ruling is domination (VII.3.1325a27–31)
and in taking their way of life to be best precisely on the ground that it is
inactive (*apraktos*) (VII.3.1325a31–2).

Aristotle's corrective to both sides is to insist that contemplation is an
activity, indeed the highest sort of activity:

> But if these things are argued rightly and happiness is to be regarded as acting
> well (*eupraxia*), the best way of life both in common for every city and for the
> individual would be the active one (*bios praktikos*). Yet the active life is not
> necessarily to be regarded as being in relation to others, as some suppose. Nor
> are those thoughts alone active that arise from activity for the sake of what
> results, but rather much more active are those that are complete in themselves
> (*autoteleis*), and the sorts of study and ways of thinking (*theôrias*) that are for
> their own sake. For acting well (*eupraxia*) is the end, so it too is a certain action
> (*praxis tis*); and even in the case of external actions, we speak of those who by
> means of their thoughts are master craftsmen as acting in the authoritative
> sense. Indeed, not even cities that are situated by themselves and intentionally
> choose to live in this way are necessarily inactive. For this [activity] can come
> about on the basis of [a city's] parts: there are many sorts of partnership that
> belong to the city in relation to one another. (VII.3.1325b13–26)[4]

It is tempting to take this to imply that contemplation (*theôria*, a term loosely
embracing a wide variety of purely theoretical virtues, including scientific

4 All references unless otherwise indicated are to the *Politics*. This and all extended
translations from the *Politics* are taken, sometimes with minor emendations, from
C. Lord, tr., *The Politics of Aristotle* (Chicago, 1984). My disagreement with Lord's
interpretation does not affect my admiration for his translation. Authors of extended
translations from other works of Aristotle are identified in the text.

knowledge [*epistêmê*], intellectual intuition [*nous*] and contemplative wisdom [*sophia*] [*EN* VI.3.1139b14–7.1141b8]) is to be the preferred activity of a best state, to which other activities are subordinated as means. If the life of the exclusively contemplative person is made politically normative, Aristotle seems to say, the best state will isolate itself, avoiding political relations with its neighbors, just as the apolitical intellectual avoids participation in public affairs. In this way the orientation to domination over other cities, as well as over one's fellow citizens, which seems to be endemic in political life, would be cut at the root.[5]

But there are difficulties with this view:

1 Aristotle nowhere concedes – indeed he flatly denies (VII.2.1324 b22–35, 3.1325a26–b11) – that politics necessarily implies domination, and that a good state must isolate itself. He says that a best state will incorporate everything for which we can wish or pray (II.6.1265a19, IV.11.1295a30, VII.3.1325b38), and that will include interactions with neighboring states whenever possible (II.6.1265a21–4, VII.6.1327 b5–7). In the long passage just quoted, moreover, the isolation of a best state seems to be conceded rather than ideal: *even if* such a state were isolated, Aristotle seems to say, rather than living a properly political life with its neighbors, it would *still* have internal political relations (see VII.2.1325a1–6).

2 Aristotle seems to deny that all the citizens of his best state will have a capacity for contemplation (VII.14.1333a24–5), even if he does say that their way of life is to be in some sense philosophical (VII.15.1334a23–4). An ideal state in which some citizens would be unable to participate in

---

5 The text of the *Politics* breaks off during a discussion of musical education. It is thus difficult to know whether Aristotle's specifications for musical education would have been, or in non-extant texts in fact was, followed by a discussion of mandatory training for contemplative virtues. Commentators who assert or imply that it was or would have been include J. Burnet, *Aristotle on Education* (Cambridge, 1903), pp. 134, and Ernest Barker, *The Politics of Aristotle* (Oxford, 1946), p. 352. W. L. Newman, in his great commentary, *The Politics of Aristotle* (Oxford, 1887–1902), is more cagey on the issue. At one point he says, "The direct education of the reason . . . will be directed to the development both of the practical and the contemplative reason, and will make the development of the latter its supreme end" (vol. III, p. xlv). This speculation tends to support the view that contemplation is a "dominant end" in Aristotle's ideal state. But he also says that *Politics* VII. 1–3 "represents the political and the contemplative lives as akin, both being rich in *kalai praxeis*," in contrast to *EN* X, which privileges contemplation (vol. I, p. 303; see Newman's interpretation of the argument of *Pol.* VII.1–3, vol. I, pp. 298–305). "Dominant end" readings of the role of contemplation in *Pol.* VII–VIII have invited criticism by Solmsen, "Leisure and Play in Aristotle's Ideal State," pp. 25–7, who points out that it is not clear that all the citizens are presumed capable of contemplative knowledge (VII.14.1333a28–30), and that we ought to infer as much from texts at hand as possible. What we can infer is that musical leisure activities are regarded as constitutive parts of the good life, rather than as instrumental to it or in subordinate to it in other ways. This already conflicts with views that make contemplation a "dominant end" in the ideal state.

the definitive good of the political community to which they belong would be very odd, particularly since in Aristotle's best state good citizens are coextensive with good persons (III.4.1277a1–5).

3 The passage quoted does not, in any case, say or imply that contemplation will be the exclusive or dominant activity in this state. Nor does it say that other pursuits are instrumental to contemplation. *It claims only that when the concept of action is properly understood, contemplation will be seen as having a more active character than instrumental activities.*

But even if these points are well taken we must still wonder how Aristotle can call contemplation an activity at all, or regard its cultivation as a kind of active or practical life. In ordinary discourse, which Aristotle usually takes as a guide to his work,[6] the contemplative and practical lives look too much like alternatives for this kind of definitional high-handedness. Aristotle himself says that the active life is the political life (VII.2.1324a40), and the political life is presumed throughout to be distinct from the life of contemplation. One way to blunt this difficulty would be to treat the instrumentally effective actions that flow from contemplation by way of applied or technical scientific expertise as the source of its practical or active character.[7] But this idea is directly contradicted by the text cited above, which claims that intrinsically good pursuits, even when unaccompanied by good effects, have a more active (*praktikos*) character than those that are in addition instrumentally valuable. Moreover, Aristotle does not in fact think that contemplation has instrumental value; or, if it does, that this increases its intrinsic worth. For God's contemplative activity paradigmatically defines this concept, and God has no instrumental activities at all (VII.1.1323b23–5, 3.1325b28–30).

6 Our understanding of Aristotle's philosophical method has been revolutionized by G. E. L. Owen's demonstration that the phenomena of which philosophical theories give accounts are, for the most part, the things people commonly and reputably say (*legomena, endoxa*). See G. E. L. Owen, "*Tithenai ta phainomena*," in S. Mansion, *Aristote et les problemes de methode* (Louvain, 1961), pp. 83–103, reprinted in J. Barnes *et al.*, *Articles on Aristotle* (London, 1975), pp. 113–26, and in G. E. L. Owen, *Logic, Science and Dialectic: Collected Papers in Greek Philosophy*, ed. M. Nussbaum (London, 1986), pp. 239–51. In M. Nussbaum, "Saving the Appearances," in M. Schofield and M. Nussbaum, *Language and Logos: Studies in Ancient Greek Philosophy in Honor of G. E. L. Owen*, (Cambridge, 1982), pp. 267–93, and in Nussbaum, *The Fragility of Goodness*, pp. 240–63, Nussbaum takes Owen's insight in a strongly pragmatic direction, according to which the point of philosophical theory is to introduce "wide reflective equilibrium" (Rawls) among our beliefs. This view does not, in my view, do sufficient justice to Aristotle's drive toward theoretical adequacy.

7 Jaeger writes, "Aristotle can combine the philosopher's ideal life with this view of the purpose of the state and society [as active] only by *representing* philosophic contemplation as itself a sort of *creative* 'action'. . . . [Aristotle] comes forward . . . to build a state in which this intellectual form of action may obtain recognition and become *effective* as the crown of all the human activities that *further* the common good" (*Aristotle*, p. 282). The words I have italicized suggest that activity retains for Jaeger too close a connection to instrumental value, since the presumption is left open that contemplation in itself is not activity, because it is not "effective."

Alternatively, it might be said that the active character of contemplation rests on an implicit invocation of Aristotle's metaphysics of *energeia*, which can forge a link between contemplation and action on non-instrumental grounds. Actions that are complete in themselves are actualizations (*energeiai*); and contemplation is the most perfect of actualizations.[8] This notion is probably intimated in the text at hand. But in the present context this metaphysical claim is premature. If the point of Aristotle's adjudication of the quarrel between the conventionally political man and the apolitical intellectual were merely to let the latter win by redefining the contemplative life as active just because intrinsically good activity (*eupraxia*) is actualization (*energeia*), the conventionally political man might fairly claim that the question has been begged. If the political man is genuinely *right*, as Aristotle says he is, in holding that the best life for states as well as individuals is an active life, the term activity (*praxis*) must mean something recognizably and genuinely active – and not just "actualization." At the very least, actualization would have to be defined and brought to bear on this issue concretely. Similarly, the exclusively contemplative man must be genuinely *wrong* in holding that the best life is inactive. There can be no objection to Aristotle backing up his substantive link between action and contemplation by a metaphysics showing that contemplation *can* be an activity *because* it is actualization. But the first-order connection must be made independently on the political level.

My own view is that in *Pol*. VII.1–3 Aristotle does not intend to privilege and politicize the contemplative life, or to redefine it stipulatively as an active life. Rather, he rejects the ways of life of both apolitical intellectuals and conventionally political men as models for the happy life of both the individual and of the best state. The claim that contemplation is an activity serves to cancel both extremes, and to construct a space in which political and contemplative engagements can fuse into a *sui generis* way of life, or rather into a pair of possible lives that have more in common with each other than either has with conventionally political or exclusively contemplative lives. Aristotle wants to demonstrate that *unless* contemplation is regarded as an activity by both contemplative and politically engaged persons, the intrinsically worthwhile, virtuous aspects of political life cannot be identified or pursued. Failure to acknowledge that contemplation is an activity will, on

---

8 On the distinction between *kinêsis* and *energeia* see J. L. Ackrill, "Aristotle's Distinction between *Energeia* and *Kinêsis*," in *New Essays on Plato and Aristotle* ed. R. Bambrough (London, 1965), pp. 121–41; but more recently and insightfully, L. A. Kosman, "Substance, Being and *Energeia*," *Oxford Studies in Ancient Philosophy*, 2 (1984), pp. 121–49. Following Kosman, an "*energeia* is the sort of thing which is perfected or completed in the very instant of its being enacted" (p. 124), and "the difference between *kinêsis* and *energeia* is the difference between a process or activity (in the broad sense) whose end and completion lies outside itself (in some other entity which it is devoted to bringing into being), and a process or activity whose end is nothing other than itself, which constitutes and contains its own ends, and is thus *enteleis* or perfect" (p. 127). Virtuous activity is, for Aristotle, an *energeia*.

this view, render both parties incapable of discerning and pursuing what is good in political life. Conversely, acknowledging this claim will reveal what contemplation and good political activity have in common (in contrast to merely instrumentally good activity) which makes them both worth pursuing for their own sake. Only when this point is appreciated, I suggest, will we be in a position clearly to see what conception of activity is presupposed in virtue of which Aristotle can, without trivialization or empty stipulation, call contemplation an activity, and why failure to acknowledge this proposition must prevent anyone from either speculating well about or approximating in practice a best or ideal state.

Note first that once it has been admitted that the contemplative life is *prima facie* a virtuous and happy way of life, the proposition that contemplation is a kind of activity is already formally entailed by the conjunction of two of the components into which Aristotle has analyzed happiness: the virtue component and the activity component. Anyone who admits that devotion to contemplation makes for a virtuously happy life (quite apart from the different question of who can live such a life, or to what extent), but who at the same time fails to acknowledge its active character must, accordingly, question either Aristotle's analysis of happiness, or his stipulation that individual happiness and the happiness of the state are parallel. (It is perhaps for this reason that at this point Aristotle interrupts the flow of his argument to justify this stipulation by a commonsense argument according to which "those who ascribe living well to wealth in the case of a single person also call the city as a whole blessed if it is wealthy," just as "those who honor the tyrannical way of life assert that the city is happiest which rules the greatest number of persons." Similarly, he concludes "if anyone accepts that the individual is happy on account of virtue he will also assert that the more virtuous city is the one that is happier" [VII.2.1324a5–13].) It follows from all these considerations that, even if we are unable at this stage fully to justify the proposition that contemplation is an activity, or even to know what that might mean, we are invited to inquire what effect failure to subscribe to this proposition might have on those wishing to speculate coherently about political ideals.

This inquiry can profitably begin by returning once more to the dialectic between the conventionally political man and his exclusively contemplative opponent to see more clearly what Aristotle thinks is right and wrong with each. Proponents of the exclusively contemplative life are explicitly apolitical. However, in their ideal of freedom from domination by external concerns, they do pick up an important element of an idea central to Aristotle's conception of the state – self-sufficiency or autonomy (*autarkeia*, I.2.1252b27–1253al). According to the powerful genetic account of *Pol.* I, a state can be distinguished from earlier forms of community, such as the family and the village, only when economic self-sufficiency is attained (I.2.1252b27–30, II.2.1261b14, III.1.1275b20–21, VII.5.1326b30). Under those conditions, political associates can cease implicitly assuming that the aim of their association is biological and economic reproduction – "mere life" – and can begin thinking of such reproduction as a means to living well (*eu zên*). To live well means to lack nothing essential to a good and happy life. That is what Aristotle means by self-sufficiency in the fullest sense, which he considers a mark of the happy life (*EE* VII.2.1238a11–13, *EN* I.7. 1097b7–21) and accordingly attributes to the gods, to philosophers, to (virtuous) friends – and to political life.[9] The political life considered from this perspective is self-sufficient precisely because, by its committed pursuit of intrinsically good things, it transcends the burdens, that is, the heteronomies and dependencies, imposed by the pursuit of necessary things. The autonomy of political life in this sense is closely connected to the availability and proper use of leisure. For leisure constitutes the contrast class to necessity, and Aristotle's analysis of the life of virtuous leisure in *Pol.* VIII is, as we shall see, a development of his discussion of self-sufficiency in *Pol.* I. We may see already, however, that self-sufficiency does not consist only in the *de facto* achievement of material plenty, but in a condition where the attitudes of political associates are no longer dominated or distorted by a means-oriented mentality – a mentality that, having inevitably arisen in a world of scarcity, can live on even in a world of great abundance, as it does in deviant states.

Important parts of this analysis are assumed by the exclusively contemplative man. He is unwilling to let his life be dominated by necessities, and he is accordingly as contemptuous of despotic masters as he is of slaves – both of whom, in his view, are caught up in a life of dependency. That is why the exclusively contemplative man, Aristotle says, sees his life as a free one (VII.3.1325a23–5). That is all to the good. The problem is that these apolitical intellectuals falsely believe that the ideal of self-sufficiency can be realized only by breaking with the political life that made such an ideal possible in the first place, arrogating to themselves the life of a god.

Why do they think this? One reason is that they are loathe to expose themselves to the contingencies that threaten social and political life. More to the point is the fact that in most actual states, self-sufficiency, as I have characterized it, will seldom have been attained, and then only fitfully. Many states will have only imperfectly emerged from the values of pre-political forms of community. Others, under the compulsion of difficulties and the defective governments they bring in train, will tend to regress toward despotic rule and devotion to mere life. In such states means are systematically confused with ends. Domination and war, or alternatively, indefinitely increased consumption and luxury, are seen as the essential point of holding and exercising power (VII.1.1323a35–7). Aristotle goes on at some length about the confusions to which people in such communities are prone (VII.2.1324a39–3.1325b11). He considers, for example, a person who proclaims the excellence and nobility of a despotic way of life on the ground that one who has absolute power always has the greatest number of occasions to do excellent deeds (VII.3.1325a34–40). This can be true, Aristotle says, only

9 For an analysis of self-sufficiency (*autarkeia*) along these lines and an enumeration of the things to which it is ascribed, see E. B. Cole, "*Autarkeia* in Aristotle," *University of Dayton Review*, 19 (1988), pp. 35–42.

for a person who fails to grasp the idea of excellent activity that he is invoking, which demands (in its virtue component) that we never sacrifice virtue for a gain in external goods (VII.3.1325b5–6), and (in its instrumental goods component) that we strictly tailor things and acts having only instrumental value, such as wealth or power, to intrinsically good purposes (VII.1.1323b7–10). There is no intrinsic value in having power over slaves (VII.3.1325a25), Aristotle says. Far less noble, therefore (indeed, positively evil) is having power over those who do not deserve by nature to be enslaved (VII.2.1324b22–40). Thus a despotic way of life can be exercised in many cases only by violating the very norms that the despot invokes to justify his way of life.

But this is not just the despot's problem. Even well-disposed politicians, living in reasonably good states, are constantly subject to these sorts of incoherences. For political life requires, by its very nature, acquisition and complex use of external goods. This being so, one may easily, if self-deceptively, come to regard these goods as one's end, and virtue as a means to acquiring them (VII.1.1323a35–b21, 13.1332a25–8). A utilitarian view of virtue such as this will be too weak actually to sustain a person's commitment to the virtue component of happiness, especially under duress or the influence of desire (*EE* VIII.3.1249a15–17).

No one is more likely to be as sensitive to these incoherences, or as repelled by them, as the exclusively contemplative person, since seen against the background of his ideal so much in the political world seems defective. He will not see much difference, therefore, between the case of the well-intended but weak political man and the despot. For his part, he would avoid both sorts of life as an impediment to happiness (VII.2.1324a36–8). But for this very reason no one is as likely as the exclusively contemplative person to fail to distinguish within the world of actual states cases that are better or more promising than others, let alone cases where the good life is genuinely prized over mere life. Instead, he may be tempted, not least because of the fact that his concerns enable him to reduce his own material needs to a minimum, to dismiss the political world as a whole and to refuse to acknowledge that it aims at or achieves any real excellence. But in so concluding, he, no less than the despot, will fail to distinguish political from pre-political life, and political rule from despotism (VII.3.1325a23–30). For to the extent that political life generally is thought to exclude intrinsic goods and to be bent toward the compulsions of mere life, the master–slave relation will be predicated of political life *as such*, where it can, through this very universalization, be rejected *in toto*.

Of even greater importance to us is the fact that the apolitical intellectual does not have any marked reason to identify his way of life as an active one. His interest is to defend it as free (VII.3.1325a21–4). Thus his dismissal of the political life identifies virtue, happiness and leisure exclusively with contemplation and fatally concedes the conventionally political man's conception of himself alone as leading an *active* life. He disputes only the latter's claim that "the man who does nothing attains no good" (VII.3.1325a22–3, 31–3). Friedrich Solmsen correctly describes this attitude when he writes that "in disgusted reaction to the injustice and subjugation of others held to be inevitable concomitants of political activity," the apolitical intellectual takes his own life to be gloriously impractical (VII.3.1325a31–2), thus identifying virtue, happiness and leisure with *inactivity*.[10] From Aristotle's perspective, the trouble with this reaction is that in his retreat from any conjunction of activity and genuine excellence, the apolitical intellectual leaves intact a defective conception of activity, which does not enable one to distinguish well between actions that are endlike and those that are at best instrumentally valuable. This bias toward an instrumental conception of activity, and away from intrinsically excellent action, reinforces the conventionally political man's tendency to regard external goods – wealth, money, power, reputation, etc. – as the end of politics, and to value the virtues only to the extent that they are useful in achieving this end (VII.1.1323a35–8). At the same time it leaves the apolitical intellectual himself incapable of acknowledging that "the actions of the just and the moderate are the realization of much that is noble" (VII.3.1325a33–4).

This situation renders *both* the apolitical intellectual *and* the conventionally political man incapable of giving an adequate account of political reality insofar as it corresponds to the analysis of *Pol.* I. For neither party will see the extent to which the acquisitive and despotical lives are antithetical to the political life properly construed (VII.2.1324a31–7, 3.1325a25–31). *A fortiori*, neither party will be in a position to think well about a best state. For we may characterize a best state as one in which the differences between mere life and good life, necessity and leisure, and domination and politics are most clearly drawn. In fact, in his retreat from politics, the apolitical intellectual may be in a worse position to make these discriminations than the conventionally practical man. For the latter *can* recognize that exercise of the moral virtues is "the realization of much that is noble." But the apolitical intellectual has foreclosed this possibility from the outset. At most, he may regard these virtues as (dubiously necessary) means to the contemplative life, in which case their exercise will not actually be a component of the happy life. If the conventionally political man is to be cured of his regressions towards greed and despotism, then, it will certainly be without the help of the exclusively contemplative person, whose prejudices assume that no such cure is possible.

Aristotle's reason for insisting that contemplation is activity now comes clearly into view. The impasse between the exclusively contemplative person and the conventionally political man can be overcome, he concludes, only if both parties acknowledge this proposition. This can be seen clearly if we represent the views just described in terms of the analysis of happiness Aristotle has imported into the *Politics* from the *Ethics*. For his part, the apolitical intellectual is strongly committed to the virtue component of this analysis. But he holds that if one's life is really focused on virtue, one will distance oneself from instrumental goods, and from the actions required to get and use them, as far as possible (VII.3.1325a24–6). The more instru-

10 Solmsen, "Leisure and Play in Aristotle's Ideal State," p. 3.

mental goods are required for engaging in a particular kind of life, he probably thinks, the more threatened is one's commitment to virtue for its own sake. A life devoted exclusively to contemplation minimizes this dependence on instrumentalities and creates a presumptively negative attitude even toward goods that are physically required (*EN* X.8.1178a24–5). The apolitical intellectual exhibits, then, an ambiguous attitude toward the instrumental goods component of Aristotle's analysis of happiness. He may admit in principle that such goods are necessary for the practice of virtue. But the plain fact is that instrumental goods are external goods and goods of the body, and, as such, are dependent on fortune's whims (VII.13. 332a31–2; *EN* I.8.1099a8). They thus create dependencies that threaten to compromise the intellectual's freedom and self-sufficiency. When confronted, therefore, with a commonly acknowledged virtue whose practice requires a significant measure of these goods, he would sooner disqualify the proposed practice as virtuous than countenance the requisite goods and the acts required to procure them (see II.5.1263b6–12). Since the virtues and practices most obviously threatened in this way are connected with the socio-political or active life, the apolitical intellectual's admitted indifference to an active self-conception leads him to define happiness and virtue in terms of an *absence* of activity. He thus in effect denies the activity component of Aristotle's analysis of happiness and so disqualifies himself, in Aristotle's view, from adequately considering the nature of the best and happiest state. For the instrumentalist conception of activity with which he is left makes it impossible for him fully to grasp and wield the distinction between despotical and political life, and to see the latter as inherently valuable.

One who takes the contemplative life to be devoted to intrinsic goods must, therefore, acknowledge the active nature of that life unless he is prepared to deny that happiness is activity of the soul in accord with virtue, and in so doing forfeit the use of concepts necessary for thinking coherently about politics. But when one who prizes contemplation for its own sake does construe it as excellent activity, he will also be able to see that noble political practice is more like contemplation than good politics is like instrumental activity. For both contemplation and the performance of excellent acts in the moral and political sphere are engaged in for their own sake. The lover of contemplation thereby distinguishes genuine from distorted politics (rather than distinguishing politics generally from contemplation) and so avoids the mistake of the apolitical intellectual, who "considers every sort of rule as a kind of mastery" (VII.3.1325a27–30).

The conventionally political man's problems are a mirror image of his contemplative counterpart's. He does well to affirm the activity and instrumental goods components of Aristotle's analysis (VII.3.1325a23). But his conception of the virtue component, even when he fully intends to praise a life devoted to the various excellences, excludes contemplative virtues on the ground that "he who does nothing does nothing well" (VII.3.1325a22). That is, the conventionally political man – perhaps noting the intellectual's own dissociation from the active life – concludes that the latter is not living a virtuous or happy life at all, since such a life consists of excellent actions. But this judgment leaves the conventionally political man with an inadequate and incomplete conception of virtue. This has important consequences. Those who pursue an exclusively political life typically mistake means for ends, treating virtue as an instrumental good useful for acquiring external goods such as power, money, and reputation, which they regard as ends. Contemplation, precisely because its value does not increase with the addition of instrumental value, and because its adepts have a strictly functional attitude toward necessities, is far less subject to this confusion. Thus if one construes contemplation as antithetical to the active life, and if one's conception of virtue does not extend to the contemplative virtues, one must become insensitive to the distinction between the inherently and the instrumentally good, on which in turn rests the distinction between mere life and political life, and thus one's ability to reflect coherently on a best state. If, however, a self-defined man of action accedes to the proposition that contemplation is an activity, even if it has no utilitarian worth – indeed precisely *because* it does not – his conception of excellent activity will enable him to distinguish well between inherently good and instrumental aspects of politics, and *a fortiori* between the latter and the values of the despot.

This puts the matter psychologically and prudentially. But Aristotle means to make the point a conceptual and normative one. In the *Eudemian Ethics* he says:

> The majority of those engaged in politics are not correctly designated politicians, since they are not truly political. For the political man is one who purposely chooses noble actions for their own sake, whereas the majority embrace the political life for the sake of money or excess. (I.5.1216a23–7, trans. Rackham)

The lesson of the present argument in the *Politics* is the same. A person will count as genuinely political only if he regards both kinds of virtue as connected to happiness through noble activity done for its own sake. This analysis does not, it is important to note, depend on the degree to which the genuinely political person is himself able to participate in contemplative activity. It is sufficient that he love learning for its own sake, pursue it as far as possible, and honor those whose learning penetrates further than his own. At the same time, an appreciation of genuine political life, so understood, requires that one whose own way of life is centered on contemplation own his political identity and the political context within which his leisured way of life arises. He must reject the apolitical intellectual's view that political life is, *as such*, an impediment to happiness and his contention that apolitical intellectualism is the "only philosophical way of life" (VII.2.1324a29). The civic life which the genuinely political person and the politically open intellectual jointly share can itself, then, be called "philosophical" with some justice. For when the *soi-disant* activist is open to contemplation, and the intellectual to political engagement, learning and contemplation can be pursued vigorously within the framework of a social life devoted to all forms of intrinsically worthwhile activities, and contemptuous of an overestimation of the merely instrumental, rather than of the political as such. The received distinction between the contemplative and political lives is not rendered void by this analysis. It is, however, reconceived in such a way that the latter is not the only kind of active life (VII.3.1325b17–21), and the former is not the only kind of philosophical life (VII.2.1324a29). The two lives arise within a common framework and diverge only as a function of each citizen trying to realize his own highest capabilities (VII.14.1333a29–30). Under these conditions, it would be jejune to ask why a person who shows contemplative ability should pay lip service to politics, since it plays no role in his actual life, or, for the same reason, why the practical man should honor contemplation. Recognizing that the excluded value does not form part of one's own happiness, and therefore one's self-interest, is relevant only when a narrow conception of self-interest is assumed. Such a conception unwittingly reveals that those asking such questions do not yet possess an adequate conception of happiness and its analytical components to pose the proper questions.

We are now in a position to see more clearly what conception of activity is presupposed by Aristotle's claim that "contemplation is an activity." When Aristotle says that "Much more active [than instrumentally good thoughts] are those thoughts . . . that are for their own sake" and that "even in the case of external actions we speak of those who by means of their thoughts are master craftsmen as acting in an authoritative sense" (VII.3.1325b17–23), he is asserting that activity is most properly predicated of pursuits that do not share in the dependency, heteronomy (the opposite of self-sufficiency, *autarkeia*) and hence passivity (the oppositive of activity) that attend merely instrumental and necessary things, persons or behaviors. Of these, activity is predicated only imperfectly and derivatively, whereas it is properly said of the practice of the moral and intellectual virtues. But while both political and contemplative pursuits are fully active by this measure, contemplation appears more paradigmatic of activity than does political engagement. It is less entangled with instrumentality, and hence potential dependency and inactivity, than are even the best political actions (*EN* X.8.1178a24–b8). That is why God's exclusively contemplative life is mentioned in this context as exemplary for life in the best state. God is perfectly happy, perfectly contemplative, perfectly active – and totally devoid of any external actions that must be performed as conditions of his proper activity or that flow from it (VII.1.1323b21–9, 3.1325b27–31). This is untrue of humans, whose proper activities depend on many such things. Nonetheless, God's life is a proper model for us. For it suggests that we should use the performance of intrinsically good actions, of which contemplation is the highest, as a measure of the natural and external goods that are necessary conditions for our own excellent activity, given the constraints of our compound nature (*EE* VIII.3.1249b17–23).[11]

---

11 At the end of *EE* Aristotle writes: "Whatever choice and possession of things good by nature will most produce the contemplation of God – whether goods of the body, or money, or friends, or other goods – this is best, and the finest principle of

This conception of the happy life falls within the range of those that in recent years have been called "inclusive ends" interpretations of Aristotelian happiness. On this view, now ascendant among scholars, Aristotelian happiness, at least in most of its formulations, countenances a lifetime of excellent activity in both the political–moral and contemplative spheres. There is a preference for contemplation, for those capable of it (VII.14. 1333a27–30), but no implication that this ranking reduces the moral virtues to mere means for contemplative activity, nor any implication that those who lack contemplative ability cannot be genuinely happy. As such, "inclusivism" contrasts with "strict intellectualism," both in a radical form, where the truly happy, contemplative person regards himself as altogether free from social obligations, and in a weaker, more plausible version, according to which moral duties are necessary conditions for, but not proper parts of, happiness.[12] Inclusivism itself has weaker and stronger versions. The weaker version is a view in which happiness is considered merely the additive sum of goods commonly regarded as constituents of the happy life, with no strong ordering principle among them. Since this countenances the unconstrained trading off of one good to realize another, it has been called the "trade-off

---

determination" (tr. Cooper). Jaeger, *Aristotle*, pp. 239–43, used this text to support his contention that the *EE* (allegedly following the *Protrepticus*) has an intellectualist or Platonic view of the good life. Cooper, *Reason and Human Good in Aristotle*, pp. 136–9, has shown that this is a false reading. The text does not privilege the contemplative over the political life, but gives a measure for valuing natural and external goods. The same principle for prizing and allocating external and natural goods appears in *Pol.* VII.1–3. On my reading it means: only by openness to contemplation can one have a proper measure of external goods, that is, use them as instruments of virtuous action rather than using virtue as an instrument to gain external goods. That such choices take into account our compound nature is implicit in Aristotle's claim in the same context that we should regard God's totally leisured, contemplative life as our exemplar, even though, being men and not gods, we are to practice the moral as well as the intellectual virtues (VII.I.1323b21–6). At VII.3.1325b28–31, moreover, Aristotle is not out to defend the view that contemplation is the only true excellence, but that it is both an excellence and an activity. Thus the view that the best state is to live an isolated life exclusively or dominantly devoted to contemplation does not receive support from the texts in which God's life is mentioned as an exemplar.

12 "Strict intellectualism" is often called a "dominant end" interpretation of Aristotelian happiness, because in recognizing the superior value of contemplation it puts at risk the value of the moral–political virtues and their practice as *constituents* of happiness. The focal text is *EN* X.7.1177a12–19, where it appears that the happy life *as such* is a contemplative one, and that the moral–political life is reduced to a "second-best" sort of happiness (X.7.1178a6–9). This view seems to imply either that the moral–political virtues are necessary means (for some obscure reason) to the contemplative life or that they may be dispensed with by the contemplative person. That is why intellectualism has usually been seen more as a problem into which Aristotle stumbles in *EN* X than his considered view. For a review of the issue, see Cooper, *Reason and Human Good in Aristotle*, pp. 148–54, especially nn. 5–10; and Ackrill, "Aristotle on *Eudaimonia*." Strict intellectualism, however, has been looked upon as Aristotle's positive ideal, come what may, by Richard Kraut, *Aristotle on the Human Good* (Princeton, 1989).

view."[13] A stronger sort of inclusivism asserts that the contemplative virtues serve as an ordering principle, according to which contemplation is to be pursued as vigorously as possible within the bounds of social obligations, which must be met first. "Moral virtue comes first," writes John Cooper, an advocate of this view. "But once moral virtue is securely entrenched intellectual goods are allowed to predominate." This has been called the "superstructure view."[14] This interpretation rightly forbids unconstrained trade-offs between the moral and the intellectual virtues. But, in several of its formulations, this account has the disadvantage of suggesting that practice of the moral or social virtues is a constraint on time that would be better spent contemplating. It has about it an air of annoying, but manageable, tension in how citizens are to allocate their time and energy among competing goods. This may be a genuine problem. But it cannot be properly resolved unless we appreciate first the degree to which Aristotle thinks that good politics and contemplative activity are mutually supportive, indeed mutually entailing, and until we are acquainted fully with the constitutional conditions under which any tension between them is minimized, that is, the conditions of an ideal aristocracy.[15]

13 Keyt dubs this "the trade-off view" in "Intellectualism in Aristotle." In these terms, Ackrill, "Aristotle on *Eudaimonia*," Nussbaum, *The Fragility of Goodness*, p. 375, and Roche, "*Ergon* and *Eudaimonia* in *Nicomachean Ethics* 1," pp. 175–94, appear to me to subscribe to this account.

14 Cooper, *Reason and Human Good in Aristotle*, p. 143. Keyt calls this view "superstructuralist" in "Intellectualism in Aristotle" because the contemplative virtues arise on a base of moral and political virtues. "Complete virtue" on this account involves an ordering principle in which contemplation is intrinsically higher than moral–political virtues, but the latter remain basic constituents of happiness. This results in "moderate intellectualism." Keyt fits this pattern, as well as Cooper, pp. 142–3, and Irwin, *Aristotle's First Principles*, pp. 616–7, n. 24. "The moral life," Keyt writes, "sets certain minimum requirements that must be satisfied before one is to engage in theoretical activity" (p. 370).

15 Can *EN* X.7 be accommodated to "superstructuralism," or is this text an exception to the inclusivist view of *EE* VIII.3 and *Pol.* VII.1–3? Cooper, *Reason and Human Good in Aristotle*, pp. 155–77, thinks it is incontestably and unfortunately strict intellectualist. Nussbaum, *The Fragility of Goodness*, pp. 375–7, and Anthony Kenny, *The Aristotelian Ethics* (Oxford, 1978), agree. Kenny is so scandalized by *EN* X.7 that he implausibly argues that most of it predates the *EE*; and Nussbaum simply regards Aristotle (with no evidence) as having noted this Platonic view in *EN* X.7 without strongly sponsoring it. Keyt, "Intellectualism in Aristotle," was the first to argue that *EN* X.7 is itself a version of "superstructuralist" inclusivism. Cooper has since retreated from his original view and argued that *EN* X.7 fits this pattern, although on different grounds than Keyt offers. See J. Cooper, "Contemplation and Happiness: a Reconsideration," *Synthese*, 72 (1987), pp. 187–216. My own view is that an ordering principle in which other good things *cannot* be intended or achieved *as* intrinsic goods unless contemplation is regarded as the highest of all goods – a view I see in *EE* VIII.3 and *Pol.* VII.1–3 – should make it easier to accommodate *EN* X.7 to some sort of inclusive ends interpretation than any conception in which contemplation is merely "added" as a culminating perfection to other virtues, as it seems to be for Cooper and Keyt, or *a fortiori* is merely an item on an unordered list of goods.

2   LEISURE, MUSIC, AND PHILOSOPHY IN ARISTOTLE'S IDEAL ARISTOCRACY

Confirmation of this interpretation of *Pol.* VII.1–3 comes from the fit between this account and the constitutional structure of the aristocracy Aristotle actually describes in the remainder of *Pol.* VII–VIII. Aristotle argues there that the norms set down in *Pol.* VII.1–3 are best embodied in a state whose way of life centers on the cultivation and exercise of the virtues proper to leisure activity, especially love of wisdom (*philosophia*) (VII.15. 1334a11–40.) If this is to be achieved, he says, the citizens must be able to take full advantage of the goods and services provided by the productive and commercial classes, while at the same time these unleisured classes are excluded from citizenship. Further, a best state must possess an educational system designed to enable its citizens to be "capable of using good things . . . in leisure" (VII.15.1334a37–8). In this section I review Aristotle's arguments for these two claims, showing how they affirm and apply the principles laid down in *Pol.* VII.1–3. I go on to suggest what these arguments imply about the relation between music and contemplation in Aristotle's ideal state, a topic that has invited conflicting views.

Aristotle begins by considering what material conditions must be presupposed (VII.4.1325b36) if a best city is to be realized (*Pol.* VII.4–7). Every state must have, or have access to, farmers to grow food, craftsmen to provide implements and weapons, and agents of both internal and external trade (VII.8.1328b6–22). Since this is to be a happy state, it must be amply provided with the material goods that enable its citizens to live well – with liberality (*eleutheriôs*), but moderately (*sôphronôs*) (VII.5.1326b33). A state living on the ragged edge of material sufficiency may look adequate to the exclusively contemplative man, whose material needs are minimal. But the fact is that this condition will generate a state always threatening to regress into a vulgar and debilitating concern with basic necessities. To prevent this, the best state must be well situated and physically well endowed so that it can produce an agricultural surplus on the private (and public) farms (VII.9.1329a19–22, 10.1330a9–13), worked by imported slaves or indigenous barbarians (VII.9.1329a25–6), which constitute the foundation of its economy. But Aristotle does not think this will suffice. A well-provisioned state must rely on imports of items it cannot itself produce (VII.6.1327 a26–9). But here we reach a problem troublesome to all aristocratic political theories. Experience suggests that an extensive supply of commodities can be acquired only by pursuing an energetic imperialistic policy, or by taking in the benefits of trade by giving free rein to the commercial classes, or by a combination of both (VII.6.1327a29–32). Pursuit of the second course will, however, shift influence in the city to people whose values, concerned as they are with external goods, are hopelessly instrumental, generating a state that cannot in principle be happy; while pursuit of the first course will tilt civic consciousness toward despotism, and will so increase the prestige of instrumental goods, especially power, that political men will come to regard domination of others as the end of the state (VII.2.1324b23–25a15). A combination of commercialism and militarism will be especially deadly. How, then, can the socio-economic substructure for a genuinely excellent state be institutionalized in a way that allows both for generous provisioning and the pursuit of intrinsically good values?

Aristotle's solution is to leave craftsmanship and commerce in the hands of foreign-born residents (*metoikoi, xenoi*), who are to dwell at a port some distance from the city proper (VII.6.1327a16–39) and who are to interact with the citizens only in a specially designed commercial meeting place, under the strict control of magistrates (VII.6.1327a37–9, 12.1331b1–4). Since these classes lead a life inescapably focused on the unleisured (*ascholia* = [lat.] *neg-otium* = [eng.] busy-ness) production, exchange and consumption of instrumental goods, they cannot share in the life of a city devoted to the pursuit of the intrinsic goods of leisure. Accordingly, they are to be totally excluded from citizenship (VII.9.1328b33–29a2, 29a19–20, 35–9). This would be unjust if this population were composed of free born natives. For just claims on citizenship derive from free birth, as well as from wealth and virtue (III.12.1283a14–22).[16] But Aristotle is envisioning a city which, whether by chance or providence, embodies "everything for which we might wish and pray" (II.6.1265a19, VII.3.1325b37, 13.1332a29–35) and so feels free to imagine a situation in which such claims are neither valid nor pressed. This solution presupposes that, like the goods they produce and procure, these craftsmen, merchants and laborers are – and are perceived by the citizens as – merely necessary conditions for the citizens' own activities, just as slaves are necessary conditions for the activities of the free members of a household (VII.8.1328a22–36, 9.1328b34–1329a2, 35–9).

This exclusion has an important consequence in applying the principles of *Pol.* VII.1–3. The citizens' perception that farmers, craftsmen and merchants are analogous to domestic slaves will intensify when such persons have no claim on citizenship. For this similarity, undamped by any need to recognize these persons as fellow citizens, will reinforce the contempt in which the citizens hold these persons and their utilitarian tasks and values. This perception will incline the citizens, as a point of aristocratic pride, to favor values and practices differing as far as possible from those of the vulgar. Overt dissociation – physical, psychological and political – of the citizens from craftsmen, merchants and laborers is, therefore, an indispensable condition under which the pursuit of the intrinsically good activities of leisure can be set afoot. For the citizens of Aristotle's best state will then be led consciously to contrast their own way of life with the busy, unleisured lives of the other classes. It follows that:

> the citizens should not live a vulgar or a merchant's way of life, for this sort of life is ignoble and contrary to virtue; nor should those who are citizens be farmers, for there is a need for leisure both with a view to virtue and with a view to political activities. (VII.9.1328b38–29a2)

---

16 *Pol.* III.9.1281a3–7, 13.1283a23–42. See David Keyt, "Aristotle's Theory of Distributive Justice," essay 11 in this volume.

Under these conditions, Aristotle does not fear to vest political power in the hands of property-owners who rule and are ruled in turn (VII.9. 1329a3–9, 14.1332b25–7.) Whatever tendencies such men might have to turn power and wealth into ends, or to regard virtue in a utilitarian light, can be countered through an educational system that reinforces the contempt for vulgar, instrumentalist values built into the fundamental structure of social experience itself. Under these conditions, those who bear arms can be entrusted with property ownership and later the full citizenship of office-holding. This will not leave the state vulnerable to revolt by honor-cherishing, but imprudent, youths (as Plato had feared). For these young citizens, whose virtues will have been developed as soldiers, can expect to hold political offices when their deliberative ability and practical wisdom will have begun to develop (VII.9.1329a12–22, 14.1332b25–40); and the same men, having internalized and protected the values of their city throughout their adult lives, will fittingly honor and symbolize those same values by serving as priests in old age (VII.9.1329a26–34). Aristotle regards this as the most natural form of the rule (by rotation) of equal over equal (VII.9.1329a15–16).

The most important function of the legislator, therefore, is to design legal and educational institutions that capitalize on the city's natural advantages, especially its exclusion of the working classes from citizenship, to produce a fully excellent way of life (VII.14.1334a2–6, VIII.3.1337b31–5). As Aristotle's remarks about natural rotational rule suggest, the value system inculcated by these legal and educational institutions is to be based on invariant principles of social and psychological development, which he has analyzed in detail in other treatises and now quickly reviews. Lower capacities, he reminds us, emerge earlier in psychological development, no less than in physical, and they exist for the sake of later, higher capacities (VII.14.1333a21–3). Thus the emotional parts of the soul develop before the rational parts, and are less choiceworthy than the latter. Similarly the part of the rational soul that gives orders to the emotional part is less choiceworthy than contemplative reason – at least for those capable of both (VII.14. 1333a16–30). Aristotle goes on to say that this psychic hierarchy is to be mirrored in the structure of social activity, according to which "war is for the sake of peace, occupation for the sake of leisure, and necessary and useful things for the sake of noble things" (VII.14.1333a33–6). The point of this important remark is that the necessary and utilitarian will prevail over the noble, as emotion will prevail over reason, unless peace is truly preferred to war; and war will indeed prevail over peace unless leisure, and the rationally virtuous practices that flourish in it, including contemplative knowledge, are preferred to all forms of occupation (*ascholia*), especially war-oriented politics and the consumer-ethic with which it is frequently and fatally linked. A legislator must above all else see that these principles inform the best constitution (VII.14.1333a37–40).

To the theoretical rationale that grounds this value system Aristotle adds a cautionary empirical tale (VII.14.1333b5–34a10). When legislators violate this hierarchy, they produce unstable and unhappy regimes. Even the legislator of the Spartans, he says, "who are commonly thought to be the best governed of the Greeks," lacked wisdom. For "he legislated everything with a view to domination and war." But the Spartans, having now lost their empire, are unhappy because "states of this sort preserve themselves only when they are warring; and when they remain at peace, they lose their edge, like iron . . . because their legislator did not educate them to be capable of being at leisure." It is relatively easy, Aristotle explains, to be virtuous under conditions of danger and duress, such as the Spartan life invites and requires, for "war compels men to be just and to behave with moderation." But when danger is past, those possessing only virtues useful in times of stress fail, "for the enjoyment of good fortune and leisure in peacetime tends to make them arrogant" (VII.15.1334a25–7). "But it is disgraceful not to be capable of using good things, and still more so to be incapable of using them in leisure, but to be seen as good men only while occupied and at war, and servile when remaining at peace and being at leisure" (VII.15.1334a36–9). For the virtues exercised under duress "have their nobility only in a necessary way, and it would be more choiceworthy if no man or city required anything of the sort" (VII.13.1332a12–15). But the virtues that enable citizens to make good use of their leisure "are noble in an unqualified way" (VII.13.1332a16–17). Happy states and their citizens will, therefore, "be most in need of love of wisdom (*philosophia*), as well as of moderation and justice, to the extent that they are at leisure in the midst of an abundance of good things" (VII.15.1334a32–4).

These arguments lead Aristotle to conclude that the natural hierarchy of psychic powers can be preserved, developed and exercised only in a state that prizes the correct employment of leisure as its highest good, and rank orders the virtues in a way that fosters precisely this goal. Leisure emerges with the increasing economic self-sufficiency of cities (I.2.1252b28–30), and comes, we may presume, to be increasingly prized. But it doesn't follow from this that every person or state conceives of leisure in the same way, or that all such conceptions are equally valuable. Indeed, only in a best state will that particular conception of leisure obtain which fully conforms to the requirements just reviewed, according to which leisure-time provides an occasion for activities in and through which the highest capacities and virtues are exercised – and in which, accordingly, leisure itself is conceived as activity.[17]

This certainly cannot be the conception of leisure that obtains in deviant constitutions or barbarian regimes. For these bear the scars of pre-political forms of association by adopting a view of leisure as passive enjoyment and freedom from work. Leisure is reserved for a ruling class that uses its power to deflect work onto others, reserving consumption and enjoyment for itself.

---

17 The distinction between a single, invariant *concept* and differing *conceptions* of it is derived from John Rawls and H. L. A. Hart. But Hart found it in Aristotle. For example, *EN* I discusses various conceptions of the concept of happiness: "The many, the most vulgar, seemingly conceive the good and happiness as pleasure. . . . Cultivated people, those active [in politics], conceive the good as honor" (*EN* I.5.1095b15–33, tr. Irwin).

Activity is construed as work, and the good life therefore as enjoyable inactivity. The world-view of such states focuses on the never-ceasing systole and diastole of production and consumption. This consumption-oriented and pleasure-loving way of life can be best observed in the way of life followed by the rulers of Asian cities, which, due to defects in human material, have never fully emerged from a conflation of economic with political life, and from a confusion between despotism and political rule properly so-called. But this ideal, in the form of the apolaustic life, or the life of enjoyment, also exercises a deleterious influence on Greek men and cities, which, for Aristotle, are by nature and circumstance capable of transcending these confusions, and are reprehensible when they do not (*EN* I.5.1095b19–21).

In contrast to the passive ideal of vulgar cities, it would at first sight seem that the possibility of correlating leisure with excellent activity occurs in dominantly military states, whose representative men self-consciously distance themselves from the values of the vulgar. Persons and cities of this sort can recognize that the biosocial function of leisure, construed as enjoyment, is to provide the rest (*anapausis*) that follows the exhaustion of effort and makes renewed activity possible (VIII.3.1337b36–38a2). They can also recognize that this cycle of work and relaxation, and the persons whose lives it dominates, is instrumental as a whole, and that this cycle is embedded within and subordinated to a higher cycle that alternates between peace and war (VII.14.1333a31–2). But, although timocratic cities do contemptuously reject the apolaustic life, they are likely to find their own paradigms of virtuous activity within the war-oriented phase of this higher cycle, since war provides the occasion for the exercise of the excellences such men value most. This gives rise to the problem to which Aristotle refers in his discussion of Sparta. The virtues practiced in such cities are not fully noble or active, since they are exercised under duress (VII.13.1332a1–19), and in times of peace there is a threat that degeneration toward laxity will set in (VII.15.1334 a34–b3). For since activity is correlated in such cities with war, and the virtues useful for peacetime are not well cultivated, the conception of leisure that becomes current will be borrowed, for the most part, from the passive pleasure ethic of the vulgar. Under such conditions, rulers can easily construe the blandishments of consumption and enjoyment as threats to the cultivation and exercise of excellence, and can therefore regard war as an antidote to the unfortunate effects of a lax peace. A conventionally political, militarily oriented city comes perilously close, therefore, to denying the self-evident principle that "war is for the sake of peace, as work is for the sake of leisure" (VII.14.1333a35–7). It tacitly assumes that where leisure is left to the whims of spontaneity, it will soon degenerate into frivolity and inactivity (VII.14.1334a6–10). Aristotle senses this underlying tension in Plato, who seeks, as I will show later, to repress it rather than transcend it. Aristotle's own aim is to break out of this dialectic altogether. Thus his citizens are to be educated "not only to be occupied in a correct fashion (*ascholein orthôs*) but also to be capable of being at leisure in a noble fashion (*scholazein dunasthai kalôs*). For this is the beginning point of everything – if we may speak of this once again" (VIII.3.1337b31–3).

This remark occurs, significantly enough, at the outset of Aristotle's extended discussion of music. Aristotle lists three possible social functions for music: amusement or play (*paidia*); character formation (*ethikê, paideia*); and leisure processes (*diagôgê en têi scholêi*) (VIII.5.1339a16–27, 1339b14, VIII.3. 1337b29). (Later, he adds a reference to "catharsis" to these "uses" or functions of music: VIII.7.1341b39). It is tempting to correlate these three functions with the different conceptions of leisure prevailing in different sorts of cities. In most states, where leisure is construed as rest from labor, the dominant function of music is play or entertainment (*paidia*) (VIII.3. 1337b29–42, 5.1339b32–3). Aristotle criticizes this as more appropriate to children than to adults, except in legitimate subordinate roles (VIII.3. 1337b35–38a2). In conventionally political cities, where leisure is construed as peace between wars, music is dominantly oriented toward character formation (VIII.5.1339a41–b4). It is, however, a mistake, Aristotle says, to think of this as the highest function of music (as Plato did). For this too is an instrumental role, whereas, he assures us, "those who in earlier times arranged that music would be in education did so not as something necessary, for it involves nothing of the sort, nor as something useful . . . but for the pastime that is in leisure (*diagôgê en têi scholêi*) . . . of free persons" (VIII.3.1338a13–23). In explanation of this conception Aristotle refers to a passage from Homer in which Odysseus, reclining after many trials in the banquet hall of Alcinoos, suggests that feasting, listening to bardic tales, remembering, reflecting and conversing are the "most gracious end (*telos chariesteron*)" and the "very best (*kalliston*)" of the good things in life (VIII.3.1338a23–31). The point is that music, considered as an end (*telos*) rather than a means, is partially constitutive of the good life itself, and that it is incumbent on the legislator of the best constitution to ensure that the citizens can engage in it, and in related leisure activities, in precisely this way.[18]

Aristotle refers positively to dithyrambs and other choral and instrumental forms (VIII.5.1340a8–14, 6.1341a14–24); provides "theatrical music" for both high and low-minded audiences (VIII.7.1342a16–28); and allows citizens past a certain age to attend satires and comedies (VII.17.1336b20). The functions of these musical or musically accompanied forms are various and overlapping. They include entertainment, catharsis, and character

---

18 *Odyssey* IX.5–16, slightly garbled by Aristotle. I disagree with Lord, *Education and Culture in the Political Thought of Aristotle*, pp. 57, 76–7, who denies that Aristotle speaks positively of this Homeric text. Lord says that for the ancients, music reduces to enjoyable play (*paidia*) and thus lacks the intensely moral dimension that Lord requires of Aristotle's theory of music. Lord concedes that this interpretation is difficult to reconcile with the text (p. 57). But this view falls on other grounds as well. Lord wants to assimilate moral learning to "adult" character formation. But Aristotle's primary interest in music is more cognitive than that, and in this light he judges the musically accompanied reflective narrative portrayed by Homer (and embodied in Homeric poetic practice itself) as an early form of reflective learning, which will be developed further into more abstract and theoretical forms of learning and knowing as culture itself matures.

development. But at least some of them qualify for the endlike leisure time processes that Aristotle sees a simple but compelling example of in Homer's scene in Alcinous' banquet hall. I cannot enter here into which forms these might be. The matter is textually tangled. It can, however, be said that all and only those forms reaching this level do so because they have a *cognitive* dimension that transcends mere entertainment, psychological catharsis, and character building by inducing reflection and learning. Aristotle says plainly that leisure processes (*diagôgê en têi scholêi*) are for the sake of practical wisdom (*phronêsis*) (VIII.5.1339a26) and learning (*mathêsis*) (VIII.5.1339a37, 6.1341 a23). This is exactly what we would expect him to say. For unless music engages rationality, the distinctive human function (*ergon*), on both the producing and receiving end, it cannot be fully endlike according to Aristotle's general principles. Thus Aristotle clearly insists that young citizens engage in music, not only for the sake of character formation, but so that they might develop ability to judge (*kritein*) musical performances correctly, especially those in which correct response is required to "respectable characters and noble actions" (VIII.5.1340a13–18). Aristotle goes on to make much of the fact that such judgments presuppose active participation in music-making from childhood, and not just the passive exposure characteristic of "Persian and Median Kings" (VIII.5.1339a35–6) – even if this active involvement brings with it some risk that technical proficiency might result in vulgar professionalism (VIII.6.1340b20–41a9). Apparently the ability to judge music implies knowing it in a technical way; and this technical knowledge is crucial to the subsequent development of both practical and theoretical knowledge. Passive reception of music, Aristotle implies, will result in little or no learning of any sort, and declines into mere play or entertainment (*paidia*). It is activity that teaches us about right action.

Thus far I have not mentioned tragedies. It is inviting to see an approval of tragedy and tragic festivals as an element of the endlike leisure processes (*diagôgê en têi scholêi*) Aristotle prizes as the highest function of music. Tragedy, especially as it is analyzed in the *Poetics*, seems to pass all the tests just laid down for cognitive relevance to virtuous activity and learning. Nonetheless, two cautionary notes are necessary. First, there is no direct mention of tragedy or tragic festivals in what remains of *Pol.* VIII. Second, use of the mention of catharsis at VIII.7.1341b39 as a link between *Pol.* VIII and the *Poetics* has been conclusively discredited.[19] The catharsis of the *Politics* is a psychological effect paradigmatically seen in people who throw themselves into the frenzy of Dionysian music (VIII.7.1342a5–16); in the *Poetics* catharsis has little directly to do with this. Although music is part of tragedy, it cannot be said that tragedy is part of music; and it is the

19 The view in question goes back to J. Bernays, *Grundzuge der verloren Abhandlung des Aristoteles über Wirkung der Tragoedie* (Breslau, 1857), reprinted in *Zwei Abhandlungen über die aristotelische Theorie des Drama*, (Berlin, 1880). A summary of arguments against this view can be found in S. Halliwell, *Aristotle's Poetics* (Chapel Hill, 1986), pp. 190–98, 353–4.

non-musical part in which tragic catharsis resides. Nor is it entirely clear that Aristotle's mention at VIII.7.1341b40 of a work on poetics refers to the *Poetics*, or to the part of it we possess. These arguments suggest that one cannot project the catharsis of the *Politics* onto the theory of tragedy in the *Poetics* and then read the latter back into the *Politics*, as has commonly been done. Nonetheless, it would be to conclude too much from these facts to think that inferences between the two works should altogether be forbidden. For recent views about tragedy, as it is independently analyzed in the *Poetics*, fit quite well into the endlike leisure activities described in *Pol*. VIII.

These connections do not, however, run directly through the concept of catharsis. Instead, they run through the concept of learning (*mathêsis*). That is because tragic catharsis, we learn in the *Poetics* (4.1448b15–16), rests on the learning involved in actively following a plot to its resolution, with the result that the experience of the tragic character, and *at the same time* the excellence of its representation (*mimêsis*), is worked through, clarified and properly judged.[20] This can be done only by those who can follow the development and resolution of the plot, and the moral deserts of its characters, with their minds no less than their (well educated) feelings. Thus tragedy affords a kind of learning which, although it is not education (*paideia*) – in fact it presupposes it – does have normative import. It sharpens and exercises practical judgement – and at the same time opens out onto a wider, more contemplative understanding of human affairs. That is just what is required of the endlike leisure processes of *Pol*. VIII. I conclude, therefore, that there is an important place for tragedy in Aristotle's ideal state as part of its leisured life.

The link between practical and contemplative wisdom just mentioned can be envisioned as follows. The activity of judging poetic representations involves, Aristotle says, an implicit, reflective grasp of the universals, both factual and normative, which govern excellent human activity (*Poet*. 9. 1451b5–11). This suggests that the technical judgment and practical wisdom called into play by musically attended forms like tragedy also have a certain

---

20 The general view of catharsis as "clarification" sketched here is argued, in various (sometimes conflicting) ways, by all of the following: H. House, *Aristotle's Poetics* (London, 1956); L. Golden, "Mimesis and Catharsis," *Classical Philology*, 64 (1969), pp. 145–53; Lord, *Education and Culture in the Political Thought of Aristotle*, pp. 156–64; Nussbaum, *The Fragility of Goodness*, pp. 240–63; R. Janko, *Aristotle's Poetics* (Indianapolis, 1987), pp. xviii–xix; and Halliwell, *Aristotle's Poetics*, pp. 173–4. This approach may be distinguished from the (false) view of G. F. Else, *Aristotle's Poetics: The Argument* (Cambridge, Mass., 1957), that the catharsis of the *Poetics* is predicated of the plot, and not of the audience. J. Lear, "Catharsis," *Phronesis*, 33 (1988), pp. 297–326, calls the "clarification" view the "educational" view of catharsis. But Lear, like many of those whose interpretation he is contesting, fails to differentiate cathartic "clarification" aimed at training feeling responses and inducing habituation (*ethismos*) – which is indeed "educational" in Aristotle's sense – from the sort of learning by cathartic clarification that awakens and exercises cognitive abilities – practical judgement and contemplative learning. The latter is *not* a matter of education (*paideia*). Nussbaum's formulation comes closest to my own.

relevance to contemplative wisdom. Art, conversation and other dimensions of endlike leisure processes (*diagôgê en têi scholêi*) undoubtedly begin with, and remain intensely concerned with, norms of human actions. But in learning about the human condition by judging the correctness of representations of it, practical wisdom itself learns a lesson vividly taught by the art we judge to be best. That lesson is that humans are not the highest beings in the cosmos, and hence practical wisdom is not the highest kind of knowledge (*EN* VI.7.1141a20–2; 38–b1). In contrast to the humanistic, sophistic insistence on the centrality of human life, tragic authors from Homer to Sophocles and Euripides teach the same lesson Aristotle does: even though human life is a worthy object of reflective attention, its value can be properly judged only when it is acknowledged that man is not the measure of all things. Nor is it a cure for this vice to underestimate and belittle man, as Plato does when he allows the Athenian Stranger to call humans playthings of the gods, a conceit against which his interlocutors rightly protest (*Laws* VII.803c–e). For both over- and underestimation of the human place in the scheme of things are vices of one who lacks practical wisdom. That is perhaps why, in the *Eudemian Ethics*, practical wisdom (*phronêsis*) is seen as a mean between overreaching cleverness and pusillanimous subordination (*EE* II.3.1221a12).

Music, from this perspective, aids in the development of practical wisdom, but it also does more than this. Proper understanding of the place of human beings, with a view to action, brings with it incipient wonder about the things that are more valuable than human beings, and that are above all worth contemplating for their own sake.[21] Accordingly, practical reason can be relied on, by its very nature, to adopt a principle of choice such that the development and exercise of contemplative capacities is prized by all citizens of a best state, and is intensively pursued by those having talent for it within the framework of a shared, leisured political life. The men of practical wisdom who rule, therefore, in Aristotle's best state will put no boundary on the intensification of leisured learning in the direction of scientific knowledge and contemplative wisdom, nor will any politically relevant contrast emerge between those who are and are not capable of such activities. For contemplative wisdom will be seen *from the perspective of genuine practical wisdom* itself as emergent from and continuous with the musical and musically attended leisure activities that occupy a prominent place in the life of a best state. Music and similar engagements will be seen, therefore, to have mediated rather than blocked or replaced this ascent toward contemplation (just as the ascent toward contemplation sustains and deepens practical wisdom itself). For these reasons, it can be argued that Aristotle is envisioning the non-musical leisure pursuits characteristic of mature civilizations, such as

---

21 Nussbaum's account of the wisdom taught by poetry, *The Fragility of Goodness*, pp. 240–63, misses this point largely because of her explicitly anthropocentric perspective. This is not unrelated to her view of philosophy as coordination of human opinions (from a human perspective). Put otherwise, if Aristotle's philosophy tries to find middle ground between Plato and Protagoras, Nussbaum inclines too far in the direction of Protagoras.

the sophisticated conversations of symposia, dialectical encounters, and philosophical lectures such as his own, as extensions of, and to some degree commentaries on, the musically accompanied leisure activities whose paradigm he sees in Homer.

Musical leisure is, therefore, an important scene for the exercise of the reflective virtues concerned with the proper employment of leisure, which Aristotle collectively calls philosophy (*philosophia*). Philosophy thus conceived does indeed, as Solmsen and Lord have argued, presuppose the broad sense of this term used by Thucydides when he speaks of the Athenians as prizing "philosophy without softness."[22] But philosophy seems in this context to imply for Aristotle something even more specific – an ascent from musical practice to practical wisdom and to contemplation, by which rationality, which marks the exercise of virtues and so happiness, is developed and intensified in increasingly profound ways. All of these cognitively rich pursuits, of which contemplative knowledge of divine and eternal things is highest, will be seen as activities in a more proper sense than those instrumental actions normally called "practical," whose dependencies, in respects explicated above, disqualify them for this status. This conception of contemplation as activity, fostered by devotion to music and other leisure activities, fully accords with the principles set forth in *Pol*. VII.1–3. For musically mediated leisure activities so construed complete the dissociation of Aristotle's citizens from the instrumentalistic conception of activity initiated by the exclusion of the working classes from citizenship. In Aristotle's best state, therefore, contemplation will indeed be seen as activity, as the prefatory argument of *Pol*. VII.1–3 requires, and this understanding of contemplation will produce precisely the political consequences demanded by that argument for a best state. The body of *Pol*. VII–VIII is thus a direct application of the principles laid down in *Pol*. VII.1–3.

This interpretation is at odds with the view, first proposed by Solmsen, according to which music is a political substitute or surrogate for contemplation, rather than a stimulus to it.[23] For, I shall argue, one cannot say this and at the same time abide consistently within the assumptions Aristotle lays down in *Pol*. VII.1–3. In saying that music is a surrogate for contemplation in *Pol*. VII–VIII Solmsen was rightly reacting to commentators, who, influenced by strict intellectualistic preconceptions about Aristotelian happiness, tended to make contemplation a "dominant end" in Aristotle's ideal state, and suggested that after completing his treatise on music Aristotle would have gone on, or in fact did go on it parts of the *Politics* now missing, to specify abstract intellectual training for all the citizens.[24] Solmsen pointed out that Aristotle implies that all citizens share in the proper good of this city and have the same education (VIII.1.1337a22–7, 2.1337a34–5), but that

22 Solmsen, "Leisure and Play in Aristotle's Ideal State," pp. 24–6; Lord, *Education and Culture in the Political Thought of Aristotle*, pp. 198–200. The reference to Thucydides is to *Peloponnesian War* II.40.1.

23 Solmsen, "Leisure and Play in Aristotle's Ideal State," pp. 25–6.

24 See note 5.

only some are capable of contemplation (VII.14.1333a27–30). He suggested, therefore, that on any commonsense view of the matter too few could possess enough contemplative ability to justify strongly orienting an entire city toward it. Accordingly, Solmsen judged the musically focused educational system outlined in *Pol.* VIII to be essentially complete, even if textually truncated. For, he claimed, private musical leisure-time pursuits – the sort of thing prized by people in Hellenistic, if not in classical, cities – are treated there as an analogue to, and substitute for, contemplation properly so-called, since it is around the interests and abilities of the majority of good men, rather than of a theoretical few, that an ideal regime must be organized. Such a state can allow its contemplative minority to develop their special capacities. But these pursuits will be treated as their peculiar form of private leisure, different but not incompatible with the musical interests of the majority, providing for whose interests is the main object of statecraft.[25]

Solmsen himself concedes that music, and adult leisure activities (*diagôgê en têi scholêi*) generally, will be indistinguishable, on this account, from mere play or entertainment (*paidia*) unless they have a moral dimension.[26] But, given his stress on the private satisfactions of the leisured class in Hellenistic cities, it is hard to see how Solmsen's own account meets this demand. In recently taking up Solmsen's suggestion, Carnes Lord has tried to meet this difficulty by holding that music substitutes for contemplation, not because of Aristotle's concern for the private enjoyments of the citizens of post-political Hellenistic cities, but because something like contemplation, though more widely shareable, is necessary to moderate the inherent aggressiveness of the political men who rule Aristotle's ideal state – their drive to dominate, which Lord holds, has an inherent tendency to undermine virtue even as it bonds politically active men in devotion to the state.[27] The assumption is that contemplation undergirds the virtuous conduct of fully contemplative persons, and that music can similarly, though less perfectly, restrain political "gentlemen" from giving way to their baser, political selves. Musical leisure is thus an integral support for and part of the *public* life of the ideal city, and not a concession to what Solmsen thinks of as a characteristically Hellenistic concern for the citizen's private sensibilities.[28] Lord has much to say about how music performs this role, assigning an especially important role to participation in "theatrical music" (VIII.7.1342a18) and tragic festivals.[29] He thus provides the moral dimension that Solmsen asks for. But in so doing he holds that for Aristotle participation in traditional Greek music, and especially in dramatic festivals, serves to provide "grown men" with a "continuing education in virtue and prudence"[30] in which tragic catharsis has the effect of controlling a range of hostile and destructive emotions

---

25 Solmsen, "Leisure and Play in Aristotle's Ideal State," pp. 25–8.
26 Ibid., p. 23, 27.
27 Lord, *Education and Culture in the Political Thought of Aristotle*, pp. 189–202.
28 Ibid., p. 202, n. 27.
29 Ibid., pp. 156–79.
30 Ibid., p. 35.

endemic among political men. On his view Aristotle's adult leisure activities are distinguished from the education of the young primarily because the cathartic function of music serves to restore and foster moral equilibrium in passionate adults.

One difficulty with this approach is that Lord has to go beyond anything Aristotle says, here or in the *Poetics*, by postulating a wider range of cathartic effects than pity and fear.[31] More importantly, there is something wrong with the very notion of education for adults. The Greek word for education, *paideia*, comes from the word *pais*, meaning child, suggesting that *paideia* is restricted to the training of the young (VIII.1.1337a11–2.1337a34, VII.14. 1333b3–4). It is true that Aristotle sometimes uses *paideia* more widely, as when he refers to "the educated person" (*EN* I.3.1094b23–95a2); and Lord cites a passage from the *Nicomachean Ethics* (X.9.1180a1–19), in which Aristotle says that adults stand in need of continued habituation in virtue.[32] But when Aristotle uses *paideia* in the sense of "educated" he refers precisely to someone who *has* profited, in childhood and youth, from good education; and at *EN* X.9.1180a1–19, where Aristotle speaks of continued habituation (*ethismos*) for adults, the term *paideia* is conspicuous by its absence – and the context, in any case, is explicitly restricted to the uneducated many (*hoi polloi*) rather than to Lord's "gentlemen." Aristotle says, moreover, that education (*paideia*) comes to an end at some point (VII.14.1333b4). Finally, at VIII.7.1341b32–42a16 catharsis, which Lord takes to be the primary instrument of adult education, is listed as a different use of music from education.

It is difficult to escape the conclusion that just as Solmsen inappropriately reduces the endlike leisure processes (*diagôgê en têi scholê*) Aristotle so prizes to mere play, so Lord reduces them to mere education. Accordingly, neither preserves Aristotle's clear differentiation between the various functions of music, and his insistence that its highest function is fully endlike. In the process the rational element of Aristotle's endlike leisure processes is deeply subverted. Lord recognizes that if there is to be an education of adults it must be an education in prudence or practical wisdom (*phronêsis*).[33] But for him, Aristotle's clear belief that proper moral habituation is a necessary condition for practical wisdom (*EN* I.4.1095b4–10; VI.5.1140b11–14) is interpreted in such a way that practical wisdom is itself rendered less an intellectual than a moral virtue.[34] For Lord's vision of adult education focuses on continued training of affective response more than on the development of autonomous rational judgment. This is a Platonic view because Plato thinks that only very few persons – those possessing contemplative virtue – have their feelings fully formed. The rest are not all that different from children. There are

31 Ibid., pp. 159–64.
32 Ibid., p. 156.
33 Ibid., p. 155.
34 Ibid., pp. 157–8. Contrast M. Burnyeat, "On Learning to Be Good," in *Essays on Aristotle's Ethics*, ed. A. O. Rorty (Berkeley, 1980), pp. 69–92.

for Plato, in any case, no autonomous agents possessing practical but not contemplative wisdom.

The consequences of Lord's analysis for the relation between action and contemplation in Pol. VII–VIII are, in any event, profoundly at odds with the thrust of Aristotle's argument. If music were conceived by Aristotle as a substitute for contemplation within the political sphere, music would be construed, from within the political sphere, as "active," that is, as political in some sense. Contemplation itself would, by contrast, be seen by those who engage in it, as well as by their fellow citizens, as inactive because it is apolitical. This would result in violating Aristotle's principle that "contemplation is activity," and would open up precisely the antinomies Aristotle seeks to preclude. "Men of action" would be unable to discriminate well between instrumental and intrinsically good activity, even if they could be led to repress the former, or to sublimate it into music. With activity conceived instrumentally, meanwhile, "men of contemplation" would dissociate themselves altogether from the sphere of action, with the result that the continuity between genuine politics and contemplation as spheres of excellent leisured activity would be at risk.

That this is in fact the upshot of Lord's interpretation is inescapably clear in his remark that:

> To speak of an active or practical life which consists in the pursuit of "speculations" which have no end beyond themselves is to speak of a way of life which is no longer "active" in any tolerable sense of the term. . . . happiness in the truest sense belongs not with activity but with leisure.[35]

It is central to Aristotle's purpose in Pol. VII–VIII to block precisely these claims. It is ironic that they appear here as an interpretation of this text.

3   ARISTOTLE'S CRITIQUE OF PLATONIC POLITICS

Lord himself admits that "the notion that grown men . . . stand in need of a continuing education in virtue or prudence may be thought to bear the stamp of Plato rather than of the mature Aristotle."[36] It certainly does. But Lord does not regard the Platonizing cast of his interpretation as objectionable. For he asserts that "Aristotle fully shares the position of Plato regarding 'the ancient quarrel between poetry and philosophy,'" namely, that "philosophy or reason could never be fully effective in political life."[37] This assurance fails, however, to take account of the fact that Plato's political theory,

35 Ibid., pp. 187–8; Lord, "Politics and Philosophy in Aristotle's Politics," p. 344. For Lord, Aristotle "manages" (Education and Culture in the Political Thought of Aristotle, p. 189) to get the citizens to think of philosophy as activity (when it really isn't?) because political philosophy is a kind of rhetoric. See ibid., p. 32. This too is part of Lord's Platonism, reflecting his subscription to the views of Leo Strauss.
36 Ibid., p. 35.
37 Ibid.

perhaps including his ideas about the social functions of art, comes in for some heavy criticism in the *Politics*. It is probable, in fact, that Aristotle's portrait of an ideal aristocracy in *Pol*. VII is directed against Plato. *Pol.* VII–VIII is generally thought to be coeval with *Pol*. II,[38] where most of Aristotle's criticisms of Plato's efforts to envision ideal states are concentrated, and is intended to portray a regime that successfully avoids precisely the defects Aristotle recognizes, rightly or wrongly, in Plato's treatments of this theme. I will conclude with a brief review of these issues.

It would be incorrect to assume that Aristotle is accusing Plato of straightforwardly denying any of the components of his own analysis of happiness. Plato's deepest insistence, like Aristotle's, is that without cultivating virtue for its own sake we cannot be happy, either individually or collectively (*Republic* IX.580b–c). Nor does Plato say that the contemplative life is exclusively the only way of embodying these principles. For Plato also holds that political life is essential to the human good, and that intellectuals should internalize a sense of responsibility to and identity with the city that nurtured them. They are linked to its fate as citizens, and ought to devote their talents to its well-being (*Rep*. VII.539e–40b). But it is one thing to say these things and quite another to devise a consistent way of achieving them.

Plato and Aristotle begin seriously to diverge at the question of what talents can bring about a city's political happiness. Plato believes that only the person of contemplative wisdom can do it (*Rep*. VI.501e, VII.529d–30c). Plato's paradoxical idea, born of his own political struggles and hatreds, is that only a person not overtly devoted to political life can be politically virtuous. The effectiveness with which virtuous people carry out their responsibilities to their city is, then, a function of their contemplative self-conception and abilities, not of what Aristotle calls practical wisdom (*phronêsis*). Good politics becomes, in effect, applied contemplation. Aristotle, on the other hand, thinks that this conception seriously misconstrues the value of contemplative wisdom itself and undermines the autonomy of political agents. In the end, it makes it impossible for Plato to construct a coherent and persuasive picture of a good society.

Plato's conception of good politics as applied contemplation unfolds under Glaucon's unquestioned assumption that of the three sorts of goods – intrinsic, instrumental and mixed – the mixed sort is best (*Rep*. II.357a–358a). This makes it possible for Plato to regard the value of contemplation as increasing as practical utility is added to its inherent worth. (This conception is also implicit in Plato's conception of God as the Demiurge.) This view implies, however, a certain impiety from Aristotle's perspective, since contemplation is a share in God's proper life, and God's life consists of contemplation unaccompanied by instrumental acts (*Pol*. VII.3. 1325b27–9; *EE* VIII.3.1249b14–21; *EN* X.7.1177b26–32). The best of all things does not, therefore, belong (except incidentally) to the mixed class. This misunderstanding has serious political consequences. For it not only obscures the

38 Jaeger, *Aristotle*, pp. 284–7.

highest paradigm of activity in accord with virtue, but, in making contemplative knowledge a tool of effective statecraft, it countenances a higher form of instrumentalism. This will intensify, rather than blunt, the latent instrumentalism of political men (auxiliary guardians or soliders) and the overt instrumentalism of the producers. For under these conditions, contemplation will be seen as active *only* on its applied side, with the result that contemplation unattended by practical benefits will be seen as inactive, and the concept of activity will be conformed to instrumentalistic and productive paradigms. On the heels of Plato's failure to recognize that contemplation is inherently active, the fruitless dialectic between the conventionally political man and the apolitical intellectual will resume, with the result that Plato will be unable to abide consistently by the analysis of individual and political happiness Aristotle lays down in *Pol.* VII.1–3.

This will be particularly true, Aristotle notes, in view of the fact that the state portrayed in the *Republic* is composed from the outset of farmers and craftsmen (*Pol.* IV.4.1291a11–23; *Rep.* II.369d), whose limitless desires lead to the combination of commercialism and militarism that Plato and Aristotle both feared. Nor in the *Republic*, as Aristotle interprets it (*Pol.* II.3.1262a4–8, 5.1264b25, IV.4.1291a11–28), does Plato cleanly dissociate the lower classes from citizenship when he begins to purify the luxurious city that soon results. On the contrary, Aristotle says, far from excluding craftsmen and farmers from citizenship, Plato makes them the political majority: "Socrates," he writes, "makes the guardians a sort of garrison, while the farmers, artisans and other classes are the citizens" (II.5.1264a25–7). But how could Plato exclude them, considering that they are *ex hypothesi*, the founders of the state? Since, then, Plato begins from a less than ideal premiss, according to which the producing classes are enfranchised *ab initio*, he is forced to conceive the problem of politics in terms of how restraint can be exercised on vulgarizing values whose potential legitimacy is granted from the outset. Plato's main concern henceforth is to find means to have his city internalize, or at least recognize, the inhibitory attitudes toward material goods best embodied in the contemplative life. In the *Republic*, the possibility of enforcing these attitudes on a political community provides motives for inviting philosophers to overcome their apoliticality and to become rulers.

Aristotle is deeply sceptical about whether this approach would work even on its own terms. Under the conditions from which Plato begins, the primary role of the ruling classes is not to develop and exercise capacities for virtuous action, but to constrain the desires and actions of the majority. To achieve this the guardians must serve as an "occupying garrison" over the many. But this arrangement will only aggravate class conflict (II.5.1264a24–35). Aristotle cannot believe, moreover, that those who bear arms, and whose love of honor will have been awakened by their domination over the other citizens, will be induced to give up their right to rule to philosophers (II.5.1264b6–9, VII.9.1329a9–12). But even if this could be arranged, the disenfranchised soldiery, now deprived of private property without possessing sufficient wisdom to be indifferent to its loss (for it was lack of that quality that kept them from becoming philosophers [*Rep.* VI.503d–e]), cannot be prevented from envying the material advantages of the very people they are charged with ruling over, and from seeking eventually to reacquire political authority to redress the situation (*Pol.* II.5.1264a17–40). For their part, the philosophical rulers are asked to leave the contemplative life for which they are fit to perform tasks whose value must always be in question in a state full of such tensions, and which they will be tempted to abandon. (It is precisely by this route that the ideal state begins to come apart in the final books of the *Republic* [*Rep.* VIII.546a–548c].)

Just below the surface in Plato's *Republic*, accordingly, there is much potential for a reversal of values in which instrumental goods are secretly preferred to intrinsic, and in which preventing ignoble acts, rather than acting freely in accord with virtue, is the actual aim of politics. Good political life, ironically, appears as a life that puts constraints on action: the activities of the craftsmen are to be constrained by the soldiers, the activities of the soldiers by the philosophers, and the philosophical life itself will appear as an inactive, but inherently preferable, alternative to the dutifully constrained, instrumentally good activity of ruling. Such a state may (like the state portrayed in the *Laws*) be moderate (*sôphrôn*) or good at repressing desires, Aristotle says, "but it is possible to live with moderation, yet wretchedly" (II.6.1265a29–32). This is not, therefore, a city of happy people (II.5.1264 b15–23). For a happy life is one in which people display their many virtues in action by using external goods well, especially in unconstrained, leisured conditions, rather than a life in which external goods are rendered scarce for fear that they will be used badly, and in which tendencies toward autonomous activity are repressed. Nor is Aristotle impressed by Plato's attempt to obviate this difficulty by first postulating an asymmetry between individual happiness and the happiness of states and then holding that trading off quanta of individual happiness is a condition for maximizing collective happiness (*Rep.* IV.420b). "It is impossible for a state to be happy as a whole," he archly remarks, "unless its parts are happy" (II.5.1264b16–20).

It is, however, not the *Republic* but the *Laws* to which we should compare Aristotle's own best state. For, as commentators have long noted, there are many parallels between the Cretan city and Aristotle's own.[39] The most important of the similarities for our purposes is that Plato's "second-best city" (*Laws* VII.807b) is founded as a colony composed exclusively of land-owning farmers. Craftsmen and merchants, and the vulgar values they bring with them, are fully excluded from any claim on membership in the city (*Laws* VIII.846d). Indeed, even external trade through an associated port is eschewed, for "it infects a place with commerce and the money making that comes with retail trade, and engenders shifty and untrustworthy dispositions in souls" (*Laws* IV.705a). Since, moreover, the actual work of farming is assigned to slaves, the citizens "dwell in the greatest leisure" (*Laws*

---

39 For instance, G. Morrow, "Aristotle's Comments on Plato's *Laws*," in *Aristotle and Plato in Mid-Fourth Century*, eds I. Düring and G. Owen (Göteborg, 1960), pp. 145–62. See also Newman, *Politics*, vol. I, pp. 433–54, especially 453–4; and E. Barker, *Greek Political Theory* (London, 1918), pp. 380–2.

VII.806d–e, VIII.832d). Under these conditions, Plato feels free to blur the boundary between farmers and soldiers, assigning both private property and the right to bear arms to a large number of land-owning citizen-soldiers, and to dispense with the permanent rule of philosopher kings.

But, Aristotle says, Plato "gradually brings the [second] city around to the other" (*Pol.* II.6.1265a1–3). His distrust of advanced economic activity, which leads him, unlike Aristotle, to eschew an associated commercial port, again raises the question of scarcity, and with it, Aristotle thinks, the spectre of political friction between rich and poor (II.6.1265a12–17). In order to blunt these tendencies, constraints are placed on the exchange of property and the acquisition of wealth (II.6.1265a39–b16) by a myth of immutable foundation and a massive code of received and unamendable laws (1264b40–65a1) as well as by the artificial isolation of the city (1265a20–25). These impersonal and inflexible institutions take the place of philosopher kings. They entail that the citizens of Plato's Cretan city are to be given the same education as those in the *Republic* – an education focused on moderation at the expense of the other virtues (II.6.1265a1, 27–31), in which musical leisure, in the form of prescribed play, serves as an inhibitory mechanism for citizens who are to retain a certain naive childishness. This is not, Aristotle thinks, the active leisured learning of genuinely mature and free adults (II.6.1265a6; see *Laws* VII.803d–804b). In the end, therefore, Aristotle suggests that there is nothing much better about the second regime (II.6.1264b26). The reason ultimately lies in Plato's continued belief that the highest function of political life is the repression of desire. Plato does not, therefore, distinguish between a genuinely good state and one that merely succeeds better than others in circumventing the assumed defects of political life generally (II.6.1265b29–33). Plato himself regards the Cretan city as "second best" to the city portrayed in the *Republic*, even though it is closer to Aristotle's own ideal, because it contains more concessions to the desires of men – for property and for political autonomy – and hence is farther from the contemplative life. These facts testify to the residual but powerful hold of the traditionally conceived contemplative ideal, with its contempt for the conventionally active or political life, on Plato, who was nonetheless passionately, indeed hopelessly, interested in politics, and whose political thought therefore twists and turns within the bounds of assumptions that cannot sustain coherent reflection on the natural potentialities of political life. This is ironic. For we are accustomed to think of Plato as more idealistic than Aristotle, and as having a higher regard for the contemplative life. But Aristotle's argument shows that Plato is actually not idealistic enough.

The very conceptions that prevent Plato from abiding in practice by Aristotle's theory of the happy life have only been avoided imperfectly by commentators. Jaeger adopted Platonic assumptions with his eyes open. For he believed that *Pol.* VII–VIII and *Pol.* II come from Aristotle's earlier maturity and retain much of the middle-Platonism Jaeger sees in Aristotle's academic writings.[40] On his view, an ideal Aristotelian state would be one in

40 Jaeger, *Aristotle*, pp. 275–82.

which only those capable of contemplation proper are, largely by chance, in a position to claim citizenship. They may then make the cultivation of contemplative virtues the focal point of their shared life, untroubled by any need to block the destabilization introduced by inferior citizens. This interpretation preserves Aristotle's view that contemplation unaccompanied by instrumentally good results is more valuable than contemplation that has practical benefits. But it does so only weakly. For the implication remains that if citizens with little or no contemplative ability *were* to be admitted, a program of "applied contemplation" would be required to maintain the state's orientation toward the good, and to keep it from degenerating into power and greed.

That is precisely what begins to happens in Solmsen's interpretation and what reaches full flood in Lord's. Once the citizens of Aristotle's ideal state are thought to be, in the main, incapable of contemplative wisdom (Solmsen), and are assumed to be political "gentlemen" (Lord), driven by the passion for power inherent (Lord says) in political life, musical culture is invoked to take the place of contemplation in diverting these less virtuous citizens from their allegedly *ineradicable* tendency to dominate others.[41] But wherever a surrogate for contemplation, and the supposed political benefits brought by its adepts, is sought, as it already is in Plato's *Laws* itself, we may detect the influence of Platonism; and wherever Platonism obtains, conflict between activity and contemplation must also arise. This conflict cannot be resolved by assigning contemplative wisdom an instrumental or technical role in the form of "applied philosophy." Aristotle's treatise on an ideal state lays out the conditions under which precisely this conflict can be transcended. What undergirds Aristotle's solution is his deep confidence in the practical wisdom (*phronêsis*) of autonomous political agents, which, for

41 Solmsen, "Leisure and Play in Aristotle's Ideal State," p. 26; Lord, *Education and Culture in the Political Thought of Aristotle*, p. 202. Lord's approach has been taken a revealing step further by P. A. Vander Waerdt, "Kingship and Philosophy in Aristotle's Best Regime." He argues that Aristotle's tendency to regard kingship, rather than rotational aristocratic rule, as the absolutely best form of government (he cites 1284b25–34, 1288a15–29, 1325b10–14, 1332b16–27) holds even for an ideal state. For all power should be transferred to one who is so far above others in point of virtue that practical matters can be left in his competent hands, with the result that almost exclusive preoccupation with musical leisure will even more successfully keep the soldiers and citizens from degenerating into the love of domination that will be awakened inevitably in every man concerned with politics except the absolutely best. Vander Waerdt says that Aristotle seems to prefer rotational rule only as a concession to his aristocratic hearers. This approach, like Lord's, shows the influence of Leo Strauss in its reiterated Platonic assumption that only the philosophers have their emotions and imaginations in hand – and can be talked to straight. Vander Waerdt confesses implicit distrust of the practical reason of non-philosophers bluntly when he says that "*Phronêsis* is by itself morally neutral, capable of securing base as well as virtuous ends" (p. 263). I can think of no proposition Aristotle would deny more strenuously.

Aristotle, does not repress, deflect or manage desire, but completes the education of desire for intrinsically good things, and prizes contemplation not because it is politically useful, but because it is inherently noble and divine.[42]

42 Many people have read and criticized this manuscript in one or another of its drafts. I would like to thank in particular Elizabeth Belfiori, Tom Brickhouse, David Charles, Norman Dahl, Mary Depew, Allan Gotthelf, Marjorie Grene, David Keyt, Fred Miller, Merrill Ring, and Nick Smith.

Bibliography on Aristotle's Politics

TEXTS, TRANSLATIONS, AND COMMENTARIES

Aubonnet, J., *Aristote, Politique*, text, French translation, and notes, 3 vols Budé (Paris, 1968).

Barker, E., *The Politics of Aristotle*, translation with introduction, notes, and appendixes (Oxford, 1946).

Dreizehnter, A., *Aristoteles' Politik*, text (Munich, 1970).

Everson, S., *Aristotle, The Politics*, Jowett's translation as revised by J. Barnes (Cambridge, 1988).

Immisch, O., *Aristotelis Politica*, text with scholia and glosses, Teubner (Leibzig, 1929).

Lord, C., *Aristotle, The Politics*, translation with introduction, notes, and glossary (Chicago, 1984).

Newman, W. L., *The Politics of Aristotle*, text, introduction, notes critical and explanatory, 4 vols (Oxford, 1887–1902 [repr. 1973]).

Rackham, H., *Aristotle, Politics*, text and translation, Loeb Classical Library (Cambridge, Mass., 1932).

Robinson, R., *Aristotle's Politics Books III and IV*, translation, introduction, and comments, Oxford Clarendon Series (Oxford, 1962).

Ross, W. D., *Aristotelis Politica*, Oxford Classical Texts (Oxford, 1957).

Sinclair, T. A., *Aristotle, The Politics*, translation. 2nd rev. edn by J. T. Saunders (Harmondsworth, 1983).

Susemihl, F. and Hicks, R. D., *The Politics of Aristotle*, text, introduction, analysis, and commentary to Books I–V [I–III, VII–VIII] (London, 1894 [repr. 1976]).

BOOKS AND ARTICLES

Aalders, G. J. D., "Die Mischverfassung und ihre historische Dokumentation in den *Politica* des Aristoteles," with discussion, in Fondation Hardt, *Entretiens sur l'Antiquité Classique IX, La "Politique" d'Aristote* (Geneva, 1964), pp. 199–244.

Adkins, A. W. H., "The Connection Between Aristotle's *Ethics* and *Politics*," *Political Theory*, 12 (1984), pp. 29–49.

Allan, D. J., "Individual and State in the *Ethics* and *Politics*," in Fondation Hardt, *Entretiens sur l'Antiquité Classique IX, La "Politique" d'Aristote* (Geneva, 1964), pp. 53–95.

Ambler, W., "Aristotle's Understanding of the Naturalness of the City," *Review of Politics*, 47 (1985), pp. 163–85.

Ambler, W., "Aristotle on Nature and Politics: The Case of Slavery," *Political Theory*, 15 (1987), pp. 390–411.

Arnhart, L., "Darwin, Aristotle, and the Biology of Human Rights," *Social Science Information*, 23 (1984), pp. 493–521.

Arnhart, L., "Aristotle's Biopolitics: A Defense of Biological Teleology against Biological Nihilism," *Politics and the Life Sciences*, 6 (1988), pp. 173–229.

Aubenque, P., "Theorie et pratique politiques chez Aristote," with discussion, in Fondation Hardt, *Entretiens sur l'Antiquité Classique IX, La "Politique" d'Aristote*, (Geneva, 1964), pp. 97–123.

Barker, E., *The Political Thought of Plato and Aristotle* (London, 1906 [repr. 1959]).

Barker, E., "The Life of Aristotle and the Composition and Structure of the *Politics*," *Classical Review*, 45 (1931), pp. 162–72.

Barnes, J., "Aristotle and Women," review of G. E. R. Lloyd, *Science, Folklore and Ideology, London Review of Books* (16–29 Feb. 1984), p. 9.

Barnes, J. "Aristotle and Political Liberty," with commentary by R. Sorabji, in Patzig, 1989.

Barnes, J., Schofield, M., and Sorabji, R., eds, *Articles on Aristotle 2: Ethics and Politics* (London, 1977).

Baumrin, B. H., "Two Concepts of Justice," *Midwest Studies in Philosophy*, 7 (1982), pp. 63–72.

Berns, L., "Spiritedness in Ethics and Politics: A Study in Aristotelian Psychology," *Interpretation*, 12 (1984), pp. 335–48.

Bien, G., *Die Grundlegung der politischen Philosophie bei Aristoteles* (Freiburg–Munich, 1973).

Bien, G., "Die Wirkungsgeschichte der aristotelischen 'Politik'," with commentary by W. Kullmann, in Patzig, 1989.

Bluhm, J., "The Place of the 'Polity' in Aristotle's Theory of the Ideal State," *Journal of Politics*, 24 (1962), pp. 743–53.

Bodéüs, R., *Le philosophe et la cité: Recherches sur les rapports entre morale et politique dans la pensée d'Aristote* (Paris, 1982).

Bodéüs, R., "Savoir politique et savoir philosophique," in Patzig, 1989.

Bonner, R. J., and Smith, G., *The Administration of Justice from Homer to Aristotle*, 2 vols (Chicago, 1930, 1938 [repr. 1968]).

Booth, W. J., "Politics and the Household: A Commentary on Aristotle's *Politics* Book One," *History of Political Thought*, 2 (1981), pp. 203–26.

Bornemann, E., "Aristoteles' Urteil über Platons politische Theorien," *Philologus*, 79 (1923), pp. 70–111, 113–58, 234–57.

Bradley, A. C., "Aristotle's Conception of the State," in *Hellenica*, ed. E. Abbott (London, 1880 [repr. 1971]), pp. 181–243.

Braun, E., *Das dritte Buch der aristotelelischen "Politik": Interpretation* (Vienna, 1965).

Braun, E., "Die Summierungstheorie des Aristoteles," in Steinmetz, 1973, pp. 396–423.

Braun, E., "Die Ursache der Pluritalität von Verfassungsformen nach Aristoteles," in Steinmetz, 1973, pp. 431–9.

Braun, E., "Eine Maxime der Staatskunst in der Politik des Aristoteles," in Steinmetz, 1973, pp. 424–30.

Brumbaugh, R. S., "Revolution, Propaganda and Education: Aristotle's Causes in Politics," *Paideia*, 2 (1978), pp. 172–81.

Burnet, J., *Aristotle on Education* (Cambridge, 1903).

Cashdollar, S., "Aristotle's Politics of Morals," *Journal of the History of Philosophy*, 2 (1973), pp. 146–60.

Chambers, M., "Aristotle's 'Forms of Democracy'," *Transactions of the American Philological Association*, 92 (1961), pp. 20–36.

Clark, S. R. L., "Slaves and Citizens," *Philosophy*, 60 (1985), pp. 27–46.

Cloché, P., "Aristote et les institutions de Sparte," in Steinmetz, 1973, pp. 336–60.

Coby, P., "Aristotle's Four Conceptions of Politics," *Western Political Quarterly*, 39 (1986), pp. 480–503.

Cooper, J. M., "Aristotle on the Goods of Fortune," *Philosophical Review*, 94 (1985), pp. 173–96.

Cooper, J. M., "Political Animals and Civic Friendship," with commentary by J. Annas, in Patzig, 1989.

De Laix, R. A., "Aristotle's Conception of the Spartan Constitution," *Journal of the History of Philosophy*, 12 (1974), pp. 21–30.

Defourny, M., "The Aim of the State: Peace," in Barnes *et al.*, 1977, pp. 195–201.

Depew, D. J., "Aristotle's *De Anima* and Marx's Theory of Man," *Graduate Faculty Philosophy Journal*, 8 (1982), pp. 133–87.

Develin, R., "The Good Man and the Good Citizen in Aristotle's *Politics*," *Phronesis*, 18 (1973), pp. 71–9.

Dreizehnter, A., *Untersuchungen zur Textgeschichte der Aristotelischen Politik* (Leiden, 1962).

Düring, I., *Aristoteles, Darstellung und Interpretation seines Denkens* (Heidelberg, 1966), pp. 474–505.

Eucken, C., "Der aristotelische Demokratiebegriff und sein historisches Umfeld," with commentary by T. H. Irwin, in Patzig, 1989.

Everson, S., "Aristotle on the Foundations of the State," *Political Studies* 36 (1988), pp. 89–101.

Ferguson, J., "Teleology in Aristotle's *Politics*," in *Aristotle on Nature and Living Things*, ed. A. Gotthelf (Pittsburgh, 1985), pp. 259–73.

Finley, M. I., "Aristotle and Economic Analysis," in Barnes *et al.*, 1977, pp. 140–58.

Finley, M. I., s.v., "Aristotle" in *The New Palgrave: A Dictionary of Economics* (London, 1987).

Fortenbaugh, W., *Aristotle on Emotion* (London, 1975), chs. 2–3,

Fortenbaugh, W., "Aristotle on Prior and Posterior, Correct and Mistaken Constitutions," *Transactions of the American Philological Association*, 106 (1976), pp. 125–37.

Fortenbaugh, W., "Aristotle on Slaves and Women," in Barnes *et al.*, 1977, pp. 135–9.

Fritz, K. von, and Kapp, E., "The Development of Aristotle's Political Philosophy and the Concept of Nature," in Barnes *et alf15.*, *1977, pp. 113–34.*

Gigon, O., *"Die Sklaverei bei Aristoteles,"* with discussion, in Fondation Hardt, *Entretiens sur l'Antiquité Classique IX, La "Politique" d'Aristote* (Geneva, 1964), pp. 245–83.

Gigon, O., "Einleitung zu einer Übersetzung der Politik des Aristoteles," in Steinmetz, 1973, pp. 181–225.

Goldschmidt, V., "La Théorie aristotélicienne de l'esclavage et sa méthode," in *Zetesis*: Melanges E. de Strycker (Antwerp, 1973), pp. 147–63.

Hamburger, M., *Morals and Law. The Growth of Aristotle's Legal Theory*, new edition (New York, 1971).

Harding, S. and Hintikka, M. B., eds, *Discovering Reality: Feminist Perspectives on Epistemology, Metaphysics, Methodology, and Philosophy of Science* (Dordrecht, 1983).

Harrison, A. R. W., "Aristotle's *Nicomachean Ethics*, Book V, and the Law of Athens," *Journal of Hellenic Studies*, 77 (1957), pp. 42–7.

Havelock, E. A., *The Liberal Temper in Greek Politics* (New Haven and London, 1957), chs 11–12.

Hentschke, A. B., *Politik und Philosophie bei Plato und Aristoteles* (Frankfurt, 1971).

Holmes, S. T., "Aristippus in and out of Athens," *American Political Science Review*, 73 (1979), pp. 113–28.

Huxley, G., "Crete in Aristotle's *Politics*," *Greek, Roman, and Byzantine Studies*, 12 (1971), pp. 505–15.

Huxley, G., *On Aristotle and Greek Society* (Belfast, 1979).

Huxley, G. "On Aristotle's Best State," in *Crux*, eds P. A. Cartledge and F. D. Harvey (London, 1985), pp. 139–49.

Immisch, O., "Der Epilog der Nikomachischen Ethik," *Rheinisches Museum für Philologie*, 84 (1935), pp. 54–61.

Irwin, T. H., "Moral Science and Political Theory in Aristotle," in *Crux*, eds P. A. Cartledge and F. D. Harvey (London, 1985), pp. 150–68.

Irwin, T. H., "Generosity and Property in Aristole's *Politics*," *Social Philosophy and Policy*, 4 (1987), pp. 37–54.

Irwin, T. H., *Aristotle's First Principles* (Oxford, 1988), chs 16–22.

Irwin, T. H., "The Good of Political Activity," with commentary by G. Striker, in Patzig, 1989.

Jaeger, W., *Aristotle: Fundamentals of the History of his Development*, tr. R. Robinson, 2nd edn (Oxford, 1948), ch. 10.

Johnson, C., "Who is Aristotle's Citizen," *Phronesis*, 29 (1984), pp. 73–90.

Johnson, C., "The Hobbesian Conception of Sovereignty and Aristotle's *Politics*," *Journal of the History of Ideas*, 46 (1985), pp. 327–48.

Johnson, C., *Aristotle's Theory of the State* (London, 1990).

Kahlenberg, K., "Beitrag zur Interpretation des III. Buches der aristotelischen Politik," in Steinmetz, 1973, pp. 102–79.

Kahn, C. H., "The Normative Structure of Aristotle's *Politics*," in Patzig, 1989.

Kelsen, H., "The Philosophy of Aristotle and the Hellenic–Macedonian Policy," *The International Journal of Ethics*, 48 (1937), pp. 1–64. Partially repr. in Barnes *et al.*, 1977, pp. 170–94.

Kelsen, H., "Aristotle's Doctrine of Justice," in *What is Justice?* (Berkeley, 1957).

Keyt, D., Review of *Aristotle's Political Theory* by R. G. Mulgan and of *Aristotle* by J. B. Morrall, *Philosophical Quarterly*, 31 (1981), pp. 68–9.

Keyt, D., "Distributive Justice in Aristotle's *Ethics* and *Politics*," *Topoi*, 4 (1985), pp. 23–45.

Keyt, D., "Three Fundamental Theorems in Aristotle's *Politics*," *Phronesis*, 32 (1987), pp. 54–79.

Kraut, R., *Aristotle on the Human Good* (Princeton, 1989).

Kullmann, W., "Der Mensch als politisches Lebewesen bei Aristoteles," *Hermes*, 108 (1980), pp. 419–43.

Kullmann, W., "Aristoteles' Staatslehre aus heutiger Sicht," *Gymnasium*, 90 (1983), pp. 456–77.

Kullmann, W., "Equality in Aristotle's Political Thought," in *Equality and Inequality of Man in Ancient Thought*, ed. I. Kajanto, *Commentationes Humanarum Litterarum*, 75 (1984), pp. 31–44.

Kullmann, W., "L'image de l'homme dans la pensée politique d'Aristote," *Les études philosophiques* (1989), pp. 1–20.

Laird, J., "Hobbes on Aristotle's *Politics*," *Proceedings of the Aristotelian Society*, 43 (1942–3), pp. 1–20.

Lange, L., "Woman Is Not a Rational Animal: On Aristotle's Biology of Reproduction," in Harding and Hintikka, 1983, pp. 1–15.

Lear, J., *Aristotle: The Desire to Understand* (Cambridge, 1988), ch. 5.

Lendle, O., "Die Einleitung des dritten Buches der aristotelischen Politika," in Steinmetz, 1973, pp. 226–41.

Lewis, T. J., "Acquisition and Anxiety: Aristotle's Case Against the Market," *Canadian Journal of Economics*, 11 (1978), pp. 69–90.

Leyden, W. von, "Aristotle and the Concept of Law," *Philosophy*, 42 (1967), pp. 1–19.

Leyden, W. von, *Aristotle on Equality and Justice: His Political Argument* (London, 1985).

Lord, C., "Politics and Philosophy in Aristotle's *Politics*," *Hermes*, 106 (1978), pp. 336–59.

Lord, C., "The Character and Composition of Aristotle's *Politics*," *Political Theory*, 9 (1981), pp. 459–78.

Lord, C., *Education and Culture in the Political Thought of Aristotle* (Ithaca, 1982).

Lord, C., "Aristotle," in *History of Political Philosophy*, eds L. Strauss and J. Cropsey, 3rd edn (Chicago, 1987), pp. 118–54.

Lord, C., "Politics and Education in Aristotle's *Politics*," with commentary by D. A. Rees, in Patzig, 1989.

Meikle, S., "Aristotle and the Political Economy of the Polis," *Journal of Hellenic Studies*, 99 (1979), pp. 57–73.

Menger, C., "The Opinion Ascribed to Aristotle that the State Is an Original Phenomenon Given Simultaneously with the Existence of Man," Appendix VII of *Investigations into the Method of the Social Sciences with Special References to Economics* (New York, 1985), pp. 220–22 (see also pp. 129–59).

Mesk, J., "Die Buchfolge in der aristotelischen Politik," in Steinmetz, 1973, pp. 1–20.

Miller, E. F., "Prudence and the Rule of Law," *American Journal of Jurisprudence*, 24 (1979), pp. 181–206.

Miller, F. D., "The State and the Community in Aristotle's *Politics*," *Reason Papers*, 1 (1974), pp. 61–9.

Miller, F. D., "Aristotle and the Natural Rights Tradition," *Reason Papers*, 13 (1988), pp. 166–81.

Miller, F. D., "Aristotle on Nature, Law and Justice," *University of Dayton Review*, Special Issue on Aristotle 19 (1988–9), pp. 57–69.

Miller, F. D., "Aristotle's Political Naturalism," *Apeiron* 22 (1989), pp. 195–218.

Miller, F. D., "Aristotle on Property Rights," in *Essays in Ancient Greek Philosophy*, eds J. Anton and A. Preus, vol. IV, (Albany, 1990).

Miller, R. W., "Marx and Aristotle: A Kind of Consequentialism," in *Marx and Morality*, eds K. Nielson and S. C. Patten, *Canadian Journal of Philosophy*, supplementary vol. 7 (1981), pp. 323–52.

Moraux, P., "Quelques apories de la politique et leur arriére-plan historique," with discussion, in Fondation Hardt, *Entretiens sur l'Antiquité Classique IX, La "Politique" d'Aristote* (Geneva, 1964), pp. 125–58.

Morrall, J. B., *Aristotle* (London, 1977).

Morrow, G. R., "Aristotle's Comments on Plato's *Laws*" in *Aristotle and Plato in the Mid-Fourth Century*, eds I. Düring and G. E. L. Owen, (Göteborg, 1960), pp. 145–62.

Mulgan, R. G., "Aristotle and the Democratic Conception of Freedom," in *Auckland Classical Studies Presented to E. M. Blaiklock*, ed. B. F. Harris (Auckland, 1970), pp. 95–111.

Mulgan, R. G., "Aristotle's Sovereign," *Political Studies*, 18 (1970), pp. 518–22.

Mulgan, R. G., "Aristotle and Absolute Rule," *Antichthon*, 8 (1974), pp. 21–8.

Mulgan, R. G., "Aristotle's Doctrine that Man is a Political Animal," *Hermes*, 102 (1974), pp. 438–45.

Mulgan, R. G., "A Note on Aristotle's Absolute Ruler," *Phronesis*, 19 (1974), pp. 66–9.

Mulgan, R. G., *Aristotle's Political Theory* (Oxford, 1977).

Mulgan, R. G., "Aristotle and the Value of Political Participation," *Political Theory*, 18 (1990), pp. 195–215.

Mulhern, J. J., "ΜΙΑ ΜΟΝΟΝ ΠΑΝΤΑΧΟΥ ΚΑΤΑ ΦΥΣΙΝ Η ΑΡΙΣΤΗ (*EN* 1135a)," *Phronesis*, 17 (1972), pp. 260–68.

Newman, W. L., "Aristotle's Classification of Forms of Government," *Classical Review*, 6 (1892), pp. 289–93.

Nussbaum, M. C., "Shame, Separateness, and Political Unity: Aristotle's Criticism of Plato," in *Essays on Aristotle's Ethics*, ed. A. O. Rorty (Berkeley, 1980), pp. 395–435.

Nussbaum, M. C., "Nature, Function, and Capability: Aristotle on Political Distribution," with commentary by D. Charles and reply by Nussbaum, in Patzig, 1989.

Okin, S. M., *Women in Western Political Thought* (Princeton, 1979), ch. 4.

Patzig, G., ed., *XI. Symposium Aristotelicum: Studien zur Politik des Aristoteles* (Göttingen, 1989).

Pellegrin, P., "La Théorie aristotélicienne d'esclavage: tendances actuelles de l'interprétation," *Revue Philosophique*, 172 (1982), pp. 345–57.

Pellegrin, P., "Naturalité, excellence, diversité. Politique et biologie chez Aristote," in Patzig, 1989.

Polansky, R., "The Dominance of Polis for Aristotle," *Dialogos*, 33 (1979), pp. 43–56.

Polanyi, K., "Aristotle Discovers the Economy," in *Trade and Market in the Early Empires*, eds, K. Polanyi, C. M. Arensberg and H. W. Pearson (Glencoe, 1957), pp. 64–94.

Popper, K. R., *The Open Society and its Enemies*, 5th edn (London, 1966), vol. 2, ch. 11.

Riedel, M., *Metaphysik und Metapolitik. Studien zu Aristoteles und zur politischen Sprache der neuzeitlichen Philosophie* (Frankfurt a.M., 1975).

Ritter, J., *Metaphysik und Politik. Studien zu Aristoteles und Hegel* (Frankfurt a.M., 1969).

Rosen, F., "The Political Context of Aristotle's Categories of Justice," *Phronesis*, 20 (1975), pp. 228–40.

Rosenberg, A., "Aristoteles über Diktatur und Demokratie (Politik Buch III)," in Steinmetz, 1973, pp. 43–65.

Ross, W. D., *Aristotle*, 5th edn (London, 1949), ch. 8.

Rowe, C. J., "Aims and Methods in Aristotle's *Politics*," *Classical Quarterly*, 27 (1977), pp. 159–72.

Sabine, G. H., *A History of Political Theory*, 4th edn (Hinsdale, 1973), ch. 5–6.

Salkever, S. G., "Aristotle's Social Science," *Political Theory*, 9 (1981), pp. 479–508.

Salkever, S. G., "Women, Soldiers, Citizens: Plato and Aristotle on the Politics of Virility," *Polity*, 19 (1986), pp. 232–53.

Salkever, S. G., *Finding the Mean* (Princeton, 1990).

Schlatter, R., "Greek Theories of Slavery from Homer to Aristotle," *Harvard Studies in Classical Philology*, 47 (1936), pp. 165–204.

Schlatter, R., *Private Property: The History of an Idea* (New Brunswick, 1951), ch. 1.

Schmid, W. T., "Aristotle on Choice: Liberty and the *Polis*," *Paideia*, 2 (1978), pp. 182–95.

Schmidt, J., "A Raven with a Halo: The Translation of Aristotle's *Politics*," *History of Political Thought*, 7 (1986), pp. 295–319.

Schofield, M., "Ideology and Philosophy in Aristotle's Theory of Slavery," with commentary by C. H. Kahn, in Patzig, 1989.

Schott, R., "Aristotle on Women," *Kinesis*, 11 (1982), pp. 69–84.

Schroeder, D. N., "Aristotle on Law," *Polis*, 4 (1981), pp. 17–31.

Schumpeter, J. A., *History of Economic Analysis* (Oxford, 1954), pp. 57–64.

Schütrumpf, E., *Die Analyse der Polis durch Aristoteles*, 2 vols (Amsterdam, 1980).

Schütrumpf, E., "Kritische Überlegungen zur Ontologie und Terminologie der aristotelischen 'Politik'," *Allgemeine Zeitschrift für Philosophie* 6/2 (1981), pp. 26–47.

Seel, G., "Die Rechtfertigung von Herrschaft in der Politik des Aristoteles," with commentary by T. Ebert, in Patzig, 1989.

Shellens, M. S., "Aristotle on Natural Law," *Natural Law Forum*, 4 (1959), pp. 72–100.

Sidgwick, H., "Aristotle's Classification of Forms of Government," *Classical Review*, 6 (1892), pp. 141–4.

Siegfried, W., "Zur Entstehungsgeschichte von Aristotles' Politik," in Steinmetz, 1973, pp. 66–95.

Siegfried, W. "Untersuchungen zur Staatslehre des Aristoteles," in Steinmetz, 1973, pp. 242–335.

Sinclair, T. A., *A History of Greek Political Thought* (London, 1951), ch. 11.

Smith, N. D., "Aristotle's Theory of Natural Slavery," *Phoenix*, 37 (1983), pp. 109–22.

Smith, N. D., "Plato and Aristotle on the Nature of Women," *Journal of the History of Philosophy*, 21 (1983), pp. 467–78.

Solmsen, F., "Leisure and Play in Aristotle's Ideal State," *Rheinisches Museum*, 107 (1964), pp. 193–220.

Soudek, J., "Aristotle's Theory of Exchange: An Enquiry into the Origin of Economic Analysis," *Proceedings of the American Philosophical Society*, 96 (1952), pp. 45–75.

Sparshott, F., "Aristotle on Women," *Philosophical Inquiry*, 7 (1985), pp. 177–200.

Spelman, E. V., "Aristotle and the Politicization of the Soul," in Harding and Hintikka, 1983, pp. 17–30.

Springborg, P., "Aristotle and the Problem of Needs," *History of Political Thought*, 5 (1984), pp. 393–424.

Stark, R., "Der Gesamtaufbau der aristotelischen *Politik*," with discussion, in Fondation Hardt, *Entretiens sur l'Antiquité Classique XI, La "Politique" d'Aristote* (Geneva, 1964), pp. 1–51.

Ste Croix, G. E. M. de, *The Class Struggle in the Ancient Greek World From the Archaic Age to the Arab Conquests* (London, 1981), pp. 69–80 and elsewhere.

Steinmetz, P., ed., *Schriften zu den Politika des Aristoteles* (Hildesheim, 1973).

Stocks, J. L., "The Composition of Aristotle's *Politics*," *Classical Quarterly*, 21 (1927), pp. 177–87.

Stocks, J. L., "*Scholê*," *Classical Quarterly*, 30 (1936), pp. 177–87.

Strauss, L., *The City and Man* (Chicago, 1964), ch. 1.

Vander Waerdt, P. A., "Kingship and Philosophy in Aristotle's Best Regime," *Phronesis*, 30 (1985), pp. 249–73.

Vander Waerdt, P. A., "The Political Intention of Aristotle's Moral Philosophy," *Ancient Philosophy*, 5 (1985), pp. 77–89.

Weil, R., *Aristote et l'histoire: Essai sur la "Politique,"* (Paris, 1960).

Weil, R., "Aristotle's View of History," in Barnes *et al.*, 1977, pp. 202–17.

Wheeler, M., "Aristotle's Analysis of the Nature of Political Struggle," in Barnes *et al.*, 1977, pp. 159–69.

Whitehead, D., "Aristotle the Metic," *Proceedings of the Cambridge Philological Society*, 21 (1975), pp. 94–9.

Willers, D., "Der Aufbau der aristotelischen Politik," in Steinmetz, 1973, pp. 96–101.

Winthrop, D., "Aristotle and Theories of Justice," *American Political Science Review*, 72 (1978), pp. 1201–16.

Winthrop, D., "Aristotle on Participatory Democracy," *Polity*, 11 (1978), pp. 151–71.

Wolff, F., "Justice et Pouvoir (Aristote, Politique III, 9–13)," *Phronesis*, 33 (1988), pp. 273–96.

Wood, E. M. and Wood, N., *Class Ideology and Ancient Political Theory* (Oxford, 1978), ch. 5.

Wormuth, F., "Aristotle on Law," in *Essays in Political Theory Presented to George H. Sabine*, eds, M. Konvitz and A. E. Murphy (Ithaca, 1948 [repr. 1972]), pp. 45–61.

Yack, B., "Community and Conflict in Aristotle's Political Philosophy," *Review of Politics*, 47 (1985), pp. 92–112.

Index Locorum

ARISTOTLE

Categoriae (Cat.)
  6.6a26 160
  8.11a15–16 160
  12.14a26–8 227
    14a29–35 127
    14b4–8 126, 229

De Interpretatione (DI)
  9. 116
  13.22b36–23a4 288

Analytica Priora (An. Pr.)
I.
    3.25b14 287
    5.26b34–6 132
    27a18–20 132
    13.32b5–6 287

Analytica Posteriora (An. Post.)
I.
    2.71b33–72a5 269
    4. 101, 113
    6. 101
    8.75b33ff. 113
    10.76b13 114
II.
    10.93b30 250
    17.99a12–14 240

Topics (Top.)
I.
    1.100b21–3 268
    3.101b5ff. 63
    4.101b19–23 251
    7. 136
    8.103b15–16 250
    15.107b13–18 248, 275
II.
    9.114a38–b1 232
    11.115b17–18 277
III.
    3.118a35–6 232
VI.
    1.139a25–7 256
    139a31–2 251
    4.141b3–14 269

    6.145a15–16 6
  13.150a18–21 137
    150a33–6 137
    150b23–6 238
VII.
    3.153a15–16 250
    153b14–15 250
    153b25–6 232
VIII.
    1.156a27–30 232

Physica (Phys.) 323–4
I.
    6.–7. 326
II.
    1.192b8–12 7
    192b13–15 130
    192b13–19 123
    192b33–193a2 269
    193a9–b18 130
    2.194a28–33 129
    194a32–3 270
    3.195a23–5 270
    4.–6. 121–2
    5.197a5–8 122
    197b1–8 122
    197b20–2 122
    6.197b34–5 258
    198a9–10 119
    7.198a22–7 121
    8. 270
    198b35–6 258, 287
    199b4 258
    199b15–18 120
    199b24–6 120
    9.199b34ff. 111
IV.
    5.213a9 188
V.
    1. 324–6
    3.226b27–8 228
VII.
    4.248b7–10 248, 275
    7.260b17–19 127
VIII.
    4.255a30–b5 125, 139
    7.260b17–19 127

261a13–14   126
9.265a22–4   126

De Caelo (DC)   289
I.
  12.   277
    281b25–7   123
    282a21–3   123
II.
  5.288a2–3   132
III.
  1.298a27–32   7, 123

de Generatione et Corruptione (GC)
II.
  6.333a20–7   275
    333b4–7   258

Meteorologica (Meteor.)
II.
  4.361a6   234

de Anima (DA)   80, 83–4
I.
  1.403a25–b7   250
    403a27–b2   7
II.
  1.413a8–9   35
  2.413a31–b1   231
    413b24–7   231
  3.414b20–32   228, 230
    415a11–12   231
  4.415a16–24   231
    416b23–5   229, 256
  5.417a21–b2   125
    417a21–418a6   139
  6.418a7–8   231
III.
  3.428b19   228
  4.429b5–9   125, 139

de Somno et Vigilia (Somn.)
  2.455b17–28   270, 291

Historia Animalium (HA)
I.
  1.486a5–8   140
    487b33–488a10   105–8, 113,
      123–4
    488a7   293
  6.490b18   109
    491a14ff.   105
II.
  1.497b31–2   292
  15.505b28   109
  17.507a19–24   292

V.
  1.539b7–14   121
  19.550b32–551a13   121
VI.
  15.569a24–b9   121
  16.   121
VII.
  10.   120
VIII.
  1.588a18–b3   124
    588b4ff.   107
    589a1ff.   108
IX.
  37.622a4   103
  40.623b5–13   133

de Partibus Animalium (PA)
I.
  1.639b19ff.   111
    640b35ff.   100
    641b12   270
    642a7ff.   111
  3.643a35ff.   105, 113
  4.644a23ff.   109
    644a31   109
    644b7ff.   105, 113
  5.645a23–6   270
II.
  1.   330
    646b10   31
    646a24–9   127, 131
    646a25–6   126
  2.648a9–11   292
  10.656a7ff.   106–7
III.
  2.663b28–9   287
  3.665a22–6   290
IV.
  8.684a32–b1   292
  10.687a7–15   248
    687a15–16   132
  12.694b12   81

de Motu Animalium (MA)
  10.703a29   33
    703a29–b2   118

de Incessu Animalium (IA)
  2.704b12–18   290
  4.705b33–706a4   290
    706a9–10   289
    706a12–13   290
    706a17–22   289
  5.706b12–16   290
  12.711a18–19   132
  19.714b8–14   292

de Generatione Animalium (GA)
I.
    1.715b25–30   121
    2.716a23   81
    8.722b   188
    18.726b24   90
    19.727b29–30   287
II.
    1.731b35ff.   116
      732b15ff.   107
      734b25ff.   100
      734b28–30   81
      735a9–11   125
      735a17–19   256
    6.742a19–22   126
III.
    10.   127
    11.762b28ff.   116
IV.
    1.765a34–b4   292
    3.   258
      767a36–b15   258
      769b8–10   258
    4.   258
      770b9–17   258
      770b11–13   287
    8.777a19–21   287

Metaphysics (Met.)   58, 80–1, 109
I.
    1.   332
    3.983a31–2   270
    8.989a15–18   126
II.
    1.993b19–21   6
III.
    3.999a6–10   228
      999a8   230
      999a13–14   229
IV.
    2.1003a33–b10   230
      1003b23–1004a2   187
    3.1005b2–5   7
V.
    4.1014b16ff.   188
      1014b26–1015a13   130
    5.1015a20ff.   111
    6.   187
      1016b31–1017a3   136
    9.1018a9–11   136
    11.1018b34–7   127
      1019a2–4   127, 137
    26.1023b34–6   136
VI.
    1.   326
      1025b25   6, 119
      1026a18–19   7

    2.   329
      1026b27–1027a17   258
      1027a8–11   287
VII.
    1.1028a34–6   230
    5.1031a12   250
    7.1032a12–13   119
      1032a15–25   122
      1032a25–32   121
    8.   329
      1032b29–32   122
      1034a5ff.   114
    9.1034a21–6   121
    10.1035b4–8   126
      1035b23–5   137
      1035b27ff.   114
IX.
    4.1047b3–6   277
    8.1049b12–17   126
      1050a4–b6   126
      1050a21   124
      1050b1–2   80
      1050b6–19   127
X.
    1.1052a15–b1   188
      1052a15–3.1054a32   187
    3.1054a20ff.   190
XI.
    7.1064a16–19   6
      1064b1–3   7
    8.1065b3–4   119
XII.
    1.1069a30–b2   278
    3.1070a6–7   121
      1070a6–9   119
    4.1070b30–4   121
    8.1073a30–5   123
      1074a38   18
      1074b10ff.   116
XIII.
    2.1077b3–4   126
      1077a36–b11   127
XIV.
    4.1091b16ff.   187

Ethica Nicomachea (EN)   5–6, 8, 58, 65,
    72–3, 75–93, 119–20, 198, 280–1,
    348, 356
I.
    1.1094a8–9   64
    2.   119, 326
      1094a18–22   191
      1094a26–b11   1
      1094a27   76
      1094a27–8   5
      1094b7–10   21
      1094b10–11   5
      1094b10ff.   115

3. 326
  1094b11ff. 112
  1094b14–15 5
  1094b14ff. 112
  1094b19–22 287
  1094b23–1095a2 373
  1094b25 130
  1095a2 5, 76, 112
  1095a5–6 308
4.1095a14–20 5, 253
  1095a17 77
  1095a19–20 252
  1095a30–b13 269
  1095b4ff. 92
  1095b4–10 373
  1095b5 6
  1095b6 76
5.1095b15–33 365–6
6.1096a19–29 248
  1096a25 113
  1096b31–1097a3 239
7. 8, 77–83, 87, 90–2
  1097b7–21 354
  1097b8–11 124, 193
  1097b11 104
  1097b14–15 202
  1097b17–20 348
  1097b22–1098a18 77, 82
  1097b23ff. 84
  1097b24ff. 80, 91
  1097b33–1098a7 80
  1098a7–20 252, 259
  1098a12–16 91
  1098a16 76, 114
  1098a16–18 6, 191
8.1098b9–12 268
  1098b30–1099a7 348
  1099a8 357
  1099a31–b8 259, 348
9.1099b20–32 72
  1099b20–5 132
  1099b29–32 124
  1100a4–5 346
10.1100b35ff. 63
  1101a14–16 6
13.1102a7–10 41, 72, 124
  1102a10–12 60
  1102a32–b5 231
  1103a3–10 271

II.
1. 27
  1103a18–b6 135
  1103a23–6 124, 295
2.1103b26ff. 112
5.1106a6–10 124
6.1106a15 82
  1106a23 91
  1106b36 191

1106b36–1107a2 145, 252
7.1107b8–21 259
9.1109b20–3 134
III.
1.1110b28–30 135
2.1111b26–9 191
3.1112a31–3 119
4.1113a22–4 191
IV.
1. 213, 259
  1119b26–7 246
  1120b4–6 220
  1120b11–20 220
2. 259
3.1124b31–1125a2 222
5.1126a31–b4 134
V. 6, 11, 158, 238, 242
1. 47
  1129a13–14 64
  1129b14–25 299
  1129b17–19 215, 300
  1129b19 81
  1129b25–7 260
  1130a10–13 260
2.1130a14–b5 215
  1130b26–9 73
  1130b30–1131a1 238
  1130b30–1131a9 300
3. 6, 247, 300–1
  1131a10–14 242
  1131a13–14 277
  1131a14–24 6
  1131a18–20 240
  1131a24–8 241–2
  1131a25–9 301, 326
  1131a27–9 124, 310
  1131a31 240
  1131b9–10 241
  1131b12–13 240
  1131b19–23 241
  1131b25 300
4. 301
  1131b25–9 238
  1131b29–31 246
  1132b31–3 158
5. 9, 156–81, 301
  1132b31–4 6
  1132b31ff. 158
  1132b31–4 300
  1132b34 177
  1133a10–13 159
  1133a16–18 30
  1133a16–22 159–60
  1133a19–26 275
  1133a23–5 167
  1133a25–31 161–2, 301
  1133a32–3 167
  1133b6–10 161–2

Éthica Nicomachea (EN) cont'd.

    1133b10–13 164
    1133b15–22 159–60
    1133b19–20 162
    1133b27–8 162, 169
  6.1134a24ff. 189
    1134a26–8 288
    1134a35–b2 304
    1134b13–15 296
  7. 11, 279–82, 285–9, 293, 296–8
    1134b18–1135a5 285–9, 296–8
    1134b18–24 260
    1134b18ff. 68
    1134b23–4 298
    1134b35–1135a5 48
    1135a4–5 288, 293, 301
    1135a5 124, 257
    1135a5–8 298
  10.1137b13 298
    1137b18 130
    1137b26–32 284, 298, 305
    1137b26 130
  11.1138a19–20 260
VI. 6
  2.1139a26–31 6
    1139b3–4 6
  3.1139b14–7.1141b8 350
  4. 119, 324
    1140a9–10 261
    1140a14–16 119
    1140a20–1 261
  5. 119
    1140b6–7 6
    1140b11–14 373
  7.1141a20–2 370
    1141a38–b1 370
  8. 7, 119
    1141b23ff. 72
    1141b24–8 298
    1141b24–33 240
    1142a17–18 7
  11.1143b6–7 131
  12.1144a34–6 135
  13. 124
    1144b1–17 148
    1144b5 125
    1144b30–1145a2 28
    1145a10–11 119
VII. 6
  1.1145a15–30 266
    1145a27–8 277
    1145b2–7 268, 282
    1145b12–13 134
  3.1146b15ff. 334
  8.1150b36 135
    1151a20–4 134
  12.1153a7–17 324
  13.1153b9–21 6

VIII.
  1.1155a1–9 193
    1155a16–21 209
    1155a22–3 189
  2.–3. 252
  3.1156b25ff. 193
  4.1157a25–9 252
    1157a30–2 258
  5.1157b19 252
  6.1158a10 193
  9.1159b25ff. 189
    1159b31 196
    1160a11ff. 103
    1160a14–30 25, 254
    1160a21–3 129
  10.1160a33–5 233
    1160a35–6 53
    1160a35–b22 235, 274
    1160b10–17 227
    1160b12–16 246
    1160b21 309
    1160b21–2 227
    1160b29–31 146
  11.1161a32ff. 67
    1161a32–4 146
    1161b5–8 17
  12.1162a16–19 128
    1162a17–18 27
    1162a17ff. 104
    1162a17–19 123
    1162a19 81
  13.1162b21–3 284
    1162b21–1163a1 298
IX.
  7.1167b16ff. 195
  8.1168b7–8 196
    1168b31–3 118, 256
    1169a17 132
  9.1169b16ff. 105
    1169b18ff. 103
    1169b3–1170b19 193
    1169b17–19 252
    1169b18–19 124
    1170a21 130
    1170b6–7 193
    1170b8–10 134
    1170b10–14 252
  10.1170b20ff. 193
    1170b29–33 16
    1171a2 252
  12.1171b32 252
X. 350, 360
  4.1174a13ff. 324
  6.–8. 115
  7. 361
    1177a12–19 360
    1177b6 76
    1177b6–12 214

1177b6–20   206
1177b26–32   375
1177b31–1178a2   23
1178a6–9   360
8.1178a14–16   124
1178a23–b3   259
1178a24–5   357
1178a24–b8   359
1178b10–12   286
1178b33–1179a13   259
9.   72–3
1179a35ff.   112
1179b20–4   135
1179b20–1180a24   124
1179b24–6   295
1179b31–4   70
1179b31–1180a5   295
1179b34–5   299
1180a1–5   40
1180a1–19   373
1180a5–14   70, 73
1180a18–24   40
1180a21–4   295, 304
1180a22   298
1180a24–6   60
1180a24–9   15
1180a29–34   71
1180a30–b13   295
1180b12–13   73
1180b23–1181b12   119
1180b28–1181b23   5
1181b6–15   71
1181b12–13   72–3
1181b12–22   6
1181b14ff.   112
1181b15   1, 73, 115
1181b15–22   70
1181b28–9   73

Magna Moralia (MM)   6, 281, 285
I.   11
33.   279–82, 285–9, 293
1194b6   189
1194b30–1195a8   285–9
34.1197b36–1198a22   124–5
II.
9.1207b31–3   6

Ethica Eudemia (EE)   6, 75, 281, 348,
361
I.
1.1214a30–1   252
1214b7–11   191
2.1214b11–27   262
5.1216a23–7   358
1216b16ff.   112

7.1217a21ff.   114
8.1217b31   113
1218a6ff.   187
1218b13   7
II.
1.1219a8   124
1219a13–18   261
1219a26–8   348
1219a35–9   346
1219a38–9   6, 259
1219b1–2   6
1219b1–12   348
3.1220b27–9   132
1221a12   370
III.
1.1229a1–2   252
1229a7   252
7.1234a23–33   124
1234a27–30   148
VII.
1.1234b22   5
2.   252
1235b34   189
1236a14–15   193
1236a17–22   230
1237a30–2   193
1237b35   193
1238a9   193
1238a11–13   354
8.1241a35ff.   195
9.1241b13–15   238, 299
1214b14–15   134
1241b32   230
10.1242a10ff.   189
1242a22ff.   103–5
1242a22–7   123–4
1242a28–9   146
1242a40ff.   104
1242b22ff.   189
1242b33ff.   189
1243b22   275
12.1244b1–1245b19   193
1244b24–6   252
1245a30–1   193
1245b19   193
VIII.
2.1248b26–38   348
3.   361
1248b26–7   6
1249a15–17   355
1249a22–b25   348
1249b14–21   375
1249b17–23   359

On Virtues and Vices
5.1250b33   209
7.1251b3   209

Politica (Pol.)
I. 4–5, 57–8, 72, 293–8, 356
    1.–2. 3, 8, 95
    1.1252a1 250
    1252a1–7 184, 191, 253
    1252a8ff. 188
    1252a18–23 140, 238
    2. 8, 9, 109–10, 118–41
    1252a7–18 123
    1252a24 96, 165
    1252a24–34 294
    1252a24–b30 23
    1252a24–1253a1 294
    1252a26–34 122, 128
    1252a30–4 143
    1252b1–4 165
    1252b5–9 145, 151
    1252b7 90
    1252b9 143
    1252b9–10 122
    1252b10 128
    1252b12 150
    1252b12–16 122, 129
    1252b19–27 96
    1252b27–30 122, 132, 203
    1252b27–34 128–31
    1252b27–1253a1 256, 353
    1252b28–30 130, 365
    1252b29ff. 102
    1252b29–30 124
    1252b30 22, 66, 118, 122, 269,
        293
    1252b31–4 130
    1252b31–43 269
    1252b32 109–10, 270
    1252b32ff. 99
    1252b32–4 25
    1252b34–1253a7 132–3, 269
    1253a1ff. 95–101, 103, 105
    1253a1–4 123
    1253a1–18 293, 296
    1253a2 118, 269
    1253a2–3 120, 258, 293
    1253a2–4 28
    1253a3–4 139
    1253a3–7 153
    1253a7ff. 99, 102
    1253a7–9 120
    1253a7–18 33, 123, 133–5
    1253a9–10 152
    1253a14–15 152
    1253a15–29 216
    1253a16 112, 147
    1253a18 82, 100
    1253a18–19 120, 138
    1253a18ff. 100
    1253a18–29 143, 153, 256, 294
    1253a18–33 136–40

    1253a19 104, 112, 127
    1253a20ff. 110
    1253a20–3 29
    1253a23 261
    1253a25 118, 269
    1253a25–6 120, 293
    1253a27ff. 107
    1253a27–9 28, 153, 258
    1253a29 115, 133
    1253a29–30 27, 125, 293
    1253a29–39 296
    1253a30–1 119
    1253a31–9 28, 294
    1253a32ff. 99
    1253a32–3 295
    1253a35–7 153
    1253a37–9 238, 295, 299
    3.–13. 3
    3.1253b3–7 128
    1253b15ff. 64
    1253b20–3 260, 268, 297
    4.–7. 9, 269
    4. 143
    1253b29–30 151
    1253b32 145, 151
    1253b33–9 17
    1254a1–7 324
    1254a5 119
    1254a8ff. 189
    5.1254a17–20 260
    1254a21–4 143
    1254a28–33 31
    1254a34–b21 269
    1254a36–7 124
    1254b4–5 146, 150
    1254b4–20 149
    1254b5–6 146
    1254b13–14 269
    1254b16–19 17, 150
    1254b16ff. 189
    1254b17–23 143–6
    1254b20 90
    1254b20–3 143
    1254b23–6 150
    1254b25–6 143, 146
    1254b27–34 42, 150
    1254b30–1 259
    1254b34–1255a2 151, 274
    6.1255a1–3 260
    1255a3–26 144
    1255a3–b4 88, 143
    1255a5–9 297
    1255a10 273
    1255a28ff. 145
    1255b3–4 42
    1255b4–15 297
    1255b9ff. 189
    1255b11–12 143, 145, 152

1255b13–14   146
7.1255b35–7   145, 259
8.–10.   156–80
8.–11.   9
8.1256b16–26   150
1256b23–6   152
1256b26–39   266
1256b32   129
9.1256b27   166
1256b27ff.   163
1256b30ff.   163
1256b36ff.   163
1256b37–8   166
1256b40–1257a5   163
1257a6–13   158
1257a6ff.   165
1257a15–41   164
1257b25–6   120
1257b1–5   166
1257b10–11   301
1257b20–35   166–7
1257b40–1258a14   167
1258a39ff.   163
10.1258a19ff.   112
1258a21–3   119
1258a40–b2   260
1258b2–8   167
1258b4   165
11.1258b9–10   64
1258b9–11   66
1258b37   36
1258b37–9   220
1258b38   143
12.1259a37–9   128
1259a39   222
1259b1   146, 149
1259b1–3   269
1259b10–11   146, 149
1259b21–1260b7   145
1259b21ff.   87
1259b25–6   143
13.   9
1259b21–1260b7   145
1259b27–8   146
1260a10ff.   87, 90
1260a12   143, 147
1260a14   90
1260a17ff.   91
1260a36–b2   36
1260b3–7   148
1260b5–7   17, 146–7
1260b8ff.   24
1260b18–19   40
II.   3–5, 10, 57–8, 72, 182–225, 347,
375, 378
1.1260b27–36   183
1260b36–1261a9   184
1261a22–4   30

2.–5.   10
2.1261a10–b16   184, 216
1261a12–b15   208
1261a20–2   187–9
1261a24–5   251
1261a29–30   189
1261a30–1   177, 300
1261a32–4   245
1261a31   6
1261b7   187
1261b7–9   189
1261b10–11   188
1261b10–15   190
1261b14   129, 353
3.1261b16   191
1261b16–1262b36   184
1261b20–30   275
1261b31–2   187
1261b33–1262a14   192
1262a4–8   376
1262a7   273
1262a14–24   192
4.1262a25–40   192
1262b7–24   215
1262b11–13   188
1262b29–35   192
1262b36   191
5.   10, 306
1262b37–1263b29   194
1262b37–1264a1   184
1263a17–21   195
1263a30–b14   201
1263a40–b5   220
1263b6–12   357
1263b7–8   195
1263b10–11   196
1263b15–22   195, 200, 219
1263b22–9   201
1263b29   195
1263b30ff.   190
1263b31–2   188
1263b39–1264a2   39
1264a1–5   277
1264a1ff.   196
1264a14–17   186
1264a17–40   377
1264a22–9   208
1264a24–35   376
1264a34–6   264
1264b5–6   268
1264b6–9   376
1264b15–25   215, 377
1264b16   197
1264b19–22   34
1264b25   376
6.1264b26   378
1264b40–1265a1   378
1265a1–3   299, 378

Politica (Pol.) cont'd.
1265a6   378
1265a12–17   378
1265a13–17   16
1265a17–18   43, 277
1265a19   350, 363
1265a20–5   378
1265a21–4   350
1265a27–32   377–8
1265a39–b16   378
1265b6–16   123
1265b25   240
1265b29–33   378
1265b35   231
1265b40–1   217
7.1266b8–14   123
1266b28–31   39
1266b38–1267a2   219
1267a37–9   219
1267b16   274
8.1267b37–9   253
1268a25   272
1268b34–8   119
1269a4ff.   116
1269a7   116
1269a9–27   298–9
1269a12–24   295
9.1269a34–b7   264
1269b12–1270a15   40
1270b11–12   5
1271a26–37   217
1271a41ff.   60
1271b2–3   251, 256–7
1271b9   273
10.   256
1271b32   299
1272a12–21   217
1272b19–22   5
11.   256
1273a15–17   246
1273a21–b7   263–4
1273a37–9   256–7
1273b10   261
12.1273b32–3   119, 296
1274b9–11   184
1274b12–15   292
1274b18–19   119, 296
III.   3–5, 10, 57–8, 298–305, 309–11
1.   326
1274b32–4   250
1274b38   42, 119, 238
1274b39–41   29
1274b41   111
1275a7–14   263
1275a14–23   264
1275a22–34   226
1275a35–b5   226–8, 232

1275b7–8   245
1275b17–19   264
1275b20–1   202, 353
2.1275b33   264
1276a17–b13   238
3.1276a23–4   256
1276a27–9   16
1276b1   250
1276b1–13   43, 119, 325–6
1276b7–8   238, 299
4.1276b16–34   88
1276b20   35
1276b34ff.   82, 88, 90
1277a1–5   351
1277a5ff.   110
1277a14–16   90
1277a25ff.   90
1277a29   90
1277b3–7   221–2
1277b3   261
1277b25–7   259
5.   268
1277b38–9   263
1278a1–3   153
1278a3   261
1278a4–6   264
1278a9–13   36
1278a12–21   220
1278a17–21   262
1278a18–21   37
1278a19–20   242
1278a21–4   37
1278a28   264
1278a28–34   243
6.   103, 107
1278b8–11   119, 238
1278b9–10   309
1278b15ff.   101–3
1278b15–30   227
1278b17–30   203, 294
1278b19–25   124
1278b19–30   42, 293
1278b19–1279a21   46
1278b20ff.   66
1278b20–5   252
1278b21ff.   102
1278b21–2   32, 227
1278b23   229
1278b23–4   47
1278b24ff.   102
1278b32–40   144, 146
1278b33–8   23
1279a3–4   35
1279a8–13   303
1279a10–16   329
1279a17–7.1279b10   1
1279a17–21   47, 67, 127, 146,

150, 227, 229, 232, 235–6,
257–8, 299
7. 10, 43, 108, 300, 310
1279a32–4 274
1279a34–b4 235
1279a35–7 53
1279a37–b4 44
1279a39–b4 46
1279a40 235
1279b4–6 230, 309
1279b4–10 270
1279b6–7 274
1279b7ff. 68
1279b9–10 320
8. 228–9
1279b11ff. 64, 112
1279b17–19 310
1279b34–1280a6 44
1280a1–6 315–16
9.–13. 247
9. 124, 310
1280a7ff. 67
1280a7–25 247
1280a14–16 303
1280a16–18 326
1280a18 6
1280a18–19 242
1280a22–1281a8 22
1280a24–5 244
1280a25–31 246
1280a25–40 250–1
1280a31–2 22, 66
1280a31ff. 102
1280a31–6 203
1280a32–4 123
1280a33–4 102, 143
1280b5 125, 259
1280b6 268
1280b10 297
1280b4–35 251
1280b6–8 250, 257–8
1280b10–12 253
1280b20ff. 159
1280b26 15
1280b28 257, 268
1280b30 313
1280b33–5 262
1280b33–1281a1 132
1280b34 24, 102
1280b34–5 22
1280b36–40 252
1280b39 66, 229
1280b39–1281a8 301
1280b40 24
1280b40ff. 102
1281a2 22
1281a2–4 252

1281a3–7 363
1281a4–8 248, 251
1281a7 125, 259
10.1281a11–13 247
1281a15 240
1281a18 240
1281a23 272
11. 3
1281a39–1282a41 51
1281a40–2 239, 271
1281a42–b2 270
1281a42–b38 322
1281b1–7 270–1
1281b15–21 270, 277
1281b21–31 271
1281b23–4 276
1281b25–8 272
1281b31 272
1281b33 272
1281b34–5 134
1281b35 270
1282a10–11 261
1282a13–14 272
1282a17 270
1282a17–23 272, 322
1282a24–b1 272
1282a25–6 276
1282a39–41 271
1282b1–6 51, 305
1282b4–6 298
1282b6–13 299
1282b10–11 40
1282b10–13 68
12.1282b14–16 119
1282b18 277
1282b18–21 242
1282b18–1283a9 247–8
1282b20 6
1282b22–3 119
1282b23 2
1282b23–1283a22 49
1282b24 240
1282b33–4 248
1283a1 248
1283a14–22 51, 249, 363
1283a16–22 124
13.1283a23–42 363
1283a33 249
1283a40–2 271, 273
1283b4–8 45
1283b13–35 273
1283b19–20 249
1283b23 273
1283b23–7 272
1283b27–8 45
1283b30–5 271
1283b36–42 232

Politica (Pol.) cont'd.
    1284a3–17   239, 274, 304
    1284a10   235
    1284a10–11   239, 277
    1284a11   53
    1284a11–17   274
    1284a13–14   304
    1284b22–34   239
    1284b25–34   276, 379
  14.   314
    1285b29–33   239, 273
  15.   302
    1285b36   273
    1286a9–11   298
    1286a17–20   298
    1286b3–7   235
    1286b3–22   45
    1286b8–22   227, 329–30
    1286b15–16   67
    1286b20–2   45
    1286b22–7   237
    1286b36   272
  16.   302
    1287a1–3   273
    1287a8–10   273
    1287a8–18   260
    1287a8–23   302
    1287a12–16   244
    1287a18   295, 299
    1287a21–2   231
    1287a29–30   231
    1287a32   303
    1287a41–b5   298, 303
    1287b5–8   284
    1287b25–6   299
  17.   3, 239
    1287b37–41   42–3, 124, 257, 260,
        300
    1287b41–1288a5   303
    1288a3   304
    1288a9–12   315
    1288a12–15   44
    1288a14   240
    1288a15–19   274, 277
    1288a15–29   379
    1288a24–9   276, 304
    1288a26–9   274
  18. 1288a32–4   235
    1288a32–41   315
    1288a35   274
    1288a36   235
IV.   4–5, 8, 11, 57–62, 65–70, 72–4,
    302, 307–22
  1.   43, 62, 65–6, 70
    1288b10–21   7
    1288b16–19   63
    1288b21   57, 62–3

    1288b28–30   308
    1288b29   65
    1288b35–8   73–4, 307
    1288b37ff.   62, 73
    1288b38–9   59
    1289a11–13   304
    1289a13–15   40
    1289a13–20   299
    1289a15–18   119, 238, 240, 309
    1289a17   229
  2.   65–6
    1289a7ff.   65
    1289a26   58
    1289a26–30   270
    1289a28–30   230
    1289a30–3   53, 124, 234–5, 256,
        274
    1289a31–3   257, 259, 265
    1289a38–b5   235
    1289a38–b11   270
    1289a39–b5   53, 300
    1289a40   235, 239
    1289b2–5   322
    1289b5–11   234
    1289b9–11   60, 74
    1289b13–14   65
    1289b20–2   65
  3. 1289b27–8   328
    1289b27–1290a13   45, 238
    1289b36–8   329
    1290a7–11   299
    1290a8   240
    1290a13–16   311
    1290a13–19   233
    1290a22–9   234
    1290a23–6   311
    1290a24–7   44
    1290a27–9   322
  4.   312–14
    1290b4   240
    1290b4–5   248
    1290b9–14   243
    1290b17–20   317
    1290b21–39   110, 238
    1290b21–1291b2   30
    1290b24   262
    1290b25–38   143, 312
    1290b38–1291b8   238
    1290b39   262
    1291a4–6   261
    1291a10–19   202
    1291a11–28   376
    1291a16   261
    1291a16–18   66
    1291a17   274
    1291a17–18   203
    1291a19–24   203

1291a24–8   110, 118, 123, 203, 256, 262, 269
1291a32–3   262
1291a33–6   18
1291b2   261
1291b7–13   233
1291b11–13   45
1291b30–7   318
1291b34–6   321
1292a6–7   303
1292a17–18   330
1292a18–21   303
1292a19–20   49
1292a28–30   55
1292a31–2   272
1292a32   304
1292a36–7   298
5.   312
1292b10   313
6.   312–14
1293a1–10   329
1293a30–3   49
7.1293a40   233
1293b1–19   239, 256
1293b2–21   309
1293b14–21   268, 314
1293b16   231
8.   309
1293b22–6   44
1293b23–7   124, 236, 257
1293b25   237
1293b33–4   311
1293b36–8   316
1293b41   240
1294a5–7   299
1294a9–11   46, 250
1294a9–25   45
1294a10   240
1294a10–11   124
1294a11–14   317
1294a21–2   249
1294a22–5   124
1294a24–5   239, 260
9.   309
1294a37–9   246
1294b3–4   246
1294b7–9   246
1294b19   231
1294b19–29   244
1294b31–4   246
1294b37–9   246
10.   314
1295a17–23   274
11.   309
1295a25–34   234, 257
1295a30   350
1295a40   304

1295a40–b1   45
1295a36   6
1295b1–3   229
1295b3   311
1295b15–18   320
1296a1–5   227
1296a7   67
1296a13–18   322
1296a22–3   234
1296a22–b2   329
1296a37–40   234
12.   60, 65
1296b15   273
1296b17–34   51
1296b24–34   43
1296b29   220
1297a9   240
13.1297a17–24   246, 298
1297a38ff.   68
1297b16–28   227, 329
14.–16.   65, 238
14.1298a3–7   272
1298a29–31   55
1298b16–18   246
1298b26–1299a1   303
1298b29   295
15.   262
1299a28–30   64
1299a34   82
1299a39   261
1299b30–8   245
1299b38–1300a1   55
1300a4–6   41
1300b31–2   243
1301a12–13   245
V.   4–5, 8, 11–12, 57–62, 65–70, 72–4, 302, 307–11, 323–45
1.   324
1301a20–5   308, 324
1301a22   325
1301a25–b1   326–8
1301a25–36   46
1301a26–7   48
1301a28–31   244
1301a34–5   244
1301a39–b1   331
1301b3–4   249
1301b5ff.   325
1301b6–10   227
1301b26–9   333
1301b29   310
1301b30–1302a8   242
1301b35ff.   67
1301b35–6   48
1301b37–9   311
1301b39–1302a2   234, 329
1302a8–15   237, 320, 322, 325

Politica (Pol.) cont'd.
  2.1302a16–18 324, 332
    1302a20–2 334
    1302a31–4 335
  3.1302b10–14 337
    1302b18–19 334
    1302b25–9 334–5
    1302b32 336
    1302b33–1303a2 32
    1302b34 336
    1302b34ff. 110
    1302b40–1303a11 334
    1303a13–14 324–5, 336
    1303a25–b3 264
    1303a28–b2 335
    1303b7–17 337
  4.1303b15 331
    1303b21–2 325
    1303b28 325
    1303b31–2 325
    1304a17–38 32
    1304b4–5 328
    1304b4–18 331–2
  5.–7. 337
  5. 314
    1304b19–20 332
    1304b23–4 343
    1304b35 320
    1305a7–28 337
    1305a18–34 329
    1305a28–32 338
  6.1305b22–39 333, 338
    1305b39ff. 333
    1306a12–19 246
    1306b6–16 335
    1306b17–21 330, 338
  7.1306b22–7 334
    1307a5–27 68, 328, 338, 342
    1307a34 222
    1307a40ff. 325
    1307b19–25 333
    1307b22–7 328
  8. 323
    1307b26–30 338
    1307b40–1308a3 331
    1308a16–18 338
    1308a24–30 343
    1308b10–19 32
    1308b20–4 40
    1309a2–3 316
    1309a15–20 320
    1309a20–6 217
    1309a21–2 240
    1309a27–32 272
    1309a28 240
  9. 323
    1309a33–7 274
    1309a36–9 67

    1309b18ff. 68
    1309b18–19 339
    1309b20–35 32
    1309b21 245
    1309b23ff. 110, 236
    1309b31–5 330
    1309b37 245
    1310a12ff. 108
    1310a12–14 40, 339
    1310a14–17 297, 304
    1310a19–36 319
    1310a22–4 320
    1310a28–36 222, 321
    1310a32–4 15
    1310a34–5 41
    1310a36–8 222
  10.–12. 309
  10.1310a40–b7 341
    1310b2–7 328
    1310b3 235
    1310b18–20 227
    1310b32–4 235
    1310b33 242
    1310b37–8 342
    1310b40–1311a8 274
    1311a2–22 342
    1311a4–6 46
    1311a9–10 46, 67
    1311a10 315
    1311a22–5 341
    1311b1–3 5
    1311b38 342
    1312a12 342
    1312a40–b9 333
    1312b1–7 310
    1312b5–6 330
    1312b25ff. 345
    1313a3–4 340
    1313a3–16 45
    1313a9–10 331
  11.1313a34–8 66, 331
    1313a38 342
    1313a39–b6 340
    1313b9–10 342
    1315a6–7 240
    1315b8–10 69
  12.1315b11–39 237
    1316a3–4 343
    1316a17–39 344
    1316a29–34 227
    1316a39ff. 344
    1316b14–15 344
VI. 4–5, 8, 11, 57–62, 65–70, 72–4,
    239, 302, 307–22, 328
  1. 60, 244
    1316b31–6 4
    1317a17 310
    1317a25 220

1317a35–8   4
1317a36–40   244
1317a40–b17   222
2.   321
  1317a23–9   43
  1317a40–b2   46
  1317a40–b17   316
  1317b2–3   245
  1317b2–11   316
  1317b3–4   242
  1317b4   310
  1317b11ff.   67
  1317b11–12   15, 250
  1317b11–17   319
  1317b17–35   55
  1317b18–38   244
  1317b30–1   245
  1317b40–1   46
  1318a4–10   318
3.1318a18–21   244, 246
4.   312–14
  1318b6–1319b32   329
  1318b16–17   320
  1318b28–30   317
  1318b39   222
  1319a27   220
  1319b4–6   4
  1319b6–11   243
  1319b30   15, 222
5.   312
  1319b37–9   4
  1319b40–1320a   284
  1320a17   45
  1320a30   240
  1320a37   240
  1320b2   240
  1320b9–14   272
6.   312
  1320b17–20   313
  1320b18–33   245–6
  1320b19–20   310
  1320b29–31   313
  1320b29–1321a1   42
  1320b22–5   246
  1321a1–2   45
  1321a2–3   49
  1321a5–21   262
7.1321a5–21   329
  1321a41–b1   67
8.   238, 262
  1321b14–18   132
  1322a29–b12   272
  1322b16–17   245
  1323a6–9   245
VII.   3–5, 8, 12, 57–61, 65, 69–74,
    111, 183, 197–8, 239, 260–70, 278,
    302, 307, 318, 346–81

1.–3.   12, 346–63, 371, 376
1.–15.   264
1.1323a14   59
  1323a14–2.1324a23   21
  1323a14–23   348
  1323a24–b21   348, 354–6
  1323a39–3.1325b11   354
  1323b7–10   355
  1323b16–18   275
  1323b21–9   359–60
  1323b22–33   348
  1323b23–5   351
  1323b29–31   260
  1323b37–1324a5   348
  1323b40–1324a2   259, 265, 348
2.1324a5   76
  1324a5–13   353
  1324a19–20   119
  1324a23–5   256–7
  1324a23–32   259
  1324a25–34   349
  1324a29   358–9
  1324a31–7   356
  1324a36–8   355
  1324a39–3.1325b11   354
  1324a40   259, 351
  1324b3–9   251
  1324b5–9   257
  1324b22–40   350–5
  1324b23–1325a15   362
  1325a1–6   350
  1325a3–4   251
  1325a5–6   355
3.1325a20   259
  1325a21–34   354–7
  1325a24–b11   349–50
  1325a25   355
  1325a34–40   354
  1325b3–5   264
  1325b5–6   355
  1325b7–10   260, 276
  1325b10–14   273–4, 379
  1325b12–26   349
  1325b14–21   259
  1325b17–23   359
  1325b27–31   359–60, 375
  1325b28–30   351
4.   326
  1325b33–4   348
  1325b36   362
  1325b37   363
  1325b38   350
  1325b37–8   277
  1325b40ff.   111
  1325b40–1326a5   118–19, 296,
    326
  1326a6–5.1326b39   16

Politica (Pol.) cont'd.
  1326a7–9   132
  1326a13   124
  1326a18–20   263
  1326a21   262
  1326a29–31   295
  1326a35ff.   110
  1326a35–7   31
  1326a35–b22   16
  1326b2ff.   100, 105
  1326b4   129
  1326b5–8   119
  1326b8–9   129
  1326b15   240
  1326b20–1   263
  1326b24   16
  1326b26–30   203
5.   326
  1326b29–30   129, 353
  1326b33   362
6.1327a11–b15   261
  1327a16–39   362–3
  1327b5–7   350
  1327b7–9   263
  1327b8   89
7.1327b20–33   39, 90
  1327b23–38   143
  1328a9–10   266
8.   238
  1328a20–5   269
  1328a21–5   118, 262
  1328a21ff.   111, 256
  1328a22   110
  1328a22–36   363
  1328a30–3   262
  1328a35   76
  1328a35–8   124, 251
  1328a37–8   259
  1328a38–41   60
  1328a38–b2   67
  1328b2–3   261
  1328b4–15   260
  1328b5ff.   89
  1328b6–22   362
  1328b12–23   30
  1328b12–13   18
  1328b13–15   262
  1328b16   111
  1328b16–17   132
  1328b20–3   261
9.1328b24–1329a25   89
  1328b33–1329a2   220, 262–3, 305, 363
  1328b34   76
  1328b34–1329a29   363
  1328b39–41   262
  1328b40–1   37

  1328b41–1329a2   262
  1329a2   76
  1329a2–5   89–90, 261
  1329a2–34   264
  1329a3–4   262
  1329a3–9   364
  1329a9–12   376
  1329a12–22   364
  1329a13–17   265
  1329a16   240
  1329a17–19   263
  1329a19   59
  1329a19–22   36, 262, 362–3
  1329a22–4   124
  1329a23–5   268
  1329a25–6   263, 362
  1329a26–34   364
  1329a27–34   18, 261
  1329a31   262
  1329a34–9   261–2
  1329a35–9   363
  1329a40ff.   151
  1329a40–b5   268
10.1329a41   261
  1329b23–5   261, 268
  1329b25ff.   116
  1329b25–35   277
  1329b41–1330a2   201, 217
  1330a2–13   217, 218
  1330a5–8   266
  1330a8–13   18, 362
  1330a16   240
  1330a25–6   143
  1330a25–30   145
  1330a25–33   41, 263
  1330a26–7   264
  1330a32–3   143–4
11.1330a34–b17   39
12.1331a30–b13   261
  1331a37–b1   40
  1331b1–4   363
  1331b4–18   262
13.1331b24–1332a27   124
  1331b26–38   42
  1331b41–1332a1   259
  1332a1–19   366
  1332a7–10   259, 348
  1332a7–25   214
  1332a7ff.   76
  1332a8   6
  1332a9–19   348
  1332a12–17   215, 365
  1332a19–40   348
  1332a22   6
  1332a25–8   355
  1332a29–35   363
  1332a28   59

1332a31–2   357
1332a36–8   270
14.1332b12–13   254
1332b16–27   239, 274, 277, 379
1332b23–7   304
1332b25–7   267
1332b25–40   364
1332b35–41   265
1333a6–16   38, 145, 221
1333a11   76
1333a11–12   28
1333a16–b3   259
1333a22–3   119
1333a24–5   350
1333a27–30   350, 359–60, 372
1333a31–2   366
1333a35–7   366
1333b3–4   373
1333b5–1334a10   364
1333b12–14   251, 257
1334a1–14   89
1334a6–10   366
15.1334a11   76
1334a11–40   259, 362
1334a16–34   214
1334a22–3   215
1334a23–4   350
1334a25–7   365
1334a32–4   365
1334a34–b3   366
1334a36–9   365
16.1335b19–26   123
1335b28   18
1335b38–1336a2   266
17.1336a4   265
1336b3–12   266
1336b11–12   40
1336b14–23   18
1336b20   367
1337a1   296
1337a5–6   39
VIII.   3–5, 8, 12, 57–61, 65, 69–70,
72–4, 183, 239, 278, 302, 307, 318,
346–81
1.1337a11–2.1337a34   373
1337a21–3   40
1337a22–7   371
1337a27–30   34, 41, 216
1337a31–2   60
1337a31–2.1337b3   40
2.1337a34–5   371
1337a38–9   271
1337b8–11   36, 220
1337b17–21   38, 221–2
3.1337b29–42   367
1337b31–5   364, 366
1337b35–1338a2   366–7

1338a13–31   367
1338b2–4   266
4.1338b9   60
1339a4   265
5.1339a16–27   367–8
1339a35–6   368
1339a37   261, 368
1339a41–b4   367
1339b9–10   36
1339b14   367
1339b32–3   367
1340a1   130
1340a8–14   367
1340a13–18   368
6.1340b20–1341a9   368
1340b42–1341a1   125, 259
1341a7–8   36
1341a10–12   36
1341a14–24   367
1341a23   368
1341b8–14   36
1341b10–17   220–1
7.1341b32–1342a16   373
1341b35   130
1341b39   367–8
1341b40   369
1342a5–16   368
1342a16–28   367
1342a18   372
1342a20   261
1342a20–2   220
1342b16   130

Oeconomica (Oec.)
I.
5.1344a25–6   145

Rhetorica (Rhet.)   81, 281
I.   11, 281
1.1354a34–b11   303
1354b5–8   240
1355a20–4   281
1355a28ff.   64
1355a30–3   64
1355a37–8   281
1355b10ff.   63
3.1358b4–5   250
4.1359a30–b2   119
7.1364a5–9   129
8.1366a2–8   124, 250
1366a4   67, 222
1366a5–6   67
10.   279–85
1368b7–9   282–4, 286
1368b27   334
1369a35–b2   287

Rhetorica (Rhet.) cont'd.
  11.1371b4–8 7
  13. 279–85
    1373b4–18 282–4, 286
    1374a23–5 284
    1374a25–b22 284–5, 298, 305
  15. 279–85, 287
    1375a27–b8 283–4, 286
    1376b9–10 297
II. 281
  1.1378a22–6 334
  12.1389b8–10 210
  13.1390a18–23 209–10
  19.1392a20–3 126
    1392b10–11 147
  23.–34. 281
III.
  18.1419b7–9 221

Rhetorica ad Alexander (Rhet. Al.)
  2.1421b35–1422a4 284

Poetica (Poet.)
  1. 7
  2. 110
  4.1448b4–24 120
    1448b15–16 369
    1449a14ff. 98
    1449a15 130
  9.1451b5–7 329
    1451b5–11 369, 373
  13.1452b36–1453a7 209
  18.1456a18–20 209

Athênaiôn Politeia (Ath. Pol.)
  3.6 295
  4. 85
  41.1 243

PLATO

Apology (Apol.)
  32a–c 245

Crito
  48b8 91

Gorgias (Gorg.) 20
  504d1–3 295
  507e6–508a8 240
  508a 321
  515a7 243

Laws 1, 3, 70, 72–3, 107, 193, 198,
  239, 299, 347, 377–9
I.
  644d1–3 303
  645a1–2 303

II. 239
III. 97, 311
  676aff. 96, 100
  677aff. 116
  679b3ff. 101
  680b 97
  680d3 97
  688a2 295
  690c1–3 303
IV. 11
  705a 377
  709a1–b2 122
  712b8–715e2 231–3
  714a1–2 303
  714b3–715d6 303
  715e7–716a3 289
  716c4–6 289
V.
  739b 196
  739b–e 185
VI.
  754d6 295
  757c 321
  765e9–758a2 240
  772a4–d4 295
  777e5–778a1 147
VII.
  794d5–795d5 292
  803c–e 370
  803d–804b 378
  806d–e 377–8
  807b 377
VIII.
  832d 377–8
  835e4–5 303
  846d377
  846d1–847b6 263
IX.
  858a7–c1 296
  875c3–d5 304
  875d4 295
X.
  888d6–890b2 121
  888d7–890d8 278, 289
  889e3–890a2 284
XI.
  920a3–4 263
XII.
  945b3–e3 272
  952d5–953d7 263

Meno
  71d1–72a5 86
  73a 87
  73c9 87
  73d 87
  77b4–5 87

Parmenides (Parm.)
132d2   278

Phaedo (Phdo.)
65d4–5   278
103b5   278, 289

Philebus (Phlb.)
20d–22b   202
26b7–10   295

Protagoras   107
327a–c   248

Republic (Rep.)   1–3, 10, 20, 107, 110,
    118, 182–225, 239, 250, 268, 275,
    306, 327, 340, 347, 376–8
I.
  348c   92
  348c5–10   79
II.
  357a–358a   375
  358e3–359b5   284
  359a1–2   253
  369aff.   96–7, 100–1
  369b5–7   202
  369c10   203
  369d   376
  369d2   203
  369d11–12   203
  370a7–b5   207
  371d5–7   261
  372a5–d5   204
  372e2–6   204
  374a–d   205
  374b6–c2   207
III.
  412b–d   205
IV.
  419a   205
  419a–421c   185, 197
  420b   206, 377
  421c2   296
  422e–423d   187
  424a   196
  443c–444a   198
  445a–b   206
V.
  451d–457c   268
  472a8–e6   2, 239
  461e   184
  461–6   186, 192
  462a–463c   184–9, 208
  462ff.   191
  464a   185
  464c–465d   195

465d–466c   206
465e–466a   197
472a8–c6   239
VI.
  484c6–d3   289
  500c2–5   289
  501b2   278, 289
  501e   375
  503d–e   376
VII.
  519d4–7   206
  519e–520a   198
  520e1–3   206
  529d–530c   375
  539e–540b   375
  540a7–b1   289
  540b2–5   206
  540c   268
VIII.   343–4
  546a–548c   377
  555–6   320
  558c   321
IX.   343–4
  580b–c   375
  586a–c   204
  588b–591d   198
  590c   191
  590c–591a   207
  592a10–b4   2, 239
X.
  597b5–7   278
  597c2   278, 289
  598a1   289
  598a1–3   278

Sophist (Soph.)   108
223d5–10   261
246b8   278

Statesman   1, 3, 44, 53, 304
276e10ff.   108
294a7–8   304
297b7–c4   304
300c9–d2   304
301d8–c4   304
302–3   234
303a–b   320, 322

Theaetetus (Theaet.)
167c4–5   2, 239
172a–b   278
174d–e   327

Timaeus (Tim.)
22c   116
37c6–38c3   278
51e6–52b2   278